Christine Schirrmacher

"Let there be no Compulsion in Religion" (Sura 2:256):

Apostasy from Islam as judged by contemporary Islamic Theologians

Religious Freedom Series (IIRF)

Vol 4

Vol. 1: Charles L. Tieszen. Re-Examining Religious Persecution: Constructing a Thelogical Framework for Understanding Persecution.

Vol. 2: Christof Sauer, Richard Howell (Hg.). Suffering, Persecution and Martyrdom: Theological Reflections.

Vol. 3: Heiner Bielefeldt. Freedom of Religion Belief: Thematic Reports of the UN Special Rapporteur 2010 – 2013.

Christine Schirrmacher

"Let there be no Compulsion in Religion" (Sura 2:256):

Apostasy from Islam as judged by contemporary Islamic Theologians

Discourses on Apostasy, Religious Freedom, and Human Rights

WIPF & STOCK · Eugene, Oregon

"LET THERE BE NO COMPULSION IN RELIGION" (SURA 2:256): APOSTASY FROM ISLAM AS JUDGED BY CONTEMPORARY ISLAMIC THEOLOGIANS: DISCOURSES ON APOSTASY, RELIGIOUS FREEDOM, AND HUMAN RIGHTS)

This edition published by Wipf and Stock Publishers in cooperation with Verlag für Kultur und Wissenschaft.

Wipf & Stock
An Imprint of Wipf and Stock Publishers
199 W. 8th Ave., Suite 3
Eugene, OR 97401

www.wipfandstock.com

PAPERBACK ISBN: 978-1-4982-9153-8
HARDCOVER ISBN: 978-1-4982-914-5

Manufactured in the U.S.A.

For David

Acknowledgement

The study at hand was accepted in 2012 by the Philosophical Faculty of the University of Bonn within the Program of Islamic Studies as a postdoctoral thesis and has since been slightly modified and updated for printing.

My sincere appreciation goes out to the reviewers and their friendly encouragement of the research project: Prof. Dr. Stephan Conermann and Prof. Dr. Eva Orthmann, Professors of Islamic Studies at the Institute of Oriental and Asian Studies at the University of Bonn, Prof. Dr. Tilman Mayer, Professor of Political Theory, History of Political Ideas, and Contemporary History at the Institute of Political Science and Sociology at the University of Bonn, Prof. Dr. Gerhard Robbers, Professor for Public Law, Ecclesiastical Law, Political Philosophy and Constitutional History on the Law Faculty of the University of Trier as well as Prof. Dr. Ursula Spuler-Stegemann, Professor of Religious Studies at Philipps-Universität Marburg. In an interview lasting several hours, Prof. Dr. Abdullah Saeed, Sultan of Oman Professor of Arab and Islamic Studies at the University of Melbourne, willingly provided information about theological as well as personal views on current developments within Islamic theology and Muslim majority societies.

Numerous additional people have provided me support in various ways, among them Max Klingberg of the International Society of Human Rights (Internationale Gesellschaft für Menschenrechte, or IGFM), Elisabeth Mundhenk, Dr. Suhail Rubin, Hermann Brecht, Dr. Petra Uphoff, Johannes Strehle, and, last but not least, my family. My family's matchless support for the project provided me with the necessary tailwind. Also I thank Open Doors International for contributing to the translation costs of this book. My sincere thanks go also to Richard McClary for the laborious English translation and likewise to Titus Vogt for his tireless efforts in preparing the type space.

The focus of the study has to do with assessing apostasy from Islam by contemporary, globally influential representatives of Islamic theology. By means of their pronouncements, they are contributors to a social climate in which the civil rights of those who think differently are proclaimed and justified, limited, or completely denied. In the process, it is not only a question of converts or representatives of secularism who frequently see themselves exposed to charges of "apostasy" in societies characterized by Islam. It likewise affects critical intellectuals and journalists, progressive scholars of the Quran and defenders of alternative interpretations of issues relating to Sharia law, agnostics and enlightened thinkers, women's rights and human rights activists as well as members of non-recognized (also Muslim) minorities. Linked to the publication of this study is my hope that universal human rights and religious freedom will continue to be placed in the focus of international politics and diplomacy in the 21st century and that they might experience increased acceptance and application.

Bonn, Germany, January 2016

Contents

Acknowledgement **7**

Contents **9**

1. Introduction **15**

1.1. Freedom of Religion – a Universal Commodity? 15

1.2. Justification of the Choice of Topic – Method 18

1.3. The State of Research 20

1.4. Why Pay Attention to the Positions Prominent Theologians Have on Apostasy? 35

1.5. The Focus of the Study 50

1.6. What is "Apostasy"? 51

1.6.1. Apostasy as Judged by Islamic Theology 51
1.6.2. What the Quran Says about Apostasy 52
1.6.3. What Tradition Says about Apostasy 56
1.6.4. Apostasy – a Multilayered Term 58
1.6.5. Opportunity for Remorse 62
1.6.6. The Measure of Punishment for Apostasy 63
1.6.7. Legal and Social Consequences of Apostasy 66

1.7. Apostasy throughout History 67

1.7.1. The Ridda Wars after Muḥammad 67
1.7.2. The Time between the Ridda Wars and Modern Times ... 68
1.7.3. Apostasy in the 20th Century 73
1.7.4. The Example of Egypt 74
1.7.5. Freedom of Religion or "Inner" Freedom of Belief? 84

1.8. Contemporary Dealings with Apostates in Muslim Majority Societies 89

1.8.1. Social Reality 89
1.8.2. The Significance of Sharia Law 91
1.8.3. The Legal Reality in Questions relating to Apostasy 94
1.8.4. The Situation in Individual Countries 96
1.8.5. Non-recognized Religious Communities 104

1.8.6. Individual Cases where Apostasy Charges Have Been Brought 108

2. Yūsuf al-Qaraḍāwī's "Moderate" Position: Religious Freedom is the Internal Freedom of Conscience 127

2.1. Yūsuf al-Qaraḍāwī: His Life and Work – Essential Principles of His Theology 127
2.1.1. An Influential Protagonist of Classical Scholarship 127
2.1.2. Family Home and School Education 132
2.1.3. Links to the Muslim Brotherhood 133
2.1.4. The Beginning of Popularity: "al-ḥalāl wa-'l-ḥarām" – 1960 139
2.1.5. Exile in Qatar 143
2.1.6. al-Qaraḍāwī and Minority Rights 145
2.1.7. al-Qaraḍāwī as the Representative of a Centrist Position 149
2.1.8. Examples of Centrist Theology and Theology of Moderation 153
2.1.9. al-Qaraḍāwī's Authority 156
2.1.10. al-Qaraḍāwī and the "Islamic Awakening" 158

2.2. The Significance of Yūsuf al-Qaraḍāwī 160
2.2.1. *ᶜālim* between the Early Days and Modernity 160
2.2.2. Offices and Committees 161
2.2.3. al-Qaraḍāwī's Use of the Media 166
2.2.4. al-Qaraḍāwī as a Transnational Scholar 169
2.2.5. Assessing al-Qaraḍāwī 179

2.3. Yūsuf al-Qaraḍāwī's Position on Apostasy in Islam 183
2.3.1. The "Centrist" Position and "Moderation" 183
2.3.2. The Lawful and the Prohibited in Islam (al-ḥalāl wa-'l-ḥarām fi 'l-islām) – 1960 185
2.3.3. Yūsuf al-Qaraḍāwīs Magnum Opus on Apostasy: The Crime of Apostasy and Punishment of Apostates in the Light of the Quran and Sunna ("ǧarīmat ar-ridda wa-ᶜuqūbat al-murtadd fī ḍau' al-qur'ān wa-'s-sunna") – 1996 188

2.3.4. The Danger of Apostasy . . . and the Battle against Dissension ("Le danger de l'apostasie . . . et la lutte contre la zizanie") – 2002 226
2.3.5. Source of the Punishment for Apostasy – 2003 228
2.3.6. The Freedom of Belief and Thought ("al-ḥurrīya ad-dīnīya wa-'l-fikrīya") – 2005 230
2.3.7. Major and Minor Apostasy – 2006 231
2.3.8. Is Apostasy a Capital Crime in Islam? – 2006 249
2.3.9. The Inviolability of Blood ("al-ḥurma ad-dimā'") – 2007 254
2.3.10. ǧihād Jurisprudence ("fiqh al-ǧihād") – 2009 256
2.3.11. Miscellaneous Comments by al-Qaraḍāwī on Apostasy 261

2.4. Conclusion: al-Qaraḍāwī's Position on Apostasy 265
2.4.1. The Missing Definition of Apostasy 266
2.4.2. Yūsuf al-Qaraḍāwī's Judgment on Apostasy against the Backdrop of His Theology 267
2.4.3. Yūsuf al-Qaraḍāwī's View of Apostasy against the Backdrop of His Life Work 269
2.4.4. Yūsuf al-Qaraḍāwī's View of Apostasy against the Backdrop of His Ancestry and Education 270
2.4.5. The Superiority of Islam 273
2.4.6. The Persecution of Apostates as an Assurance of Peace 274
2.4.7. The Question of the Necessity of an Islamic State 277
2.4.8. What does "Moderate" Mean in the Question of Apostasy? 280
2.4.9. Outlook 283

3. Abdullah Saeed's "Progressive" Position: Unlimited Religious Freedom 287

3.1. Abdullah Saeed: His Life and Work – Essential Principles of His Theology 287
3.1.1. An Influential Academic and Advisor 287
3.1.2. Publications 293
3.1.3. Abdullah Saeed's Position within Islamic Theology 296
3.1.4. Target Audience and Potential for Reception 303

3.2. Abdullah Saeed's Significance 306
3.2.1. Offices and Committees 307
3.2.2. Advisory Activities for the Australian Government 309
3.2.3. Use of the Media 311
3.2.4. Abdullah Saeed as a Transnational Scholar 313

3.3. Abdullah Saeed's Position on Apostasy in Islam 313
3.3.1. Freedom of Belief in Islam ("A Fresh Look at Freedom of Belief in Islam") – 1994 313
3.3.2. Civil Rights Held by non-Muslims in an Islamic State ("Citizenship Rights of Non-Muslims in a Islamic State") – 1999 319
3.3.3. Abdullah Saeed's Primary Work on Apostasy: Freedom of Religion, Apostasy and Islam – 2004 325
3.3.4. "The Quranic Case against Killing Apostates" – 2011 361
3.3.5. "Hadith (*ḥadīṯ*) and Apostasy" – 2011 363
3.3.6. Miscellaneous Comments by Abdullah Saeed on Apostasy 367

3.4. Results: Abdullah Saeed's Position on Apostasy 382
3.4.1. Abdullah Saeed's Scrutiny of Final Judgments 382
3.4.2. Abdullah Saeed Holds Fast to the Quran as God's Revelation 384
3.4.3. Criticism of the Abuse of Power and Encrustation 387
3.4.4. Abdullah Saeed's Hopes for the Future 389
3.4.5. Abdullah Saeed – Crossing the Borders between Cultures 391
3.4.6. A Comparison between Abdullah Saeed's Position and Yūsuf al-Qaraḍāwī's Position 393
3.4.7. Outlook 398

4. Abū l-Aᶜlā Maudūdī's "Restrictive" Position: Religious Freedom is Self-Abandonment 401

4.1. Abū l-Aᶜlā Maudūdī: Life and Work – Essential Principles of His Theology 401
4.1.1. Influential Politician and Activist 401
4.1.2. Maudūdī's Parental Home, Formal Education, and Journalism 407

4.1.3. Jamā'at-i-Islāmī 414
4.1.4. The Rule of God and "Theodemocracy" 422
4.1.5. Maudūdī's Criticism and Acceptance of the Spirit of the Age 426
4.1.6. Maudūdī's Understanding of *ǧāhilīya* and *Jihād* 428
4.1.7. Maudūdī's Agitation with the Aḥmadīya Movement 431
4.1.8. Criticism of Maudūdī 438

4.2. Abū l-Acla Maudūdī's Significance 439
4.2.1. Maudūdī's Influence as a Theologian 440
4.2.2. Maudūdī's Influence as an Author 442
4.2.3. Maudūdī's Influence in the Islamist Movements of the 20th Century 445

4.3. Abū l-Acla Maudūdīs Position on Apostasy from Islam 464
4.3.1. Maudūdī as an Architect of a Homogeneous Society 464
4.3.2. Abū l-Acla Maudūdī's Main Work on Apostasy: The Punishment of Apostates according to Islamic Law ("murtadd ki sazā islāmī qānūn mēn̲") – 1942/1943 466
4.3.3. The Rights of non-Muslims in an Islamic State ("Islāmī ḥukūmat mēn̲ ḏimmīyōn̲ kē ḥuqūq") – 1948 504
4.3.4. The Aḥmadīya Question ("Qādiyānī mas'ala") – 1953 507
4.3.5. "Let there be no compulsion in religion" (Sura 2:256) – 1955 514
4.3.6. Human Rights in Islam – 1976 521
4.3.7. Maudūdīs Other Remarks on Apostasy 535

4.4. Conclusion: Abū l-Acla Maudūdī's Position on Apostasy 536
4.4.1. The Prohibition against Apostasy on the Way to an Islamic Social Order 536
4.4.2. Maudūdī's Blueprint for a Homogeneous Society 538
4.4.3. The Islamic State as a Model of Hierarchy and Authority 540
4.4.4. The Islamic State as a Precondition for Piety 542
4.4.5. Comparison of the Positions Held by Abū l-Acla Maudūdī, Yūsuf al-Qaraḍāwī and Abdullah Saeed 543
4.4.6. Outlook 552

5. Concluding Remarks: Paths to an Increase in Religious Freedom? 557

6. Bibliography 565

6.1. Sources 565
6.1.1. Sources Relating to Yūsuf al-Qaraḍāwī 565
6.1.2. Sources Relating to Abdullah Saeed 568
6.1.3. Sources Relating to Abū l-A^clā Maudūdī 574

6.2. Secondary Literature 578

6.3. Internet Articles and Internet Documents not Ascribed to an Author 614

6.4. Abbreviations 618

1. Introduction

1.1. Freedom of Religion – a Universal Commodity?

Why is it that up to the present day, "apostates" – progressive Muslim intellectuals, converts, and members of non-recognized minorities – are socially ostracized, discriminated against according to civil law, persecuted, and taken into custody and imprisoned in Muslim majority countries, although in hardly any of these countries a law against falling away from Islam exists? Indeed, why is this the case even though in virtually all of these countries the constitutions ensure religious freedom? Why are apostates acquitted in court in some places but then have to go underground lest they lose their life in broad daylight? Who are the participants accounting for the creation of such a social climate in which apostasy, criticism of religion, and criticism of the local form of Islam appear to be crimes deserving death? And which preconditions have to be fulfilled in order for Muslim proponents of complete religious freedom to increasingly find a hearing in society and theology?

"Religious freedom in Islam: that's a big topic" – Patricia Crone formulated it in this manner in 2007 in her ceremonial address upon the opening of the 30th German Congress of Oriental Studies in Freiburg, Germany.[1] Topics such as positive and negative religious freedom as a component of the canon of human rights, the question of the right to change one's religion, and how authoritative Muslim theologians assess falling away from Islam (in Arabic: *radd* or *irtidād*) against the backdrop of their Sharia-based prohibitions as well as the social and legal position of "apostates" in Muslim majority countries are in point of fact a relevant and multi-layered and yet overall scarcely treated topic within Islamic studies.[2] Indeed, in part it is apparently "a delicate topic to raise."[3]

---

1 Patricia Crone. "Islam and Religious Freedom." Ceremonial address upon the occasion of the opening celebration of the 30th German Orientalist Convention (30. Deutscher Orientalistentag), 24.9.2007. http://orient.ruf.uni-freiburg.de/dotpub/crone.pdf (15.4.2014).

2 David Cook's statement in 2006 still makes sense today: "Apostasy from Islam and conversion to it are topics in which serious research is scanty." David Cook.

The vague notion frequently circulates that Islam forbids apostasy, indeed that apostates and converts from Islam to another religion are threatened with death. Where and with which justification this can be the case, however, in light of the known fact that there is no codified Sharia lawbook? Additionally, where does the justification come from when primarily Arab states call upon the Sharia as the source of legislation yet only apply it in locally valid catalogues of criminal law – and even at this point predominantly only in civil law? Where is the justification when scarcely any state has a prohibition against apostasy in its constitution or legislation? From a first glance at the wording of the constitutions of numerous Muslim majority countries, which are expressly committed to religious freedom, the conclusion could be drawn that in the final event religious freedom in such states reaches much farther than is initially supposed.

The fact that this is, however, not the case becomes clear very quickly to whomever deals with what are from location to location extremely varied but almost universally strained and in part dramatic situations facing critical intellectuals, artists, progressive Quranic scholars, journalists and secularists, agnostics or confessing atheists, enlightened thinkers, women's and human rights activists, converts to other religions, and members of non-recognized minorities. The spectrum of limitations and pressure varies greatly from country to country and ranges from discrimination via legal disadvantages to societal ostracism and all the way to public condemnation, from arbitrary incarceration to threats and even death. What is, however, the cause and basis for all of this if no Sharia-orientated legislation on this question exists locally at all? Is it the widespread problematic nature of education? Does it have economic causes? Is it the misuse of power and political position?

If the state and legislative structures are not the deciding lever in the machinery which sets these side effects in motion as they relate to those who think differently, the question is to be asked as to the role public opinion makers play, particularly as it relates to the position of influential rep-

---

"Apostasy from Islam: A Historical Perspective" in: *JSAI* 31 (2006), pp. 248-288, here p. 248.

3 According to Anh Nga Longva's formulation on the occasion of the conspicuously small number of relevant scholarly publications on the topic of apostasy: Anh Nga Longva. "The Apostasy Law in Kuwait and the Liberal Predicament" in: *CD* 14/3 (2002), pp. 257-282, here p. 258.

resentatives of Islamic theology, for they exert a great degree of influence on society via a large number of channels. Worldview transfer and the transfer of the history of ideas in theology and law, and above all in society, which proceeds from them are together the central focus of this study. In which direction do influential theologians mould the societal climate with respect to the treatment of outsiders? Do these theologians justify and intensify outsiders' possession of fewer rights due to their comments and opinion statements? Do they and their rationale account for a balancing counterweight in the difficult legal situation minorities and those who think differently face? Or do they even advocate more civil rights and liberties than the legal frameworks provide?

Over the past decades there have been an increased number of cases of escape and desire for asylum, and the mishandling and execution of certain critical intellectuals, authors and Quranic scholars, apostates and converts has been covered in press reports in the Western media. Research into all known cases, however, is more difficult than it might appear at first glance: It is only seldom that the precise circumstances and motives leading to this arrest or that case of death can be investigated from a distance. In part, one finds that the local press does not report at all or presents an official standard version of a spying offense instead of the facts, or it refers to the involvement of the person concerned in drug dealing, or it presents involvement in some other morally offensive behavior or activity which is subversive to the state under the existing legal framework. The result is that from the outside it is often difficult to obtain a clear picture.

For that reason what one has here – while taking into account a number of prominent examples of the persecution of apostates which have already been academically investigated – is less the question of the consequences of apostasy as the central issue, but rather the points of departure with respect to the aspect of the history of the development of ideas. Why are apostates in Muslim majority countries under such strong fire in the first place? To ask this is to pose the question of the position contributors to this sort of societal climate have, a social climate in the shadows of which either civil rights and liberties and diversity of opinions can flourish or where intolerance, threats, and discrimination of those who think differently can blossom. For that reason the attitudes of influential representatives of Islamic theology as they relate to apostasy and to dealing with apostates are what take the center stage of this investigation.

1.2. Justification of the Choice of Topic – Method

The presentation and comparison of the voices of influential theological Muslim voices in the 20th century comprise the focus of this investigation. Prior to being able to present an overall picture of Muslim contemporary theology on what has up to this point been a largely neglected topic, individual perspectives have to be worked out, compared with each other, and their influence on politics and society illuminated. Thus the topic of apostasy in no way only involves theological debate, as initially may appear to be the case. Rather, on the basis of the particular influence of the three protagonists presented herein, it also involves society and politics: Apostasy thus becomes a topic which extends far beyond universities' lecterns of and mosques' pulpits.

It is not only theologians who still today call for the death penalty for apostates who are the target of this study (although this position is defended up to the present day and for that reason will also be taken into account). Rather, equal weight will be given to the moderate position of affirming personal freedom of conscience as well as the uncompromising defense of complete religious freedom along with the simultaneous thoroughgoing rejection of the death penalty for falling away from Islam.

Three main positions toward apostasy will be introduced by means of the publications of three contemporary theologians of the 20th century. The first selection factor was the respective worldwide prominence of the individual and their shaping influence on the global *umma*; a second criterion was that all three scholars have intensively addressed the topic of apostasy in their publications and have published at least one independent work on the topic. A third criterion dealing with the issue was their national and international social and political influence, such that not only theologians but simultaneously global players on the international stage of politics and society are presented. Fourthly, it has to do exclusively with theologians who enjoyed a traditional education and do not follow a dialogue which is essentially critical of the Quran or Islam or would be considered liberal in their theological leanings. At the same time, having chosen three theologians from Egypt/Qatar, the Maldives/Australia, and India/Pakistan, a narrowing of the field of view by a one-sided regionalization has been avoided and an arch has been built from the Arabian world to Asia and, through the diverse spheres of activity these protagonists pursue, all the way to Europe.

All three theologians presented here assume the unqualified divine inspiration of the Quran and the timeless validity of its ordering principles for politics and society. And yet – in part by using the same line of reasoning – they come to very different conclusions in their points of view on apostasy and apostates.

Initially, after an overview on the assessment of apostasy and the treatment of apostates throughout history, from the early days of Islam up to modern times, the respective main writings of the three authors will be analyzed as will all their further statements on the topic of apostasy and religious freedom. The various positions resulting from analyzing their work will be explicated, and their respective justifications for or against religious freedom will be presented against the backdrop of their biography and theology. Due to the authors' origins, which will be seen to be in different regions, and due to their influence on politics and society, the major statements from their works will be assessed by taking into account these authors' national and international reception. The conclusions of the individual chapters comprise a comparison of the elucidated texts and positions against the backdrop of questions posed as to whether and under which conditions the advocates of complete religious freedom could have a greater forum for the propagation of their thinking in the future.

In 2008 a number of articles by the Armenian Journalist and editor Hrant Dink were published, who has critically analyzed the Turkish-Armenian relationship in a number of his writings. He made the Young Turks' government's genocide of Armenians at the beginning of the 20th century under the Ottoman Empire a subject of public discussion. He was shot in broad daylight in Istanbul in 2007. His articles were published posthumously and carry the title *Von der Saat der Worte*[4] (English translation of the title: *On the Sowing of Words*). In the process, these articles are reminders of the frequently undervalued social and political impact of the spoken or written word, which are fortified via influential protagonists in societal and political forums, over the media or religious communities, and as a result bear fruit far beyond the tightly framed bounds of direct speech and script.

When it comes to the topic of apostasy, we are also dealing with the sowing of words – at this point words sown by Muslim scholars – who by

---

4 Hrant Dink. *Von der Saat der Worte*. Verlag Hans Schiler: Berlin, 2008.

the positions they take, which will be shown herein, exercise influence on the destiny of many other people in their society in both a positive and a negative sense. For that reason, when apostasy is judged by representatives of Muslim theology, it is in no way purely a theological question as it could initially appear to be from a Western perspective. Rather, it is a topic of great social relevance and of a considerable explosive nature due to its repercussions all the way into the political realm and legislation.

1.3. The State of Research

On the whole, the topic of apostasy within the context of Islam has been treated only sparsely up to the present time,[5] even if the topic of Islam and religious freedom can occasionally be a topic of public lectures before audiences made up of specialists.[6] The study at hand[7] is above all centered on essays of an introductory nature, which, however – like the few books published on the topic – predominantly consider the legal assessment of apostasy in the early times of Islamic history and, in some cases, name or describe some concrete cases of apostasy in Islamic history and place them in central focus. There is little knowledge to be gained on the topic of apostasy from the few treatments dealing with what unclearly differentiates apostasy from heresy[8] or heterodoxy[9] in Islamic history. Up to now, the

---

5 Publications for the topic of likewise interesting disciplines such as religious sociology and psychology, respectively, are for instance an essay by Raoul J. Adam. "Relating Faith Development and Religious Styles: Reflections in Light of Apostasy from Religious Fundamentalism" in: *APS* 20 (2008), pp. 201-231, are not regarded here as are the basic considerations on the definition of the role of religions in society and the state in, for example, Roger Trigg. *Religion in Public Life: Must Faith be Privatized?* Oxford: Oxford University Press, 2007.

6 According to, for example, Patricia Crone in her Ceremonial address upon the occasion of the opening celebration of the 30th German Orientalist Convention 2007: Crone. Islam.

7 For this research paper, all available primary as well as secondary sources have been included until 2012; from 2012 to 2014 relevant publications have also been taken into account.

8 For example, that applies to essays by Bernard Lewis. "Some Observations on the Significance of Heresy in the History of Islam" in: *SI* 1 (1953), pp. 43-63 and by Alexander Knysh. "'Orthodoxy' and 'Heresy' in Medieval Islam: An Essay in Reassessment" in: *MW* 83/1 (1993), pp. 48-67.

available treatments have above all been concentrated on the following areas:

a) Investigations on the Topic of Human Rights: Publications on the topic of human rights in the Islamic context, on Islam-based definitions of human rights as well as on human rights declarations by Islamic organizations are already available in large numbers.[10] However, in doing so questions of religious freedom and apostasy are generally only treated at the margins. For instance, this is the case in the basic study by Ann Elizabeth Mayer, *Islam and Human Rights. Tradition and Politics*[11] or done so more briefly by Anne Duncker, *Menschenrechte im Islam. Eine Analyse islamischer Erklärungen über die Menschenrechte*[12] (English translation of the title: *Human Rights in Islam. An Analysis of Islamic Declarations on Human Rights*). From a Muslim point of view, Abdullahi Ahmed An-Na'im's work *Toward an Islamic Reformation. Civil Liberties, Human Rights, and International Law*[13] is one of the best known on this topic, which, howev-

---

9 For instance in Werner Ende. "Wer ist ein Glaubensheld, wer ist ein Ketzer?" in: *WI* 23-24 (1984), pp. 70-94.

10 Mentioned only representatively here: Kevin Dwyer. *Arab Voices. The Human Rights Debate in the Middle East.* Routledge: London, 1991; Sami A. Aldeeb Abu-Sahlieh. *Les musulmans face aux droits de l'homme. Religion & droit & politique. Étude et documents.* Verlag Dr. Dieter Winkler: Bochum, 1994; Lorenz Müller. *Islam und Menschenrechte. Sunnitische Muslime zwischen Islamismus, Säkularismus und Modernismus.* Deutsches Orient-Institut: Hamburg, 1996; Heiner Bielefeldt. *Philosophie der Menschenrechte. Grundlage eines weltweiten Freiheitsethos.* Wissenschaftliche Buchgesellschaft: Darmstadt, 1998; Alexandra Petersohn. "Islamisches Menschenrechtsverständnis unter Berücksichtigung der Vorbehalte muslimischer Staaten zu den UN-Menschenrechtsverträgen." Dissertation, Rheinischen-Friedrichs-Wilhelms-Universität, Bonn (University of Bonn, Germany), 1999; Carsten Jürgensen. *Demokratie und Menschenrechte in der arabischen Welt. Positionen arabischer Menschenrechtsaktivisten*, Nomos: Baden-Baden, 1999; Paul M. Taylor. Freedom *of Religion. UN and European Human Rights Law and Practice.* Cambridge University Press: Cambridge, 2005.

11 Ann Elizabeth Mayer. *Islam and Human Rights. Tradition and Politics.* Westview Press: Boulder, 1995[2].

12 Anne Duncker. *Menschenrechte im Islam. Eine Analyse islamischer Erklärungen über die Menschenrechte.* Wissenschaftlicher Verlag: Berlin, 2006.

13 Abdullahi Ahmed An-Na'im. *Toward an Islamic Reformation. Civil Liberties, Human Rights, and International Law*, Syracuse University Press: New York, 1990; also comp.: Abdullahi Ahmed An-Na'im (ed.). *Human Rights in Cross-*

er, hardly touches on the question of apostasy. Christian Stahmann, in his dissertation "Islamische Menschenrechtskonzepte. Islamische Menschenrechtskonzepte und das Problem sogenannter 'islamischer' Menschenrechtsverletzungen in Pakistan seit 1977" (English translation of the title: "Islamic Conceptions of Human Rights. Islamic Conceptions of Human Rights and the Problem of so-called 'Islamic' Human Rights Violations in Pakistan since 1977"),[14] indeed goes into the problem of apostasy, yet he does not treat it as a distinct topic. Rather, he addresses it in connection with the discussion of human rights concepts as defined by Islam within the framework of his specialized area, social ethics. He primarily concentrates on the reception of the idea of human rights thinking in Pakistan beginning with the term of office of Zia ul-Haqq. Stahmann seizes upon the most important areas of conflict arising as they compare with the United Nations' Universal Declaration of Human Rights.

In order to evaluate the various positions of Muslim theologians and intellectuals on the topic of human rights, the dissertations by Lorenz Müller, entitled "Islam und Menschenrechte: Sunnitische Muslime zwischen Islamismus, Säkularismus und Modernismus" (English translation of the title: "Islam and Human Rights: Sunnite Muslims between Islam, Secularism, and Modernism")[15] and Gudrun Krämer's study "Gottes Staat als Republik: Reflexionen zeitgenössischer Muslime zu Islam, Menschenrechten und Demokratie"[16] (English translation of the title: "Theocracy as a Republic: Reflections of contemporary Muslims on Islam, Human Rights, and Democracy") as perhaps the most comprehensive study on this topic, are worthy of mention. In 1991 Martin Forstner published a foundational and in the years that followed oft quoted essay entitled "Das Menschenrecht der Religionsfreiheit und des Religionswechsels als Problem der islamischen Staaten" (English translation of the title: "The Human Right of Religious Freedom and a Change of Religion as a Problem for Is-

---

Cultural Perspectives. A Quest for Consensus, University of Pennsylvania Press: Philadelphia, 1992.

14 Christian Stahmann. *Islamische Menschenrechtskonzepte. Islamische Menschenrechtskonzepte und das Problem sogenannter "islamischer" Menschenrechtsverletzungen in Pakistan seit 1977*, Ergon: Würzburg, 2005.

15 Müller. *Islam*.

16 Gudrun Krämer. *Gottes Staat als Republik: Reflexionen zeitgenössischer Muslime zu Islam, Menschenrechten und Demokratie*. Nomos: Baden-Baden, 1999.

lamic States").[17] In that essay he illuminated the topic of apostasy against the backdrop of Islamic human rights declarations such as the 1990 Cairo Declaration on Human Rights in Islam and the Universal Islamic Declaration on Human Rights from 1981 and contrasted the understanding of tolerance in classic Islamic theology with the 1948 United Nations' Universal Declaration of Human Rights.

Other publications such as, for instance, the anthology by Johannes Schwartländer entitled Freiheit der Religion. Christentum und Islam unter dem Anspruch der Menschenrechte (English translation of the title: Freedom of Religion. Christianity and Islam under the Claims of Human Rights combine the topic of human rights and human dignity with basic considerations on what is a unilinear definition of religious freedom and the lack of a possible exit from the Islamic community of belief in Muslim majority countries.[18] In his presentation of classic Islamic regulations carrying the title Crime and Punishment in Islam Law, which addresses the genesis of Islamic law as well as the practical application of it in the period from the 16th to the 20th century, Rudolph Peters briefly ranks apostasy among the ḥadd offenses but does not go into more detail with additional content.[19]

b) Studies of the Social and Legal Status of Minorities in Muslim majority Societies: Apart from studies which treat the status of minorities in certain segments of Islamic history[20] or within Islamist discourse, concentrating mostly on classic legal texts and reclaiming the *ḏimma* model unchanged for modernity,[21] the more comprehensive studies primarily con-

---

17 Martin Forstner. "Das Menschenrecht der Religionsfreiheit und des Religionswechsels als Problem der islamischen Staaten" in: *Kanon. Kirche und Staat im Christlichen Osten. Jahrbuch der Gesellschaft für das Recht der Ostkirchen*. Verlag des Verbandes der wissenschaftlichen Gesellschaften Österreichs: Wien, 1991, pp. 105-186.

18 Johannes Schwartländer. *Freiheit der Religion. Christentum und Islam unter dem Anspruch der Menschenrechte*. Matthias-Grünewald-Verlag: Mainz, 1993.

19 Rudolph Peters. *Crime and Punishment in Islamic Law. Theory and Practice from the Sixteenth to the Twenty-First Century*. Cambridge University Press: Cambridge, 2005, pp. 64-65.

20 See, for example, Khaled Abou El Fadl. "Islamic Law and Muslim Minorities: The Juristic Discourse on Muslim Minorities from the second/eighth to the eleventh/seventeenth Centuries" in: *ILS* 1 (1994), pp. 141-187.

21 This is for instance explained by Uriah Furman. "Minorities in Contemporary Islamist Discourse" in: *MES* 36/4 (2000), pp. 1-20, here pp. 13+19.

centrate on the legal position of non-Muslim minorities in various countries. Thus Johanna Pink, in her dissertation "Neue Religionsgemeinschaften in Ägypten. Minderheiten im Spannungsfeld von Glaubensfreiheit, öffentlicher Ordnung und Islam" (English translation of the title: "New religious Communities in Egypt. Minorities in the Conflict Area of Freedom of Belief, Public Order and Islam"), dealt with the social and legal status of those minorities in the Egyptian state which do not belong to the *people of the book* as well as their theological assessment in Muslim and Christian discourse.[22]

Eliz Sanasarian treats the politics of the country of Iran with respect to its non-Muslim minorities for the first ten years after the Iranian Revolution,[23] and Petra Uphoff investigates Iranian penal and civil codes beginning with the Iranian constitution and legislation in her dissertation entitled "Untersuchung zur rechtlichen Stellung und Situation von nichtmuslimischen Minderheiten im Iran" (English translation of the title: "Investigation of the legal Position and Situation of non-Muslim minorities in Iran) in order to discern the legal position of Bahā'ī, Zoroastrians, Jews, various Christian groups, the Ahl al-ḥaqq, the Mandeans, the Yezidi, and Iranian ethnic minorities as well as converts from Islam to other religions.[24]

c) Individual Charges of Apostasy against Prominent Personages: The entire course of isolated claims of apostasy, which have received strong echoes through press reports, have been documented: In his dissertation in the field of theology, Gereon Vogel dedicates himself to the case of Salman Rushdie in his work "Blasphemie. Die Affäre Rushdie in religionswissenschaftlicher Sicht. Zugleich ein Beitrag zum Begriff der Religion" (English translation of the Title: "Blasphemy. The Rushdie Affair from the

22 Johanna Pink chose the Bahā'ī, the Aḥmadīya, Jehovah's Witnesses, the Seventh Day Adventists, and the Mormons for her investigation of the legal and social position of non-recognized minorities in Egypt from: Johanna Pink. *Neue Religionsgemeinschaften in Ägypten*. Ergon: Würzburg, 2003; on the Bahā'ī additionally more detailed: Johanna Pink. "A Post-Qur'ānic Religion between Apostasy and Public Order: Egyptian Muftis and Courts on the Legal Status of the Bahā'ī Faith" in: *ILS* 10/3 (2003), pp. 409-434.

23 Eliz Sanasarian. *Religious Minorities in Iran*. Cambridge University Press: Cambridge, 2000.

24 Petra Uphoff. *Untersuchung zur rechtlichen Stellung und Situation von nichtmuslimischen Minderheiten im Iran*. Internationale Gesellschaft für Menschenrechte: Frankfurt, 2012.

Viewpoint of Religious Studies. Simultaneously a Contribution to the Concept of Religion").[25] Jörn Thielmann did his doctorate with a study entitled "Naṣr Ḥāmid Abū Zaid und die wiedererfundene ḥisba. Šarī'a und Qānūn im heutigen Ägypten" (Translation of title: "Naṣr Ḥāmid Abū Zaid and the re-discovered ḥisba. Šarī'a and Qānūn in present day Egypt") about the case of Naṣr Ḥāmid Abū Zaid, coming to terms with the charges, the court case, and the judgment against the backdrop of the resuscitation of the historical instrument of the *ḥisba* charge in Egypt on the last two decades of the 20th century.[26]

The scholar and politician Maḥmūd Muḥammad Ṭāhā, who was publicly executed in 1985 on account of apostasy, also belongs to the best known cases of the persecution of apostasy in the 20th century. His orientation had an apologetic thrust and was predominantly limited to the political power games among Sudanese political powers at the end of the 20th century. Abdullahi Ahmed An-Na'im, who was arguably the most prominent student of Maḥmūd Muḥammad Ṭāhā, already depicted this most famous case of condemnation on the account of apostasy to date in his 1986 essay "The Islamic Law of Apostasy and its Modern Applicability. A Case from the Sudan"[27] and in āhā's major translated and published work shortly thereafter entitled *The Second Message of Islam*.[28]

However, in his essay "The Islamic Law of Apostasy and its Modern Applicability. A Case from the Sudan," An-Na'im only deals with the Islamic side of this case in a brief summary form. He primarily deals with the historically preceding legal developments in the Sudan in the case of Ṭāhā[29] and only depicts Ṭāhā's disputed opinions with a few strokes,

---

25 Gereon Vogel. *Blasphemie. Die Affäre Rushdie in religionswissenschaftlicher Sicht*. Peter Lang: Frankfurt, 1998.

26 Jörn Thielmann. *Naṣr Ḥāmid Abū Zaid und die wiedererfundene ḥisba. Šarī'a und Qānūn im heutigen Ägypten*, Ergon: Würzburg, 2003.

27 Abdullahi Ahmed An-Na'im. "The Islamic Law of Apostasy and its Modern Applicability. A Case from the Sudan" in: *Religion* 16 (1986), pp. 197-224.

28 Mahmoud Mohamed Taha. *The Second Message of Islam*, Translation and Introduction by Abdullahi Ahmed an-Na'im. Syracuse University Press: Syracuse, 1987.

29 The background of Islamification of Sudanese law is described in most detail by Aharon Layish; Gabriel R. Warburg. *The Reinstatement of Islamic Law in Sudan under Numayrī. An Evaluation of a Legal Experiment in the Light of its Historical Context, Methodology, and Repercussions*. E. J. Brill: Leiden, 2002.

which in the end became the trigger for the case of apostasy undertaken against him.[30] Against the backdrop of Ṭāhā's biography, as well as the politico-religious development in the Sudan at the end of the 20th century, Annette Oevermann, in her pathbreaking study *Die "Republikanischen Brüder" im Sudan* (Translation of the title: *The "Republican Brothers" in the Sudan*) analyzes the theoretical and methodical approach of Ṭāhā's central views and the potential for conflict between Ṭāhā and the Sudanese political-religious elite.[31]

d) Individual Essays or older Treatments of the Topic of Apostasy: Up to the present day, Samuel M. Zwemer's post-colonial treatment from a Christian perspective is seldom missing from the list of literature on the topic of apostasy. His work, entitled *The Law of Apostasy in Islam*,[32] combines a theoretical discussion of the topic with respect to the Quran and tradition by taking Islamic legal texts into account and by naming practical examples of dealing with apostates in various countries.[33]

Most essays on the topic of apostasy restrict themselves to a limited geographic region or period of time,[34] for example the description of the attempts by British diplomacy to place permanent protection for converts to Christianity at the High Porte in the Ottoman Empire in the middle of the 19th century.[35] In one of the more foundational essays from 1976/1977 entitled "Apostasy in Islam," Rudolph Peters and Gert J. J. De Vries address the topic of apostasy from an Islamic legal perspective. In addition,

---

30 An-Na'im. "Law".

31 Annette Oevermann. *Die "Republikanischen Brüder" im Sudan. Eine islamische Reformbewegung im Zwanzigsten Jahrhundert*. Peter Lang: Frankfurt, 1993.

32 Samuel M. Zwemer. *Das Gesetz wider den Abfall vom Islam*, C. Bertelsmann: Gütersloh, 1926.

33 An advance copy with parts of the second chapter appeared in 1924: Samuel Zwemer. "The Law of Apostasy" in: *MW* 14 (1924), pp. 373-391. Comp. the shorter treatment by F. H. Ruxton, which likewise appeared at the beginning of the 20th century. "The Convert's Status in Maliki Law" in: *MW* 3 (1913), pp. 37-40.

34 For instance, also according to the tracing over a very tight frame of possible motives for the conversion of individuals and the manner of dealing with the topic of apostasy in the Ottoman Empire at the middle of the 19th century in Selim Deringil. "There is no Compulsion in Religion: On Conversion and Apostasy in the Late Ottoman Empire: 1839-1856" in: *CSSH* 42/3 (2000), pp. 547-575.

35 See on this: Turgut Subaşı. "The Apostasy Question in the Context of Anglo-Ottoman Relations, 1843-1844" in: *MES* 38/2 (2002), pp. 1-34.

they address the question of the definition as well as the penal and civil legal consequences of apostasy according to classic Sharia law and then, in a second section, cover the problematic issue of apostasy using the example of groups not recognized under Sharia law, such as the Bahā'ī and the Aḥmadīya.[36] The authors come to the astonishing conclusion – also against the backdrop of the second half of the 1970s – that there is "no evidence that apostates are still killed nowadays in Islamic countries."[37] They draw this conclusion although the writers name a number of members of the *ᶜulamā'* in the modern age who speak out in an unqualified manner in favor of applying the death penalty.

Besides there are short articles in the *Encyclopaedia of Islam* and the *Encyclopaedia of the Qur'ān* by W. Heffening under the heading "Murtadd,"[38] and by M. Lecker under the heading "al-Ridda"[39] – the latter treating the apostate movement of settled as well as nomadic Arab tribes on the Arabian Peninsula which began before Mohammed's death and was drawn out beyond the time of Abū Bakr's caliphate. There is also the work by Wael Hallaq on "Apostasy"[40] and Frank Griffel, likewise under "Apostasy."[41] Besides those, Joel Kramer offers a summary of the historically ascertainable evidence for dealing with apostates in the early days of Islam and in early legal literature.[42] Furthermore, Lutz Wiederhold restricts himself to a discussion of the prohibition on blasphemy in Shaf'i legal literature.[43]

---

36 Rudolph Peters; Gert J. J. De Vries. "Apostasy in Islam" in: *WI* 17 (1976-1977), pp. 1-25.

37 Ibid., p. 13.

38 W. Heffening. "Murtadd" in: *EI*/2, Vol. VII. E. J. Brill: Leiden, 1993, pp. 635-636.

39 M. Lecker. "Al-Ridda" in: *EI*/2, Vol. XII, Suppl. E. J. Brill: Leiden, 2004, S. 692-695.

40 Wael Hallaq. "Apostasy" in: *EQ*, Vol. 1. E. J. Brill: Leiden, 2001, pp. 119-122.

41 This new edition was available to me in the online version: Frank Griffel. "Apostasy" in: *EI*/3 http://referenceworks.brillonline.com/entries/encyclopaedia-of-islam-3/apostasy-SIM_0044?s.num=7 (15.4.2014).

42 Joel Kraemer. "Apostates, Rebels and Brigands" in: *IOS* 10 (1980), pp. 34-73, here pp. 36-48.

43 Lutz Wiederhold. "Blasphemy against the Prophet Muḥammad and his Companions *(sabb al-rasūl, sabb al-ṣaḥābah)*: The Introduction of the Topic into Shāfiᶜī Legal Literature and its Relevance for Legal Practice under Mamluke Rule" in: *JSS* 42/1 (1997), pp. 39-70.

In his article "The Interpretation of Qur'anic Text to Promote or Negate the Death Penalty for Apostates and Blasphemers," Declan O'Sullivan illuminates the different interpretations of the relevant texts from the Quran and tradition on apostasy by representatives of Islamic theology.[44] Finally, in his essay "Apostasy as Objective and Depersonalized Fact: Two Recent Egyptian Court Judgments," Baber Johnson primarily describes the charge of apostasy against Naṣr Ḥāmid Abū Zaid as an internal crisis within the world of Egyptian scholarship.[45]

Deviating from common Western academic discourse, the article by Syafa'atun Almirzanah entitled "On Human Rights and the Qur'anic Perspective: Freedom of Religion and the Rule of Apostasy" is above all a confirmation of Islam's ability to be reconciled with religious freedom and seen as a "polyinterpretable religion."[46] In a similar vein, Saira Malik comments on the most important Quranic passages and texts of tradition on the topic of apostasy.[47] Sherazad Hamit articulated his position on the death penalty upon the condemnation of the Afghan convert Abdur Rahman at the beginning of 2006[48] as did Niaz A. Shah on what in his view is the inherent Quranic principle of religious freedom and reconcilability with UN-defined human rights.[49] These authors formulate what is a basic rejection of all sorts of possible justification of capital punishment for apostates from the Quran and *sunna*.

In very similar fashion, the 1994 article "Religious Freedom and the Law of Apostasy in Islam,"[50] by Mahmoud Ayoub, joins in with his own

---

44 Declan O'Sullivan. "The Interpretation of Qur'anic Text to Promote or Negate the Death Penalty for Apostates and Blasphemers" in: *JQS* 3/2 (2001), pp. 63-93.

45 Baber Johansen. "Apostasy as Objective and Depersonalized Fact: Two Recent Egyptian Court Judgments" in: *SoR* 70/3 (2003), pp. 687-710.

46 Syafa'atun Almirzanah. "On Human Rights and the Qur'anic Perspective: Freedom of Religion and the Rule of Apostasy" in: *AJ* 45/2 (2007), pp. 367-388, here p. 370.

47 Saira Malik. "An Analysis of Apostasy/*irtidād*: Considerations for Muslims in Contemporary Western Societies" in: *JILC* 11/3 (2009), pp. 211-223.

48 Sherazad Hamit. "Apostasy and the Notion of Religious Freedom in Islam" in: *MIJ* 1/2 (2006), pp. 31-38.

49 Niaz A. Shah, "Freedom of Religion: Koranic and Human Rights Perspectives" in: *AJHL* 6/1-2 (2005), pp. 69-88.

50 Mahmoud Ayoub. "Religious Freedom and the Law of Apostasy in Islam" in: *ISCH* 20 (1994), pp. 75-91.

viewpoint on the debate: In addition to the fact-based treatment of the topic, he delivers his own judgment on the question of the justification of the death penalty for apostasy. Therein, he accepts neither the commonly quoted Quran passages nor the texts of tradition as justification for the punishment of apostasy:[51] He initially reports on classic Sharia legal texts on the topic of apostasy and in the process differentiates between Sunnite and Shiite legal scholars before concluding that the actual sense of the regulations of Islamic law on apostasy is always to want to offer the apostate a way out via the remaining uncertainty about the inner attitude of the person instead of condemning him.

According to Ayoub, in the case manifest apostasy, this "way out" consists of calling upon the accused to utter the Islamic confession of faith. Even if this individual is an apostate and internally harbors completely other thoughts, his confession to Islam should be satisfactory, and the judge should not insist further. Ayoub appears to not take into account that presumably there is hardly a convert to another religion or an adherent of a non-recognized minority who would want to say the Islamic confession of faith.[52] Additionally, the following applies for Ayoub: "Apostasy was never a problem for the Muslim community," since the few apostates executed were executed for political (not religious) reasons.[53] Admittedly, Ayoub grants the following for the second half of the 20th century: "Apostasy has become a thorny issue for both Western missionaries and secular human-

---

51 Ibid., pp. 82-84.

52 At this point Mahmoud Ayoub possibly rather has the doubter or the atheist in mind rather than the convert. He explains that also a Jew who believes in the oneness of God only has to confirm the sending of Mohammed with his own words and then counts as a Muslim and that there would thus be a way for adherents of monotheistic religions to avoid punishment: ibid., p. 90.

53 Mohammed Talbi, Professor for Medieval Islamic History in Tunis and a member of the honorary board of the "Association Nationale pour la Défense de la Liberté Religieuse" (International Association for the Protection of Religious Freedom) even goes so far as to maintain: "I do not know, thoughout the history of Islam, of any application of the law condemning the apostate to death. This law is mostly theoretical" – which in this pointed emphasis, in spite of a low number of executions administered by the state on account of apostasy, is still incorrect: Mohamed Talbi. "Religious Liberty: A Muslim Perspective" in: *ISCH* 11 (1985), pp. 99-113, here p. 108 and Mohamed Talbi. "Religionsfreiheit – eine muslimische Perspektive" in: Schwartländer, *Freiheit,* p. 65.

ists and for many Western-educated Muslim intellectuals as well," especially since Muslims have combated against one another with the weapon of charges of apostasy.[54]

Susanne Olsson's 2008 essay, "Apostasy in Egypt: Contemporary Cases of *Ḥisbah*," has to do with the topic of combating unpopular opponents within the Muslim community with the increasingly utilized weapon of the charge of apostasy in Egypt in the 1980s and 1990s[55] Similarly, Roswitha Badry treats this topic in her work "Das Instrument der Verketzerung, seine Politisierung und der Bedarf nach einer Neubeurteilung der Scharia und der Apostasiefrage im Islam" (English translation of the title: "The Instrument of branding Someone as a Heretic, its Politicization, and the need for a new Assessment of Sharia and the Question of Apostasy in Islam"). Badry recognizes that up to the present days there is a distinct preponderance of a "pre-modern, traditional" viewpoint of apostasy which as a consequence condemns apostates.[56]

Bülent Ucar points out in his article, for which he exclusively takes Turkish sources besides using secondary literature from the Western context, that with respect to the intra-Islamic discussion on apostasy about the justification of the death penalty in Turkey, there are "self-appointed extremists"[57]. He takes a position insofar as he judges the present day insistence on the necessity of the death penalty for apostates as outdated. This is due to the idea that capital punishment can only be understood in connection with actions which are hostile to the state or which are "warlike acts" which as a general rule apostates no longer have in mind. Additionally, a prohibition on changing religions goes against the exercise of free will,

---

54 Ayoub. "Freedom".

55 Susanne Olsson. "Apostasy in Egypt. Contemporary Cases of Ḥisbah" in: *MW* 98/1 (2008), pp. 95-115.

56 Roswitha Badry. "Das Instrument der Verketzerung, seine Politisierung und der Bedarf nach einer Neubeurteilung der 'Scharia' und der Apostasiefrage im Islam" in: Thorsten Gerald Schneiders (ed.). *Islamverherrlichung. Wenn die Kritik zum Tabu wird.* VS Verlag: Wiesbaden, 2010, pp. 117-129, here p. 124.

57 Bülent Ucar. "Die Todesstrafe für Apostaten in der Scharia. Traditionelle Standpunkte und neuere Interpretationen zur Überwindung eines Paradigmas der Abgrenzung" in: Hansjörg Schmid u.a. (ed.). *Identität durch Differenz? Wechselseitige Abgrenzungen in Christentum und Islam.* Verlag Friedrich Pustet: Regensburg, 2007, pp. 227-244, here p. 229.

which God, who is just, intended for humankind. This is also an example of a mixture of scholarly treatment and personal opinion.[58]

Silvia Tellenbach's 2001 essay "Die Apostasie im islamischen Recht" (English translation of the title: "Apostasy under Islamic Law") is more strongly oriented towards actual cases of apostasy.[59] She initially treats the classic legal doctrine on apostasy in order to then point out the contradictory situation. On the one hand, in modernity one finds that most Islamic states are committed to religious freedom in their constitutions. On the other hand, however, this ends at the desire to turn from Islam. Tellenbach mentions what is alongside the call made by contemporary scholars for capital punishment for apostate, in her view, a moderate position which has been advocated since the 1950s. It seeks to desist from punishment in the case of what is effectively privately held unbelief. Anne F. Broadbridge's essay from 2006, entitled "Apostasy Trials in Eighth/Fourteenth Century Egypt and Syria: A Case Study,"[60] details a number of cases of executions of apostates in Cairo and Damascus at the time of Mamluk rule, while Declan O'Sullivan, in his paper entitled "Egyptian Cases of Blasphemy and Apostasy against Islam: *Takfir al-Muslim*" (the prohibition against attacking those accused) turns his attention to a number of cases of apostasy in modern Egypt.[61] David Cook's essay from 2006, called "Apostasy from Islam: A Historical Perspective"[62] focuses on depictions of the early days of Islam as well as a number of individual cases of apostasy up to the 14th century but does not take up the discussion and concrete incidents relating to modern times.

---

58 Ibid., pp. 243-244.

59 Silvia Tellenbach. "Die Apostasie im islamischen Recht," 2006. http://www.gair.de/pdf/publikationen/tellenbach_apostasie.pdf (15.4. 2014). The essay originally appeared in Italian under the title "L'apostasia nel diritto islamico" in: *Daimon – Annuario di diritto camparato delle religioni* 1 (2001), pp. 53-70.

60 Anne F. Broadbridge. "Apostasy Trials in Eighth/Fourteenth Century Egypt and Syria: A Case Study" in: Judith Pfeiffer; Sholeh A. Quinn (ed.), *History and Historiography of Post-Mongol Central Asia and the Middle East. Studies in Honor of John E. Woods*. Harrassowitz: Wiesbaden, 2006, pp. 363-382.

61 Declan O'Sullivan. "Egyptian Cases of Blasphemy and Apostasy against Islam: *Takfir al-Muslim* (Prohibition against Attacking those Accused)" in: *IJHR* 7/2 (2003), pp. 97-137.

62 Cook. Apostasy.

Only very few papers go into the last mentioned approach and turn their attention to the concrete description of apostates and the actual extent of religious freedom in individual regions or states. Launching from the few remarks in the Quran and tradition on the topic of apostasy and the 1948 UN Universal Declaration of Human Rights, for instance, Sami A. Aldeeb Abu-Sahlieh explicates the contradiction between the constitutionally guaranteed religious freedom and the actual prohibition on turning away from Islam in numerous Muslim majority states.[63] He treats a number of laws which have consequences for family law, and briefly names individual cases such as the execution of Maḥmūd Muḥammad Ṭāhā in the Sudan as well as Farağ Fūda in Egypt and additionally names individual advocates and opponents of the death penalty for apostasy. Individual authors, such as Anh Nga Longva and Egdunas Racius, have dealt with the presentation of individual charges of apostasy at the end of the 20th century,[64] for instance Mandana Knust Rassekh Afshar addressed the case of Abdur Rahman in Afghanistan.[65]

e) Books published on the Topic of Apostasy: Only a few of the more comprehensive publications place the topic of apostasy as such in the center, but up until now they have almost exclusively dealt with the early days of Islam up to the late Middle Ages. Yohanan Friedmann's study *Tolerance and Coercion in Islam. Interfaith Relations in the Muslim Tradition*, organizes dealings with apostates in the early days of Islam within the framework of classic Islamic theology and how it has been positioned with respect to tolerance and the assessment of other religions.[66] In his essay

---

63 Sami A. Aldeeb Abu-Sahlieh. "Le Délit d'Apostasie aujourd'hui et ses Conséquences en Droit Arabe et Musulman" in: *ISCH* (20) 1994, pp. 93-116.

64 Longva. "Apostasy Law"; Egdunas Racius. "Limits of Application of the Šarī'a in Modern Kuwait: The Case Study of Apostasy of Ḥusayn Qambar ᶜAlī, a Convert from Islam to Christianity" in: SAI 7 (1999), pp. 5-21.

65 Mandana Knust Rassekh Afshar. "The Case of an Afghan Apostate – The Right to a Fair Trial between Islamic Law and Human Rights in the Afghan Constitution." http://www.mpil.de/shared/data/pdf/knust,_case_of_an_afghan_apostate.pdf (26.7.2011).

66 Yohanan Friedmann. *Tolerance and Coercion in Islam. Interfaith Relations in the Muslim Tradition*, Cambridge University Press: Cambridge, 2003, especially pp. 121-159.

"Die Anwendung des Apostasieurteils bei aš-Šāfiʿī und al-Ġazālī"[67] (English translation of the title: "The Application of Judgments against Apostasy in aš-Šāfiʿī und al-Ġazālī") and later more comprehensively in his detailed study entitled "Apostasie und Toleranz im Islam. Die Entwicklung zu al-Ġazālīs Urteil gegen die Philosophie und die Reaktionen der Philosophen" (English translation of the title: "Apostasy and Tolerance in Islam. The Development up to al-Ġazālī's verdict against Philosophy and the Reaction of Philosophers"), Frank Griffel directs his primary concentration at the condemnation of new Platonic and Aristotelian philosophy at the beginning of the 12th century,[68] while in the center of a study published under the pseudonym Ibn Warraq and entitled "Leaving Islam. Apostates Speak out," 25 autobiographical pieces depict the various motives prior Muslims from all parts of the world have for their turning from Islam.[69] Based on Ibn Warraqs publications and other databases, Mohammad Hassan Khalil and Mucahit Bilici, in their essay "Conversion out of Islam: A Study of Conversion Narratives of Former Muslims," depict in short form the motives for conversions and their various contexts.[70]

A certain exception to specific studies is the legal dissertation by Katharina Knüppel entitled "Religionsfreiheit und Apostasie in islamisch geprägten Staaten"[71] (English title translation: "Religious Freedom and Apostasy in Countries characterized by Islam"). The tension between a Sharia-based understanding of human rights and religious freedom and a UN-defined stands in the center of the Knüppel's work. After a presentation of the emergence and main features of Islamic law from the perspective of jurisprudence, the author, exclusively using sources in German, English, and French, comes to discuss the topic of apostasy in the final

---

67 Frank Griffel. "Die Anwendung des Apostasieurteils bei aš-Šāfiʿī und al-Ġazālī" in: Stefan Wild; Hartmut Schild (eds.). *Akten des 27. Orientalistentages: Norm und Abweichung*. Ergon Verlag: Würzburg, 1998, pp. 353-362.

68 Frank Griffel. *Apostasie und Toleranz im Islam. Die Entwicklung zu al-Ġazālīs Urteil gegen die Philosophie und die Reaktionen der Philosophen*. E. J. Brill: Leiden, 2000.

69 Ibn Warraq (ed.). *Leaving Islam. Apostates Speak Out*, Promotheus Books: Amherst, 2003.

70 Mohammad Hassan Khalil; Mucahit Bilici. "Conversion out of Islam: A Study of Conversion Narratives of Former Muslims" in: *MW* 97/1 (2007), pp. 111-124.

71 Katharina Knüppel. *Religionsfreiheit und Apostasie in islamisch geprägten Staaten*. Peter Lang: Frankfurt, 2010.

third of her study. There she initially sketches out classic Islamic law, with its civil law consequences in the case of apostasy and finally, by means of a number of examples, sketches out dealings with apostates in selected Muslim majority countries.

By far the most detailed analysis of the situation regarding the topic of apostasy is the study published in December 2011 by Paul Marshall and Nina Shea entitled *Silenced. How Apostasy & Blasphemy Codes are Choking Freedom Worldwide*. It treats numerous charges of apostasy relating to individual countries, and it also goes into international conflicts which have to do with the topic of apostasy; the study does not, however, go into Islamic theology and its representatives in the past and present.[72]

f) Textual Studies on the Basis of the Positions on Apostasy taken by Muslim Scholars: Only very few studies place the writings of contemporary theologians on apostasy in the center of their research and classify the argumentation of these writings and their significance in the context of the authorship and the history of their literary reception:

One of the few examples is the essay by Armin Hasemann published in 2002 entitled "Zur Apostasiediskussion im Modernen Ägypten" (English translation of the title: "On the Discussion of Apostasy in modern Egypt"), which in large part dealt with Maḥmūd Muḥammad Mazrūᶜa's 1994 document *aḥkām ar-ridda wa-'l-murtaddīn min ḫilāl šahādatay al-Ġazālī wa-Mazrūᶜa*.[73] In this document Maḥmūd Muḥammad Mazrūᶜa published his own position as well as that of the preacher and prior Muslim Brotherhood activist Muḥammad al-Ġazālī, with which Mazrūᶜa primarily justified the murder of the Egyptian intellectual and journalist Farağ Fūda in broad daylight on June 8, 1992 as an act of self defense. The murder came only days after a group of al-Azhar students openly accused Fūda of blasphemy. The second part of the essay addresses the definitions of apostasy in early legal literature and their consequences under criminal law. In the final pages there is an outlook to the 19th and 20th centuries in which, Hasemann supposes, there is still a majority of Azhar scholars who could be seen to prin-

72 Paul Marshall; Nina Shea. *Silenced. How Apostasy & Blasphemy Codes are Choking Freedom Worldwide*. Oxford University Press: Oxford, 2011.

73 Armin Hasemann. "Zur Apostasiediskussion im Modernen Ägypten" in: *WI* 42/1 (2002), pp. 72-121.

cipally lean in Mazrūᶜa's direction.[74] This is the case even if there are voices of "moderate Islamic reform," and Hasemann specifically mentions Rašīd Riḍā, Muḥammad ᶜAbduh, Maḥmūd Šaltūt, and (the Pakistani judge) S. A. Rahman.[75] They viewed the execution of an apostate solely on the basis of his apostasy as unwarranted. On the other hand, he did not distance himself from a Sharia-based justification of the death penalty per se.

From this overview it becomes clear that the writings and positions of influential theologians on the topic of apostasy have up until now almost remained unnoticed, although through their statements they play a key role in the production of a social climate working either in favor of or to the disadvantage of apostates. Furthermore, in today's media age, these ideas are imparted throughout the world over the internet, radio, and television, in addition to the traditional book market and mosques.

1.4. Why Pay Attention to the Positions Prominent Theologians Have on Apostasy?

In order to be able to more closely illuminate the argumentation and, alongside that, the effects of the writings of influential theologians in producing a social climate with respect to the question of apostasy, three contemporary 20th century theologians who have theological as well as sociopolitical influence will be introduced: Examining Yūsuf al-Qaraḍāwī (1926-), Abdullah Saeed (1960-), and Abū l-Aᶜlā Maudūdī (1903-1979) means that different regional areas, namely the Middle East, parts of Asia, Australia, and Europe will all be brought into focus.

The three theologians named could be designated global players. They have gained their reputation through their geographically broad publication

[74] This is all the more the case when al-Azhar repeatedly came forth with legal opinions denouncing intellectuals and scholars as apostates. These statements were off the beaten path of the common al-Azhar theological line of thought and affirmed that the apostate was to be punished with death according to tradition. Comp. on this: Sabine Damir-Geilsdorf. "Der islamische Fundamentalismus und seine muslimischen Gegner" in: Wolfgang Achtner; Holger Böckel; Doris Kreuzkamp (ed.). *Notwendige Fundamente – gefährlicher Fundamentalismus? Giessener Hochschulgespräche & Hochschulpredigten der ESG*, *WS* 03/04, Gießen 2004, pp. 71-95, here p. 90.

[75] Hasemann. "Apostasiediskussion", here p. 113.

activity on several continents, through the translations of their writings into numerous languages, on the basis of their offices and positions in influential as well as political committees, their economic independence, their cooperation with government institutions, their influence on political processes, and their influence based on their recourse to modern media in order to strengthen the wide range of influence they exert.

All three theologians are not only authors, scholars, and preachers who exercise limited local influence on their listeners in the mosque or in the lecture hall. Rather, they are also successful messengers of their concerns. They present these concerns to a global circle of listeners in a manner enhanced by modern media. They personally train decision makers, consult them, and exert lasting influence on politics and society through their expertise and networking with local and supra-regional powers that be. It is this connection to society and politics in particular which makes them interesting protagonists on the stage of contention over the ever increasingly insistent call raised for comprehensive freedom of religion and freedom of speech.

Given their statements on apostasy and their influence as theologians on politics and society, they contribute to the shaping of the social climate responsible for the evaluation and treatment of apostates in situ. All three dramatis personae have published independent works on the topic of apostasy which take the center position in my textual analysis and are complemented by the integration of other publications by the authors on the topic of religious freedom, freedom of speech, human rights, and minority rights. In the process, it appears absolutely essential to me to break down the works of the three authors on apostasy in detail in order to understand the differences in what in part are, at first glance, their very similar sounding arguments. It is also important to classify their positions against the backdrop of their biographical background and their complete works as authors and to compare them with each other.

Yūsuf al-Qaraḍāwī (1926-) can, on the basis of his numerous as well as influential offices around the globe, on the basis of the large number of book publications of around 120 titles, his *fatāwā*, articles, public addresses, sermons, and his broad teaching and consulting activity for various banks and financial institutions, his enduring media presence with his own television program on al-Jazeera, and his extensive use of the internet with a number of his own web sites nowadays, perhaps count as the most influential Sunnite theologian alive today.

With his classic training in Islamic theology and jurisprudence at al-Azhar, where he received his doctorate in 1973 with a dissertation on alms-giving (*zakāt*), his activity and influence as founder of a number of scholarly committees such as the European Council for Fatwa and Research (ECFR) and the International Union of Muslim Scholars (IUMS), and his ideological rootedness in the Muslim Brotherhood, he is effective not only as a multiplier for these institutions but also as one of the most important architects of "minority rights" (*fiqh al-aqallīyāt*). He permanently promotes his method of interpretation of "centrism and moderation" (*fiqh al-aqallīyāt*) and thus offers Muslim youth, in the Western diaspora in particular, a paradigm for action and identity which marks him off not only as a theologian but also as a socio-political personality very concertedly embroiled in the debate concerning modernity. He also markets his positions on what is "allowed" and what is "forbidden" with a great authority and media impact.

Although Yūsuf al-Qaraḍādawī has been a strong presence journalistically as well as over other media, in recent years he has increasingly become the focus of academic studies. In the beginning, these studies more generally treated his biography, his offices, and his media presence, while in the meantime, after publications about his personal profile became more numerous, they have concentrated on individual aspects of his work.

Among the comprehensive individual investigations which have been published as monographs or collective volumes, there is Nadia Wardeh's master's thesis from 2001 entitled "Yūsuf al-Qaraḍāwī and the 'Islamic Awakening' of the late 20th century." It places al-Qaraḍāwī's concept of "Islamic awakening" in the center of her study.[76]

In his 2005 study going by the title "Islamische Ethik und moderne Gesellschaft im Islamismus" (English translation of the title: "Islamic Ethics and Modern Society in the Islamism of Yusuf al-Qaradawi"), Wendelin Wenzel-Teuber deals with all of al-Qaraḍāwī's works up to the year 1995 in a type of overview of al-Qaraḍāwī's political ethics – in my opinion,

76 Nadia Wardeh. "Yūsuf al-Qaraḍāwī and the "Islamic Awakening" of the late 20th century," M.A. thesis atMcGill University: Montreal, 2001.

however, not very focused if viewed thematically.[77] In 2006 a study was done by Florian Remien, likewise designed as a master's thesis. It offered a comparison of Yūsuf al-Qaraḍāwī's, Tariq Ramadan's und Charles Taylor's stock taking of Muslims' current situation in European society. He illuminates this with respect to al-Qaraḍāwī against the background of the Islamic awakening of the Muslim minority.[78]

In 2009 Samuel Helfont published a detailed monograph on Yūsuf al-Qaraḍāwī at the University of Tel Aviv's Moshe Dayan Center for Middle Eastern and African Studies. It was entitled "Yusuf al-Qaradawi, Islam and Modernity" and addressed al-Qaraḍāwī's relationship to modernity, to *ǧihād*, to non-Muslims, to democracy, and to the status of women. However, he limited himself to non-Arab source texts, meaning that he did not consider Yūsuf al-Qaraḍāwī's numerous Arabic publications.[79]

On the basis of Arabic texts, Carsten Polanz's master's thesis, "Yūsuf al-Qaraḍāwīs Konzept der Mitte bei der Unterscheidung zwischen Jihad und Terrorismus nach dem 11. September" (English translation of the title: "Yūsuf al-Qaraḍāwī's Concept of Centrism in the Differentiation between Jihad and Terrorism after September 11") grappled with al-Qaraḍāwī's concept of *wasaṭīya* as it applied to differentiating between terrorism and *ǧihād*.[80]

Bettina Gräf has intensively dealt with varous aspects of al-Qaraḍāwī's life and work in the collected volume published together with Jakob Skovgaard-Petersen in 2009 entitled *Global Mufti. The Phenomenon of Yusuf al-Qaradawi*[81] and most recently in 2010 in her dissertation "Medien-Fatwas@Yusuf al-Qaradawi. Die Popularisierung des islamischen Rechts (English translation of the title: "Media-Fatwas@Yusuf al-Qaradawi. The

---

77 Wendelin Wenzel-Teuber. *Islamische Ethik und moderne Gesellschaft im Islamismus von Yusuf al-Qaradawi*. Dr. Kovač: Hamburg 2005.

78 Florian Remien. *Muslime in Europa: Westlicher Staat und islamische Identität. Untersuchungen zu Ansätzen von Yūsuf al-Qaraḍāwī*, Tariq Ramadan und Charles Taylor. EB-Verlag: Schenefeld, 2007.

79 Samuel Helfont. *Yusuf al-Qaradawi, Islam and Modernity*. Moshe Dayan Center for Middle Eastern and African Studies: Tel Aviv University, 2009.

80 Carsten Polanz. *Yūsuf al-Qaraḍāwīs Konzept der Mitte bei der Unterscheidung zwischen Jihad und Terrorismus nach dem 11. September 2001*, EB Verlag: Berlin, 2010.

81 Jakob Skovgaard-Petersen; Bettina Gräf (ed.). *Global Mufti. The Phenomenon of Yusuf al-Qaradawi*. Hurst & Company: London, 2009.

Popularization of Islamic law").[82] The first named collection of essays treats al-Qaraḍāwī's formal and informal connections with influential institutions – in particular the connections with al-Azhar and the Muslim Brotherhood. It also addresses his position of authority and his influence in Europe as well as in the media, his position with respect to women's rights, his concept of centrism *(wasaṭīya)*, and finally his interpretation and application of Islamic law according to the principle of *maṣlaḥa*.

What is more, there are a number of essays which have appeared on the al-Qaraḍāwī phenomenon: In his treatise "Fiqh al-Aqalliyyat: A Legal Theory for Muslim Minorities", Shammai Fishman analyzed al-Qaraḍāwī's concept of minority rights *(fiqh al-aqallīyāt)*. Fishman makes al-Qaraḍāwī out to be one of the founders of this right at the beginning of the 1990s.[83] Jörg Schlabach, in his master's thesis, *Scharia im Westen. Muslime unter nicht-islamischer Herrschaft und die Entwicklung eines muslimischen Minderheitenrechts für Europa* (English translation of the title: "The Sharia in the West. Muslims under non-Muslim Rule and the Development of Muslims' Minority Rights in Europe") dealt with, among others, Yūsuf al-Qaraḍāwī's particular legal understanding.[84]

This topic was addressed in more depth and put into a study by Sarah Albrecht in her investigation entitled *Islamisches Minderheitenrecht. Yūsuf al-Qaraḍāwīs Konzept des fiqh al-aqallīyāt* (English translation of the title: *Islamic Minority Law. Yūsuf al-Qaraḍāwī's Concept of fiqh al-aqallīyāt*),[85] while Ursi Schweizer's monograph *Muslime in Europa. Staatsbürgerschaft und Islam in einer liberalen und säkularen Demokratie* (English translation of the title: *Citizenship and Islam in a liberal and secular Democracy*) deals with, among others, al-Qaraḍāwī's statements on the relationship of Islamic religious adherence and citizenship as well as

---

82 Bettina Gräf. *Medien-Fatwas@Yusuf al-Qaradawi. Die Popularisierung des islamischen Rechts*, Klaus Schwarz: Berlin, 2010.

83 Shammai Fishman. "Fiqh al-Aqalliyyat: A Legal Theory for Muslim Minorities," Research Monographs on the Muslim World, Series No. 1, Paper No. 2, October 2006. Hudson Institute: Washington, 2006, pp. 1-18.

84 Jörg Schlabach. *Scharia im Westen. Muslime unter nicht-islamischer Herrschaft und die Entwicklung eines muslimischen Minderheitenrechts für Europa*. Lit Verlag: Berlin, 2009.

85 Sarah Albrecht. *Islamisches Minderheitenrecht. Yūsuf al-Qaraḍāwīs Konzept des fiqh al-aqallīyāt*, Ergon: Würzburg, 2010.

his notion of the question of Muslims' political participation in democracies.[86]

In addition, there are numerous essays and shorter articles which have appeared and which deal with the person and various aspects of al-Qaraḍāwī's life and work: Again, those which can be named in particular include Bettina Gräf, who addressed al-Qaraḍāwī in a number of articles – on the characterization of al-Qaraḍāwī as a reformer, for instance[87] – as well as spending a part of her master's thesis on a *fatwā* on political Islam[88] and on al-Qaraḍāwī's internet presence,[89] in particular his page IslamOnline.[90]

Furthermore, Anne Sofie Roald goes into al-Qaraḍāwī's political influence in the media,[91] Barbara Stowasser into his *fatāwā* on women's rights,[92] and Janet Kursawe discusses the partly contradictory position al-Qaraḍāwī holds between extremism and liberalism.[93] Ermete Mariani treats al-Qaraḍāwī's immense authority through market globalization and globalization of the media;[94] similar work has been done by Jakob Skovgaard-Petersen, who points in particular to al-Qaraḍāwī's omnipresence due to

---

86 Ursi Schweizer. *Muslime in Europa. Staatsbürgerschaft und Islam in einer liberalen und säkularen Demokratie*, Klaus Schwarz: Berlin, 2008.

87 Bettina Gräf. "Yūsuf al-Qaradāwī: Das Erlaubte und das Verbotene im Islam" in: Katajun Amirpur; Ludwig Ammann (eds.). *Der Islam am Wendepunkt. Liberale und konservative Reformer einer Weltreligion*. Herder: Freiburg, 2006, pp. 109-117.

88 Bettina Gräf. *Islamische Gelehrte als politische Akteure im globalen Kontext. Eine Fatwa von Yusuf ᶜAbdallah al-Qaradawi. Diskussionspapiere 93*, Klaus Schwarz Verlag: Berlin, 2003.

89 Bettina Gräf. "Sheikh Yūsuf al-Qaraḍāwī in Cyberspace" in: *WI* 47 (2007), pp. 403-421.

90 Bettina Gräf. "IslamOnline.net: Independent, interactive, popular" in: *AMS* 4 (2008).

91 Anne Sofie Roald. "The Wise Men: Democratization and Gender Equalization in the Islamic Message: Yūsuf al-Qaraḍāwī and Aḥmad al-Kubaisī on the Air" in: *Encounters* 7/1 (2001), pp. 29-55.

92 Barbara Stowasser. "Old Shaykhs, Young Women, and the Internet: The Rewriting of Women's Political Rights in Islam" in: *MW* 91/1&2 (2001), pp. 99-119.

93 Janet Kursawe. "Yusūf ᶜAbdallāh al-Qarāḍawī (sic) (Yusuf Abdallah al-Qaradawi)" in: *Orient* 44/4 (2003), pp. 523-530.

94 Ermete Mariani, "Youssef Al-Qaradawi: Pouvoir Médiatique, Économique et Symbolique" in: Frank Mermier (ed.). *Mondialisation et nouveaux médias dans l'espace arabe*. Maisonneuve & Larose, Paris, 2003, pp. 195-203.

his extensive use of the media.[95] Noah Feldman illuminates al-Qaraḍāwī's notion of the Sharia and his understanding arising out of it as far as the relationship between Islam and democracy are concerned.[96] Ana Belén Soage treats al-Qaraḍāwī as an influential and leading figure for the Muslim community, which as its own authority acts to sanction at some points and reprove at others,[97] as well as al-Qaraḍāwī's membership in the Muslim Brotherhood.[98]

Wendelin Wenzel-Teuber emphasizes al-Qaraḍāwī's own interpretive sovereignty in questions of Islamic law,[99] and Nina Wiedl, within the framework of her investigation of *da^cwa* in Europe, goes into al-Qaraḍāwī's attitude towards the permanent residency of Muslims in Europe.[100] The most recent publication on al-Qaraḍāwī could be the investigation *Islamist Rhetoric. Language and culture in contemporary Egypt* which is a comparative analysis of a number of publicly effective exponents of Islamic theology and preaching by Jakob Høigilt, who therein analyzes the significant linguistic stylistic tools in al-Qaraḍāwī's works.[101]

None of the publications named up to now deal with al-Qaraḍāwī's attitude towards the topic of apostasy. What exists on this topic up to the present time is only a portion of an essay by Gudrun Krämer entitled

---

95 Jakob Skovgaard-Petersen. "The Global Mufti" in: Birgit Schaebler; Leif Stenberg (ed.). *Globalizsation and the Muslim World. Culture, Religion and Modernity.* Syracuse University Press: New York, 2004, pp. 153-165.

96 Noah Feldman. "Shari'a and Islamic Democracy in the Age of al-Jazeera" in: Abbas Amanat; Frank Griffel (eds.). *Shari'a. Islamic Law in the Contemporary Context*, Stanford University Press: Stanford, 2007, pp. 104-119.

97 Ana Belén Soage. "Shaykh Yusuf Al-Qaradawi: Portrait of a Leading Islamic Cleric" in: *MERIA* 12/1 (2008), pp. 51-68.

98 Ana Belén Soage. "Yusuf al-Qaradawi: The Muslim Brothers' Favorite Ideological Guide" in: Barry Rubin (ed.). *The Muslim Brotherhood. The Organization and Policies of a Global Islamist Movement.* Palgrave Macmillan: New York, 2010, pp. 19-37.

99 Wendelin Wenzel-Teuber. "Yūsuf al-Qaraḍāwī – Wenn ein arabischer Fernsehprediger das Denken übernimmt" in: Thorsten Gerald Schneiders (ed.). *Islamverherrlichung. Wenn die Kritik zum Tabu wird*, VS Verlag: Wiesbaden, 2010, pp. 277-285.

100 Nina Wiedl. *Da'wa – Der Ruf zum Islam in Europa.* Verlag Hans Schiler: Berlin, 2008, pp. 134-172.

101 Jakob Høigilt. *Islamist Rhetoric. Language and culture in contemporary Egypt.* Routledge: London, 2011.

"Drawing Boundaries: Yūsuf al-Qaraḍāwī on Apostasy."[102] In the second, shorter segment of the essay, after a presentation of al-Qaraḍāwī's life and work, the author summarizes a number of statements made in his work *ǧarīmat ar-ridda wa-ᶜuqūbat al-murtadd fī ḍau' al-qur'ān wa-'s-sunna* dating from 1996. An actual presentation, classification, and evaluation of the position al-Qaraḍāwī takes on apostasy, however, is not available. An essay, likewise from the pen of Gudrun Krämer, on al-Qaraḍāwī's assessment of non-Muslims under the heading "New fiqh applied. Yusuf al-Qaradawi on Non-Muslims in Islamic Societies," altogether deals only shortly with al-Qaraḍāwī's position on apostasy.[103]

Abdullah Saeed (1960-), who was born on the Maldives, was educated in Pakistan and completed the first portion of his studies up to the receipt of his B.A. in Arabic and Islamic Studies in Saudi Arabia. Thereafter, he moved to Australia and received his doctorate. Since 2003 he has held a position as the Sultan of Oman Professor of Arab and Islamic Studies at the University of Melbourne and is the Director of the Centre for the Study of Contemporary Islam at the University of Melbourne.

Up to the present time, Abdullah Saeed has published and edited close to 20 independent works, among them works on the interpretation of the Quran, on the theory of political rule, on Islam in Australia and Indonesia, and on Islamic finance, on which a comprehensive monograph entitled *Islamic Banking and Interest* was published by the prestigious publisher E. J. Brill.[104] Additionally, he has published a four volume Arabic grammar. A number of his books have been translated into Italian, Portuguese, and Indonesian. Furthermore, he has published numerous collected volumes and a number of academic articles on the topics of Islamic family law, questions related to the integration of Muslims in Western societies, human rights, Quranic hermeneutics, the role of the *ᶜulamā'* in modern societies, financial affairs as well as on *iǧtihād* (independent reasoning) and Jihādism and on the question of the justification of suicide attacks.

---

102 Gudrun Krämer. "Drawing Boundaries: Yūsuf al-Qaraḍāwī on Apostasy" in: Gudrun Krämer; Sabine Schmidtke (eds.). *Speaking for Islam. Religious Authorities in Muslim Societies*. E. J. Brill: Leiden, 2006, pp. 181-217.

103 Gudrun Krämer. "New fiqh applied. Yusuf al-Qaradawi on Non-Muslims in Islamic Societies" in: *JSAI* 36 (2009).

104 Abdullah Saeed. *Islamic Banking and Interest. A Study of the Prohibition of Riba and its Contemporary Interpretation*. E. J. Brill: Leiden, 1996.

With his brother, the former Attorney General of the Maldives, Hassan Saeed, he composed a detailed work on the topic of apostasy in Islam. It is entitled *Freedom of Religion, Apostasy and Islam*,[105] in which the unconditional call is made to revise apostasy legislation found in classical Islamic law and in which complete freedom of religion is justified from source texts of Islam.

Abdullah Saeed's significance lies on the one hand in his widespread activity in a number of countries in Asia, of which his numerous invitations, conference addresses as well as his publications on the three continents of Europe, Australia, and Asia bear eloquent witness. His connections to Indonesia appear to be particularly intensive. Additionally, he consults the Australian government with respect to questions of integration of the Muslim minority, and his publishing of domestic studies in cooperation with various governmental institutions means that his expositions have international reach. Since the translation of his work appears to have just begun, the apex of Abdullah Saeed's prominence and influence still lie ahead. No publications exist on the person and work of Abdullah Saeed as well as on his view of apostasy.

Abū l-Aᶜlā Maudūdī (1903-1979) counts as one of the most prominent and consistent masterminds for an Islamic state, and he has engaged himself politically for its realization since India was divided and Pakistan was formed in 1947. His writings, in which he trumpets a constitution and societal order thoroughly molded by Islam, in which Islam alone should be the sole identity and basis of the legal system and of legislation. His political engagement played a significant role in the definition of Pakistan as an Islamic state. One finds in part that his documents reach into the present and provide a framework for configuring the relationship to non-Sunnite minorities (e.g., the Aḥmadīya movement) and define the extent to which religious freedom and human rights extend for those who think differently.

Abū l-Aᶜlā Maudūdī's opinions, which he disseminated in sermons, books, radio addresses, legal opinions, letters, and pamphlets as well as in his commentary on the Quran, *Tafhīm al-Qur'ān*, which has been translated into several languages, were reinforced by the founding of *Jamā'at-i-Islāmī* in 1941. It was initially active as a movement, then as a lobbying

[105] Abdullah Saeed; Hassan Saeed. *Freedom of Religion, Apostasy and Islam*. Ashgate: Aldershot, 2004.

group, and, beginning in 1957, also as a political party for the formation of an Islamic state. Additionally, as its *amīr*, Abū l-Aᶜlā Maudūdī, exercised continuing influence through the formulation of the first Pakistani constitution in 1956.

An additional field of intensive influence came when Maudūdī was speaker and ringleader of one of numerous *ᶜulamā'*, which brought agitation against the Aḥmadīya movement from 1953 onwards and had its dramatic crowning moment in 1974 when the Aḥmadīya were excluded from the Islamic community due to Maudūdī's close connections to the Muslim World League. The head of the government in the 1980s, Zia ul-Haqq, who was massively supported and advised by Maudūdī and the *Jamā'at-i-Islāmī,* extended and exacerbated the *Blasphemy Laws* which have up to the present day led to a flood of arbitrary charges, imprisonments, and violence against the weakest members of the society – above all adherents of the Aḥmadīya movement, Christians, and converts. This denouncing of the minority Aḥmadīya movement, cast in the form of concrete laws, had already been given a comprehensive ideological-theological justification in 1953.

Abū l-Aᶜlā Maudūdī is frequently labeled the most influential Islamic activist and theologian of the 20th century.[106] His influence can be traced up to the present Islamist and jihādistic movements. This pertains particularly to his understanding of the sovereignty of God *(ḥākimīyat allāh)*, which actually sees the implementation of Islam as first coming through its societal and political implementation. Maudūdī authored 138 independent works,[107] of which a number of them were translated into numerous languages such as French, Russian, Arabic, Persian, Indonesian, and Malaysian. The translated works in English and Arabic, in particular, as well as his even more popular multi-volume commentary on the Quran entitled

---

106 For instance according to Abdul Rashid Moten. "Islamic Thought in Contemporary Pakistan: The Legacy of ᶜAllāma Mawdūdī" in: Ibrahim Abu-Rabi' (ed.). *The Blackwell Companion to Contemporary Islamic Thought*. Blackwell Publishing: Malden, 2006, pp. 175-193, p. 177.

107 According to the count by Qazi Zulqadr Siddiqi; S. M. Aslam; M. M. Ahsan, "A Bibliography of Writings by and about Mawlānā Sayyid Abul Aᶜlā Mawdūdī" in: Khurshid Ahmad; Zafar Ishaq Ansari (eds.). *Islamic Perspectives. Studies in Honour of Mawlānā Sayyid Abul Aᶜlā Mawdūdī*, The Islamic Foundation: London/Saudi Publishing House: Jeddah, 1979, pp. 3-14.

Tafhīm al-Qur'ān continue to have an effect up into the third and fourth generations of Muslim immigrants in Western countries.[108]

Maudūdī's understanding of an integrated Islam and of a state oriented towards the Sharia as a basic prerequisite for the implementation of Islamic faith has been able to become deeply rooted through the connection of Maudūdī's person and literature with Sayyid Quṭb, Rūḥollāh Khomeinī, Ḥassan al-Bannā, and ᶜAbdallāh Yūsuf ᶜAzzām up to his protegé Usāma bin Lādin in Islamism and parts of Jihādism. For that reason, Maudūdī stands here not only as a journalist and theologian but rather as a political activist at the center of this study. Through his intensive political influence, he molded the ideological foundations of Pakistan long after his death.

There are predominantly Urdu language biographies from the viewpoint of adherents on Abū l-Aᶜlā Maudūdī's life and work which have been produced up to this point.[109] Examples are the biography by Syed As'ad Gilani, published originally in Urdu in 1962 and released in Arabic and English in 1978 with the title *"Maududi". Thought and Movement* and which include a number of Maudūdī's own testimonials.[110] Among the rather hagiographical depictions, one can also count the commemorative publication *Islamic Perspectives. Studies in Honour of Mawlānā Sayyid Abul Aᶜlā Mawdūdī*, released in the year of Maudūdī's death, 1979, by the British Islamic Foundation in cooperation with the Saudi Publishing House.[111] There is also Sarwat Saulat's depiction of Maudūdī's life and work entitled *Maulana Maududi*.[112]

---

108 Thus up to this day, the *Jamā'at-i-Islāmī, founded by* Abū l-Aᶜlā Maudūdī, dominates the British Islamic scene via "missions" works it started. Comp. on this the information in David Rich. "The Very Model of a very British Brotherhood" in: Barry Rubin (ed.). *The Muslim Brotherhood. The Organization and Policies of a Global Islamist Movement.* Palgrave Macmillan: New York, 2010, pp. 117-136, here p. 117.

109 Mir Mustansir noted relevantly in 1985: "A number of biographies of Mawdūdī have been written, most of them in Urdu and practically all of them of poor quality." Mustansir Mir. "Some Features of Mawdudi's Tafhīm al-Qur'ān" in: *AJISS* 2 (1985), pp. 233-244, here p. 233.

110 The publisher indicates that Gilanis' work involved the first biography of Maudūdī ever: Farooq Gilani. "Publisher's Note" in: Syed As'ad Gilani. *'Maududi'. Thought and Movement.* East & West Publishing Company: Karachi, 1978^5, p. XIV.

111 Ahmad; Ansari (eds.). *Perspectives.*

112 Sarwat Saulat. *Maulana Maududi.* International Islamic Publishers: Karachi, 1979.

Additionally, more comprehensive depictions of Maudūdī's biography and work include, for instance, three studies by Riaz Ahmad. The first, dating from 1969, is about Maudūdī as *homo politicus*. It expounds his political theories and spheres of influence and is entitled *The Concept of the Islamic State as found in the Writings of Abul A'la Madūdī*.[113] The second study dates from 1976 and is entitled *Maulana Maududi and the Islamic State*.[114] The third study is from 2004 and is entitled *Islam and Modern Political Institutions in Pakistan. A Study of Mawlana Mawdudi*.[115] Seyyid Vali Reza Nasr addresses Maudūdī's role as an activist in the diverse Islamic movement of the 20th century, initially in his essay "Mawdudi and the Jama'at-i Islami: The Origins, Theory and Practice of Islamic Revivalism"[116] and then more in detail in 1996 in his study *Mawdudi and the Making of Islamic Revivalism*.[117] In 2010, what was originally conceived as Sheikh Jameil Ali's doctoral dissertation at the University of Kashmir was published. It is entitled *Islamic Thought and Movement in the Subcontinent. A Study of Sayyid Abu A'la Mawdudi and Sayyid Abul Hassan Ali Nadwi*.[118] In it, Ali above all concerns himself with Maudūdī's understanding of the role of Islamic community as a political entity and its implementation in the *Jamā'at-i-Islāmī* movement.

Both of the newest academic depictions of Maudūdī's biography and works available in Germany are the 2011 study by Roy Jackson entitled "Mawlana Mawdudi and Politcal Islam,"[119] which critically addresses

---

113 Riaz Ahmad. *The Concept of the Islamic State as found in the Writings of Abul A'la Madūdī*. Ph.D. Thesis, op. cit., 1969.

114 Dr. Sayed Riaz Ahmad. *Maulana Maududi and the Islamic State*. People's Publishing House: Lahore, 1976.

115 Sayed Riaz Ahmad. *Islam and Modern Political Institutions in Pakistan. A Study of Mawlana Mawdudi*. Ferozsons Ltd.: Lahore, 2004.

116 Seyyid Vali Reza Nasr. "Mawdudi and the Jama'at-i Islami: The Origins, Theory and Practice of Islamic Revivalism" in: Ali Rahnema (ed.). *Pioneers of Islamic Revival*. Zed Books: London, 1994, pp. 98-124.

117 Seyyid Vali Reza Nasr. *Mawdudi and the Making of Islamic Revivalism*. Oxford University Press: Oxford, 1996.

118 Sheikh Jameil Ali. *Islamic Thought and Movement in the Subcontinent. A Study of Sayyid Abu A'la Mawdudi and Sayyid Abul Hassan Ali Nadwi*, D. K. Printworld Ltd: New Delhi, 2010.

119 Roy Jackson. *Mawlana Mawdudi & Political Islam. Authority and The Islamic State*. Routledge: London, 2011.

Maudūdī's theology and life work as well as the post doctoral thesis (German: Habilitationsschrift) by Peter Hartung entitled *A System of Life – Maudūdī and the Ideologisation of Islam*, which illuminates the important elements of Maudūdī's theology against the backdrop of the 20th century ideologies which flowed into this theology.[120]

Additionally, there are around 70 individual articles available about different aspects of Maudūdī's life and work. They are in part critically distanced and in part written from the perspective of adherents and admirers,[121] and only the more significant ones will be briefly mentioned here:

In 1980, H. Mintjes, with a work entitled "Mawlana Mawdudi's Last Years and the Resurgence of Fundamentalist Islam,"[122] illuminated the last three years of Maudūdī's life and his significance as a key figure in international Islamism. Eran Lerman, in his 1981 essay entitled "Mawdudi's Concept of Islam,"[123] expressly explained the Marxist body of thought found in Maudūdī's theology and political ideology. In 1983, Charles J. Adams' "Mawdudi and the Islamic State"[124] grappled essentially with the significant positions within Maudūdī's theological and political worldview. A. Rashid Moten, in his 1984 essay "Pure and Practical Ideology: The Thought of Mawlana Madudi (1903-1979)"[125] illuminated a number of foundational topics across works which characterize Maudūdī's life and work, such as Maudūdī's understanding of Islam and politics, his notion of commerce and history, his justification of the necessity of a revolution and an Islamic movement. In 1985, Mustansir Mir's "Some Features of Mawdudi's Tafhīm al-Qur'ān"[126] dealt with Maudūdī's content and mode

---

120 Jan-Peter Hartung. "A System of Life. Maudūdī and the Ideologisation of Islam". Hurst: London, 2013

121 As an example of a particularly well worked out hagiographic presentation of the person and work of Mawdūdī see for instance Malik B. Badri. "A Tribute to Mawlāna Mawdūdī from an Autobiographical Point of View" in: *MW* 93/3-4 (2003), pp. 487-502.

122 H. Mintjes. "Mawlana Mawdudi's Last Years and the Resurgence of Fundamentalist Islam" in: *al-mushir* 22 (1980), pp. 46-73.

123 Eran Lerman. "Mawdudi's Concept of Islam" in: *MES* 17/4 (1981), pp. 492-509.

124 Charles J. Adams. Mawdudi and the Islamic State" in: John L. Esposito (ed.). *Voices of Resurgent Islam*. Oxford University Press: New York, 1983, pp. 99-133.

125 A. Rashid Moten. "Pure and Practical Ideology: The Thought of Mawlana Madudi (1903-1979)" in: *IQ* 28/3 (1984), pp. 217-240.

126 Mir. "Features", in: *AJISS* 2 (1985), pp. 233-244.

of action between 1942 and his 1972 commentary on the Quran. In 1997, Seyed Abbas Araghchi's essay entitled "Islamic Theo-Democracy: The Political Ideas of Abul A'la Mawdudi" discussed Maudūdī's concept of political dominion.[127] In 2003 Zeenath Kauser illuminated significant differences between Maudūdī's concepts of democracy and rule and those of the West.[128]

In 2003, a collection of essays sympathetic to Maudūdī appeared as a "special issue" double edition of the journal *The Muslim World* and addressed the Maudūdī phenomenon The more significant essays treat the following aspects:

In his essay entitled "Mawdūdī's Critique of the Secular Mind," Tārik Jān grapples with Maudūdī's relationship to Western secularism and to Western ideologies such as Darwinism, Hegelianism, and Marxism.[129] In his treatment "Mawdūdī's Concept of Sharīᶜah," Anis Ahmad addresses Mawdūdī's frequent commitment to the necessity of a comprehensive application of the Sharia as well as his understanding of the Sharia.[130] M. Kamal Hassan illuminates the dissemination of Maudūdī's literature in a work entitled "The Influence of Mawdūdī's Thought on Muslims in Southeast Asia: A Brief Survey"[131] in Asian states with populations where there is a Muslim majority such as Malaysia, Indonesia, or Brunei Darussalam as well as in Southeast Asian societies with Muslim minorities, such as the Philippines, Thailand, Singapore, Cambodia, Vietnam, Myanmar, and Laos. In his treatment "Mawdūdī and the Transformation of Jamāᶜat-e-Islāmī in Pakistan,"[132] Abdul Rashid Moten addresses the transformation and development of the political movement of the *Jamācat-i-Islāmī*, which was founded by Mawdūdī. It acted for over thirty years as a political

---

127 Seyed Abbas Araghchi. "Islamic Theo-Democracy: The Political Ideas of Abul A'la Mawdudi" in: *IJIA* 8/4 (1997), pp. 772-797.

128 Zeenath Kauser. "Mawdudi on Democracy: A Critical Appreciation" in: *IQ* 47/4 (2003), pp. 303-331.

129 Tārik Jān. "Mawdūdī's Critique of the Secular Mind" in: *MW* 93/3-4 (2003), pp. 503-519.

130 Anis Ahmad. "Mawdūdī's Concept of Sharīᶜah" in: *MW* 93/3-4 (2003), pp. 533-545.

131 M. Kamal Hassan. "The Influence of Mawdūdī's Thought on Muslims in Southeast Asia: A Brief Survey" in: *MW* 93/3-4 (2003), pp. 429-464.

132 Abdul Rashid Moten. "Mawdūdī and the Transformation of Jamāᶜat-e-Islāmī in Pakistan" in: *MW* 93/3-4 (2003), pp. 391-413.

sounding board and as a multiplier and large support network for Mawdūdī's political activities. Omar Khalidi, with his "Mawlāna Mawdūdī and the Future Political Order in British India," attends to Mawdūdī's stance towards the partitioning of India,[133] and Fathi Osman occupies himself with the reception and dissemination of Mawdūdī's writings in Arabic speaking countries in his essay "Mawdūdī's Contribution to the Development of Modern Islamic Thinking in the Arab-Speaking World."[134]

Abdul Rashid Moten is likewise basically favorably disposed yet not uncritical regarding Mawdūdī's person and work in his 2006 essay entitled "Islamic Thought in Contemporary Pakistan: The Legacy of cAllāma Mawdūdī",[135] which also mentions the significant points of Mawdūdī's ideology, such as his view of an Islamic economy or his notion of the necessary revolution against the backdrop of the partitioning of Pakistan. M. Abdul Haq Ansari, in his 2006 article "Mawdūdī's Contribution to Theology," elucidates the main features of Mawdūdī's methodology and epistemology,[136] and Asma Afsaruddin analyses Mawdūdī's use of theological terms and content as being political and ideological at their core in her 2007 treatment "Mawdūdī's 'Theo-Democracy': How Islamic is it really?"[137]

It is also not Mawdūdī's biography, his complete works, and his conception of statehood which stand in the center of interest for the author with respect to Abū l-A^{c}lā Maudūdī. Rather, it is his understanding of religious freedom and apostasy as well as his notion of human rights and minority rights. His position on the topic of apostasy has up to this point not become a subject of academic investigation. Sajjad Idris has approached this subject area with his essay dating from 2003 and entitled "Reflections on Mawdūdī and Human Rights."[138] However, the author does not take into account Mawdūdī's actual publication on this topic, "Islam and Human

133 Omar Khalidi. Mawlāna Mawdūdī and the Future Political Order in British India" in: *MW* 93/3-4 (2003), pp. 415-427.

134 Fathi Osman. "Mawdūdī's Contribution to the Development of Modern Islamic Thinking in the Arab-Speaking World" in *MW* 93/3-4 (2003), S. 465-485.

135 Moten. "Thought".

136 M. Abdul Haq Ansari. "Mawdūdī's Contribution to Theology" in: *MW* 93/3-4 (2003), pp. 521-531.

137 Asma Afsaruddin. "Mawdūdī's 'Theo-Democracy': How Islamic is it really?" in: *OM* 87/1 (2007), pp. 301-325.

138 Sajjad Idris. "Reflections on Mawdūdī and Human Rights" in: *MW* 93/3-4 (2003), pp. 547-561.

Rights."[139] Rather, he limits itself to a number of aspects of his understanding of the superiority of Islam with respect to minority rights, human rights, and women's rights.

Apart from a few lines stating Mawdūdī's stance on apostasy in summary form in Tim Green's unpublished master's thesis "Factors affecting Attitudes to Apostasy in Pakistan,"[140] Anne-Liv Gamlem comes closest to the topic in her 2008 master's thesis entitled *Islamic Discourse of Difference: A Critical Analysis of Maulana Mawdudi's Texts on Kāfirs* and *Dhimmīs*.[141]" By means of two of Mawdūdī's texts, she grapples with his description and assessment of "non-believers" and of "wards". Otherwise, publications on Mawdūdī's assessment of apostasy and freedom of religion do not exist as of yet.

1.5. The Focus of the Study

The focus of the following study – from the viewpoint of the orientation as well as with respect to its breadth – consists of the interpretation of the three main writings of the mentioned authors on the topic of apostasy and the appraisal of them as well as their classification into the theology of the individual protagonists. Up to now, none of these writings – or writings of comparably influential protagonists – have been comprehensively appraised on the basis of their content, classified according to the context of their development and the theology of the authors, illuminated on the basis of their social relevance, and compared with differing positions found within the debate on apostasy. The lives and work of the three theologians are only presented in summary manner as background for the discussion about the respective sphere of activity and circle of influence of the authors.

It is precisely renowned theologians and the institutions for which they speak that are the co-actors in the production of a social climate in which –

---

139 Abu A'la Mawdudi. *Human Rights in Islam*. The Islamic Foundation: London, 1976/1990².

140 Tim Green. *Factors affecting Attitudes to Apostasy in Pakistan*, unpublished M.A. Thesis in the area of "Islamic Societies and Cultures," School of Oriental and African Studies: London, 1998, pp. 21-22.

141 Anne-Liv Gamlem. *Islamic Discourse of Difference: A Critical Analysis of Maulana Mawdudi's Texts on Kāfirs* and *Dhimmīs*. Masteroppgave i Sør-Asiastudier. Institutt for kulturstudier og orientalske språk: Universitetet i Oslo: Høsten 2008.

strengthened by the dispensation of justice, the media, and politics – rejection or perhaps the justification and advocacy of complete religious freedom in the sense of the 1948 UN Universal Declaration of Human Rights are able to thrive.

For that reason, the question to be asked is whether and how a climate of discourse emerges through the cooperation of theologians and activists who characterize the defense of "true" Islam as their main field of work. It is a climate of discourse which, apart from the political or economic influencing factors that can only be mentioned at the margins here, contributes to the sense of injustice or perhaps contributes to the lack of a sense of injustice in light of a condemnation or even the killing of an apostate in broad daylight. The focus of this study thus lies with the question of which contents these amplifiers transport onto the topic of apostasy (and with that, indirectly on the question of religious freedom and human rights) and in which way their theological perspectives in politics and society are expressed and become operative.

1.6. What is "Apostasy"?

1.6.1. Apostasy as Judged by Islamic Theology

The fact that members of the *umma* turn away from the faith and the question of judging this fact as well as the practical intercourse with apostates is something that has links back to the early days of Islam. On the basis of Muḥammad's battle for recognition as an apostle of God, a legislator, and a political leader, this question has been bound to theological, social, and political aspects from the very beginning. There is no doubt within Islamic theology that the turning away of individuals and entire groups from the community of Muslims was something which was condemned. What the main reason was is a heatedly disputed matter, whether it was a theological judgment of the apostates or whether social or political reasons were in the foreground. Additionally, there is also the disputed question of which penalties were threatened or imposed.

As early as in the Quran there are sanctions defined for certain offenses; the hardest sanctions have to do with those who, as post-Quranic theology and law formulate it, infringe upon God's law and, with that, transgress "absolute norms commanded or prohibited,"[142] that is, the borders *(ḥadd, Pl. ḥudūd)* of human law. Such offenses draw particularly high penalties from lashings to the amputation of a hand or a foot and all the way up to execution. With the ordering of the death penalty, what is generally a decision over life and death to which God is entitled (Sura 4:29) is conferred upon humankind.

Whether apostasy falls under the *ḥudūd* offenses is quite disputed within present day Islamic theology. However, it was unambiguously affirmed in the early days of Islam by the overwhelming number of theologians and by the four Sunnite legal schools as well as by the Shiite school. "*Falling away from the faith* is viewed as the greatest wrong, and it is the gravest sin which a human can commit."[143] According to the rationale, as with the other five *ḥadd* offenses of adultery, slander with respect to adultery, grand larceny, mugging, and the consumption of alcohol or wine, there is great harm, so that to combat this offense is absolutely essential.[144]

1.6.2. What the Quran Says about Apostasy

On the basis of how Islam frequently imposes a prohibition on apostasy and the elaborations of many a theologian that the prohibition on apostasy is unambiguously derivable from the Quran, one could assume that the Quran contains clear directions which order the execution of an apostate. That is, however, not the case, and thus one of the reasons for the intra-Islamic discussion about it:

The Quran uses several overlapping terms for the circumscription of unbelief (*kufr*) and turning away from belief (*ridda* oder *irtidād*). He mentions the "sacrilegious people" (*fāsiqūn*) as well as the hypocrites (*munāfiqūn*). It also mentions people who were devout and became unbelieving, without, however, actually giving a definition of one of these groups.

It is apparent that the individual who has turned his back against Islam has lapsed into unbelief and has made himself guilty of apostasy. Indeed,

---

142 Adel El Baradie. *Gottes-Recht und Menschen-Recht. Grundlagenprobleme der islamischen Strafrechtslehre*. Nomos: Baden-Baden, 1983, p. 97.

143 Adel Theodor Khoury (trans.). Der Koran, Arabisch-Deutsch. Übersetzung und wissenschaftlicher Kommentar. Gütersloher Verlagshaus: Gütersloh, 1995, Vol. 6, p. 361 (emphasis in the original).

144 This justification is discussed by Peters. *Crime*, p. 53.

the Quran uses the root of the term "unbelief," *k-f-r*, 482 times,[145] which in at least 19 verses is used in the sense of turning away or committing apostasy.[146] However, the terms *ridda* and *irtidād* themselves never actually occur in the Quran. There are only formulations which in a general manner pick as a central theme people's turning away (from Islam) and becoming unbelievers after they have been believers. The Quran unambiguously labels this as going astray (e.g., Sura 3:90).

A number of Quran verses speak about "straying" (*ḍalla*; Sura 2:108), without mentioning a punishment at all. Others exclusively mention the punishment of hell (Sura 4:115) or the "curse of God, of his angels, and of all mankind," (*la^cnat allāh wa-'l-malā'ika wa-'n-nās*; Sura 3:86-87). Other verses unspecifically broach the issue of God's wrath and punishment in this world as well as in the afterlife (Sura 9:74), without, however, setting down a concrete measure of punishment.

Furthermore, a number of Quran verses apparently imply a free choice for or against the acceptance of Islam (Suras 2:256; 3:20; 6:104; 16:9; 109:6); other verses, in turn, call for believers to forgive those who canvass for apostasy (e.g., Sura 2:109). These are particularly the verses which opponents of the death penalty quote as objections to legitimately justifying a worldly penalty.

Admittedly, there are also verses in the Quran which serve advocates as arguments for the death penalty for apostasy. In this connection, Sura 2:217 is quoted most frequently, a verse which charges the individual with the reprehensible action of leading another to apostasy: Such action is seen as more reprehensible than manslaughter. However, Sura 2:217 also only threatens the apostate with the punishment of eternal hell in the next life (*wa-ūlā'ika aṣḥāb an-nār hum fīhā ḫalidūna*). It does not mention a punishment in this life:

> "They ask thee concerning fighting in the prohibited month. Say: 'Fighting therein is a grave (offence); but graver is it in the sight of God to prevent access to the path of God, to deny Him, to prevent access to the sacred mosque,

[145] For a Quranic definition of "unbelief" see for instance Camilla Adang. "Belief and Unbelief" in: *EQ*, Vol. 1, E. J. Brill: Leiden, 2001, pp. 218-226; on the variations in the definition of *kufr* see Charles J. Adams. "Kufr" in: *OEMIW*, Vol. 2, Oxford University Press: Oxford, 1995, pp. 439-443.

[146] According to Hallaq. "Apostasy", pp. 119-122.

> and drive out its members.' Tumult and oppression are worse than slaughter. Nor will they cease fighting you until they turn you back from your faith if they can. And if any of you turn back from their faith and die in unbelief, their works will bear no fruit in this life and in the hereafter; they will be companions of the fire and will abide therein."[147]

Likewise, Sura 3:80+86-91 indeed also says that God does not guide those who turn away from belief, will not forgive them, and that a massive punishment awaits them; however, there is no defined punishment in this life in this key verse on apostasy; one could also understand these verses as an admonition for a timely turning back and acceptance of Islam in this life.

A certain assumption is shown in Sura 9:74 in this respect, which mentions a grievous penalty in this life and in the Hereafter (*ᶜaḏāban alīman fī 'd-dunyā wa-'l-āḫira*) – without, however, defining the penalty in this life in any more detail. Also, the formulation which follows directly, which says that this individual who has become unbelieving has "none on earth to protect or help them" leaves it an open issue as to which consequences will be drawn.

The accent is shifted in Sura 4:88-89. Here one sees that it initially speaks about "hypocrites" (*al-munāfiqūn*) who want everyone else to become as unbelieving as they are. And then it says:

> "But if they turn renegades, seize them and slay them wherever ye find them; and (in any case) take no friends or helpers from their ranks."

Sura 9:11-12 also has to do with those who have attached themselves to the Muslim community – verse 11 mentions remorse, ritualistic prayer, and the giving of alms as characteristics of their new affiliation. Then, however, they "violate their oaths" (*nakaṯū aimānahum*): They should be fought as "the chiefs of unfaith" (*fa-qātilū a'immat al-kufr*). From these verses in particular as well as with the hindsight of the incipient and, in the final event, militarily defeated movement of apostasy on the Arabian Peninsula which started shortly prior to Mohammed's death,[148] the so-called

---

147 http://www.sacred-texts.com/isl/quran/00227.htm (15.4.2014).

148 More precise circumstances and protagonists are for instanced discussed by Tilman Nagel. *Mohammed. Zwanzig Kapitel über den Propheten der Muslime.* Oldenburg: München, 2010, pp. 193-198.

Ridda wars, numerous theologians derive political peril to the Muslim community from the disloyal actions of apostates.

Additional verses which are drawn upon to condemn apostates indeed argue that this way of turning away or of luring others away is basically wrong (Sura 4:167), since it is Satan who instigates such thoughts (Sura 47:25). They point to the damage, the misery, or the futility and invalid nature of their actions (Suras 5:21; 7:147; 8:73; 33:19; 47:1) and mention God's wrath and the penalty of hellfire as a consequence of turning away (Suras 5:5; 9:74; 88:24). However, they do not formulate concrete punishment in this life or even order criminal prosecution of the apostate. For instance, Sura 4:115 threatens the individual who "contends with the Apostle"[149] (*man yušāqiq ar-rasūl*) with the punishment of hell. Sura 4:137 warns the apostate that he cannot expect forgiveness from God (likewise Sura 4:168).

Among the most frequently quoted verses is Sura 16:106-107+109; it is a passage which speaks about an individual who was once a believer, and it mentions the "wrath from God" (*ġaḍab min allāh*) and a "dreadful penalty" (*ᶜaḏāb ᶜaẓīm*) as a consequence. While Sura 16:106 speaks in a general sense about the penalty (likewise Sura 48:16), verse 109 explicitly refers to the punishment "in the hereafter" (*fī 'l-āḫira*).

On the basis of these textual findings, advocates of religious freedom argue primarily with the text of the Quran itself: Indeed, the Quran denounces turning away from (Islamic) community and vocalizes warnings about the error, the separation from the community of believers, and the punishment of God. Yet, one can recognize neither a process for establishing what apostasy is nor for conducting criminal proceedings nor for determining a measure of punishment from these verses. Therefore, the advocates of the death penalty for apostasy cannot call upon the authority of God's revelation.[150]

---

149 According to the translation in Scheich ᶜAbdullāh aṣ-Ṣāmit; Frank Bubenheim; Nadeem Elyas (trans.) *Der edle Qur'ān und die Übersetzung seiner Bedeutungen in die deutsche Sprache*. König-Fahd-Komplex zum Druck vom Qur'ān (sic): Medina, 2005, p. 97.

150 For instance, according to the former Chief Justice of the Supreme Court, Islamabad, Vice Chancellor of the University of Punjab and Director of the Institute of Islamic Culture Lahore: Shaikh Abdur Rahman. *Punishment of Apostasy in Islam*. Institute of Islamic Culture: Lahore, 1972², pp. 10-13.

1.6.3. What Tradition Says about Apostasy

In comparison to the Quran, the recording of post-Quranic tradition marked a clear shift in emphasis: Instead of the threats of punishment in hell in the afterlife for apostasy from Islam, one finds in *aḥādīṯ*, with more frequency, more clarity of content, and with an explanation of criminal proceedings that revenge for apostasy is dealt with in the here and now.[151] Apparently, there is a progression from the composition of the Quran to the recording of tradition, of an indeterminate announcement of God's wrath in the here and now to a transfer of the punishment into the present life. This progression is visible, while the threat of a punishment in the afterlife is hardly a topic in tradition as far as apostasy is concerned.[152] Tradition expressly uses the term "apostasy" (*ridda*) for turning away from Islam and reports the execution of individual apostates, calling multiple times for the administration of the death penalty for apostates. Disparagement of Muḥammad is also expressly condemned in the *ḥadīṯ* literature beginning in the 8th century.[153]

The most significant and, as far as advocates of the death penalty are concerned, most frequently quoted tradition in this context, which serves as the most prominent argument for justifying the (from the viewpoint of advocates) obligation to execute apostates, is the dictum traceable back to Muḥammad: "Whoever changes his Islamic religion, kill him"[154] (*man baddala dīnahu fa-'qtulūhu*).[155] However, this tradition falls under the *aḥādīṯ al-aḥad*. Thus, those theologians who essentially reject the justification for killing an apostate do not allow it as an argument for the justification of the death penalty.[156]

---

151 Heffening. "Murtadd", p. 635.

152 As emphasized by Griffel. *Apostasie*, p. 50.

153 According to Wiederhold. "Blasphemy", p. 43.

154 This tradition is traced back to Ibn ᶜAbbās; Buḫārī (istitābat al-murtaddīn, bāb 2, Vol. 9, Buch 84, No. 57) mentions it, among others, and likewise Ibn Māǧa (ḥudūd, bāb 2) as well as al-Nasā'ī (taḥrīm ad-dam, bāb 14). Comp. the overview of the texts of tradition in A. J. Wensinck. *Concordance et Indices de la Tradition Musulmane*, 7 Vols., E. J. Brill: Leiden, 1936-1969, here Vol. I, p. 153 und Vol. V, p. 287.

155 For a list of the passages and most frequent formulations found in tradition also see Heffening. "Murtadd", p. 635.

156 Aibek Ahmedov suggests that Muḥammad did not command to execute any apostate as long as he was only changing his religion and did not commit political trea-

Furthermore, a number of additional texts from tradition are drawn upon for the discussion about the legitimacy of the death penalty, such as one traced back to a report by Ibn ᶜAbbā and ᶜĀ'iša. This came after Muḥammad allowed the execution of each individual who distanced himself from the community and left Islam.[157] Also, there is a tradition frequently cited by advocates of the death penalty with only three cases where it is allowed to shed the blood of a Muslim. Stemming from Buḫārī, they are, namely, apostasy occurring after accepting Islam, the case of adultery, and killing which does not represent blood vengeance.[158] Based on the authority of Buḫārī, this tradition is frequently quoted as a weighty argument for the duty to execute in the case of apostasy.

Tradition, in contrast to the Quran, makes detailed statements, including reference to the type of punishment: As a general rule, the texts provide for the beheading of apostates with the sword; other traditions call for other punishments, such as crucifixion or banishment.[159] ᶜAbbās handed down the tradition that when ᶜAlī banished a number of non-believers or, more specifically, heretics, that earned him the criticism of Anās b. Mālik (died 795).[160]

On the other hand, opponents of the punishability of apostasy have cited that there are also reports in tradition where Muḥammad gave amnesty to apostates or, as the case may be, accepted their confession of remorse and where no worldy punishment followed their apostasy.[161]

---

son: Aibek Ahmedov. "Religious Minorities and Apostasy in Early Islamic States: Legal and Historical Analysis of Sources", in: *JISP* 2/3 (2006), pp. 1-17, here p. 13.

157 Thus handed down by Buḫārī, Muslim, and indeed others; comp. The numerous passages in W. Heffening. "Murtadd" in: *EI/2*, Vol. VII, 1993, pp. 635-636, here p. 635.

158 Buḫārī, Vol. 9, Book 83, No. 17; comp. on this the statements by Khoury (trans.). Koran, Vol. 6, p. 361.

159 This text is for instance found in Nasā'ī, taḥrīm ad-dam, bāb 11 et al.; comp. W. Heffening. "Murtadd" in: *EI/2*, Vol. VII. E. J. Brill: Leiden, 1993, pp. 635-636, here p. 635.

160 Buḫārī, istitābat al-murtaddīn, bāb 2 et al.; see Heffening. "Murtadd", p. 635.

161 Comp. for instance the exposition of a text in Yohanan Friedmann. *Tolerance and Coercion in Islam. Interfaith Relations in the Muslim Tradition*. Cambridge University Press: Cambridge, 2003, pp. 125+131.

1.6.4. Apostasy – a Multilayered Term

Although the Quran and tradition repeatedly take up the topic of aspostasy – and at least in a number of cases tradition brings up apostasy with the threat or order to administer the death penalty – neither in the Quran nor in the *aḥādīṯ* is there an unequivocal definition of what apostasy from Islam (*al-ruǧūᶜ ᶜan dīn al-islām*[162] oder *qaṭᶜ al-islām*) actually means[163] and which preconditions there are for its conclusive determination. With that said, the most important question remains unanswered. It is a question present over the course of Islamic history and has to do with the very controversially discussed topic of which actions or attitudes make an individual an unbeliever.[164]

Over the course of centuries, many key elements of apostasy were brought together – leading the way is the association of some being next or similar to God, i.e., in the final event a denial of the center of Islamic theology, the *tauḥīd*. However, at no point in the normative texts nor in the case of one of the theologians is there a complete listing of all hallmarks of apostasy or a comprehensive definition of the same.[165] All definitions are up to this day have either been insufficiently comprehensive or vague. For that reason, only a very limited consensus has been achieved among scholars throughout the entire span of history.[166] The lack of a classical scholar's hierarchy, at least in Sunnite Islam, has also in part contributed to this.

As one of the conditions for the determination of apostasy, for example, the Malikite legal school has formulated that the person in question would have to have been "a good Muslim", since it can only be a question of true unbelief if the individual had beforehand been doubtless about the

---

162 According to the formulation of the Egyptian Court of Cassation in the case of Abu Zaid. The apostate turns from Islam and towards unbelief, which is recognizable by his statement or his actions: Kilian Bälz. "Submitting Faith to Judicial Scrutiny through the Family Trial: The 'Abū Zayd Case'" in: *WI 37/2* (1997), pp. 135-155, here p. 146.

163 Thus also Peters; De Vries. "Apostasy", p. 3.

164 According to Griffel, aš-Šāfiᶜī let the speaking of the confession of faith count as a way to differentiate between belief and unbelief, i.e., according to his opinion, no one could request more than the *šahāda* as a proof of belief: Griffel. "Anwendung", p. 356.

165 A number of conditions which in the case of apostasy have to be fulfilled, are mentioned by, for example, Ayoub. "Freedom", p. 88 and Peters; de Vries. "Apostasy", p. 3.

166 Comp. the expositions by Johansen. "Apostasy", pp. 690-692.

Muslim faith in word and deed.[167] It goes without saying that such a formulation is one which can be very ambiguously characterized and has the potential of being misused.[168] Additionally, on the basis of the lack of a definition which is unequivocal, the term sometimes is blurred with the terms for unbelief or blasphemy (*kufr*), heresy (*ilḥād*), hypocrisy (*nafāq*) or polytheism (*širk*).[169]

It is precisely this missing definition which makes the charge of *ridda* a sharp weapon in the hands of scrupulous rulers or influential scholars and opinion makers in the battle against unwelcome political or theological opponents.[170] Through its vagueness, the charge of apostasy can also be expanded to areas which originally have nothing to do with turning away from Islam.[171] Recent events in Pakistan show that very restrained criticism of the country's blasphemy laws are seized upon with the charge of apostasy and death threats or, more specifically, can lead to the killing of high ranking officials. An example is the killing of the Pakistani Minister for Minorities, Shabaz Bhatti, on March 2, 2011.[172]

---

167 According to Peters; De Vries. "Apostasy", p. 6 with reference to Abū ᶜAlī Muḥammad Ibn Muḥammad al-Ḥaṭṭāb, *Mawāhib al-ǧalīl li-šarḥ muḫtaṣar Ḫalīl*, Ṭarābulus: Maktabatt al-Naǧāḥ, no year provided (Reprint of the Cairo edition 1329 h.), Vol. 6, p. 279f.

168 Martin Forstner lists a number of the characteristics of apostasy mentioned in Islamic legal literature. Forstner. "Menschenrecht", p. 113f.

169 Appropriately referred to by Mark S. Weiner. "Religious Freedom and the Rule of the Clan in Muslim Societies" in: *RFIA 9/2* (2011), pp. 39-45, here p. 39.

170 Abdullahi Ahmed an-Na'im for instance principally rejects the justification of sharia penalties, which were established during Muḥammad's time at Medina: "Sharia was *constructed* by Muslim jurists" (emphasis in the original). An-Na'im holds the sharia as such to not be of divine origin and points to the possibility of misuse as early as the case of the conflict between Sunnis and Shiites: an-Na'im. *Reformation*. pp. 184-186.

171 Thus according to Mathias Rohe, the call for a new interpretation of the classical (legal) sources can "in the extreme case" likewise expose their advocates in the Sudan or Afganistan to charges of apostasy such as that individual who as a Muslim in Canada rejected the religious arbitration of the Islamic Institute of Civil Justice: Mathias Rohe. *Das islamische Recht. Geschichte und Gegenwart*. C. H. Beck: München, 2009, pp. 304+323.

172 Comp for instance the report "Pakistan: Christlicher Minister ermordet" at: http://www.igfm.de/news-presse/aktuelle-meldungen/detailansicht/?tx_ttnews%5Btt_news%5D=1124&cHash=5e123624fab76a858610a6a1a39a42c3 (15.4.2014).

A far-reaching consensus has existed from early days onward that a distancing from Islam in word or deed counts as apostasy, even if the person involved only expresses it out of fun or acted in an associated manner. Likewise, the permanent, deliberate non-observance of the Five Pillars of Islam is apostasy, in particular failure to fulfill the duty to pray which cannot be explained by a Sharia-defined reason for hindrance (such as illness, travel, or other acceptable reasons). Additionally, every conviction which contradicts the basic teachings of Islam can generally be understood as apostasy, such as denying the existence of God or denying the oneness of God (*tauḥīd*), a declaration of the invalidity of the Sharia, or declaring that what is allowed is forbidden or for declaring that what is forbidden is allowed.[173]

Naturally, the veneration of another being next to God and the blaspheming of God, as well as the denigration of, reviling of, or ridiculing the prophets, in particular Muḥammad, is considered to be apostasy.[174] Also, to deny the sending of the prophets, to disrespect the Quran through offensive denial of its authority as well as to reject its commands and prohibitions is considered apostasy. Furthermore, apostasy exists in the case of contaminating and destroying a copy of the Quran or not acknowledging the commands of the Sharia about which common agreement exists (for instance the prohibition of *zinā'*). Battling against Islam (*muḥāraba*) and its adherents is, as a general rule, defined as a form of unbelief or apostasy; likewise and conversely, apostasy is seen in the eyes of a number of theologians as a form of battle against Islam. On the other hand, according to the understanding of a number of theologians, the return of a Jew or Christian to his original faith should not be judged as apostasy if the use of illegitimate means, such as coercion, had led to a conversion to Islam in the first place.[175]

---

173 For instance according to Khoury (trans.). Koran, pp. 94-98.

174 Tilman Nagel concludes with respect to judging an insult of Muḥammad as apostasy "that this was the prevailing opinion in the 8th century." Tilman Nagel. *Allahs Liebling. Ursprung und Erscheinungsformen des Mohammedglaubens*, 2 vols., R. Oldenburg: München, 2008, here Vol. 1, p. 187.

175 Also according to Wael B. Hallaq. *Sharīʿa. Theory, Practice, Transformations.* Cambridge University Press: Cambridge, 2009, p. 319.

Apostasy should be confirmed by two credible male witnesses who make matching statements about the acts or the words of the apostate.[176] That makes it possible to throw the gates wide open to condemn a person as an apostate who continues to see himself as a believing Muslim. Over the course of history, expressly distancing oneself from Islam or, more specifically, demonstrating a complete conversion to another religion, has for the most part not been considered necessary in order to fulfill the elements of the offense of apostasy,[177] and that makes the practice of *takfīr* (declaring another person to not be a believer) possible in the first place.

The practice of *takfīr* shifts the judgment for turning away from Islam to the decision making realm allotted to a third party who can also legally judge an apostate against his will and expression of intent, making him a passive recipient of a (death) penalty by scholars or the powers that be. If *takfīr* is pronounced by influential members of the society – for instance by personalities from within public life – the justification of the judgment and its corresponding announcement effect are shifted to the middle of society, and there are perhaps dramatic consequences. If *takfīr* is directed against people of low social status, such as has frequently appeared to be the case in Pakistan since the enactment of blasphemy laws in the 1980s, there hardly seems to be a realistic chance to turn away such a charge because in many cases procedures for the taking of evidence do not follow the rule of law.

Beginning with the basic assumption that Islam is the only uncorrupted, pure revelation of God while all other religions, due to their polytheistic belief, have either basically taken the wrong track (such as Hinduism) or perhaps have, at least over the course of time, been distorted and for that reason have been abrogated (such as Judaism or Christianity), according to the majority opinion, actual punishment is only threatened in the case of apostasy from Islam. Punishment is not, however, threatened with the change between Judaism and Christianity, whose adherents have limited rights in Muslim majority states.[178] If a Jew or a Christian becomes a fol

[176] Thus summarized by Adel Theodor Khoury. *Toleranz im Islam*. Chr. Kaiser Verlag: München, 1980, p. 111.

[177] Pointed out by, for example, Baradie. *Gottes-Recht*, p. 123.

[178] However, according to the opinion of a number of legal scholars, such a conversion does not remain without consequence and for instance entails banishment. Comp. the presentation of a discussion in Friedmann. *Tolerance*, pp. 146-148.

lower of Zoroastrianism, he should be reprimanded but not killed.[179] If a Muslim believer becomes a Jew or a Christian, he can, however, in no case become a *ḏimmī* – with his life and property protected in principal – but is rather to be considered an apostate. He is considered to be outlawed and can claim no legal status at all. He also enjoys no legal protection.[180]

1.6.5. Opportunity for Remorse

Most theologians grant the apostate a period to demonstrate remorse (*istitāba*), which frequently is set at three days. After that time, he should be beheaded by sword.[181] However, he should not be tormented.[182] According to the understanding of Malikites and Hanbalites, if he offends the angels, the Quran, Muḥammad, or Islam, he should be immediately killed without the opportunity for remorse. In the case of the criminal offense of blasphemy against God, the individual should first of all have the opportunity for remorse.[183]

If he demonstrates remorse, he should twice say the *šahāda* with its declaration of belief in God, as a convert does. The individual thus counts as having returned to Islam.[184] Likewise, the refusal of the individual suspected of apostasy to say the *šahāda* can be classified as unequivocal proof of apostasy.[185]

---

179 Comp. the remarks in Khoury. *Toleranz*, p. 112.

180 Comp. the remarks in Uphoff. *Untersuchung*, p. 355.

181 However, there are also sources from tradition which provide contrary information: Heffening. "Murtadd", p. 635.

182 There are, however, reports, for instance from the 14th century, which tell of different methods of torture to which an individual condemned for apostasy was publicly subjected to prior to his being killed. Comp. in particular the depiction of the torture and execution of Fatḥ al-Dīn Aḥmad al-Baqaqī, who was charged with non-observance of Ramadan, consumption of alcohol, sodomy, defiling a copy of the Quran as well as ridiculing a number of verses of the Quran. In spite of his having confessed belief in Islam a number of times, he was convicted of apostasy: Broadbridge. "Apostasy Trials", pp. 363-366.

183 According to Uphoff. *Untersuchung*, p. 59.

184 For example, Naṣr Ḥāmid Abū Zaid reports that at the beginning of his apostasy trial in Cairo in the middle of the 1990s the case could have been ended prematurely by his uttering the *šahāda* before the court but that he did not want to concede the right to this "inquisition" to the court: Nasr Hamid Abu Zaid. *Ein Leben mit dem Islam*. Herder: Freiburg, 1999, pp. 174-175.

185 This is pointed out by Friedmann. *Tolerance*, p. 121.

Malikites and Hanbalites accept no form of remorse and return to Islam. Hanafites (who, however, call for the death penalty for insulting Muḥammad[186]) and Shafi'ites speak out for the acceptance of remorse on the part of the accused. A portion of the Shafi'ites, however, grant no possibility for remorse if the involved person has turned to a special, non-standard group, such as the Bahā'ī or Aḥmadīya. The Twelver Shiites differentiate between an apostate born as a Muslim (*murtadd fiṭrī*) who does not have to be prompted to express remorse, and an apostate not born as an Muslim (*murtadd millī*) where this is the case. With that said, as Yohanan Friedmann has observed, apostasy is the sole *ḥadd* offense which can be eliminated[187] even if not all scholars concede this[188] and a number of them want to administer the punishment despite the confession of remorse.[189]

1.6.6. The Measure of Punishment for Apostasy

Given the current state of research, it is presently not possible to sketch a comprehensive picture of whether and to which extent apostasy was punished by death in the early days of Islam. In addition to the corresponding legal literature, up to the present there have primarily been reports about individual cases of apostasy which have been reviewed. However, they do not provide a complete picture of the early days and the Middle Ages.

On the basis of reports from tradition, it appears indubitable that punishment for apostasy was practiced in the early times of Islam.[190] However, whether this was widespread or not cannot be claimed for certain. David Cook supposes that the number of apostates was indeed much higher than is documented according to the knowledge provided by sources, but most apostates were de facto not punished.[191]

According to Sharia law, only individuals who are of majority age (*bāliġ*), in complete possession of their mental faculties (*ᶜāqil*), and not un-

186 Uphoff. *Untersuchung*, p. 61.

187 Friedmann. *Tolerance*, p. 127.

188 In particular this is not in the event of repeated apostasy: Comp. the discussion on this ibid., pp. 143-144.

189 Tilman Nagel states that not all theologians in the early days viewed penitence as canceling the punishment: Nagel. *Liebling*, p. 187.

190 For the depiction of a case from the time shortly after Mohammed's death see for instance ibid., p. 181.

191 Cook. "Apostasy", p. 278.

der coercion (*muḫtār*) could be threatened with the death penalty, i.e., an individual who is neither mentally handicapped nor of minor age nor acting under coercion. Hanafites and Malikites also absolve individuals of their guilt if they acted while in a state of drunkenness.[192]

There has been consensus since the middle of the 7th century, as Frank Griffel sees it, that adult male apostates have to be executed.[193] This finds expression in the *fiqh* literature of the four Sunni legal schools as well as in the most important Shiite school from the 8th century onwards.[194] If the in-

---

192 The exception clause of mental incapacity was repeatedly attempted over the course of history. Anne F. Broadbridge explains for the Mamluk courts of the 14th century that the attempt to save the defendant in this manner prior to execution was generally unsuccessful: "In fact, execution could only be avoided if partisans of the accused managed to prove him insane, although usually even these attempts were unsuccessful." Anne F. Broadbridge. "Apostasy Trials in Eighth/Fourteenth Century Egypt and Syria: A Case Study" in: Judith Pfeiffer; Sholeh A. Quinn (eds.). *History and Historiography of Post-Mongol Central Asia and the Middle East. Studies in Honor of John E. Woods*. Harrassowitz: Wiesbaden, 2006, pp. 363-382, p. 369. In the tug of war regarding the Afghan convert Abdur Rahman in 2006, in addition to the efforts of international diplomacy, the sharia-based justification of his mental incapacity saved him from the administration of the death penalty, which according to Afghan law would have been compulsory in the case of proven apostasy. Comp. for instance the report: Berlusconi: "Rahman in Italien eingetroffen," 30.3.2006. http://www.faz.net/artikel/C31325/religionsfreiheit-berlusconi-rahman-in-italien-eingetroffen-30070029.html (15.4.2014). In the middle of the 1990s, the Kuwaiti convert Ḥusain Qambar ᶜAlī, as an on-site field study revealed, was labeled "insane" and a "lunatic," "a case for psychiatry" by a number of people who were well-intentioned and wanted to avert his death sentence: Anh Nga Longva. "The Apostasy Law in the Age of Universal Human Rights and Citizenship. Some Legal and Political Implications." The Fourth Nordic Conference on Middle Eastern Studies: The Middle East in Globalizing World (sic). Oslo, 13.-16.8.1998. http://www.hf.uib.no/smi/pao/longva.html (15.4.2014).

193 Griffel. "Apostasy".

194 Beginning in the 8th century the term *irtidād* was exclusively used discursively for apostasy from Islam: Wael Hallaq. "Apostasy" in: *EQ*, Vol. 1. E. J. Brill: Leiden, 2001, pp. 119-122, here p. 119. This is also the time – from the middle of the 8th century onwards – by which the training of judges was professionalized: Baber Johansen. "Wahrheit und Geltungsanspruch: Zur Begründung und Begrenzung der Autorität des Qadi-Urteils im Islamischen Recht" in: *La Giustizia nell'Alto Medioevo (Secoli IX-XI)*, April 11-17, 1996, Vol. 2. Presso la Sede del Centro: Spoleto, 1997, pp. 975-1065, here p. 988.

dividual falls away from Islam, he has forfeited his life.[195] The common punishment is beheading by sword. There are, however, reports of drowning and stoning.[196]

The administration of the death penalty on apostates is granted to the ruler; an execution by an unauthorized party is, however, not an offense. Rather, it is only a rash action for which the offender is not punished. He only receives a *ta'zīr* punishment, e.g., a reproach.[197] This is due to the idea that the killing of an apostate is principally a duty (*wāğib* oder *farḍ*) and not only a possibility among many.[198] Since according to the Sharia an offender only takes his legal right into his own hands and does not break the law per se, the culprit does not thus commit a murder.[199] Furthermore, he is also not obliged to pay a blood price as would normally be required in the case of manslaughter.[200]

According to the understanding of Hanbalites, Shafi'tes, and Malikites, women are to be killed too in the case of apostasy. In contrast, Hanafites plead for their incarceration and daily punishment[201] since they do not pre-

---

195 "An apostate is *de jure* dead . . . An apostate has nothing to choose but the re-embracing of Islam or the sword. . .," for Islam is not a "personal relationship between man and Allāh", but rather involves the entire society and state; there, however, "the Kingdom of Heaven" has to become visible, and that is made impossible in the case of high treason. Mohammad Iqbal Siddiqi. *The Penal Law of Islam*. International Islamic Publishers: New Delhi, 1994, pp. 106+109.

196 A number of examples are mentioned by Heffening. "Murtadd", p. 635.

197 This is for instance also confirmed by Abdul Qader 'Oudah Shaheed. *Criminal Law in Islam*. 3 Vols. International Islamic Publishers: New Delhi, 1991, here Vol. 2, pp. 257-258, who reminds the overhasty executor of a penalty since he usurped the "competent authority." He can only be punished for that, and according to 'Oudah Shaheed he has not committed a murder. Should the responsible authorities neglect to punish the apostate, his murder should not generate any penalty at all for: "under the Islamic Sharia, the killing of an apostate is an obligation imposed upon every individual rather than a right" (ibid., p. 259). If he does not act, he must himself be punished, because laws contrary to the sharia are invalid (ibid., p. 260).

198 According to Safia M. Safwat. "Offences and Penalties in Islamic Law" in: *IQ* 26/3 (1982), pp. 149-181, here p. 169.

199 This is emphasized by Peters. *Crime*, p. 39.

200 So summarized in Hallaq. "Apostasy", p. 122.

201 Khoury. *Toleranz im Islam*, pp. 112.

sent a threat to the Islamic community.[202] The Twelver Shiites advocate their chastisement at daily prayer times,[203] and Malikites only advocate delaying the execution of women who are pregnant or who are nursing their children.[204]

1.6.7. Legal and Social Consequences of Apostasy

If there is hardly any consensus about preconditions for apostasy and respecting the legitimacy of a charge, this applies all the more with regard to the legal and social consequences of apostasy. It has likewise remained disputed throughout what has been a varied history as to who actually is in the position to judge a case of apostasy and who is justified to punish apostasy – in particular on the basis of the separation between spiritual and worldly rule according to the reigns of the four rightly guided caliphs from 661 A.D. onwards.

The most severe Sharia-based consequence defined appear in the area of civil law. According to the understanding of Hanbalites, Malikites, and Shafi'its, the possessions of the apostate are handed over to the state. Hanafites advocate distributing possessions accumulated prior to apostasy to the family and advocate distributing possessions acquired after committing apostasy to the state.

The apostate's marriage, be it as husband or wife, automatically ends by dissolution[205] (*fasẖ*) on account of apostasy, for it is illegal (*bāṭil*). The children of the apostate have to be taken from him, and contracts he is party to are invalid. He can no longer inherit or bequeath and may not be buried in a Muslim cemetery using Islamic burial rites.[206] In any event, an apostate's children remain Muslim and have to be raised as such. If both

---

202 For further explanations see Friedmann. *Tolerance*, p. 137.

203 Accoring to Safwat. "Offences", p. 169.

204 Adel Theodor Khoury. "Abfall vom Glauben im Koran und im Rechtssystem" in: Adel Theodor Khoury; Peter Heine; Janbernd Oebbecke. *Handbuch Recht und Kultur des Islams in der deutschen Gesellschaft*. Gütersloher Verlagshaus: Gütersloh 2000, pp. 237-242, here p. 239.

205 In a number of countries, for example in Pakistan, special regulations where the marriage is not dissolved due to apostasy on the part of the wife, in order to not allow a path to divorce to be opened via a (alleged) conversion.

206 On the civil law consequences of apostasy comp. the information in Peters; De Vries. "Apostasy", p. 635.

parents are apostates, the children have to continue to attend Islamic religious instruction. As adults they receive identification papers which – for instance in Egypt – label them as Muslims. They may only enter into Islamic marriage, and their children count legally as Muslims. In a number of states, a married couple which has converted or a converted parent is threatened with having one's own children taken away. This means that even in the case of apostasy of both parents, the Islamic community is not numerically reduced as apostasy cannot continue into the next generation.

1.7. Apostasy throughout History

The roots of the problematic issue of apostasy and its varied theological treatment thus already lie in the time of the recording of the Quran and tradition. From the beginning onwards, this topic was interwoven with political factors. This was all the more the case when, at the latest with Muḥammad's death in 661 A.D., a number of Arab tribes who saw themselves only personally bound to Muḥammad rose up against Muslim rule.

1.7.1. The Ridda Wars after Muḥammad

These battles in the early days of Islam, which have gone down in history with the term *ḥurūb ar-ridda*, lasted from 632 until the beginning of 634. Within research the reasons are disputed. Was this a "hangover of pre-Islamic customs", whereby a "formal protective relationship" to an influential community was lost through increased alienation?[207] The conclusion that the killing of those who turned away reflected customary Arabic law is excluded by Frank Griffel.[208] Did it rather have primarily to do with rejecting the collection of taxes, with a revolt against Islam as a religion, or the rule coming from Medina, or were there various local catalysts?[209]

The fact remains that the wars against these apostates punished those who apostatized with death. The first Caliph Abū Bakr spearheaded the efforts and in so doing was presumably the first military leader (after

[207] This is entertained by Hasemann. "Apostasiediskussion", p. 37.

[208] Griffel. *Apostasie*, p. 68.

[209] These points are mentioned by Wael Hallaq, who supposes for four of the six centres of resistance religiously defined reasons: Hallaq. "Apostasy", pp. 120-121.

Muḥammad), who had punished apostates with death[210] and this can be traced back to a number of factors.[211] However, it has been supposed that probably not all of those who committed apostasy had actually converted to Islam prior thereto. Thus, at their root, these battles would have hardly had religious motives in any basic sense of the word.[212]

One motive for the rigorous persecution of apostates in the early days of Islam might have been to turn away dangers confronting the young Islamic community. However multilayered the individual justifications might have been for the Ridda wars: Through this event, apostasy has become anchored in the collective consciousness of the *umma* as endangering the community and has thus legitimized military action against apostates up to the present day.[213]

1.7.2. The Time between the Ridda Wars and Modern Times

From the time subsequent to the Ridda wars, the 8th century, there are only a few individual cases where the death penalty was administered to apostates. David Cook sees the reason for this in the fact that in the course of Abbasid rule, namely from the end of the 8th century onwards, criminal prosecution and application of the death penalty began. He also sees the defensive measures against apostates in the time of the Umayyads and the early time of the Abbasids to have primarily been limited to an intellectual debate.[214]

A hallmark of this development is without doubt the fact that in the 8th century the term *irtidād* also came to exclusively be used for apostasy.[215] One has thus supposed that Hišām Ibn ᶜAbd al-Malik was executed in Kufa or that Wāsiṭ was executed in 742 or 743 on account of propagating

210 Ibid., p. 121.

211 A depiction of the specific circumstances of the *ridda* wars see for instance at Syed Barakat Ahmad. "Conversion from Islam" in: C. E. Bosworth et al. (ed.). *The Islamic World from Classical to Modern Times*. The Darwin Press: Princeton, 1989, pp. 3-25, here pp. 9-11.

212 According to Hallaq. "Apostasy", pp. 120-121.

213 The impact of this "upon the collective Muslim psyche" is referred to by Hallaq. ibid., p. 121.

214 However, he qualifies that it is not possible to set a precise time for when executions of apostates began: Cook. "Apostasy", pp. 256+276-277.

215 Hallaq. "Apostasy", pp. 119.

Mu'tazilite convictions. In 784 the Iranian poet Bašār Ibn Burd was killed on account of apostasy, and in 922 al-Ḥusayn ibn Manṣūr al-Ḥallāǧ was executed on account of blasphemy.[216] A number of additional individual cases had to do with Christians said to have been executed on account of their conversion and then subsequent return to the Christian faith: Kyros is mentioned from the year 769. He was burned, and in 795 Saint Elias was executed in Damascus. In 806 Saint Bacchus was executed in Fusṭāṭ. Two additional cases are known from the 10th and 14th centuries,[217] and also sources from the 11th century in Spain under Muslim rule tell us about the application of the death penalty for apostasy.[218]

From the 9th century onwards, a time in which the execution of apostates became historically accessible, the captives, who more or less voluntarily converted to Islam, later again frequently turned away from their new religion.[219] It is reported that establishing the truth – the truth of whether apostasy was involved – occured on the basis of the self-confession of the individual involved, i.e., if they spoke "words of unbelief" (*kalimāt al-kufr*). What exactly these "words of unbelief" were is something for which there was no exact definition prior to the 12th century. Prior to the 12th century, it appears that legal experts (for that reason?) were rather hesitant to judge between belief and unbelief.[220] This was due to the fact that the inner life of a person was frequently considered to not be accessible for judgment by other people, with the result that many scholars appear to have postponed the question to see if the person involved caused uproar and rebellion. That appeared to be clearer judged.

As early as from the commencement of the 9th century, there were complaints that the charge of apostasy was applied as a weapon against unwanted opponents. Thus, for example, Abū Ḥāmid Muḥammad ibn Muḥammad al-Ġazālī (d. 1111) became agitated about the exaggerated

216 According to Ahmad. "Conversion", p. 15.

217 These examples are mentioned by Adel Theodor Khoury. *Christen unterm Halbmond. Religiöse Minderheiten unter der Herrschaft des Islams*. Herder: Freiburg, 1994, pp. 101-102.

218 Comp. the analysis of a *Fatwā* from this time by David Wasserstein. "A *Fatwā* on Conversion in Islamic Spain", in: *SMJR* 1 (1993), pp. 177-188.

219 David Cook makes the following judgment about the 9th century: "However, after this period apostasy becomes very widespread": Cook. "Apostasy", p. 256.

220 An exception appears to have been the Khāriǧites, who practiced *takfīr* and supposedly carried out executions: Olsson. "Apostasy", p. 95.

practice of *takfīr* among theologians, which supposedly led to debates more than executions.[221]

It therefore appears that in those first centuries after the Ridda wars, the topic of apostasy seemed to have been less of a political dispute and more something having primarily to do with a theological set of questions.[222] Charges of unbelief against a representative of a deviating theological understanding appeared in many cases to have had few practical consequences, even if individual cases have been handed down entailing measures of punishment such as prison sentences as well as the death penalty.[223]

Tilman Nagel mentions the Malakite scholar al-Qāḍī ᶜIjāḍ (d. 1149) as the first one to call for the death penalty for those who "spread indecent things about Muḥammad or who place into question all the questions of consummated faith and of profane life." He also argued that such statements shake the foundation of Muslim community; that is a view to which the Hanbalite theologian Ibn Taymīya (d. 1328) and the Shafi'it scholar Taqī ad-Dīn as-Subkī (d. 1355) later subscribed.[224] After the 12th century, what develops among the Mamluks and Ottomans in particular are comprehensive lists with definitions of the "words of unbelief" which are shown to grow as time progresses.[225] From the 12th and then in particular from the 14th centuries onward, there are a number of cases of executions of apostates which have been handed down.[226] Information about the ap-

---

221 According to Bernard Lewis. *Die politische Sprache des Islam*. Europäische Verlagsanstalt: Hamburg, 2002, p. 144 with source citations. Michael Chamberlain also explains that from the end of the 12th century to the middle of the 14th century, at least in Mamluk governed Damascus, there was no sign of the exercise of state force in order to combat heresies: Michael Chamberlain. *Knowledge and Social Practice in Medieval Damascus, 1190-1350*. Cambridge University Press: Cambridge, 1994, p. 168.

222 That likewise applies to the discourse about heresy as it is closely related to the apostasy discussion. The representatives – and that also involves the Shiite opposition – were viewed in the early days of Islam in many cases first as political and then later, however, more strongly as religious special groups: Lewis. "Observations", pp. 43-47.

223 Ibid., pp. 59-60.

224 Tilman Nagel. *Das Islamische Recht. Eine Einführung*. WVA-Verlag Skulima: Westhofen, 2001, p. 295.

225 According to Johansen. "Apostasy", pp. 691-695.

226 Comp. the list of around one dozen cases between the 12th and the 18th century in Cook. "Apostasy", pp. 257ff. + 275 as well as detailed depictions of individual

proximate numbers could probably only be provided by detailed studies about specific periods of time for specific regions.

By all appearances, the general fact is that the significance of the topic of apostasy in the first centuries of Islamic history, as far as numbers are concerned, appears to have been limited. Whether each individual who in the early days advocated a deviating viewpoint was executed is, in the face of the majority structure of Muslims and non-Muslims in the newly conquered areas as well as the numerous theological divisions within the *umma* is, in my opinion, more than questionable. That would mean that there never was an early time of "ideal" Islam in which every appearance of unbelief and apostasy was categorically persecuted and directly punished with execution.

Present day advocates of the punishment of apostates strongly refer to this alleged early time in order to legitimate their notion. At this point they primarily refer to tradition, according to which report Muḥammad and the four rightly guided caliphs themselves called for the death penalty for apostates and are said to have brought about its application. On the grounds of the spotty nature respecting the body of source material, the logical conclusion for Armin Hasemann is immediately suggested that in the history of Islam "apostasy from Islam [has] numerically never [been] a significant phenomenon."[227] David Cook, on the other hand, does not accept this conclusion due to the low number of known examples of apostasy and conversions. He supposes that these prominent cases, along with a missing systematic appraisal, could only be the tip of the iceberg requiring additional research.[228]

At the threshold to modernity in the Ottoman Empire, from which up to now only individual cases of execution for apostasy have been reviewed,[229] the relationships for non-Muslims can be seen to change with respect to the classic *ḏimmī* model: Beginning in 1453, with the introduction of the millet system, a "strictly controlled tolerance" ruled in the empire, the "Pax Ot-

cases executions relating to apostasy under Mamluk rulers in: Broadbridge. "Apostasy Trials", pp. 363-382.

227 Hasemann. "Apostasiediskussion", p. 72.

228 Cook. "Apostasy", p. 279.

229 Ahmad supports the daring thesis that in the Mogul Empire there was only one case of apostasy and that is was of a (purely) political nature: Ahmad. "Conversion", p. 15.

tomana".[230] In 1839 the decree Hatt-i Sharif by Sultan Abdülmecid I assured all Ottoman subjects the protection of life, honor, and possessions, independent of their religion. In 1844, due to the appeals of European powers, the Ottoman Sultan abandoned the death penalty for apostates from Islam in the Treaty of Küçük Kaynarca.[231] The negotiations which led to this treaty were co-determined by two events which occurred only a short time prior thereto. These were the execution of a 20-year-old Armenian in Istanbul in 1843 and the killing of a young Greek in Bilecik near Bursa as a consequence of apostasy.[232]

The British envoy to the court of Sultan Abdülmecid I (1839-1861), Stratford Canning, had especially intensively championed the cause of prohibiting the execution of apostates at the High Porte with the support of the diplomatic representatives of Austria, Russia, Prussia, and France. After a longer diplomatic tug of war, in which the British envoy Stratford Canning attempted in vain to move the Sublime Porte to change legislation with respect to the treatment of apostates, and during which time there was no desire to be bossed around by Europe's envoys,[233] Sultan Abdülmecid finally granted a decree on March 21, 1844 in which the Sultan stated that he would give support to the Sublime Porte with respect to their intention to take "effective measures" and prevent the persecution and execution of Christians who counted as apostates. Additionally, the Sultan personally gave Stratford Canning his word that in his domain neither Christianity nor Christians and their religion would be persecuted.[234] Conclusion of this development was seen in the Islahat Fermani, the Reform Edict of 1856. It placed Muslims and non-Muslim citizens on equal legal footing[235] but did not, however, explicitly name the topic of apostasy.[236]

---

230 Ahmet Mumçu. "Die rechtliche Lage der nichtmuslimischen Bürger im Osmanischen Reich im 19. Jahrhundert" in: *Kanon* 12 (1994), pp. 85-103, here p. 87.

231 James P. Piscatori. *Islam in a World of Nation-States*. Cambridge University Press: Cambridge, 1986, p. 52.

232 Comp. the detailed depiction of these two cases in: Subaşı. "Apostasy", pp. 4-9.

233 This complicated conflict situation, which received additional importance throughout the then current cases of apostasy is referred to by Deringil. "Compulsion", p. 559.

234 Subaşı. "Apostasy", pp. 23-24.

235 Mumçu assumes the turning point to not be until 1859, however, the time from which apostates were no longer executed in the Ottoman Empire: Mumçu. "Lage", pp. 94-95+98.

236 Deringil refers to this: "Compulsion", p. 556.

In Egypt, from 1825 and 1835, there are reports of two cases where women apostates were executed.[237] After that, it appears that with the exception of two cases of stoning, caused by the conversion of Ṣaḥibzādah ᶜAbd al-Laṭīf (1903) and Maulawī Niʻmat Allāh (1924)[238] to the Aḥmadīya movement in Afghanistan, there were only a very few known cases of executions of apostates for around 150 years.[239] Above all, there were no cases which virtually came about due to scholarly decisions by outsiders and – in contrast to cases from the early days of Islam – not from the self-confession of the persons involved.[240]

1.7.3. Apostasy in the 20th Century

Thus, while Islamic history seems to give the appearance that on the whole apostasy is not a frequent problem and that on the threshold to modernity there are only specific cases of "documented executions on account of apostasy . . . in the first half of the 19th century,"[241] apostasy's problematic nature basically took a new and thoroughly dramatic turn in the 20th century. There are several operative regional and trans-regional reasons for this. In any event, the following applies to Muslim majority countries: "Globalization is making an impact upon religion."[242]

---

237 Comp. the depiction of both cases in Peters; De Vries. "Apostasy", p. 13.

238 These two examples are mentioned by Ahmad. "Conversion", p. 16.

239 The accusations made against a preacher of Babism in Iraq, who was charged under Ottoman jurisdiction in the province of Baghdad as an apostate and sentenced to forced labor but not executed, are reported on by Said Amir Arjomand. "Religious Human Rights and the Principle of Legal Pluralism in the Middle East. Legal Perspectives" in: Johan D. Van der Vyver and John Jr. Witte (eds.). *Religious Human Rights in Global Perspective*. Martinus Nijhoff Publishers: Den Haag, 1996, pp. 331-347, here pp. 338-339. The founder of the movement, the Bāb himself, suffered death by an execution commando in 1850 owing to the instigation of Shiite scholars and his refusal to recant his teaching.

240 Johansen judges that between 1843 and the 1980s "apostasy trials based on published opinions of writers or scholars had practically disappeared in the Middle East": Johansen. "Apostasy", p. 690.

241 Tellenbach. *Apostasie,* with reference to a case Edward William Lane depicts: Edward William Lane, *An Account of the Manners and Customs of the Modern Egyptians*: *Written in Egypt during the years 1833-1835*. Charles Knight & Co: London, 1836.

242 Roald. "Men", p. 31.

According to the predominant understanding of classical theology consonant with Sharia law, the set of problems surrounding the prescribed punishment of an apostate appears to have returned in modernity. Stated more precisely, this has occurred at the end of the 20th century and has done so with increased vehemence. Furthermore, it leads to the question of the reasons and the fundamental mechanisms of this resuscitation of the alleged early Islamic punishment of apostasy.

In particular, the question of apostasy became enmeshed with social and above all political issues at the beginning of the 20th century. Indeed, over the course of the 20th century it became increasingly political. Remarkably however, punishment for apostasy did not find its way anywhere into the legal codification of Muslim majority countries up to the middle of the 20th century.

The early days of Islam are in the 20th century used increasingly by advocates of the death penalty in order to show that the persecution of apostates has "always" been practiced and is, by the way, an act of duty within Islam. This is due to the idea that apostasy is a capital crime and that according to Sharia law, judgment with respect to *ḥudūd* offenses is not forgone. In modern times, apostasy is equated with treason, insurrection, the revocation of political loyalty, and revolution by pointing to the Ridda wars and the apostasy of the Ḫāriǧītes.

1.7.4. The Example of Egypt

Egypt, one of the centers of Sunnite Islam scholarship, plays a central role with respect to there being a revival in charges of apostasy made in modernity. It is the birthplace of one of the most important and nowadays most influential Islamist movements, the Muslim Brotherhood, and at the same time it is the arena for intensive socio-political as well as economic influence exercised by European colonial powers up to the middle of the 20th century.

As early as the 1970s, one can recognize what was the beginning of increasing Islamization in societies marked by Islam. Above all in Egypt, there were clearly perceptible tensions in the debate over how to justify a more secular orientation in political life or legitimate a more strongly Islamic orientation in political life.[243] This secularization debate, which was

[243] For example, this development is referred to by Armando Salvatore in *Islam and the Political Discourse of Modernity*. Ithaca Press: Reading, 1997, pp. 199-200.

closely tied to the perception and judgment of apostasy, can be considered a manifestation of the so-called Islamization and a mirror of the battle between modernists, traditionalists, and reformists.[244] These battles over the ideological direction within politics had effects on the apostasy debate, among others.

In particular, beginning in the 1980s there were an increasing number of charges and cases recorded relating to apostasy,[245] whereby the cases which became a topic in the international press were by far not the only ones. Armin Hasemann counted more than 50 charges relating to apostasy from Islam pending before the courts in Egypt alone in his essay published in 2002 –[246] alone these cases open up a larger field of research. Naturally, questions arise as to the historical and political background of these suddenly occurring and numerous suits against apostasy as well as questions relating to comparisons with pre-modern times, the early 20th century, and the dawn of the 21st century.

Wolf-Dieter Lemke sees the central explanation of the 20th century Egyptian worldview conflict in Egypt's forfeiting its almost unchallenged religious and spiritual leadership in the 18th century and the loss of political influence by the *ᶜulamā'*. These conflicts arose between an ancestrally and traditionally oriented scholarly elite which continued to view itself as the "rightful speakers and spiritual leaders of Egyptian Muslims" into the 20th century[247] and a European-instructed stratum of educated people in post-colonial Egypt.

Along with long-lasting political, economic, social, and legislative influence from the side of colonial powers, with nation building, and the far-reaching marginalization of Islamic law and its confinement to the area of civil law as well as the foundational restructuring of the traditional educa-

---

244 As subsumed by Hasemann. "Apostasiediskussion", p. 72.

245 On the better known cases in modernity there are, for example, Maḥmūd Ṭāhā's condemnation to death by hanging in 1985, the *fatwā* against Salman Rushdie in 1989 linked to a death threat, the assassination of Farağ Fūda in 1992, the divorce case against Naṣr Ḥāmid Abū Zaid in 1993, the assassination of Nağīb Maḥfūẓ in 1994, and the *fatwā* against Taslima Nasreen in 1994 which likewise was linked to a death threat.

246 Hasemann. "Apostasiediskussion", p. 117.

247 Wolf-Dieter Lemke. *Maḥmūd Šaltūt (1893-1963) und die Reform der Azhar. Untersuchungen zu Erneuerungsbestrebungen im ägyptisch-islamischen Erziehungssystem*. Verlag Peter Lang: Frankfurt, 1980, p. 20.

tion system with a far-reaching deprivation of power once held by the *ᶜulamā'*, these scholars in large part forfeited their traditional position and a large portion of their spheres of influence in the administration of justice and education. They were also robbed of more and more of this influence through changed curricula and the establishment of European-shaped educational facilities. Furthermore, since they were still holding onto their time-honored self-conception, their traditional education, and their theological positioning, the gulf steadily grew between the claims of Islamic law and theology and their complete application epitomized by scholars and the reality of a changing society less and less informed by Islamic values.

This development was supposed to have been stemmed from reforms initiated by Maḥmūd Šaltūt at al-Azhar in 1961. The connection between the world of scholarship and society was to be reestablished, at least with respect to the education of the *ᶜulamā'*.[248] This reform, however, was primarily a formal correction of the direction being taken, since in the theological or, as the case may be, worldview positioning of theology no foundational reconciliation between traditional scholarship and modernity took place.

Since in the following centuries, irrespective of the final ending of the colonial era in Egypt's socio-political orientation, neither the thrust in the direction of modernity strengthened, nor the self-image and the basic worldview orientation of the *ᶜulamā'* saw essential change, the conflict continued unresolved. On the one hand, it even intensified through opposing developments such as the founding and influence exercised by the largest Islamic movement, the Muslim Brotherhood, from 1928 onwards. On the other hand, there was progressive secularization within politics and society all the way to alliance with the communist-socialist bloc powers. Public calls for the application of the death penalty for apostasy by a number of *ᶜulamā'* in the last third of the 20th century can be interpreted in this connection as a dramatic and public protest against this lost influence in order to transfer with one beat of the drum religiously founded judgments and the claim of their social validity into the public consciousness and the public sphere.

---

[248] The role of Azhar scholars in politics and society in modern Egypt is illuminated by, for instance, Malika Zeghal in *Gardiens de l'Islam. Les oulémas d'Al Azhar dans l'Égypte contemporaine*. Presses de la Fondation Nationale des Sciences Politiques: Paris, 1996.

This influence has ironically been reclaimed with the aid of secular judges, who have been called upon to support the calls of traditional as well as Islamist leaders of opinion. For this reason Kilian Bälz has made the calls for validation and application of Islamic law in post-colonial Egypt out to be a means of affirming identity and the return to a national legal culture. And these call have not solely come from the Islamist camp.[249]

The charge of apostasy has reached a level of significance over the course of the 20th century as far as legal practice is concerned. It has also reached a level of significance for the public and social climate as well as for the definition of civil rights for intellectuals, journalists, and scholars. This has been shown by the renewed and reclaimed influence of theology or, as the case may be, by a part of theology on society and politics. From this perspective it is before the background of the great significance how influential *ᶜulamā'* judge the question of apostasy in their writings and which consequences they call for in dealing with apostates.

Susanne Olsson finds a need for the preservation of Muslim identity in Egypt to be of significant importance for the increase in charges of apostasy in Egypt over the last two decades of the 20th century. From her viewpoint, Globalization and Westernization, as external factors, are just as much the catalysts as are the internal prevailing difficult social, political, and economic circumstances in Egypt. She sees the significant cause in the ambitions of the actors to achieve political influence over the community and politics as well as in the attempt of opinion leaders "to monopolize 'the sacred.'" In this rivalry what is at stake is defining the alleged true Islam and achieving legitimacy, whereby the charge of apostasy becomes an instrument of power.[250]

Baber Johansen supposes that another causal factor for the emergence of a religious class, which takes a basically distanced attitude to the government and calls for the complete application of the Sharia, is the failure of the state with respect to the economic development, the establishment of social justice and cultural integration as well as the apparent military weakness which developed as shown through the wars lost in the 20th cen-

249 Kilian Bälz. "Die 'Islamisierung' des Rechts in Ägypten und Libyen: Islamische Rechtsetzung im Nationalstaat" in: *RabelsZ* 62 (1998), pp. 437-463, here p. 439.

250 Olsson. "Apostasy", pp. 96+108-110.

tury.[251] Or, as Barry Rubin formulated it in summary form with respect to the years prior to 1990, "Arab regimes had failed at home and abroad."[252] The course of domestic and foreign policy of Ǧamāl ᶜAbd an-Nāṣir had shown itself to be a dead end by the end of his term as President in 1970, and it left the country on the losing side.[253] The begin of Anwar as-Sādāt's term of office, who used religious and even Islamist groups such as the Muslim Brotherhood to level the Nasserite era, marked a turning point and granted the meaning and staging of charges of apostasy a brand new direction.

It was as early as the early 1970's that seeds spread primarily by Sayyid Quṭb germinated and reduced Egyptian society to a community persisting in the *ǧāhilīya*. At the top was a "pharaoh" who made compromises with Western governments and ideologies and thereby conceded Egypt's identity. The result was, among others, the founding of more militant movements than the Muslim Brotherhood, for example the *takfīr wa-'l-hiǧra*, which found favorable conditions in the shadows of a repressive regime and its socio-political failure.[254]

It should come as no surprise that the Islamist spectrum hardly formulated any tolerant assessment of apostasy.[255] The increased number of charges, their increased vehemence, and the condemnation of apostates was in no way limited to this sphere of people or to groups becoming increasingly militant, such as *takfīr wa-'l-hiǧra*, which continued the Quṭb legacy. A not necessarily militant part also spilled into the established halls of scholarship and via them into the center of society. This development,

---

[251] Johansen. "Apostasy", p. 698.

[252] Barry Rubin. *The Long War for Freedom. The Arab Struggle for Democracy in the Middle East*. John Wiley & Sons: Hoboken, 2006, p. 24.

[253] This is emphasized by, among others, by Amy Ayalon in *Egypt's Quest for Cultural Orientation*. The Moshe Dayan Center for Middle Eastern and African Studies: Tel Aviv University, 1999, p. 14.

[254] Comp. on this the analysis of the situation in Egypt in the final third of the 20th century in Omar Ashour's *The De-Radicalization of Jihadists. Transforming armed Islamist movements*. Routledge: London, 2009, pp. 9-10.

[255] Although there are also some advocates of religious freedom within the movement of the Muslim Brotherhood: Noha El-Hennawy. "Islamist Presidential Candidate Declares Conversion Permissible", 16.5.2011. http://www.egyptindependent.com//news/islamist-presidential-candidate-declares-conversion-permissible (15.4.2014).

for which the increasing number of apostasy lawsuits at the end of the 20th century are a sign, enables conclusions to be drawn with respect to the unresolved internal tensions and unanswered questions regarding the justification and essential orientation of politics and the role of religion in the judiciary and society.

Armin Hasemann thus supposes to primarily see an effort by scholars to disassemble the regime by way of the numerous legal cases of apostasy in the last two decades of the 20th century in Egypt. This regime was subject to strong criticism by public uproar via radical forces as well as by secularists. The result was that between all the fronts involved, the government had all policy options taken away. When it was then incapable of acting autonomously, the government was publicly exposed to derision.[256]

As a matter of fact, against the backdrop of the burgeoning Islamism beginning in the middle of the 20th century, the topic of apostasy cannot be separated from the increased politicization of religion and can be interpreted as an attempt on the part of Islamists to create tensions in order to be able to call upon the government to apply the Sharia as it is anchored in the constitution. This is all the more so after the Sharia, which since 1971 had been defined as a source of legislation in Egypt, was declared in 1980 to be the essential source of legislation.[257]

Islamic protagonists were thus able to officially call upon the constitution and profess that in the punishment of apostates one was only dealing with the application of that which was national law anyway. For that reason, an analysis of cases of apostasy from the last three decades cannot avoid attention to inner-Islamic positioning and mutual demarcation between secularization, globalization, and the call for "Islamic awakening" (*ṣaḥwa*) by Islamic movements.[258]

---

256 Hasemann. "Apostasiediskussion", p. 119.

257 For a more detailed comment comp. Baber Johansen. "Zwischen Verfassung, kodifiziertem Recht und Šarīʿa: Die Apostasiegesetzgebung und Rechtsprechung einiger arabischer Staaten" in: Silvia Tellenbach; Thoralf Hanstein (eds.). *Beiträge zum Islamischen Recht IV*. Peter Lang: Frankfurt, 2004, pp. 23-43.

258 Comp. on the "new Egyptian Islamist school" of the late 1970s and the early 1980s Raymond William Baker. "Building the World in a Global Age" in: Armando Salvatore; Mark LeVine (eds.). *Religion, Social Practice and Contested Hegemonies. Reconstructing the Public Sphere in Muslim Majority Societies*. Palgrave Macmillan: New York, 2005, pp. 109-133, here p. 114ff.

Through the perceptible failure on the part of state power to cope with existing economic and social problems in the labor, residential, and educational sectors, the Islamic opposition has been brought onto the scene, which has proclaimed the complete application of Sharia law (including criminal prosecution of apostates) as a way to progress, justice, affluence, and peace. An expression of this has been legislative changes that came about during this time in a number of Muslim majority countries and which also included changes for the question of apostasy: Thus for instance the Sudan and Yemen passed apostasy laws in 1994 with penalties for apostasy from Islam, and after a change in criminal law, Iran threatens "case facts disparaging the prophet" with the death penalty.[259]

Furthermore, in Egypt there is an additional distinctive feature which have given legal cases on account of apostasy an unforeseen boost: the revival of *ḥisba* complaint. Jörn Thielmann mentions the legitimacy of condemning contemporary intellectuals as apostates through the aid and new definition of what was first taken over in the 11th century from predecessors in antiquity and Islamicized as the office of the *muḥtasib* – a preserver of public order, above all one who oversaw the market[260] who supervised sale agreements[261] – and calls it an "invention of tradition"[262]: At this point an alleged "original" Islamic institution is "revived" which at the time of the emergence of Islam demonstrably did not exist and never at all was found in this form as a moral authority for judging the personal belief convictions of Muslims. In its revitalization, the *ḥisba* is above all interpreted by dependence upon Sura 3:110 (*al-amr bi-'l-ma^crūf wa-'n-nahy ^can al-munkar*) as a duty for every individual in order to avert harm to the community and to promote the good.[263]

---

259 Comments thereto in: Silvia Tellenbach. "Neues zum iranischen Strafrecht" in: *ZAA* 18 (1998), pp. 38-42.

260 Cl. Cahen; M. Talbi. "ḥisba" in: *EI*/2, Vol. 3. E. J: Brill: Leiden, 1986, pp. 485-489, here p. 486.

261 According to Khurshid Ahmad in his introduction to Ibn Taymīya's treatment: *al-ḥisba fi 'l-islām: al-Shaykh al-Imām Ibn Taymīya. Public Duties in Islam. The Institution of Ḥisba*. The Islamic Foundation: London, 1982, pp. 7.

262 Thielmann. *Abū Zaid*, pp. 197+36ff.

263 Comp. on the restriction of human rights, women's rights and freedom rights by filing a *ḥisba* complaint The Center for Human Rights Legal Aid (CHRLA). "From Confiscation to Charges of Apostasy. The Implications of the Egyptian Court Decision Ordering the Divorce of Dr. Nasr Hamed Abu-Zeid from his Wife,

As soon as during the 19th century, the office of the *muḥtasib* as a supervisor over the market, who primarily mediated disputes between traders and to a limited degree could take action against violations of the correct execution of transactions,[264] was continually losing significance and at the beginning of the 20th century "had disappeared in almost all Islamic countries."[265] The possibility, indeed the duty for an office to conduct moral supervision over the Muslim community, had never existed in history in this manner. Now, in the course of *ḥisba* cases in the 20th century – which are historically not more precisely defined – this duty was "again" invoked.[266] This particularly supports the agenda of Islamist individuals. Their attempts involve putting their own governments under pressure by pointing to the mandatory implementation of the Sharia as a source of legislation as mentioned in the constitution. Yūsuf al-Qaraḍāwī, who is imputed to belong within the Islamist spectrum, also points to this difference between what is required and what reality is and the necessity for a course correction:

> We call for Islam but we do not act accordingly. We recite the Quran, but we do not implement its directives (*aḥkāmahu*). We purport love to the Apostle (*ḥubb ar-rasūl*) (May God's blessing and peace be upon him), but we do not hold to his *sunna*. We document in our constitutions that Islam is the state religion (*dīn ad-daula huwa 'l-islām*), but we do not grant it the entitled position it has in the dispensation of justice (*ḥukm*), legislation (*tašrīᶜ*), and with respect to (our) orientation (*tauǧīh*) . . . And for that reason we have to begin with reform (*iṣlāḥ*) within ourselves and our societies in line with God's directive before we call for calm (*hudū'*) as well as the safeguarding of wisdom, discretion, and moderation (*iltizām al-ḥikma wa-'s-sakīna wa-'l-iᶜtidāl*) from our youth."[267]

Since 20th century Egyptian law as well as the constitutions of most Muslim majority countries do not make it directly possible to bring charges on

Dr. Ibthal Younis" in: *Dossier. Women Living Under Muslim Laws* 14-15 (1996), pp. 33-44.

264 According to Bälz. "Faith", p. 139.

265 Thielmann. *Abū Zaid*, p. 59.

266 According to Thielmann. ibid., p. 149.

267 Yūsuf al-Qaraḍāwī. *aṣ-ṣaḥwa al-islāmīya baina 'l-ǧumūd wa-'t-taṭarruf. dār aš-šurūq: al-Qāhira*, 2005², p. 20.

account of apostasy, the gravest consequences arise for the apostate through social ostracization. From a legal perspective, this is above all the case in civil law, since the apostate can no longer take possession of an inheritance and may no longer enter into a legal marriage with a Muslim woman or maintain a marriage. This is due to the fact that, according to Sharia law, he is no longer party to a valid marriage.

In a 1963 case concerning this matter, the Egyptian court of cassation decided that a "legal separation of married people . . . is merely a consequence of apostasy according to civil law" and with that does not affect "the freedom of belief as an internal affair of the individual."[268] Furthermore, the case of divorce brought against the Quran scholar Naṣr Ḥāmid Abū Zaid (1943-2010) was based upon the charge of apostasy, since "apostasy is tantamount to death, and the deceased does not possess any place for marriage."[269] Indeed, in legislation there is no offense of apostasy, so that no direct charge is possible on account of apostasy from Islam. The punishment of the apostate is, however, possible via civil law where apostasy is substantiated and can by all means resort to the effective tools of ostracization and discrimination of those who think differently by forced divorce, disinheritance, and removal of children.

By linking an alleged law existing from the time of Muḥammad's life with the *ḥisba* charge, which was little known to the public, through the well known verse from the Quran "*al-amr bi-'l-maᶜrūf wa-'n-nahy ᶜan al-munkar*" (Sura 3:110), it was possible for Abū Zaid's accusers to make his condemnation as an apostate and thus his forced divorce appear to some extent to be an Islamic duty. It therefore served to repel something supposedly reprehensible from society or, as advocates of the *ḥisba* charge formulated it, to defend "Islam."[270]

Among the standard repertoire of Islamists as a manner of self-legitimization,[271] there is an emphasis on the duty to ward off things detri-

268 According to the reasons for the judgment by the court of cassation found in Thielmann. *Abū Zaid*, pp. 85+195.

269 According to Thielmann. ibid., p. 137 from indictment No. 591/1993 at the Giza Civil Court against Abū Zaid.

270 According to Thielmann in his analysis of inner-societal mechanisms which enabled Abū Zaid's conviction in the middle of the 1990s in Egypt: ibid., pp. 225+212.

271 In all probability it is not mere historical interest that the Islamic Foundation located in London published an English translation of the document *Taqī ad-Dīn*

mental to the society. Owing to limited possibilities for objective acquisition of information in countries with restricted access to the press and to a diversity of opinions as well as due to widespread conspiracy theories[272] and numerous negative internal political, social, and economic developments, this meets with much credibility.

By emphasizing an apparent proto-Islam tradition and teaching, which reclaims the practice of the death penalty for apostates since the time of Muḥammad and the four rightly guided caliphs, there is an appearance of continuity through the omission of the theologically diverse and regionally manifold outcomes of Islamic history, by which the present day call for the application of the death penalty for apostasy seems to be a concern of "proto-Islam". With this said, the call to apply a Sharia-based punishment for apostates as something tied to the early days of "true" Islam becomes a means for the *ᶜulamā'* to renew their claim for regaining lost social and political influence as well as providing options of legally valid actions. It is also a *shibboleth* of the desire and will to recapture an alleged ideal Islamic past.

In the apostasy debate it is less a matter of true Islamization of law than it is the use of an instrument of power in order to oppress undesirables as well as to determine a measurement for orthodoxy to which all statements by artists, academics, and intellectuals should be subordinated. The wish thereby is to achieve a definition of what true Islam is. In this scenario al-Azhar, which on the one hand has stood under closer state control since there were far-reaching reforms in 1961 and, on the other hand, has simultaneously remained the most important institute of learning and the most significant mouthpiece for classical scholars, plays an important role as a "third force in the space between the government and the Islamist opposition."[273]

Aḥmad Ibn Taymīyas, al-ḥisba fī 'l-Islām with the title *Public Duties in Islam: The Institution of the Hisba* in 1982. In the foreword the publisher Kurshid Ahmad who is not only the Vice President of *Jamā'at-i-Islāmī* and chairman of the Institute of Policy Studies in Islamabad but also the most important trustee of Maudūdīs bequest justifies the necessity of the *ḥisba* with a verse from Sura 3:110 (ibid., p 9).

272 According to Pink. *Religionsgemeinschaften*, pp. 411+414.

273 On the role played by al-Azhar comp. Steven Barraclough. "Al-Azhar: Between the Government and the Islamists" in: *MEJ* 52/2 (1998), pp. 236-249, here p. 236.

1.7.5. Freedom of Religion or "Inner" Freedom of Belief?

Through the influence of European colonial powers and the partial implementation of European legal codification, Sharia provisions were only partially utilized in marital and family law and no longer in criminal law nor in procedural and commercial law. Sharia came to serve a function as an alibi or torso. At the same time, most constitutions of countries of Arabic character in the 20th century guaranteed religious freedom. The 1971 Egyptian Constitution was, for example, one of the earliest and most comprehensive. On the one hand, it did not concretely define to which areas and forms of expression within issues of religion this freedom extended. However, on the other hand, it did not define the possible limits or, more specifically, the matters of fact relating to apostasy,[274] which had already no longer been punishable under the 1913 Constitution.[275]

Sharia law only still existed with respect to family law. A charge of apostasy was thus actually only possible as a *ḥisba* charge with the justification of warding off injury to the community, as if it was a matter of a political offense of insurgency or rebellion. It was not until January 1996 that there was a law forbidding individuals from directly bringing a *hisba* charge before a court. This law was passed in order to "fight intellectual terrorism and to safeguard intellectuals from tempting to bring moral and psychological damage upon themselves."[276] Beginning in May 1996 *ḥisba* charges were only accepted if the accuser could make a personal and direct interest in the charge credible. Every attempt at a charge from an uninvolved third party can now no longer be punished.

There is a differentiation between an inner – and according to the majority opinion possibly differing – personal conviction for which freedom of belief (*ḥurrīyat al-ᶜaqīda*) exists, and the external membership in a religious community, where there is no free choice for Muslim believers, thus a situation absent of religious freedom (*ḥurrīyat ad-dīn*). This differentiation appears today to be the key to an understanding of the effective degree of freedom in questions of belief and religion, but it is also so with respect

274 Johansen. "Apostasy", p. 696.

275 According to Hasemann. "Apostasiediskussion", p.110.

276 According to the explanation in al-Ahram dated January 30, 1996 of law No. 3/1996, published in: *al-Jarīda al-Rasmiyya* No. 4 dated January 29, 1996; quoted in Bälz. "Faith", p. 141.

to individual freedom of opinion in numerous Muslim majority countries.[277]

Public order, which is defined through Islam as the state religion, has to be maintained according to this understanding under all circumstances. The well-being of the public order, which forbids high treason or rather exposure to corroding infiltration, is essentially superordinated to the interests of the individual.[278] Egypt, it is argued, is in the final event an Islamic state and not a secular one.[279] In this way there is a differentiation between the private person, who is alone responsible to God, and the public person, who is subject to the state and its jurisdiction.[280]

It is precisely this understanding of the reduced freedom of what is solely an internally embraced conviction which is actually defined as freedom: It is the recommendation to not allow one's own worldview positions to get through to the outside or, as the case may be, to evade any additional interrogation by saying the Islamic creed (*šahāda*), which Mahmoud M. Ayoub expresses as the recommended course of action for judges when a defendant is brought before a judge on account of apostasy.[281]

This understanding of the inseparability of the areas of internal, personally gained convictions, and external membership has its precursor in Islamic history[282] and was the force behind modern constitutions.[283] In the

---

277 This is formulated in summary form by Saeed; Saeed. *Freedom*, pp. 95-96 for die positions of Maḥmūd Šaltūt, Ǧamāl al-Bannā, and Muḥammad Sayyid Ṭanṭāwī.

278 According to Forstner as an upshot of the lesson on criminal law from the 1954 execution of the member of the Muslim Brotherhood ᶜAbd al-Qādir ᶜAuda: "Menschenrecht ", pp. 116-117.

279 According to the argumentation of the Egyptian Appellate Court in the case of Abū Zaid, quoted in Bälz. "Faith", p. 150.

280 This conclusion was drawn by Thielmann. *Abū Zaid*, p. 204.

281 "The principle in all this is not to find a way to punish a would be apostate, but rather to find a way out for him or her." Ayoub. Freedom, p. 90.

282 With respect to representatives of the Mu'tazila in the 10th and 11th centuries, Patricia Crone thus makes a differentiation between the publicly practiced religion and the internal convictions which on the one hand allows religious freedom (limited to the internal) and on the other hand does not allow any violation of the publicly practiced religion: Crone. "Islam."

283 Largely according to Mustafa Erdogan in the new formulation of the Turkish Constitution from 1980, which according to his understanding defined the religion of each individual to substantially be a "feeling" which is a private matter of each individual's conscience: Mustafa Erdodan. "Religious Freedom in the Turkish Con-

definition of belief and unbelief, the concept of what was "internal" (*bāṭin*) or, more specifically, the acknowledgment of a non-accessible, appraisable conscience was already a parameter of Egyptian jurisprudence prior to the dawn of modernity.[284]

In past centuries, scholars were already discussing whether it is right and at all possible to clearly judge the (internally embraced) unbelief of a person, which many theologians throughout the course of history have cringed. Where apostasy counts as a danger for the stability of the state, the (lack) of internal conviction has been transformed into what is from the side of the state a tangible offense of rebellion and insurgency. In such case, condemnation on account of apostasy is no longer an attack on one's personal domain of the conscience or a limitation on religious freedom: The call for the death penalty is then a necessary defense, an act of self-defense, for the sake of the *umma*.[285]

At the same time, the death penalty for apostasy has never officially been abolished from within the history of Islamic theology, and the principal justification of its punishment was never placed into question by influential scholarly committees or institutions. This made the 20th century revival of the death penalty as a proto-Islamic matter possible in the first place. Precisely this discrepancy between the effectively appropriate right and the right "truly set by the law" is, for instance, expressed by a member of the leadership of the Muslim Brotherhood, ᶜAbd al-Qādir ᶜAuda (1906-1954). He was professionally active as a judge until 1950)[286] and did not understand the (Egyptian) law's failure to mention the death penalty as permission for apostasy in any way. He also affirmed the justification to punish where no written law existed:

> "Je ne suis pas contre la liberté de croyance, mais je ne permets pas que ces croyances (non-kitabi) (sic) soient pratiquées, faute de quoi nous aurons des

---

stitution" in: *MW* 89/3-4 (1999), pp. 377-388, here p. 378, unfortunately without a source citation.

284 According to Johansen in "Apostasy", pp. 687f.

285 Ibid., pp. 694-695.

286 For a summary of ᶜAuda's political conceptions comp. for instance Krämer. *Staat*, pp. 196-206.

gens qui adoreront les vaches, sans pouvoir les interdire en raison de la constitution."[287]

Hence the guaranteed "freedom of belief" (*ḥurrīyat al-iᶜtiqād* or *ḥurrīyat al-ᶜaqīda)* in the Egyptian Constitution does not mean, for example, religious freedom (*ḥurrīyat ad-dīn* or *ḥurrīyat al-iᶜtiqād ad-dīnī*) in a comprehensive sense.[288] Rather, it is only freedom of inner thought and conviction. Thus, inner thought and conviction becomes clear in religious practice and open membership in groups such as the Bahā'ī,[289] which do not belong to the legally recognized religious communities in Egypt.

"The fundamental right to freedom of belief," which always stands under the qualification of maintaining public order and propriety, which, according to the understanding of the Supreme Court, is oriented towards the Sharia and is to be determined by it, is in reality "legally completely meaningless."[290] This is because an internally embraced conviction does not represent a legally enforceable dimension. In contrast, restrictions and discrimination with respect to access to higher offices in the army, universities, or administration for members of non-recognized religious groups are suited for producing a social climate in which there is at least a multi-class system among the citizens of a state. In this climate, disdain, contempt, ostracization by certain individuals, and even imprisonment and condemnation of such a citizen by the state finds its justification, and an appeal to the constitutionally based guarantee of religious freedom does not help an individual along at all.

With the separation into an internal and an external sphere of religious freedom, confession of belief was made into an act of the state. Furthermore, the offense of sedition was made into harm to the community by a

---

287 Sami Awad Aldeeb Abu-Sahlieh. *L'Impact de la Religion sur l'Ordre Juridique, Cas de l'Egypte, non-musulmans en Pays d'Islam.* Editions universitaires, Fribourg, 1979, p. 266, quoted in *Travaux préparatoires de la constitution de 1953* (op. cit., without year) Vol. 1, p. 90.

288 According to Pink. *Religionsgemeinschaften*, p. 173.

289 It is also stated accordingly by Hans-Georg Ebert that "the phenomenon of religious freedom is understood more strongly as (inner) freedom of belief than as (external) freedom of confession by the Muslim side. Hans-Georg Ebert. *Das Personalstatut arabischer Länder. Problemfelder, Methoden, Perspektiven.* Peter Lang: Frankfurt, 1996, p. 49.

290 As summarized by Pink in *Religionsgemeinschaften*, pp. 186-187.

certificate of baptism or by the stroke of the pen: Publications in word and writing now counted as weapons of modernity to the detriment of the *umma*, which had to be warded off via punishment administered to the apostate. This led to an eruption of a vast number of cases of apostasy which turned out rather harshly against feminists and intellectuals, artists and theologians, scientists and writers in the 1980s and 1990s, even with the simultaneous commitment to religious freedom as anchored in the constitution. In particular, this occurred as one saw noticeable resistance against Europeanization and the displacement of Islamic law in the first third of the 20th century.[291]

Therefore, according to this understanding, Abū Zaid's condemnation "on account of apostasy . . . [was] not in contradiction to freedom of belief (*ḥurrīyat al-ᶜaqīda*), despite his holding to Islam. The constitutionally-based guarantee of the freedom of belief was thereby not affected," for the "conviction of belief (*iᶜtiqād*) is hidden within the individual and not accessible to the judiciary."[292] For that reason, the punishment of this attack on Islam does not contradict the personal freedom of the accused.

In the process, the court makes a differentiation between falling away from the faith, which it judges, and the person and his most deeply held convictions, which it does not judge. It separates them from each other as if one has nothing to do with the other and as a worldly court declares itself to be the highest authority over belief and unbelief. The court does so by elevating the writings of an individual who himself is a confessing Muslim to something destructive to the Muslim community, thus making such undertaking a political act.[293]

This climate concretely expresses itself in Egypt in often made calls in the press nowadays to move against acknowledged religious communities not seen as revealed religions. On the other hand, in newspapers counted as falling within the Islamist spectrum, such action, especially in the middle of the 1980s and less so in the 1990s, was seen as applying *ridda* laws and the death penalty for apostates for the protection of the majority religion.

291 Bälz names as an example the demand brought forward by the Muslim Brotherhood in the 30's to bring Sharia law to bear: Bälz. "'Islamisierung'", p. 439.

292 Thielmann. *Abū Zaid*, p. 190.

293 According to Johansen summarizing the court decision on apostasy beginning in the 1980s last century: Johansen. "Apostasy", pp. 688+705.

This also had effects upon adherents of non-acknowledged religious communities such as Bahā'ī.[294]

In 1986, a call was made by a member of the Muslim Brotherhood for the Egyptian government to bring before Parliament an existing legal draft in existence since 1977 which was to make apostasy from Islam punishable. After this did not happen, the individual indicated that he would himself bring a draft of the law into Parliament which would stipulate the execution of apostates by hanging,[295] an event which likewise offers an insight into the social climate at the start of increased legal cases of apostasy in the 1980s and 1990s in Egypt.

1.8. Contemporary Dealings with Apostates in Muslim Majority Societies

1.8.1. Social Reality

The question of dealing with apostates in Muslim majority countries at the beginning of the 21st century is not unilinear, and a universal answer cannot be given for all religions.[296] There are laws in existence which make apostasy directly punishable in only the fewest of countries, let alone punishment which involves the threat of the death penalty. Thus, while there appears to be some clear hesitation with respect to anchoring the condemnation of apostasy in the legal texts of the individual countries, the apostate, the confessing atheist or critic, the journalist or progressive Quranic scholar, the women's rights or human rights activists, the convert, or the member of a non-recognized minority, by making his worldview position known, is confronted with different consequences depending on the local situation:

---

294 Examples in Pink. *Religionsgemeinschaften*, pp. 320ff.

295 Comp. the description of this incident in Forstner's "Menschenrecht", pp. 105-106.

296 Detailed studies on the situation of apostates in each particular country are still lacking. The most richly detailed depiction of the situation in individual states and regions with what is simultaneously the most comprehensive collection of individual cases is in my opinion the study published in December 2011: Paul Marshall; Nina Shea. *Apostasy*.

These consequences could likewise contain social questions such as ostracization, discrimination and being disadvantaged, the loss of employment and one's residence as well as social death, thus legal consequences including forced divorce, disinheritance, or the removal of children and even physical death which in a number of states is by all means a real consequence presented by apostasy from Islam, or, more generally, a consequence of an undesired religious or worldview position.

This reality of far-reaching consequences alongside constitutionally guaranteed religious freedom is shown, for instance, in the case of the Kuwaiti convert Ḥusain Qambar ᶜAlī in the middle of the 1990s. As a consequence of a custody battle for his children and the fact that his conversion to Christianity thereby became publicly known, he was first charged in May 1996 by a Sharia court with apostasy and found guilty. However, in spite of the low court recommendation to condemn him to death, he was not executed. Instead, he received a passport shortly before his court case was taken up again and was able to leave the country.

The Constitution of Kuwait, which does not contain a passage on apostasy, is formulated as follows in Article 35 with respect to religious freedom: "Freedom of belief is absolute." However, it restricts this statement by including the following: "The State protects the freedom of practising religion in accordance with established customs, provided that it does not conflict with public policy or morals."[297] Qambar ᶜAlī, who had been excluded by his family from succession with respect to inheritance and had been increasingly threatened in public, went underground after the court case out of fear of attempts on his life, lost his family, his employment, and his home. He emigrated temporarily to the USA but later returned to Kuwait.[298]

It is not uncommon that one's own family or society participates in ostracization and persecution, and in part there are participants on the side of the state, such as the police or security forces.[299] The worldview justification

---

297 Kuwait – Constitution, Adopted: 11.11.1962. http://www.servat.unibe.ch/icl/ku00000_.html (15.4.2014).

298 Comp. the depiction of the case in: Racius. "Limits", pp. 5-21 as well as in Longva's "Apostasy", p. 14.

299 The latter is for instance expressly mentioned by Maurits S. Berger in "Apostasy and Public Policy in Contemporary Egypt: An Evaluation of Recent Cases from Egypt's Highest Courts" in: *HRQ* 25 (2003), pp. 720-740, here p. 722.

for this comes predominantly from the mouth of imams, mullahs, or scholars. Among them are a number who use their influence in Muslim majority countries to implant in society the sense of duty to kill apostates as a command of Islam. For that reason, they have to be viewed as a driving force in the call to follow the Sharia in light of the far-reaching lack of governmental legislation against apostasy and regarding the punishment of apostasy.

The condemnation or execution of apostates, in particular when it serves one's own retention of power, occurs in part with state knowledge or approval. In other cases, it occurs with state participation or more specifically by state order. Frequently, the involved party is not officially charged and condemned on account of apostasy but rather on account of insurgency, causing division within society, disruption of societal peace,[300] degrading the reputation of the nation, or on account of alleged offenses, such as espionage, adultery, drug dealing, or high treason.[301] In other cases, the individual accused of apostasy is executed in broad daylight during the course of the legal investigation or after his acquittal.[302]

1.8.2. The Significance of Sharia Law

By reducing Sharia law to marital and family law and by adopting western legal norms over the course of colonization and nation building, what

300 This is referred to for the Egyptian context by Berger, ibid.

301 This is also emphasized by Mayer in *Islam*, pp. 146 with reference to Bahā'ī charges in Iran on account of such crimes.

302 Pakistan in particular has repeatedly had reports of deadly attacks on accused individuals who have been charged with apostasy and blasphemy: Thus, for instance, the 44 year old teacher and short story author Niamat Ahmar was charged with blasphemy after he not only made multiple calls for peace and brotherliness in his publications, but also as a member of the teaching staff tried to expose the misuse of money and resources in his school. On January 6, 1992 he was killed by a knife attack conducted by Farooq Ahmad prior to the trial in the offices of the District Education Officer in Faisalabad. Farooq Ahmad stated that it was "the 'religious duty' to punish and kill" Ahmar. After the murder of Ahmar, public cheering broke out in his hometown of Miani while at the same time the investigations were delayed. Comp. this report as well as the presentation of additional cases of extra-legal executions and cases of death of those detained after charges were brought on account of apostasy and blasphemy in Pakistan in Chaudhry Naeem Shakir's "Fundamentalism, Enforcement of Shariah and Law on Blasphemy in Pakistan" in: *al-mushir* 34/4 (1992), pp. 113-129, here pp. 114+115.

emerged in most Muslim majority countries were typically contradictory conceptions of legality: On the one hand, there is the written law, which, in particular as far as criminal law is concerned, shows hardly any echo of classical Sharia law. For example, religious courts of justice were abolished in Egypt in 1956; since that time the administration of justice has basically had a secular orientation.

On the other hand, the constitution by all means makes reference to the Sharia. Indeed, this reference has been intensified over the past three decades. Thus, in Egypt in 1980 a constitutional change resulted in the Sharia's being declared the primary source of legislation without this being concretely reflected in penal legislation. Legislation does not mention a word about apostasy, whereby the creation of a corresponding societal climate can apparently allow the thought of individual duty to implement Sharia law to indeed arise.[303]

The tug of war for influence on legislation between religious and secular powers in Egypt in the second half of the 20th century also became clear by the fact that at that time several committees within the government and at al-Azhar presented drafts for Sharia-compliant legal codification.[304] However, they achieved no actual significance and in 1985 were finally put aside.[305]

Next to politics and society, there is thus a third force in the persecution of apostates. It is the influential group of established traditional theologians and scholars from mosques and universities, who for the most part preach a universal applicability of Sharia law even if they do not call for the practical implementation of Sharia law. This means that the contradiction between the written, valid law and Sharia law which is preached as proper and yet invalid is continually made a topic. In particular, this hap-

303 Comp. several examples in chapter 1.8.6.

304 Thus from the side of al-Azhar University in 1978 there was a legal draft formulated and approved by the Egyptian State Council (*mağlis ad-daula*) which designated apostasy as a punishable act for which the imposition of the death penalty was to be possible: Ian Edge. "A Comparative Approach to the Treatment of Non-Muslim Minorities in the Middle East, with Special Reference to Egypt" in: Chibli Mallat; Jane Connors (eds.). *Islamic Family Law*. Graham & Trotman: London, 1993, pp. 31-53, here pp. 48-49.

305 As summarized by Alexander Flores in "Ägypten" in: Werner Ende; Udo Steinbach (eds.). *Der Islam in der Gegenwart*. C. H. Beck: München, 2005^5, pp. 477-489, here p. 479.

pens due to the fact that over the course of Islamic history, Sharia law has not been referenced solely by influential scholars with respect to validity in the theological sphere and declared to be principally invalid or superseded in the politico-social realm.

Therefore, the Sharia remains a permanently present quantity via its prominently referenced position in constitutions. However, its influence on legislation and politics has not been further defined. Thus, from the viewpoint of Islamist forces, it is a completely undervalued quantity. The awareness that "real" Sharia law stands above worldly law is especially kept alive by religious scholars. On the other hand, concrete legislation only makes general reference to the fact that behavior against the Sharia, for instance apostasy, is viewed as reprehensible in the public consciousness. This consciousness is additionally kept alive by formulations of law which make reference to inappropriate behavior, even if done so in a very vague form. An example is Law 95, dating from 1980. It was drafted by President Anwar al-Sādāt and adopted by the People's Assembly. It prohibits "shameful conduct" and for that reason is called "*qānūn al-ᶜaib*" (Law of Shame) in colloquial speech.[306]

For example, it is clear from the prohibition against missions work by adherents of other religions which commonly exists: In arguably all Muslim majority countries, this prohibition is justified from classical Sharia law. For a start, there is reference to the *ḏimmī* prohibition, which is against the Islamic community's being reduced in size when people are lured away.[307] It is seen as an infringement against the *ordre public*, or public order, and thereby is considered to be socially corrosive and unacceptable, even if a prohibition on mission work is not regulated by law. In a number of countries that is the case, for example in Morocco, where Article 220 II of the Moroccan Penal Code, by threat of a prison term of six months to two years and a fine of 200-500 dirhams, prohibits the neediness of an individual from being exploited by offering forms of aid and soliciting believing Muslims away from Islam.[308] Against the backdrop of application of the law, however, there is no doubt that the prohibition against solicitation is the core of the law, especially since the charge of exploiting the neediness with the simultaneous widespread economic need of a good

306 According to Edge's "Approach", p. 49.
307 As formulated by Khoury. *Christen*, p. 94.
308 Forstner. "Menschenrecht", p. 114.

portion of the population could hardly be effectively rebutted in any specific case.

1.8.3. The Legal Reality in Questions relating to Apostasy

Thus the paradoxical situation arises – Abdullahi an-Na'im calls it "an extremely serious ambivalence"[309] – that the constitutions of a number of Muslim majority countries expressly convey the right to religious freedom,[310] and yet there is no true positive or negative religious freedom in any direction. Rather, there is only the freedom to convert to Islam. In the process, on the basis of frequent dramatic consequences for the apostate, the question of the justification of religious freedom not only has a religious dimension. Rather, there are also social and political consequences. The fact that neither classic nor contemporary Islamic theology has ever brought forward a generally accepted definition of apostasy means that the very changeable filling of this term allows application to all sorts of situations.[311]

Several hundred individual cases where charges on account of apostasy have been made could be listed here. However, they yield only little additional knowledge in a study of the history of ideas. Additionally, research into these cases from a scholarly point of view is not unproblematic. This is due to the fact that verifiable information or, more specifically, reports and

[309] Abdullahi Ahmed An-Na'im. Religious Minorities under Islamic Law and the Limits of Cultural Relativism in: *HRQ* 9 (1987), pp. 1-18, here p. 14.

[310] A number of examples from corresponding passages of text in the constitutions of Syria, Jordan, Algeria, Yemen, Mauretania, and Morocco guaranteeing religious freedom can be seen in Abu-Sahlieh. "Délit", pp. 96ff.

[311] For instance the Saudi scholar Abdul Rahman al-Barrak condemned the publication of two authors as apostasy in a *fatwā* who, deviating from his own opinion, had published an article in the Saudi newspaper Al-Riyadh. A few days later there were 20 additional Saudi scholars who had associated themselves with Abdul Rahman al-Barrak's viewpoint in an open letter. al-Barrak declared Aba Al-Kheil and Abdullah bin Bjad Al-Otaibi to be unbelievers and called upon them to repent; otherwise they were to be executed. Comp. the following depiction of the case: Former Qatar University Dean of Islamic Law Dr. Abd Al-Hamid Al-Ansari in AAFAQ Article Responds to Fatwa Calling for Two Saudi Writers' Killing. MEMRI Special Dispatch No 1888, 7.4.2008. http://www.memri.org/report/en/0/0/0/0/0/0/2699.htm (15.4.2014).

opinions from various sides are in many cases not obtainable. The local press frequently does not report. Alternatively, it reports the case from a perspective which does not place the focus on the injury to religious freedom. Rather, it emphasizes the potential danger that emanates from this person or his "offenses" which have otherwise allegedly made him guilty.

Therefore, in the following I limit myself to a paradigmatic depiction summarizing a number of known cases of apostasy which have already been soundly worked through in a scholarly manner. Also, there are a number of heretofore unknown cases where there is a favorable foundation as far as available literature is concerned. In doing so, the cases have to do with situations where confessing Muslims who continue to consider themselves as believers are looked upon as having become apostates in the eyes of others.[312] There are also cases where individuals have performed a turning away from Islam, for example through conversion.

Finally, groups are to be mentioned in this connection which, as post-Quranic religions, enjoy no official recognition within Islamic theology, possess no legal status within a number of Muslim majority states, and which count as apostates simply due to their religious affiliation. This affects the Aḥmadīya movement in a particular way, as in 1974 it was excluded from the National Assembly of Pakistan upon the initiative of Saudi Arabia. For that reason, adherents of the Aḥmadīya movement in Pakistan are no longer allowed to call themselves Muslims, can no longer make calls to come to prayer, and their meeting places may no longer be designated as mosques. They count as apostates per se and have no right to exercise their religion.

Likewise affected are in some locations the Bahā'ī, which like the Aḥmadīya suffer from sui generis mistrust due to the fact that the story of their emergence is post-Quranic and – depending on the geographic region – suffer from discrimination and even threats upon their lives. There are a number of studies having to do with the situation this group faces.[313] As

---

312 Thus the judgment of the Egyptian Attorney General in November 1987 that a group of 28 members under the leadership of a former al-Azhar Sheik were apostates because this individual taught that the basis of Islam should only be the Quran and not the *sunna* or other sources. This example is mentioned by Forster. "Menschenrecht", p. 106.

313 Comp. in particular the studies by Sanasarian. *Minorities*; Pink. *Religionsgemeinschaften* and Uphoff. *Untersuchung*.

unwelcome individuals who think differently, they are frequently subject to the Islamist practice of being declared unbelievers because they do not share the politicized position Islamists have, and *takfīr* is thus attributed to them.

1.8.4. The Situation in Individual Countries

An official charge of apostasy is possible on the basis of a formulation in the penal code in only a few Muslim majority countries. In most of these countries, argumentation relating to an infringement rests upon the idea of *ordre public*. That means that along with apostasy or, as the case may be, conversion, there is an automatic interpretation of presumed criticism of Islam as a state religion[314] and that, respectively, there is criticism of the Sharia as the most important or sole source of legislation, essentially undermining the foundations of the Islamic state. More specifically, it is interpreted as an attempt to overthrow or to split the nation or even to collaborate with foreign powers. Regardless of a commitment to religious freedom in a number of constitutions in Muslim majority countries, even if a criminal provision on apostasy is lacking – neither unlimited religious freedom with the opportunity to convert to any faith nor immunity from prosecution can be assumed for apostates. The "World Report 2012" of "Human Rights without Frontiers International" mentions eight countries where apostasy is punishable by the death penalty today: Afghanistan, Iran, Malaysia, Mauretania, Saudi Arabia, Somalia, Sudan and Yemen; in Jordan and Egypt, the apostate will according to this report most probably suffer from a form of "social death" and will be outlawed.[315] The Washington-based Think Tank "Pew Research Center for the People and the Press" adds to these eight countries where apostasy is punishable by the death penalty another 12 countries where apostasy is punishable in principle, e.g. by applying Muslim family law: Pakistan, Bahrain, Qatar, UAE, Oman, Egypt, Syria, Iraq, Jordan, Nigeria, Maldives and the Comoro Islands.[316]

---

314 This is pointed out by Tellenbach. "Apostasie".

315 Willy Fautré; Jan Nils Schubert; Vaiya, Alfiaz (eds.). *Freedom of Religion or Belief.* World Report 2012. Human Rights Without Frontiers Int.: Brussels, [2013]

316 "Which Countries Still Outlaw Apostasy and Blasphemy?" http://www.pewresearch.org/fact-tank/2014/05/28/which-countries-still-outlaw-apostasy-and-blasphemy/, 28.5.2014 (10.6.2014).

Since the Sharia counts in a number of cases as a significant or even the sole source of legislation,[317] a judgment can also be justified on principle as in agreement with the foundations of Sharia law or, alternatively if called for by established representatives from the realms of theology, jurisprudence, or the government. This is also so when a legal provision is missing, even when, notably, in the area of Egyptian penal law no legislation oriented towards Sharia law exists. Thus, Article 1 §2 of the Egyptian Criminal Code reads as follows:

> "In the absence of applicable text of law (sic), the judge may rule according to customary law *('urf)*. In the absence of customary law, according to Islamic *sharia'a*. And finally, in the absence of all the above, according to natural law *(qanun tabi'i)* and the rules of justice *(qawa'id al-'adala)*."

If the judge does not apply these principles, he can even be prosecuted for contempt of justice.[318]

Furthermore, the choir of voices of influential theologians is thoroughly dissonant. Owing to what the current events are, they can position themselves in novel and diverse ways. Thus, the Grand Mufi of Egypt, ^{c}Alī Ğum^{c}a, basically rejected a sentencing for apostasy enforced by the state on July 21, 2007 in the course of the public discussion surrounding the sensational case involving the journalist Muḥammad Hegazy. He had converted to Christianity in 1998. Hegazy had applied for new personal identification documents in 2007 with his changed religious affiliation and thereby made his conversion public. Just two days later, on July 23, 2007, ^{c}Alī Ğum^{c}a, revised his own statement and declared the punishment of an apostate as legal.[319] At the same time, the Minister for Religious Affairs at

[317] The Constitution of Egypt of September 11, 1971 mentioned Islam as the state religion in Article 2. A 1980 constitutional amendment narrowed this formulation to the effect that the Sharia is the primary source of legislation.

[318] According to the wording and the rationale in: Ahmed Seif al-Islam Hamad. "Legal Plurality and Legitimation of Human Rights Abuses. A Case Study of State Council Rulings Concerning the Rights of Apostates" in: Baudouin Dupret; Maurits Berger; Laila al-Zwaini (eds.). *Legal Pluralism in the Arab World.* Kluwer Law International: Den Haag, 1999, pp. 219-228, here p. 221.

[319] Ramadan Al Sherbini. "Top cleric denies 'freedom to choose religion' comment," 24.7.2007. http://gulfnews.com/news/region/egypt/top-cleric-denies-freedom-to-choose-religion-comment-1.191048 (15.4.2014).

that time, Maḥmūd Ḥamdī Zaqzūq[320] (b. 1933), confirmed the principal legality of the death penalty.[321]

There are three concrete possibilities which exist to punish apostasy with legal assistance in various countries.[322] A few countries immediately introduced laws relating to this and allow for punishment for apostasy from Islam.[323] Among them are, for instance, Northern Sudan, which unambiguously established the death penalty for apostasy in Article 126 of the 1991 Sudanese Penal Code.[324]

"1. Every Muslim who advocates the renunciation of the creed of Islam, or who publicly declares his renouncement thereof by an express statement or conclusive act, shall be deemed to commit the offence of apostasy.

2. Whoever commits apostasy shall be given a chance to repent during a period to be determined by the court; if he persists in his apostasy, and is not a recent convert to Islam, he shall be punished to death.

---

320 Maḥmūd Ḥamdī Zaqzūq had publicly declared his attitude towards apostasy a number of years before: Mahmoud Zakzouk. "Fragen zum Thema Islam". Shorouk Intl. Bookshop: [Cairo], 2004, p. 108.

321 According to the report of the International Society for Human Rights: Egypt: "Muslim Authorities Call for Beheading of Convert. Minister for Religion Approves Death Penalty for Defection from Islam – The ISHR Appeals to President Mubarak to Protect Converts," 30.8.2007. http://www.ishr.org/Detailansicht.861+M5b2895cd995.0.html (15.4.2014).

322 With this arrangement I am following the study based on the survey on religious freedom in various Muslim majority states and entitled *No Place to Call Home. Experiences of Apostates from Islam. Failures of the International Community.* Christian Solidarity Worldwide: New Malden, 2008, pp. 43ff.

323 For that reason. the occasionally formulated assumption that apostasy is not punished with death anywhere and exclusively has social consequences, along with a general assertion such as, for example, postulated by Longva, is inappropriate: "Nowadays, in societies where conversion from Islam is still viewed as a crime, apostates are no longer executed but are deprived of the right to remain married to their Muslim spouse(s), to retain guardianship over their Muslim-born children, to inherit, and their right to dispose of properties . . ." Longva. "Apostasy", p. 260. Longva additionally expresses the following on the death penalty: "This question no longer has practical relevance, since . . . apostates are no longer executed" (ibid., p. 260).

324 On March 22, 1991 the Sudanese government under Ḥasan al-Turābī passed a penal code based on Sharia standards, which is still in force.

3. The penalty provided for apostasy shall be remitted whenever the apostate recants his apostasy before his execution."[325]

Yemen, which has declared the Sharia to generally be the source of all legislation, also has a similarly sounding regulation in its 1994 Yemeni Penal Code.[326] Likewise Malaysia, in Kelantan's Syariah Criminal Code II enacted in 1993, Section 23(1) prescribes the death penalty for apostasy if the offender refuses to return to Islam and to repent. The State of Terengganu passed a similar law in 2002, the Syariah Criminal Offence (Hudud and Qisas) Enactment.[327] Some other federal states of Malaysia threaten the apostate with punishment or re-education in one of the rehabilitation centers.[328]

The second category includes countries in which admittedly no codified sanction against apostasy exists. However, on the basis of a general legislative orientation towards Sharia law, it is principally possible to punish apostates, be it by fines, imprisonment, or death. These countries include Saudi Arabia, which does not possess any codified penal code but in Article 26 of its Basic Law of Governance contains the following: "The State shall protect human rights in accordance with the Sharia."[329] This makes the protection of human rights outside of the Sharia, e.g., for apostates, impossible. A special case is represented by Pakistan, which admittedly has no direct legal provision addressing a change of religion. However, clauses were added to the blasphemy laws in 1991. As a consequence,

---

[325] Quoted in Abdelfattah Amor. "Addendum 2 of the Interim Report on the Elimination of all Forms of Religious Intolerance relating to a Visit to the Sudan." United Nations General Assembly, Fifty-first session, Agenda item 110 (b). 11. November 1996, A/51/542/Add.2. http://un.org/documents/ga/docs/51/plenary/a51-542 add2.htm (15.4.2014).

[326] Peters labels the penal codes of Yemen and Sudan the sole penal codes which directly call for the death penalty for apostasy: Peters. *Crime*, p. 168.

[327] Comp. the comprehensive presentation of the judgment on apostasy in Malaysia in Saeed; Saeed. *Freedom*, pp. 123ff.

[328] Mohamed Azam Mohamed Adil. "Law of Apostasy and Freedom of Religion in Malaysia" in: *AJCL* 2/1 (2007), pp. 1-36.

[329] Quoted in Herbert Baumann; Matthias Ebert (eds.). *Die Verfassungen der Mitgliedsländer der Liga der Arabischen Staaten*. Berlin Verlag: Berlin, 1995, pp. 618.

the death penalty has to be imposed upon every individual convicted of blaspheming Muḥammad.[330]

It is a similar case in Somalia, Mauritania (Article 306 of the 1984 Penal Code),[331] and in Iran, where according to §513 of the Iranian Penal Code the individual who slanders religion (meaning Islam) can be punished with imprisonment and lashings of the whip or, insofar as the act is judged to be a "blaspheming of the Prophet," with death.[332] Since 1996, through a change to penal law, an insult to Muḥammad is under the threat of the death penalty, but up to now the Iranian Penal Code does not contain a paragraph explicitly calling for the death penalty in the case of apostasy from Islam. There have, however, been advances in this direction:

On September 9, 2008, the Iranian Parliament (*Majlis*) voted in favor of a legal draft on "apostasy, heresy and witchcraft" which allowed for the death penalty for apostasy.[333] Up to this date (2016), it has not been presented to the Guardian Council for approval. If that occurs, the Guardian Council has to decide on the law presented to it in a very short time. If the law is passed, that would be the first time codification of the criminal offense of apostasy in Iran.

And yet that does not mean that apostasy in Iran remains without consequences[334] or is exempt from punishment: Article 167 of the Islamic Re-

330 Comp. the wording of the law at http://www.pakistani.org/pakistan/legislation/1860/actXLVof1860.html (15.4.2014).

331 The wording of the penal code of Mauretania expressly labels apostasy in stating that the "crime d'apostasie, soit par parole, soit par action, de façon apparente ou évidente . . . s'il ne se repent pas . . . il est condamné à mort en tant qu'apostat . . . Toute personne coupable du crime d'apostasie . . . sera . . . punie de la peine de mort." Quoted in Samir Kahlil Samir. "Le Débat autour du Délit d'Apostasie dans l'Islam contemporain" in: John J. Donohue; Christian W. Troll (eds.). *Faith, Power, and Violence. Muslims and Christians in a Plural Society, Past and Present.* Pontificio Istituto Orientale: Rom 1998, pp. 115-140, here p. 117.

332 According to the report by Amnesty International: Dieter Karg. "Besitz der Satanischen Verse," http://aidrupal.aspdienste.de/umleitung/2000/deu06/080?print=1 (15.4.2014); a legal framework which Petra Uphoff confirms for the year 2008: Uphoff. *Untersuchung*, p. 55.

333 The text appeared with the date 11.12. 2007 on the page of the Iranian Ministry of Justice http://maavanews.ir/tabid/38/Default.aspx (14.5. 2011).

334 Comp. the list of repressive measures against converts, opposition members, and minorities in Iran in the annually published situation report: *Amnesty International*

public of Iran Constitution stipulates that a judge has to base his judgment on Islamic sources or, more specifically, on valid *fatāwā* in cases where a law covering a particular issue is lacking.[335] Additionally, according to Article 170 of the Constitution, no judgment can be made which contradicts the laws of Islam.

The currently valid penal code of Iran is codified in the "Islamic Penal Law" dated July 30, 1991. Since that time it has provisionally been in force and is at present prolonged every two years. However, it is not part of the legislative penal code passed by the Parliament of Iran. It formulates the following in Articles 225.7 and 225.8: "Punishment for an (. . .) [male] apostate is death . . . The highest penalty for apostate women (...) is lifelong imprisonment. During this time of punishment her living conditions will be made difficult as directed by the court and attempts will be made to guide her to the right path . . ." Rūḥollāh Khomeinī adds the following as an interpretive provision: "She is to receive lashing at the five times of daily prayer, and her quality of life and amount of food, clothing, and water have to be reduced until she demonstrates remorse."[336]

Article 226 of the Iran Penal Code additionally permits the killing of an apostate without charges and court proceedings. Furthermore, according to Article 295 of the penal code, the executor administering the death penalty on an apostate or a person held to be an apostate is not punished.

Up to now, the term *murtadd* only appears in Article 26 of the Iranian Press Law as a slanderer of Islam and of its values.[337] However, in Iran it is

---

Report 2011. Zur weltweiten Lage der Menscherechte. S. Fischer: Frankfurt, 2011, pp. 205-211.

335 Thus Hossein Soodmand in Mashad was brought to court on December 3, 1990 for his lapsing from Islam 30 years prior and in spite of the lack of a corresponding paragraph in the Iranian penal code was sentenced to death by hanging on account of apostasy with reference to Sharia law: Alasdair Palmer, "Hanged for being a Christian in Iran," 11.10.2008. http://www.telegraph.co.uk/news/worldnews/middleeast/iran/3179465/Hanged-for-being-a-Christian-in-Iran.html (15.4.2014).

336 Max Klingberg. "Abfall vom Islam in der Islamischen Republik Iran. Rechtslage nach der Präsidentschaftswahl vom 12. Juni 2009." Unpublished report, International Society for Human Rights (ISHR): Frankfurt [2010] (copy from the ISHR collection).

337 Uphoff. *Untersuchung*, p. 141.

> "perfectly clear to every Iranian that the death penalty stands in the case of apostasy. Moreover, conversion counts as an attack on the Islamic state and the Islamic community and is to be punished as 'war against God.'"[338]

At least since 2009, the onset of the "Green Revolution", converts from Islam to Christianity and similarly many women's rights activists[339] have been especially severely persecuted, their private meetings dissolved, and the members of house churches sentenced to long periods of imprisonment or even condemned to be executed. Since 1979, apostates have repeatedly been brought before courts in Iran under the explicit charge of apostasy – but also under other charges.[340]

Since the death penalty can be administered in Iran for numerous offenses such as murder, drug smuggling, terrorism, warring against God (*Mohareb*), armed robbery, highway robbery, subversion, obtaining weapons, treason, embezzlement and the misappropriation of public funds, forming gangs, insults against and desecration of institutions of Islam or holy individuals (which, for example, counts essentially as a given through missions work by converts) as well as for rape, homosexuality, sexual relationships between a non-Muslim and a Muslim as well as adultery,[341]

---

338 Summarized for the situation in Iran: Uphoff. ibid., p. 140.

339 The public condemnation of women's rights activists as apostates has also been used in other countries as as a weapon to discredit them. Thus, in 1990 in Saudi Arabia, upon the stationing of US troops in the course of the Second Gulf War, several dozen women got behind the wheel and drove through the streets of Riyadh. They were labeled apostates. In Morocco the charge was brought specifically in the run-up to measures for the legal and social equality of women which led to the issuance of the *Moudawana*: For these and other examples see Nancy Gallagher's "Apostasy" in: *EWIC*, Vol. 2, pp. 7-9, here p. 7; for the last example comp. the more comprehensive explanation of the debates in the run-up to the adoption of the *Moudawana*, in which the link to the charge of apostasy was raised, in Anna Kristina Virkama's *Discussing Moudawana. Perspectives on Family Law Reform, Gender Equality and Social Change in Morocco*. M.A. Thesis, University of Joensuu/Finnland, Faculty of Social Science, 2006, pp. 12-15.

340 Thus summarized by Uphoff. *Untersuchung* p. 137ff.; see ibid. the 2008 submitted draft for a change in legislation on "Apostasie, Ketzerei und Zauberei" ("Apostasy, Heresy, and Magic"), p. 146ff.

341 According to a list of offenses presently carrying the death penalty taken from documentation from within the country gathered by German government institutions, June 2010 (copy from private collection).

charges against apostates are possible at any time under the claim of one of these offenses.

For instance, human rights organizations reported on the imprisonment of Yousef Nadarkhani, mentioning his conversion to Christianity in 1996 and on September 22, 2010 his sentencing to death on account of apostasy and conducting missionary activities. Nadarkhani had been the pastor of a house church with 400 members in Rasht in the Gilan Province. Nadarkhani's wife was also imprisoned and sentenced to lifelong imprisonment (she was, however, later released), and Nadarkhani's lawyer Mohammad Ali Dadkhah was convicted and sentenced in July 2011 to pay a fine, receive lashings, serve a 9 year term of imprisonment, and undergo a 10-year occupational ban as a lecturer and lawyer. The governor of Gilan labeled Nadarkhani a "rapist," "extortionist," and "Zionist."[342] After several international protests, among others by members of the German Parliament, Nadarkhani was released unexpectedly,[343] even though it should be kept in mind that a larger number of people continue to be imprisoned in Iran under the charge of apostasy.[344]

In a third category of countries one finds that apostasy is not directly punishable. However, the apostate can either be punished via civil law (forced divorce, disinheritance, removal of children) or another offense can be brought against the individual, such as exercising force upon or enticing Muslims to take up another religion (for instance in Algeria), the destruction of national unity, or "denigrating the Government of the Republic of Turkey" (Article 301), which can be punished according to the respective penal law catalogs.[345]

---

[342] Comp. the earlier reports of the International Society for Human Rights: http://www.igfm.de/Iran-Todesstrafe-fuer-Pastor-Youcef-Nadarkhani.2942.0.html and http://www.igfm.de/Detailansicht.384+M5a9eccbb165.0.html (13.10. 2011).

[343] "Islamische Republik Iran: Freispruch und Haftentlassung für Pastor Youcef Nadarkhani", 10.9.2012, http://www.igfm.de/ne/?tx_ttnews%5Btt_news%5D=1762&cHash=743035d888280393bb9157a2fed6dede (15.4.2014).

[344] Comp. the names of house church leaders presently imprisoned in Iran: Fautré; Schubert; Vaiya (eds.). *Freedom*, pp. 108-109.

[345] Comp. the remarks in the study: *No Place*, pp. 47-49.

1.8.5. Non-recognized Religious Communities

Apart from individual persons who, for instance, through the abuse of power, unfavorable circumstances, chance, a lack of rule of law, envy, thirst for profit seeking, and revenge are able to be charged with apostasy, the problem of apostasy can also be a threat to entire people groups who, for example, belong to a non-recognized religious community. Included are post-Quranic religious communities such as the Bahā'ī or the Aḥmadīya, whose adherents are not counted among the "people of the book" and thus from the viewpoint of many theologians have no claim to be recognized as do Jews and Christians.

In various Muslim majority countries, adherents of the Bahā'ī religion have for that reason had to struggle with legal as well as social difficulties: Thus, there is a report from 1962 of a number of teachers condemned to death who had become Bahā'ī in Morocco but were condemned on charges of rebellion, of creating criminal gangs, and of destroying religious practices. This was a charge which the court of appeals reduced to the charge of apostasy.[346]

The Bahā'ī are counted among those religious communities subject to the charge of apostasy due solely to the fact that they emerged in the 19th century. Their founder, Sayyid (oder Mīrzā) ᶜAlī Muḥammad, labeled himself the "promised Mahdi" in 1844 in Iran. In 1848, his adherents declared the Sharia to no longer be valid and declared the words of the founder, the "Bāb", to be God's revelation. The execution of the founder took place in 1850 and the persecution of the community began, out of which roots the Bahā'ī religion developed under the new leader of the movement, Mīrzā Ḥusayn ᶜĀlī. Today the group comprises between three and one-half[347] and seven million people.[348]

In Iran the position of the Bahā'ī, for whom the numbers of adherents fluctuate between 150,000 and 500,000 people,[349] has been very difficult

---

[346] According to the report by Peters; De Vries. "Apostasy", pp. 13-14.

[347] According to the numerical data in Uphoff's *Untersuchung*, p. 280 from internal publications of the Bahā'ī.

[348] Johanna Pink assumes "six to seven million" Bahā'ī: Johanna Pink. "A Post-Qur'ānic Religion between Apostasy and Public Order: Egyptian Muftis and Courts on the Legal Status of the Bahā'ī Faith" in: *ILS* 10/3 (2003), pp. 409-434, here pp. 409-410.

[349] According to Uphoff. *Untersuchung*, p. 280.

since the outbreak of the Islamic Revolution in 1979. They have "had to count on intensified persecution," and leading members were sentenced to 20 years of imprisonment in August 2010.[350] As early as during the first six months after the outbreak of the Revolution, there were around 200 Bahā'ī individuals out of the leadership ranks of the religious community who were executed, allegedly likewise 15 members of the National Spiritual Council who have been missing for years. Their community has been forbidden in Iran and their facilities dissolved, their possessions seized, their religious sites and cemeteries destroyed, and numerous Bahā'ī arrested, tortured, and killed. From the point of view of the Iranian government, Bahā'ī are heretics, spies for Israel, and agents of Zionism. On the basis of advanced persecution and an unchanging situation, the elimination of their community in Iran is definitely possible.[351]

Bahā'ī do not have a legal status in Iran, i.e., they have no civil rights or state protection. That concretely means that as victims of crime they receive no compensation, thus the killing of a Bahā'ī leaves the culprit unpunished. It also means that access to university is made enormously difficult if not impossible.[352] They may not occupy any positions in government services[353] nor may they hold higher positions in the armed forces. They may not receive business licenses, nor are they allowed to appear in court as a witness. Furthermore, they may not receive an inher-

---

350 According to the report: *Amnesty International Report 2012*, p. 218.

351 Comp. the comprehensive report with several examples of executions of Iranian Bahā'ī: "The Bahā'ī Question. Cultural Cleansing in Iran," http://news.bahai.org/documentlibrary/TheBahaiQuestion.pdf (15.4.2014).

352 Due to international pressure, it is supposed that beginning in 2004 for the first time since the Iranian Revolution broke out, Bahā'ī have principally been granted admission to study; however, they have gradually been excluded or have not been granted admission to study after having taken the entrance exam: According to Uphoff. *Untersuchung*, p. 286f. Reports, which are based on observations made on site by German government institutions in June 2010, speak of "character tests" which the applicants for study have to go through as well as speaking of a frequently general exclusion of Bahā'ī from studies (copy from private collection).

353 According to documentation ascertained by German government institutions in June 2010, this restriction even applies in Iran for the minority of Sunni Muslims there, who on account of their confession likewise are discriminated against. For example, until now the construction of their own mosque in Teheran has been forbidden, although it is supposed that around 1.5 million Sunnis live in greater Teheran.

itance, are refused education and professional practice as a lawyer, receive no state pension payments, and may not visibly exercise their faith.

Bahā'ī do not receive a birth certificate or identification papers, which makes legal exit from Iran impossible, and the same applies to state recognition of their marriages. If married people live together as a couple according to the rites of Bahā'ī, they can be arrested for prostitution and custody of their children can be lost. Similarly, their children have to leave school if their status is discovered.

Bahā'ī are essentially not entitled to indemnification payments or blood money: Thus it became known that on July 6, 1997 the military serviceman Shahram Rezai was shot in the head in a premeditated manner by his superior near Rasht. After it was learned that the victim was a member of the Bahā'ī, the superior was exempted from the normal payment of blood money. However, he was requested to reimburse the public treasury for the three bullets which he used for Rezai's murder.[354]

Bahā'ī are also frequently suspected of serving imperialism, Zionism, or foreign powers; *Fatāwā* unanimously proclaim that membership in the Bahā'ī community is unbelief and that Muslims who accept this faith commit apostasy. Even if the death penalty is rarely made a topic of discussion in this connection,[355] and it is seldom directly called for with respect to the Bahā'ī,[356] there have now and again been arrests (admittedly short-term).[357] Until the very recent past, Bahā'ī were often not allowed to enter their religious affiliation in their personal identification card and thus were not able to conclude a legal marriage in Egypt. Marriages in foreign

---

[354] For the depiction of this bizarre incident as well as a number of additional cases and a list of concrete measures in Iran since the end of the 19th against the community of Bahā'ī see Uphoff's *Untersuchung*, p. 287-288.

[355] Every now and then over the past decades the call came for the death penalty for apostasy in connection with non-recognized religious communities in the media, for instance in Egypt: Pink. *Religionsgemeinschaften*, p. 320; see also p. 104.

[356] In spite of the condemnation of Bahā'ī as unbelievers and apostates, the prevailing number of muftis dealing with this issue have avoided making the consequence of the death penalty a topic of discussion: According to Johanna Pink on the basis of an analysis of 15 *fatāwā* from the years 1910 to 1998 on the community of Bahā'ī in Egypt: Pink. "Religion", pp. 418+429.

[357] Pink mentions five cases of arrest and indictment between the 1960s and 2001 on account of mere affiliation in the Bahā'ī community: Ibid., pp. 413+418+426-430.

countries are albeit hardly recognized in Egypt.[358] Without appropriate documents, Bahā'ī are not allowed to enroll their children in school, to open a bank account or to establish a company.[359] The 1960 presidential decree, which commanded the seizure of their possessions, the punishment of their community activities, and the dissolution of their congregations is still in force.[360] In March 2010, the highest administrative court allowed Bahā'ī to no longer have to provide their religious affiliation in their personal identification card – and the Minister of the Interior expanded this to include the members of all religions.[361] Whether this will actually reduce discrimination against the Bahā'ī remains to be seen.

The Aḥmadīya in Pakistan also have as little claim to assured legal status. By a decision by the National Assembly of Pakistan, they have been declared to belong to the non-Islamic minority.[362] The declaration by th group's founder, Mīrzā Ġulām Aḥmad, to be a prophet commissioned by God, he infringed upon the generally recognized understanding of the Quran and Islamic theology that Muḥammad was sent as the final prophet in history, as the "seal of the prophets." The Aḥmadīya movement was excluded from the Islamic community in 1974, and in 1976 Saudi scholars openly labeled Aḥmadīya adherents "non-believers." They count as apostates in Pakistan and have been severely persecuted for decades.[363]

---

358 Pink. *Religionsgemeinschaften*, p. 123.

359 Marshall; Shea. *Apostasy*, p. 64.

360 Johanna Pink. "Der Mufti, der Scheich und der Religionsminister. Ägyptische Religionspolitik zwischen Verstaatlichung, Toleranzrhetorik und Repression" in: Sigrid Faath (ed.). *Staatliche Religionspolitik in Nordafrika/Nahost. Ein Instrument für modernisierende Reformen?* GIGA Institut für Nahost-Studien: Hamburg, 2007, pp. 27-56, here p. 51.

361 *Amnesty International Report 2010. Zur weltweiten Lage der Menschenrechte.* S. Fischer: Frankfurt, 2010, p. 72. The 2011 Amnesty International report does not contain any additional statements thereto.

362 See regarding this the opinion of the Aḥmadīya movement by Munir D. Ahmed: "Ausschluss der Ahmadiyya aus dem Islam. Eine umstrittene Entscheidung des Pakistanischen Parlaments" in: *Orient* 1 (1975) pp. 112-143.

363 The "Gesellschaft für bedrohte Völker" (The Society for Threatened Peoples) even speaks of "pogroms" against this faith community: "Verfolgung von Muslimen und Christen stoppen." http://www.gfbv.de/inhaltsDok.php?id=317 (15.4.2014). Also comp. the list in numerous legal suits of apostasy in the following US report, which estimates that from1986 bis 2006 35% of the cases had to do with members of the der Aḥmadīya movement in spite of their small proportion of the popula-

1.8.6. Individual Cases where Apostasy Charges Have Been Brought

Individual cases which demonstrate the unclear nature of cases of apostasy will be described in the following.[364] They will make the malleability of the term clear, the misuse of power in this connection, and the frequent and sheer impossibility of credibly warding off charges when a defendant still views himself as a Muslim. Also, as a non-believer, there is a difficulty in successfully insisting upon the constitutionally guaranteed religious freedom.

Initially, charges brought against unknown individuals who have been crushed by accusations of apostasy or blasphemy will be outlined. Then, the same will be done with a number of cases in which there were prominent victims. All of the examples make clear that in addition to the religious dimension of the topic there are social as well as political dimensions as well.

Mehdi Dibaj – 1983

Mehdi Dibaj, an Iranian convert to Christianity and pastor of an evangelical congregation in Babol, was arrested on account of apostasy in 1983 and held for nine years without trial. His wife was charged with adultery on account of his apostasy and her divorce judicially decreed.[365] Dibaj spent two years in solitary confinement, and several times he was collected and taken for mock executions. Around ten years later, in December 1993, he was officially charged with apostasy, found guilty by a Revolutionary Court,[366] and sentenced to death. The sentence, however, was never carried

tion: Refworld. The Leader in Refugee Decision Support Pakistan: "Conviction of Ahmadis under Ordinance XX or the Blasphemy Laws and their Prevalence; Penalties handed out." http://www.refworld.org/cgi-bin/texis/vtx/rwmain?page=country&category=&publisher=IRBC&type=&coi=Pak&rid=&docid=47d654712d&skip=0 (15.4.2014).

364 The specifics regarding the years after the names designate the year the (first) charge was made on account of apostasy and more specifically the beginning of the legal proceedings with respect to apostasy.

365 See the description of the case in Sanasarian's *Minorities*, pp. 124-125.

366 The judgment of the Court of Justice, File No 1690/69 K7, Verdict No 1766/72 dated December 21 1993 formulated as an indictment: "Mr Mehdi Dibaj . . . is ac-

out. At that time his conversion from Islam to Christianity already lay 45 years in the past.[367] Dibaj was released from prison on January 16, 1994. After a short time, he vanished from the street without a trace on June 24, 1994. The police reported on July 5, 1994 that his corpse had been found in a forest west of Teheran.[368]

Akbar Ganji – 2000

The Iranian journalist and author Akbar Ganji was arrested together with 17 additional intellectuals and journalists on April 22, 2000 upon his return to Iran after participating in a cultural conference organized by the Heinrich Böll Foundation from April 7 to April 9, 2000. A number of speakers had made critical statements about the Iranian regime at the conference. Ayatollah Mesbah-Yazdi supposedly accused Akbar Ganji of apostasy.[369]

Prior to his participation at the conference, Ganji had already composed a number of articles critical of the regime. In these articles he had accused senior representatives within the authority apparatus of multiple killings of journalists and Iranian citizens, the so-called "Chain Murders" of the

cused of apostasy & cursing the prophet of Allah (Mohammed) and all the saints and insulting Ayatollah Khomeini . . ." (copy from private collection).

[367] According to the accused himself in his "Schriftliche Verteidigung von Mehdi Dibaj, dem Gericht für die Verhandlung am 3. Dezember 1993 übergeben" (copy, op. cit., without specification of the year and from private collection).

[368] An original source, which is available to the International Society for Human Rights (ISHR), Frankfurt, and compiled by a high-ranking cleric from the Iranian Ministry of Justice on the basis of information from the Supreme Court of Iran, names (supposedly within the period of time beginning with the outbreak of the Islamic Revolution) up to 2000 14 individuals by name who were executed unofficially on account of apostasy but officially on account of other offenses. Most of them had converted to Christianity, but at the same time there are also conversions to Buddhism and the Bahā'ī religion (copy of the document from the collection of the ISHR).

[369] According to Dieter Karg within the framework of an expert opinion on asylum subsequent to the above mentioned conference of the Heinrich-Böll Foundation in April 2000: "Asylgutachten. Gefährdung von Teilnehmern an der Iran-Konferenz der Heinrich Böll-Stiftung in Berlin vom 7.-9. April 2000," 29.8.2000. http://www.amnesty.de/umleitung/2000/deu06/100 (15.4.2014). Also comp. Christiane Hoffmann. "Willkommene Munition. Streit im Iran um eine Konferenz in Berlin" in: *FAZ*, 20.4.2000, No. 94, p. 5.

1990ies. During the trial, Ganji was charged, among others, with "propaganda against the Islamic state order", "activities against national security" and "collecting classified state documents for the purpose of creating turmoil".[370] In 2001, Ganji was sentenced to 6 years' imprisonment. He entered into an open-ended hunger strike and finally, after 63 days and on the edge of death, was moved to a hospital on March 17, 2006 and finally released from Evin prison.[371]

Muhammad Younus Shaikh – 2000

The case of Muhammad Younus Shaikh is completely different: It makes clear just how strongly the charge of apostasy can be used as an instrument of power against an individual:

Dr. Muhammad Younus Shaikh, a physician trained in Pakistan and Great Britain and Professor of Anatomy at the Homeopathic Medical College in Islamabad, a human rights activist, and, as a founder of the movement known as "The Enlightenment", a representative of reform Islam, had expressed his objection to Pakistani support of the "freedom fighters" in Kashmir at a conference of the South Asia Union on October 1, 2000.[372] He also spoke out in favour of recognizing the present line of demarcation between Pakistan and Kashmir as an international border, whereupon one of the Pakistani officers present allegedly responded with threats to Shaikh.

Just a few days later, Shaikh was suspended from his activity at the Homeopathic Medical College and during the same evening was charged with blasphemy according to § 295-C by a student who had connections to the Pakistani government. He is said to have uttered "blasphemous remarks" about Muḥammad on October 2, 2000 between the hours of 12:00

---

370 Comp. the following report: Gesundheitszustand/Haft ohne Kontakt zur Aussenwelt/ Iran, 23.3.2006. Iran: Akbar Ganji, 45jähriger Journalist. http://www.am nesty.de/umleitung/2006/mde13/029 (15.4.2014); comp. also the proceedings of the conference: Heinrich-Böll-Stiftung (ed.). *Iran nach den Wahlen. Eine Konferenz und ihre Folgen*. Westfälisches Dampfboot: Münster, 2001, p. 211.

371 Comp. the disscussion and different contributions, the documentation of the conference, the courtroom protocols and sentences: Heinrich-Böll-Stiftung (ed.). *Iran*.

372 According to depiction by Riaz Hassan. *Inside Muslim Minds*. Melbourne University Press: Carlton, 2008, p. 29.

and 12:40 p.m.[373] and maintained that neither Muḥammad, prior to his calling as a prophet at around the age of 40, nor his parents knew the cleanliness laws of Islam and for that reason could have neither followed the command to circumcise nor to remove hair from the armpits because they were not yet Muslims.[374]

After the charges against Younus Shaikh, the group called "Movement for the Finality of the Prophet" led an angry mob into the streets which threatened to set the college and the police station on fire.[375] In spite of his attesting to his innocence, Shaikh was arrested on October 4, 2000 and held until August 2001 (according to statements released this was for his own protection) in solitary confinement. The case was not conducted by Judge Safdar Hussain Malik of the Lower Court in the regional prison in Islamabad. Rather, for fear of attacks by extremists, it was held in the Adyala Prison Rawalpindi behind closed doors. Shaikh's lawyers were put under pressure and likewise threatened with a case of apostasy.

After almost 11 months of imprisonment, Shaikh was sentenced to death on August 18, 2001 as well as to the payment of 1 million rupees by the Islamabad Additional District and Sessions Court. In the course of the appeals procedure, his application to be released on bail was rejected on January 16, 2002. This, however, was presumably done to protect him from being executed in broad daylight.

In July 2002, after an additional 15 months of solitary confinement, the case was again tried. There was no lawyer who dared come to Shaikh's defense. On October 9, 2003, around three years after the charges had been filed, the court finally judged that the judgment by the first order court was invalid. Younus Shaikh, however, was not released. Rather, the case was sent back to the lower court. Three hearings were scheduled for November

---

373 Comp. the comprehensive report according to the later release of the accused: "Younus Shaikh Free! International Humanist and Ethical Union." The World Union of Humanist Organizations, 23.1.2004. http://iheu.org/dr-younus-shaikh-free/ (15.4.2014).

374 It is supposed that this statement was foisted upon Shaikh in part or in toto in order to be able to give a reason for an apostasy trial for the unambigous offense of sacrilege against the Prophet. The direct trigger for the suit was arguably Shaikh's utterances regarding the conflict in Kashmir as well as his founding the reform movement "The Enlightenment" in 1990 against which the conservative powers wanted to take action in this way.

375 According to the report in Marshall; Shea. *Silenced*, p. 98.

2003, and on November 21, 2003, after over three years of imprisonment and the loss of his entire existence, the defendant was quietly released with the explanation that his accusers had made false statements. Immediately thereafter, however, he received asylum in Switzerland since a *Fatwā* had been released calling for his murder.[376]

M. Yousaf Ali – 2002

Muslims who have no intention of leaving Islam can also be charged with blasphemy if they represent ideas which are thorns in the side of the powers that be: On June 11, 2002, the 60 year old journalist at the *Daily Pakistan* and former army officer, M. Yousaf Ali, was sentenced first to 35 years of imprisonment and later to death, In fact, this occurred on the basis of a report made by a witness claiming that Ali had said that he considered himself to be Muḥammad.

The charge against him stemmed from the year 1997, when he was arrested for the first time. He was finally released on bail in 1999. In 2000 the case began again, albeit behind closed doors. Pressured by local religious extremist organizations, M. Yousaf Ali, who counted as a moderate in his opinions and was known to be an opponent of extremism, was labeled a "liar," "unbeliever," and "apostate" and charged with adultery, fraud, and blasphemy.

In the middle of June 2002, upon his relocation to another cell in Kot Lakhpat, Lahore's central jail, he was shot four times and killed by another prisoner apparently waiting for him. The assassin allegedly called out: "It was your duty but I have done it." No evidence was ever brought forth for the religious opinion with which M. Yousaf Ali was charged, that he claimed to himself be Muḥammad. Investigations later revealed that upon

[376] After describing the Younus Shaikh's case, Ursula-Charlotte Dunckern points out that in Pakistan there have been numerous times when those suspected of apostasy have been killed prior to their legal proceedings: Ursula-Charlotte Dunckern. "Allah will deinen Tod" in: *Der Freitag*, 21.9.2001. http://www.freitag.de/autoren/der-freitag/allah-will-deinen-tod (15.4.2014).

the occasion of a religious gathering, he merely stated: "I feel the presence of the Prophet Mohammed here."[377]

Hamid Pourmand – 2004

In September 2004, the military officer Hamid Pourmand, who had converted to Christianity around 25 years earlier, was arrested and charged with apostasy along with 85 additional Protestants at a conference in Karaj, Iran, west of Teheran. He was moved to a military prison in November 2004 and thereafter found guilty of espionage by a military court. He had been charged with activity in a political party, which is not allowed for members of the military. In February 2005, however, he was accused of membership in an "underground church" in which many Muslims had become Christians.

He was sentenced to three years of imprisonment due to the fact that he kept his conversion secret and misled the army with respect to his religious affiliation. His lawyer was also not able to rebut the charges with documents clearly indicating that his superior had known about his conversion prior to his promotion to a higher position, since, for instance, he had been released from the obligation to fast during Ramadan. Pourmand was placed under pressure to recant his conversion, was threatened several times with execution, and finally dishonourably discharged from the army. He lost his income, his rights to a pension, and his house. In the middle of 2006, Hamid Pourman was suddenly released from the Evin Prison in Teheran without any further explanation.[378]

Mohammed Hegazy – 2008

On August 2, 2007, the then 24-year old journalist Mohammed Hegazy (b. 1983), who had converted from Islam to Christianity in 1999 and shortly after his conversion at the age of 16 was tortured by the domestic secret

---

377 Barbara G. Baker. "Blasphemy 'Convict' shot dead in Pakistani Jail," 14.6. 2002. http://www.worthynews.com/462-blaspemy-convict-shot-dead-in-pakistani-jail?wpmp_switcher=mobile (15.4.2014).

378 Comp. the report of Amnesty International: "Prisoner of Conscience Appeal Case. Hamid Pourmand: Imprisonment Due to Religious Belief." http://www.amnesty.org/en/library/asset/MDE13/060/2005/en/26a13a09-d4a7-11dd-8a23-d58a49c0d652/mde130602005en.html (15.4.2014).

police, SSIS, filed a suit against the Egyptian Minister of the Interior, Habib al-Adly. He did so because it had been made impossible for him to have his religious affiliation changed on his identity card from "Muslim" to "Christian". This is the first example of such a case,[379] and it made Hegazy into perhaps the best known convert in Egypt.

The immediate occasion for his case was the fact that Hegazy had to marry his wife, who likewise had converted to Christianity, according to Muslim fashion due to the impossibility of his being able to officially leave Islam. Also, the imminent birth of his daughter in January 2008 would have meant that she in turn would have been legally Muslim although both parents were in the meantime practicing Christians. Hegazy's lawyer received numerous death threats and charges that brought him into court. Hegazy was taken into custody several times, and in 2002 he was taken in broad daylight by the state security and, with the official statement that he had published a number of poems, was tortured for three days in Port Fouad. After that, he was subjected to a hearing before the state security court and again imprisoned on account of "disrupting the peace," the "dissemination of propaganda which violates laws," and "endangering public security."[380]

On January 29, 2008 Judge Muhammad Husseini rejected Hegazy's application to change his religious affiliation. He did so by referring to Article 2 of the Egyptian Constitution and its reference to the Sharia as the primary source of legislation, such that this state of affairs justified the prohibition on leaving Islam.

Hegazy went underground after his apartment was broken into several times. On account of numerous death threats, he remains nowadays in the underground with what in the meantime is his family of four. A number of attacks have been made on him and his family, and one death has resulted from these actions. Hegazy's father has filed – as has his father-in-law – for a forced divorce of the pair as well as the removal of custody rights over the children. Hegazy's father-in-law has shown a commitment to re-

379 According to Stephanie Winer. "Dissident Watch: Mohammed Hegazy" in: *MEQ*, Winter 2006, p 96. http://www.meforum.org/2631/dissident-watch-mohammed-hegazy (21.7.2011).

380 Max Klingberg. "Mohammed Hegazy. Hintergrundinformationen, Stand 28.4.2010." International Society for Human Rights (ISHR): Frankfurt: [2010], p. 2 (copy of an unpublished report from ISHR collection).

trieving his daughter, "and if it has to be, then dead."[381] The Hegazy family does not possess travel documents, and in the meantime all lawyers have given up on defending Hegazy for fear of attacks. There are 300 intellectuals, writers, and lawyers who have signed a petition directed at the public and asking that Hegazy be provided no support.

After the Grand Mufti of Egypt, ᶜAlī Ǧumᶜa, made it known that the punishment for an apostate is something that is God's issue in the afterlife,[382] there was public resistance to this: On August 25, 2007 Sheik Yūsuf al-Badrī publicly confirmed the legitimacy of Hegazy's death penalty in a television program. In so doing, he aligned himself with the former Dean of the Department for Women at al-Azhar, Suad Saleh. The longstanding Minister of Religious Affairs, Maḥmūd Ḥamdī Zaqzūq (b. 1933), likewise expressly confirmed the legality of the death penalty in the case of open apostasy.[383] "Because he was spreading confusion in the state and had infringed upon its order,"[384] this was seen as high treason punishable by death. A new court case was started in 2009 but was postponed due to international interest on the part of the media.[385]

. . . and similar Cases

There are a large number of similar cases known from various countries, and they make it clear just what abuse of power there is as well as how difficult the non-transparency of charges of apostasy against unwanted critics is.[386]

---

381 Hegazy's father-in-law commented in this manner in a press interview: "Todesstrafe für Muslim, der Christ wurde," 16.8. 2007. http://www.welt.de/welt_print/article1109387/Gelehrter_Todesstrafe_fuer_Muslim_der_Christ_wurde.html (15.4.2014).

382 Winer. "Mohammed Hegazy", p. 96.

383 According to the report: "Ägypten: Muslimische Autoritäten fordern Enthauptung von Konvertiten," 31.8.2007. http://www.kath.net/detail.php?id=17614 (15.4.2014).

384 Zakzouk, *Fragen*, p. 108.

385 Comp. the description of the case in, for example, the study: *No Place*, p. 79 as well as the depiction in the hertofore unpublished report by Klingberg. "Mohammed Hegazy."

386 Comp. for instance the report about the charge of apostasy against Mahmoud Metin and Arash Basirat, who were taken into custody in Shiraz on May 15, 2008: "Zum Christentum übergetreten: Herr Mahmoud Matin, 52jähriger Bauingenieur,

For example, the case of the Christian-Pakistani trader Martha Bibi, who is from the village of Kot Nanka Singh near Lahore, is marked by the abuse of power. In December 2006, building materials had been borrowed from her business for the construction of a mosque, and until the end of January 2007 she repeatedly asked in vain that they be returned. After a Muslim neighbour became enraged, holding that Martha Bibi had slighted Muḥammad, a crowd of people came to her house in order to set her on fire. She was able to flee and was arrested on account of blasphemy on January 23, 2007.[387]

In Afghanistan, accusations of blasphemy were brought against Ali Mahaqiq Nasab on October 5, 2005. He was the publisher of the women's magazine *Women's Rights* at the time. The accusations were due to the fact that in one of his publications the penalties for theft and adultery had been criticized as being harsh. A speaker for the Supreme Court confirmed that the arrest was based on charges filed by a Muslim scholar from Kabul and owing to the publication of content allegedly directed against Islam. In spite of their acquittals, a number of journalists in similar situations have had to leave the country after being released from prison. This has been on account of the acute danger to their lives, for instance in 2003 in the case of the publisher of the weekly newspaper *Aftab Afghanistan*.[388]

Herr Arasch Basirat, 44 Jahre," 17.8.2008, Zum Christentum übergetreten: Herr Mahmoud Matin, 52jähriger Bauingenieur, Herr Arasch Basirat, 44 Jahre, 17.9.2008. http://www.amnesty.de/urgent-action/ua-151-2008-2/drohende-todes strafe (15.4.2014) as well as the report about the charges against several men on account of sorcery and apostasy: "Ali Hussain Sibat, 46-jähriger libanesischer Staatsbürger, zweiter Mann nur bekannt als 'Magier der TV-Moderatorinnen'," 9.12. 2009. http://www.amnesty.de/urgent-action/ua-328-2009/todesurteil-wegen-hexerei (15.4.2014).

387 According to the report: "Pakistan: Aus Rache der Blasphemie bezichtigt. Baumaterialien für Moscheebau ausgeliehen, nach Forderung auf Rückgabe Blasphemie vorgeworfen. Fünffache Mutter inhaftiert." http://www.igfm.de/ne/?tx_ttnews%5Btt_news%5D=2169&cHash=3c03817d73f67cdda032a8494513cd6c (15.4.2014).

388 As reported by the "Gesellschaft für bedrohte Völker" (The Society for Threatened Peoples): "Kritische Stimmen gegen Islamisierung nicht zum Schweigen bringen! Afghanistan: Freilassung eines wegen Gotteslästerung verhafteten Journalisten gefordert," 5.10.2005. http://www.gfbv.de/pressemit.php?id=304&highlight=blasphemie (15.4.2014).

On March 11, 2007 the Turkish citizen Sabri Bogday, who ran a hairdresser's salon in Jeddah, Saudi Arabia, was arrested. In a court case conducted behind closed doors, Bogday was sentenced to death for insulting Islam and cursing God in public, which can be interpreted as apostasy in Saudi Arabia. He had neither an interpreter nor a lawyer assigned to him.[389]

In addition to being subjected to arbitrariness and a lack of rights, victims of charges of apostasy and blasphemy complain of the use of violence, torture, threats, and the incarceration of family members as well as psychological force such as intimidation, mock executions, psychological torture, and confinement in a darkened cell. In addition there is "social execution", such as the frequent loss of one's employment, the loss of one's residence and family as well as being cast out and ostracized.[390]

Maḥmūd Muḥammad Ṭāhā – 1968

The prelude to a list of very well known charges of apostasy is the case against the elderly reform scholar and politician Maḥmūd Muḥammad Ṭāhā in Khartoum, Sudan. The first time that Ṭāhā was charged with apostasy and taken to court was in 1968. This supposedly occurred less due to specific religious statements than due to leftist statements on sociopolitical topics.[391]

According to Ṭāhā's interpretation, what is considered Meccan Islam is a message of freedom and equality of all people, a type of secular humanism,[392] which he labeled the "second message of Islam."[393] As early as 1945 he founded the "Republican Party" *(al-ḥizb al-ǧumhūrī)*.[394] It had the

---

389 Comp. the report by Amnesty International: "Urgent Action. Todesstrafe/Unfaires Gerichtsverfahren. Saudi-Arabien, Sabri Bogday, 30-jähriger türkischer Staatsbürger", 23.4.2008. http://www.amnesty.de/umleitung/2008/mde23/014 (15.4.2014).

390 Comp. the detailed description of additional cases in Egypt in O'Sullivan's "Cases", pp. 97-137.

391 For an explanation of his most important theses see: Mahgoub El-Tigani Mahmoud. *State and Religion in the Sudan. Sudanese Thinkers*. The Edwin Mellen Press: Lewiston, 2003, pp. 75ff.

392 As formulated by Vogel in *Blasphemie*, p. 30.

393 Comp. Taha's own explanations in his document: Taha. *Message*.

394 On the genesis and orientation of the movement comp., for instance, An-Na'im's "Law", pp. 204ff.

goal of producing an independent, federalist Sudanese republic which later passed over into the movement of the "Republican Brothers" and "Sisters" (*al-iḫwān* and *al-aḫawāt al-ǧumhūrīyūn*). He called for a "radical reformulation" of the Sharia[395] by including the complete equality of women, and he did so at a time when Sudan saw more and more advancement in the direction of Islamization.

Knowing full well that according to Sudanese law a court case regarding apostasy was not lawful, Ṭāhā ignored the subsequent court hearings and the call by the judge to repent and reverse his direction.[396] In 1972 al-Azhar condemned Ṭāhā in a *Fatwā* against apostasy, in 1975 the Muslim World League expressed itself similarly in an official opinion, and in 1976 a number of Sudanese Salafite scholars and adherents of the Muslim Brotherhood aligned themselves with the opinion in a letter to the President Ǧa'far Muḥammad an-Numayrī.[397]

After President Numayrī signed a law regarding the nationwide application of the Sharia and the transformation of the Sudan into an Islamic Republic, Ṭāhā was again charged. He was "sentenced to death with the approval of the Islamic World League on account of apostasy and sedition"[398] in the final weeks of Numayrī's presidential administration and publicly executed on January 18, 1985.

Article 247 of the Sudanese code of criminal procedure actually specifies that it is not allowable to administer the death penalty to an individual beyond the age of 70. The exceptions, however, are *ḥadd* offenses. For that reason, the attempts of the persecutors were directed at Ṭāhā's position towards Islamic law, declaring them to be expressions of apostasy from Islam and thus asserting that they were *ḥadd* offenses.

However, the execution was then ordered on the basis of Article 96 of the criminal code, the "undermining of the constitution and warmongering against the state,"[399] since the criminal code did not have a paragraph that would have allowed execution for apostasy. Thus, for political ends the

395 Oevermann. *Brüder*, p. 10
396 Ibid., pp. 59+64-66
397 Comp. the translation of both texts in Oevermann's *Brüder*, pp. 67-68.
398 Müller. *Islam*, p. 241.
399 According to Oevermann. *Brüder*, p. 95.

law was adapted for the situation by the outgoing government.[400] According to Annette Oevermann, the Muslim Brotherhood and the Islamic World League were pulling all the strings in the background.[401] The result is that Ṭāhā probably has to be above all be seen as a victim of the course of Islamization the country was treading.[402]

Salman Rushdie – 1989

A lot has been written about the pronouncement of the *fatwā* or, more specifically, the *ḥokm*[403] by Rūḥollāh Khomeinī on February 14, 1989 upon the publication of *The Satanic Verses*[404] by Salman Rushdie, a writer who was born in India and grew up in Great Britain. This was preceded by book burnings, demonstrations, and the killing of six people in Pakistan.[405] With Khomeinī's announcement of Rushdie's condemnation on account of defaming the Quran, Islam, and Muḥammad, the author, as well as all people who were involved in the production, printing, distribution, translation, and sale of the book were threatened with death.

Rushdie's case is one of the first and most famous cases of the condemnation of a literary figure in a Muslim family due to apostasy. It also involved a head of state, who was at the same time the supreme religious authority of Iran and declared someone to be an outlaw. This head of state and supreme religious authority called upon anyone to administer the death penalty. In so doing, all Muslims around the world belonging to the *umma* were made accessories, the world was made the courtroom, and the street the place of execution. This demand was later reinforced by a bounty

---

400 Also according to Aharon Layish and Gabriel R. Warburg, who recognize therein primarily a measure to secure the survival of the regime as well as a warning to other potential critics: Layish; Warburg. *Reinstatement*, p. 59.

401 Oevermann. *Brüder*, pp. 99-100.

402 According to An-Na'im. "Law", p. 210.

403 The discussion about the classification of the text as a *fatwā or ḥokm* comp. in: Vogel. *Blasphemie*, pp. 184-186.

404 For an explanation of the contents of Rushdies Roman see for instance William Shepard. "Satanic Verses and the Death of God: Salmān Rushdie and Najīb Maḥfūẓ" in: *MW* 82/1-2 (1992), pp. 91-111.

405 According to Mehdi Mozzafari. "The Rushdie Affair: Blasphemy as a New Form of International Conflict and Crisis" in: *TPV* 2 (1990), pp. 415-441, here p. 415.

amounting to millions[406] and offered by a religious foundation with which Khomeinī's sons were supposed to have been connected.[407]

Farağ Fūda – 1992

The case of the well known author and intellectual Farağ Fūda counts among the most famous cases of persecution where there was official toleration by the state as well as unofficially supported persecution and execution of an intellectual on account of apostasy.

Fūda was killed in broad daylight on June 8, 1992 in Cairo by two members of the *al-ğamāᶜa al-islāmīya* group after having been openly accused for a period of time by various people of apostasy and unbelief. For his part, he had challenged notable representatives of Islam to refute his theses.[408] Among his theses were, for instance, the claims that Sharia law and emulating the habits and customs from the time of the origin of Islam were ineffective in improving Egypt's numerous social problems.[409] Freedom of speech, democracy, an improved legal position for the Coptic minority as well as the separation of religion and politics were additional demands which gained Fūda embittered rejection and hatred in certain circles.

The actions were first preceded by a *fatwā* from the chairman of the al-Azhar *fatwā* committee on February 1, 1990, which generally rejected the

---

406 It has admittedly been questioned whether Khomeinī's actual goal was at all the killing of Salman Rushdie: For example, Mehdi Mozzafari joins in this notion: "The Rushdie Affair: Blasphemy as a New Form of International Conflict and Crisis" in: *TPV* 2 (1990), pp. 415-441, here p. 439.

407 According to Vogel. *Blasphemie*, p. 191.

408 Ana Belén Soage traces the escalation of words prior to Fūda's murder: Ana Belén Soage. "Faraj Fowda, or the Cost of Freedom of Expression" in: *MERIA* 11/2 (2007), pp. 26-33.

409 For instance formulated by Fūda in his document: *Farağ Fūda. al-ḥaqīqa al-ġā'iba*. dār wa-maṭābiʿ al-mustaqbal al-Iskandarīya: 2003², in which he states that justice (*al-ᶜadl*) in a society comes about neither through the rectitude of a judge nor through that of the citizens nor through the "application of the Sharia" (*bi-taṭbīq aš-šarīᶜa*) (ibid., p.28). This alone is not at all the "actual essence of Islam" (*ğauhar al-islām*) (ibid., p. 31).

administration of *ḥadd* penalties for apostasy.[410] However, two years later, on June 3, 1992, a second *fatwā* was issued which contained personal detractions, threats, and a condemnation of Fūda's as a blasphemer of God and an apostate. It was initiated by a group of Azhar scholars. Five days later Fūda's murder took place in broad daylight.

The responsible members of the al-Azhar teaching staff were not able to carry out the execution of an individual who, according to their opinion, was guilty. They were unable to move the state to apply the death penalty on account of apostasy, but by virtue of their office and by appealing to their religious authority, they were able to personally convince the attacker,[411] as he admitted in a later hearing, that Fūda's murder was a religious duty.[412] With that said, the not to be underestimated influence of the *ᶜulamā'* on society, which can influence public opinion without judicial or executive features,[413] is clearly shown in this case.

The al-Azhar scholars legitimated declaring the unofficial defendant to be an outlaw as well as his execution by enlisting religious justification.[414] According to Malika Zeghal, this was the first time that a statement by a member of the *ᶜulamā'* led to the direct use of violence against someone who was differently minded.[415] Fūda's murder was preceded by a hearing by state security as well as a public debate at the Cairo Book Fair in Janu-

---

410 According to M. Najjar. "The Debate on Islam and Secularism in Egypt" in: *ASQ* 18/2 (1996), pp. 1-21, here p. 6.

411 In connection with the murder of Farağ Fūda, Sami A. Aldeeb Abu-Sahlieh formulates it as follows: "Les actes de ces intégristes sonst très souvent légitimés par les autorités religieuses officielles, et en premier lieu par al-Azhar." Abu-Sahlieh. Délit, p. 101.

412 According to Rubin. *War*, p. 1.

413 As formulated by Ami Ayalon regarding the actions of the *ᶜulamā'* in Fūda's case: ". . . aired with much authority, these views had the dangerous potential of inspiring the radical Islamist groups and providing justification for their violent actions." Ayalon. *Quest*, p. 24.

414 Tamir Moustafa names the legitimation of the action by al-Azhar scholars and the instigation of its being carried out by members of the Islamist spectrum's "division of labor": Tamir Moustafa, "Conflict and Cooperation between the State and Religious Institutions in Contemporary Egpyt" in: *IJMES* 32 (2000), pp. 3-22, here p. 21.

415 Zeghal. *Gardiens*, p. 318.

ary 1992 in front of an audience of 30,000[416] spectators regarding the question of whether the state should have a civil or a religious character. At this debate Fūda had strongly attacked the former noted Muslim Brotherhood activist Muḥammad al-Ġazālī.

In the subsequent legal proceeding before the Supreme Security Court in Cairo against Fūda's murderer, Muḥammad al-Ġazālī, "who was at that time one of the most prominent religious figures in Egypt and the Arab world and also a member of the influential Islamic Research Academy (IRA) at Al-Azhar,"[417] was called to submit an opinion.

In his opinion, al-Ġazālī called for the exclusion of every apostate from the community and his condemnation to death by the ruler as well as the unconditional application of *ḥadd* punishment. He continued by adding that the individual who prematurely kills an apostate indeed commits presumption of administrative office. However, Islam does not provide for a punishment for this. After all, it only offsets the "disgrace" which exists due to the state's not having administered the appropriate punishment.

al-Ġazālī used degrading words when, with reference to the apostate, he said such an individual acts "as a germ in society . . . who spits out his poison and spurs people on to leave Islam."[418] Fūda did not keep his apparent unbelief to himself. Rather, he made it publicly known and thus undermined Islam, which ultimately promotes Zionism and colonialism, as to al-Ġazālī.[419]

---

416 This number is mentioned by Alexander Flores. "Secularism, Integralism, and Political Islam: The Egyptian Debate" in: Joel Beinin; Joe Stork (eds.). *Political Islam. Essays from Middle East Report.* University of California Press: Berkeley, 1997, pp. 83-94, here p. 86.

417 He is thus characterized by O'Sullivan. "Cases", here p. 106.

418 Comp. al-Ġazālī's address on June 22, 1993 in: Hartmut Fähndrich. "Der Kasus Farag Foda" in: *Du. Islam – Die Begegnung am Mittelmeer.* 1994, pp. 55-56, here p. 56. Raymond William Baker comments on al- Ġazālī's commentary in the following manner: "He . . . was vilified when his testimony was distorted in tendentious ways as a justification of the assassins" (Raymond William Baker, *Islam without Fear. Egypt and the New Islamists.* Harvard University Press: Cambridge 2003, p. 190). If one reads the wording of al-Ġazālī's address, one asks, however, in which respect ít was *not* a justification of the murder of an apostate and to what extent al-Ġazālī's commentary was supposedly "distorted."

419 According to O'Sullivan as summarized from press reports: O'Sullivan, "Cases", p. 107.

The Egyptian scholar Muḥammad Mazrūᶜa expressed himself even more aggressively, holding that Fūda's killing was necessary to maintain Muslim community since the state apparently does not have the will to act. For that reason, the defendants were not seen as guilty.[420] What followed was indeed a legal proceeding against Fūda's assailants. They were subsequently condemned and executed for murder, but there were also public demonstrations which expressed overt joy and sympathy for the offender, such as by the then leader of the Muslim Brotherhood, Mā'mūn al-Huḍaybī.[421]

Naṣr Ḥāmid Abū Zaid – 1993

The Egyptian linguist, literary scholar, and Quranic scholar Naṣr Ḥāmid Abū Zaid (1943-2010), who called for a new Quranic hermeneutic, was publicly charged with apostasy in the middle of the 1990s. His new hermeneutic had taken into account the social and political conditions at the time of the emergence of Islam on the Arabian Peninsula. In 1993 the same preacher and former activist for the Muslim Brotherhood, Muḥammad al-Ġazālī, who during the legal proceedings against Farağ Fūda's murderer had spoken out about the need to administer the death penalty to apostates, together with *aš-Šaᶜb*, a body associated with the Muslim Brotherhood, publicly condemned this "blind little apostate"[422] (*kuwayfir maġrūr*).[423] Likewise, an additional scholar, Dr. ᶜAbd aṣ-Ṣabūr Šāhīn, who had earlier

---

420 Hasemann describes and analyzes in his essay entitled "Zur Apostasiediskussion im Modernen Ägypten" Muḥammad Mazrūᶜa's arguments which justify in detail why in the case of Farağ Fūda the notion of apostasy was involved: Hasemann, "Apostasiediskussion". Comp. Mazrūᶜa's arguments in detail in his work: *Muḥammad Mazrūᶜa. aḥkām al-ridda wa-'l-murtaddīn min ḫilāl šahādatai al-Ġazālī wa-Mazrūᶜa*. Cairo 1994. Additionally, Mazrūᶜa's commentary appeared in: *Aḥmad as-Suyūfī. muḥākamat al-murtaddīn. al-malaff al-kāmil li-šahādatai al-Ġazālī wa-Mazrūᶜa fī qaḍīyat Farağ Fūda wa-kāffat rudūd al-afᶜāl allatī fağarat qaḍīyat ar-ridda*. Cairo, 1994.

421 Comp. the mention of a number of names expressly welcoming Fūda's execution in Soage's "Faraj Fowda", pp. 30-31.

422 Quoted in Thielmann. *Abū Zaid*, p. 128.

423 The diminutive form of the additional stigmatization of a scholar on account of apostasy: According to Thielmann. *Abū Zaid*, p. 128, with reference to Peters; De Vries. "Apostasy", p. 4.

tried to prevent Abū Zaid's appointment as a professor,[424] condemned him publicly as an apostate.[425]

In the same year, 1993, a group of lawyers had submitted a complaint against Abū Zaid to the court of first instance, the chamber for civil matters. It contained a petition for divorce to be carried out against him and his wife on grounds of apostasy.[426] The primary objective was to first of all remove him from the teaching staff of the university. A book publication by Ismā'īl Sālim ᶜAbd al-Āl, an assistant professor at *Dār al-ᶜulūm,* even called for the death of the apostate Abū Zaid.[427]

The case was dismissed by the court of first instance in 1994. However, in a court of second instance, although Abū Zaid had been made a full professor at Cairo University, the court of appeals judged that Abū Zaid was a heretic and had to repent. Otherwise, he would be considered to be living in a state of adultery with his wife.[428] In 1996 the Egyptian Court of Cassation confirmed the judgment in a third and final instance.

One of the plaintiffs, Yūsuf al-Badrī, had already called for Abū Zaid's death in 1995. The jihadist group *al-Ǧihād* issued a *fatwā* calling for Abū Zaid's death.[429] The forced divorce from Abū Zaid's wife was ordered by the court such that Abū Zaid had to flee into Western exile and had lived in the Netherlands since 2004 till his death in 2010. Hence it was the first time that a charge of apostasy on the basis of academic writings about the Quran became effective via the indirect route of family law and in the final event was life threatening for the person concerned.[430] Politics and society were not predominantly responsible for this justification and expression of violence. The cause also did not lie in the lack of education, in Western influence, or in desperation arising due to poverty. At this point it was influential theologians, and a number of them belonged to the most significant Sunnite teaching and educational institution, al-Azhar. They publicly and effectively propagated their ideology that it is necessary to kill those who think differently. This had as its consequence the killing of Farağ Fūda.

424 According to Zeghal. *Gardiens*, p. 318.
425 Olsson. "Apostasy", p. 104.
426 Thielmann. *Abū Zaid*, p. 131.
427 Ibid., p. 151.
428 Ibid., p. 205.
429 Olsson. "Apostasy", p. 105.
430 Bälz. "Faith", p. 154.

Ṭāhā Ḥusain – 1926, Nağīb Maḥfūẓ – 1994, and Nawāl al-Saʿadāwī – 2002

Ṭāhā Ḥusain (1889-1973), who had become blind during childhood, was an ancient history professor at Cairo University since 1921, a professor for Arab literature since 1925, and was also a literary figure with multiple doctorates who served as Education Minister. Due to the publication of his book *fī 'l-šiʿr al-ğāhilī* (*On Pre-Islamic Poetry*), he was labeled an apostate by al-Azhar.[431] The book appeared in 1926 and, among others things, was based on the thesis that the Quranic narratives of Ibrahim und Isma'il were myths.[432] He was threatened with removal from the university, with the result that he had to delete the corresponding passages and release the book under a new title.[433]

An attempt on the life of Nağīb Maḥfūẓ was made on October 14, 1994. He was a literary figure and intellectual who was the first Arab language author to win the Nobel Prize for Literature in 1988. He was also an advocate of a democratic, liberal social order with the simultaneous separation of state and religion. Extremists had charged him with apostasy and blasphemy, primarily on account of his originally published short story "Children of Our Village" (*awlād ḥāratinā*), which was able to be first released in Egypt in 2006. According to extremists' opinion, Maḥfūẓ was an "atheistic Marxist and an enemy of Islam."[434] After being presented with the Nobel Prize in 1988, a *fatwā* was issued by extremists which called for Nağīb Maḥfūẓ's blood to be spilled and to execute him as an apostate and an unbeliever as a result of his having composed the short story.[435]

---

431 See the description in his autobiography in E. H. Paxton (trans.) *An Egyptian Childhood. The Autobiography of Taha Hussein.* George Routledge & Sons: London, 1932, pp. 15-16.

432 Tilman Nagel relates Ḥusain's conflict-laden literary statements to his study of classical philology in France: Tilman Nagel. "Abkehr von Europa. Der ägyptische Literat Ṭāhā Ḥusain (1889-1973) und die Umformung des Islams in eine Ideologie" in: *ZDMG* 143 (1993), pp. 383-398, here pp. 386-389.

433 According to Najjar. "Debate", p. 3.

434 For reasons for these charges see for instance Fauzi M. Najjar's "Islamic Fundamentalism and the Intellectuals: the Case of Naguib Mahfouz" in: *BJMES* 25/1 (1998), pp. 139-168, here pp. 141ff. (quote p. 143).

435 According to the writer's own depiction: Ibid., p. 160.

A publication ban was also placed upon the works of the physician, lecturer, and literary figure Nawāl al-Saᶜadāwī. She has been awarded multiple honorary doctorates and literary and friendship prizes. Her involvement in women's and human rights issues and her socio-critical positions as well as her statements regarding the pre-Islamic origins of individual rites of pilgrimage, such as kissing the black stone, or the compulsive wearing of a veil have resulted in occasional publication bans by the Egyptian government (for instance at the 2001 Cairo Book Fair). She was briefly arrested under the presidency of Anwar al-Sādāt.[436] However, she was released after Ḥusnī Mubārak assumed office. Over the course of several years, she appeared as the only woman on the death list of jihādist organizations. At times Nawāl al-Saᶜadāwī has left Egypt,[437] teaching in the USA from 1992-1997 and publishing a number of her books abroad.

In 2002 she was the first woman to be charged with apostasy by a lawyer and threatened with divorce; however, she was able to ward off a verdict. In 2007 she had to defend herself before the Cairo public prosecutor after being charged with apostasy and heresy by al-Azhar. Owing to this, she was stripped of her Egyptian nationality and all her writings were banned. In 2008 the case was decided in her favour.[438]

It is clear that in addition to state laws and social conditions, the Islamic world of academia is involved in the production of a worldview climate which vis-à-vis apostates is either marked by acquiescence and toleration or by distrust and rejection. In order to shed more light upon the creation of this climate, the next three chapters will serve to introduce three influential representatives of Islamic theology and their understandings of apostasy, religious freedom, and human rights by means of their own publications.

---

436 Comp. the interpretation of her period of imprisonment in al-Saᶜadāwī's own writings in Mary Jane Androme's "Nawal El Saadawi's Memoirs from the Women's Prison: Women Closing Ranks" in: Ernest N. Emenyonu; Maureen N. Eke (eds.). *Emerging Perspectives on Nawal El Saadawi*. Africa World Press: Trenton, 2010, pp. 79-91.

437 Comp. the autobiographical depiction of al-Saᶜadāwī's taking leave of her children in January 1993 when she along with her husband Sherif Hetata temporarily traveled to North Carolina: Nawal El Saadawi. *A Daughter of Isis*. Zed Books: London, 1999, pp. 12-13.

438 According to information on al-Saᶜadāwī's life and work on her home page http://www.nawalsaadawi.net/ (15.4.2014).

2. Yūsuf al-Qaraḍāwī's "Moderate" Position: Religious Freedom is the Internal Freedom of Conscience

2.1. Yūsuf al-Qaraḍāwī: His Life and Work – Essential Principles of His Theology

Yūsuf al-Qaraḍāwī (b. 1926), is "one of the world's most respected Islamic scholars"[1] at the present time. Furthermore, given his diverse statements on apostasy, he is of particular interest. His global influence is practically unparalleled. There is no doubt that not only his political opinions achieve a hearing around the world. One instance is his expression of congratulations on February 18, 2011 on Taḥrīr Square in Cairo to the insurgents of the Egyptian Revolution, which he considered to be an inevitable triumph of believers and God's punishment on an oppressive, pharaoh-like regime.[2] Likewise, al-Qaraḍāwī's theological opinions, among them his statements on the topic of apostasy, are prominently observed in the global context and exercise a significant amount of influence on the spiritual climate of the *umma* around the world.

2.1.1. An Influential Protagonist of Classical Scholarship

Yūsuf al-Qaraḍāwī is listed here as a representative of a "centrist position", which neither completely rejects the death penalty for apostasy nor essentially advocates it. This position is frequently designated to be "moder-

1 Alexandre Caeiro. "Transnational ulama, European Fatwas, and Islamic Authority. A Case Study of the European Council for Fatwa and Research, in: Martin van Bruinessen; Stefano Allievi (eds.). *Producing Islamic Knowledge. Transmission and Dissemination in Western Europe*. Routledge: London, 2011, pp. 121-141, here p. 124.

2 Yahya M. Michot. "Qaradawi's Tahrir Square Sermon: Text and Comments," http://www.onislam.net/english/shariah/contemporary-issues/interviews-reviews-and-events/451341-the-tahrir-square-sermon-of-sheikh-al-qaradawi.html?Events= (3.7.2011).

ate".[3] After a presentation and evaluation of all of al-Qaraḍāwī's statements on the topic of apostasy, the question of the extent to which his advocacy of the death penalty for apostates means that this modifier is legitimate will be answered in a subsequent assessment.

Yūsuf al-Qaraḍāwī's global influence can be perceived by looking at many factors. Thus, he has received a number of awards and honors. Already in 1994 he received the "King Faisal International Prize" for Islamic Studies from the King Faisal Foundation,[4] a prize endowed with 200,000 in award money. Additional honors were the "Sultan Hassanal Bolkiah Award for Islamic Jurisprudence" in 1997, awarded by the Sultan of Brunei, and the "Tokoh Ma'al Hijrah Award" from the Malaysian government in 2009.[5] In 2000, al-Qaraḍāwī was named by the crown prince of Dubai and the Defense Minister of the United Arab Emirates, Sheik Ḥamdān Ibn Rāšid Āl-Maktūm, as the recipient of the "Dubai International Holy Quran Award" and named the "Islamic Personality of the Year". This award carried prize money of 1 million Dirhams.[6]

In a ranking of the 500 most influential Muslims, he came in under the "Top 50" in 2010, and he achieved a spot of 14 in the individual rankings. Only 6 heads of state, led by the then ruling Saudi King ᶜAbdullāh Ibn ᶜAbdul ᶜAzīz, as well as five scholars – all of whom were members of state religions institutions or state directed religious institutions – filled in the spots before him with two exceptions:

---

3 Roughly Marc Lynch's thought, who labels al-Qaraḍāwī an "avowed moderate": Marc Lynch. *Voices of the New Arab Public. Iraq, Al-Jazeera, and Middle East Politics Today*. Columbia University Press: New York, 2006, p. 87. Lynch does not judge al-Qaraḍāwī to be liberal, yet surely as a bulwark against Osama Bin Laden, indeed considering whether he is not actually a "a democrat" (ibid.).

4 Profile: "Shaykh Yusuf al-Qaradawi." Minaret Research Network. *The IOS Minaret*, an Online Islamic Magazine. An Initiative of Institute (sic) of Objective Studies, New Delhi, India. Vol. 5/20, 1.-15.3.2011. http://www.iosminaret.org/vol-5/issue20/pofile.php (15.8.2011).

5 See for instance the overview at: http://mjc.org.za/index.php?option=com_content&view=article&id=190:biography-shaykh-al-qaradawi&catid=51:the-world-of-islam&Itemid=75 (15.8.2011).

6 Eman Abdullah. Qaradawi honored as Islamic Personality of the Year. 17.12.2000. http://gulfnews.com/news/gulf/uae/general/qaradawi-honoured-as-islamic-personality-of-the-year-1.437003 (3.2.2011).

The one personality ranked higher than al-Qaraḍāwī, who is not rooted in a state institution, is the former supreme leader of the Muslim Brotherhood, Mohammed Badie. The other holds the same position in his own movement, Fethullah Gülen from Turkey. Amr Khaled, the star preacher of pop-Islam from Egypt, is listed after al-Qaraḍāwī,[7] which might well have granted al-Qaraḍāwī some satisfaction.[8] Although al-Qaraḍāwī's health status is supposedly not the best, given that in the meantime he is 90 years old,[9] honors are not being yanked away: On September 12, 2011, the *Gulf Times* reported the opening of the Al-Qaradawi Centre for Islamic Moderation and Renewal in Qatar by Sheik Mozah Nasser al-Misnad, Board Member of the Qatar Foundation.[10] The task of the center is, among others, to collect and document al-Qaraḍāwī's works.

Al-Qaraḍāwī, is labelled "a movement of one person,"[11] "a phenomenon,"[12] or the "pope of the Islamic World"[13] by his critics. By those who

---

7 Joseph Lumbard; Aref Ali Nayed (ed.) *The 500 Most Influential Muslims 2010.* The Royal Islamic Strategic Studies Centre: (Amman), 2010. http://www.rissc.jo/docs/0A-FullVersion-LowRes.pdf (5.8.2010).

8 Comp. the presentation of the strained relationship between Amr Khaled und al-Qaraḍāwī as well as his derogatory judgement about what is in his opinion Amr Khaled's lack of theological competence and scholarship in Lindsay Wise. "Amr Khaled vs Yusuf Al Qaradawi: The Danish Cartoon Controversy and the Clash of Two Islamic TV Titans." http://www.tbsjournal.com/wise.htm (23.8.2010).

9 A report in "The Pensinsula" on May 15, 2011 mentioned al-Qaraḍāwī's temporary relocation to a hospital: http://www.thepeninsulaqatar.com/qatar/152345-yusuf-qaradawi-in-hospital.html (13.10.2011); die AhlulBayt News Agency reported that al-Qaraḍāwī suffered a stroke in the spring of 2011: http://abna.ir/data.asp?lang=3&Id=237256 (13.11.2011).

10 Riham el-Houshi. "Qaradawi Centre Vows to Fight Extremism," In: *Gulf Times*, 12.9.2011. http://www.gulf-times.com/site/topics/article.asp?cu_no=2&item_no=314242&version=1&template_id=57 (13.10.2011).

11 Reuven Paz. "The Coronation of the King of the Golden Path: Sheikh Qaradawi becomes Imam Al-Wasatiyyah and a School and Movement by Itself," Global Research in International Affairs (GLORIA) Center: The Project for the Research of Islamist Movements (Prism), Occasional Papers Vol 5/3 (2007). www.e-prism.org/images/PRISM_no_3_vol_5_-_Qaradawi_-_August07.pdf (10.8.2010).

12 Noah Feldman. "Shari'a and Islamic Democracy in the Age of al-Jazeera," in: Abbas Amanat; Frank Griffel (eds.). *Shari'a. Islamic Law in the Contemporary Context.* Stanford University Press: Stanford, 2007, pp. 104-119, here p. 104.

13 According to Motaz al-Khateeb with reference to ᶜAbd al-Razzāq ᶜĪd: Motaz al-Khateeb. "Yūsuf al-Qaraḍāwī as an Authoritative Reference (Marjiᶜiyya)" in:

reject such superlatives, he still has to be recognized as one of the most influential Islamic-Sunni scholars of the present day, if not the most influential living Islamic scholar of all. This is due to the great number of offices and positions he holds, his professional expertise in a number of disciplines within Islamic theology and law, his large number of books published on the topics of politics, social order and religion, his innumerable sermons, addresses, and *fatāwā*, his global unresting travel and lecturing activity which he has maintained over the course of decades, his professional use of the media – which earned him the titles of a "TV titan"[14] and the "greatest star of contemporary Islam"[15] – as well as his ability to root traditional Islamic law and its deontology as a feasible ethico-societal guidance system in modern times.

On the one hand, Yūsuf al-Qaraḍāwī islamicizes modernity primarily with interpretations supported by his own authority and his application oriented interpretation of legal questions. He does so since he judges things from the perspective of classical theology and presents all the questions arising nowadays from this perspective. At the same time, he is modernizing Islamic law by demonstrating viable methods for applying traditional regulations through modified implementation and thus providing Islamic law a current meaning.

Especially by virtue of his immense influence and high level of authority, al-Qaraḍāwī, a grandson of Islamic reform theology dating from the 19th century in Egypt,[16] and by virtue of the media he uses as a means to communicate to the *umma* around the world, he is one of the most interesting contemporary scholars and opinion makers regarding the question of judging apostasy today. Especially in the question of apostasy, the traditional understanding rooted in the sharia of the unconditional necessity of applying the death penalty meets modern times, in which the diversity of

Jakob Skovgaard-Petersen; Bettina Gräf (eds.) *Global Mufti. The Phenomenon of Yusuf al-Qaradawi*. Hurst & Company: London, 2009, pp. 85-108, here p. 86.

14 Wise. "Amr Khaled".

15 According to Ermete Mariani. "Cyber-Fatwas, Sermons and Media Campaigns: Amr Khaled and Omar Bakri Muhammad in Search of New Audiences," in: Martin van Bruinessen; Stefano Allievi (ed.). *Producing Islamic Knowledge. Transmission and Dissemination in Western Europe*. Routledge: London, 2011, pp. 142-168, here p. 145.

16 al-Khateeb. "al-Qaraḍāwī", p. 85.

religions and worldviews have long since been a reality. At least in Western countries, in which Muslims nowadays live permanently and in great numbers, positive as well as negative religious freedom, the opportunity to change religions, and openly acknowledged irreligion are all self evident. This circumstance alone places an indirect query upon the classical Islamic position and its call for the death penalty in the case of apostasy.

Under the circumstances, can a scholar who takes a leading role in committees around the globe and has international experience at his disposal really suggest that everyone who turns away from Islam should be condemned to death? How would such a call work in reality in a Western context (which, however, only knows al-Qaraḍāwī from his visits)? How would such a message be accepted in a global context? Can or would the globally operating, traditionally educated scholar want to distance himself from classical Sharia law to the point that compatibility between teaching and reality would become possible? Is the al-Azhar scholar al-Qaraḍāwī looking for the application of Sharia law in a mitigated form or for its suspension in Western modernity, or is he calling modernity to apply Sharia law?

There is no way to doubt that an utter condemnation by al-Qaraḍāwī with respect to the call made under classical Sharia law for the death penalty for apostates could have immense influence. He is indeed one of the magnifying, or burning, glasses within Islamic scholarship whose positions – which earlier were only accessible to a small circle of students – find acceptance and resonance in today's *umma* around the world due to the globally available media. However, insistence on the death penalty for apostates – all the more since it involves a famous personality such as al-Qaraḍāwī – has nowadays vastly more influence than any statement made by a scholar in earlier times would have had if he issued non-public *fatāwā* in his mosque, preached before the local community, or published mostly for a small circle of readers.

This is particularly clear when it comes to the medium of the internet: There one finds that through the accessible and simultaneously impersonal establishment of contacts, there are by far more and completely new categories of people – such as women – who are participants in discourses which are conducted very openly. Specifically, the impersonal media of the internet makes very personal queries possible. The internet becomes a type of online mosque, in which in a virtual respect the believer sits at the feet of a scholar and asks for counsel and guidance.

al-Qaraḍāwī's life and work, owing to his specialization in a number of disciplines within Islamic theology and law as well as in his numerous publications and circle of activity in various international committees, the media, and the public, offer an approach to different subject matter areas. There are a number of them, such as his position on minority rights[17] or regarding Islamic "awakening"[18] which have already been treated in detail in literature. Nowhere has al-Qaraḍāwī's attitude toward religious freedom and apostasy been treated up to now, and here it will be brought into line within the framework of his theology and his international activity.

2.1.2. Family Home and School Education

Yūsuf ᶜAbd Allāh al-Qaraḍāwī was born in 1926 in Ṣafṭ Turāb. He later wrote in his biography that Ṣafṭ Turāb was a "modest village"[19] near al-Maḥalla al-Kubrā in the province of al-Gharbiya in the Nile Delta in Lower Egypt, and most of the people lived in poverty. Far away from the large cities such as Cairo or Damascus which, as he notes, brought forth scholars such as Aḥmad Amīn or Muḥammad Sayyid Ṭanṭāwī, he came to the world in a remote patch of the world where there were five mosques. However, there was "neither water nor electricity, neither paved roads nor associations of any kind, neither libraries nor museums or the like."[20] There was no hospital and no bus station. There was only a Quran school and an elementary school. His father fed the family by farming; however, his father died when Yūsuf was two years old.[21] The result was that he grew up in his uncle Aḥmad's house. His uncle was an illiterate and likewise lived on modest means.[22]

---

17 Albrecht. *Minderheitenrecht.*

18 Wardeh. *al-Qaraḍāwī.*

19 In the following I quote from al-Qaraḍāwī's three volume autobiography, which in my opinion has not been analyzed anywhere: Yūsuf al-Qaraḍāwī. *Ibn al-qarya wa-'l-kuttāb. malāmiḥ sīra wa-masīra*, Vols. 1-4. dār aš-šurūq: al-Qāhira, 2002-2011, here Vol. 1, pp. 15+23.

20 Ibid., pp. 22+15.

21 al-Qaraḍāwī later ascribed what was from his point of view an avoidable death from kidney disease to the "incompetence of medicine in those days": Ibid., Vol. 1, p. 105.

22 Ibid., Vol. 1, p. 105.

When al-Qaraḍāwī was 4 years old, he began instruction in the Quran, and at the age of seven he began school lessons in the state elementary school. Already prior to his tenth birthday, he himself reports that he had learned the Quran by heart and had received an award in a Quran competition. "I was less than 10 years old . . . and ever since then I was known in the village as the preacher Yousuf."[23] When he was 12 he completed his state elementary school education, and at the age of 14 he is said to have sometimes assumed the tasks of the imam. As early as the age of 20, he was holding lectures on Islamic jurisprudence.[24]

Before that, however, in 1939, at 13 years of age, he was able to enroll at the al-Azhar's "Institute for Religious Basics" *(al-maᶜhad ad-dīnī)* in Ṭanṭā in the Nile Delta. This occurred after a sheik appeared one day in the village, did not introduce himself by name to anyone there, and, after a conversation with the young Yūsuf, recognized his gifting.

After the sheik called on al-Qaraḍāwī's uncle to discuss further school attendance for Yūsuf, and the uncle described the poverty of the family to the sheik, al-Qaraḍāwī later said that the sheik had been "sent from heaven." In an intensive discussion about al-Qaraḍāwī's further school education, a suggestion was made to al-Qaraḍāwī's uncle in the following words: "This child has to go to al-Azhar!" It is downright "*ḥarām*", if the child is not instructed there.[25] After some hesitation, the uncle agreed. This was after the visitor was able to dispel his concerns regarding the costs and the young Yūsuf made assurances to get by with a minimum of financial support. It was in this manner that al-Qaraḍāwī came to Ṭanṭā, where he very successfully completed his studies and for the first time composed verse as well as drama about the Quranic prophet Yūsuf.

2.1.3. Links to the Muslim Brotherhood

When al-Qaraḍāwī was in his first year of studies in Ṭanṭā, Ḥassan al-Bannā, the founder and first leader of the Muslim Brotherhood, visited the

---

[23] According to al-Qaraḍāwī about himself upon the occasion of his being named the "Islamic Personality of the Year" in 2000 by the Crown Prince of Dubai and the Defense Minister of the United Arab Emirates, Sheikh Ḥamdān Ibn Rāšid Āl-Maktūm: Abdullah. "Qaradawi".

[24] According to Soage. "Shaykh Yusuf Al-Qaradawi: Portrait", p. 52.

[25] al-Qaraḍāwī. *Ibn al-qarya,* Vol. 1, pp. 149+148.

city. He made such a lasting impression on al-Qaraḍāwī that from that point onwards, al-Qaraḍāwī took advantage of every opportunity to listen to him.[26] If, as al-Qaraḍāwī later wrote in his autobiography, one could speak in other cases of "love at first sight", in his case one would indeed have to speak about "fondness from the first word onwards" *(ḥubb min awwal kalima)*.[27]

al-Qaraḍāwī has always counted al-Bannā among those who had the greatest influence on his life and thought. He was also the one who led him onto the way of "moderation."[28] Individuals who count as additional role models for his intellectual work are Taqī ad-Dīn Ibn Taymīya (1263-1328),[29] whose understanding, is supposed to have shaped al-Qaraḍāwī with respect to, inter alia, his assessment of apostasy. Additionally, there are Rašīd Riḍā (1865-1935) and Muḥammad ᶜAbduh (1849-1905). Furthermore, al-Qaraḍāwī himself mentions names such as Bahī al-Ḫūlī, Abū Ḥāmid al-Ġazālī (d. 1111), ᶜAbdallāh Dirāz, and Maḥmūd Šaltūt (1893-1963).[30]

In 1942 or 1943,[31] al-Qaraḍāwī not only became a member of the Muslim Brotherhood. He also became an activist for them. As an activist, he

---

26 Ibid., Vol. 1, p. 160.

27 Ibid., Vol. 1, p. 242.

28 According to al-Qaraḍāwī in a personal interview: Joyce Davis. "Between Jihad and Salaam," *Profiles in Islam*. Macmillan: Houndmills, 1997, p. 227.

29 Ibn Taymīya was also a defender of "moderation between the extremes, as Simon Wolfgang Fuchs has shown: Simon Wolfgang Fuchs. *Proper Signposts for the Camp. The Reception of Classical Authorities in the Ǧihādī Manual al-ᶜUmda fī Iᶜdād al-ᶜUdda*. Ergon Verlag: Würzburg, 2011, p. 32.

30 Wendelin Wenzel-Teuber summarizing in an overview of al-Qaraḍāwī's works up to the year 1995: Wendelin Wenzel-Teuber. *Ethik*, p. 37.

31 Jakob Skovgaard-Petersen mentions 1941 as the year when al-Qaraḍāwī joined the Muslim Brotherhood: Jakob Skovgaard-Petersen. Yūsuf al-Qaraḍāwī and al-Azhar in: Jakob Skovgaard-Petersen; Bettina Gräf (ed.) *Global Mufti. The Phenomenon of Yusuf al-Qaradawi*. Hurst & Company: London, 2009, pp. 27-53, here p. 31; on the other hand, Husam Tammam mentions 1942: Husam Tammam. "Yūsuf al-Qaraḍāwī and the Muslim Brotherhood" in: Jakob Skovgaard-Petersen; Bettina Gräf (eds.) *Global Mufti. The Phenomenon of Yusuf al-Qaradawi*. Hurst & Company: London, 2009, pp. 55-83, here p. 76; Gudrun Krämer mentions "1942-43": Gudrun Krämer. "Drawing Boundaries: Yūsuf al-Qaraḍāwī on Apostasy" in: Gudrun Krämer; Sabine Schmidtke (eds.). *Speaking for Islam. Religious Authorities in Muslim Societies*. E. J. Brill: Leiden, 2006, pp. 181-217, here p. 186.

soon fell into conflict with the Egyptian state powers. As early as 1948, he was jailed for the first time, in Ṭanṭā. In 1949, after al-Bannā's execution, he was first moved to a detention center near Cairo and then, however, released. The result is that he was able to begin studying theology (*ᶜulūm ad-dīn*) within the theological department at al-Azhar (*uṣūl ad-dīn*) and was able to complete those studies with a *ᶜālimīya* degree in 1954.[32]

During his studies at al-Azhar, he made repeated and insistent demands for reform, such as demanding the acceptance of female students and introducing English into the curriculum.[33] As early as 1952/53, he founded a student organization within the department, participated in protests against the British protectorate power, and upon the instruction of the then leader of the Muslim Brotherhood, Ḥasan al-Huḍaybī, travelled during the same year to Upper Egypt, Syria, Jordan, Lebanon, and the Gaza Strip to recruit for the organization.

At the beginning of 1954, al-Qaraḍāwī was again jailed, initially for a short time. After an attempted assassination of the head of the Free Officers, Ǧamāl ᶜAbd an-Nāṣir, the responsibility for which was placed upon the Muslim Brotherhood, he was again incarcerated in the fall of 1954 with many thousands of members of the Muslim Brotherhood. This time he was incarcerated for almost 20 months,[34] until the middle of 1956, in a military prison.

There, under the presidency of Ǧamāl ᶜAbd an-Nāṣirs, he was subjected to severe conditions of imprisonment, torture, and was made an involuntary witness to the humiliation and execution of others. As he later recalls in his autobiography, all the inmates in these penitentiaries, without exception, were subject to mistreatment, torture of a "physical and psychological, corporal and mental, active and passive" kind.[35] With drastic wording, al-Qaraḍāwī depicts the numerous ailments suffered by the prisoners due to the conditions of imprisonment and the deceit of the guards[36] as well as the various types of "torture and torment" (*at-tankīl wa-'t-*

---

[32] On his early academic career see Basheer M. Nafi. Fatwā and War: "On the Allegiance of the American Muslim Soldiers in the Aftermath of September 11" in: *ILS* 11/1 (2004), pp. 78-116, here pp. 97f.

[33] According to Skovgaard-Petersen. "Mufti", p. 155.

[34] According to Wenzel-Teuber. *Ethik*, p. 39.

[35] al-Qaraḍāwī. *Ibn al-qarya*, Vol. 2, p. 115.

[36] Ibid., Vol. 2, pp. 151ff.

ta^c^dīb) encountered by the inmates, whom he calls "the pious Muslims" *(al-mutadayyinūna al-muslimūna)*.[37] "Yes, certainly," according to al-Qaraḍāwī, "the dogs were friendlier and more compassionate than those who descended from human beings!"[38] And again and again, he reports, confessions were extorted with the aid of torture. "There were a number of tormented individuals," as described by al-Qaraḍāwī,

> "from whom there were no secrets or acts to be found out, as they imagined. And yet there was no way around a confession. Sometimes they admitted imaginary meetings as a type of vice so that no hands would be laid upon them, but woe to him, indeed, woe to him, if they discovered his lies. A number of them had by all means secrets and activities to admit, but they wanted to protect their brothers from prison, from mistreatment, and from the expected punishment."[39]

Thus al-Qaraḍāwī impressively depicts for the reader the senselessness of the mistreatment in order to find out the truth. One can suppose that within these events al-Qaraḍāwī experienced in his younger years lie a reason why he later has so often distanced himself from every type of extremism. Also, in particular in the apostasy debate, he has repeatedly had strong objections to responding to the innocent with basic mistrust und insinuations. Still, many years later al-Qaraḍāwī appears to have his periods of imprisonment before his eyes. In his writings he has repeatedly denounced "the torture of people in prisons and detention centers" as an act "of the greatest contemptibleness."[40]

In 1956 al-Qaraḍāwī was freed on the condition that he refrain from public sermons, teaching, and every type of political engagement.[41] To begin with, he worked in the Ministry of *Waqf*, and in 1957 he received a degree from the department for Arabic languages in the area of language and literature. In the same year, he was able to register with the theological department at al-Azhar with a focus on the Quran and *ḥadīṯ*. The prohibition on preaching was temporarily loosened, but soon after that, in 1959,

---

37 Also comp. the depiction in his work: *aṣ-ṣaḥwa al-islāmīya*, p. 100.

38 *al-Qaraḍāwī. Ibn al-qarya*, Vol. 2, p. 115.

39 Ibid.

40 As quoted by Bettina Gräf from his *Fatwā* "Der politische Islam" ("al-islām al-siyāsī"): Gräf. "Gelehrte", pp. 32+36.

41 As summarized by Samuel Helfont: *al-Qaradawi*, p. 36.

after he had begun to preach in a mosque on the Nile island of Zamālek in Cairo, it was renewed.

He composed his dissertation on the topic of the giving of the *zakāt* and its meaning for combating social problems. It was entitled "*fiqh az-zakāt. dirāsa muqārina li-aḥkāmihā wa-falsafatihā fī ḍau' al-qur'ān wa-'s-sunna.*" However, owing to his activities for the Muslim Brotherhood and their clashes with the Egyptian state power, he did not receive his doctorate until 1973. He received his doctorate under the presidency of Anwar al-Sādāt,[42] when after Ǧamāl ᶜAbd an-Nāṣir's death a "whiff of freedom blew through.[43]

Throughout his entire life, al-Qaraḍāwī has maintained a special relationship with the Muslim Brotherhood, indeed al-Qaraḍāwī could perhaps be considered its most successful protagonist and most influential propagandist of all.[44] The fact that in a number of his views he deviated from the Muslim Brotherhood's spiritus rector, Sayyid Quṭb,[45] did not detract from his role. In spite of a number of signs of respect for Quṭb in his books, he expressed himself very frankly in part.[46]

al-Qaraḍāwī, still one of the most important reference values for the movement today,[47] never took an official leadership position in the hierar-

---

42 There must have been particular satisfaction in his doctorate becoming a reality, not only when considering his modest background but also given his repeated inprisonment and torture in Egyptian military prisons, the impossibility of his receiving academic recognition under the presidential administration of Ǧamāl ᶜAbd an-Nāṣirs, despite having achieved the best results in his studies as well as his longlasting exile in Qatar; in any case, he depicts the process of receiving a belated doctorate and final admission into the teaching staff of al-Azhar with great satisfaction and in complete detail in his autobiography: *Ibn al-qarya,* Vol. 3, pp. 275ff.

43 Ibid., p. 269.

44 At least according to Tammam. "al-Qaraḍāwī", p. 59.

45 Roxanne Euben and Muhammad Qasim Zaman even label al-Qaraḍāwī as "one of Qutb's severest critics from within the Islamist camp"; Roxanne Euben; Muhammad Qasim Zaman. *Princeton Readings in Islamist Thought. Texts and Contexts from al-Banna to Bin Laden.* Princeton University Press: Princeton, 2009, here p. 16.

46 For example, he criticizes Quṭb in detail and very clearly in his work: *al-iǧtihād wa-'l-muᶜāṣir baina 'l-inḍibāṭ wa-'l-infirāṭ.* al-Qāhira: dār at-tauzīᶜ wa-'n-našr al-islāmīya, 1994, p. 101ff.

47 Also according to Brigitte Maréchal. *The Muslim Brothers in Egypt. Roots and Discourse.* E. J. Brill: Leiden, 2008, p. 147.

chy, although it was many times offered to him.[48] At the end of the 1970s, he was declared to be the "spiritual leader of the Muslim Brotherhood.[49] In his 1999 book *al-iḫwān al-muslimūn*, al-Qaraḍāwī explained that for a number of years there had been no institutional links with the Muslim Brotherhood, neither inside nor outside of Egypt, since he had not wanted to limit his sphere of activity to the members of the Muslim Brotherhood. al-Qaraḍāwī's sphere of influence was to become more extensive than this movement.[50]

Nevertheless, the Muslim Brotherhood has considered him to be their "spiritual framer" (*munaẓẓir*) and their "legal expert" (*muftī*), and he has not been in disagreement with many of their views.[51] Thus, al-Qaraḍāwī has exercised influence inside and outside of the movement with his position. His position was institutionally independent of the Muslim Brotherhood, yet still ideologically rather closely tied to it. On the one hand, he was able to clearly distance himself from the movement in various questions,[52] while their constituency alone secured steadily high print runs for his books.[53] al-Qaraḍāwī himself has emphasized that those with the Muslim Brotherhood were the "first" who had read his books.[54] al-Qaraḍāwī's educational path as well as his ideological home with the Muslim Brotherhood are of extreme significance for his point of view with respect to apostasy.

Up to the present day, al-Qaraḍāwī exercises significant influence via his publications: The number of *fatāwā* from his pen is not to be overlooked, and in addition to his close to 120 book titles, he has composed addresses, articles, tracts, sermons, plays, and poetry. The sum of the books he has sold numbers in the hundreds of thousands at least, and many of his published books have been translated into European, African, and

48 For instance, when the position of supreme leader *(al-muršid al-ᶜāmm)* of the Muslim Brotherhood was offered to him in 1976: Skovgaard-Petersen. "al-Qaraḍāwī", in: p. 37.

49 Formulated according to Kursawe. "al-Qarāḍawī" [sic], p. 525.

50 Yūsuf al-Qaradāwī. *al-iḫwān al-muslimūn. 70 ᶜāman fi 'd-daᶜwa wa-'t-tarbiya wa-'l-ǧihād*. Maktabat wahba: al-Qāhira, 1999, p. 287.

51 Ibid.

52 See, for example, Khaled *Abou El Fadl. Rebellion and Violence in Islamic Law*. Cambridge University Press: Cambridge, 2003, p. 199.

53 The former aspect is emphasized by Soage: "al-Qaradawi", p. 21.

54 al-Qaraḍāwī. *al-iḫwān*, p. 287.

Asian languages. Translation activity into the global language of English as well as into Asian languages, such as Indonesian, where there is a large Muslim readership, appears to have really just begun. The result is that in spite of his advanced age of 90, he has possibly not yet reached the peak of his popularity.

2.1.4. The Beginning of Popularity: "al-ḥalāl wa-'l-ḥarām" – 1960

As early as 1959, upon the instigation of Dr. Bahī in the name of the General Institute for Islamic Culture at al-Azhar (*al-idāra al-ᶜāmma li-t-taqāfa al-islāmīya*), al-Qaraḍāwī began[55] to compose the book which up to this day has remained his most popular, most translated, most quoted, and most widespread book *The Lawful and the Prohibited in Islam* (*al-ḥalāl wa-'l-ḥarām fī 'l-islām*). With this book, he quasi anticipated his later role for the *umma*, since here, on the basis of numerous everyday questions, he most notably responded to Muslims in a migration context by drawing the lines between what is forbidden and what is allowed as it is derived from the Quran and the *sunna*.

Interestingly, a comparison between the edition translated into German entitled *Erlaubtes und Verbotenes im Islam*[56] (English translation of the title: *The Lawful and the Prohibited in Islam*), dating from 1989, and Qaraḍāwī's original version *al-ḥalāl wa-'l-ḥarām fī 'l-islām* from 1960 reveals numerous additions by Ahmad von Denffer, who expands and explains what are in part rather brief remarks in the Arabic original at a number of places, in part giving al-Qaraḍāwī's statements a completely new direction and set of assertions. Thus, for instance, the following is allowed in the German translation of *Erlaubtes und Verbotenes im Islam* insofar as it relates to the husband in the case of rebellion by the wife according to Sura 4:34: "If that also fails [what is meant is admonishing the wife and punishing her with sexual disregard] he may hit her lightly with the hands, whereby he should avoid the face and other sensitive places."[57]

---

[55] According to al-Qaraḍāwī himself in the foreword: *al-ḥalāl wa-'l-ḥarām*, p. 5.

[56] Jusuf al-Qaradawi. *Erlaubtes und Verbotenes im Islam*. SKD Bavaria: München, 1989

[57] Ibid., p. 175.

al-Qaraḍāwī's own words in the original Arabic version read as follows, however:

> "And if this is not suitable and not that [admonishing the wife and her disregards], then he should try chastisement by hand (*ğarriba at-ta'dīb bi-'l-yad*), flanked by fierce (or agonizing) blows (*muğtanaban aḍ-ḍarb al-mubarriḥ*), but keep them away from her face. This is the therapy (*ᶜilāğ*) which is suitable for many a woman in some cases according to a set measure."[58]

Also later Arabic editions, such as, for example, the editions of 1974, 1980 and 1993 contain exactly the same formulation in Arabic; i.e., al-Qaraḍāwī maintained his original statement over the course of a number of decades and did not modify it.[59]

A translation published in English in Delhi in 1998, however, as the inside cover title indicates, is a reprint of a non-dated edition by American Trust Publications and likewise contains a euphemistic variation which comes close to the German translation: ". . . it is permissible for him to beat her lightly with his hands, avoiding her face and other sensitive areas"[60], such that the conclusion is suggested that the original Arabic wording is as with Ahmad von Denffer in the German translation, deliberately softened at this point.

Approximately in the middle between the German and the Arabic wording is a French-Moroccan co-production of a French translation which instructs the husband, when he notices "signes de fierté ou d'insubordination" in her, he can "educate" his wife "by hand." This translation says nothing about "light blows", but rather limits itself to indicating that the blows should not be "really fierce":

> "Si cela [admonishing the wife and separating oneself from her in the marriage bed] s'avère inutile, il essaie de l'éduquer avec sa main tout en évitant de la frapper durement et en épargnant son visage. Ce remède est efficace

58 al-Qaraḍāwī. *al-ḥalāl*, 1960, p. 145.

59 al-Qaraḍāwī. *al-ḥalāl*, 1974^{8}, p. 215; al-Qaraḍāwī. *al-ḥalāl*, 1980^{13}, p. 198; al-Qaraḍāwī. *al-ḥalāl*, 1993, p. 400.

60 Yusuf al-Qaradawi. *The Lawful and the Prohibited in Islam* (*Al-Halal Wal Haram Fil Islam*). Hindustan Publications: Delhi, 1998, p. 205.

avec certaines femmes, dans des circonstances particulières et dans une mesure déterminée."[61]

In 2004, al-Qaraḍāwī gave an interview in which, upon receiving an inquiry, he greatly softened his chastisement of wives: "L'homme n'a pas à battre sa femme . . . en plus, battre sa femme a ici un sens symbolique" – a formulation which, however, with such blunt words and against the background of his prior close to 40 years of directions to chastise wives "with fierce blows" has to be interpreted as opportunistic evasion.[62]

There are a number of basic viewpoints found in his work *The Lawful and the Prohibited* which have accompanied him throughout his entire life and which also still appear in his recently composed writings: For one thing, there is his opinion that committing to only a single school of religious law is out of the question for him, since that would mean that al-Qaraḍāwī would have to leave his intellectual abilities unutilized.[63] As a consequence of that, he emphasizes at this point that the aspiration of "Islamic legislation" (*tašrīᶜ al-islāmī*) should be directed at "easing" people's everyday life.[64]

The relevance of *al-ḥalāl wa-'l-ḥarām fī 'l-islām* lies significantly in its character as a type of practical handbook on the application of Islam in the 20th century in non-Islamic societies. As early as this, al-Qaraḍāwī interpreted the Sharia in a manner whereby there could be situations in which out of pure necessity, given the circumstances, there are exceptions to an otherwise general set of rules – e.g., circumstances like an approaching death due to starvation or dependency upon starting to work in a restaurant in the face of a lack of alternatives.[65]

---

61 Docteur Youcef Quardhaoui (sic). *Le Licite et l'Illicite en Islam*. Okad Editions: Paris/Ets. Rayhane: Maroc, 1990, p. 172.

62 Comp. the text of the entire interview at: Xavier Ternisien. *Al-Qaradāwi* (sic) *l'Islam à l'Écran* in: *Le Monde*, 31.8.2004, viewable at http://www.lemonde.fr/cgi-bin/ACHATS/ARCHIVES/archives.cgi?ID=2227aac3529430e8246cc12167f181f9497f22456afa40ac (16.10.2011).

63 al-Qaraḍāwī. *al-ḥalāl*, 1960, p. 7.

64 Ibid., p. 9.

65 Ibid., pp. 13+30.

Already in this early work by al-Qaraḍāwī, his position of moderation, practicability, and alleviation are clear.[66] Likewise, there is al-Qaraḍāwī's basic position that in the case of doubt one should be restrained with the judgment of *ḥarām* instead of too quickly declaring that what is actually allowed is prohibited. This is so that only things will be forbidden which Allah has expressly declared in a text (*lā ḥarām illā mā warada naṣṣ ṣaḥīḥ ṣarīḥ min aš-šāriᶜ bi-taḥrīmihi*).[67] In all other cases, where a prohibition has not unmistakably been delivered to people, those possibilities in question may be taken advantage of since they are deemed to be allowed.

To set up too many unilateral prohibitions is deemed by al-Qaraḍāwī to be wrongly understood piety, which exaggeratingly takes things too precisely.[68] That is an attitude which he has strongly criticized throughout his life. However, he does not name any transparent criteria in that work nor later on that would itself be applicable to others with respect to prohibitions or alleviations, respectively. Rather, he above all decides on the basis of his own authority what it means to take things too precisely and what the indispensable regulations of Islam are.

At the same time, neither in his work *al-halāl wa-'l-ḥarām fi 'l-islām* nor in later works is it a matter of for him to utter liberal views in any actual sense or to countenance what classical Islamic jurisprudence views as *ḥarām*. Indeed it is not even to sanction what indirectly stands in connection to it.[69] To be sure, Islam, according to al-Qaraḍāwī, has narrowly limited what is prohibited, but what has been prohibited has to be abided by under all circumstances.[70]

---

66 With that, al-Qaraḍāwī expands the possibilities for alleviation and compromise shown by classical scholars by orienting lifestyle towards the respective necessities (*ḍarūra*), constraints (*ikrāh*), and general well-being (*maṣlaḥa*) in a non-Islamic area. For this, Khaled Abou El Fadl mentions a number of examples from classical theology: Khaled Abou El Fadl. "Islamic Law and Muslim Minorities: The Juristic Discourse on Muslim Minorities from the second/eighth to the eleventh/seventeenth Centuries" in: ILS 1 (1994), pp. 141-187, here pp. 178-179.

67 al-Qaraḍāwī. *al-ḥalāl*, p. 15.

68 Ibid., p. 19. This thought is elaborated upon further later in his work *aṣ-ṣaḥwa*, p. 164ff.

69 al-Qaraḍāwī. *al-ḥalāl*, 1960, pp. 23-29.

70 Ibid., p. 30.

2.1.5. Exile in Qatar

In 1961[71] al-Qaraḍāwī relocated to Qatar where today, around 55 years later, he still has his residence. An immediate reason for his relocation was his initial four year candidature at al-Azhar for a position abroad.[72] In the process, he removed himself from what were additional threats of persecution in the 1960s on account of his links to the Muslim Brotherhood.[73] These links would have brought him into conflict with the Egyptian state power.[74] In Qatar, al-Qaraḍāwī initially received a four-year position. After that, the Egyptian government demonstrated an interest in his return and in 1965 stated that the time of his being "on loan" (*iᶜāra*) to Qatar had elapsed and he should return to Egypt.[75] This was a request which al-Qaraḍāwī, however, in no way wanted to fulfil.

In Qatar, it is uncertain whether al-Qaraḍāwī had already been recognized as the rising star of scholarship and his potential for the construction of an educational system was seen, or whether it was because al-Qaraḍāwī had built up good relations with the ruling house, or whether there were other agreements: The fact is that representatives of the Egyptian government first requested al-Qaraḍāwī's return and officially filed with the state of Qatar for him to be handed over. Government representatives, however, rejected this. al-Qaraḍāwī commented as follow: "May Allah repay them richly."[76] This is due to the fact that the justification was that al-Qaraḍāwī was indispensable. These "attempts" by the Egyptian state to repatriate al-Qaraḍāwī therefore ended "with a failure" (*bi-'l-iḫfāq*) due to the "courageous attitude of Qatar" (*mauqif qaṭar aš-šuǧāᶜ*), as al-Qaraḍāwī pointed out with satisfaction.[77] Thus, his position abroad remained secure for the moment.

---

71 al-Qaraḍāwī mentions this date himself in an autobiography: *Ibn al-qarya*, Vol. 2, p. 299; Without a source citation, Barbara Stowasser mentions 1962 as the year of al-Qaraḍāwī's move: Stowasser, "Shaykhs", p. 109; Likewise Soage, "al-Qaradawi", p. 20.

72 According to Krämer. "Boundaries", p. 189.

73 Also according to Skovgaard-Petersen. "al-Qaraḍāwī", p. 36.

74 In 1962 he was supposedly held in solitary confinement for 50 days by the Egyptian secret service: Wenzel-Teuber. *Ethik*, p. 40.

75 al-Qaraḍāwī. *Ibn al-qarya,* Vol. 3, p. 16.

76 Ibid.

77 Ibid.

Qatar then issued temporary permission to al-Qaraḍāwī to continue to travel internationally and granted him citizenship in 1969, so that he was permanently beyond the grasp of Egypt.[78] al-Qaraḍāwī was thus independent of Egyptian politics and the media there, insofar as direct control of his speaking, preaching, and publication activity was concerned. Nevertheless, in Qatar he was still close enough to his homeland to be able to consistently comment on developments in Egypt[79] without being surrendered to the political and theological establishment – to the establishment of al-Azhar, for instance.

In 1961, Qatar possessed neither independence nor radio nor television nor newspapers. In the 50 years which followed, Qatar passed through a process of dramatic transformation. Indeed, it was not only via the change from agrarian subsistence farming conducted by a primarily tribally shaped population to a rapid urbanization and extensive dependence on oil production. Rather, it was change experienced through concessions in the realm of what had been limited freedom of expression. It was within this framework that al-Qaraḍāwī was first able to wholeheartedly develop his activities. This includes the fact that Qatar was the first Arab state to go online[80] and likewise made the significant step of establishing the news broadcaster al-Jazeera in 1996. With the start of al-Jazeera, Qatar attempted to accommodate a population pushing to be politically informed and increasingly seeking a right to have a say in a relatively open culture of discourse.[81] Up to the present day, this is an exception in the Arabic realm. [82]

---

78 Also according to Anne Sofie Roald from a personal interview with al-Qaraḍāwī from 1998: Roald. "Men", p. 34.

79 He did this in detail in his book Yūsuf al-Qaraḍāwī. *al-ḥall al-islāmī, farīda wa-ḍarūra*. Maktabat wahba: al-Qāhira, 2001[5], pp. 8-38, in which he dealt critically with the revolutions of 1919 and 1952 and what was from his point of view only Egypt's alleged independence; he lamented the present "fiasco" (*fašal*) in the areas of morality, commerce, and the military, among others, as well as with respect to freedom and optimism on the part of youth.

80 According to Grey E. Burkhart; Susan Older. *The Information Revolution in the Middle East and North Africa*. Rand Corporation: Santa Monica, 2003, p. 36.

81 al-Jazeera's "Code of Ethics" mentions for instance as guidelines for its reporting "honesty, courage, fairness, balance, independence, credibility and diversity," as well as "respect" and "transparency" and the reminder: "Endeavour to get to the truth." Quoted in: Sarah Jurkiewicz. *Al-Jazeera vor Ort. Journalismus als ethische Praxis*. Frank&Timme: Berlin, 2009, p. 135.

al-Qaraḍāwī was made director of the newly founded school of higher education for religious studies *(al-maᶜhad ad-dīnī at̲-t̲ānawī)* in Doha in 1961, and he was founder of the Department for Islamic Studies of the Pedagogical Faculty. In 1977 he was made deacon of the Faculty for Sharia and Islamic Studies which he set up, and in 1980 he was made Director of the "Seerah and Sunnah Center at Qatar University". Up to the present day, he is also the Director of the Bibliographical Center of the Prophet at the University of Qatar.

From Qatar he has participated in innumerable conferences in Arabic and Western countries as well as in Asia. He has established quite a few umbrella organizations designed to represent Muslim interests in Western countries and has taken key positions in numerous financial institutions. He has become an omnipresent authority via multiple websites which were started with close links to him as an individual, via numerous television appearances, and due to his production of books, other writings, and *fatāwā*.

2.1.6. al-Qaraḍāwī and Minority Rights

One focus of al-Qaraḍāwī's literary activity is his occupation with how Muslim minorities are positioned in non-Islamic societies.[83] He counts as one of the most influential representatives of the rights for Muslim minorities in the Western Diaspora,[84] the *fiqh al-aqallīyāt*. This area of minority

---

82 A detailed analysis of the social reality of Qatar in comparison with the neighboring states is for instance found in Andrew Rathmell; Kirsten Schulze. "Political Reform in the Gulf: The Case of Qatar" in: *MES* 36/4 (2000), pp. 47-62, here pp. 52-53.

83 It catches one's eye, as Uriah Furman appropriately observes, that there is almost complete silence on the part of al-Qaraḍāwī with respect to the position of non-Islamic minorities in Islamic societies. When al-Qaraḍāwī speaks about minorities, he primarily contrasts Islam's toleration with alleged oppression, injustice, persecution, and the extermination of those who think differently by representatives of other religions and worldviews: Uriah Furman. "Minorities in Contemporary Islamist Discourse" in: *MES* 36/4 (2000), pp. 1-20, here pp. 1+9; an example of this is for instance his work: Yūsuf al-Qaraḍāwī. *ġair al-muslimīn fī 'l-muǧtamaᶜ al-islāmī*. Maktabat wahba: al-Qāhira, 2005[4].

84 He addresses the particular situation of Islamic minorities in non-Islamic societies in articles, *Fatāwā*, and, as Ana Belén Soage comments, in his work financed by

law, which was discussed as early as the beginning of the 1990s at international conferences,[85] is based on two foundational assumptions:

1. The global nature of Islam (*ᶜālamīyat al-islām*), which justifies Muslims' permanently staying in the diaspora.

2. The search for solutions according to the intentions of Islamic law (*maqāṣid aš-šarīᶜa*). On that basis, interpretation of the law is allowed according to the requirements of life in non-Islamic society and allows development of corresponding forms of relief for this situation.[86]

In the process, an "opening" is possible as well as the choice of what is the best respective solution in order to "profit" from it.[87] The precondition for this is that the Muslim minority is aware of its special identity, i.e., that it awakens out of its passivity and wishes to mold non-Islamic society.

Through the establishment of minority law, al-Qaraḍāwī practices *iğtihād*, by which he has used *fatāwā* to take positions on all questions which

---

the Saudi World League: Yūsuf al-Qaraḍāwī. *fī fiqh al-aqallīyāt al-muslima. ḥayāt al-muslimīn wasaṭ al-muğtamaᶜāt al-uḫrā*. al-Qāhira: Dār aš-šurūq, 2001: Soage. al-Qaradawi, p. 21.

[85] Sarah Albrecht mentions the beginning of the 1990s as the beginning of the debate and cites one of the conferences organized by the "Union des Organisations Islamiques de France" (UOIF) in 1992 which addressed the topic of the permanent presence of Muslims in non-Islamic foreign countries and already contemplated the necessity of minority rights. Yūsuf al-Qaraḍāwī participated in this conference: Sarah Albrecht. *Islamisches Minderheitenrecht. Yūsuf al-Qaraḍāwīs Konzept des fiqh al-aqallīyāt*. Ergon: Würzburg, 2010, pp. 19f. Jörg Schlabach mentions in his study *Scharia im Westen. Muslime unter nicht-islamischer Herrschaft und die Entwicklung eines muslimischen Minderheitenrechts für Europa*. Lit Verlag: Berlin, 2009, pp. 66+154 with reference to Nuh Ha Mim Kellers essay: "Which of the Four Orthodox Madhhabs Has the Most Devloped Fiqh for Muslims Living as Minorities?" http://www.masud.co.uk/ISLAM/nuh/fiqh.htm (15.4.2014) the year 1994 as the time at which Ṭāhā Ğābir al-ᶜAlwānī brought minority rights into public debate for the first time. However, in the mentioned essay, Nuh Ha Mim Keller only points out that he heard about these minority rights for the first time from Ṭāhā Ğābir al-ᶜAlwānī; Ṭāhā Ğābir al-ᶜAlwānī's own publication on this topic also does not mention a concrete date for the introduction of minority rights into the discourse among scholars: Taha Jabir al-Alwani. *Towards a Fiqh for Minorities. Some Basic Reflections*. International Institute of Islamic Thought: London, 2003. However, one can well assume that it is from the beginning of the 1990s.

[86] Thus summarized on minority rights by Fishman. Fiqh.

[87] See also al-Qaraḍāwī's explanations in his work: Yūsuf al-Qaraḍāwī. *ṯaqāfatunā bain 'l-infitāḥ wa-'l-inġilāq*. dār aš-šurūq: al-Qāhira, 2000, pp. 9ff.

only arise in the diaspora. In the process, he defends the position that Muslims should be granted forms of relief in this particular situation since they find themselves in a position of weakness.

Via minority law, Muslims in the diaspora are, independent of whether they are more or less religiously oriented, reminded of their Muslim identity as a decisive criterion for what they belong to. Through a connection to their original culture, they should find themselves more strongly bound to Islamic society than to Western society.

The goal of addressing minority rights is to preserve Muslim believers for the sake of the Islamic community, even if they are permanently living in a non-Islamic environment. For that reason, the idea behind the granting of special regulations for the diaspora situation is not in itself to grant farther-reaching civil rights and liberties. This is due to the fact that it is not freedom per se which is the goal of this manner of legal interpretation. Rather, it has to do with an application of Islamic law in a non-Islamic state that is closer to reality – and thus more able to be practiced. Therefore, minority rights offer in themselves no point of contact for less dogmatic interaction with other worldviews and, respectively, the freedom to change one's religion. Instead, what is demonstrated through minority rights is that Islam, as a universal message applicable to all societies and areas of life, is fit for the future as a legal sytem.

At the same time, what al-Qaraḍāwī has in mind is the future of the *umma* for generations beyond the current one. Only a youth who is convinced of Islam, one who has understood the universal message of Islam and put it into practice, is capable of propagating Islam, i.e., capable of *daᶜwa*:

> "Muslims in the West should be sincere callers to their religion. They should keep up in mind that calling others to Islam is not only restricted to scholars and sheikhs, but it goes far to encompass every committed Muslim."[88]

Minorities are challenged anew in the life they pursue and through their decision to be located in a particular place, and they are thus vulnerable, for "in diaspora, however, Islam becomes yet another stigma of foreign-

[88] Since the relevant article by al-Qaraḍāwī cannot be retrieved on the internet, I have quoted from: Uriya Shavit. "Should Muslims integrate in the West?" in: *MEF* 4/14 (2007), pp. 13-21.

ness, a sign of the other."[89] al-Qaraḍāwī attempts to convert this new situation of potential weakness into a strengthening of the *umma*. Through a breakdown of Islamic deontology into indispensable basics and adaptable commands of Islam, he conveys a new self-awareness for the *umma* by not pressing towards non-compliance – i.e., towards separation and retreat – but by providing a justification for the necessity of their permanent differentness in a non-Muslim society.[90]

He does not encourage becoming a consummate part of the host society. Instead, he is primarily calling for the preservation of Muslim identity.[91] In the process, as a representative of a type of Islamic awakening, he is at the same time conveying "certainty, morality and stability"[92] in a Western environment that misses precisely that. With a newly defined Islamic identity, minority rights draw a non-negotiable dividing line with respect to the host society and at the same time provide a justification. Through this Muslims from different background and with different orientations become a new community especially charged with the *daʿwa* mandate,[93] where adherence to Islam is treated as the sole decisive criterion for their life in Western society. The top priority, as far as loyalty is concerned, is the *umma*, which occurs in this global form in the first place thanks to the idea of minority rights.

89 Peter Mandaville. *Transnational Muslim Politics. Reimagening the umma.* Routledge: London, 2001, p. 115.

90 This opinion is likely not al-Qaraḍāwī's personal insight; rather, it emerges from the soil of his classical education as a scholar. In the early days, Muslim legal experts viewed the following as applicable in non-Muslim areas: "Muslim jurists disapprove of full integration, and one senses their view that a Muslim should retain an independent identity as well as some form of separate existence." El Fadl. "Law", p. 178.

91 Likewise Sayyid Quṭb, who called upon his adherents to realize a better future through the active design of the here and now with the assistance of a comprehensive expression of Islam, defined "the identiy of Muslims by their substantial differentiation to the 'rest of the world'": according to Sabine Damir-Geilsdorf. *Herrschaft und Gesellschaft. Der islamistische Wegbereiter Sayyid Quṭb und seine Rezeption.* Ergon: Würzburg, 2003, p. 360.

92 Suha Taji-Farouki; Basheer M. Nafi (eds.). *Islamic Thought in the Twentieth Century.* I. B. Tauris: London, 2004, p. 9.

93 On reviving thinking about *daʿwa* in Europe by 20th century Muslim theologians comp. Nina Wiedl's study: Wiedl. *Da'wa.*

2.1.7. al-Qaraḍāwī as the Representative of a Centrist Position

al-Qaraḍāwī is perceived as the most important representative of a centrist position (*wasaṭīya*), of moderation (*iᶜtidāl*),[94] and of balance (*tawāzun* bzw. *taᶜādul*)[95] between rigid strictness and liberal interpretation,[96] between blind compliance to a certain legal school and the easy going dismissal of traditional conceptions within the *umma*, between rigidification and arbitrariness, between literal Salafism and liberalism, between extremism and secularism. In a number of his writings, he warns against exaggeration which is not favourable for the purposes of Islam and at the same time intensively utilizes this "label" of moderation in order to convey a positive picture of Islam in public.[97] The *wasaṭīya* is, according to al-Qaraḍāwī, a satisfactory method,[98] for it means:

> "balance between intellect and revelation, between matter and spirit, between rights and duties, between individualism and collectivism, between inspiration and responsibility, between text and *iǧtihād*, between the [ideal] model and reality, between the constant and the changeable, between earlier receipt of inspiration and the orientation of focussing sights on the future."[99]

al-Qaraḍāwī substantiates his approach of "moderation and justice" with verses from the Quran, such as Sura 2:143: "Thus have we made of you an umma justly balanced, that ye might be witnesses over the nations, and the messenger a witness over yourselves . . ." Furthermore, he underpins his approach of moderation with the *aḥādīṯ*: There one finds emphatic warn-

---

94 Comp his remarks on the concept of *wasaṭīya* and *iᶜtidāl* in his work: Yūsuf al-Qaraḍāwī. *fiqh al-ǧihād. dirāsa muqārana li-aḥkāmihī wa-falsafatihī fī ḍau' al-qur'ān wa-'s-sunna*. Maktabat wahba: al-Qāhira, 2009[1], Vol. 1, pp. 29ff.

95 In this he principally follows representatives of reform Islam such as al-Bannā, Muḥammad Abdūh, and Rašīd Riḍā: Gudrun Krämer. *Hasan al-Banna*. Oneworld Publications: Oxford, 2010, p. 115.

96 For a number of topics where al-Qaraḍāwī seeks to strike a balance comp. Wardeh. *al-Qaraḍāwī*, p. 34.

97 According to Bettina Gräf, who gives an overview of the specific application of the term first used in the 20th century, *wasaṭīya*, particularly by al-Qaraḍāwī: Bettina Gräf. "The Concept of Wasaṭiyya in the Work of Yūsuf al-Qaraḍāwī" in: Jakob Skovgaard-Petersen; Bettina Gräf (ed.) Mufti, p. 224.

98 al-Qaraḍāwī. *ṯaqāfatunā*, p. 12.

99 Ibid., p. 30.

ings against "exaggeration in religion" (*al-ġulūw fī 'd-dīn*). The Prophet even repeated three times that no believer should be "meticulous," for they who acted "in word, deed, or perception" (*fī 'l-qaul au fī 'l-ᶜamal au fī 'r-ra'y*) "perished" (*halaka al-mutanaṭṭiᶜūna*).[100] ᶜĀ'iša also handed down that the Prophet, when there were two possibilities, preferred the milder solution as did the generation of the companions of the Prophet.[101] Additionally, he announced the sending of a reformer of religion at the beginning of each century – at this point the question could definitely arise as to whether al-Qaraḍāwī perhaps understands himself to be this reformer.[102]

This search for practical solutions in modernity lifted al-Qaraḍāwī into an outstanding position of authority and power to provide direction as a legal scholar. Whoever by his scholarship defines the possibilities and boundaries available for bridge building between early Islam and modernity has made himself indispensible in spite of the present loss of importance of classical scholars. This is due to his becoming the authority for what is prohibited and what is allowed.

For al-Qaraḍāwī, there is no alternative to the way of "alleviation" (*taysīr*), since the Sharia has not been communicated in order to aggravate humanity's existence and to make compliance impossible. Rather, it has been given to show mankind practical ways of exercising his religion. al-Qaraḍāwī quotes sayings of Mohammed with reference to renowned authorities, such as Aḥmad Ibn Ḥanbal, ᶜAbdallāh Ibn ᶜUmar, or Abū Ǧa'far Muḥammad aṭ-Ṭabarī, with which he allowed his adherents to simplify things so that commands could be fulfilled.[103]

al-Qaraḍāwī quotes the following from the Quran: "God intends every facility for you; he does not want to put you to difficulties" (Sura 2:185). Therefore, it does not involve release from God's commands. Rather, it has to do with the correct emphasis, which is decisive in order to differentiate what is important from what is unimportant. The result is that the appropriate perspectives are preserved. Furthermore, there is an additional motive for his vigorous advocacy of striking a balance as the sole practicable option in his pragmatic conception of things. That motive has to do with the idea that people are not in the position of permanently treading the ex-

---

100 al-Qaraḍāwī. *aṣ-ṣaḥwa al-islāmīya*, p. 164.

101 This explanation is for instance referred to by Fishman. *Fiqh*, p. 10.

102 This is considered by Soage. "Shaykh Yusuf Al-Qaradawi: Portrait", p. 57.

103 al-Qaraḍāwī. *aṣ-ṣaḥwa al-islāmī*, pp. 35ff.

treme path and holding to it, and for that reason the way of moderation is the sole alternative.[104]

For al-Qaraḍāwī, however, "alleviation" does not only mean balancing the extremes. Rather, it also means declaring a number of things as allowable under the special conditions of migration which in classical Sharia law are clearly forbidden. It is not a matter of declaring something to be invalid or for weakening the Sharia in itself. Rather, it has to do with preserving Muslim youth from being ruined by secularism and atheism by showing a practical application of Islam. Thus al-Qaraḍāwī gives a female convert to Islam the advice, for example, to not separate from the non-Muslim husband – which is what classic Sharia law would provide for in this case. Rather, the advice is to remain with him, in order to use this way to possibly win him over to Islam,[105] for: "Necessities make what is forbidden permissible."[106]

Extremists, on the other hand – which al-Qaraḍāwī neither defines in more detail by name or institutionally – exempt themselves from others's criticism, position themselves with their – falsely arrogated – *iǧtihād* at eye-level with the four rightly guided caliphs and set themselves up as absolute with their erroneous beliefs. At the same time, they mistrust others and suspect them of all possible offenses and sins, from which the dead themselves are also not exempted. They fast, pray, and follow religious rituals in an extreme manner.[107] al-Qaraḍāwī probably alludes to his own ex-

---

104 Ibid., pp. 23f.

105 Owing to its particular significance for Western countries, this *fatwā* was supposedly adopted into the French selected collection of al-Qaraḍāwī's fatāwā entitled "La femme convertie doit-elle séparer de son mari qui demeure incroyant?": *Yūsuf al-Qaraḍāwī (sic). Fatwā Contemporaines.* Maison d'Ennour: Paris, 2009, pp. 1031-1036. A closer explanation and evaluation of this *fatwā* see Caciro. "ulama", p. 134-136.

106 According to al-Qaraḍāwī in an interview in October 2010: "Shari'ah Staff. Islamists Should Participate in Every Election in Pursuit of Reform," Sheikh Qaradawi's first interview with Onislam.net. http://www.onislam.net/english/shariah/contemporary-issues/interviews-reviews-and-events/449388-sheikh-qaradawis-first-interview-with-onislamnet (15.4.2014).

107 According to Joyce David in a summary of an interview of al-Qaraḍāwī conducted by her in Qatar in the mid 1990ies: David. Jihad p. 224.

periences when he notes that non even the educated Muslim scholar escapes the accusations of these extremists.[108]

Extremism, which in the end is the result of misdirected thought, makes a person eccentric, obfuscates the view the individual has of himself as well as the view he has of others, obscures the actual goals of the Sharia as well as the special circumstances of the respective epoch and causes bigotry, intolerance, and rigidity. People in other life situations and new converts are pushed too far, especially as they are harshly regarded and rudely treated by these extremists. The peak is reached when extremists, from the position they hold, charge others with alterations, laxity, and deviation from Islam. Such mental terrorism is just as intimidating as physical terrorism[109] (is al-Qaraḍāwī defending himself against his literal Salafi opponents?).

Sagi Polka assigns seven characteristics to this position at the center of the spectrum – "centrism", as it is also called.[110] It is the way

- of pursuing the middle between *taǧdīd* und *salafīya*, with the goal of blending tradition and modernity,
- of emphasizing the all-embracing nature of Islam in the areas of religion, society, politics, legislation, and culture,
- of balance between the unshakeable basic doctrines of Islam and the interpretable rules for daily life so that *iǧtihād* becomes possible,
- of the differentiation between divine commands and Islamic legislation,
- of emphasizing the significance of human reason, which does not present a contrast to tradition and what can be learned from the past
- of the gradual introduction and application of Islamic law, and
- of learning from others' experiences, also from non-Muslim communities and countries.

William Baker mentions, among others, the endorsement of change via dialog and debate instead of through means of force as characteristics of

108 al-Qaraḍāwī. *aṣ-ṣaḥwa al-islāmīya*, pp. 35ff. + 43.

109 Ibid., pp. 27ff.+35ff.

110 Sagi Polka. "The Centrist Stream in Egypt and its Role in the Public Discourse Surrounding the Shaping of the Country's Cultural Identity" in: *MES* 39/3 (2003), pp. 39-64, here pp. 42-44.

the way of the middle, the expressed toleration of different positions, the call to action in society, judging politics as a spiritual sphere, the translation of ethic and religious duties in principles of societal responsibility and participation, and, finally, openness for global dialog.[111] al-Qaraḍāwī unites all of this in his person, as he himself summarizes:

> "The Islam which we refuse is the one which calls to fatalism (jabriyya) in creed, formalism (shakliyya) in worship, negativism (silbiyya) in behaviour, superficiality (saṭḥiyya) in thought, literarity (ḥarfiyya) in interpretation, literalism (ẓāhiriyya) in jurisprudence, and external appearance (maẓhariyya) in life (sic)."[112]

al-Qaraḍāwī's centrist path will now be illustrated with a number of examples:

2.1.8. Examples of Centrist Theology and Theology of Moderation

Integration

Concerning the integration of Muslims in non-Islamic societies, it is neither a matter of foundational non-compliance nor of complete adaptation, neither of forced implementation of Islam in every individual aspect and at all costs, nor of the surrender of Islamic identity and of assimilation into a non-Islamic environment. al-Qaraḍāwī instead calls upon Muslims in the diaspora to safeguard their identity, to fulfill the duties of faith, to build a united community with other Muslims, to acquire knowledge about Islam, and to stand up for the rights of the *umma* and above all for *daᶜwa*:[113]

---

[111] Raymond William Baker. "Invidious Comparisons: Realism, Postmodern Globalism, and Centrist Islamic Movements in Egypt" in: John L. Esposito. *Political Islam. Revolution, Radicalism, or Reform?* Lynne Rienner Publishers: Boulder/Colorado, 1997, pp. 115-133, here p. 123.

[112] Remarks by al-Qaraḍāwī's upon the occasion of a personal meeting, quoted in: Roald. "Men", p. 36.

[113] According al-Qaraḍāwī's own summary at: Yusuf al-Qaradawi. "Duties of Muslims Living in the West," 27.5.2007: http://www.islamonline.net/servlet/Satellite?cid=1119503544980&pagename=IslamOnline-English-Ask_Scholar/FatwaE/FatwaEAskTheScholar (15.4.2014).

> "In summary, al-Qaraḍāwī promotes the maintenance of a collective Muslim religious identity and interaction with society . . . The maintenance and promotion of an essentially understood Islamic identity or personality, which is determined by confessions and duties, can be understood as the highest goal of his project."[114]

Women

On the one hand, al-Qaraḍāwī views women as particularly commissioned members of the society. On the other hand, he judges them as unreliable and in need of guidance, when for instance he rejects testimony by women in criminal proceedings when seeking a court verdict.[115]

On one hand, he advocates women's involvement in politics, and on the other hand, he holds to the classic dress code including the headscarf and the pillars of marital Sharia law with respect to the obligation to provide support on the part of the husband and the duty to obey on the part of the wife. On the one hand, he expressly endorses women's receiving an education and being allowed to have their own bank account.[116] On the other hand, the man is to remain the decision making authority to which the wife is subordinate.

On the one hand, al-Qaraḍāwī, affirms that the woman has the right to be treated well by her husband. On the other hand, he endorses polygamy[117] as well as the right of the man to "manual chastisement" (*ta'dīb bi-'l-yad*) in order to break her resistance.[118] The last position in particular is emphasized with the assertion: "Some women enjoy the beating."[119]

---

114 Summarized according to Schlabach. *Scharia*, p. 116.

115 For an analysis of his position between pragmatism and gender equity comp.: Barbara Freyer Stowasser. "Yūsuf al-Qaraḍāwī on Women" in: Jakob Skovgaard-Petersen; Bettina Gräf (eds.) *Global Mufti. The Phenomenon of Yusuf al-Qaradawi*. Hurst & Company: London, 2009, pp. 181-211.

116 al-Qaraḍāwī has repeatedly condemned locking women up in homes and denying them education by the Taliban in Afghanistan as un-Islamic. In an interview in 1998 he reported that his four daughters have degrees in nuclear physics, chemistry, engineering, and genetics. For quotes from the interview see El Fadl. *Rebellion*, p. 95.

117 Yusuf al-Qaradawi. "Does Inability to treat Wives equally prohibit Polygamy?" 27.7.2004. http://www.islamonline.net/servlet/Satellite?pagename=IslamOnline-English-Ask_Scholar%2FFatwaE%2FFatwaEAskTheScholar&cid=1119503548826 (15.4.2014).

118 al-Qaraḍāwī. *al-ḥalāl*, 1960, p. 145.

ǧihād

On the one hand, al-Qaraḍāwī rejects the September 11, 2011 attacks as well as al-Qaida operations as terrorism. On the other hand, he endorses suicide attacks as "operations of martyrdom" as defense in Palestinian areas.[120] Even (Palestinian) women are permitted to participate in *ǧihād* and in attacks,[121] in an emergency even without the permission of their husbands or parents and also without *ḥiǧāb*.[122]

Civilians should, on the one hand, be spared in *ǧihād*. On the other hand, he declares the society of Israel to be a military society in every respect[123] and with that declares all people there to be combatants who do not have to be spared.[124] In the question of the legitimacy of *ǧihād*, al-Qaraḍāwī is more radical than other Sunni scholars, indeed even surpassing a number of Saudi scholars. On the other hand, he is not actually a defender of Jihādism, since he does not hold that suicide attacks are fundamentally and everywhere justified.[125]

---

119 Steven Stalinsky; Y. Yehoshua. "Muslim Clerics on the Religious Rulings Regarding Wife-Beating." MEMRI: The Middle East Media Research Institute, 22.3.2004. http://www.memri.org/report/en/0/0/0/0/0/0/1091.htm (15.4.2014).

120 On al-Qaraḍāwī's advocating operations of martyrdom in Palestine as the "most noble manner of *jihād* on the path of God and as legitimate intimidation" for the benefit of the Islamic community see Mariella Ourghi. *Muslimische Positionen zur Berechtigung von Gewalt. Einzelstimmen, Revisionen, Kontroversen*. Ergon: Würzburg, 2010, pp. 108ff., here p. 109.

121 He has commented extensively in his *ǧihād* Theology: al-Qaraḍāwī. *fiqh al-ǧihād*. Vol 1, pp, 115-126.

122 Yusuf al-Qaradawi. "Palestinian Women Carrying out Martyr Operations," 6.11.2006. http://www.islamonline.net/servlet/Satellite?pagename=IslamOnline-English-Ask_Scholar/FatwaE&cid=1119503545134 (15.4.2014).

123 For example, al-Qaraḍāwī formulates it in this manner in his *fatwā: fī mafhūm al-kufr wa-'l-kāfir wa-mauqif minhū*: *"al-muǧtamaᶜ al-isrāʾīlī muǧtamaᶜ ᶜaskarī kulluhū"*: Yūsuf al-Qaraḍāwī. *min hady al-islām. fatāwā al-muᶜāṣira*. 4 Bde., Dār al-qalam li-n-našr wa-'t-tauzīᶜ bi-'l-Kūwait/al-Qāhira, 2009[11], Vol. 4, pp. 790-797, here p. 795.

124 Yūsuf al-Qaraḍāwī: "Israeli society was completely military in its make-up and did not include any civilians." "Qaradawi criticizes al-Azhar for Condemning Jerusalem Attacks." http://www.islamonline.org/English/News/2001-12/05/article6.shtml (5.2.2011).

125 For an analysis of al-Qaraḍāwī's position on the question of the legitimacy of *ǧihād* and his attitude toward terrorism see Polanz. *al-Qaraḍāwīs Konzept*.

Apostasy

Also when it comes to the topic of apostasy, al-Qaraḍāwī pursues a middle course. On the one hand, he does not really distance himself from the order to punish apostates by the death penalty. On the contrary, he emphasizes that the application of *ḥadd* punishment, as it is formulated in the Quran and in tradition and as in his eyes it was applied by Mohammed and the companions of the Prophet for the protection of society, is not negotiable.

At the same time, he attaches certain conditions to the dictate of capital punishment for apostasy and emphasizes that the execution of an apostate is not possible in every case and not without careful examination. His position of moderation in regard to the punishment of apostasy has to do with the fact that he grants the possibility of not performing the execution of an apostate in certain cases, when it is a matter of the *forum internum*, the innermost core of being, the area of freedom of thought and conscience in a person not determinable by law and not visible.

2.1.9. al-Qaraḍāwī's Authority

In spite of this principal negotiability and modifiability of the application of certain legal norms and the practical alleviation of its enforcement, al-Qaraḍāwī is not speaking about a self service use of the word. He neither wants to surrender the message of Islam to individual arbitrariness nor to the judgment of the ignorant. He therefore considers it completely wrong when Muslims in the Diaspora choose information sources and references not authorized by scholars, especially when the multimedia world and the diaspora situation offers many self-named advisors a forum for presentation and claims to what in al-Qaraḍāwī's eyes is unjustified guidance.

Specifically, it is the depersonalized form of advice in the worldwide web which never allows true piece of mind with respect to who is wearing the gown of scholarship and who is using an impressive internet presence to underpin his self-pronounced authority. It requires that those who are able to teach, the *ᶜulamā'* as al-Qaraḍāwī repeatedly emphasizes, be able to differentiate between that which cannot be given up in doctrine and practice and that which is subordinate, and it requires that they be able to accordingly instruct the *umma*.[126] It necessitates an intermediary between the

[126] Summarized thus by Salvatore. *Islam*, p. 205.

specialist scholarship of the authorities and the instruction-dependent end consumer, whose role al-Qaraḍāwī himself occupies when he raises the claim of representing correctly understood Islam and its appropriate interpretation and application for the present time and circumstances.

However, for al-Qaraḍāwī it is not a matter of weakening the claim of Islam in itself, or of liberalizing the law of Islam or of Europeanizing it. The claim of having a comprehensive lifestyle and orientation for all of temporary existence according to the Quran and the *sunna* remain indispensable for him,[127] even as he claims the right about how this is to be put into practice in the Western context. Where moderation and alleviation are endorsed, in the final event he decides by virtue of his learning and the authority which derives from it. He submits scholars from the past to a critical examination and reevaluation with regard to the question of what is today still able to be practiced and in which manner. At the same time, he extracts himself from all critical examination through his absolute judgments.

al-Qaraḍāwī frequently uses terminology such as tolerance, democracy, and human rights, but he fills them with content corresponding to guidelines from Sharia law. He repeatedly reclaims terms from Western modernity – e.g., the term tolerance – in order to present their contents as actually Islamic or as having been brought to consummation in the house of Islam. In his book Buch *ġair al-muslimīn fī 'l-muǧtamaᶜ al-islāmī*, al-Qaraḍāwī explains with respect to tolerance towards other religions, for instance, that there are different gradations. In Islam, however, the highest degree of tolerance is expressed, since only Islam offers non-Muslims complete religious freedom. Only in Islam does a "spirit of tolerance" inhere (*rūḥ as-samāḥa*), which leads to a situation where finally all thinking, all attitudes, feelings, and actions by Muslims are shaped by tolerance. This tolerance is not to be produced through legislation and legal practice, and for that reason it is exclusively practiced in Islamic society.[128]

---

127 He expounds this rather lengthily in his book: *al-ḥall*, pp. 39-72: There he mentions areas of spirituality and morality, education and culture, community, commerce, and the military, domestic and foreign policy as well as legislation as those areas which with the aid of the implementation of a comprehensive form of Islam have to be reconfigured.

128 al-Qaraḍāwī. *ġair al-muslimīn*, pp. 47-49.

Thus, from al-Qaraḍāwī's perspective, Islam offers precisely the correct amount of freedom of opinion and religious freedom. Admittedly, the content-based definition of freedom of opinion is determined within the framework of the Sharia, which according to al-Qaraḍāwī's interpretation contains the freedom to convert to Islam. However, it of course tolerates no openly recognizable apostasy from Islam.

2.1.10. al-Qaraḍāwī and the "Islamic Awakening"

al-Qaraḍāwī not only has the individual in view when, for example he issues *fatāwā* for living in the diaspora in the West and offers solutions conforming to the Sharia. He has also called upon the Islamic community, the *umma*, as a whole, to conduct an "Islamic awakening" (*aṣ-ṣaḥwa al-islāmīya*), to conduct a "return to the inherent nature and provenance" (*ᶜauda ila 'l-fiṭra wa-'r-ruǧūᶜ ila 'l-aṣl*),[129] as well as to actively mold their life circumstances. This is a thought which had already been expressed by significant representatives of reform theology, such as Muḥammad Abdūh, in the 19th century.

When members of the Islamic community fulfill the duties of their faith and let Islam holistically take effect in their lives, only then will they be in a position to make this awaking happen, They are in turn only in the position for this if they are instructed by "trustworthy scholars" (*min ṯiqāt al-ᶜulamā'*) who unite "a wealth of knowledge" *(saᶜat al-ᶜilm)* with the "fear of God and moderation" (*waraᶜ wa-'l-iᶜtidāl*).[130] The precondition for the production of a healthy *umma* and its suitable disposition and attitude, in particular among Muslim youth, is therefore the imparting of knowledge and education. The directions for an "awakening" must for that reason not be placed in the hands of lay people or extremists. Rather, what is required is the *ᶜulamā'* as teachers, "the only legitimate leaders *and* interpreters of the "awakening".[131] Only then can the awakening effect self-assurance within the *umma* and respect among non-Muslims.

What in the meantime is a large number of Muslims in Eastern and Western Europe – al-Qaraḍāwī mentions a number of 50 million people – is allowing them to increasingly achieve self-confidence and their true

---

129 al-Qaraḍāwī. *aṣ-ṣaḥwa al-islāmīya*, p. 156.

130 Ibid., p. 161.

131 Salvatore. *Islam*, p. 203 (emphasis in the original).

identity: "This made them regain pride in their Islamic identity, realize that they were an integral part of the Islamic Umma."[132] The goal al-Qaraḍāwī has is that this large Islamic community achieve globally respect and acknowledgment so that the entire world grasps the message and truth of Islam. On the basis of respect for the *umma*, world powers will then negotiate on an equal footing and abandon their ambitions for dominion with respect to Muslim majority countries.

In this way, the Islamic awakening becomes a "self-defense mechanism",[133] which will overcome the split within the Muslim community and win back its lost honor. From the point of view of al-Qaraḍāwī's efforts at reinvigorating Muslim youth, it seems hard to imagine that he could grant permission to individuals to freely choose their religious affiliation, which would make renewed and deeper rootedness of Muslim youth in their faith an impossibility.

For al-Qaraḍāwī, this awakening has to manifest itself in seven major areas:

1) In the education of youth, which has to be equipped with the correct instruction and protected from false ideologies,
2) through the change of political systems by implementing new political bearers of responsibility, by rejecting totalitarianism and dictatorship, despotism, and the denial of civil rights, and instead by establishing political freedoms and a true democracy through consultation (*šūrā*) – saturated with Islamic values,
3) in the area of social work,
4) in the economy
5) in *ǧihād* as service for the holistic implementation of Islam,
6) in the media and in the proclamation of Islam, so that its teaching is disseminated, and
7) in the areas of knowledge and learning, since al-Qaraḍāwī is of the opinion that most people have insufficient knowledge of Islam.[134]

132 According to al-Qaraḍāwī, quoted in: Anas Osama Altikriti (trans.) European Council for Fatwa and Research. *First Collection of Fatwas*. no date provided, see 3 www.e-cfr.org/data/cat30072008113814.doc (15.4.2014).

133 Wardeh. *al-Qaraḍāwī*, p. 70.

134 Summarized in this manner by ibid., pp. 72ff.

In all of these areas al-Qaraḍāwī has garnered his own competence and qualifications and has produced a considerable number of books and writings. The consequence that he considers himself to be one of the key people to bring about this "awakening" is strongly suggested.

2.2. The Significance of Yūsuf al-Qaraḍāwī

2.2.1. *ᶜālim* between the Early Days and Modernity

Through his manifold activities over the past decades, al-Qaraḍāwī has developed a far-reaching range of significance. This is based upon his classical scholarly education and his numerous publications and offices he has held. Modern channels of communication transmission are used to pass on his views to the global *umma* in a manner adapted for the public and in a manner that effectively reaches the public. However, he does not only exercise influence on the masses, which for their part are neither scholars with classical educations nor have biographies which are rooted in the Near East.[135]

With his application of the eternally valid Sharia law to the demands of modernity, without declaring everything either as allowable or as forbidden, al-Qaraḍāwī makes it clear that it is possible in modernity and in Western societies to be a believing Muslim and simultaneously a progressive, educated citizen. He thus maintains and justifies the timeless and universal validity of Islam anew, presenting it as superior to all other systems of society and ways of life. In this way he strengthens the identity of the Muslim minority, to which Islam is at all times in the position to give practical direction. At the same time, he has worked to animated classical Islamic law anew and to present it as unchangingly meaningful. He thus relieves it of the suspicion of historical rigidification and irrelevance.

al-Qaraḍāwī seeks reconstruction of a type of Islamic society similar to the very first Muslim community, in which he as scholar plays a prominent role, of course. This is all the more the case since in Western societies there are no Islamic educational facilities comparable to the classical institutes of learning such as, in particular, al-Azhar, no state appointed muftis

---

[135] Apart from a one-year stay at al-Azhar, Remien mentions Tariq Ramadan, exclusively educated at Western institutions, as an example for this: Remien. *Muslime*, pp. 8+34.

nor distinguished preachers in large mosques. For that reason, al-Qaraḍāwī's prominent role also sheds light upon what has until now been a scarcely developed independence for the Islamic community in the West. The Islamic community in the West has theologically largely continued to be nourished from the Near East. The question thus arises as to whether al-Qaraḍāwī, through the authoritative instructions he gives for all areas of life, and which do not foresee empowering the independent formation of judgments, will not permanently incapacitate the *umma* when it comes to making decisions.[136]

2.2.2. Offices and Committees

al-Qaraḍāwī's influence is not just based on his scholarship, which has an effect through his books and *fatāwā*. Rather, it is also based on the numerous committees and institutions,[137] above all located in Europe, which he chairs and in which founding he was involved. This appears to apply to almost all the larger Islamic institutions or associations of Muslim scholars in Europe since the 1980s. Basically, these are institutions founded by him or founded with his involvement and are a practical result of his understanding of the leading role of the united and self-assured *umma* in the diaspora, which is being trained for the global implementation of a holistic Islam.[138]

European Council for Fatwa and Research (ECFR)

The European Council for Fatwa and Research (*al-maǧlis al-urūbbī li-l-iftā' wa-'l-buḥūṯ*) was founded upon the occasion of a constituent meeting of the Federation of Islamic Organizations in Europe (FIOE) with the as-

---

[136] Tariq Ramadan speaks in connection with the continuing dependence of Muslims stemming from Europe on the directions of a Near Eastern scholarly aristocracy of its "infantilization": Ibid., p. 40.

[137] al-Qaraḍāwī is supposed to have had the USA more strongly in the focus of his activities, which, however, only faced difficulties already at the end of the 1990s and, owing to the stricter security measures following the 2001 terror attacks, were no longer able to develop: Wiedl. *Da'wa*, p. 142.

[138] Comp. al-Qaraḍāwīs strategic deliberations for a global standard in Sylvain Besson. *La Conquête de L'Occident. Le projet secret des islamistes*. Éditions du Seuil: Paris, 2005, pp. 78ff.

sistance of al-Qaraḍāwī und Faysal Mawlawi, on March 29 and 30, 1997 in London.[139] The European Council for Fatwa and Research has its base in Dublin. The goal and mandate is the production of a common platform for scholars for drafting expert opinions and counselling Muslims in the diaspora.[140] The ECFR has dedicated itself to providing Sharia-based explanations and imparting practical rules for life through *fatāwā* and counselling, attuned to the circumstances present in non-Islamic societies.[141] The ECFR has utilized a minority rights approach since 2004.[142]

The mandate of the ECFR is not only the service of Muslims in the diaspora. Rather, it is also the creation of a platform for the reclamation and exercise of transnational authority, unity, and authority to instruct, especially through English and French translations of *fatāwā* issued by the ECFR, whereby virtually all Muslims in Europe are supposedly being reached. al-Qaraḍāwī is the founder and is up to the present day the chairman of the ECFR.[143] This emphasizes that he is promoting the progress of Islam in the West with the aid of *fatāwā* issued there, "to silence those ignorant and vile voices." The council can thus speak with one voice for all of Europe, "to prevent controversy and intellectual conflicts . . . wherever possible."[144]

Through instruction provided by the ECFR, Muslims should be strengthened by the application of a method of moderation and of foregoing violence[145] in order to neither shed their Islamic identity nor to only

139 According to Caeiro. "ulama", p. 123.

140 Schweitzer, for example, describes in detail the goals of ECFR: Schweitzer. *Muslime*, pp. 35ff.

141 Whether the destination of the ECFR is "to integrate Muslims into European societies," as Alexandre Caeiro believes, is surely dependent upon the definition which one applies to the term integration. Alexandre Caeiro. "The Power of European Fatwas: The Minority Fiqh Project and the Making of an Islamic Counterpublic" in: *MES* 42 (2010), pp. 435-449, here p. 436.

142 According to *Fishman. Fiqh*, p. 12.

143 According to Albrecht. *Minderheitenrecht*, pp. 45.

144 According to the introductory statement with a description of the oritentation of ECFR: Altikriti (trans). Council.

145 Violence could, according to the ECFR, be utilized in order to eliminate "oppression, military occupation, or ethnic cleansing"; according to Schweizer' summary of the statements of the ECFR: Schweizer. *Muslime*, p. 43.

halfheartedly preserve it:[146] "Migration is correct, in fact compulsory, if the destination allows the Muslim more means of performing religion than the land of origin."[147]

The financing for the ECFR is based on donations, bequests, funding from foundations and from the sale of a journal;[148] financing especially resides with Scheik Ḥamdān Ibn Rāšid Āl-Maktūm's al Maktoum Charity Foundation in Dubai.[149]

There are 34 scholars from various countries which today belong to the Council, among them the Grand Mufti of Bosnia and Herzegovina, Mustafa Cerić. The scholars are indeed predominantly but not exclusively resident in Europe. At the present there are 14 scholars who come from non-European countries, 12 of which are from Arab countries in the Near East and Northern Africa.[150] That means that the ECFR is not genuinely an institution established by Europeans for Europeans. Rather, it is at least in part an import and a Near Eastern-Northern African voice in Europe.

International Union of Muslim Scholars (IUMS)

al-Qaraḍāwī is up to this day the chairman of the International Union of Muslim Scholars (*al-ittiḥād al-cālamī li-culamā' al-muslimīn*) (also referred to as: IUMS), which was co-founded by him in 2004 and is located in Dublin. The IUMS links scholars of all schools of religious law. However, it does not only want to be a forum for scholars. Rather, by observing the principle of moderation it administers a role as an international conflict mediator. Thus, a number of its members travelled to Afghanistan in 2001, for instance, in the run-up to the blowing up of the Buddha statues of Bamiyan in an effort to prevent their being destroyed.[151]

---

146 Altikriti (trans.) Council.

147 European Council for Fatwa and Research: *Fatwas of European Council for Fatwa and Research*. Kairo: Al-Falah Foundation 2002, quoted in: Schweizer. *Muslime*, p. 39.

148 These sources of financeing are mentioned by Schweizer. *Muslime*, p. 37.

149 Albrecht. *Minderheitenrecht*, p. 26.

150 The countries of origin of the individual scholars is mentioned by Caeiro. "ulama", p. 125.

151 According to Alexandre Caeiro; Mahmoud al-Saify. "Qaraḍāwī in Europe, Europe in Qaraḍāwī? The Global Mufti's European Politics" in: Jakob Skovgaard-

Furthermore, the IUMS seeks engagement that establishes a platform of unity, a platform for efforts to strengthen the faith, for recognizing the dangers for the spread of Islam in a globalized world, and for the representation of Muslim minorities in Western countries.[152] Sunnis, Shiites, Zaydites and Ibadites are all represented in the IUMS, such that the unity of the *umma* is already being tried in this committee in a model-like manner. This unity has been formulated by al-Qaraḍāwī as a condition for the exercise of influence in Europe.

Federation of Islamic Organisations in Europe (FIOE)

Since the middle of the 1980s, al-Qaraḍāwī has been the main engine and the supreme authority of the Federation of Islamic Organisations in Europe (FIOE),[153] initially located in London and since 2007 located in Brussels, and the Union des Organisations Islamiques en Europe (UOIE), which were both founded in 1989. The French branch was founded in 1983 as the "Union des Organisations Islamiques de France" (UOIF). These organizations are deemed to be closely related to the Muslim Brotherhood and up to this day dominated by it.[154]

The UOIF appointed al-Qaraḍāwī to be a member of the academic advisory board of the "Institut Européen des Sciences Humaines" (IESH) in Château-Chinon, which opened in 1990. Its goals, among others, are described in the following manner: "The education of Muslim leadership has been made its task (imams, teachers, researchers, etc.), who have profound religious knowledge and a deep understanding of the European context."[155]

Petersen; Bettina Gräf (eds.) *Global Mufti. The Phenomenon of Yusuf al-Qaradawi*. Hurst & Company: London, 2009, pp. 109-148, here p. 132.

152 http://www.iumsonline.net/index.php?option=com_content&view=article&id=550&Itemid=86 (15.4.2014).

153 See the website http://www.fioe.org (15.4.2014).

154 According to, for example, Lorenzo Vidino. "Aims and Methods of Europe's Muslim Brotherhood" in: *Current Trends in Islamist Ideology*, Vol. 4, Hudson Institute: Washington, 2006, pp. 22-44, here pp. 36f.

155 http://www.iesh.org/index.php (15.4.2014).

The Finance Sector

Beyond scholarly and representative committees, al-Qaraḍāwī has continuing influence in the financial and banking sector. Since the 1970s, he has been a consultant for various Islamic banks and financial institutions.[156] For instance, he was the chairman of the supreme expert panel and supervisory board of the International Association of Islamic Banks. He has the chairman of the Islamic Society of Boston, which was founded in 1981. He has been one of the largest partners of the al Taqwa Bank on the Bahamas, which has been ascribed to the Muslim Brotherhood,[157] and has been active for the Qatar National Bank, the Qatar International Islamic Bank, and the Faysal Bank in Bahrain and Pakistan. Furthermore, he was the chairman of the aid organization Union of Good, which was established in 2000 in Saudi Arabia. It is an umbrella organization for about 50 Islamic fundraising institutions around the world. It is suspected of financing terrorism and of being linked to HAMAS. Beyond Saudi Arabia, al-Qaraḍāwī is supposed to have good contacts in Sudan and Iran.[158]

Up to this day, al-Qaraḍāwī is a member of, or in many cases was the founder of, numerous additional Islamic educational, *zakāt*, and charity institutions in countries such as Qatar, Pakistan, Sudan, Kuwait, Saudi Arabia, Egypt, Jordan, Great Britain, and France, which have the collection of donations for Palestinian territories[159] counted among their activities.[160]

Additional Offices

Furthermore, al-Qaraḍāwī is a member of the Āl al-Bayt Foundation's (*maǧma*ᶜ *buḥūṯ al-ḥaḍāra al-islāmīya)* Royal Centre for Islamic Civiliza-

156 For a list of his positions in the financial sector see Mariani. "Al-Qaradawi", here pp. 201f.

157 For instance according to an analysis by Lorenzo Vidino. "The Muslim Brotherhood's Conquest of Europe" in: *MEQ* 12/1 (2005), pp. 25-34. http://www.meforum.org/687/the-muslim-brotherhoods-conquest-of-europe (16.7.2011).

158 According to Kursawe. "al-Qarāḍawī " (sic), p. 526.

159 Regarding the necessity of *ǧihād* with the goal of driving away "enemies" and "freeing the country" of Palestine, the situation of which is particularly close to his heart, he comments at length, inter alia, in his work *al-islām wa-'l-*ᶜ*unf*. dār aš-šurūq: al-Qāhira, 2005, pp. 31 ff.

160 For a list of the respective organizations see Tammam. "al-Qaraḍāwī", p. 67.

tion Studies. The Āl al-Bayt Foundation is located in Amman. He is also a member of the Board of Trustees of the International Islamic University in Islamabad, a member of the Islamic International Media Foundation in Islamabad, and a member of the Organization for Islamic da^cwa in Khartoum. He is the founder of the International *Wasaṭīya* Center in Kuwait (*al-markaz al-ᶜālamī li-l-wasaṭīya*) and is involved in the *Wasaṭīya* Forum (*muntadāṣ'l-wasaṭīya li-l-fikr wa-'ṯ-ṯaqāfa*), which started in 2002 in Amman. Furthermore, he is a member of the International Fiqh Academy (IFA) (*maǧmaᶜ al-fiqh al-islāmī ad-duwalī*), the Organization of the Islamic Conference in Jeddah (*munaẓẓamat al-mu'tamar al-islāmī*), and the Muslim World League's *(rābiṭat al-ᶜālam al-islāmī)* Fiqh Academy (*al-maǧmaᶜ al-fiqhī al-islāmī*) in Mecca.[161]

Additionally, al-Qaraḍāwī was chairman of the Islamic Scientific Council of a number of Algerian universities and institutions. He is also reported to have been a faculty member of, and up to 2003 the Chairman of the Board of Trustees of, the Islamic American University (IAU) in Michigan, a subsidiary of the Muslim American Society.[162] Furthermore, al-Qaraḍāwī is a member of the board of trustees of the Centre of Islamic Studies in Oxford. Initiatives with a narrower scope in which al-Qaraḍāwī has been represented appear to be the International Islamic Charitable Association in Kuwait, which are traceable back to his initiative, as well as the Qatar Islamic Fund for Zakāt and Ṣadaqa, of which he was the Chairman and founder.[163]

As a member of the Islamic Literature Association in Cairo, al-Qaraḍāwī is involved in the publication of periodicals, such as the *Oxford Journal of Islamic Studies* and *al-manār al-ǧadīd*, the latter being a publication which has apparently been published in Cairo since 1998.[164]

2.2.3. al-Qaraḍāwī's Use of the Media

Qatar began a radio station in 1970, for which al-Qaraḍāwī immediately began to produce religious programs.[165] Beginning in 1996, al-Qaraḍāwī

---

161 Also comp. the list of his offices in Albrecht. *Minderheitenrecht*, p. 67.

162 On the webpage http://www.muslimamericansociety.org (15.4.2014) al-Qaraḍāwī nowadays shows up neither on the board of trustees nor on the faculty.

163 According to Krämer. "Boundaries", pp. 191-193.

164 Sarah Albrecht. *Minderheitenrecht*, p. 46.

165 According to Helfont: *Qaradawi*, p. 45.

appeared on the program "The Sharia and Life," *(aš-šarᶜīa wa-'l-ḥayāt)* produced in Doha by the broadcaster Al Jazeera. This program has been significantly responsible for al-Qaraḍāwī's popularity and global authority. He appears weekly in the program with the clothing and habit of the traditional scholar and debates with a second participant who represents a differing opinion. In the process, there is a deviation from the classical constellation of the scholarly monologue, but the authority of scholarship is not abandoned. In contrast, since al-Qaraḍāwī lectures in the language of scholars[166] and with intensive regard to acknowledged source texts, he underlines his claim to convey instruction to the entire *umma*, which the medium of television reaches.

After the addresses, the audience can call and direct their questions to both guests on the program so that a discussion forum arises about the applicability of Islamic rules of life in a non-Islamic environment.[167]

Above all through this program, which reaches an audience of millions, al-Qaraḍāwī has become a type of omnipresent TV mufti and *ᶜālim*, whose greatest capital is "the personal rectitude and integrity . . . which is attributed or acribed to him"[168]: namely that of a leader who is influential, judicious, and simultaneously devoted to people's concerns, someone who dispenses praise and reproach, endorses and condemns, recommends and rejects, and in the process calls upon people to take courageous positions, to exhibit reasonable behaviour, to maintain "Islamic" standards, and in this manner to create a completely own community with its own rules of life.

---

166 Muhammad Qasim Zaman also emphasizes this: "What we have here is a language that seeks multiple audiences, an intelligibility across local cultures. It remains a language of the 'ulama'." Muhammad Qasim Zaman. "The Scope and Limits of Islamic Cosmopolitanism and the Discursive Language of the 'Ulama'" in: Miriam Cooke; Bruce B. Lawrence (eds.). *Muslim Networks from Hajj to HipHop*. The University of Carolina Press: Chapel Hill, 2005, pp. 84-104, here p. 102.

167 The audience, who report back with questions or comments on the program, were, at least in the early years beginning in 2000, about 2/3 from Europe and 1/3 from Arab countries. As a reason for this, Skovgaard-Petersen notes a lack of competent teachers in Europe: Skovgaard-Petersen. "Mufti", p. 157.

168 Thus formulated by Birgit Krawietz, in particular for the authority of the mufti: Birgit Krawietz. "Der Mufti und sein Fatwa. Verfahrenstheorie und Verfahrenspraxis nach islamischem Recht" in: *WO* 26 (1995), pp. 161-180, here p. 170.

In 1997, with www.qaradawi.net, al-Qaraḍāwī started the first personalized Arab website of a scholar with the support of the Qatari Al-Balāgh-Cultural Society.[169] It placed the person of al-Qaraḍāwī completely in the center. In 1999 both the English and the Arabian versions of www.islamonline.net were started, and they are both located in Doha. al-Qaraḍāwī was involved in the founding of both. At least in the past, IslamOnline as well as al Jazeera are said to have received support from the Emir of Qatar. In its early days, al-Jazeera is said to have received $US 130 to $US 150 mio.[170]

IslamOnline.net was originally started as a *zakāt* service by the IT specialist Maryam al-Ḥağarī and her Qatari teacher for Sharia law, Ḥāmid al-Anṣārī. It was begun at Qatar University with initial financing from the Qatar Foundation.[171] What is involved is a website partly supervised in Qatar and partly supervised in Cairo, however, in which al-Qaraḍāwī has his say with his own opinions. He also answers specific questions and publishes excerpts and summaries of his talks, writings, and books.

Its entire orientation is that of an advisory page which brings together the opinions of experts from various fields[172] such as theology and law, sociology and political science, psychology, and medicine, economics, and art regarding questions of politics, society, and personal piety. Also, a number of what are to a certain extent differing answers are by all means able to be presented in the process.[173]

However, where several scholars take responsibility for joint opinions, they convey agreement on the part of several authorities to the questioner and carry with them greater authority than one individual's opinion. al-Qaraḍāwī describes the orientation and goal of the IslamOnline project as the "Jihad of our era,"[174] as a project for the propagation and defense of

---

169 For detailed information see Gräf. "Sheikh Yūsuf", p. 407.

170 According to the staement in Jurkiewicz. *Al-Jazeera*, p. 19.

171 According to Gräf on the basis of Interviews with both individuals: Gräf. "IslamOnline.net" and in more detail in her dissertation: *Medien-Fatwas*, pp. 252ff.

172 According to Gräf. "IslamOnline.net".

173 Referred to, for example, by Vit Šisler: Vit Šisler. "Islamic Jurisprudence in Cyberspace. Construction of Interpretative Authority in Muslim Diaspora" in: R. Polčák; M. Škop; D. Šmahel (eds.). *Cyberspace 2005 Conference proceedings*. Masaryk University: Brno, 2006, pp. 43-50.

174 From a brochure on the first anniversary of IslamOnline and quoted in: Gräf. "IslamOnline.net".

Islam, which does not exclude that these pages also serve "the worldwide dissemination of a completely personal religious conviction, of the self-actualization and self-dramatization" of al-Qaraḍāwī.[175]

In the meantime, the website www.islamonline.net offers only texts in Arabic; on www.onislam.net Arabic as well as English texts are published,[176] on which al-Qaraḍāwī is strongly present with interviews and commentaries. This page also offers counseling and advice on everyday questions, information on Islam, comments on current events, discussions of legal and religious issues, politics and society. There is also a section called "OnIslam Africa" which publishes numbers of texts in the African language Yoruba.[177]

2.2.4. al-Qaraḍāwī as a Transnational Scholar

Besides seeing al-Qaraḍāwī's significance through the offices he holds and his use of the media, it is also visible through the role he plays for the Muslim community. This can be deduced from the climate he creates through his commentaries and publications, which in turn is important for the topic of apostasy.

A Beacon in an Era of Arbitrariness

Through his utterances on all the topics of every day life, al-Qaraḍāwī has become a beacon of orientation in a time when there is increasing fragmentation within the authority of classical scholars.[178] In modernity there is also a measure of arbitrariness with respect to the application of Islamic law. Through his clear instruction on the practical implementation of Islamic law, he conveys clear guidelines for life's layout as a Muslim believer. Especially given the lack of a higher teaching authority and an

---

175 According to Florian Harms on *daʿwa* driven on the internet by Muslim aktivists: Florian Harms. "Der Prophet ruft aus dem Cyberspace. Formen islamischer Mission im Internet" in: Matthias Brückner; Johanna Pink. *Von Chatraum bis Cyberjihad. Muslimische Internetnutzung in lokaler und globaler Perspektive*. Ergon Verlag: Würzburg, 2009, pp. 169-212, here p. 194.

176 http://www.onislam.net/english/; http://www.onislam.net/arabic/ (15.4.2014).

177 http://www.onislam.net/english/onislam-africa.html (15.4.2014).

178 On the fragmentation of authority among scholars see for instance Dale F. Eickelman; James Piscatori. *Muslim Politics*. Princeton University Press: Princeton, 1996, pp. 131-135.

only comparatively poorly educated theological hierarchy of scholars within Sunni Islam – as well as the specific circumstances in modernity such as the global reach of new media –he has to work at the same time to maintain his influence, particularly as he finds himself in a competition of conviction with charismatic, and yet often less theologically trained, opinion leaders and their notions.

Conducive for al-Qaraḍāwī's influence is up to the present day his location in Qatar, where he is effectively withdrawn from what is most assuredly an anticipated conflict with respect to his positions between politics and al-Azhar, between the Muslim Brotherhood and the Egyptian state and its directives. On the other hand, on the grounds of this situation in Egypt, he is unable to resort to any state or religious institutions in order to add any weight to his influence. This means that his influence only reaches as far as he can claim recognition of his authority by achieving a following and expressions of approval.

Traditional Scholars in Cyberspace

By means of the media, al-Qaraḍāwī offers traditional scholarship – underscored by corresponding clothing and his demeanor – as well as newly interpreted content and direct public addresses.[179] Via the broadcaster al Jazeera this happens "with great effectiveness in the Arab world."[180] He thus oversteps the borders of his regional influence and becomes an omnipresent and omnicompetent authority:[181] The pre-digital separation between a center of Islam and its periphery is suspended by the complete

---

179 On these media authorities created by the internet, the newly established connection between traditional content in modern garb, and the change in the classical manner of conveying knowledge comp. Gary R. Bunt. *Islam in the Digital Age. E-Jihad, Online Fatwas and Cyber Islamic Environments*. Pluto Press: London, 2003, pp. 135ff.

180 Abdo Jamil Al-Mikhlafy. *Al-Jazeera. Ein regionaler Spieler und globaler Herausforderer*. Schüren: Marburg, 2006, p. 167.

181 The competition for influence on a fragmented Muslim public through the use of media is particularly pointed out by Dale F. Eickelman: "Clash of cultures? Intellectuals, their publics, and Islam" in: Stéphane A. Dudoignon; Komatsu Hisao; Kosugi Yasushi (eds.) *Intellectuals in the Modern Islamic World*. Routledge: London, 2006, pp. 289-304, here p. 290.

globalization of cyberspace.[182] Through his ministry, and via new channels of the media, al-Qaraḍāwī has won back influence which traditional scholars had increasingly lost since the 19th century due to the decreased significance of religious education.[183]

al-Qaraḍāwī is, however, not only a traditional scholar and not only reclaims the past. Rather, he seeks to claim the present, which he interprets anew "in light of the Quran and sunna."[184] He also seeks to claim the future by equipping youth and commissioning them for the future.

All-encompassing Competence with a Comprehensive Claim

In his own person, al-Qaraḍāwī embodies that which he finds to be a prerequisite for coping with modernity: comprehensive scholarship in a number of disciplines, which alone justify *iǧtihād*, i.e., offering qualified opinions on all the significant topics of daily life. In the process, he does not remain with the traditional topics of Islamic theology.[185]

Repeatedly, he emphasizes that pseudo-scholars cannot claim any authority for themselves. And specialists who only master one discipline can easily mislead others.[186] Precisely on the basis of the freedom of choice in

---

182 Particularly pointed out by Gary R. Bunt. "The Digital Umma" in: Amyn B. Sajoo (ed.). *A Companion to the Muslim World.* I.B. Tauris Publishers: London, 2009, pp. 291-310, here p. 309.

183 See Muhammad Qasim Zaman. "The Ulama of Contemporary Islam and their Conception of the Common Good" in: Armando Salvatore; Dale F. Eickelman (eds.). *Public Islam and the Common Good.* Brill: Leiden, 2004, pp. 129-155, here p. 129.

184 Numerous of his book titles, among them also his treatment of apostasy: Yūsuf al-Qaraḍāwī. *ǧarīmat ar-ridda wa ʿuqūbat al-murtadd fī ḍau' al-qur'ān wa-'s-sunna.* Maktabat wahba: al-Qāhira, 2005[3], were provided with an addendum in order to emphasize that his writings are not mere treatments by a scholar but rather a position derived from authoritative Islamic sources.

185 He thus expresses himself in his writing: al-Qaraḍāwī. *al-iǧtihād*, pp. 9ff.+39ff. on topics such as organ transplantation or abortion. However, he also treats traditional areas of folk Islam, such as the questions of whether amulets, necromancy, sorcery, astrology, veneration of graves, and the blessings of stones and trees are allowed in Islam Yūsuf al-Qaraḍāwī. *ḥaqīqat at-tauḥīd. Maktabat wahba*: al-Qāhira, 2006[8], pp. 52ff.

186 al-Qaraḍāwī. *aṣ-ṣaḥwa al-islāmīya*, p. 172.

the search for information, he emphasizes the duty to seek counsel from authorities.

al- Qaraḍāwī addresses himself indiscriminately to all Arab speaking Muslims via www.qaradawi.net, and via IslamOnline he uses the world language of English beyond that to address the worldwide IslamOnline community. Nowhere is it recognizable that he has a particular emphasis upon his national background or that he has a tendency to limit his following to Egypt or Qatar. Sunnis are fond of visiting his sites more than any others, but Shiites as well are among his audience,[187] which in light of the sharp demarcation between Sunnis and Shiites on many another web pages catches one's eye all the more. Due to the fact that al-Qaraḍāwī himself does not belong to any of the four known Sunni legal schools and that following one specific legal school is not necessary, he appoints himself to be an interdenominational scholar.

Architect of the Umma

It is not al-Qaraḍāwī's goal to call for the overthrow of governments in Europe or to violently tear down the legal systems there. His goal is instead to achieve change from within by strengthening the Muslim community, whose members are to transmit the convictions learned through education and instruction and through solicitation within their surroundings. The change pursued by al-Qaraḍāwī works from inside to outside, from the bottom to the top. For him it is not a matter of revolution. Rather, it has to do with reform rooted in the Sharia. It is not about an overthrow. Rather, it is about renewal and a course correction.

It is not modernity that rules over him and the *umma*. Rather, it is he – and more specifically comprehensive Islam which he preaches – that rules over modernity. By emphasizing the necessity of unity within the *umma* and the inclusion of various standpoints, al-Qaraḍāwī' creates the unity which he calls for in his own person. Only the completely a-religious individual or the literal Salafist would supposedly not see himself as represented by al-Qaraḍāwī' – both are within the *umma* clear minorities.

Due to the the fact that al-Qaraḍāwī claims to give Muslims guidance in Muslim majority countries as well as in the diaspora in the Western world, he has created a new type of global *umma*, which throughout Islam-

---

[187] According to Roald. "Men", p. 50.

ic history had never become visible in this way. It has first emerged through its claim that in the final analysis it is entitled to give instructions to all Muslims in all life situations and in all geographic areas, independent of their place of residence and their national or denominational roots.[188]

He gathers Muslims of various backgrounds and types into an *umma*, not, however, by taking up arguments, dealing with them, and searching for compromise. Rather, he does this by conveying his opinion authoritatively as a go-between and as allegedly the only appropriate one that has opinions which are superior to others' opinions. As support for his argumentation, he quotes those who share his opinion in a particular point, but he does not seriously deal with contrary opinions.[189] al-Qaraḍāwī uses his sources selectively, indeed in part in a manipulative manner,[190] in order to justify his position.[191] He repeats himself often, from earlier publications. Yet, he can slightly alter his statements after years, contradicting himself when compared to earlier statements and statements made elsewhere.[192]

An individual can indeed decide the degree to which he wants to become an active designer of this *umma*, the degree to which he wants to limit himself to being a silent user of the internet, or, alternatively, the degree to which he wants to enter into contact with the scholar.[193] al-

---

188 Gary R. Bunt speaks about "creating a cohesive electronic identity in cyberspace for Islamic political agendas and concerns." Gary R. Bunt. *Virtually Islamic. Computer-mediated Communications and Cyber Islamic Environments*. University of Wales Press: Cardiff, 2000, p. 102.

189 Also according to Muhammad Qasim Zaman. "The Ulama of Contemporary Islam and their Conception of the Common Good" in: Armando Salvatore; Dale F. Eickelman (eds.). *Public Islam and the Common Good*. Brill: Leiden, 2004, pp. 129-155, here p. 173.

190 That becomes particularly clear when he expresses himself in a derogatory manner about other religions, for example, about Judaism or Christianity or the wrongdoings on the part of Jews and Christians throughout history and draws upon the one-sided derogatory statements by other Muslim apologists as allegedly objective sources. Comp. on this, for example: al-Qaraḍāwī. *ġair al-muslimīn*, pp. 76ff.

191 Comp. for an explanation of al-Qaraḍāwī's pattern of argumentation Helfont. *Yusuf al-Qaradawi*, pp. 66ff.

192 The inconsistent nature of statements made by al-Qaradawi is also mentioned by Mariani: ". . . ses positions étant souvent contradictoires ou du moins paradoxales." "Al-Qaradawi", p. 197.

193 The various possibilities for rapprochement between questioners and authority is pointed out in particular by Jon W. Anderson. *Muslim Networks, Muslim Selves in*

Qaraḍāwī insists, however, that the actual membership of all Muslims in the diaspora is an *umma* which gives believers their true identity and in the final event conveys the idea that they have no home in Western society. He therefore reduces the believer down to dealing with the question of whether that individual practices Islam completely and appropriately and views his living environment from the perspective of whether the living environment enables him to do so.

Pragmatic Intermediary between Liberalization and Petrification

An additional source of al-Qaraḍāwī's authority lies in the fact that he not only imitates traditional legal judgments and does not simply preach forbiddance of the technical and social achievements of modernity. Instead he seeks a pragmatic way of alleviation for believers and approves of the emergence into modernity. He rejects the Westernization of believers just as he does a softening of the comprehensive claim of Islam and the sacrifice of Islamic identity and practice in favor of modernity.

In this way, he acknowledges societal change as well as a change in Muslim behaviour on the condition that indispensable principles and content is preserved. He legitimates the acceptance of modernity without adopting it uncritically. For al-Qaraḍāwī, with his creation of *homo islamicus modernus*, it is nothing less than a matter of an alternative to the Western civilization which spans the globe, whereby he himself is the point man for that alternative.

On the one hand, due to the the fact that al-Qaraḍāwī acknowledges the unlimited authority of the Quran and the *sunna*, and at the same time, in modernity and in times of migration, seeks a practical way to preserve the moral and ethical guidelines, he wants to win over secularly oriented powers as well as religiously oriented powers to his form of understanding. He seeks to win secularly oriented powers by reminding them of their actual identity and by showing them a way to implement forms of behaviour based upon Islam which do not demand of them that they make a complete break with modernity. He seeks to win religiously oriented Muslims by

Cyberspace: Islam in the Post-Modern Public Sphere. NMit Working Papers (sic) on New Media & Information Technology in the Middle East. http://www.mafhoum.com/press3/102S22.htm (15.4.2014).

unreservedly holding fast to the authority of classic sources and scholars from the early days.

Bridge Building between Secular and Religious Forces
An Activist und Preacher of Daᶜwa

al-Qaraḍāwī does not only see his task to be to instruct the *umma* in their migration. Rather, he also charges them with the duty of *daᶜwa*. al-Qaraḍāwī does not content himself with warning youth against assimilation, the seductive influence of secularism, and atheism. Rather, he declares the *daᶜwa* to be a duty of all Muslims in the diaspora.

He has warned of the passivity of retreat and has charged Muslims with making a comprehensive effort for Islam[194] so that young people, in particular, can receive a new self-awareness as envoys and no longer be perceived as (a potentially disdained) minority. This task also justifies a longer stay in Western countries and at the same time answers the question of justifying a permanent stay in a non-Islamic area.[195]

If the *daᶜwa* mandate were to be implemented, then an environment characterized by Islam should gradually emerge. The entire political and social climate of the West and its understanding of democracy, human rights, and women's rights would change for the benefit of Islam so that the superiority of Islam would be recognized. al-Qaraḍāwī views the past expulsion of Islam from Europe as a defeat, but he prophesies a new conquest: "I maintain that the conquest this time will not be by the sword but by preaching and ideology . . ."[196]

---

194 Caeiro formulates al-Qaraḍāwī's viewpoint on the responsibility for social engagenemtn on the part of the Muslim minority as follows: "For the Egyptian scholar, the Muslim is a *political animal* by definition" (emphasis in the Original). Caeiro. "ulama", p. 132.

195 According to Shavit, there are also other theologians in the 20th century who have defended the view that essentially allows this, for example Saudi Arabia's longtime supreme legal expert, Abd al-ᶜAzīz bin ᶜAbdallāh bin Bāz: Shavit. "Muslims".

196 The corresponding *fatwā* can no longer be retrieved via IslamOnline; the above mentioned quote can now only be found at: "Leading Sunni Sheikh Yousef Al-Qaradhawi and Other Sheikhs Herald the Coming Conquest of Rome," MEMRI Special Dispatch No. 447, 6.12.2002. http://www.memri.org/report/en/0/0/0/0/

Muslims should take up leading positions in the West by studying sciences such as mathematics, astronomy, physics, chemistry, geology, oceanography, desert studies, physiology, and biology. Such courses of study are no longer only an option. Rather, it is "an inescapable obligation" in order to have a network of specially trained experts to be able to enter into competition with others and to respond to the needs of Muslims in society.[197]

Mentor of Youth

One of al-Qaraḍāwī's primary goals is to teach Islamic youth so that they can become the people upon whom hopes are pinned and become the avant-garde of Muslim society and of Europe:[198]

> "I am trying to help the youth build themselves mentally through culture, spiritually and religiously through worship, morally by virtue, physically through sports, and socially by serving everyone in society, through clinics and dispensaries."[199]

Educated and equipped youth would then be capable of bringing renewal to the rest of the world and to the *umma*.[200] al-Qaraḍāwī has already recommended the construction of a boarding school, has drafted a curriculum, and has pleaded for teaching staff who are neither extremists nor liberals.[201] The reform theologian Rašīd Riḍā had already pursued a similar thought. With financial support of 4,000 Pounds[202] annually, inter alia, he

---

0/0/774.htm (15.4.2014), among others with reference to similar sounding remarks by al-Qaraḍāwī, inter alia, in various broadcasts on al-Jazeera.

197 Yusuf al-Qaradawi. "Deserting Worldly Sciences for Religious Studies," 4.2.2010. http://www.onislam.net/english/ask-the-scholar/morals-and-manners/social-manners/170426.html (15.4.2014).

198 These thoughts are discussed in more detail in his work: *al-iḫwān*, pp. 32ff.

199 According to al-Qaraḍāwī as summarized in a personal interview: Davis. *Jihad*, p. 230.

200 On the targeted renewal, *wasaṭīya*, and minority rights al-Qaraḍāwī comments in detail in his work: *al-awlawīyāt al-ḥaraka al-islāmīya fi 'l-marḥala al-qādima*. Maktabat wahba: al-Qāhira, 1990, pp. 13ff, 107ff, 139ff.

201 Wardeh. *al-Qaraḍāwī*, p. 73.

202 This sum is mentioned by Umar Ryad. *Islamic Reformism and Christianity. A Critical Reading of the Works of Muḥammad Rashīd Riḍā and His Associates (1898-1935)*. E. J. Brill: Leiden, 2009, pp. 162-163.

established an educational institution on Roda Island near Cairo in the Nile through the "Sublime Porte" (or High Porte) from 1912 onwards. It was called the "Center for the Propagation of Islam and Leadership" (*dār ad-dacwa wa-'l-iršād*) and had as its goal[203] to train up especially capable pupils for tasks of leadership as well as to be messengers of Islam. In the final event, the idea was to choose a caliph from that circle of legal scholars capable of *iğtihād* and to unite the Muslim world under his leadership.[204]

Authority for the Homeless

In a time where there is much choice with respect to one's own life orientation, on the basis of the dislocation of the community in the diaspora in a non-Islamic society as well as the anonymous options for contact on the internet, one can assume that the feeling of obligation to follow certain scholars and specifically to observe their *fatāwā* is less strongly pronounced than in a personal situation of counsel given in a mosque or in an institute of learning in Near Eastern societies.

al-Qaraḍāwī has attempted to recreate this lost personal connection to his hearers that has resulted through the media, and he has tried to do this by addressing topics relating to numerous areas of life – e.g., questions relating to financial matters, marriage, child rearing, matters of dress, professional life, and inheritance matters – and thus making himself indispensable for the daily life of his hearers. He not only produced this link via the intellect. Rather, he did so via an emotional path, by repeatedly ornamenting his treatments with clichés from Arabic poetry still generally highly regarded in Arab society, which he had been composing since his early youth.[205]

---

203 However, the establishment had to be closed after the outbreak of World War I: W. Ende. "Rashīd Riḍā" in: *EI/2*, Vol. VIII. E. J. Brill: Leiden, 19, pp. 446-448, here p. 447.

204 According to Malcolm H. Kerr. *Islamic Reform. The Political and Legal Theories of Muḥammad cAbduh and Rashīd Riḍā.* University of California Press: Berkeley, 1966, p. 183.

205 al-Qaraḍāwī intersperses numerous verses in his autobiography: al-Qaraḍāwī. *al-qarya*, e.g., Vol. 1, pp. 306ff.

Apologist and Link between Worlds

al-Qaraḍāwī cannot be accused of giving a one-sided dark picture of the West as enemy territory for Muslims. Indeed he emphasizes peculiarities of Islamic theology as distinguished from Christian and Jewish theology and leaves no doubt where the truth lies for him. However, he turns against the conclusion that a basic hostility between Muslims and Christians follows from that.

On the contrary, he calls for "the spirit of mercy and tolerance towards the People of the Scripture," for "some hardcore Muslims claim there are no common grounds at all between us and Jews and Christians as long as we deem them infidels who corrupted the words of Allah."[206] al-Qaraḍāwī submits further that "the People of the Scriptures" are still closer to Muslims than are "pagans" and "atheists" so that he recommends forming a common front against the advocates of atheism, promiscuity, pornography, materialism, nudism, sexual arbitrariness, abortion, homosexuality, and same-sex marriages.[207]

al-Qaraḍāwī has recreated himself as the link par excellence: He combines tradition with modernity, early Islam with Islamic Awakening, and the Near East with the West.

> "Le cheikh Qaradawi se place au point de jonction de trois mondes qu'il contribue à réunir au niveau transnational: les médias de masse, la finance islamique et la religion."[208]

He has not only maintained the truth of the all-encompassing nature of, and the timelessness of Islam. He has wanted to bring it about with the help of modernity and prove it. For that he has claimed modernity for himself by defining it anew and determining how it is to look in the future.

---

206 Yūsuf al-Qaraḍāwī. "Bringing Religions closer: Is that possible?" http://www.onislam.net/english/ask-the-scholar/dawah-principles/dawah-to-non-and-new-muslims/174432.html?New_Muslims= 29,05.2004 (15.4.2014).

207 Ibid.

208 Mariani. Al-Qaradawi, p. 203.

2.2.5. Assessing al-Qaraḍāwī

al-Qaraḍāwī – a Moderate Reformer?

In light of this dazzling diversity of activities and al-Qaraḍāwī's personality, it is not surprising that the assessments of him widely vary, depending upon the viewpoint of the observer and according to the comparisons and reference points:[209] They vary from a classification of his person as liberal,[210] as moderate,[211] to his being a misguided pseudo-scholar,[212] "the public enemy No. 1 for Ahlu-s-Sunnah wa-l-Jama'ah," a heretic who spreads unbelief *(kufr)* and misleads people towards unbelief,[213] as one who works on the destruction of Islam,[214] and as "an infidel, an apostate, and a heretic."[215] Others have considered him to be a reform-oriented expositor,[216] while even others have viewed him as "fundamentalist,"[217] as a scholar who has misused the religion of Islam in order to label suicide attacks as heroic defenses of Islam,[218] or as one of the "sheikhs of death."[219]

---

209 Carsten Polanz points out how dependent the term "moderation" is on the corresponding comparative parameters: Polanz. a*l-Qaraḍāwīs Konzept*, p. 21.

210 For example, he is classified among representatives of liberal Islam by Charles Kurzman. *Liberal Islam. A Sourcebook*. Oxford University Press: Oxford, 1998, pp. 196-204.

211 He is labelled as "one of the contemporary world's leading moderate Islamic thinkers and activists" by Nadiah Wardeh: *al-Qaraḍāwī*, p. ii.

212 For example, according to the website run by Salafists: http://www.allaahuakbar.net/jamaat-e-islaami/qaradawism/reading_in_qaradawism.htm (5.8.2010).

213 According to the "Kulturinstitut der Italienischen Islamischen Gemeinschaft" which positioned itself in 1999 against Wahhabism and advocated Jewish-Christian-Islamic dialogue: http://www.amislam.com/qaradawi.htm (3.8.2010).

214 For example, according to the Salafist side http://www.thenoblequran.com/sps/sp.cfm?subsecID=NDV16~articleID=NDV160003~pfriend= (15.4.2014).

215 Syrian jihadist scholar Abu Basir Al-Tartusi: "Sheikh Youssef Al-Qaradhawi is an Apostate," MEMRI Special Dispatch No 2162, 24.12.2008. http://www.memri.org/report/en/print3018.htm (15.4.2014).

216 John L. Esposito. "Practice and Theory. A Response to 'Islam and the Challenge of Democracy' in: *BR* April/May 2003.

217 Kursawe. "al-Qarāḍawī" (sic), p. 529.

218 Mona Eltahawy, who criticizes classifying al-Qaraḍāwīs as a "moderate," speaks on the basis of his foundational advocacy of suicide attacks of a "lionization of death among too many Palestinians," which has led to considering this means of

The question of whether al-Qaraḍāwī can be designated as moderate, modern, or even as a reformer can be answered with "both . . . and," or answered with a question about the standpoint of the viewer. In comparison to a clear advocacy of Jihādism and terror such as al-Qaida und the Taliban, al-Qaraḍāwī's message is moderate. In comparison to literal Salafist positions on the limitation of women's rights and the rejection of that which supposedly contradicts early Islam, al-Qaraḍāwī sounds revolutionary and open-minded. Nevertheless, he has not become an advocate for women's rights and human rights.

The Sharia remains his standard, which he interprets traditionally and as a matter of principle holds to be valid in all areas. This includes corporal punishment, the application of which he unmistakably repeatedly calls for.[220] His conceptual framework consists exclusively of the Quran and the *sunna* and its interpretation by leading scholars. By returning to their practice, he hopes for a renewal of society. For that reason, one could consider him to be associated with Salafism or even labeled a reformed Salafist.[221]

---

battle to be an increasingly legitimate weapon against "Zionist" and "occupying forces": Mona Eltahawy. "Qaradawi damages Palestine's Cause by turning Global Issue into Islamist Weapon" in: Joshua Craze; Mark Huband (eds.) *The Kingdom. Saudi Arabia and the Challenge of the 21st Century*. Hurst & Company: London, 2009, pp. 286-290, here p. 288.

219 al-Qaraḍāwī is mentioned by name and labeled in this manner in a 2004 petition from scholars with more than 2,500 signatures of Muslim intellectuals from 23 countries. It was directed at the then UN General Secretary, Kofi Annan: "Stop Terror Sheikhs, Muslim Academis Demand" in: *Arab News*, 30.10.2004. http://www.arabnews.com/node/257332 (15.4.2014).

220 For instance in his work *ġair al-muslimīn*, p. 87.

221 According to Sarah Albrecht, he considers himself to belong to the *Salafīya* tradition: Albrecht. *Minderheitenrecht*, pp. 40-41. However, for *Salafīya* he represents rather nontypical notions, such as, for example, that singing and listening to music are allowed; yet at the same time, he labels his relationship to the *Salafīya* as good: Huda al-Salih. Al-Qaradawi: "I Call for making Sufism into Salafi, and making Salafi into Sufi" in: Al-Sharq al-Awsat Online, Thursday, 23.12.2010, quoted in: "Shaykh Yusuf al-Qaradawi on Muslim Brotherhood, Salafi Tendency, Shiism, Women." http://www.biyokulule.com/view_content.php?articleid=3171 (15.4.2014).

Criticism of al-Qaraḍāwī

Above all, al-Qaraḍāwī's basic advocacy of *ğihād* has been critically assessed.[222] Indeed he at times exclusively views it as a defensive struggle only justified in Islamic countries, neither allowing attacks on minorities there nor attacks on Muslims by Muslims.[223] On the other hand, he then makes quite a number of exceptions,[224] in particular with respect to suicide attacks in Palestine. Other points of criticism are his advocacy of the chastisement of wives. His condemnation of homosexuality and apostasy, his call for the death penalty for adulterous relationships,[225] his advocacy of polygamy, and in part his inflammatory anti-Jewish utterances have also been criticized. It is not only Western scholars who voice criticism of al-Qaraḍāwī. There are also Muslim authors who have published a number of books in which they deal critically with al-Qaraḍāwī.[226]

There is also some criticism of al-Qaraḍāwī with respect to his travels. While the USA banned al-Qaraḍāwī's entry into the United States in 1999 on account of his support of HAMAS and again in 2001, a wave of criticism arose in London in 2004 when al-Qaraḍāwī visited the European Council of Fatwa and Research (ECFR) and in connection with this trip

---

222 A number of statements by al-Qaraḍāwī on this topic are summarized by David Bukay: David Bukay. *From Muhammad to Bin Laden. Religious and Ideological Sources of the Homicide Bombers Phenomen.* Transaction Publishers: New Brunswick, 2008, pp. 297-302.

223 Samuel Helfont summarizes al-Qaraḍāwīs view of *ğihād*: Helfont. *al-Qaradawi*, pp. 87-88.

224 He thus allows women and children to participate in armed battle and declares the killing of occupying forces, such as US forces in Iraq and any kind of militant action in Chechnya to be just justified: comp. his comprehensive explanations in his work: Yūsuf al-Qaraḍāwī. *fiqh al-ğihād*, pp. 1082ff; 1186ff.; also comp. the evidence in the article: "Reactions to Sheikh Al-Qaradhawi's Fatwa Calling for the Abduction and Killing of American Civilians in Iraq." MEMRI Special Dispatch No. 794, 6.10.2004. http://www.memri.org/report/en/0/0/0/0/0/0/1231.htm (15.4.2014), as well as further confirmation in Polanz. *al-Qaraḍāwīs Konzept*, p. 70 and the explanations of Helfont. *al-Qaradawi*, pp.79; 83.

225 al-Qaraḍāwī. *al-ḥalāl*, 1960, p. 237.

226 Although al-Qaraḍāwī also has good relations with Saudi Arabian scholars, there are supposedly above all literal Salafists who do not share his positions and who have composed over 30 works refuting him. Comp. this information in: Tammam. "al-Qaraḍāwī", p. 83.

cofounded the International Union of Muslim Scholars (IUMS) in Ireland. Upon the occasion of the reception of al-Qaraḍāwī by the Mayor of London, Ken Livingstone, who is said to have labelled al-Qaraḍāwī as "moderate,"[227] this was countered by strong protests from various groups, among them Muslim women's rights activists[228] as well as the Gay and Lesbian Humanist Association.[229]

al-Qaraḍāwī was openly criticized for his advocacy of suicide attacks in Israel, his (at least at that time) approving attitude towards female circumcision as well as his advocacy of chastisement of disobedient wives, his call for beating homosexuals, and his anti-semitic utterances.[230] When in 2008 al-Qaraḍāwī wanted to again travel to Great Britain, a visa was denied with the justification that his visit would endanger the peace and security of the country. al-Qaraḍāwī attributed this to the work of the "Zionist lobby."[231]

Criticism has also been voiced by literally oriented Salafists who view his concept of *wasaṭīya* as too broadminded, while for his part al-Qaraḍāwī is condemned for being extremist. Specifically they bring the charge that al-Qaraḍāwī is a "a despicable Muftee, who utters kufr," who has reclaimed scholarship for himself and "has embarked upon changing the religion of Allah, misguiding the ummah with his straying verdicts." He is said to have adapted to modernity and the West and has thus betrayed Islam. In short, he is an apostate, and this deserves the death penalty.[232] al-

---

227 According to Rich "Model", p. 125.

228 On the protests of the "Middle East Centre for Women's Rights" in London see: "Statement by the Middle East Centre for Women's Rights on the Terrorist Attacks in London" in: Al-Nisa 9, August 2005, pp. 12ff. http://www.mecwr.org/resources/Al-Nisa9-+English-+Aug+05.pdf (31.7.2010).

229 See the following for the position of the Gay and Lesbian Humanist Association: http://www.galha.org/briefing/qaradawi.html (31.7.2010).

230 For a collection of critical media reports on this stay by al-Qaraḍāwī in London see: http://www.london.gov.uk/media/mayor-press-releases/2005/01/mayor-responds-to-dossier-on-al-qaradawi, 11.1.2005 (15.4.2014).

231 According to al-Qaraḍāwī in an interview with Asharq alawsat: Turki al-Saheil. "A Talk with Shaikh Yusuf al-Qaradawi" in: *Asharq alawsat*, 8.4.2008. http://www.aawsat.net/2008/04/article55259331 (15.4.2014).

232 "Dr. Yusuf Qaradawi a man who is wearing the gown of knowledge and the title of 'muftee' has embarked upon changing the religion of Allaah (tabdeel) and misguiding the ummah with his straying verdicts." For instance the website

Qaraḍāwī's work is also a thorn in the side of literal Salafist scholars because he allows a permanent stay in a non-Islamic territory, something which is strictly rejected by Salafists.[233]

2.3. Yūsuf al-Qaraḍāwī's Position on Apostasy in Islam

2.3.1. The "Centrist" Position and "Moderation"

In light of the immense significance and the vast reach of this globally active theologian, the question arises as to how al-Qaraḍāwī positions himself with respect to the topic of religious freedom, and how he does so not only based on purely academic interest. The question of the freedom to choose with regard to one's own religion is a barometer for measuring personal as well as political civil rights and liberties. At the same time, it is one of the central human rights questions. A glance at the global map shows that where, on balance, the freedom to choose in questions of religion does badly, one mostly finds that only limited political as well as personal civil rights and liberties exist.

For the implementation of such civil rights and liberties, it is not only favorable political conditions which are of great significance. Rather, what is also of great significance is their derivation by opinion leaders from the realm of politics, society, and religion. This is due the fact that they provide the justification for political action based upon a perspective found in the history of ideas, even before the political framework for these civil liberties is produced. Although it is not always recognizable at first glance from a Western perspective, it should not be underestimated how authoritative Islamic theologians are involved in Muslim majority countries by exercising influence in the creation of a social climate. This is clear in examples such as the defense of the assassins of the literary figure Farağ Fūda by established theologians such as Muḥammad al-Ġazālī and Muḥammad Mazrūʿa in 1992. They had argued in court before the Egyptian Supreme Constitutional Court that the killing of Fūda, who was in

http://www.thenoblequran.com/sps/sp.cfm?subsecID=NDV16~articleID=NDV160002~articlePages=1 (15.4.2014).

233 According to Sarah Albrecht for both influential Saudi Arabian legal experts Ṣāliḥ al-ʿUṯaimīn (1925-2001) and ʿAbd al-ʿAzīz ʿAbd Allāh Ibn Bāz (1910-1999): Albrecht. *Minderheitenrecht*, p. 33.

their opinion the apostate (only a few days after a *fatwā* advocating execution of apostates was issued from the side of al-Azhar),[234] was a duty of the citizenry in order to maintain Muslim community,[235] for which they received much applause.[236]

For that reason, the force of influence theologians unfold deserves attention with respect to the practical consequences to be drawn from their opinions. Scholars either provide arguments which can serve as justification for advocating the death penalty – or even vigilante justice – or as the rationale for moderation and civil rights and liberties upon which soil tolerance and pluralism flourish. This is visible, for instance, when an author, intellectual, theologian, or journalist expresses himself critically on questions of religion, government, or social order and are accused in public of apostasy or blasphemy and their contribution to a discussion is interpreted as a threat.

Precisely for reasons of al-Qaraḍāwī's popularity, his appearance as a classical scholar, and his far-reaching influence, his pronouncements on the question of conversion and apostasy from Islam carry special weight all the way into politics and society. The utterances of one of the most prominent, if not today one the most influential, opinion leaders within Sunni theology doubtless receive a hearing.

al-Qaraḍāwī has repeatedly addressed the topic of apostasy over the course of many years. A number of times he has tended to make statements on the margins and in connection with other topics, while in other texts apostasy stands in the focus of his treatment. In a number of texts he tends to treat apostasy more from a theological standpoint, while in others it is treated more as a social and political problem. In a number of texts he calls for immediate action against apostasy, while in others he leaves consequences in his commentaries open. In part he clearly differentiates between tacit apostasy – concealed from the world – which through doubt and estrangement from Islam exclusively takes place within the heart of the involved individual and openly propagated apostasy. Openly propagated apostasy gives rise to unrest and upheaval in the Muslim community, and, for that reason, must absolutely be avenged. In a number of texts, he does

234 Comp. the presentation of the public threats and official statements preceding Fūda's killing in Soage. "Faraj Fowda".

235 Comp. the explanation of the argumentation in Hasemann. "Apostasiediskussion".

236 Comp. the detailed depiction of the case in Section 1.8.6.

not differentiate between these varied forms of apostasy.[237] Indeed, he deals with the entire topic in a few sentences without making a difference with respect to the respective form of apostasy (defensive or offensive) and how to deal with apostates (removal of the individual's doubts or punishment).

al-Qaraḍāwī has basically not revised his viewpoint on apostasy over the course of the last 50 years.[238] He has expanded and modified it numerous times, and depending on the occasion he has placed different focuses on his reasoning and thus judged apostasy here and there stronger as a theologian or as an activist. He is sometimes excursive in his argumentation, indeed even contradictory in a number of statements – above all in detailed questions – but an essential break from statements made on this topic as early as 1960 or a foundational rethinking regarding this question is nowhere to be seen.

2.3.2. The Lawful and the Prohibited in Islam (al-ḥalāl wa-'l-ḥarām fi 'l-islām) – 1960

As early as in his early work *al-ḥalāl wa-'l-ḥarām fi 'l-islām*[239] – which is simultaneously his most influential and most highly circulated book[240] – al-Qaraḍāwī mentions the relationship between Muslims and non-Muslims and apostasy from Islam in his penultimate chapter. At that point, he broaches the topic of three offences in all brevity which present an exception to the sanctity of life and for which the death penalty applies. Among

---

[237] In a text published on IslamOnline in 2003, for starter the Maroccan scholar Sheik Abdul Bari az-Zamzamy called for the general adminstration of the death penalty for apostates, with which al-Qaraḍāwī concurs with a very general statement: "All Muslim Jurists agree that the apostate is to be punished . . . The majority of them go for killing." "Group of Muftis. Source of the Punishment for Apostasy," 26.7.2003, http://www.onislam.net/english/ask-the-scholar/crimes-and-penalties/apostasy/169569.html (15.4.2014).

[238] Wenzel-Teuber certifies that at different times his thinking indicates various emphases on the same topic. However, in the essenial features of his thinking, there are no significant developments." Wenzel-Teuber. *Ethik*, p. 41f.

[239] al-Qaraḍāwī. *al-ḥalāl*.

[240] Tammam proceeds on the assumption that this work by al-Qaraḍāwī has appeared in 30 editions up to now and in over 20 languages: "al-Qaraḍāwī", p. 58. Comp. also Section 2.1.4.

them are murder, extra-marital relationships, and "apostasy from Islam after willingly accepting it" (*ḫurūǧ ᶜalā dīn al-islām baᶜda 'd-duḫūl fīhi*).[241]

No one is forced into Islam, according to al-Qaraḍāwī, but if it does happen, it is unthinkable to leave Islam as "the Jews" supposedly did at the time of Mohammed. al-Qaraḍāwī refers at this point to the frequently quoted tradition of Buḫārī and Muslim, according to which the blood of a Muslim can be spilled in three cases: in the case of murder, extra-marital relations, and apostasy from Islam.[242]

Overall, however, al-Qaraḍāwī remains obscure in these statements; the reader is left to draw his own conclusions. al-Qaraḍāwī remains vague when he implies that an individual has a free decision to accept Islam. He does this without considering that the majority of all Muslims, as children of Muslim parents or of a Muslim father, do not demonstrate their own personal autonomous responsibility when they enter Islam, and that this hardly can be evaluated as a voluntary acceptance of Islam.

al-Qaraḍāwī remains above all indeterminate when he – upon the occasion of a later expansion of this work[243] – gives the reminder that the death penalty may only be imposed by an authority or a ruler (*walīy al-amr*). Is al-Qaraḍāwī pointing to a worldly power? In which countries or under which circumstances could such a process even take place at all, since by far all Arab countries are Muslim majority countries, in spite of a general acknowledgement of the Sharia as one or even as the sole source of their legislation, limit application of Sharia law primarily to issues of marital and family law? From this declaration, it becomes clear that al-Qaraḍāwī views *ḥadd*-punishments as an indispensable component of the Islamic administration and application of justice.[244] However, it is not clear how they could be concretely applied in the case of the three offenses named by him – among them apostasy.

---

241 al-Qaraḍāwī. *al-ḥalāl*, p. 237.

242 Ibid., pp. 237-238.

243 The first edition (al-Qaraḍāwī. *al-ḥalāl*, 1960) does not yet contain the following remarks; they are added in later editions: al-Qaraḍāwī. *al-ḥalāl*, 1974⁸, p. 342; see also al-Qaraḍāwī. *al-ḥalāl*, 1980¹³, p. 318.

244 In numerous works, al-Qaraḍāwī emphasizes that the administration of *ḥudūd* punishments belong to the indispensable components; this is a "necessity" (*ḍarūra*); he argues in this manner, for example, in his document: Yūsuf al-Qaraḍāwī. *al-islām wa-'l-ᶜalmānīya waǧhan li-waǧh*. Maktabat wahba: al-Qāhira, 2006², p. 67.

al-Qaraḍāwī expressly warns against self-administered justice by "individual persons" (*al-afrād*) in the case of these three offenses deserving death. At this point, he expresses a warning with the justification that individuals are not granted the right to make such a judgment. That would lead to a situation where one and the same person is "judge" (*qāḍin*) and "executor" (*munaffiḏ*) and that would, in turn, have "chaos" (*fauḍa*) as the consequence. It is not the death penalty per se – also for apostasy – that is objectionable for al-Qaraḍāwī. Rather, it is the viewpoint that in vigilante justice too close an interrelation between accusation and judgment arises and the reins of responsibility are taken out of the hands of scholars.

It is not the victim that is in the center of al-Qaraḍāwī's considerations; instead, he appears to be concerned about the idea that the case of wrongfully presumptuous authority to decide combines the office of judge and executioner too closely and that scholars' vested decision-making authority would be forfeited. The actual objectionable point for al-Qaraḍāwī is thus more the procedure than the judgment and the outcome of the proceedings, namely the death of the person charged.

With this short report, the consequences from what has been said remain fully open. On the one hand, al-Qaraḍāwī' calls for the death penalty, which authorized powers are to impose, but he gives no indication as to how a court could concretely apply this order in the face of what in most countries is a situation where Sharia law is not the valid penal law. Given that, his call is either carefully stated, given the memory of earlier suffered repression by Egyptian state power, or else it is unrealistic. In the worst case, someone who wants to see Sharia law applied could consider it as freedom to act since the unconditional validity of Sharia law has been expressly confirmed by al-Qaraḍāwī. Since at this point there is no corroboration with warnings from the Quran and the *sunna*, it would also mean ignoring admonitions with respect to the consequences of vigilante justice.

What is the goal of al-Qaraḍāwī's remarks on the necessity of imposing the death penalty on apostates? Since he denies self administered justice, the call for the death penalty for apostasy is in the final event utopian, since neither in Western countries nor in most Muslim majority countries would court proceedings for apostasy be conceivable. Does al-Qaraḍāwī only want to submit a scholarly position, without concretely delivering directions on how to act? In light of the handbook nature of this work, with its numerous examples from everyday life – from plucking one's eyebrows to cosmetic surgery and all the way to playing chess and keeping watch-dogs – this is scarcely illuminating.

If one does not want to insinuate that al-Qaraḍāwī is making a direct call to implement Sharia law, if necessary in opposition to legislators, then it supposedly at least involves clearly determining the obligatory handling of such offenses even if no concrete directives for action arise from it. Thus, in the final event, the consequences from al-Qaraḍāwī's instructions for the treatment of apostates is largely left to the reader – and for that reason contain a certain potential danger.

In the event of murder, al-Qaraḍāwī follows the guidelines of classical Sharia law for *qiṣāṣ* offenses (offenses which require retaliation or the payment of blood money) in accordance with Sura 2: 178-179. He explains how retribution for murder can be called for by those surviving and suggests that the relatives be able to have retributive justice with respect to the culprit "so that their hearts experience healing" and are "freed from all desire for revenge." Is such retributive justice in the case of the disgrace of apostasy likewise possible so that "hearts experience healing"?[245]

2.3.3. Yūsuf al-Qaraḍāwīs Magnum Opus on Apostasy: The Crime of Apostasy and Punishment of Apostates in the Light of the Quran and Sunna ("ǧarīmat ar-ridda wa-ᶜuqūbat al-murtadd fī ḍau' al-qur'ān wa-'s-sunna") – 1996

Occasion and Significance of the Document

al-Qaraḍāwī' magnum opus on the topic of apostasy, with the title *ǧarīmat ar-ridda wa-ᶜuqūbat al-murtadd fī ḍau' al-qur'ān wa-'s-sunna* (The Crime of Apostasy and Punishment of Apostates in the Light of the Quran and Sunna) and a length of almost 75 pages, was initially published in 1996 in this form and since that time has experience multiple print runs. However, significant portions of this document were not composed for the first time in 1996. The second half of the work (pp. 44-73) is a verbatim copy of a segment published in 1993 in al-Qaraḍāwī's work *malāmiḥ al-*

[245] al-Qaraḍāwī. *al-ḥalāl*, 1974^{8}, p. 342.

muğtama^c al-muslim allaḏī nanšuduhū, in which he likewise dealt with the topic of apostasy.[246]

He again used this portion of his work for a publication on IslamOnline in 2002, without any additional explanations or making it known that it was an abstract from two publications which had appeared previously.[247] At a later time he again used this text – likewise without making this fact recognizable – when he published a *fatwa* on apostasy on his website www.qaradawi.net with the heading *ḫuṭūra ar-ridda wa-ᶜuqūbat al-murtadd* and under the category *fatāwā wa-aḥkām*.[248] The question at this point – whether contrived or actually posed to al-Qaraḍāwī – refers to the killing of an apostate, one who does not promote his apostasy but rather had only informed a friend about it. Does one have to punish the assassin for murder?

More clearly than at other points, al-Qaraḍāwī goes into the problem of premature execution of apostates in his *fatwā ḫuṭūra ar-ridda wa-ᶜuqūbat al-murtadd*. He emphasizes that the guilty individual would first have to confirm his apostasy (which would not be the case here), should receive an opportunity for remorse, and finally that the administration of punishment may not simply lie in the hands of "any people." Rather, this is placed with the *ḥākim* (judge or ruler), thus meaning that there is no justification for vigilante justice. A large part of the above mentioned text connects to al-Qaraḍāwī's work *ğarīmat ar-ridda wa-ᶜuqūbat al-murtadd fī ḍau' al-qur'ān wa-'s-sunna*.[249] The *fatwā* closes with an explanation of the acts of penance which are to be rendered in the case of unjustified killing: The guilty individual has to pay blood money and has to observe a fast of an additional two months.

In the face of al-Qaraḍāwī's numerous omissions on apostasy in these various passages, it is remarkable that in 1996 he apparently considered it

---

[246] Yūsuf al-Qaraḍāwī. *malāmiḥ al-muğtamaᶜ al-muslim allaḏī nanšuduhū*. Maktabat wahba: al-Qāhira, 1993, pp. 29-46.

[247] Yūsuf al-Qaraḍāwī. *al-muğtamaᶜ al-muslim wa-muwāğahat ar-ridda*. 28.2.2008. http://mdarik.islamonline.net/servlet/Satellite?c=ArticleA_C&cid=1175010105612&pagename=Zone-Arabic-MDarik%2FMDALayout (3.8.2010).

[248] Today the text is found on the Arabic Webpage OnIslam: Yūsuf al-Qaraḍāwī. *ḫuṭūra ar-ridda wa-ᶜuqūbat al-murtadd*, 27.3.2006. http://www.onislam.net/arabic/ask-the-scholar/8397/8320/43372-2004-08-01%2017-37-04.html (15.4.2014).

[249] With some gaps, al-Qaraḍāwī uses the text from his work: *ğarīmat ar-ridda*, pp. 44-63.

necessary to devote an entirely independent work with the title *ǧarīmat ar-ridda wa-ᶜuqūbat al-murtadd fī ḍau' al-qur'ān wa-'s-sunna* to the topic of apostasy,[250] even if he used earlier texts for it. It is remarkable because the significance of the topic – if one considers the very low number of openly confessing atheists, agnostics, and converts from Islam to other religions – it hardly appears necessary to take such a firm position on this question.

If, however, reference is also made to a number of events immediately preceding the publication of this writing, then there are a number of reasons for its being composed that come under consideration. Accordingly, there were numerous apostasy cases at the end of the 1980s and at the beginning of the 1990s in Egypt, launched above all against artists, authors, theologians as well as against human rights and women's rights activists.[251] It is possible that al-Qaraḍāwī, who is originally from Egypt, composed his writings upon the occasion of widely discussed cases there as a sort of aid in establishing his argumentation. It is also the case that in 1996 the intensive disputes surrounding Salman Rushdie's *Satanic Verses* from the end of the 1980s, the 1992 murder of the intellectual Faraǧ Fūda, and the assassination attempt on the writer Naǧīb Maḥfūẓ in 1994 lay only a few years back.

Especially Fūda's murder, which took place in broad daylight, made waves of public discussion swell in Egypt. Within the circles of al-Azhar and the public, there were arguments as to the legitimacy and even the obligation to execute an apostate, particularly including those made by Maḥmūd Muḥammad Mazrūᶜa[252] and which were debated all the way into courtrooms. And last but not least, the case of Naṣr Ḥāmid Abū Zaid can be mentioned in this connection, who from 1993 onwards drew great attention to himself.

Against this backdrop, it is not only explicable why al-Qaraḍāwī devoted one entire treatise to apostasy. Rather, it is also explicable why this document, in contrast to a number of others from his pen, is strongly char-

250 al-Qaraḍāwī. *ǧarīmat ar-ridda*.

251 In 2002 Hasemann counts exclusively for Egypt more than 50 claims before court on account of Islam in the ten prior years: Hasemann. "Apostasiediskussion", p. 117.

252 According to Krämer. "Boundaries", p. 201.

acterized by socio-political features and reflects comparatively little in the way of theological argumentation.[253]

Implied from the perspective of al-Qaraḍāwī's basic considerations regarding the guidance and education of youth and their attachment to the *umma*, as well as due to his specialization in Sharia law, the topic is primarily interesting to him from the perspective of Islamic law. This is due to the fact that for him reality has to be measured against Sharia law. Additionally, this concern is of interest for al-Qaraḍāwī in the course of his efforts relating to *da^cwa* and the dissemination of Islam worldwide. For him it is a world view dispute having to do with the central question of who will shape the *umma* and which values will be appropriated. For that reason, al-Qaraḍāwī views every worldview which is not Islamic or does not advocate the comprehensive socio-political view of Islam he favors to be a form of apostasy.

This document on apostasy is additionally of interest because the topic in itself would be appropriate for dealing on a critical level with questions or objections against Islam, thereby argumentatively presenting Islam as a convincing alternative to competing schemes such as secularism or atheism. It would also be suitable for bridge building – as in the case of minority rights – or more specifically for finding a synthesis between realities in the Islamic and Western life realms and for al-Qaraḍāwī's presenting himself as a representative of a "moderate" Islam.

Generally speaking, however, this is not what happens. In al-Qaraḍāwī's writings, it is not a question of bridge building or reconciling reality (Muslims nowadays live in large numbers in Western societies with complete positive as well as negative religious freedom) with the classic Sharia claim (turning away from Islam is legally impossible and is prosecuted).

---

[253] A theologically stronger document which had only little in the way of socio-political argumentation was put forth by al-Qaraḍāwī in 1978 in: *ẓāhirat al-ġulūw fī 'l-takfīr. Dar al-ǧihād/dār al-i^ctiṣām* [al-Qāhira, 1978], in which he also took up the topic of apostasy. It is worth noting that he indeed speaks there at two points (pp 24+33) of the "decision" by the judge (*ḥukm*) (pp. 24+33) as well as of the "punishment for the apostate" (*^cuqūbat al-murtadd*) (pp. 34); however, he mentions the death penalty and the duty to explicitly execute the apostate as little as the danger for the remaining Muslim society which proceeds from the apostate while both these topics – the sentence and the potential danger – clearly stand in the foreground in his work: *ǧarīmat ar-ridda*.

Just as it is in my opinion wrong to want to recognize true moderation in al-Qaraḍāwī's draft of minority rights, is would be just as displaced to want to make out a moderate course with respect to al-Qaraḍāwī's notion of apostasy: For al-Qaraḍāwī, when it comes to the treatment of apostasy, it primarily has to do with uncovering the destructive influences which in his opinion act upon Islamic society from the outside and are carried into the society. It also has to do with resisting such bodies of thought and not with a constructive dispute with the realities of modernity.

At no point does al-Qaraḍāwī grapple with individual arguments of those who doubt, religiously distant secularists or atheists, agnostics, or converts to another religion; indeed, the motive and considerations of such skeptics appear to in no way interest al-Qaraḍāwī. If he were to discuss this at eye level, then these considerations could enter into rivalry with al-Qaraḍāwī's convictions.[254] However, if al-Qaraḍāwī allowed grounds of conscience for turning from Islam and more specifically for preferring another religion or no religion, that would relativize his postulate of the unrivaled truth of Islam which is clear to every person.

Thus al-Qaraḍāwī, who himself might have never heard arguments from doubters or converts, does not use a single line to engage any deliberation as to why someone would not only fall away from Islam. Nor does he say anything as to why someone would take the step out of the community of Muslims and make his apostasy known through conversion to another religion in spite of what under certain circumstances has dramatic consequences for the individual personally, with respect to the individual's family, and with respect to the individual's social standing. To turn away from Islam necessarily means wickedness, decadence, and betrayal; no other interpretation exists for al-Qaraḍāwī. For that reason, all occurrences of this kind have to be combated as a type of threat to the community.

At no point in this work by al-Qaraḍāwī and in the scattered remarks he makes about apostasy in his other remaining works are there any glimmers of understanding or mild occupation with the thoughts of doubters or an understanding for the arguments of apostates, much less an intensive occupation with them. In al-Qaraḍāwī's work *ǧarīmat ar-ridda wa-ᶜuqūbat al-*

---

254 Justification as for instance formulated by the Kuwait convert Ḥusain Qambar ᶜAlī with respect to his religious conversion: "I have found God elsewhere," do not even arise on the margins of any of al-Qaraḍāwī's publications. Anh Nga Longva. "Apostasy and the Liberal Predicament," *ISIM Newsletter*, 8 (2001), p. 14.

murtadd fī ḍau' al-qur'ān wa-'s-sunna, it is not a matter of an equitable weighing up of the pros and cons of various worldviews or of convincing doubters. Rather, it is a matter of a renewed confirmation of the validity of Sharia law. Thus al-Qaraḍāwī remains bound to an internal discourse serving his own confirmation, without including outside arguments and more specifically without even addressing the viewpoints of the others at all.

The Title of the Work

The title of the work itself, *ğarīmat ar-ridda wa-ᶜuqūbat al-murtadd fī ḍau' al-qur'ān wa-'s-sunna*, points to the orientation and the characteristic style of the writing's contents. It is not a matter of apostasy as such, and just as little is it an explanation of the possible reasons for it, or a weighing up of the pros and cons. Instead, the title includes charges and sentencing: In the case of apostasy it is a matter of a "crime." The suffix is "and the Punishment of the Apostate" gives the single clear indication of the fitting way to deal with an apostate. Charges and condemnation continue to move ahead via God-given authority, thus according to (or "in light of") the Quran and the *sunna*.

It is thus not a matter of the individual opinions of the author: Rather, it is a discussion of the set of problems having to do with apostasy according to sources of divine authority. At the same time, the term *ğarīma* can also mean "offense" or "sin". With that said, there is a hint made with respect to the theological dimension of the question. The choice of this term points to the fact that al-Qaraḍāwī not only wants to treat apostasy as an offense in the here and now. Rather, from a theological perspective, it is judged to be a crime.

Topic and Content

In the foreword, al-Qaraḍāwī begins by declaring that the topic of apostasy is frequently addressed; however, it is done in an unqualified manner. This means that either it proceeds from incorrect guidelines – by assuming for instance that the Quran does not speak about this "crime" and that tradition only contains one verse regarding it – or that the topic is not adequately reasoned through by not distinguishing between concealed apostasy and apostasy that is made public.

al-Qaraḍāwī continues self-assuredly that nothing less is at stake important to him than to set forth "the truth" (Arabic: *al-ḥaqq*).[255] As with respect to other questions within al-Qaraḍāwī's topical spectrum – legal questions such as minority rights, religious concerns such as the obligation to make the *zakāt* contribution or socio-political questions such as the teaching on *ǧihād* – he approaches the topic of apostasy with great authority: He possesses a competence enabling him to make judgments which bring light into the obscurity of the diversity of opinions, and he knows how to lay out the sources in a binding fashion.

As early as in the foreword of the work, al-Qaraḍāwī points to what in his opinion is the drama underlying the topic of apostasy. Apostasy is not only in the position to bring *fitna* (turmoil, strife) into the community – a term pregnant with meaning which he arguably chooses with forethought – indeed even civil war (*ḥarb ahlīya*) can be sparked off by apostasy, which could lead a country to perish.[256] At the outset, al-Qaraḍāwī does not introduce the topic of apostasy as an incidental issue. Rather, he highlights its particular significance against the backdrop of the necessity of averting a danger and avoiding damage which, if it is not effectively warded off, would lead the Islamic community into the abyss.

In a qualifying manner – although he up to this point has not lost a word on the actual punishment of apostates – al-Qaraḍāwī points out in the introduction that in the case of an individual who makes no attempt to bring the community to commit apostasy, action could be limited to mere incarceration. An attempt to lead him back to Islam is appropriate in order to remove the "fogginess and darkness from his thinking" (*labs wa l-ġabaš ᶜan fikrihi*).[257]

However, al-Qaraḍāw does not discuss how that could happen: Via arguments? Via insistence? Via threats? Or via promises? al-Qaraḍāwī speaks indirectly of the possibility for repentance by granting a period of time for reflection and implicitly speaking against what other theologians have expressed as intransigent action of immediately executing an individual who has inwardly fallen into doubt. Despite this, al-Qaraḍāwī leaves no doubt that with respect to the result sought after – that the doubter has to

255 al-Qaraḍāwī. *ǧarīmat ar-ridda*, p. 6.
256 Ibid.
257 Ibid., p. 7.

return to Islam as quickly as possible – there can be, as far as al-Qaraḍāwī is concerned, no discussion.

The Confession of the Umma

After this introduction, al-Qaraḍāwī goes far afield in order to first of all lay out the character of the Islamic confession (*ᶜaqīda*). The foundation of the confession is God and prophethood as the Quran and *sunna* describe them. The term *ᶜaqīda* (confession, belief, doctrine) occupies a key position in this book by al-Qaraḍāwī: Throughout the entire text, he places the protection of the community and holding fast to this confession in the center, which he views as the crux of the matter with respect to the identity of the community.

Because al-Qaraḍāwī presents the *šahāda* as the first and most important formulation of the *ᶜaqīda*,[258] for that reason, among others, the term *ᶜaqīda* has such great significance. The *ᶜaqīda* is thus closely linked with the cause of the existence of the Islamic community (*umma*) and its essence. Along the lines of this essential confession, in what follows al-Qaraḍāwī summarizes the foundational characteristics of this confession, similar to an abridged form of dogmatics.

al-Qaraḍāwī first of all derives the obligation for permanent membership in the community of believers from the essence and the lordship of God. Prior to that, he explains the essence of the Islamic community, which lives by protecting and maintaining this confession and which is embodied in belief in God, the angels, the (revealed) books, the messengers, and the Final Judgment.[259] Foundational elements of this confession are of course the belief in one God and the prophethood of Muḥammad. al-Qaraḍāwī lingers for a while on a description of God and his actions as the omnipotent Creator and the eternal Lord of heaven and earth, who does not procreate and is not the result of procreation.[260]

After that, on the basis of the omnipotence of God, al-Qaraḍāwī explains the essence of humanity, the essence of all of his creation, and the

[258] According to W. Montgomery Watt. "ᶜAḳīda" in: *EI*/2, Vol. I. E. J. Brill: Leiden, 1986, pp. 332-336, here p. 332.

[259] al-Qaraḍāwī. *ǧarīmat ar-ridda*, p. 9.

[260] Ibid., p. 11.

essence of all creatures, who are servants of God and are his possession.[261] For that reason, according to al-Qaraḍāwī, God, the Omnipotent One, has a right to claim "worship and unlimited obedience" (*al-ᶜibāda wa-'ṭ-ṭāᶜa al-muṭlaqa*).[262] He brings about all things, also bringing about people's submission to him and devotion to him in love. For that reason, according to al-Qaraḍāwī, the *šahāda* also means that humankind is not to exercise obedience and submission to anyone or anything else other than God and his commands alone.[263] In the course of his work, he repeatedly reverts to the thought of the unlimited omnipotence of God in contrast to the only limited self-determination of his creatures.

In what follows, al-Qaraḍāwī discusses what the confession means with respect to the unique oneness of God, the *tauḥīd*,[264] and which consequences are implied from his point of view: There is no other who is Lord besides him, as protector and as ruler. At this point it is already clear that for al-Qaraḍāwī there is no true separation between a religious and a worldly sphere and that belief (or confession) is in no way an affair which can be limited to the religious realm.

In a similar manner, he considers ideologies – such as secularism or more specifically laizism,[265] materialism, communism, or Marxism – to be comprehensive worldviews, which not only convey incorrect contents. Rather, in the eyes of their adherents, they are "a philosophy for all of life and a comprehensive confession" (*falsafat ḥayāt kāmila wa-ᶜaqīda šāmila*), or, as others say, "religions without revelation" (*adyān bi-ġairi waḥy*). They convey to people a completely different view of the world, history, life, humanity, and God.

Having said that, such worldviews and ideologies cover not only a part of people's life and worldview orientation. Instead, they covers one's entire existence. In the same way, in al-Qaraḍāwī's eyes, belief in God and, more specifically, confessing Islam means a comprehensive demand on or seizure of the individual. It occurs through the acknowledgment of the

261 Ibid., p. 12.
262 Ibid., p. 13.
263 Ibid., p. 14.
264 Ibid., p. 15ff.
265 The dispute with laicism is viewed by al-Qaraḍāwī as so decisive that he dedicates an entire work to it: al-Qaraḍāwī. *al-islām wa-'l-ᶜalmānīya*.
266 al-Qaraḍāwī. *ğarīmat ar-ridda*, p. 41.

lordship of God and the orientation of all spheres towards God's revelation – such as legislation and the administration of justice. According to the way al-Qaraḍāwī discusses it, the confession was this holistic and effective in the first Muslim community, and it should take this position again today.[267]

On the one hand, monotheistic belief for al-Qaraḍāwī requires the rejection of idolatry, but it also calls for the same rejection of whatever rule does not stem from God but is exercised by individuals over other individuals. For that reason, the *tauḥīd* is a liberation of people from subjugation and slavery (or servitude) *(taḥrīr al-insān min al-ḫuḍūᶜ wa-'l-ᶜubūdīya).* Above all, however, it is a liberation from subjugation to other people. If God is inimitable and his dominion absolute, then the individual who is liberated by the revelation of God, the Creator, may only subject himself to him, the Creator, but not to any creature nor to any system produced by mankind.

The Freedom of Submission

For al-Qaraḍāwī this "liberation" of the individual is not freedom *towards* something – towards the freedom of choice in the sense of an autonomous decision in questions of belief and which would also include the freedom to have no confession of faith – but rather it is only the freedom *from* something, namely from pre-Islamic polytheism and the unduly and spuriously claimed dominion of mankind over others.

This also becomes clear in al-Qaraḍāwī's *fatwā* "Religion and Freedom" *(ad-dīn wa-'l-ḥurrīya)*, in which he first of all establishes that Islam brought forth and established true freedom in all important realms. Prior to the proclamation of Islam, people were enslaved with respect to their thinking, politics, society, religion, and commerce; however, humankind is born free and has the right to freedom. When Islam then appeared, it brought the freedom of belief (*ḥurrīyat al-iᶜtiqād*), freedom of thought (*ḥurrīyat al-fikr*), and the freedom of speech and to express criticism (*ḥurrīyat al-qaul wa-'n-naqd*). People have never been forced to its acceptance. Thus, al-Qaraḍāwī quotes "Let there be no compulsion in religion . . ." (Sura 2:256). Once, however, people have taken this step with complete conscience and deliberately turned to Islam, then turning back is

[267] Ibid., p. 42.

no longer possible. Otherwise, the punishment for apostasy has to be applied,[268] for God does not desire that belief becomes a "toy" (*ulʿūba*).

In this connection, for al-Qaraḍāwī the term "freedom" therefore above all means liberation from pre-Islamic slavery as well as from all other systems which could be established over the course of history and which deviate from Islam. For him, freedom is coterminous with Islam. al-Qaraḍāwī again emphasizes freedom of thought and freedom of speech at the end of the *fatwā*, but he does not deal with the question of how things look from the viewpoint of an individual who thinks differently or from from the standpoint of someone who deliberately would like to leave Islam.[269]

When al-Qaraḍāwī expresses himself so firmly about the freedom of Islam in his writing on apostasy entitled *ǧarīmat ar-ridda* as well as in his *fatwā ad-dīn wa-'l-ḥurrīya*, he still, in light of such an authoritatively presented directive from a scholar, leaves the question open as to whether his interpretations of the commands are as infallible as the revelation of God itself. If they are not, then the authority of the interpretations is in the final event a human one, and they could even be viewed as an example of the enslavement of people by people, which al-Qaraḍāwī here denounces.

Additionally, there is a consideration that apparently does not come into focus for him, i.e., that people are able to set up the very rule over other people he denounces. This is done by setting down as binding which guidelines they have to follow as minorities in non-Islamic societies and which compromises they may make. The possibility that al-Qaraḍāwī's authority and position could be the embodiment of this unjustifiably presumed upon rule of people over people – by, for example, his pronouncing a death sentence upon one individual with all peace of mind and enthusiastically calling down God's blessing in the case of another individual – is something which al-Qaraḍāwī completely blocks out.

Indeed, also when he quotes Sura 9:31 in connection with these considerations on the exercise of authority,[270] he does so by stating in a condemning way that besides Jesus Christ, Jews and Christians had taken "scholars" (*aḥbār*) and put them in God's place as lords. This, he says, is precisely a

---

[268] Wherein this "punishment (*ʿuqūba*) consists is, however, not made concrete by al-Qaraḍāwī at this point.

[269] al-Qaraḍāwī. *min hady al-islām*, Vol. 1, pp. 701+702.

[270] al-Qaraḍāwī. *ǧarīmat ar-ridda*, p. 20.

sign of their unbelief. However, al-Qaraḍāwī does not in any way make a connection with his own position of authority.[271]

In the process, al-Qaraḍāwī declares himself to be the absolute authority. He presumes for himself, without self-critical reflection or debate with competing scholars and their opinions, a position where he is in complete agreement with God's revelation. He also sees himself justified in exercising this authority over other people. This absolute attitude pervades al-Qaraḍāwī's entire writing on apostasy.

By the way, this work is pervaded by what was introduced at the beginning as a dichotomous model and interpretive pattern of interpretation corresponding to the very strong Islamist pattern of argumentation: Here are the believers who follow God's revelation, and there are the unbelievers and enemies who have lapsed into ideologies of human origin. Here is the rule of God, and there is servitude arising from human origins. Here is true monotheism, and there is polytheism and the presumptuous authority of humankind. Here is the community of believers, and there are the unbelievers. Here are the blasphemers who will occupy hellfire, and there are the believers who bring about good and achieve peace on the basis of their loyalty to God's law. Here are those who worship idols, and there are those who stand on the side of God. Here are those who autonomously rebel and produce turmoil, and there are those who submit to God's rule and who form the perfect community of believers.

In connection with the rule of God, as al-Qaraḍāwī states further that it is not only a matter of the sole legitimacy of worshiping God and the rejection of worshiping people or idols. Rather, it is also a matter of God's having the exclusive claim to the hearts of humanity. For that reason, the true believer submits only to God, while the polytheist (*al-mušrik*) splits his loyalties.

---

[271] Also with other topics al-Qaradāwī blocks out the connection between his *fatwā* contents and his own person and family, respectively. Thus, Barry Rubin points out, with reference to Sayyid al-Qimnī, that in his *fatwā* the killing of American and British civilians in Iraq is indeed declared as allowed at a time when one of his sons and one of his daughters were attending American universities; also, one son was at the American University in Cairo and three daughters were at British schools at the time; however, he apparently assumed that they were in freedom and security and did not want to be sacrificed in a suicide bombing. Barry Rubin labeled this ambiguity a "high level of hypocrisy": Rubin. *War*, p. 131.

At this point, the argument for exclusivity with respect to affiliation, obedience, submission, the following of commands, and authority is introduced. Furthermore, explanations highlighting the unconditional necessity of rejecting every authority (*ḥukm*) and every command (*amr*) as well as every system (*niẓām*) and every right (*qanūn*), every ordinance (*waḍᶜ*) und every custom (*ᶜurf*), every emulation (*taqlīd*) and every program (*manhağ*), every conception (*fikra*) and every value (*qīma*) which does not arise from God's revelation are man-made, so that no room remains for autonomy and freedom of choice.

Whoever strives for freedom of choice and thereby suspends and forbids God's decrees – hereunder al-Qaraḍāwī also expressly lists *ḥadd* punishments – has rejected God's rule and placed himself in the position of God.[272] The desire for autonomy is in al-Qaraḍāwī's opinion incompatible with a holistic approach to Islam because to him it embodies independent authority and, with that said, humanity's self-aggrandizement instead of the fear of God.

al-Qaraḍāwī continues with the explanation of Mohammed's prophethood, which he labels as necessary for rightly guiding humanity. In this way, people were informed of God's revelation, his divine standards and values. Through Mohammed, the seal of the prophets, God's standards have been communicated to people, with the result that oppression and lack of knowledge has been eradicated and people can obtain knowledge about life after death and the reckoning that occurs pursuant to the good and evil works done in this life.

In the following section,[273] al-Qaraḍāwī links obedience towards the messenger of God with obedience towards God himself, but here, with respect to later argumentation, he excludes that there could be a difference or contradiction between what God himself has communicated to humankind and what he has communicated by means of his revelation through Muḥammad, the seal of the prophets. The rug is thus forehandedly pulled out from under the argument frequently brought by those who are critics of the death penalty for apostasy, which is that God himself never ordered the execution of apostates in the Quran. For when obedience towards God is equated with obedience towards Muḥammad, then the order to execute

---

272 al-Qaraḍāwī. *ğarīmat ar-ridda*, pp. 19-20.

273 Ibid., pp. 25ff.

apostates, which is exclusively found in tradition, is equated with the text of the Quran with respect to its authority.

As an argument that people do not possess the choice of deciding either for or against the ordinances of the messenger Muḥammad, al-Qaraḍāwī uses Sura 33:36, in which resistance towards Mohammed is basically condemned as unwarranted, or verses such as Sura 4:80, which directly relates obedience towards God to obedience towards Mohammed: "Whoever obeys the messenger, he indeed obeys Allah ..."

The Sin of Autonomous Striving

Those who are obedient to God are contrasted with "the hypocrites" (*al-munāfiqūn*),[274] who stand for those who deliberately turn against God and his messenger to their own ruin, who reject his requirement to proclaim that which is ordained by God and instead turn to idols. Whoever turns from God's message in this way, "making [his ears] deaf" (Arabic: *aṣamma)* and orients himself towards philosophy, is thereby – as al-Qaraḍāwī implies – deliberately acting against his better knowledge and has erringly strayed "from the right faith" (*maraqa min ad-dīn*).[275] This is due to the fact that he is not following or observing what God has sent down.

Here, in pointing to any type of deviation, non-acknowledgment, or distancing from God's revelation, there is a connection made to Quranic judgments about unbelievers as "hypocrites" (*al-munāfiqūn*), as "blasphemers" or "the unjust" (*aẓ-ẓālimūn*), as the "godless" or those who "do evil" (*al-fāsiqūn*). Also, their personal responsibility, or more specifically the deliberate nature of their actions as a result of arrogance are likewise condemned with reference to Sura 2:34 as is their refusal to submit themselves. When apostasy is equated with wickedness or hypocrisy, then the background of Quranic argumentation can be presupposed to be known without detailed justification of the culpability of the actions.

Already at this point, al-Qaradāwī poses the question[276] as to whether unbelief grows even more if the unbeliever leaves the religious community (*al-milla*). al-Qaraḍāwī grants that this question is disputed and that there are various positions with respect to it. However, in the end he judges that

[274] Ibid., p. 26ff.

[275] Ibid., p. 29.

[276] Ibid., p. 31-32.

those who are deficient in their exercise of religion, who put off their repentance, and delay forgiveness are only making themselves guilty of "smaller unbelief" (*kufr aṣġar*).

Whoever makes himself his own standard and underestimates what God has revealed – someone who thus behaves arrogantly and freely decides what is allowed and what is forbidden – makes himself become guilty of "greater unbelief" (*kufr akbar*), such as *people of the book*. They are placed in warning-like manner before the eyes of Muslims. In particular, this is the case where an individual considers God's revelation to be the reason for "backwardness" (*taḫalluf*) and "reactionism" (*raǧʿīya*). Thus, this is an individual who arrogantly places himself above God's revelation and looks down upon it.

Autonomy and one's own freedom to decide in light of God's revelation and its comprehensive call upon a person's life, thought, and person's action are thus for al-Qaraḍāwī what is actually objectionable and inappropriate behaviour towards the Almighty. At this point, the reader encounters the ample and well known notion in Islamist discourse that God's rule necessarily permeates all areas of life and that unconditional obedience to God's rule and his regulations is required.

This holistic notion of the comprehensive nature of God's system of regulations also becomes clear when shortly thereafter al-Qaraḍāwī speaks about the necessity for all people to decide between two alternatives, leaving no additional possibility open: either Allah or idols, either Islam or "pre-Islamic heathenism" (*ǧāhilīya*), either God's rule (*ḥākimīya*) or humankinds' self determination. This is terminology which is clearly reminiscent of Abū l-Aʿlā Maudūdī's concept of God's rule (*ḥākimīya*) and Sayyid Quṭb's dichotomous conceptualization, with which Quṭb spoke out as the ruling spirit of the Muslim Brotherhood for the unconditional necessity of establishing an Islamic state.[277] al-Qaraḍāwī takes up this terminology and uses it in spite of the essential criticism which he primarily exercised elsewhere upon Quṭb's conceptions of *ǧāhilīya* and *ǧihād*.[278]

---

[277] See Damir-Geilsdorf. *Herrschaft*. al-Qaraḍāwī mentions Sayyid Quṭb in addition to Abū l-Aʿlā Maudūdī as a source for these remarks on "God's rule": al-Qaraḍāwī. *ǧarīmat ar-ridda*, e.g., p 35; most frequently he refers in this sense, however, to Ibn Taymīya (1263-1328).

[278] Thus for example in his work *al-iǧtihād*, pp. 101 ff., in which al-Qaraḍāwī states in detail that for him – unlike for Sayyid Quṭb – an Islamic society which is not

Thus, autonomy and the freedom of choice have exclusively negative connotations for al-Qaraḍāwī and are equated with rebellion and decay, with turning away from God and his regulations, indeed with unbelief. For that reason, this autonomy does not fit to believers, according to al-Qaraḍāwī. This is due to the fact that they belong to Islam and live under the rule of God and his messengers, so that they call out: "We hear you and we obey you!"[279]

This does not mean that non-Muslims should be forced to turn to Islam. It is here that al-Qaraḍāwī quotes the verse from the Quran: "Let there be no compulsion in religion . . ." (Sura 2:256).[280] Non-Islamic religious communities by all means possess a right to exist. However, it means that the Muslim community possesses a set orientation, thus, for example, that it is neither Jewish nor Christian, that it neither wanders about without a leader, that it is neither secular nor liberal, that it is neither marked by Marxist nor communist traits, that it does not fall into idolatry but instead holds fast to belief in monotheism, and that it surpasses all other confessions but itself is surpassed by none other.[281]

al-Qaraḍāwī now describes the essence of Muslim community by contrasting it with Western society and a number of worldviews. Muslim community is thus not attached to deism or to Aristotle's or Plato's philosophy. In the final event, they are based on atheism or self-determination. The foundation of the Islamic community is not nationalism, existential-

comprehensively practicing Islam is not an unbelieving society; rather, it is an ignorant one requiring direction and education but not condemnation (p. 123). Indeed, at the same time he presents Quṭb as a highly venerated martyr, as an "honorable man" (*raǧūl ᶜazīz*) and "beloved friend" (*ḥabīb*) (p. 101); he, however, by all means distances himself from the core of Quṭbs thinking with respect to the heathen Egyptian society. Comp. remarks on this topic by Gräf. *Medien-Fatwas*, p. 112.

279 al-Qaraḍāwī. *ǧarīmat ar-ridda*, p. 34.

280 al-Qaraḍāwī does not mention that in classical theology this verse is hardly taken to be an argument for a free decision for or against Islam – in particular from the side of those who are not *people of the book*: "Q 2:256 . . . which in modern times is often adducted as proof of Muslim tolerance of other religions, is considered by most exegetes to have been abrogated by the so-called sword-vers (Q 9:5. . .) and other passages that call for an all-out war against the unbelievers." Adang. "Belief", p. 224.

281 al-Qaraḍāwī. *ǧarīmat ar-ridda*, pp. 37-38.

ism, nor patriotism. For that reason, it also does not look outside of the Quran for orientation, standards, or legislation. Likewise,

> "the Muslim community [is] not one in which God, the Highly Exalted One, his revelation, and his messengers are denigrated, where people remain silent in the face of this overt unbelief and are incapable of punishing a renegade unbeliever or stemming a shameless heretic,"[282]

such that this sort of individual can continue to disperse his wickedness unhindered. Muslim community distances itself from destruction and places borders before those who would like to inflict damage upon it. It is not defenseless, but rather employs means in order to preserve itself.

At this this point, al-Qaraḍāwī declares it to be a duty on the part of the Muslim community "to stop a shameless heretic" (*yazǧarū zindīqan fāǧiran*) and punish a "rebellious unbeliever" (*murtaddan kāfiran*). Such an approach is not merely an optional action for him. al-Qaraḍāwī explains such a course of action against heretics – whom he does not define more specifically – and apostates as coming directly from the character of the Muslim community, which has no other choice than to act in this manner. The true Muslim community has to move against apostates, which indirectly implies the conclusion that where there is unquestioned toleration of heretics and apostates true Islamic community cannot occur. Since the Islamic confession of faith is the foundation of Islamic community, there can be no deviation from it – which would be the case where apostates are tolerated. This would mean the forfeit of the character of Islamic society. Tolerance and permissiveness at this point become signs of self-abandonment.

Forbidding Apostasy as a Way of Averting Danger

In what follows, al-Qaraḍāwī turns his direct attention to the topic of apostasy,[283] which he criticizes right at the start as destruction of the confession – thus implicitly criticizing it as destruction of the lifeblood of the Muslim community. He explains that from his point of view the Muslim community is permanently in a state of threat of "brutal invasions and evil attacks"

282 Ibid., p. 40.

283 Ibid., pp. 44ff.

(*ġazawāt ᶜanīfa wa-hağamāt šarisa*), the goal of which is "to exterminate it to its roots" (*ilā iqtilāᶜihī min ğuḏūrihī*). For al-Qaraḍāwī, the question of how one deals with the problem of apostasy is a question of the struggle for existence, not a minor issue.

al-Qaraḍāwī mentions the Christianization that accompanied colonial rule which, as he states, was put into gear and concluded by the USA with the help of freeing up "US$ 1 billion." He compares this initiative of Christianization with a communist invasion. Both times the goal was the destruction of Islam and the infiltration of youth. In addition, there was the invasion of laicism, which al-Qaraḍāwī, as he has thoroughly done in his work *al-islām wa-'l-ᶜalmānīya wağhan li-wağh*, regards as an essential danger for the Islamic community:

There he explains that laicism is a foundational attack upon religion (*ad-dīn*), one which also is directed against the "welfare of the community" (*maṣlaḥat al-umma*).[284] Laicism particularly opposes the confession (*al-ᶜaqīda*), reverence to God (*al-ᶜibāda*), morality (*al-aḫlāq*), and the Sharia. Also, with that said, it opposes Islam itself.[285] From this it becomes clear that al-Qaraḍāwī, in an argumentum e contrario of his holistic Islamist view, understands a non-religiously based worldview to likewise comprise all areas of life just as the religion of Islam does.

The dangers facing the continued existence of Islamic community thus always penetrate from outside. Muslim believers are the victims of conquests by non-Islamic worldviews. As a result, believers are in danger of being wrested from the Islamic community, whereby its continued existence and its stability are thrown into question. At no point in al-Qaraḍāwī's entire work *ğarīmat ar-ridda* is there any mention with respect to an individual's turning from Islam of his own accord without influence from the outside. There is no mention that perhaps the individual might even join another religious community. This is not to even mention the thought that a Muslim believer could turn to another religion specifically due to having negative experiences within the Islamic community.

The resolute defense against an outside threat to the community's existence is indispensable for its self-preservation "in order to defend its survival" (*li-kai yuḥāfiẓa ᶜalā baqā'ihi*). For that reason, the apostate has to

[284] al-Qaraḍāwī. *al-islām wa-'l-ᶜalmānīya*, pp. 74ff.+82ff.

[285] Ibid., pp. 93-108.

be contained from the very beginning, when it first appears. Otherwise, it will spread "like fire through chaff" (*kamā . . . an-nār fi 'l-hašīm*).[286] Combating the first signs is essential so that a great fire does not ensue from the sparks that takes the entire community with it.

The Punishment of Apostasy

In what follows, al-Qaraḍāwī – after providing a comprehensive introduction – for the first time explicitly and relatively abruptly speaks about the punishment of apostasy: execution. This apparently does not require any actual justification in the eyes of al-Qaraḍāwī, since according to him, with respect to the necessity of punishment for the apostate among scholars of Islam, there is no dissension at all. Indeed he does concede that there is dissension as to the appropriate sentencing, but the majority of scholars favor the killing of the culprit, which by the way is also the opinion of all – not individually listed at this point – eight schools of legal thought.[287] Additionally, according to al-Qaraḍāwī, the killing of the culprit is mentioned in numerous traditions.

In the course of the discussion regarding one tradition attributed to the son-in-law and cousin of Muḥammad, ᶜAlī, which reports that he is supposed to have burned apostates alive, and the criticism conveyed by Ibn ᶜAbbās for this manner of execution, al-Qaraḍāwī emphasizes that in the text only the manner of punishment was rebuked and not the death penalty in itself.[288] From this, the reader can indirectly conclude that al-Qaraḍāwī himself advocates the execution of apostates.

Apostasy as Warfare

al-Qaraḍāwī then refers to Ibn Taymīya – and this can be considered to be the sole factor calling for moderation with respect to al-Qaraḍāwī's attitude toward apostasy in his entire work – in order to explain that these two types of apostasy are to be differentiated: a type of apostasy for which repentance is possible and therefore does not have to be punished, and an-

---

286 al-Qaraḍāwī. *ǧarīmat ar-ridda*, p. 45.

287 Astonishingly enough, al-Qaraḍāwī does not only mention the four recognized Sunni legal schools at this point.

288 al-Qaraḍāwī. *ǧarīmat ar-ridda*, p. 48.

other type of apostasy which is synonymous with "warfare against God and his Messenger" *(muḥārabat allāh wa-rasūlihī)*.[289] This means that there has to be a distinction between one who only has doubts within himself, and another one who has an influence upon others either verbally or in writing and tries to convince them of his newfound notions.

Whoever is not afraid of trying on the surface to win others over to his apostasy brings *fitna* upon the community, damages it on the whole and not only the one or the other individual. By publicizing his apostasy, it is al-Qaraḍāwī's view that such an individual can no longer be considered to be a simple unbeliever; instead, he actively conducts war against Islam and the *umma*, against God and his messenger.[290] That means his non-Islamic confession, his publicly stated doubts, his refusal to publicly practice Islam, and his joining another religious community would immediately and without any additional action be considered war against Islam and destruction of the *umma*.[291]

As a consequence, what remains as personal free space is only the deep internal questioning that an individual entertains regarding the truth of Islam which is never allowed to get through to find public expression as manifested closer examination of Islam or its emphatic refusal – either by criticism or non-practice. al-Qaraḍāwī does not discuss the question of the extent to which the pressure of being forced to remain in the Islamic community and the practice of the Five Pillars in the face of continued doubts represents hypocrisy.

This differentiation between religious practice which in any event has to be externally maintained and if necessary has to be maintained by coercion, on the one hand, and granting a certain freedom for what is possibly a deviating internal conviction, on the other hand, which may not cause the boat of community to capsize through a form of offensive confession is not a newly developed viewpoint which al-Qaraḍāwī puts forth. Rather, it was already propagated centuries ago, for instance in the 10th and 11th centuries, by the Muᶜtazila.[292]

289 Ibid., p. 50.

290 Ibid., p. 53.

291 A similar argumentation is used by Ibn Taymīya, one of al-Qaraḍāwī's role models, for whom "the endurance of the divinely ordained community is endangered by affronts to Mohammed." According to Nagel. *Liebling*. Vol. 1, p. 195.

292 Crone. "Islam".

This has also been defended by prominent personalities in modern times, e.g., the long time Egyptian Minister for Religious Affairs, Maḥmūd Ḥamdī Zaqzūq (b. 1933). He concedes that every individual has the freedom to hold his own convictions: "every individual is free to choose his belief and has the right to his own opinions, even the atheist." Zaqzūq continues to state that no one may hinder him in this situation, although the person has to maintain the strictest silence. He is protected with respect to freedom of opinion "as long as he keeps his thoughts to himself and does not disseminate them among other people in order to bring them into confusion with respect to their moral values."[293]

If, however, he speaks about his (wrong) opinions, "he infringes upon the general state order" and "is subject to punishment," whereby Zaqzūq initially leaves it open as to which punishment he considers to be appropriate. When in what follows he makes it known that deviating conceptions of belief are equated with "high treason," it becomes clear that openness with respect to one's own doubts or a turning from Islam is in his view put on a level with insurrection and resistance against the state order:

> "He can even be charged with high treason, which is punishable by death, and this not because he has discarded his faith. Rather, it is because he has spread confusion in the state by his thoughts and has impinged upon its order."[294]

In conclusion, Zaqzūq cites "Muslim scholars" on this topic. They explain that apostates were not executed on account of their lapsing in the faith. Rather, it was because they were "enemies of Islam" – in this way Zaqzuq appears, as does al-Qaraḍāwī, to view a confession by an apostate as warfare against the Islamic state.

The fact that al-Qaraḍāwī allows this separation between practiced religion and (possibly deviating) convictions as an area of freedom is one more indication that he is a classical scholar who, as far as coping with modernity is concerned – and dealing with doubters and apostates – orients himself towards the guidelines of classical theology instead of acknowledging modernity's circumstances: the reality of free competition

[293] Zakzouk. "Fragen".
[294] Ibid.

among worldviews and religions and (at least in the virtual world) unrestricted encounters with people who try to solicit new adherents.

This attitude was taken by the Egyptian Court of Cassation in the 1996 trial of Naṣr Ḥāmid Abū Zaid in connection with his falling away from Islam. According to the Court of Cassation, Abū Zaid's conviction as an apostate was not said to contradict the religious freedom established by the Egyptian Constitution. This is due to the fact that religious freedom is limited to the internal realm of the individual since it is not justiciable. Religious freedom does not allow an individual to renounce Islam and to identify oneself as an apostate;[295] this is an opinion which has also been defended under similar legal conditions outside of Egypt.[296]

At this point, al-Qaraḍāwī in turn refers to Ibn Taymīya, whom he quotes to the effect that the "oral warfare" or, literally, "warfare with the tongue" (*muḥāraba bi-'l-lisān*) is more damaging than "physical warfare" *(muḥāraba bi-'l-yad)*, and more damaging than the tongue is what a "writing instrument" wreaks (*al-qalam*), since it can disseminate what is bad over a large area.[297]

The Sentencing for Apostasy

When al-Qaraḍāwī continues on and turns his attention to the sentencing for apostasy, he initially draws upon the meaning of the confession (*ᶜaqīda*) for Muslim community, the "foundation of its identity" *(asās huwīyatihī)*, the "point around which life is centered" (*miḥwar ḥayātihi*), and the "breath of life for its existence" (*rūḥ wuǧūdihi*). For that reason, it is unthinkable for al-Qaraḍāwī to demonstrate any indulgence towards someone who rattles these foundations.

al-Qaraḍāwī continues to explain that openly declared apostasy shakes society at its foundations since it destroys the holiest values of community – here al-Qaraḍāwī in particular mentions faith and the willingness to sacrifice,[298] and elsewhere its unity. It is in any case unacceptable to make religion into a toy (*ulᶜūba*), into a religion which one joins today and which

[295] Comp. the opinion of the court in Thielmann. *Abū Zaid*, pp. 220-221.

[296] For example, Baber Johansen mentiones Tunisia: Johansen. "Apostasy", pp. 705+708-709.

[297] al-Qaraḍāwī. *ǧarīmat ar-ridda*, p. 53.

[298] Ibid., p. 56.

one leaves (again) tomorrow" *(yadḫulu fīhi al-yauma wa-yaḫruǧu minhū ġadan)*[299] as was reported of the Jews (at Muḥammad's time) in Sura 3:72.

It appears to not dawn on al-Qaraḍāwī that only the smallest number of people have become adherents of Islam due to freely considering it on their own and as a self-made choice. Rather, almost all of them have been born as children of a Muslim father and since that time have counted as Muslims according to Sharia law. They are thus not the product of self-made deliberations to "join today" and then to fall away from the faith tomorrow. Rather, without making an individual choice, they have become part of a religious community which does not operate on the basis of membership but which, at least in Arab states, operates on the basis of corresponding ancestry and on the basis of personal status law and for children of the community does not have any alternative to adherence to Islam.[300]

As a result, the question of apostasy is only infrequently a matter that actually occurs where a prior convert to Islam later wishes to leave Islam (e.g., after divorce from a Muslim spouse). In the majority of cases, it is a matter of an individual born into an Islamic family who would like to leave this religion at a later time, or it might be someone who only harbors doubts about and objections to certain aspects of Islam but neither declares his irreligion nor conversion.

These constellations are not addressed at any point by al-Qaraḍāwī. In his treatise, al-Qaraḍāwī is not at all interested in the individual and his freedom to decide, as one usually sees in characteristically Western debates about religious freedom. For al-Qaraḍāwī, the sole point of reference is the Muslim community as a politico-religious commonwealth and its interests, which have to be protected.

299 Ibid., pp. 54; 55.

300 The Egyptian Court of Cassation argued in the same characteristic style in 1996 in the case of the charge of apostasy against Naṣr Ḥāmid Abū Zaid, with the conclusion that in accepting Islam its commands on apostasy have to be accepted and that a turning away from Islam, as was taken as given in the Court of Cassation for Abū Zaid, is not admissable; also at this point not a single word was said that the "acceptance" of Islam is in most cases not based on an individual decision but simply the consequence of birth into a religious community: comp. the explanation of the argumentation of the Court of Cassation in detail in Thielmann. *Abū Zaid*, pp. 219ff.

At the same time, it is striking how distanced and practically detached al-Qaraḍāwī is when treating this topic;[301] after all, he is speaking here about a group of people who have not committed any other "offense" than no longer sharing a certain worldview or, more specifically, religion for which they as a general rule have never decided for in the first place. Thoughts, which in light of the capital punishment for this offense can be recognized in the author as sympathy, are sought for in vain in this work.

There is also another work by al-Qaraḍāwī, *Non-Muslims in Islamic Society*,[302] in which al-Qaraḍāwī only deals with conversion in one direction, namely conversion to Islam. Conversion to Islam occurs when God rightly guides an individual and opens his heart to the "truth." According to al-Qaraḍāwī, if this does not happen, these people cannot be forced into Islam. For him, this once again counts as a demonstration of the unsurpassed tolerance Islam exhibits.[303] The reverse case, where someone does not convert to Islam on the basis of his own convictions but rather counts as a Muslim from the time of birth due to the religious affiliation of his father is not treated at any point in this work dealing with the question of the relationship between Jews, Christians, and Muslims.

Comparison: Freedom of Expression from an Islamic Perspective - 2002

For purposes of comparison, an additional text published in English – and thus assuredly directed at a Western audience – will be drawn upon to present al-Qaraḍāwī's views on freedom of opinion. It dates from 2002, is entitled "Freedom of Expression from an Islamic Perspective," and in it al-Qaraḍāwī argues quite similarly to his major work on apostasy.[304]

---

301 Jacob Høigilt analyzes the stylistic means employed by al-Qaraḍāwī which he uses with the goal of producing distance to his readers and hearers in order to exercise greater authority: Høigilt. *Rhetoric*, p. 66+77+143+153.

302 al-Qaraḍāwī. *ġair al-muslimīn*.

303 Ibid., p. 19.

304 This text has originally been dated back to 2002 : Yusuf al-Qaradawi. "Freedom of expression from an Islamic perspective," 1.4.2012. http://www.onislam.net/english/ask-the-scholar/shariah-based-systems/imamate-and-political-systems/174717-freedom-of-expression-from-an-islamic-perspective.html?Political_Systems= (15.4.2014).

Internal contradictions also become clear in this text on freedom of speech, which arise between al-Qaraḍāwī's position as it is shaped by Sharia law and the realities of the 21st century: for instance, the contradiction between the assertion he holds regarding how liberal Islam is in its society shaping and comprehensive form, and the reality of the denial of extensive civil rights and liberties by prevailing Muslim theologians. al-Qaraḍāwī repeatedly emphasizes that "Islam stresses the principle of freedom," indeed that Islam has itself first established these freedoms: "Islam came to establish the freedom of belief, freedom of thought, freedom of speech, and freedom to criticize."[305]

From al-Qaraḍāwī's point of view, these comprehensive civil rights and liberties have not been a development. Rather, they are "a heavenly principle" revealed by God. Of course, there are conditions attached in this regard: "But this freedom is guaranteed on the condition that religion should not be toyed with, and people's honor and dignity should not be transgressed upon."

At this point, al-Qaraḍāwī leaves it open as to what these final limitations and the ambiguous terms of "honor" and "dignity" mean in this connection. However, from the context of al-Qaraḍāwī's position on apostasy, one can gather that when it also comes to the topic of freedom of opinion, it cannot be a matter of truly granting freedom of speech and freedom to express critique to those who think differently. Rather, it is only to concede these standpoints to those who promote and support Islam.

This also becomes clear in the way that al-Qaraḍāwī calls upon "all Muslims" to take their duty seriously to reinvigorate Islam and to implement it in everyday life. He continues by stating that Islam in no way limits freedom of speech: "It is not a characteristic of Islam to muzzle freedom of speech." Indeed, freedom of speech and the freedom to express critique become a duty if this is in the interest of the *umma* and is in order to promote what is good and to ward off what is bad for the *umma*. Are terms being utilized here in a text which is at least directed at a Western audience, terms such as "freedom of speech" and the freedom to express critique in order to campaign for Islam in a context where the term "Islam" is possibly linked with a completely different connotation?

---

[305] Ibid.

It can be indirectly concluded from al-Qaraḍāwī's words that freedom of speech has its quietus at that point where it no longer lies in the "general interest" of the *umma* and which does not promote what is good from the point of view of Sharia law. One cannot speak of true freedom of opinion and freedom of speech under these conditions. Rather, one can only speak of civil rights and liberties within the framework of the Sharia – which would in any event exclude turning away from Islam under the pretext of promoting the "good" of the community.

Apostasy as Giving up the Duty of Loyalty

In his work *ǧarīmat ar-ridda wa-ᶜuqūbat al-murtadd fī ḍau' al-qur'ān wa-'s-sunna*, al-Qaraḍāwī turns his attention to what are in his opinion the destructive effects of apostasy and emphasizes that only an apostate who propagates his apostasy and calls upon others to follow his example has to be punished by death. What initially might appear to be a certain expression of moderation in comparison with those theologians who call for the death penalty in any event in the case of apostasy, on closer inspection there is indeed little room for non-prosecution of doubters, secularists, and converts:

First of all, an apostate or doubter who never is allowed to speak about his thoughts, due to the sole fact that making a topic of his thoughts would be interpreted as propaganda, is condemned to a sort of internal emigration or to formalism and hypocrisy in the exercise of religion, which al-Qaraḍāwī does not address as a topic at any point in his entire work. In one of his remaining works on the position of non-Muslims in Islamic society, *ġair al-muslimīn fī 'l-muǧtamaᶜ al-islāmī*,[306] al-Qaraḍāwī argues quite similarly: Non-Muslims have to respect the feelings of Muslims and are not allowed to "offend" (*sabba*) Islam, which offers them protection and security, by propagating religions and worldviews which run counter to the prevailing religion of the state involved.[307] Also at this point, al-Qaraḍāwī insinuates that the openly led discussion and the unimpeded exchange of convictions, or more specifically the free competition of worldviews and religions represent a political act of treason.

[306] al-Qaraḍāwī. *ġair al-muslimīn*.
[307] Ibid., p. 45.

Secondly, in his treatment of apostasy al-Qaraḍāwī mixes up the role of the persecutor and the persecuted and misplaces the cause of punishment in the realm of responsibility of the victim of execution: His execution, as he explains here, is to be considered as a defensive measure on the part of the community and solely serves its self-preservation. At its core, apostasy is not a religious act but rather a political act, "treason towards the fatherland" (*al-ḫiyāna li-l-waṭan*) and the "most monstrous offense" (*ğarīma kubrā*). Also, whoever is a citizen (of a country) cannot arbitrarily change his country loyalty whenever it pleases him. According to al-Qaraḍāwī's view, this "exchange of loyalty (or: protective relationship), of identity and of affiliation" *(taġayyur li-l-walā' wa-tabdīl li-l-huwīya wa-taḥwīl li-l-intimā')* is a matter of apostasy from Islam.[308]

By no means is it a matter of an attitude which only involves the intellect (*mauqif ᶜaqlī*), as al-Qaraḍāwī emphasizes it. Instead, the apostate shifts his entire loyalty and affiliation to a new home and a new community by breaking with the "house of Islam": It is in a religio-political regard that al-Qaraḍāwī uses the significant term of the *umma* instead of reverting to the neutral – and in remaining works the term mostly used – *muğtama*. The apostate thus runs into the camp of the enemy with his entire being.[309]

The guilt of the apostate does not only lie in his actions, as al-Qaraḍāwī here again emphasizes. Rather, it primarily lies in his downright provocation of a reaction from the community, by speaking, writing, or taking actions which trigger the undermining of the *umma* so that the *umma* has to act if it does not want to perish.

In the process, the unbelief of the apostate has to be unobjectionably demonstrated and may not be subject to any doubt.[310] If, however, it is substantiated, then it is impossible to remain indifferent towards such

[308] al-Qaraḍāwī. *ğarīmat ar-ridda*, p. 56. It stands to reason that this comprehensive understanding of the *umma*, which is not only a religious but also a political and social community, means that al-Qaraḍāwī's spiritual home can be supposed to be the Muslim Brotherhood. Krämer points out that Ḥasan al-Bannā also judges apostasy from Islam similarly: "... to abandon one's religion was to forsake one's identity, betraying both nation and community." Krämer. *Hasan al-Banna*, p. 106.

[309] al-Qaraḍāwī. *ğarīmat ar-ridda*, p. 56.

[310] In a number of his works, al-Qaraḍāwī has expressed warnings against hastily judging a believer as non-believer and thereby practicing illegitimate *takfīr*. As early as at the end of the 1970s he dedicated his own treatment to this problematic set of issues: al-Qaraḍāwī. *ẓāhirat al-ġulūw*.

apostasy. Whoever remains inactive in such a situation brings the entire community into the danger of of being exposed to *fitna* (turmoil, civil war, attack). In turn, al-Qaraḍāwī uses the term *fitna*, an emotionally and strongly connoted expression from Islamic theology and history, which points to the danger of decomposition and breakdown of the community.

al-Qaraḍāwī goes on to say that if the apostate is left unchecked, others will likewise be misled to apostasy and indeed "in particular those people who are weak and naïve" *(ḫuṣūṣan min aḍ-ḍuᶜafā' wa-'l-busaṭā' min an-nās)*. The umma, which is weakened in this way, will be inevitably torn and succumb to a confrontation which will spread to a "bloody struggle" *(irāᶜ damawī)*, indeed even to the point of "civil war" *(ḥarb ahlīya)* and which will relentlessly destroy everything" *(ta'kulu al-aḫḍar wa-'l-yābis)*.[311] At this point al-Qaraḍāwī again reverts to very emotional notions in order to depict the dramatic nature of the situation and to point to the alternatives of battling for self-preservation and destruction.

It is apparent that as a problem having to do with the individual, al-Qaraḍāw at best considers the topic of falling away from the faith as something at the margins. Instead, it is the community and its interests which occupy the central position. Doubts or a rejection of Islam which could arise without influence from outside does not even come into al-Qaraḍāw's range of vision. He always turns towards the dangers from the outside which could be exercised by different worldviews on Islam and its adherents. For that reason, al-Qaraḍāwī treats apostasy as an offense which places the Islamic community into question, splits it, shakes it to its foundations, and in the end will destroy it. The result is that he considers drastic measures to stem the danger facing the community as a whole to be a necessary reaction to such corrosive efforts.[312]

Apostasy is virtually the opposite of that which al-Qaraḍāwī embodies in his own life's work: efforts to preserve the Islamic community by producing unity among all Muslims – also between those who live in the diaspora – and their rootedness in the traditional values and commands of the Sharia. Granting freedom to commit apostasy from Islam would allow gaps to arise in the wall of the firmly established community of all Muslims. It would also convey to them that a reinterpretation of the stipula-

---

311 al-Qaraḍāwī. *ǧarīmat ar-ridda*, p. 57.

312 Such are his arguments in his work: Yūsuf al-Qaraḍāwī. *al-ḥurrīya ad-dinīya wa-'t-taᶜaddudīya fī naẓār al-islām*. maktab al-islāmī: Bairūt, 2007, p. 41ff.

tions of the Quran and *sunna* – according to their interpretation of al-Qaraḍāwī as a reformed Salafist theologian – was a completely operable way.

The Example of Afghanistan

al-Qaraḍāwī now comes around to speak about Afghanistan, which serves in this as in many other of his works as an illustration of his remarks on the dangers of apostasy. As al-Qaraḍāwī presents it, it has namely been the case in Afghanistan that there have been a number of cases of apostasy. Also, as a consequence, there has been severe turmoil, fatalities, and warfare. For him, it is clearly evident what a destructive impact turning away from Islam has.

al-Qaraḍāwī begins by saying that accepting the "confession of Communism" (*al-ᶜaqīdat aš-šuyūᶜīya*), by a number of Afghans who had begun studying in Russia began what finally led to *ǧihād* against those who had turned from Islam and to communism.[313] The civil war lasted ten years, ruined the country and its peoples, and had as a consequence the death of millions. It left behind many disabled people, wounded, orphans, widows, and families who had lost their children. All of that, al-Qaraḍāwī states, would not have happened if one had immediately seized the evil of apostasy at the roots and pulled them out instead of indifferently remaining silent. Only because these apostates were not punished severly at the beginning were these "murderous battles" (*al-ḥurūb aḍ-ḍarūs*) able to run rampant and bring so much misery to the people.[314] Scenarios such as the Soviet invasion of Afghanistan and the war which followed are before al-Qaraḍāwī' eyes when he deals with the topic of apostasy.

---

[313] With the understanding that an approach towards communism is to be equated with apostasy from Islam is something that does not stand alone for al-Qaraḍāwī. The Academic Counselor for Islamic Law at al-Azhar University and member of the paliamentary committee on elaborating Sharia law, Ibrāhīm Aḥmad al-Waqfī, defends in his treatment *tilka ḥudūd Allāh. aš-šuᶜūn ad-dīnīya*: ad-Dauḥa/Qaṭar, 1977, p. 271 without limitation that the individual who "is convinced of the foundations of communism" is an apostate.

[314] al-Qaraḍāwī. *ǧarīmat ar-ridda*, pp. 57-58.

Caution about Premature Judgment

Against the backdrop of these devastating events in Afghanistan, al-Qaraḍāwī states, on the one hand, that one should not unjustly suspect anyone of apostasy and should be very careful with this judgment. On the other hand, if apostasy is demonstrated, then this has to have legal and social consequences, such as, for example, the separation of the apostate from his wife and his children. For that reason, the individual who issues a *fatwā* about the apostasy of a prior believer has to be absolutely competent in order to be able to clearly differentiate between someone who is only temporarily plagued with doubts and someone who has produced unequivocal facts, for example, by disparaging or ridiculing God, his revelation, his messenger, or the Sharia.[315]

If the apostate is finally convicted, it is imperative that the relevant judge, who belongs to the *ahl al-iǧtihād* (thus able to independently reach just findings) pronounces a severe judgment exclusively according to the law of God, which is derived from the Quran and the *sunna*. In no case may he dispense justice if he is an ignorant individual or if he makes arbitrary judgments. Such an individual is, according to al-Qaraḍāwī, in danger of hell fire, since "it won't do" (*lā yaǧūzu . . . hāḏā 'l-amr*) that someone who prematurely judges, has a radical tendency, or who is equipped with too little knowledge could be the individual pronouncing judgment.[316]

It becomes clear here that al-Qaraḍāwī only acknowledges reaching a verdict and dispensing justice if it involves a scholar of Islamic theology as the judge capable of reaching independently just findings, *iǧtihād*. He does not mention the study of jurisprudence at a state law school as the decisive criterion, nor profound knowledge of the laws of the state and its criminal rules. Also, it is not work experience in the judiciary that serves as qualification enabling him to come to just decisions. Rather, it is solely his knowledge of the "law of God" according to the Quran and the *sunna*, out of which he is to derive his judgments. This is his key qualification.

Whoever possesses this knowledge of the law of God, he will, as one could conversely conclude, pronounce a righteous judgment; that such a

---

[315] Sayyid Quṭb's brother, Muḥammad Quṭb, completely similarly judges contempt for the Sharia to be a form of apostasy: Damir-Geilsdorf. *Herrschaft*, pp. 296-297.

[316] al-Qaraḍāwī. *ǧarīmat ar-ridda*, pp. 60-61.

jurist could err is not something which al-Qaraḍāwī ever considers either in this work or in his remaining works.

The Opportunity to Repent

al-Qaraḍāwī now discusses whether an apostate should receive the chance to turn back prior to his execution. He does not explicitly speak in favour of providing a time for reflection. Indirectly, however, it can be taken from his argumentation that he advocates such a stance since he cites that the vast majority of jurists – he quotes Ibn Taymīya by name – approve of such a period of reflection.

Additionally, he again discusses in a tempering manner that doubts can temporarily overcome a believer, which does not mean there is manifest apostasy. The "hearts of creatures" can after all not be truly probed (*naqaba ᶜan qulūb al-ḫalq*),[317] with the result that a person has to come to a judgment according to an outer appearance; if someone thus holds fast to his confession, then he also has to continue to be viewed as a believer.[318] If, however, he clearly commits apostasy, then he has to be condemned to death and executed without leniency.

Objections against the Death Penalty for Apostates

At this point al-Qaraḍāwī grapples with a number of counterarguments against execution of apostates. However, he does not allow any basic counterargument, such as a justification from the Quran and the Sunna in favour of positive or negative religious freedom. He also does not deal at all with the contents of Western human rights declarations. Instead, he enters into a type of inner-Salafist scholarly discourse in which he primarily discusses interpretive variations and critical points with respect to the legal relevance of certain tradition which has been handed down. Thus, he takes up the objection that the Quran does not mention the punishment of the death penalty, that in justifying the death penalty one has to lean on tradi-

---

317 Ibid., p. 62.

318 At this point al-Qaraḍāwī differs, for example, from Sayyid Quṭb, whom ho often criticizes, who under certain circumstances wants to consider the apostate condemned who views himself as a Muslim and who utters the confession of faith: According to Damir-Geilsdorf. *Herrschaft*, p. 83.

tion, and that the corresponding *aḥādīṯ* on the basis of its contestable position as *aḥādīṯ al-āḥād* do not allow the administration of a *ḥadd* punishment.

It is not surprising to the reader at this point in the work that al-Qaraḍāwī rejects this opinion with reference to tradition and Muḥammad's practice as well as the Prophet's companions. As he states it, they ordered and carried out the killing of apostates at the time of the four rightly guided caliphs. Likewise, he does not leave any doubt about the legitimacy of the use of only modestly authorized traditions for Sharia-based argumentation, since otherwise, as he reasons, 90% or even 99% of the traditions would not be usable as legally binding texts.[319] All significant legal scholars additionally agree with respect to the necessity of punishing apostates, with the result that for al-Qaraḍāwī there cannot be any discussion at all about it.

Here he again quotes his most important source in this work, Ibn Taymīya, who, like al-Qaraḍāwī himself has fought for an intellectual reorientation of the *umma* and for that reason has likewise contended primarily for an orientation towards the Quran and the *sunna* instead of propagating the commitment to only one school of legal thought.[320] Ibn Taymīya has also particularly warned of conducting warfare "with the tongue" (*bi-'l-lisān*), which has worse consequences than conducting manual warfare (*bi-'l-yad*). At this point al-Qaraḍāwī cites Sura 5:33, a verse which calls for the killing or more specifically the crucifixion of those individuals who "wage war against God and his messenger." If, according to al-Qaraḍāwī's implied argument, conducting warfare with weapons against God and his messenger is to be punished by death, then how much more reprehensible is "warfare with the tongue," apostasy.[321]

Apostasy of a Ruler

In what is his last longer section, al-Qaraḍāwī eventually turns his attention to the question of what happens if a ruler leaves Islam. al-Qaraḍāwī

319 al-Qaraḍāwī. *ǧarīmat ar-ridda*, pp. 63-64.

320 As summarized by Basheer M. Nafi. "The Rise of Islamic Reformist Thought and its Challenge to Traditional Islam" in: Suha Taji-Farouki; Basheer M. Nafi (eds.). *Islamic Thought in the Twentieth Century*. I. B. Tauris: London, 2004, pp. 28-60, here p. 30.

321 al-Qaraḍāwī. *ǧarīmat ar-ridda*, p. 66.

becomes very passionate at this point. He castigates what is for him a particularly severe criminal act and uses emotional terms without, however, using concrete names of people in particular countries. Is this condemnation, made with verve, of apostate leaders a late riposte relating to al-Qaraḍāwī's incarceration as a member of the Muslim Brotherhood in Egypt in the 1950s? In any case, al-Qaraḍāwī's clearly aloof attitude to those rulers is recognizable in this section, who according to his understanding inadequately apply the law of God.

Apostasy committed by a ruler is, as far as al-Qaraḍāwī considers it, the most dangerous variety of apostasy (*aḫṭar anwāʿ ar-ridda*). Since in such case the ruler, who is actually there to serve and protect the society and should prosecute the apostates, finds that he has himself contracted the disease which he actually should eradicate. Furthermore, he then himself spreads the iniquity. It is he who "opens windows and doors" (*yaftaḥa lahum an-nawāfiḏ wa-'l-abwāb*) for apostates and, instead of combating them, provides them with rewards. He perverts the natural order by offering protection to the enemies of God, while he is inimically inclined towards (true) believers. It is he who holds the confession and the Sharia in low esteem and follows neither their commands nor prohibitions. With that said, he also insults Islam. Indeed, he acts in a way that is to be equated with a "destruction of Islam" (*ibṭāl al-islām*).[322]

On the other hand, holding fast to the duties of belief – that which thus is necessary and self-evident – is held to be a "crime" (*ǧarīma*) and "extremism" (*taṭarruf*) for such a ruler, given that his foundation consists of a wrong orientation. At the same time, he prosecutes those who conduct *daʿwa* for Islam. He stigmatizes the (compulsory) prayer of men in the mosque and the *ḥiǧāb* of women, which for al-Qaraḍāwī are self-evident duties of believers. Nevertheless, such a ruler continues to sail under the flag of Islam while he simultaneously profits from its destruction. In this way, he hollows Islam from the inside out.[323]

Is al-Qaraḍāwī alluding to the Egyptian regime? It was the Egyptian regime that severely persecuted the Muslim Brotherhood during the administration of Ǧamāl ʿAbd an-Nāṣir. The Muslim Brotherhood was conducting intensive *daʿwa* and preaching work at that time, and the regime threw many of its adherents into jail and had them tortured and executed.

322 Ibid., p. 68.
323 Ibid., p. 68.

This assumption seems to be rather strongly suggested. The duty of wearing a veil has always been one of the first demands of Islamist mentors and movements, and the large mosque gatherings in Egypt at the time of Ǧamāl ᶜAbd an-Nāṣir were a sign of protest and a demonstration of the strength of their movements. By intensively regulating the courses at al-Azhar, the government attempted to defuse permanent areas of tension between al-Azhar and the Egyptian government from the time of the Coup of the Free Officiers in 1952. At the same time, the government exercised more and more control over activities, preachers, and contents of the preaching of the other Egyptian mosques, which brought considerable criticism upon the state leadership and al-Azhar. In particular, the government used al-Azhar for the legitimization of Egyptian governmental power during the rule of President an-Nāṣir.[324] The thought is also suggested that al-Qaraḍāwī is alluding to this area of tension between the government and the Muslim brotherhood, whose plaything he himself became in the 1950s.

In the following years, the Egyptian government more and more sought to exercise stronger control over the financial resources of al-Azhar. In the final event, it established a law whereby it determines the sheik of al-Azhar. In 1961, Naṣr finally comprehensively reorganized this most important Sunnite educational institution and assigned it to the Ministry of Religious Endowments, thus significantly reducing its independent scope. This development, which al-Qaraḍāwī himself experienced until his emigration to Qatar in 1961, comprises one part of the background of his critical observations about state powers that are in a number of his works. That is perhaps here also the case.[325]

At this point, al-Qaraḍāwī does not express himself regarding the question of how just rule should otherwise look. Should it be a caliphate according to his view? How could it be set up? Which role should legal scholars and theologians play?

Indeed, as al-Qaraḍāwī comes to an end in this chapter, Islam was not able to be destroyed in spite of these attempts to drive back and stigmatize true believing Muslims as well as in spite of the efforts of Western colonial

[324] For the detailed description of this state's coopting of al-Azhar see Moustafa. "Conflict", pp. 4-9.

[325] Also comp., for example, his absolutely clear criticism of the Egyptian regime of the 1950s in his work: *aṣ-ṣaḥwa al-islāmīya*, p. 25ff.

powers. However, the "war" from within against Islam was a more difficult opponent than the colonialists ever could have been.

Intellectual Apostasy

At the end of his writing, al-Qaraḍāwī treats the topic of intellectual wrestling for the hearts and heads of people, the question of what it is that influences people and who is allowed to shape their convictions: This is an issue of "intellectual apostasy" (*ar-ridda al-fikrīya*) which hides itself well and disguises itself so well that can only be discovered with difficulty. One can justifiably maintain that it is al-Qaraḍāwī's life work to fight this form of apostasy in the many bodies in which he works. His efforts are for the affirmation of the complete validity of the Sharia and of its unreserved observance, be it in the financial sector, be it in the area of *daᶜwa*, or be it with respect to minority rights, the precise goal of which it is to preserve the Islamic minority from a deviation from Islam and the *umma* from a hollowing out of its internal world view.

This life work is placed into question if the principal validity of classically interpreted Islamic law becomes the object of discussion and is undermined through contrasting messages in public. For that reason, al-Qaraḍāwī writes in this section, he has to occupy himself with and wrestle with this form of apostasy daily *(kulla yaumin)*. When it comes to this form of apostasy, it is essentially a matter of the question of orientation towards the law of God or ruin.

al Qaraḍāwī discusses this type of apostasy as a form which, on the basis of its inconspicuous progression, is not recognized as such for a long time. Quietly and clandestinely "is slinks into minds" (*yatasallala . . . ila 'l-ᶜuqūl*) and only becomes apparent at a later time in its entirety. Its method of destruction is not "with handweapons" (*bi-'r-raṣāṣ yadawī*) but rather with slow-acting poison (*bi-'s-samm al-baṭī'*) wrapped in "honey and sweets" (*al-ᶜasal wa-'l-ḥalwā*). Whoever administers this poison to others is a "professional criminal" (*muǧramīn muḥtarifīn*).[326]

This secretly advancing apostasy, which is disseminated in newspapers, magazines, books, and television programs, is for al-Qaraḍāwī the actual enemy. It is more dangerous than the apostasy which is as visible as the light of day, since it does not stridently draw attention to itself. However, it

326 al-Qaraḍāwī. *ǧarīmat ar-ridda,* p. 71.

continuously unfolds its effect and has a broad radius of activity. This form of "hypocrisy" (*nifāq*) is more threatening than "overt disbelief" (*al-kufr aṣ-ṣarīḥ*).

al-Qaraḍāwī labels it as his duty to combat this clandestine apostasy, which takes the thinking of people captive, with its own weapons, i.e., through a worldview struggle. This serves to uncover that which is hidden and capture its apparently impressive outposts to the point that they are dismantled by the actions of the "people of truth" (*ahl al-ḥaqq*).[327] He undoubtedly counts himself among these people. This is especially the case since, as he emphasizes in his closing words, he is certain of God's help in this task. Thus, despite the immediately preceding and drastic warnings of the effects of the "poison" of false worldviews, the book ends with optimistic words stating that the truth will triumph over falsehood.

Evaluation: Yūsuf al-Qaraḍāwī's Argumentation

al-Qaraḍāwī follows in this work, as he does in his remaining works, no scientific and critical procedure. He does more preaching than scientific deduction. His approach is more to states authoritatively without discussing contrasting opinions at eye level.[328] Whatever does not fit into his context is blocked out; whatever in the history of Islam serves the purpose of his argument is drawn upon. If he quotes opponents or the writings of "unbelievers", then this is done selectively with a single quote taken out of context to undergird his argument.

However, he also does not constructively deal with Muslim scholars and authors who principally share his position. He only uses them at those points where they emphasize his opinion. Otherwise, he persists in the position of the classical scholar, who at best weighs interpretive variations against each other, for instance the variations of texts belonging to tradition. Yet he never places their justification into question and does not allow any other context for their interpretation.

Nowhere can one find an open review where an argument's pros and cons are presented and where there is an expressed justification for basic alternative opinions or a self-critical disclosure of his own position. In-

[327] Ibid., p. 73.

[328] Also according to Høigilt on the basis of an analysis of al-Qaraḍāwī's language: Høigilt. *Rhetoric*, p. 62.

stead, al-Qaraḍāwī emerges as his own authority, enabling himself to decide between right and wrong with clearly set parameters not disclosed to the reader but only comprehensible to al-Qaraḍāwī himself. He instructs his readers from his own highly perched citadel[329] unreachable to others, and he does not offer them an insight as to how he arrives at his conclusions. Furthermore, he does not even hint at the possibility of his own fallibility.

Through the frequent use of the Quran and *sunna* quotes, he implies that all of his statements are the direct result of his occupation with both of these sources, yet in the process he remains silent about the fact that with respect to these same sources there are essentially divergent interpretations and conclusions from the pens of other theologians. He puts forth his view of things as simply "the" view of Islam and at the same time takes upon himself the claim to want to speak for all Muslims who take the faith and its practice as seriously as he does.

His writing on apostasy makes it unmistakably clear that the apostate who endangers the community has to be executed and that undoubtedly this proceeds from the Quran and tradition.[330] al-Qaraḍāwī does not make any specific statements as to the procedure by which apostasy is determined and can be demonstrated, with the exception of some general pointers. For instance, he points out that laicism and communism are essentially forms of apostasy and that their adherents are for that reason considered apostates.

A certain sense of moderation can only be recognized in the few sentences in which al-Qaraḍāwī makes room for the possibility that an apostate does not have to be executed under particular circumstances. Rather, there is, in certain instances, a "mild form of apostasy (*ar-ridda al-muḫaffifa*) which makes correction and admonition necessary instead of direct punishment.[331]

---

329 Høigilt formulates it as follows: "al-Qaraḍāwī writes himself into the role of the moral and intellectual hero." *Rhetoric*, p. 65.

330 Since al-Qaraḍāwī treats the question of apostasy solely under the aspect of averting a danger, it is not surprising that he has not put forth any writing which could have taken up the topic in a positive manner, e.g., under the heading of human rights or structuring peaceful coexistence in a multi-religious society.

331 al-Qaraḍāwī. *ǧarīmat ar-ridda*, p. 6.

Should the individual suspected of apostasy be subjected to an official inquiry? Should he be demanded to say the confession of faith? Who is entitled to judge whether it is only a matter of doubts or whether it is indeed true apostasy which is involved and which injures the community? Is the ruler of a country authorized? In the face of the warnings al-Qaraḍāwī's makes with respect to a regime which no longer applies the law of God and battles against true Islam and its representatives, this hardly appears to be his preference. Legal scholars and theologians? Even this is not explicitly expressed by al-Qaraḍāwī'.

In spite of his demands for the death penalty, al-Qaraḍāwī's treatment on apostasy thus remains very imprecise with respect to its practical application. It appears to be more of a sermon, a forceful warning against apostasy. More specifically still, it appears to be drafted as the explanation of a position derived from the Quran and tradition more than it is a scholarly treatment or concrete guideline for action.

With respect to possible courses of action, the reader is largely left to his own conclusions. In light of the clearly formulated necessity for the execution of an apostate, and the fact that in the far number of Muslim majority countries it is futile to expect to bring the individual before a court, should things be taken into one's own hands? Should the individual be brought before a non-governmental Sharia court? Or should a person use his own hands against such individual? Is he not simply fulfilling the law of God if he implements the Sharia without ambiguity? Indeed, is he not obligated to unconditional obedience towards the law of God, desiring not to be counted among the hypocrites and unbelievers who deviate from it?

Nowhere does al-Qaraḍāwī call for vigilante justice. On the contrary, he repeatedly litters his writing with warnings against that. Likewise, he warns against unjustified suspicion and premature judgment against the ignorant. Addmittedly, he only limits the circle of people who can speak judgment regarding an apostate but does not scrutinize his sentencing and execution per se. And are these arid words of warning fitting against vigilante justice – when compared with the justified and emotional appeals from the Quran and tradition to save the *umma* from such "offenses" as apostasy – and able to protect an apostate from the mob on the street?

Has not al-Qaraḍawī himself argued that the pen, which to a large extent carries the message of its author, can cause more damage than hand weapons ever could?[332] Is it justified to absolve scholars such as al-Qaraḍāwī from responsibility for planting bodies of thought of intolerance and condemnation in the minds of people which have effects on politics and society? Are role models with a reach such as al-Qaraḍāwī uninvolved if an intellectual climate of intolerance and persecution toward those who think differently is produced and a critical intellectual, atheist, or convert is persecuted or even killed for apostasy by members of his or her family or society?[333]

2.3.4. The Danger of Apostasy . . . and the Battle against Dissension ("Le danger de l'apostasie . . . et la lutte contre la zizanie") – 2002

In 2002 al-Qaraḍāwī published a text about the dangers of apostasy which, given the conflict potential underlying this topic, threaten the community.[334] In his work "Le danger de l'apostasie . . . et la lutte contra la zizanie," al-Qaraḍāwī principally concentrates on the effects which apostasy has on the Islamic community. At the same time, the apostate as an individual stands less in the foreground. Apostasy is capable, through its dif-

332 Ibid., p. 53.

333 The former deacon for Islamic law at Qatar University also makes this same connection. Upon the occasion of the condemnation of two authors of a newspaper article in the Saudi newspaper *al-Riyadh* as apostates by the Saudi scholar Abdul Rahman Al-Barrak, he warned against the consequences of statements by using these words with respect to the premature condemnation of other Muslims as unbelievers: "And if an ignorant person believed what that researcher wrote and assassinated one of the scholars who was labeled an(d) (sic) infidel, because the researcher made the shedding of his blood licit, there is no legal blame on the researcher who instigated the crime and misled the killer." "Former Qatar University Dean of Islamic Law Dr. Abd Al-Hamid Al-Ansari in AAFAQ Article Responds to Fatwa Calling for Two Saudi Writers' Killing." MEMRI Special Dispatch No 1888, 7.4.2008. http://www.memri.org/report/en/0/0/0/0/0/0/2699.htm (15.4.2015).

334 Yūsuf al-Qaraḍāwī. "Le danger de l'apostasie . . . et la lutte contra la zizanie," 30.12.2002. http://www.islamophile.org/spip/Le-danger-de-l-apostasie-et-la.html (15.4.2015). This text represents what was originally an Arabic language communiqué by al-Qaraḍāwī; it is, however, no longer able to be retrieved such that the French translation is the only accessible source.

ferent evaluation to the mere fact of its existence, to stir up "strife" within the Islamic community; for that reason, it is of significant importance to al-Qaraḍāwī to lead the *umma* to a harmonious position on this question so that the *umma* remains screened off from instability.

al-Qaraḍāwī also expressly positions himself in this text as *ᶜālim*, someone who disposes over the necessary knowledge in order to authoritatively answer this question, something which with respect to apostasy is undoubtedly lacking among many people. He places himself above those who, on the basis of their lack of knowledge, are misled and prematurely form an opinion regarding apostates. However, he also places himself above those in power who come to the defense of apostates or, as the case may be, bring guilt of apostasy upon themselves. He himself belongs to those "savants très versés dans la science religieuse et les spécialistes de cette question qui savent distinguer . . ."

The threat, caused by Christian mission, colonization, the communist invasion, laicism, and atheism, which proceed from apostasy, place the spiritual identity of the Islamic community in question ("son idendité spiritual"). For that reason, it is a basic danger. al-Qaraḍāwī views it as a type of test, and putting up resistance is a valid response.

On the one hand, al-Qaraḍāwī clearly warns against judging an individual prematurely who is only suspected of apostasy but who has not fallen away from Islam at all. Likewise, one should treat an individual similarly to the one who has not publicly admitted his apostasy. Indeed, according to al-Qaraḍāwī, no one is called to conduct research into an individual's conscience or to want to look into a person's heart. Likewise, one would as little seek to lay one's hand on an apostate. On the other hand, al-Qaraḍāwī decidedly warns against neglecting the problematic topic of apostasy as well as covering up apostasy and wanting to protect it, for secretly active apostasy belongs to the most dangerous that there could ever be for the Islamic community. Whoever has clearly departed from Islam may by no means continue to be treated as a Muslim believer, for he destroys Islam from the inside.

With that said, al-Qaraḍāwī again positions himself as the representative of a central position. However, it is a central position which unambiguously advocates the application of the death penalty in the case of proven apostasy without any alternative. This is due to the fact that even in this text al-Qaraḍāwī leaves no doubt that the sole appropriate answer to proven apostasy, which is demonstrated when the apostate speaks about his apostasy and shows no remorse, is the death penalty. It is "the greatest crime in the eyes of Islam" ("le plus grand crime aux yeux de l'Islam"), and the apostate does nothing less than make himself guilty of a political offense. In making a change of religion, he runs over to the enemies of the community, "He in fact conducts a war against Islam and against the community" ("Il mène de fait une guerre contre l'Islam et contre la Communauté"). Such matters have to be stemmed with all resoluteness, whereby al-Qaraḍāwī also does not explain in this text in which manner the apostate should receive his just punishment.

2.3.5. Source of the Punishment for Apostasy – 2003

A further position statement on the problematic issue of apostasy is represented by al-Qaraḍāwī's rather short *fatwā* entitled "Source of the Punishment for Apostasy," which dates from 2003.[335] An unnamed individual turned to "IslamOnline" asking for information as to why an apostate has to be executed, where, after all, the text (supposedly what is meant here is the text of the Quran) does not require that the death penalty be administered upon the apostate: "I cannot find any verse stating such a punishment for an apostate." Why does the "Sheikh" then speak about this punishment? Is it mentioned in the tradition of the Prophet? The question is directed at a "group of muftis."

As a response, the "prominent Moroccan scholar Sheikh Abdul Bari Az-Zamzamy is quoted. He emphasizes the particular tolerance found within Islam with the words: "Islam . . . gives the freedom of thinking to people, with full respect to their mentalities and way of thinking."[336] However, Islam is not a man-made religion. Rather, it is the religion of God, and it is unthinkable with respect to it that it could be exposed to prejudiced critique: "subject to scrutiny or biased criticism" (here one could logically supplement this with: by apostates), as az-Zamzany continues. In addition, apostasy causes total disruption and confusion in the Muslim community." With that said, according to az-Zamzany, such severe pun-

335 Group of Muftis. "Source".

336 Ibid.

ishment for apostasy was determined in order to prevent anyone from even considering such a step.

az-Zamazany causally traces the severe punishment for apostasy back to a "Jewish conspiracy against Islam," because after what was allegedly a massive wave of conversions of Jews in the early days of Islam these same individuals fell away in great numbers. The goal was to produce confusion and the desire to throw people off the right path. The reader is not exposed to the concrete historical events surrounding the incident. What remains is the impression of behaviour by a group of Jews which is underhanded and damaging to the community of Muslims.

What carries on from here is a short position statement by "Sheikh 'Attiyah Saqr," the prior head of the *fatwā* committee at al-Azhar. He points out that argumentation is deceptive which maintains that the punishment for apostasy is not mentioned in the Quran, for it is recorded in the not highly reputable as well as in the irreproachable chain of transmission of tradition.

Finally, in comparison to the far less well known names, there is a last answer from the most weighty authority, al-Qaraḍāwī. For starters, he emphasizes that "all Muslim jurists agree" that apostates are to punished. They only differ with respect to their notions as to the degree of penalty. However, there is a majority among them who speak out for killing the apostate, thus for administering the death penalty.

al-Qaraḍāwī continues on the topic with quotes on the most well known *aḥādīṯ*. He refers to the Prophet's *ḥadīṯ* "Whoever changes his religion, kill him" and cites various sources, such as Ibn ᶜAbbās und aṭ-Ṭabarānī. He also quotes a known tradition traceable back to Muḥammad:

> "The blood of a Muslim individual who bears witness that there is no god but Allah and that I am the messenger of Allah, is not to be shed except in three cases: in retaliation (in murder crimes), married adulterers (and adulteresses), and the one who abandons his religion and forsakes the Muslim community."

Finally, al-Qaraḍāwī refers to ᶜAlī ibn Abī Ṭālib, who after a period of three days to reconsider had a number of his own adherents who were unwilling to change their ways burnt at the stake for worshiping him (instead of God).

This is not really a matter of an actual opinion statement on the part of al-Qaraḍāwī with respect to the topic of apostasy. Rather, it solely has to do with a number of incidental observations. However, it also becomes evident which statements are obviously substantial for al-Qaraḍāwī on this question: There are no mitigating deliberations pondered or to be made. Rather, without exception, there is a call for the death penalty for the apostate, whose condemnation is apodictically pronounced.[337]

2.3.6. The Freedom of Belief and Thought ("al-ḥurrīya ad-dīnīya wa-'l-fikrīya") – 2005

In February of 2005, in a series of broadcasts entitled *aš-šarīᶜa wa-'l-ḥayāt*, there was a program which was broadcast touching upon the area of apostasy.[338] In this program, in which al-Qaraḍāwī was one of the two regularly invited guests, he initially discusses the topic of freedom, with which an individual is endowed by virtue of being created by God. This is just as much the case as with the individual's own will and mind. From that, freedom is something which cannot be wrested from anyone. In religion, al-Qaraḍāwī emphasizes, there is no coercion. For that reason, the individual is free in his choice. However, every belief and every community has to care for its own preservation so that it does not perish and experience damage due to *fitna*.

At this point, al-Qaraḍāwī again refers to Afghanistan and the example of the war against the Soviet Union in 1979 in order to illustrate the devastating consequences of apostasy. According to al-Qaraḍāwī's point of view, everything began with apostasy. He emphasizes anew that a separation from religion also means a separation from one's own community. In other words, this is treason against one's homeland.

---

337 In his video message dealing with the necessity to defend Islam by executing the apostate, published 05.2.2013, al- Qaraḍāwī turns out to be quite apodictic: http://www.youtube.com/watch?v=huMu8ihDlVA (15.4.2013).

338 al-Qaraḍāwī. "al-ḥurrīya ad-dīnīya wa-'l-fikrīya" Transcript of the program *aš-šarīᶜa wa-'l-ḥayāt* dated February 6, 2005. http://www.qaradawi.net/site/topics/article.asp?cu_no=3841~version=1~template_id=105~transparent_id=16 (6.2.2011). Since the text accessible to me is a transcript of the verbal statements made during the program, there are a number of uncompleted sentences as well as the use of formulations utilizing dialect which rob the statements of their unambiguousness; additionally, al-Qaraḍāwī left a few statements unclear, for example, without taking a clear position in every case in response to the questions from the moderator and the viewers.

Upon being asked by the moderator, al-Qaraḍāwī again emphasizes that the punishment for apostasy from Islam is not a punishment for internally turning away. Rather, it is for the *fitna*, which occurs through the change of loyalty. This also includes the inescapable social consequences such as separation from wife and children as well as the loss of community. All the while, the administration of the death penalty is not necessary in every case. Rather, it is "only" necessary if the apostate splits the community.

Furthermore, al-Qaraḍāwī lectures that most of the scholars vote for the execution of an apostate. Some, however, contest that it can be seen as derived from the Quran and have expressed doubt regarding the authority of the traditions in question. al-Qaraḍāwī rejects this with a list of numerous texts from the *aḥādīṯ*. Finally, he turns to the question of the possibility of changing one's ways and repenting in the case of apostasy, which al-Qaraḍāwī answers by pointing to the lack of agreement among scholars. In the final event, he assigns the decisive roles to "capable *ᶜulamā'* and Sharia judges who have to enforce the judgments made about apostasy.

In light of the fact that in his remaining writings al-Qaraḍāwī hardly ever clearly names the consequences of his call for the death penalty for apostates, the final statements are unusually concrete. However, the steps to its implementation are not mentioned at this point.

2.3.7. Major and Minor Apostasy – 2006

Besides al-Qaraḍāwī's stand-alone work on the topic of apostasy, *ǧarīmat ar-ridda wa-ᶜuqūbat al-murtadd fī ḍau' al-qur'ān wa-'s-sunna*, there is a second, longer text he wrote on this topic: a *fatwā* apparently only published in English and dating from 2006. It is entitled "Apostasy. Major and Minor."[339] It has a length of about eleven pages of text.

[339] Yusuf al-Qaradawi. "Apostasy, Major and Minor." 13.4.2006. http://www.onislam.net/english/shariah/contemporary-issues/islamic-themes/413125.html (15.4.2014).

Fatwā for a Western Audience?

Publishing a text in English is all the more noteworthy, given that al-Qaraḍāwī himself has not published any of his works in English. English language works have above all been later translations from Arabic which have been released through publishing houses in Great Britain and the USA and through institutes such as, for example, the International Institute of Islamic Thought in the USA. If one sees a longer and more comprehensive text on the topic of apostasy, it seems reasonable to conclude that this text is first and foremost directed at an audience consisting of Western readership.

The *fatwā* carries the date of April 13, 2006. At this time the case of Abdur Rahman, an Afghan convert who had been condemned to death on account of apostasy, was just two weeks old. Consequently, it appears to be conceivable that this text represents al-Qaraḍāwī's direct opinion statement on this case of apostasy. This case created quite a stir in the international press.[340]

The Pashto convert Abdur Rahman, who had converted to Christianity in Pakistan in 1990, had unsuccessfully sought asylum in Europe. In 2001, after the end of Taliban rule, he returned to Afghanistan. His wife divorced him in Afghanistan on account of his conversion. While the subsequent custody battle surrounding both of the daughters was ongoing, in-laws reported him to the police on account of his conversion. In March 2006, he was arrested in Kabul and sentenced to death on account of apostasy.[341] Although the Afghan constitution guarantees religious freedom, it at the same time also stipulates that all laws have to be in line with the Sharia.

After the case became known, an intensive discussion regarding this case and the question of the justification of the death penalty for apostates emerged in the international media. Representatives involved in international diplomacy and politics were also involved. Following international pressure, the charges against Abdur Rahman were referred back to the prosecuting authorities on March 26, 2003, whereby refuge was taken in a

---

[340] In his work: al-Qaraḍāwī. *ǧarīmat ar-ridda*, p. 60, al-Qaraḍāwī had in all brevity already taken a stand on the Salman Rushdie case.

[341] Comp. for instance the report: Matthias Gebauer. "Im Knast der armen Teufel." Spiegel Online, 27.3.2006. http://www.spiegel.de/politik/ausland/0,1518,408290,00.html (15.4.2015).

"legal loophole" that declared Abdur Rahman to be of unsound mind. With that, the death penalty was able to be suspended according to Sharia law. Abdur Rahman himself rejected this as an explanation for his conversion, while hundreds of demonstrators under the leadership of Muslim scholars called for Abdur Rahman's execution. At the end of March 2006, it was announced by the court that an investigation into the case had demonstrated that procedural errors had occurred. The defendant was released from prison on March 28, 2006, arrived in his country of asylum, Italy, on March 29, and has been living there since then at an undisclosed location.[342]

When al-Qaraḍāwī published his *fatwā*, this case lay only a few weeks in the past and was surely fresh in the minds of the public. Is it a coincidence that shortly thereafter al-Qaraḍāwī released such a comprehensive opinion piece on this topic composed in English? Is it a coincidence that the destructive role of missionaries was singled out in particular with respect to the threat to Islam and that Abdur Rahman had, as it were, fallen victim to their efforts in Pakistan through his conversion? Was it unintentional that the text went into detail regarding the role of communism, which through the Soviet invasion in 1980 brought war and destruction to Afghanistan or that secularism and its destructive force were addressed? In al-Qaraḍāwī's eyes, these are two worldviews which are to be completely rejected but under which sphere of influence Abdur Rahman has lived for the past 16 years in Western countries.

Indeed, at no point does the text make reference by name to Abdur Rahman's case. If, however, the text is in a certain sense a response to this incident, then it supposedly serves to confirm anew what in al-Qaraḍāwī's eyes is an appropriate Sharia law standpoint on the question of apostasy. It is then also an elucidation and justification before a Western public which has demonstrated its lack of understanding, indeed in part expressing dismay in numerous opinion pieces regarding Abdur Rahman's case.

The text takes up a number of thoughts, which in al-Qaraḍāwī's work *ǧarīmat ar-ridda wa-ᶜuqūbat al-murtadd fī ḍau' al-qur'ān wa-'s-sunna*

---

[342] The Italian journalist Gabriele Torsello was kidnapped on October 12, 2006 in order to exchange him for Abdur Rahman; however, he was later released: According to Paul Marshall; Nina Shea. *Silenced. How Apostasy & Blasphemy Codes are Choking Freedom Worldwide*. Oxford University Press: Oxford, 2011, p. 107.

had already been touched upon, indeed in part involving almost verbatim repetition. However, the text of this *fatwā* is considerably more political in its composition and provides only a few theological justifications as well as quotes from the Quran and tradition in vastly fewer numbers than in al-Qaraḍāwīs work *ǧarīmat ar-ridda*.

On the one hand, in this text al-Qaraḍāwī also does not allow a free change of religion and does not deviate from the lawfulness of the execution of apostates as the Sharia punishment. On the other hand, from the fact that in the title "minor" apostasy, which is only briefly touched upon in al-Qaraḍāwī's Werk *ǧarīmat ar-ridda*, one can recognize an attempt to come before the Western public with a "moderate" text after the uproar of Abdur Rahman's case.

al-Qaraḍāwī's *fatwā* on "major" and "minor" apostasy is broken down into seven segments.[343] Initially it involves an explanation of what apostasy actually is, and after that a list of examples from the history of Islam as to which punishments have been carried out on apostates. Thereafter, one finds a definition of "minor" and "major" apostasy as well as a comprehensive presentation of the reasons why apostasy is so harshly punished within the Islamic community. After that, what follows is a list of the criteria by means of which an apostate is clearly identified. The final three segments treat frequent objections against the lawfulness of the death penalty for apostates, the special case of the apostasy of a ruler, and "hidden apostasy".

---

343 al-Qaraḍāwī also differentiated between slight and major apostasy in an interview with the newspaper al-Ahram al-Arabi, which appeared on July 3, 2007. If personal apostasy is no longer only limited to the individual, according to al-Qaraḍāwī, and it is rather the case that the apostate calls upon others to take the same step and the entire community is thereby affected, then the social cohesion and the foundations of community are affected. These apostates have to be comabated just as Abū Bakr battled apostates. This apostasy "is the gravest danger to society." Unfortunately only a few excerpts from the interview were at my disposal: A. Dankowitz. "Accusing Muslim Intellectuals of Apostasy." MEMRI: The Middle East Media Research Institute, 18.2.2005. http://www.memri.org/report/en/0/0/0/0/0/114/1321.htm (15.4.2015).

The Role of the Muslim Community

Right from the beginning of the text, al-Qaraḍāwī points out the foundational meaning and drama of the topic by characterizing apostasy as a threat to the Islamic faith:

> "The greatest kind of danger that faces Muslims is that which threatens their moral aspect of existence, i.e., their belief . . . apostasy from Islam is regarded as one of the most dangerous threats to the Muslim community."[344]

Apostasy appears here as a deliberate attack, as "the ugliest intrigue the enemies of Islam have plotted against Islam" in order to entice Muslims away from their faith.

al-Qaraḍāwī depicts the Muslim community as a victim of having been undermined by horrible sieges and aggressive attacks from without. Among these, one finds, for instance, the invasion of Christian missionaries under the protective hand of Western colonial lords. An additional invasion has consisted of the powers of communism, "that . . . made every effort to put an end to Islam" as well as "the . . . most dangerous and cunning kind . . . the secular invasion." This aggression also has the goal of undermining "true Islam" and to countenance things which are not inherent to Islam. In the face of such numerous attacks on Islam, a defense of the Muslim community is a duty of all Muslims. This is due to the fact that it is "extremely dangerous" to recognize apostasy in the Muslim community but to undertake nothing against it.

al-Qaraḍāwī first becomes concrete at this point by pointing out – in a manner similar to that found in his principal work on apostasy *ǧarīmat ar-ridda* – that "all" Muslim legal experts are in agreement that an apostate has to be punished; there are only differing opinions with respect to the type of punishment. However, as al-Qaraḍāwī emphasizes, the majority of Muslim legal experts, including the four Sunni and four Shiite schools of legal thought, defend the notion that the apostate has to be executed.

al-Qaraḍāwī cites early Islamic authorities on tradition as well as the companions of the Prophet in support of this point of view. Also, he cites a number of *aḥādīṯ,* which call for the death penalty for apostates and, accordingly, the lawfulness of the execution of apostasy. Upon the occasion

344 al-Qaradawi. "Apostasy."

of an *ḥadīṯ* by ᶜAlī Ibn Abī Ṭālib, al-Qaraḍāwī briefly goes into the discussion of the contested lawfulness of burning apostates alive according to a number of reports by Ibn ᶜAbbās. At this point, however, he in no way expresses doubts regarding the lawfulness of the death penalty per se.

Neither in this *fatwā* nor in his remaining works in which he concerns himself more in detail with the topic of apostasy does al-Qaraḍāwī lecture or justify the notion of other Muslim scholars who advocate granting positive as well as negative religious freedom. It is possible that he does not hold such advocates of increased civil rights in worldview questions, who would have to be among the scholars known to him, to be authorities worthy of discussion. Since he does not ever mention the free choice of religion as a position nor mention its advocates, his reference to various scholarly opinions regarding the type of punishment for apostasy has a purely rhetorical character and offers no text-based alternative to what is for him the necessity of the death penalty for apostates frequently documented with *aḥādīṯ*.

"Major" and "Minor" Apostasy

In the second section of his *fatwā*, in which on the whole al-Qaraḍāwī rather closely follows the argumentation of his work entitled *ǧarīmat*, he goes into the question of whether each apostate should be executed without exception. Initially he points to a report from Muḥammad's time, according to which an apostate was killed who not only fell away from Islam but also insulted and killed a Muslim. A further apostate not only turned away from Islam. Rather, he also disseminated negative information about Islam: "He also sought to spread falsehood and slander."

At this point, the influence played by Ibn Taymīya on al-Qaraḍāwī is again clear when al-Qaraḍāwī reports that Ibn Taymīya differentiates between two different types of apostasy. Namely, this differentiation is between a form of apostasy with which the apostate does no damage to the Muslim community and apostasy by which the apostate conducts war against God and his messenger and spreads harm throughout the country. The result is that his repentance is not accepted if he falls into the hands of Muslims. For al-Qaraḍāwī, included among the apostates who fall into the category of conducting war are those who speak with others about their newly acquired convictions.

> "Apostates who call for apostasy from Islam have not only become disbelievers in Islam but have also become enemies of Islam and the Muslim nation. They, by doing so, fall under the category of those who wage war against Almighty Allah and His Messenger and spread mischief in the land."[345]

Again, al-Qaraḍāwī cites by way of example the way the companions of the Prophet dealt with apostates in early Islamic history. In a footnote, he mentions that apostasy does not have to be followed by execution in every case and that under certain circumstances one can desist. The decision about it – and that which in comparison to his statements in his work *ǧarīmat ar-ridda* is worthy of remark – would lie with government representatives:

> "Putting the apostate to death is not a binding ruling to be followed in every case. Rather, it is a decision for those in authority in the government to take; if it orders that the apostate be executed, it must be put into effect, and vice versa."[346]

Does al-Qaraḍāwī specifically have the situation in Afghanistan in mind, where Abdur Rahman's death penalty had been announced by the Afghan government? Is he saving on his critical remarks about rulers who do not follow God's law due to the fact that Afghanistan expressly avows that "no law can be contrary to the beliefs and provisions of the sacred religion of Islam" in Chapter 1, Article 3 of its Constitution ratified on January 27, 2004?[347]

Finally, al-Qaraḍāwī turns to Ibn Taymīya's differentiation between "major" and "minor" apostasy, with which he also aligns himself. al-Qaraḍāwī makes it clear that the decisive question for him with respect to the measure of punishment is whether the apostate is to be classified as a hostile combatant. A hostile combatant is someone who tries to publicly win people over by speaking to them or producing writings, whereby such an individual would make himself guilty of the "major" form of apostasy:

---

345 Ibid.

346 Ibid.

347 Comp. "Die Verfassung der islamischen Republik Afghanistan" (The constitution of the Islamic Republic of Afghanistan) dated 27.1.2004: http://www.mpipriv.de/files/pdf4/verfassung_2004_deutsch_mpil_webseite.pdf (5.5.2014).

> "The apostate . . . is to be . . . severly punished by the death penalty," for "Apostates who call for apostasy from Islam have not only become disbelievers in Islam but have also become enemies of Islam and the Muslim nation."[348]

This means that for al-Qaraḍāwī the spoken word already represents an active and politically subversive action with the goal of destroying the community. This amounts to the equivalent of an armed attack: "waging war against something may be done by already attacking it or by speaking against it." This is underscored by al-Qaraḍāwī by his subsequently determining that the written word has more influence than the spoken word. It is for this reason that the individual who tries to promote apostasy from Islam in written form is seen far more to be an enemy of Islam than a person who only speaks about it and in turn does this to a greater extent than those who are silent about it.

The Punishment for Apostasy

What is involved in the third section is the measure of punishment for apostasy, and this is quite similar to al-Qaraḍāwī's major work on apostasy, *ğarīmat ar-ridda*. al-Qaraḍāwī' initially argues using the central position of the faith as the identity of the Islamic community: "Belief is the basic foundation of its identity, pivot, and spirit of its life." For that reason, from the standpoint of pure self protection, the Islamic community cannot allow anyone to subvert this identity. Rather, the unity of the Muslim community has to be protected. Whoever turns their back on Islam suspends the five foundations of the Sharia, which is precisely trying to maintain Islam via its moral teaching and its law: religion, life, progeny, humankind's spirit (or reason), and their possessions.

al-Qaraḍāwī begins here as he did in his earlier statements on this topic, which is to say he argues exclusively from an inherently Islamic legal perspective which does not at all take into account the possibility of an individual decision on faith independent of membership in a family or group. al-Qaraḍāwī emphasizes that in the end Islam would not force anyone to belong and would also not force an individual to accept or leave another religion. Those who accept Islam had to have been convinced of it and

---

348 al-Qaradawi. "Apostasy".

cannot just simply leave it. A certain break in the argumentation can be located at this point when al-Qaraḍāwī insists that the state of being convinced is of great significance for membership in Islam, while he simultaneously does not allow the lack of conviction as a reason for turning away from Islam.

Additionally, as al-Qaraḍāwī underscores again at this point, Islam does not call for the execution of the apostate. Rather, it only calls for the execution of those who speak openly about their apostasy or calls upon others to take the same step. Whoever keeps his doubts to himself will be punished by God in the life hereafter, but his execution in this world is not required even if a discretionary punishment in this world is possible.[349]

In his work *ǧarīmat ar-ridda*, al-Qaraḍāwī does not treat this group of covert apostates in detail. According to al-Qaraḍāwī's opinion, Islam does not intend to use execution with this group of covert apostates. He gives more space to this group in his *fatwā* than in his major work on apostasy – and that applies all the more when one takes into account the limited length of the entire text. It is possible that the clear limitation on the general permission to perform executions found within this English language text can be understood as an attempt at moderation in view of the background of Western readers.

As a further argument, al-Qaraḍāwī cites that each community here on earth is based on foundations worthy of protection. Whoever violates these and defects to the enemy is charged with having committed "a severe crime". At this point al-Qaraḍāwī introduces the term "loyalty". An apostate commits treason, for he gives up loyalty to his own community. "People who apostasize . . . pay allegiance, heart and soul, to its enemies,"[350] which al-Qaraḍāwī substantiates with an *ḥadīṯ* text.

al-Qaraḍāwī makes a careful reminder regarding the case where there are doubts regarding the defendant's offense. In this case, the decision has to fall in the favour of the defendant. On the other hand, neglecting to effectively punish apostasy endangers the entire Muslim community, for duc to this there could be further members misled to take the same step. Then these apostates could build a group which could take action against Muslims: ". . . forming a group hostile to the Muslim nation and seeking the

[349] However, according to classical Sharia law, in certain cases the death penalty can be ordered as a discretionary punishment.

[350] al-Qaradawi. "Apostasy".

help of its enemies against it." The consequence would be confrontations and finally the destruction of community: "Intellectual, social, and political disputes and disintegration," whereupon the shedding of blood or a destructive civil war could follow.

Therefore, in the final event al-Qaraḍāwī views an apostate as a disease risk which has to be kept at a distance from the community. Furthermore, he views apostasy as an indirect danger of war, as a catalyst for social and political tensions which could likely be qualified for destroying the Islamic community. At this point, there is nothing left that is recognizable as having to do with moderation. For al-Qaraḍāwī, the apostate has neither civil rights nor any rights to exist. He is a walking danger who in the interest of the community has to be eradicated as soon as possible. After the moderate words about the above mentioned exception for "covert apostates", at this point at the latest the reader has to recognize that for al-Qaraḍāwī it is not a matter of true moderation in condemning apostatsy. Rather, he steadfastly clings to the principal legitimacy of the death penalty.

As an illustration of this scenario of the destroyed community, al-Qaraḍāwī again uses the example of the Soviet invasion of Afghanistan. This began, as he explains, when Afghan Muslims were in the Soviet Union for studies and were recruited by the Communist Party. They gave up their faith and turned to communism. These apostates rose to central positions of power in Afghanistan after their return because Afghans sorely neglected this danger of apostasy. In the final event, believing Afghans inaugurated a campaign of *ǧihād* against the apostates who called upon Soviet troops for assistance. A ten-year civil war ensued. Afghanistan would have otherwise been spared this war and destruction.

It is not the independent decision on the part of the individual which is the actual starting point of apostasy. Rather, it is the enticement of an entire group by unbelieving representatives of secularism. al-Qaraḍāwī argues that apostasy did not essentially occur on account of the decision of Afghan Muslims. Instead, the main driver came as solicitation from without that was exercised upon the Muslim community. Therefore, what occurred was an "attempted seizure" of believers by unbelievers in a foreign country in order to ultimately destroy the community of Muslims (in Afghanistan).

Assessing an Apostate

In the fourth section, al-Qaraḍāwī sets up four basic rules for dealing with apostates and summarizes the legal consequences of a change in religion. He mentions the mandatory divorce of the apostate from his wife and separation from his children as well as "a material punishment," which he does not further define. According to al-Qaraḍāwī, doubts about the fact of apostasy have to be excluded, for labeling a believer as an unbeliever "is one of the most horrendous things."

Labelling someone as an unbeliever may only happen if there is no alternative to it.[351] For that reason, only distinguished scholars can pronounce such a judgment in the form of a *fatwā* about another person. The Muslim ruler should carry out the punishment in accordance with the sentence reached by Muslim legal scholars. Judges in such proceedings have to be in the position to carry out *iğtihād* or to search for qualified legal scholars who can bring the truth to light instead of reaching a wrong decision, because in the latter case the judge would be condemned to hellfire.

al-Qaraḍāwī takes up a central position in the question of the justification of who is allowed to condemn an apostate: The Muslim ruler makes the judgment in accordance with Islamic legal scholars, i.e., both work together in order to reach a just decision. On the one hand, this presupposes the influence of legal scholars on the administration of justice, and, on the other hand, it presupposes the judge's recourse to counsel. At this point, what is in part recognized in other texts to be a clear distance between al-Qaraḍāwī and those in power is nowhere to be found.

al-Qaraḍāwī then turns his attention to the question of whether an apostate should have the opportunity to repent. Again, he invokes Ibn Taymīya, who advocates this. al-Qaraḍāwī implicitly agrees with his position, since

---

351 al-Qaraḍāwī had already warned against the premature condemnation of individuals who were still believers in his work: *aṣ-ṣaḥwa al-islāmīya*, p. 47. There he refers to the members of the Egyptian Jihādist movement *takfīr wa-'l-hiğra*, who immediately label those who turn their back on their group as apostates. al-Qaraḍāwī warns against the negative consequences of such careless actions, points to the Sharia law consequences of apostasy (such as divorce and the removal of children, the seizure of possessions as well as the necessity of the death penalty for the apostate), and impressively warns that non-substantial charges have no justification and only cause harm.

that is the way that apostates can regain clarity and "overcome their state of confusion" in order to recognize Islam as the true religion. The authorities have to accept this confession of remorse, he emphasizes, while only God can judge inner stirrings. However, as al-Qaraḍāwī qualifies it, the case would be different for those whose apostasy rested upon a desire to serve the enemies of Islam or whose apostasy rested upon a concrete act – may God (immediately?) punish such an individual severely.

al-Qaraḍāwī concludes the paragraph with a warning against vigilante justice relating to apostasy. On the one hand, those who take justice into their own hands in this manner are unqualified and unauthorized to act on their own. On the other hand, it involves the misuse of power, because they plunge into being muftis, public prosecutors, judges, and police officers all in one. From al-Qaraḍāwī's perspective, vigilante justice is thus not to be opposed because the punishment is inappropriate. Rather, it is opposed because the proceedings do not correspond to the guidelines of the Sharia.

Objections against the Punishment of Apostates

al-Qaraḍāwī treats a number of objections against the imposition of the death penalty for apostasy in this section. Acccording to its contents, this section also leans rather strongly on his work *ğarīmat ar-ridda*; al-Qaraḍāwī adds nothing significant to what is said in that other work. In *ğarīmat ar-ridda* as well as here he passes judgment immediately in the introductory phrase. There he says that those who oppose the death penalty for apostates only possess inadequate knowledge in religious questions: "Writers . . . who are not versed in religious knowledge." When individuals oppose the death penalty, it exclusively involves a lack of information distinguishable in the case of other persons and not in the case of al-Qaraḍāwī. It is not a matter of a serious objection worthy of discussion.

To begin with, the objection that the death penalty is not mentioned in the Quran but rather in a number of weakly documented traditions is again made a topic at this juncture. al-Qaraḍāwī points out that the texts which advocate the execution of apostates are authentically transmitted texts which through the practice of the companions of the Prophet at the time of the four rightly guided caliphs possessed legitimacy and are additionally better documented than the traditions on the punishment of the consumption of alcohol.

Additionally, according to al-Qaraḍāwī, 95%, indeed 99% of the *aḥādīṯ* are not better documented than those on the prosecution of apostates, and these had after all been transmitted by numerous companions of the Prophet. al-Qaraḍāwī also ties in a number of statements about the reliability of those *aḥādīṯ*, which were not confirmed by the largest number of deliverers of tradition.

And finally, as al-Qaraḍāwī emphasizes, the vast majority of Muslim legal scholars in all the Sunni and Shiite schools of legal thought agree not only with respect to the punishment of apostates but also with respect to the application of the death penalty. A number of scholars in the early days of Islam seized upon verses such as Sura 5:33 as instructions for the treatment of apostates, which threatened those with execution who conducted war against God and his messenger: Likewise, according to Sura 9:74, "the hypocrites" are to be punished with the death penalty. Although in the end al-Qaraḍāwī does not again emphasize that he considers the application of the death penalty to be correct, it is clear from the context that with respect to the basic necessity of the application of the death penalty, there is no other option for him.

Apostasy by those in Power

al-Qaraḍāwī, in accordance with his remaining publications on apostasy from Islam, designates the apostasy of a ruler as the most dangerous form of apostasy there is. This is because the ruler is the individual who should actually protect the Muslim community and fight apostasy. According to al-Qaraḍāwī, however, in reality the evil is that numerous rulers not only do not fight apostasy but rather openly or covertly tolerate it, welcome it, and indeed additionally protect its protagonists and award them honors.

These leaders, who confront the faith in a hostile manner, scarcely esteem the Sharia and spurn the members of the family of the Prophet as well as the caliphs and the great scholars. They would maintain – and at this point al-Qaraḍāwī in turn clearly leans upon his work *ğarīmat ar-ridda* – that the holding of prayers in mosques for men and the veil for women is extremism and would try to prevent the emergence of a Muslim mindset, "a true Muslim mentality," while they would persecute "true callers" to Islam as well as those movements which pursue a resuscitation of Islam. He continues by calling upon the denunciation of this form of apostasy demonstrated by such rulers who only try to maintain an external Islamic appearance but in reality are very shrewdly and simultaneously destroying Islam.

The toleration and honoring of apostates by errant rulers is what in the end makes them apostates. At this juncture, al-Qaraḍāwī not only describes the marks of apostasy or discusses the appropriate measure of punishment for it. Rather, he also actively condemns those who, according to him, tolerate and promote apostasy. With that said, he immediately exercises the authority called for regarding "reputable scholars" mentioned above and makes judgments relating to who counts as an apostate.

That al-Qaraḍāwī is referring here to the tensions between adherents of the Muslim Brotherhood and Egyptian state powers in the 1950s, when viewed against the background of the ban on preaching he experienced in the 1950s and the reorganization and strengthening of state control over al-Azhar through several reforms in 1961 onwards, appears all the more probable when he laments in the following that the rulers adorned themselves with religious scholars who flattered the rulers and in the process were only mouthpieces for the political authorities. If scholars live on the benevolence of those who rule, who is there to punish the rulers for their unbelief or for their apostasy? In this manner, the entire populace is misled while it should actually be led by true scholars who deserve their title.

According to al-Qaraḍāwī, the case in the past was that colonialism had the destruction of Muslim identity as its goal. However, it did not achieve its goal. The war, which admittedly is being conducted by a number of "secularist rulers" and by secular Muslim immigrants, is both more fierce and more dangerous. al-Qaraḍāwī is of the opinion that the Muslim majority countries find themselves in a war-like confrontation in which nothing less is at stake than their existence and identity.

That al-Qaraḍāwī elaborates more on his thoughts on apostasy among those who rule than in his major work on apostasy demonstrates that ten years after composing his major work, this charge against illegitimate rulers occupies him more than ever before. When rulers "adorn" themselves with scholars who should actually be their critics but in reality are only their mouthpieces, then neither the rulers nor the scholars are doing justice to their mandates. They are not in the position to provide the people with correct leadership. That al-Qaraḍāwī even speaks about "punishment" for "secular" rulers indicates that he views academics – presumably including himself – to be in a position marked out over against the holders of power as the actual guide and decision-making entity to provide correct leadership to the people. The result is that the conclusion of this section could also be interpreted as a threat.

Concealed Apostasy

The final segment is dedicated to the topic of people who conceal their apostasy, people who fight against religion and whose attacks are conducted full of craftiness "against everything that is religious." These apostates do not fight with weapons. They advance more cleverly and have their form of apostasy take possession of the minds of people in the way that a malignant tumor takes possession of a body. al-Qaraḍāwī complains that "reputable scholars" would by all means be able to perceive who these apostates are. However, they would be unable to act because these apostates are well established "professional criminals", hypocrites, whose activities might have long remain unrecognized and whose domicile will be hellfire.

al-Qaraḍāwī labels their pernicious activities as "intellectual apostasy." They are rampant in the media, which operates daily on people as well as in legislation and are by far more dangerous than apostasy which is openly disseminated, particularly since they are constantly active. For that reason, there is in his opinion "the positive religious obligation for Muslims to launch war against such a hidden enemy."[352] For that reason, "respectable scholars" from within the realm of law are necessary in order to win the battle of intellectual apostasy being conducted in the media, with the result that in the final event the victory can be won with God's aid.

Evaluation

Throughout the entire text, al-Qaraḍāwī uses a language which in large parts speaks of, threats, violence, conducting war, and destruction. He lays out a black and white scenario in which there are only two sides: On one side there are the friends of God, and on the other side are their enemies. His judgments are hard, and his points of view are absolute. He claims for himself the position of defender of Islam: He belongs to the respectable scholars to whom he attributes a key role in the defense of Islam and who

[352] al-Qaradawi. "Apostasy".

argue in accordance with Islam as it is correctly understood. Overall, his tone is apodictic, even if he gives a surprisingly large amount of space to the "minor" form of apostasy in this text. However, this changes nothing with respect to the unconditional necessity of executing an openly recognizable apostate.

He imploringly warns the reader of the great danger of apostasy as if it is a fatal illness or a destructive invasion, the end of the identity, stability, and health of the Muslim community. There is no understanding for, indeed not even comprehension for, the point of view of doubters or converts, no equitable integration of contrary points of view, no open-ended evaluation, no critical self-reflection, and no mention of the possible social or individual consequences of such persecution and execution of people who turn their backs on Islam.

The single clear declaration of a certain level of moderation is found in the warnings against the premature condemnation of a believer as an apostate[353] and the rejection of the execution of people who only harbour internal doubts about Islam (their prosecution and execution by those holding power in Muslim majority countries, let alone Western countries, would also admittedly be unthinkable).

Quite similarly, there is a question with respect to the assessment of apostasy that was directed at the *European Council for Fatwa and Research*, which is closely linked institutionally with al-Qaraḍāwī himself. It can indirectly be dated 1997. The answer is given that the execution of a guilty individual would solely be the matter for an Islamic state but that many of the pious forefathers *(salāf)* defended the notion that only those individuals are to be executed who publicly declare their turning away from Islam, who through that bring divisiveness to the Islamic community and the name of God, his Prophet, and more specifically drag the name of all Muslims through the mud. These individuals destroy the rights of others as well as the entire state and the nation. An execution protects and pre-

[353] al-Qaraḍāwī also leans upon his role model, Ibn Taymīya, when it comes to a hasty handling of the instrument of *takfīr*: According to Sibylle Wentker. "Historische Entwicklung des Islamismus" in: Walter Feichtinger; Sibylle Wentker (eds.). *Islam, Islamismus und Islamischer Extremismus*. Böhlau Verlag: Wien, 2008, pp. 45-60, here p. 51.

serves the entire nation from evil, but it in no way means the abolition of personal freedom of belief and of the freedom of expression.[354]

From the viewpoint of its contents, al-Qaraḍāwī's *fatwā* "Apostasy: Major and Minor," leaned very heavily upon his major work dating from 1996, and much of his argument was taken directly from it. However, the overall assertion of the text is more strongly socio-politically weighted. If the text were actually a position piece on the case of Abdur Rahman, it would be more of a political manifesto than a position piece by a scholar or preacher.

With this text, al-Qaraḍāwī maneuvers towards the topic of apostasy while remaining exclusively within the argumentative pathways of traditional scholars. That is to say, he indeed takes up a number of critics' arguments against the death penalty. He does not do so, however, in order to truly discuss them. Rather, they serve him as foils comprising the background against which he constructs his advocacy of the death penalty and which he presents as the sole appropriate point of view. Additionally, al-Qaraḍāwī goes as little into the arguments of the basic advocates of religious freedom as well as those who would reject a form of Islam which is both politically and socially comprehensive in scope. al-Qaraḍāwī refutes those who are sweeping critics who only slightly deviate from his views. He does this solely by repeatingly confirming the lawfulness of his own position and by making selective reference to authorities from early Islamic history (the companions of the Prophet, the deliverers of tradition, and the four rightly guided caliphs) and assuring that they are in agreement with his positon.

From the standpoint of contents, Ibn Taymīya's influence is clear, as al-Qaraḍāwī mentions him multiple times. There is also a proximity to the Muslim Brotherhood's Islamist body of thought[355] as well as a basic reformed Salafist orientation. Included in that is al-Qaraḍāwī's judgment of state leadership, which departs from true Islam when it does not truly implement the Sharia. Likewise included are his remarks on the oppositional role of the scholar who disapproves of the pretension of leadership of unqualified state rulers. Furthermore, the oppositional role of scholars calls

354 Comp. the text of the ECFR: Altikriti (trans.) Council.

355 For a summary of the conservative Islamist discourse see, for example: Salwa Ismail. "Confronting the Other: Identity, Culture, Politics, and Conservative Islamism in Egypt" in: *IJMES* 30 (1998), pp. 199-225, here pp. 203-210.

for an uncompromising application of the death penalty for apostates and charges that an open declaration of apostasy is tantamount to conducting war. In addition to that, there are conjured up black and white enemy stereotypes, the exclusive reference to early Islamic authorities as models for condemning modernity, and the dismissing of the reality of 20th century multireligiously characterized societies where there is both conversion to and from Islam in every part of the world.

Were it not for the few pointers relating to the 20th century, the argument is argued here in such classic scholarly style and by employing such scholarly jargon that this text could be 500 years old. As regards contents, the sole point at which al-Qaraḍāwī really goes into modernity is recognizable where he mentions that the media is a tool for the dissemination of unbelief and for the promotion of apostasy. It is specifically in this area that he has made the utmost effort in order to give his points of view on classical theology and jurisprudence a hearing before a worldwide audience.

al-Qaraḍāwī attributes a special role to Islamic scholars – thus including himself – in this ideological battle for the survival of Islam. They appear to be the saviors and preservers of the Muslim community, to be those who would be able to differentiate truth from lies, discern right from wrong, hypocrisy from true faith, and to give direction to the powers that be as to how to deal with the problem of apostasy.[356]

While al-Qaraḍāwī at least scrutinizes all other opinions or, as is more frequently the case, judges them to be groundless, he thus takes up for himself the infallible point of view standing above all criticism and all scrutiny.[357] He not only addresses himself towards his adherents, all Egyp-

[356] With this, al-Qaraḍāwī ascribes to himself the comprehensive role which al-Bannā' awarded to the avant-garde of the reformers of Islam. They were not only to be missionaries, but rather ones who achieve power and authority so that they would be legislatively, educationally, judicially, and executively active and assist Islam to be comprehensively implemented. If these reformers do not aspire after power, they commit an "Islamic crime," according to al-Bannā: Abd al-Monein Said Aly; Manfred W. Wenner. "Modern Islamic Reform Movements: The Muslim Brotherhood in Contemporary Egypt" in: *MEJ* 36/3 (1982), pp. 336-361, here p. 340.

[357] al-Qaraḍāwī is in good company with Sayyid Quṭb, who according to Roxanne Euben and Muhammad Qasim Zaman consciously positioned himself similarly, in this certainty that one's own interpretation of Islam is in agreement with the sources of revelation: Euben; Qasim Zaman (ed.). *Readings*, p. 14.

tians, and all Sunnis. Rather, he addresses himself to all Muslims without exception, for whom he authoritatively – "papally" one might be tempted to say – determines the obligatory judgment and treatment of apostates. When Dale F. Eickelman and Jon W. Anderson make the globalization of the media responsible for the blurring of the lines between local, regional, and international perspectives, the consequences of which are a pluralization of political and religious points of view,[358] then al-Qaraḍāwī's authoritative demeanor can be classified as an attempt to limit this pluralization for the benefit of his own authority.

To everyone he assigns dualistic attributes such as good or evil, believing or unbelieving. This dualism allows him to describe rulers who do not act against apostasy – and by this he must actually mean the rulers of all Muslim majority countries who do not make an effort to pursue court proceedings against apostasy – as corrupt, narcissistic, incapable, and in the end apostate. There is not even the slightest indication of a limited positive characteristic or conduct which he would concede to them, while the "distinguished scholars" tower above all other protagonists as the sole hope in this contest between truth and falsehood.

al-Qaraḍāwī places the authentic Islam of the early days, which they know, preach, and want to assert, in contrast to pseudo-Islam. It is hypocrisy and apostasy which has caused the Muslim community to essentially become unhinged. If apostasy endangers "religion, life, posterity, reason, and possessions as well as "unity and identity," then everyting is at stake. Whoever is essentially threatened has to defend himself against an enemy who will become overwhelming as soon as one neglects to curb that enemy's actions.

2.3.8. Is Apostasy a Capital Crime in Islam? – 2006

Only about 14 days after the publication of al-Qaraḍāwī's comprehensive *fatwā*, the topic of "apostasy" was again treated under the title "Is Apostasy a Capital Crime in Islam?" on IslamOnline.net.[359]

---

[358] Dale F. Eickelman; Jon W. Anderson. "Print, Islam, and the Prospects for Civic Pluralism: New Religious Writings and their Audiences" in: *JIS* 8/1 (1997), pp. 43-62, here p. 47.

[359] Jamal Badawi. "Is Apostasy a Capital Crime in Islam?" 26.4.2006 http://www.onislam.net/english/shariah/contemporary-issues/islamic-themes/425673.html (15.4.2014).

It is possible that this position piece was published as an additional contribution to Abdur Rahman's case of apostasy since it strongly emphasized the freedom granted by Islam, be it in relation to freedom of conscience, religious freedom, or freedom of religious practice. The thought that this renewed position statement on the topic of apostasy is supposed to serve as a line of argument for a moderate position at IslamOnline appears to be strongly suggested.[360]

The content of this article speaks in favor of this, but also, for instance, the fact that on the internet frequently criticized IslamOnline position statements seem to disappear from the web. A still clearer indication of this is the fact that the final wording of the text makes observations on the question of which consequences public insistence on "a certain" (what is meant here is: classical) position from the scholarly world of Muslims has. It also makes observations on whether the call of Islam and of Muslims can thereby be enhanced. This is the case since up to now the call of Islam and of Muslims has been affected via inappropriate depictions. In particular, the text emphasizes that no one is allowed to take the law into his own hands – which by all means can be interpreted as a warning against executing Abdur Rahman or other converts.

al-Qaraḍāwī does not make comments in this text. Rather, his voice is only heard via quotes from his publications. And yet, since it incorporates al-Qaraḍāwī's rejection of the freedom to change religions in a statement on religious freedom, it thus falsely conveys the impression that this is also al-Qaraḍāwī's point of view.

The introduction stems from Jamal Badawi, who is introduced as "Muslim intellectual – Canada." Badawi initially explains that the majority of Muslim theologians share the opinion that apostasy is a capital crime. Indeed the Quran grants comprehensive civil rights and liberties when it

[360] That is suggestive of a further opinion on the case of Abdur Rahman on IslamOnline, in which is argued to the effect that al-Qaraḍāwī represents the following opinion: "Islam does not execute the apostate who does not proclaim his apostasy or call for it." Such apostates are (only) threatened with punishment in the life hereafter if they persist in their condition of apostasy. Additionally, there are three further scholars who are quoted who likewise reject punishing apostates in this life, such that the impression arises that on IslamOnline there are no advocates who endorse the execution of apostates: "Afghan Tried for Christianity, West Concerned." http://www.islamonline.org/English/News/2006-03/21/article09.shtml (14.4.2011).

comes to conscience, belief, and worship, but according to his opinion, however, the Quran is silent on the question of the punishment of apostasy. For that reason, people are free to orient themselves as they wish concerning their worldview, as long as they do not commit a crime or break the law. Therefore, falling away from Islam and committing a crime are two topics which are independent of each other, as far as Badawi is concerned. For al-Qaraḍāwī, on the other hand, manifestly falling away represents in itself an open declaration of war against the Muslim community.

According to Badawi, Islam's message of peace is incompatible with the thought that a person would have to convert to Islam against his will or would have to remain a Muslim. Also, even if an individual has accepted Islam, that person should not be forced to remain with this religion against his will. That would lead to hypocrisy, which is more dangerous for the destruction of the community than is apostasy: "Hypocrisy is a greater danger to the community than apostasy in itself. Hypocrites may implode the Muslim community from within."[361]

Anyway, Badawi continues, a solid textual basis is not found for the imposition of the death penalty for apostasy: The Quran says nothing about the death penalty for apostates, and the traditions which make a topic of this penalty are only "weak" aḥādīṯ and for that reason not legally binding. On the contrary, Badawi quotes a tradition from the "authentic" ḥadīṯ collection by Buḫārī, which specifically does not mention that Muḥammad ordered the killing of an apostate in connection with such a case.

The argument that apostasy in itself represents an act of treason and for that reason alone is to be punished is not held by Badawi to be cogent: For him, the question in point of fact is whether along with apostasy there are other crimes against the state which are involved. This means that at this point Badawi's argumentation is diametrically opposed to that of al-Qaraḍāwī and does not hold apostasy alone to be a crime or, at most, it holds it to be an offense which is directed solely at God. With that said, he implies that apostasy is stripped of any necessity for worldly punishment: "And if it were an offense, it would be an offense that goes surely against God."[362]

---

361 Badawi. "Apostasy".

362 Ibid.

In what follows, Badawi integrates al-Qaraḍāwī's statements on the topic of apostasy from his *fatwa* "Apostasy: Major and Minor" into his position piece. He refutes al-Qaraḍāwī's position in a non-confrontational manner. Rather, he takes up his argument that a number of texts of tradition call for the death penalty for apostasy. This textual finding is given a new interpretation by Badawi, to the effect that tradition does not call for the death penalty for mere apostasy but rather for apostasy which includes criminal actions such as murder, armed robbery, or other crimes which harm the community. (al-Qaraḍāwī had in contrast argued that an openly recognizable turning away is precisely the conscious crime which makes the death penalty necessary.)

From Badawi's perspective, it is instead to be assumed that Buḫārī's tradition (only) calls for the death penalty for apostasy in connection with an additional criminal act. According to Badawi, Ibn Taymīya presumably drew precisely this conclusion from the text (of all people Ibn Taymīya, al-Qaraḍāwī's chief witness!). As a consequence, it is demonstrated for Badawi that the threat of the death penalty is only directed against such individual who dedicates himself to battling against the Islamic community after committing apostasy:

> "Hence, the person who abandons his religion and the Muslim community . . . is meant to be the person who apostasizes from Islam and then fights against Allah and His messenger, not the person who merely becomes an apostate."[363]

Badawi now continues by defusing the well known tradition "Whoever changes his religion, kill him." For example, he deftly quotes al-Qaraḍāwī's *fatwā* "Apostasy: Major and Minor" at the point where al-Qaraḍāwī argues that this saying by Muḥammad had already been interpreted by ᶜUmar to mean that Muḥammad was not speaking with divine authority but rather only as a lead of the community of all Muslims. With that said, this saying by Muḥammad would only have been a pragmatic guideline for his community and not, however, a permanently valid legal guideline, which by the way would also agree with al-Qaraḍāwī's recommended interpretation of this tradition.

---

363 Ibid.

Badawi continues by stating that the remaining reports of tradition which order the death penalty have not made its application mandatory. For that reason, as Badawi ends, the conclusion is imperative that from the Quran and the *sunna* no direct obligation for the application of the death penalty in the case of apostasy can be derived. This is the case as long as there is no other crime associated with apostasy and the community is not thereby endangered. Individual apostasy, however, which does not fulfil these preconditions, can go unpunished, can be ignored, and thus does not play any role.

Badawi emphasizes that the situation nowadays is different compared to the time of Islam's origin, when the Islamic community was endangered by the apostasy of a number of its members. Times change, and new circumstances have necessitated a changed treatment of this problem. Badawi simultaneously protests against the charge of liberalism. By no means do the indispensable components of the Sharia have to be sacrificed in order to earn the title of "moderate or open-minded."

However, according to Badawi, would such an insistence on a special historical point of view really heighten the standing of Islam and of Muslims, a standing which has already been greatly damaged? And finally – and it is at this point that Badawi again turns towards al-Qaraḍāwī – warnings have already been expressed by al-Qaraḍāwī that in dealing with and in judging apostasy an immense level of attention is required and that only individuals in positions of great authority and knowledge are justified at all in making pronouncements in this matter.

It is apparent that in his opinion piece Badawi purposely misunderstands al-Qaraḍāwī in order to turn al-Qaraḍāwī's thoughts to his own advantage without, however, being confrontational towards al-Qaraḍāwī. He allows al-Qaraḍāwī to emerge as one of his witnesses for the justification of religious freedom and freedom of expression, which al-Qaraḍāwī never justified in this manner. Badawi selectively quotes al-Qaraḍāwī out of context as corroboration for his own position, without making this clear at all. In a comparison of all of al-Qaraḍāwī's publications on the topic of apostasy, it can be clearly established that he has never essentially revised his opinion on this topic. In each case he calls for the imposition of the death penalty, given the precondition of proven apostasy, as something which is derived from the Quran and tradition. Additionally, al-Qaraḍāwī expresses himself very authoritatively, while Badawi only says that he "suggests" certain interpretations.

Accordingly, the intent behind this misleading depiction of al-Qaraḍāwī's position on apostasy remains opaque – besides the supposition that the publication of this text, which in English has been available to a large readership, primarily has to do with presenting religious freedom by an Islamic theologian in a positive manner.[364] This supposition is supported by the authorial details at the end of the article, which introduce Jamal Badawi as Professor of Management and Religious Studies at Saint Mary's University in Halifax, Canada. Thus, he is introduced as being from a living and teaching environment in which every position which does not advocate either positive or negative religious freedom appears to be simply inconceivable.

2.3.9. The Inviolability of Blood ("al-ḥurma ad-dimā'") – 2007

Within the category "Sermons and Lectures" (*ḫuṭab wa-muḥāḍarāt*) on www.qaradawi.net, al-Qaraḍāwī released what was originally supposedly an orally presented opinion piece on the question of the lawfulness of *qiṣāṣ* punishments (crimes for which Sharia law envisages retaliation according to the principle of parity).[365] Since, according to various texts of tradition, one of the exceptions where the shedding of blood goes unpunished is the killing of an apostate, al-Qaraḍāwī makes reference to this topic in a relatively comprehensive manner in the text.

---

364 A correspondingly moderate statement on the question of the punishment of apostates in Islam by Dr. Jamal Badawi is found in the transcript of a "Live dialogue" carrying the title "Apostasy in Islam: Any Chance in the Contemporary Context?" dated March 27, 2006 on IslamOnline. There Dr. Badawi answers detailed questions on apostasy to the effect that he indeed grants that there are scholars who call for the death penalty, but he himself does not want to go along with such a demand, for apostasy does not fall into the category of *ḥudūd* offenses: "... I am personally fully convinced that the only ground for capital punishment for the apostate is only when apostasy is coupled with some other serious crimes such as high treason or murder." http://livedialogue.islamonline.net/livedialogue/english/Browse.asp?hGuestID=Gz9HCK (14.4.2011).

365 Yūsuf al-Qaraḍāwī. "ḥurma ad-dimā'", 25.10.2007. http://www.qaradawi.net/new/articles/1267-2012-02-05-19-28-41 (5.5.2014).

al-Qaraḍāwī initially quotes a number of Quranic verses and texts from the corpus of tradition in which the sanctity of marriage, the sanctity of possessions, and the sanctity of the blood of Muslim believers are addressed. He underscores the serious meaning of the topic with the statement: "God has forbidden the killing of any individual person." al-Qaraḍāwī then comes to speak about the exception: extramarital relationships (*zinan*), the killing of an individual (*qatl*), and apostasy (*ḫurūǧ ᶜan dīn allāh*). With respect to apostasy, al-Qaraḍāwī reverts to a known formulation from other texts, namely that Islam forces no one to enter the faith; however, whoever has once decided for this faith is subject to its laws and commandments; he is not allowed to make a "plaything" (*malᶜaba*) of religion and enter it or leave as he wishes.

In the process, the conditions for imposing the penalty, for instance the presence of a sufficient number of witnesses, have to be observed so that "anarchy does not creep in" due to a lack of evidence or mere rumors (*dabbat al-fauḍā*). For that reason, the implementation of *qiṣāṣ* punishments rest in the hand of an "Imam"; if this individual confirms the charge, then the person involved has to be executed.

In this text al-Qaraḍāwī indeed addresses the question of the severity of the punishment. However, he does not do so in order to seriously cast doubt upon its justification. Rather, it has to do with the fact that these severe punishments prevent the spread of wickedness and the destruction of community and ward off other similar acts. For that reason, al-Qaraḍāwī is not seriously contemplating the thought of giving into the call on the part of a number of people to abolish these retaliatory punishments. On the other hand, he also turns against those to whom the *qiṣāṣ* punishments do not appear sufficient and who only thirst after revenge. At this point, he again introduces his concept of *wasaṭīya*, which by definition he interprets as a centrist concept and presents as an appropriate answer with respect to sentencing.

However, the "center" is not that which is moderate, for instance in view of the fact of the 1948 United Nations Human Rights Declaration or, more specifically, what protects the health and the life of the involved individual by suspending the death penalty. Rather, it is that which al-Qaraḍāwī declares to be the center: indispensable Sharia law including *ḥudūd* punishments. al-Qaraḍāwī does not define in more detail who the "imam" could be who would be entitled to carry out these punishments and how in light of this fact it is to be put into practice since there is hardly any country where the death penalty can be legally imposed as a penalty for apostasy. However, that the *qiṣāṣ* punishments are indispensable and have to be applied in order to protect the community from damage is what doubtless remains as the essence after reading this text. In the final event, the centrist concept stands for an uncompromising application of Sharia punishments and, from al-Qaraḍāwī's point of view, is for the benefit of humanity.

2.3.10. ğihād Jurisprudence ("fiqh al-ğihād") – 2009

After numerous publications over the past decades, al-Qaraḍāwī submitted his lifework, comprising close to 1,500 pages, with the title *fiqh al-ğihād* and representing a comprehensive explanation and justification of the doctrine of *ğihād*.[366]

That in connection with his comprehensive exposition of *ğihād* he would also come around to talk about the topic of apostasy is an indication of the characteristic style of his argument: The fact that the topic of apostasy is at all posed in connection with the individual rules of *ğihād* makes it clear that al-Qaraḍāwī possesses a comprehensive understanding of *ğihād*. For him, *ğihād* includes military, commercial, social, cultural, mental, and moral *ğihād*.[367] The focus in this work lies in the way al-Qaraḍāwī has incorporated set pieces of text from numerous earlier publications – in part literally. Topically, there are at times dramatic warnings against the decomposition of the *umma* and of awareness of the danger which threatens the Islamic community. Preventive measures to take are also made a topic. It is interesting to observe that in this work on *ğihād* the death penalty for apostasy is treated at the margins only insofar as it slips into the text as a given. However, its justification is not actually discussed or justified.

al-Qaraḍāwī treats the topic of apostasy rather comprehensively in the fourth section of the first volume as it relates to the rank *ğihād* holds against "injustice and the abhorrent within" (*martaba ğihād aẓ-ẓulm wa- 'l-munkar fī 'd-dāḫil*),[368] whereby in spite of rather comprehensive consideration of the topic, al-Qaraḍāwī does not on the whole become more con-

---

[366] al-Qaraḍāwī. *fiqh al-ğihād*. The work appeared in a third edition in 2011.
[367] In the introduction al-Qaraḍāwī explains this: Ibid., Vol. 1, p. 11.
[368] Ibid., Vol. 1, pp.169-192.

crete than in his earlier writings. Also at this point, as in his remaining statements on this topic, he again outlines the picture of a threatened community which has to provide care and vigilance so that it does not succumb to destruction. Right at the beginning, he speaks of protecting the community from "doom" *(ḍayāᶜ)*, "collapse" *(inhiyār)*, and "decay" *(tafakkuk)* which ensues if one does not pay attention to the foundations of community. Also at this point, it is less the individual who comes into the field of vision and more the community as a whole, behind which interests and concerns all individualism and every personal need has to retreat.

To begin with, al-Qaraḍāwī circles around the topic of the "battlegrounds" (or "battlefields") of *ǧihād (mayādīn al-ǧihād)*, where it is a matter of the conflict over right and wrong as well as wickedness and oppression. al-Qaraḍāwī expresses himself by referring to verses from the Quran and tradition in very general terms about those who commit injustice and wrongdoings, and he emphasizes that resistance against depravity, tyranny, and evil are the duty of every individual believing Muslim with "hand, tongue, and heart."[369]

In a second step, this "injustice" and this "wickedness", as a danger from the inside of the community, are linked to the necessity of *ǧihād*. Indeed, combating inward wickedness appears to be a prerequisite for conflict with unbelief: *ǧihād* with the "hand, with the tongue, and with the heart" is called for, since ". . . from the viewpoint of Islam, *ǧihād* against injustice and wickedness on the inside has to precede *ǧihād* against unbelief and enemies on the outside."[370]

If the community does not intervene against the wickedness – al-Qaraḍāwī names at this point, among others, moral offenses such as extramarital relationships (*zinan*) or the consumption of intoxicants – and they spread unobstructed, then Allah will retaliate and punish the community. Actions are thus unconditionally required for self-protection,[371] and indeed above all to protect against heretical novelties and deviations on an intellectual level (*al-ibtidāᶜāt wa-'l-inḥirafāt al-fikrīya*), such as liberalism, secularism, or Marxism.[372]

---

369 Ibid., Vol. 1, pp. 169-179, here p. 171.
370 Ibid., Vol. 1, pp. 169-179, here p. 173.
371 Ibid., Vol. 1, pp. 169-179, here p. 176-177.
372 Ibid., Vol. 1, pp. 169-179, here p. 179.

Now he gets around to speaking about his actual topic in this chapter, apostasy, as well as about *ǧihād* against apostasy from Islam, which represents the most wicked stage of unbelief and the most dangerous form of wickedness of all. This is due to the fact that apostasy threatens the confession (*ᶜaqīda*) and with it the actual identity of the community. We find here excerpts from earlier writings by al-Qaraḍāwī on apostasy, for example the warning against how "the Jews" at the time of Muḥammad threatened the Islamic community by swiftly entering and exiting Islam, by playing a game with Islam that serves as a warning up to the present day.[373] Whoever is plagued with doubts should turn to a trustworthy scholar in order to find release but should not think that the solution will be found in turning away.

In the following, al-Qaraḍāwī comments on apostasy as a political offense: Whoever leaves the faith but tells no one about this will be repaid in the afterlife. However, whoever takes their apostasy to the outside world commits a "putsch" against he community (*inqilāb*) and perpetrates treason. Such a reversal in membership from one umma to another umma is not acceptable since this behaviour runs rampant and finally threatens the whole existence of the entire community.[374] For that reason, according to al-Qaraḍāw, the Quran calls for battle against apostasy and apostates.

al-Qaraḍāwī paints an even gloomier picture when he continues by describing the apostasy of an entire community as a "revolution" *(ṯaura)* against Islam, the *daᶜwa*, the *umma* and the state as was experienced by the Islamic community in the *Ridda* Wars. Had Abū Bakr not been so steadfast, the Islamic community would have perished at that time. For that reason, the apostasy of individuals has to categorically be opposed before it takes control of an entire group or community. The worst evil of all arises when apostasy infects a part of the community and no one opposes it.

al-Qaraḍāwī now specifically points out the unity among scholars with respect to punishment for apostates as has been suggested by various traditions. This is done even though there is not unanimity among all scholars

373 Ibid., Vol. 1, p. 180.

374 Ibid., Vol. 1, pp. 181-182.

and a number of scholars underscore the necessity of the call to repentance and return to Islam.[375]

al-Qaraḍāwī's prime example of apostasy follows. It has to do with a number of Afghans' who turned to communism when they took up studies in Russia. This brought about a ten-year civil war, around two million fatalities, and much suffering – only because apostasy was not opposed from the beginning. There is a second example in addition to Afghanistan, and it is known from almost all of al-Qaraḍāwī's writings on apostasy. What is provided here, however, consists only of a few snippets of information from existing set portions of text originating at a 1978 conference in Colorado, where it was said that $1 bn had been appropriated for the Christianization of the Islamic world.[376]

Since that time – and here, for the first time, al-Qaraḍāwī expands his spectrum of argumentation when compared to earlier treatments on the topic of apostasy respecting the dangers of Christian mission – Christianization has been conducted "with all its might in Muslim countries" suffering from "poverty, illness, ignorance, war, and catastrophe." In spite of the successes of these efforts, Christianization has deliberately been presented as a failure in order to win more financial support to numb Muslims and to choke their resistance.[377] For that reason, an intensification of the battle against apostasy is indispensable for the fortification of the Muslim community and the defense against such dangers. At the same time, *da^cwa* has to advance.

After these comments, al-Qaraḍāwī again turns to his familiar chains of argument by borrowing from a number of sections in his main writing on apostasy, *ǧarīmat ar-ridda*. In what follows, the particularly reprehensible apostasy on the part of a ruler as well as concealed apostasy, which is more effective than an openly demonstrated turning away from religion, are

---

375 In contrast to his other works, here al-Qaraḍāwī refers to the precise locations of these works of tradition in accordance with academic citation method: Ibid., Vol. 1, pp. 182-183.

376 In Chapter 10 of his *ǧihād* theology, he comes back to this conference and explains that missionary invasion is an element of the military and political attack by Western Imperialism and that for that reason, the use of violence against missionaries and converts who betray the *umma* and collaborate with the enemy is also justified: Ibid., Vol. 2, pp. 1129+1123ff.

377 Ibid., Vol. 1, pp. 184-187.

mentioned. This is more effective than the openly demonstrated turning away from religion. Without any additional indication, he inserts these word for word (along with two additional three-line addendums which are likewise not identified as such).[378]

al-Qaraḍāwī newly formulates the conclusion of this segment[379] by making a number of concrete suggestions with respect to the prevention of the elaborately described dangers to the community. The solution does not lie in retreat but rather in involvement on a broad scale: He thus considers it indispensable to establish an academic center where capable men should be schooled in apologetics so that they would be in the position to defend the *umma* in a special way. But beyond that, the young generation also has to be collectively equipped for this ideological battle.

al-Qaraḍāwī suggests the establishment of high level institutes in which the most capable people in the country should be accepted on the basis of how they stand out with respect to their faith and manner of living. Their specialization in various ideologies and philosophies is absolutely essential in order to adequately conduct the battle for the minds of people and to ward off Western notions which are harmful to Islamic society and the concealed apostasy that has already seeped in. Islamic society can thus win back the avant-garde role it forfeited a long time ago.

At this point, al-Qaraḍāwī exclusively treats the topic of apostasy from the aspect of aggression from without which is brought upon the Islamic community. Also in this work there are no observations as to what could at all move an individual to doubt or to turn from Islam. According to al-Qaraḍāwī's conviction, if this happens, then it happens owing to the targeted application of "poison"[380] with the goal of splitting the Muslim community and finally destroying it. Against the backdrop of remarks at the beginning of the chapter on the impossibility of tolerating wickedness and decay within the Muslim community, indeed, given the remarks by al-Qaraḍāwī that the *umma* would thereby draw the wrath of God, the statements in the second part of the section can definitely be interpreted as a call to action in the sense of saving one's own community.

---

378 al-Qaraḍāwī. *ǧarīmat ar-ridda*, pp. 68-73 is quoted in al-Qaraḍāwī. *fiqh al-ǧihād*, Vol. 1, pp. 187-190.

379 Ibid., pp. 191-192.

380 Ibid., Vol. 1, p. 189.

If one compares this lifework by al-Qaraḍāwī with what he first produced, *al-ḥalāl wa-'l-ḥarām fī 'l-islām*, dating from 1960, one sees that he has neither essentially revised his point of view with respect to apostasy nor has he taken account of the changing world with its increasingly loud calls for religious freedom and personal civil rights and liberties in Muslim majority countries. He has also not taken account of the Muslim minority in Western countries where there is comprehensive religious freedom. His warnings seem inflexible and dogmatic, indeed sterile and remote in the face of numerous dangers and possible invasions by corruptive ideas along the firmly established front of orthodoxy, all of which have to be held back at the camp gates with all one's might. To this end, al-Qaraḍāwī utilizes numerous set pieces of text from earlier works and adds them here in varying order and length, all the while subjecting the topic to no foundationally new considerations even after 50 years.

2.3.11. Miscellaneous Comments by al-Qaraḍāwī on Apostasy

Who in al-Qaraḍāwī's eyes is an apostate? Other Muslims with liberal notions? Groups on the margin within the Islamic community and non-acknowledged minorities? Converts or atheists? What exactly is it that makes someone who has fallen away into an apostate? Where is the line drawn between the doubting believer and the apostate? At no juncture does al-Qaraḍāwī provide a complete overview or comprehensive definition of those who for him are clearly apostates. He primarily treats the topic with the aid of catch phrases instead of with the aid of content-related arguments.

Apart from treatments in which al-Qaraḍāwī primarily occupies himself with apostasy, he dedicates himself to this topic in a number of additional writings via passing remarks. Without further discussion, he lines up a number of groups as apostates. This involves adherents of worldviews such as secularism or communism and more specifically adherents of religions such as Judaism or Christianity, whereby their condemnation would supposedly meet with the unqualified endorsement of a majority of his audience. At the same time, he noticeably holds back when it comes to groups where condemnation as apostates would in all probability also reap criticism.[381] al-Qaraḍawı defines orthodoxy not primarily by reference to

---

[381] He thus first of all mentions in his work: al-Qaraḍāwī. *ẓāhirat al-ġulūw*, pp. 20-21 the "communists," who in spite of the "apparent contradiction with a confession of

membership in groups or individual circumstances but rather above all on the basis of a coarse picture to which he attributes everything that can be represented as false and objectionable with the stroke of a pen (such as the rejection of the lawfulness of *ḥudūd* punishments) without having to occupy himself with it in depth.

For al-Qaraḍāwī, apostasy not only amounts to a strict turning away from Islam and turning to another religion. It is not only existent when a Muslim believer breaks with Islam or turns away from the devout practice of his religion. There are other ways of behaving and other worldviews which are considered by al-Qaraḍāwī to be apostasy, for from his point of view the following applies:

> "Islam . . . is a comprehensive system dealing with all spheres of life; it is a state and a religion, or government and a nation; it is a morality and power, or mercy and justice; it is a culture and a law or knowledge and jurisprudence; it is material and wealth, or gain and prosperity; it is Jihad and a call, or army and a cause and finally, it is true belief and worship."[382]

According to al-Qaraḍāwī, whoever embraces secularism by necessity sacrifices the holistic claims of the Sharia, renounces divine leadership, and rejects God's commands. For that reason, the call for secularism among Muslims is tantamount to a repudiation of Islam and is equivalent to atheism, and the acceptance of secularism is "downright apostasy."

The problematic internal nature of secularized Muslim societies is not something al-Qaraḍāwī confronts in this context. Instead, he insists that an individual who accepts secularism in the place of the Sharia clearly makes

---

Islam, its laws, and its values" believe in it as a "philosophy" and a "way of life" and consider every religion to be an opium for people; furthermore, he mentions "secularists" or laicists, respectively, who openly reject the revealed law of God; then he presumes, by not only mentioning the Druses and the Christians but also the Isma'ilites and "similar groups of Bāṭinīya" – thus a part of the Shia which he otherwise always attempts to pocket among his followers – which by referring to "Imām Ġazālī" and Ibn Taymīya he designates as "unbelievers" as is done with Jews and Christians; finally, he names the Bahā'ī, who like the Aḥmadīya movement did not ackowledge Muḥammad as the seal of the prophets.

382 He summarily formulates it so in: Yusuf al-Qaradawi. "How Islam views Secularism." 22.6.2002. http://www.onislam.net/english/ask-the-scholar/ideologies-movements-and-religions/175438-how-islam-views-secularism.html?Religions= (5.5.2014).

himself guilty of apostasy from Islam,[383] particularly since al-Qaraḍāwī sees secularism or more specifically laicism as linked with Christianity. Whoever for himself "accepts laicism . . . has repudiated revelation" (*al-laḏī yaqbalu al-ᶜalmānīya . . . yankaru al-waḥy*).[384] Nothing remains of that individual's Islam "except the name" (*illā ismuhu*).[385]

For al-Qaraḍāwī, secularism and laicism comprise the negative counterpart to the Islamic awakening, the *daᶜwa*, and the consequential and increasingly intensive penetration of society with Islam that he seeks. Furthermore, he seeks the gradual generation of a truly Islamic society completely oriented towards the Quran and tradition. With this condemnation of secularism as a form of atheism and apostasy, al-Qaraḍāwī finds himself in accordance with a known pattern of Islamist argumentation.

According to Fauzi Najjar, the common translation of the term secularism (*al-ᶜalmānīya*) has been "worldly" and "non-religious" since the end of the 19th century. The connotation became increasingly negative up to the 20th century, and it reached a point where secularism and atheism have become interchangeable terms. Also, for large parts of Islamism, secularists have become coterminous with unbelievers and apostates.[386] From this perspective, there can be no acceptance and subjection to the Western secular way or life in the diaspora. The transformation of the situation of the diapsora should not proceed through the use of force, and yet the active conversion of non-Islamic society into Islamic society through *daᶜwa*, education, and instruction is essential.

al-Qaraḍāwī repeatedly links the question of knowledge and practice of true religion with the functioning of a clear sense of reason, and apostasy is linked with the state of mental confusion, out of which the foundering individual has to be freed so that, for instance, he does not enter into hell

---

383 Ibid. and in: al-Qaraḍāwī. *aṣ-ṣaḥwa al-islāmīya*, pp. 89-90.

384 al-Qaraḍāwī. *al-islām wa-'l-ᶜalmānī*, p. 67.

385 Ibid. Interesting at this point is that al-Qaraḍāwī indeed mentions some of the social consequences of apostasy (for instance, that an apostate's wife and children are removed) and explains that judgment is pronounced on him, but he does not explicitly mentioned the death penalty at all.

386 This development is sketched out by Fauzi M. Najjar, who mentions some examples from recent Egyptian history: Najjar. "Debate", pp. 2-4.

fire[387] as a polytheist for whom there is no forgiveness with God[388] in the afterlife.

Individual reason is for al-Qaraḍāwī essentially a suitable instrument for acknowledging God,[389] while "doubts (about Islam) confound his thinking" (*šubuhāt balbalat fikrahū*).[390] An individual has to be freed from these doubts. Then he can recognize the truth and beauty of Islam anew.

al-Qaraḍāwī makes a further remark on apostasy in connection with a *fatwā* on the question of the rightfulness of an organ donation for a non-Muslim. If it has to do with saving the individual's life, al-Qaraḍāwī judges without differentiating between an openly confessing apostate and an individual who doubts in all quietness. The organ donation is indeed allowed, not however, if the recipient is a non-Muslim combatant or an apostate: "As he is no more than a traitor to his religion and his people and thus deserves killing."[391]

In 2003 al-Qaraḍāwī mentioned in all brevity and in a form which largely agrees literally and on the basis of content with the last chapter of his work entitled *ǧarīmat ar-ridda wa-ᶜuqūbat al-murtadd fī ḍau' al-qur'ān wa-'s-sunna* the question of "intellectual apostasy," which in his opinion is visible in forms of the modern media – newspapers, books, radio, and television. This type of consistently propagated and disseminated intellectual apostasy is, according to al-Qaraḍāwī, "more dangerous than openly announced apostasy," for advocates of this "falsehood" are "professional criminals" and "hypocrites," "whose abode will be in the lowest level of the Hell-Fire."[392]

---

387 al-Qaraḍāwī treats the "massive wickedness" (*ẓulm ᶜaẓīm*) and the "disgrace" (*mahāna*) of polytheism (*širk*) in detail in his writing *ḥaqīqat*, pp. 88 ff.

388 al-Qaraḍāwī argues in this manner, inter alia, in his document *ẓāhirat al-ġulūw*, pp. 23-24+ 38.

389 This also becomes clear in his writing: *ḥaqīqat*, in which he dedicates a separate section to the knowledge of God achieved with the aid of reason (pp. 9ff.).

390 al-Qaraḍāwī. *al-iǧtihād*, p. 113.

391 Yusuf al-Qaradawi. "Donating Organs to non-Muslims." 24.6.2002. http://www.onislam.net/english/ask-the-scholar/health-and-science/medicine/174946 (5.5.2014).

392 Yusuf al-Qaradawi. "Fatwa on Intellectual Apostasy." 24.3.2003. http://www.onislam.net/english/ask-the-scholar/crimes-and-penalties/apostasy/175287.html (5.5.2014).

al-Qaraḍāwī dedicates himself particularly intensively to neutralizing this intellectual apostasy through his work with the media and public relations work. His goal is to protect Islamic society from these attacks: "Intellectual apostasy . . . needs a wide scale attack at the same level of strength and thinking . . . Here comes the role of erudite scholars."[393]

At the end of the text, al-Qaraḍāwī uses drastic words to again denounce the prison conditions and the methods of torture to which many other members of the Muslim Brotherhood must have been subjected during their incarceration in Cairo in 1954. The lines between his charge of apostasy and of unbelief are fluid at this point. Can anyone who would strip Muslims of their humanity and drag their faith through the mud in such a manner still be considered a believer?

After a description of the methods of torture and of the torments of the detained individuals, al-Qaraḍāwī concludes that people who subject believing Muslims to such torture are no longer to be included within Islam. For him, what is present is unambiguously unbelief (*kufr*). Due to such activity, the torturers as well as those who command their actions are guilty of apostasy. Whoever associates with unbelief has himself become an "unbeliever" *(kāfir)*.[394]

2.4. Conclusion: al-Qaraḍāwī's Position on Apostasy

When one considers how severe the topic of apostasy is on the basis of its consequences – the death penalty or at least social consequences – then it is astounding that in the final event, insofar as content is concerned, al-Qaraḍāwī treats the topic in a unilinear fashion and ultimately almost superficially while not affording it any modern content-related discussion in the proper sense.

He sermonizes, but he does not differentiate. He addresses the topic lock, stock, and barrel but does not specifically debate it. Rather, he argues against it as an abnormal attitude condemned by the Sharia which is exclusively brought about by the activities of others and has to be combated. The entirely various situations in Muslim majority countries are not taken into account by al-Qaraḍāwī, and he does not spend a single word going

393 Ibid.

394 al-Qaraḍāwī. *aṣ-ṣaḥwa al-islāmīya*, p. 100.

into the circumstances of modernity and its multi-religious societies. For that reason, to a certain degree his addresses remain sterile and distanced.

2.4.1. The Missing Definition of Apostasy

Who is an apostate in al-Qaraḍāwī's eyes? Although he has dedicated more than one work to this topic, this question cannot be given an unambiguous answer. This is due to the fact that nowhere does al-Qaraḍāwī mention a binding definition of an apostate. Where is the line between a doubter accepted by the community and an apostate whom the authorized scholar should condemn to death? Which signs of an apostate are unambiguous so that at least a scholar can identify them correctly? The permanent neglect of prayer, its deliberate refusal, or does there have to be a public proclamation made that prayer is not mandatory? The deviation from what is allowed out of ignorance, as a tactic, as premeditated, or out of rebellion?

At no point does al-Qaraḍāwī mention the unambiguous signs of an apostate by name. It would be very simple in the case of a convert to another religion. That a Muslim believer could choose another religion of his or her own accord is not mentioned and dealt with anywhere by al-Qaraḍāwī. Only the activities of foreign powers and organizations are elucidated,[395] their goal being, from his point of view, that of soliciting for Christianity and destroying Islam.

It indeed becomes clear that al-Qaraḍāwī considers secularists, communists, Jews, and Christians to be unbelievers and – as far as it relates to prior Muslims – as apostates and likewise those who propagate points of view via the media which are contrary to the Quran and *sunna*, caliphs, companions of the Prophet, acknowledged theologians from the formative period, and the Sharia. Nowhere, however, does al-Qaraḍāwī provide the reader with a compilation of those worldviews which oppose Islam and the holistic understanding propagated by al-Qaraḍāwī.

Therefore, the highly important question of where the border between an apostate and a believer runs is in the final analysis left vaguely addressed by al-Qaraḍāwī as it relates to what can lead to *takfīr* and to the suspicions which he downright opposes. al-Qaraḍāwī concentrates above all on an explanation of the sentencing – for instance the lawfulness of the

---

[395] He mentions it thus in his work: *ǧarīmat ar-ridda*, p. 45, that in the USA in 1978 $1 bn was made available to Christianize Muslims.

death penalty, about which he does not lead an impartial discussion – and a depiction of how ruinous apostates' influence is on an Islamic society if its effects on the self-protection of the community are not stemmed in a timely manner. For that reason and due to the nature of the case, it cannot readily be a question of how someone who doubts Islam can overcome his doubts. For that to happen, al-Qaraḍāwī would have to grapple with inquiries of Islam with respect to doctrine and practice, which at no point in his writings on apostasy appear to be his interest.

2.4.2. Yūsuf al-Qaraḍāwī's Judgment on Apostasy against the Backdrop of His Theology

al-Qaraḍāwī's position on apostasy and his judgment regarding dealing with apostates cannot be isolated from considering al-Qaraḍāwī's classical education as a theologian and his position as an *éminence grise* for the Muslim Brotherhood. It is to be expected that al-Qaraḍāwī's position on apostasy moves within a prescribed framework of theological argumentation, which on the one hand includes his holding firmly to the unchanging validity of Sharia law and *ḥadd* punishment.[396] On the other hand, however, it includes his opening ways of practicability and of moderation and mitigation within the framework of his *wasaṭīya* discourse, which al-Qaraḍāwī views as a

> "balance between divine revelation and human reason . . . between spirit and matter, between reason and the heart, between this world and the afterlife, between rights and duties."[397]

Precisely due to the fact that for al-Qaraḍāwī the renewal of Islam all the way to an overhaul of modernity comprise the cornerstone of his apologet-

---

[396] al-Qaradāwī affirmed this anew in an interview on al-Jazeera on the justification of *ḥadd* punishments, in which he in particular pointed to the legitimacy of cutting off the hand directly behind the wrist and in all brevity also confirmed the death penalty for apostacy. Mostafa Al-Khateeb. "Hudud (Penalties) in Contemporary Legal Discourse. A Review of Sheikh Qaradawi's Program on Hudud on Al-Jazeera." http://www.onislam.net/english/shariah/contemporary-issues/interviews-reviews-and-events/450554-hudud-in-the-contemporary-fiqhi-discourse.html?Events= (5.5.2014).

[397] al-Qaraḍāwī. *al-islām wa-'l-ʿalmānīya*, p. 31.

ic, theology, and in the final event his entire life work, he cannot behave indifferently to falling away from Islam. He can also not take up a position which is based on positive and negative religious freedom. For decades, his entire effort has been directed at – in his opinion – alienated and drifting Muslim youth in the Western environment so that they recapture their Islamic identity and bind themselves to it regardless of their national and denominational extraction. This is in order for them to become convincing ambassadors of Islam in modernity.

In the light of this goal of strengthening and advancing Islam, especially in the diaspora, in al-Qaraḍāwī's opinion an intentional turning from Islam can find neither understanding nor justification nor substantiation. Such a freedom to turn away from religion would be an oppositional program to the self-reassurance and strengthening of the Islamic community in the diaspora he intends. However, al-Qaraḍāwī recognizes no grounds for a laissez-faire stance towards an apostate in Muslim majority countries, since as a representative of a reform-Salafist Islam he above all finds his frame of reference in classic scholars from the early days of Islam and in their interpretation of the Quran and the *sunna*.

Within this framework, a separation between the state and the social and private areas within religion is rejected. From this perspective, apostasy cannot be judged as a private affair. Rather, it always also involves society and the public sphere. Therefore, it is not surprising that in al-Qaraḍāwī's argumentation, it is not the individual and his interests but rather the protection of the *umma* which stands in the foreground.

Additionally, a "return" to the complete practice of the Quran and the *sunna* comprises the ways and means for social awakening that, as a reformed Salafist, al-Qaraḍāwī would like to launch and channel through his extensive activities and numerous conduits. For that reason, if the Quran and the *sunna* demand the killing of an apostate, then from al-Qaraḍāwī's point of view, obedience towards this clear direction is a precondition to promoting the stabilization of the society. As al-Qaraḍāwī sees it, this naturally includes the application of *ḥudūd* punishments. There is no sorrow whatsoever to be noted for the victim in the mentioning of them, even if it involves dismemberment or execution by stoning.[398]

---

398 al-Qaraḍāwī notes for instance in this manner in his book: *al-ḥall*, p. 39, which for most people wrongly represents that the extent of the "Islamic solution" (*al-ḥall al-islāmī*) is cutting off the hand of the thief, whipping or stoning the licentious,

A certain concession is made by al-Qaraḍāwī – admittedly this is also not in contradiction with but rather following the role models of classical theology – for the internally embraced doubts which no other person is able to investigate. As Gudrun Krämer states with respect to the right to freedom of thought: "Thoughts are thus free and their evaluation is left entirely to God – their declaration, however, is not."[399]

On the other hand, this concession relating to a category of the most internal thoughts and deliberations of a person could be interpreted as an attempt at a comprehensive seizure of the thought world of an individual. al-Qaraḍāwī's entertaining whether it is allowed to have secret internal doubts about Islam in his publications also makes him a judge of an individual's most private thoughts and simultaneously sets down what is private and what is public.

2.4.3. Yūsuf al-Qaraḍāwī's View of Apostasy against the Backdrop of His Life Work

If al-Qaraḍāwī were to advocate complete religious freedom, he would not be able to maintain his theological doctrinal system of *wasaṭīya*. If Islamic minorities in non-Islamic areas had the freedom to change religion, thus not being bound to Sharia law in this question – then with which justification should they then follow the remaining Sharia law as precisely as possible? If individuals receive Sharia-based directions from al-Qaraḍāwī and the committees such as the European Council for Fatwa and Research with respect to numerous details about their exercise of religion, from the care of their bodies to food intake, from leisure time activities to the keeping of animals, from marital law to the giving of alms, from questions of divorce all the way to the duty of wearing a head scarf, then why should a question that is as important for the maintenance of the *umma* as apostasy be ex-

and administering the remaining *ḥudūd* punishments. Indeed there can be "no doubt" (*lā raiba*) about it that these commands are "a firm component of the Islamic solution" (*ğuz' aṣīl min al-ḥall al-islāmī*). He immediately adds the following to this unmistakeable formulation in order to exclude every further error: "This is unavoidable" (*lā budda minhū*); however, *ḥudūd* punishments are only a part of the Islamic solution, which is much more comprehensive.

399 Krämer. *Gottes Staat*, p. 151.

cluded – especially when the Quran and tradition offer al-Qaraḍāwī crystal clear instructions?

His life work is to firmly root the Muslim minority in the *umma* by a modified application of Islamic law in a non-Islamic environment so that their identity is preserved and their own family and community are protected by the establishment of an Islamic environment. How could enticing believers away with foreign worldviews be passively tolerated?

To not grant inherent civil rights to Islam would mean giving up the identity of the *umma* as a community of the true *ᶜaqīda*, endangering youth and the survival of the Muslim family, making the task of *daᶜwa* impossible, and promoting the detrimental assimilation of the *umma* to the non-Islamic environment. The *umma's* permission to worldview self-determination would be the equivalent of permitting them to give up their identity. Affirming positive as well as negative religious freedom would tear gaps in the firmly established Muslim defense community which precisely needs unity and cohesion in order to compensate for its position of weakness in the diaspora.

By giving up the identity of the community, the right to stay in non-Islamic countries is lost as well as the mission of the Islamic minority, i.e., the permission to turn away from Islam would either cause al-Qaraḍāwī's principle of *wasaṭīya* to collapse or would lead him to have to distance himself from the timeless validity of Sharia punishment of execution in the case of apostasy. However, this would be incompatible with his education and orientation as a scholar in the classical tradition or would mark him a liberal. With that, he would be an uninfluential outsider in scholarly committees.

2.4.4. Yūsuf al-Qaraḍāwī's View of Apostasy against the Backdrop of His Ancestry and Education

In the face of al-Qaraḍāwī's judgment of apostasy, one could come to the conclusion that he clearly breaks from renowned institutions such as al-Azhar, which in most cases can be perceived as moderate. However, this is not so clearly the case. There have repeatedly been scholars from al-Azhar who have come forward with calls for the death penalty for apostates. Indeed, the 1978 draft charter of the Academy for Islamic Studies of the al-Azhar University counts apostasy in §59 among *ḥadd* offenses and sets down in §71 that the head of state is not able to grant a pardon in the case of apostates.[400]

In addition to a number of moderate statements on the part of quite a number of scholars, al-Azhar has on numerous occasions also allowed its members to make statements which expressly advocate the execution of the apostate. The result is that indirect complicity from the side of this institution in connection with charges of *takfīr* and attacks on supposed apostates in Egypt at the end of the 20th century cannot be ruled out.[401]

It is a sobering fact that a scholar such as al-Qaraḍāwī, to whom the attribute "moderate" is also not uncommonly ascribed in professional publications, assumes with great self-certainty the common practice of administering the death penalty to apostates from the early days of Islam onwards as he likewise does for today.[402] He assumes it as a necessity and a matter of course without regard to the unstable basis of the unclear body of source material from Muḥammad's time. Meanwhile, he pays attention to large parts of the time of the Abbasids and the Umayyads.[403] He critically grapples as little with the sources as with its opponents. Rather, he produces an ideal past that never was in order to justify his uncompromising attitude toward apostasy at the present time.

al-Qaraḍāwī's background plays a role in the popularity of his works insofar as he almost universally makes his presentations in his books and addresses in an easily understandable Arabic. This does not limit his listening audience to the scholastic aristocracy. Rather, he also makes his thinking accessible to individuals who indeed bring along some education but do not absolutely need to be theologians or academics.

The success of al-Qaraḍāwī's writings and addresses are conditioned by the fact that his works present his hearers and readers a clear notion of what is "right". His frequent simplifications, which only allow apparent

---

400 According to Krämer. Ibid., p. 155.

401 This share of the blame is also emphasized by Damir-Geilsdorf. *Herrschaft*, pp. 279-280+368.

402 Comp. his video message of 2013 when al-Qaraḍāwī postulates the application of the death penalty for apostates without any restriction: http://www.youtube.com/watch?v=huMu8ihDlVA (5.5.2014).

403 David Cook judges this period of Islamic history after the *ridda* wars as follows: "One can say that all the necessary laws were in place for the punishment of apostates; however there does not seem to have been any machinery to enforce them." Cook. "Apostasy", p. 278.

and very brief, superficial admission of counterarguments in his remarks and do not allow any true discussion on a contrary position, may not appeal to the critical intellect as much as an individual seeking orientation. al-Qaraḍāwī, who himself comes from a modest background, speaks in an understandable language and knows the questions of his constituency, and he calls his constituency to observe the commands of the Sharia and to adhere to a lifestyle which is pleasing to God.

If one listens to addresses by al-Qaraḍāwī or interviews with him (at least those in recent years), it becomes clear that his manner of speaking alone has not been the foundation of his popularity. More frequently than finding clearly structured concepts and clean inferences, one finds half sentences and in part unclear expressions and conceptual leaps in argumentation placed within urgent calls and authoritatively stated judgments. It is not a brilliant orator whom one hears speaking here, not someone who knows how to mesmerize and draw people in with his polished rhetoric, his clearly structured and incisively conveyed content: A good portion of the effect appears instead to be due to the scholarly habitus, the aura of authority of a rather distance, academically operating manner of lecturing[404] with the clothing of the *ᶜālim* which underscores what is said and the integration of dialectical idioms when he expresses his disapproval of others.[405] If, for instance, one follows him in the program explained above, *al-ḥurrīya ad-dīnīya wa-'l-fikrīya*, which is dated February 6, 2005, the fact that al-Qaraḍāwī appeared on the program at all and made comments on this topic presumably had more influence than the later transcript of the program, which was not linguistically polished.

---

[404] Jacob Høigilt explains al-Qaraḍāwī's use of numerous impersonally formulated declaratory phrases and sentences, which have the effect of producing distance to the listener and which lend greater weight to his authority as an individual entitled to issue instructions to all Muslims: Jacob Høigilt. "Varieties of Persuasion in Modern Forms of Islamic Proselytizing in Egypt" in. *RMM* 124 (2008), pp. 243-262, here pp. 248-251.

[405] Comp. the analysis of Andreas Kaplony on the use of dialectical speech in his TV show: *aš-šarīᶜa wa-'l-ḥayāt*: Andreas Kaplony. "Fernseh-Philologie: Form, Sprache und Argumentation einer Sendung von aš-Šarīᶜa wa-l-ḥayāt mit Yūsuf al-Qaraḍāwī". In: Ulrich Marzolph (ed.). Orientalistische Studien zu Sprache und Literatur. Festgabe zum 65. Geburtstag von Werner Diem. Harrassowitz: Wiesbaden, 2011, pp. 417-434, here p. 426f.

2.4.5. The Superiority of Islam

As with the topic of *wasaṭīya* and of minority rights (*fiqh al-aqallīyāt*), it is apparent that al-Qaraḍāwī also does not lose sight of the thought that Jews and Christians or secularists and communists belong to inferior religions or worldviews above which Islam towers. For this reason, changing to another religion or to no religion is not a question of a choice between equals. Rather, in the case of al-Qaraḍāwī, it is exclusively a question of obedience or rebellion, true or false, and good or evil.

Civil rights, which do not expressly preserve the classic Sharia-oriented interpretation, and pluralism and the equality of different religions and worldviews are unthinkable to al-Qaraḍāwī. This is due to the fact that it is not grounded on the basis of classic Islamic theology, and for that reason it is equivalent to endangering the society all the way up to civil war. Autonomous exemption from the law of God by an individual is for that reason pretension and has to be avenged as soon as possible before poison and destruction are able to spread into the community.

al-Qaraḍāwī's exceedingly deprecatory attitude towards the State of Israel, his unreserved advocacy of suicide attacks in Palestinian territories, his calls to kill Jews wherever it is possible,[406] and his broad disdain of Christianity[407] and abhorrence of Jews shine through[408] in his writings on apostasy. With respect to the Jews in particular, no dialog may occur with Jews except "with the sword and the rifle."[409]

---

406 According to a statement by the"Invesitgative Project on Terrorism," a consulting institution for the US Congress as well as various security agencies of the USA, al-Qaraḍāwī is supposed to have called for the killing of Jews of the "Muslim Arab Youth Association" (MAYA) in Toledo in 1995: http://www.investigativeproject.org/profile/167 (5.5.2015).

407 From al-Qaraḍāwī's point of view, it is not only the deploring corruption of Christianity that makes it an inferior religion; rather, it is the fact that Christianity carries out a separation between religion and the state (*al-faṣl baina 'd-dīn wa-'d-daula*), thus being based on the objectionable thought of laicism, while Islam has come in order to fashion the entire life of humankind: al-Qaraḍāwī. *al-islām wa-'l-ᶜalmānīya*, pp. 47+66-67.

408 This attitude towards Jews and Christians is, inter alia, made clear in his work: al-Qaraḍāwī. *ġair al-muslimīn*, pp. 76-85. In this work, he presents Christian church history as a single stringing together of acts of violence and injustice.

Beyond that, however, "the Jews" repeatedly and principally serve al-Qaraḍāwī as negative examples of unbelief, stubbornness, and their inexcusable rejection of Muḥammad[410] as well as the corruption of their Scriptures[411] serve as examples of their wiliness and lack of allegiance. There is no question that al-Qaraḍāwī does not view other religions, and more specifically their adherents, as coequal with Islam and Muslims but also worldviews such as secularism and communism are only considered from a disparaging perspective. Already for that reason he cannot summon up understanding or any sympathy for a conversion. Why should Muslims choose the worse – and in addition to that the clearly wrong – alternative?

2.4.6. The Persecution of Apostates as an Assurance of Peace

Against the backdrop of unconditional advocacy of Sharia law, the persecution, arrest, and massive use of force againat apostates for only changing their worldview appears to al-Qaraḍāwī to not be patently disproportionate. And yet he does not view the (from his standpoint necessary) killing of an apostate to actually be an application of force in the sense of aggression. Rather, it is the required reaction to an offense which has already been committed against God and the community. For that reason, for al-Qaraḍāwī apostasy needs to be fought because it is a matter of an act of self-defense and of legitimate self-protection.

al-Qaraḍāwī primarily speaks about the topic of force in connection with the misorientation of Islamist groups by many a self-named imam and sheik. He also addresses it in connection with an erroneous handling of the Sharia as well as in connection with oppression, corruption, and undemo-

---

409 Yusūf al-Qaraḍāwī formulated it in this manner in a program from the series *aš-šarʿīa wa-'l-ḥayāt* on al-Jazeera on July 13, 2004, quoted in: Sheikh Yousef al-Qaradhawi. "There is No Dialog between Us and the Jews Except with the Sword and the Rifle." MEMRI Special Dispatch No. 753, 27.7.2004. http://www.memri.org/report/en/0/0/0/0/0/0/1181.htm (5.5.2014). There is likewise a reference in the report "Leading Muslim Cleric Under Fire for Meeting Israeli Chief Rabbi" on: AP Worldstream, 7.1.1998, quoted in: http://www.investigativeproject.org/profile/167 (5.5.2014).

410 According to, for example, his writing: *ǧarīmat ar-ridda*, p. 27.

411 al-Qaraḍāwī writes in this manner al-Qaraḍāwī in ibid., p. 32, that God marks the *people of the book* "with a stamp bearing wickedness, unbelief, and sacrilege" because they reject the sending of God's message and have chosed another law.

cratic political structures.[412] Never, however, does a connection with the administration of Sharia punishment make the execution of apostates appear to him to be in any actual sense something that falls into the category of the use of force.

Furthermore, in relation to other topics such as the question of the justification of suicide attacks in Palestine or the use of force against the American occupational troops in Iraq, al-Qaraḍāwī has expressly advocated the use of force to benefit the self-defense obligation.[413] This principle of commitment to self-preservation also shines through with respect to the treatment of apostates: Apostasy is not a personal transgression for al-Qaraḍāwī. Rather, it is a crime against the state equivalent to espionage.

By studying al-Qaraḍāwī's writings, it is apparent that he is conversant enough with life in Western society and Western constitutions to be aware of the fact that a general call for the execution of every apostate would bring about a flurry among reporters and Western governments and would be simply impracticable. Nowhere does he express himself concretely on how to proceed and by whom an individual who not only turns secretly and internally from Islam but someone who openly stands up for his new belief or who confesses to be an atheist should be condemned to death and executed.

Should the Islamic community in this case break the laws of the host country, although what is involved here is not a matter of "oppression, military occupation, or ethnic cleansing?"[414] Or would the forced toleration of apostasy possibly have to do with a form of "oppression" of the Muslim minority? Should the minority, under the leadership of Sharia scholars, sit in judgment of the apostate? Who would then carry out the sentence? In light of the uncompromising advocacy of *ḥadd* punishments, it hardly appears conceivable that al-Qaraḍāwī could bring himself to a position where

---

412 Summarized according to Schweizer on al-Qaraḍāwī's justification of the use of violence: Schweizer. *Muslime*, p. 52.

413 As in an interview with the London-based newspaper *Asharq alawsat* dated September 2, 2004, quoted in in: "Reactions to Sheikh Al-Qaradhawi's Fatwa Calling for the Abduction and Killing of American Civilians in Iraq." Memri Special Dispatch No. 794, 6.10.2004. http://www.memri.org/report/en/0/0/0/0/0/0/1231.htm (5.5.2014).

414 The ECFR, which is under al-Qaraḍāwī's chairmanship, mentions these three cases where the use of violence is legitimate, as summarized by Ursi Schweizer from its releases: Schweizer. *Muslime*, p. 43.

he accepts apostasy in Western societies, at least as long as he sees himself obligated to the traditional interpretation of classical Sharia law.

Since the Islamic minority would not be able to find a hearing before a court in a Western democracy, all that remains if one has to unconditionally satisfy Sharia law is either moral (admittedly legally ineffective) condemnation or vigilante justice. Since at the same time al-Qaraḍāwī holds firmly to the unreserved necessity of killing the openly confessing apostate, vigilante justice within the Islamic community would be the logical consequence and more specifically the only viable implementation of al-Qaraḍāwī's so insistently made call. In practice, the threat to converts by family and society is much more intense and more frequent than the threat of legal judgment from the side of the state. Do the opinions of scholars mentioned here produce a public climate promoting vigilante justice or at least one which does not oppose the imposition of such?

With al-Qaraḍāwī's remarks on the topic of apostasy as well as with his other statements, what remains uncertain is how the ideal Islamic community he wishes to produce by means of his directions should actually look. He indeed gives numerous, and not always consistent, detailed answers to the questions of what is "forbidden" and what is "allowed", but he does not build a complete structure of what is to be rejected from Western civilization. He delivers no key as to which principles he follows for what is forbidden and what is allowed. For that reason, he himself remains the indispensable arbiter of what is "forbidden" and "allowed", and his continuing authority remains indispensable.

Additionally, al-Qaraḍāwī does not formulate a vision of the future and have a vision of how the global *umma* should look if it were strengthened internally by fortification and in terms of numbers by means of the spread of Islam. Under whose authority should the *umma* stand? Under the leadership of a caliph or under the leadership of scholars? Does al-Qaraḍāwī hope that in the future Muslim politicians in Western society will be able to partially embed Islamic law? Which laws would non-Muslims enjoy? In that al-Qaraḍāwī still owes answers to these questions, he does not differentiate himself from the majority of Islamist representatives who have up to now drafted numerous visions of the future of a truly Islamic society but also up to now have put forward precious little in concrete form as to the implementation of a truly Islamic society.

How could al-Qaraḍāwī's notion of dealing with apostates be concretely introduced in Western societies? It can be concluded that al-Qaraḍāwī hopes that by pervading Western societies with Islam and by Western societies' recognition of the superiority of Islam, the circumstances will change so that even there the execution of apostates could be recognized as just and necessary. Along with that, the number of Muslims would rise so sharply due to successful *da^{c}wa* work and Islam would be so positively perceived that doubters and converts would not openly confess to their rejection of Islam (this, however, has shown itself even in societies such as Saudi Arabia or Afghanistan to not be the case).

2.4.7. The Question of the Necessity of an Islamic State

In contrast to Mawdūdī und Quṭb, al-Qaraḍāwī appears to nowhere explicitly speak out for the establishment (by force if need be) of an Islamic state as a necessary precondition for a comprehensive implementation of Islam.[415] Ibn Taymīya has also argued that a state is indeed a necessary institution, but Muḥammad never installed an Islamic state. Thus this does not have to be a priority objective.[416] al-Qaraḍāwī frequently quotes the authority Ibn Taymīya, and following Ibn Taymīya, al-Qaraḍāwī nowhere – also in his writings on apostasy – calls for the implementation of a truly Islamic government or the overthrow of an existing regime.[417]

On the contrary, in the course of his position statement on the question of whether it is appropriate to revolt and to against Muslim powers overthrow the government, al-Qaraḍāwī expressly answers this in the negative. Instead, for al-Qaraḍāwī the solution to reshaping society lies in the establishment of an Islamic consciousness, of a reorientation towards Islam in

415 Also according to Gräf in her analysis of al-Qaraḍāwī's *fatwā* "Der politische Islam" (al-islām al-siyāsī): Gräf. *Gelehrte*, p. 15.

416 According to Qamaruddin Khan (sic) summing up the writings of Ibn Taymīya: Qamaruddin Khan. *The Political Thought of Ibn Taymiyah*. Adam Publishers & Distributors: New Delhi, 2009, pp. 54-55.

417 Khaled Abou El Fadl summarizes Ibn Taymīya's attitude on this with the following words: "Ibn Taymiyya . . . advocates disengagement from all violent political conflicts; Muslims should not support rulers and should not support rebels either . . . In summary, Ibn Taymiyya opposes rebellion, not out of an unreserved fidelity to those in power, but out of fidelity to the ideal of order and stability." Abou El Fadl. Rebellion, pp. 275+277-278.

all areas, and of a vitalization of belief so that in this way a truly Islamic society comes into being.[418]

For that reason, what is needed in order to effectively take Islamification forward is above all the *da^cwa*, for which the Muslim society has to be made capable through instruction.[419] Indeed, al-Qaraḍāwī even speaks of a "factory of missionaries" in which he would like to reshape al-Azhar.[420] At this point, one could assume that there is influence by the founder of the Muslim Brotherhood, Ḥasan al-Bannā, who endorsed believing Muslims' co-creation of their surroundings:

> "His aim was . . . to *form* the self and *reform* the community in order to render them useful and effective – for the ideal Islamic order to be established in the here and now."[421]

al-Qaraḍāwī does not hold much of the classic division of scholars in the world into *dār al-islām* and *dār al-ḥarb* t[422] against the backdrop of his assumption that it is not forbidden but rather a mission to live in non-Muslim areas and to proclaim Islam there. Indeed, for him the holistic implementation of the Sharia and the complete permeation of society with the values of Islam are absolutely essential. However, this should not occur with disregard for the valid local laws or through the use of force. In the case of

---

418 This also demonstrates a clear orientation towards Ibn Taymīya: "Ibne Taymiyah (sic) . . . points out that faith, and not the state, is the foremost consideration in religion and that the state is a necessary consequence of the acceptance of faith and not vice versa. Prof. Qamaruddin Khan (sic). *Thought*, p. 55.

419 al-Qaradawi. "Freedom".

420 Yūsuf al-Qaraḍāwī. *risālat al-Azhar*. *al-Qāhira*: Maktabat Wahba, 1984, without an indication of the page, quoted in Jakob Skovgaard-Petersen. "Yūsuf al-Qaraḍāwī and al-Azhar" in: Skovgaard-Petersen; Gräf (eds.) *al-Qaradawi*, p. 49.

421 Krämer supposes the influence of European and American streams of thought from the 19th century at this point, which preached an continuation of development and a higher ethical development through discipline, moderation, control, and self denial, such that for al-Bannā Islam could become "the most potent source of empowerment" for this higher development. Krämer. *Hasan al-Banna*, pp. 108-113 (quote p. 113).

422 As Nina Wiedl also concludes. "Dawa and the Islamist Revival in the West." http://www.hudson.org/content/researchattachments/attachment/1179/20100108_ct9forposting.pdf (5.5.2014).

Quṭb, however, this is a logical conclusion of his understanding of "heathen" society.[423]

According to al-Qaraḍāwī's understanding, the realization of Islam occurs less through the establishment of a state structure[424] than through the implementation of Islam in all matters. As a start, the "confession" (*ᶜaqīda*) of the society has to be Islamic. Thereafter, societies' "mottos" *(šiᶜārāt)*, its "doctrines" (*mafāhīm*) and "thinking (*afkār*), its "customs" (*mašāᶜir*) and "trends" (*nazaᶜāt*), its "morals" (*aḫlāq*) and "upbringing" (*tarbiya*), its "traditions" (*taqālīd*) and "rules of conduct" (*ādāb*), and after that "in a final step" (*aḫīran*) also the "laws" (*qawānīn*) and "religious commands"(*šarīᶜāt*) have to be Islamic.[425]

For that reason, al-Qaraḍāwī calls upon people to even live the "Islamic" life when this state does not (yet) exist. Indeed, the ruler is not uninvolved in the implementation of a comprehensive form of Islam: It is his task to apply Sharia law. Therefore, in the case of apostasy, for instance, it is his task to carry out the punishment. As far as al-Qaraḍāwī is concerned, however, the dispute is in the final event rather in the world of thought and ideas, in the media, and on account of the media's influence in the minds of people instead of in the constitutions of the individual states. It is precisely these thoughts and ideas in the minds of people which he wants to shape with his writings.

With respect to the question of the societal order, as far as al-Qaraḍāwī is concerned it is a matter of an intellectual dispute about which worldview should be propagated via the media. For that reason, he uses the media in order to combat "intellectual apostasy" with correct doctrine and his personal authority. This battle is especially necessary in light of the weakness of the Islamic community.

As far as al-Qaraḍāwī is concerned, the key to overcoming this weakness lies in a comprehensive practice of Islam (he shares this conception

---

[423] Comp., for example, the concept of the heathen society in Sayyid Quṭb in his work: Sayyid Quṭb *maᶜālim fī 'ṭ-ṭarīq*, no location provided, 1964.

[424] In his writing: *min fiqh ad-daula fī 'l-islām*. Dār aš-Šurūq: al-Qāhira, 2009[5], pp. 88f. al-Qaraḍāwī explains that Islam possesses a political character and then elaborates on how an Islamic state should behave towards pluralism, democracy, or the participation of non-Muslims or women in government.

[425] al-Qaraḍāwī. *al-ḥall*, p. 39.

with other Islamist spokesmen, such as Sayyid Quṭb[426]) and in a complete implementation of Sharia law in order to retrieve Islam – rightly understood – from its alleged marginalized position.

As he sees it, for instance, the secularism which has been introduced into Islamic society is guilty for this marginalized position. It has taught what is rejected by al-Qaraḍāwī, separation between religion and the state and between legislation and authority.[427] For that reason, the return to a comprehensive implementation of Islam is the solution for him, not the establishment of an "Islamic" form of government, or of legislation or a state apparatus which carries the label "Islamic" in front of it and, in the process, disregards God's law. The actual problem is, in al-Qaraḍāwī's view, that the Islamic community has not comprehensively implemented Islam and in spite of their belief have borrowed from paganism and materialism.[428]

Therefore, the Islamic state is not a condition for a God-pleasing life for al-Qaraḍāwī, while it is a precondition for Maudūd. As far as al-Qaraḍāwī is concerned, this state grows out of a change in everyday life which has become oriented towards Islam. However, the state does not first have to be installed before people are able to put their belief into practice.

2.4.8. What does "Moderate" Mean in the Question of Apostasy?

When the topic of apostasy comes up, the line between freedom and self-determination has been reached for al-Qaraḍāwī. He indeed does not – and this applies particularly to shorter allusions to this topic – call explicitly for execution with each individual mention of the topic of apostasy. And yet he makes it clear that the apostate has to be punished. From the numerous passages where he labels the application of *ḥudūd* punishments as an indispensable duty, it is clearly recognizable which punishment, according to his understanding, has to be administered in the case of apostasy from Islam. Additionally, at no point does he express himself as adverse to or

426 According to Damir-Geilsdorf. *Herrschaft*, p. 62.
427 al-Qaraḍāwī. *aṣ-ṣaḥwa al-islāmīya*, pp. 88-89.
428 Wardeh. "al-Qaraḍāwī", p. 43.

even only distanced from the death penalty when it comes to the question of apostasy.

In other, shorter statements on this topic, al-Qaraḍāwī limits himself to the emphasis on the duty to perform executions,[429] while in more detailed statements he differentiates more strongly between apostates who internally lean towards another belief and those who openly confess them. Indeed he rejects that Muslims should be suspicious of one another and scrutinize the beliefs of others without cause. However, on the other hand, he leaves no doubt about the idea that when there is a public appearance of apostasy, the person in question has to be executed. Who is it, however, who defines the line between false mistrust, secret doubts, and demonstrated apostasy?

In spite of his being anchored in the theology of *wasaṭīya*, it is difficult to consider al-Qaraḍāwī's conception of the question of apostasy to be moderate. For that reason, his notion counts as a centrist position because al-Qaraḍāwī does not wish to make internally reached convictions regarding the correctness of another religion or no religion, which are never made visible to the outside world, punishable by the death penalty. Certainly, such a concession to a purely hypothetical freedom of thought, which no state and no institution can after all control, is by no means what the 1948 UN Declaration on Human Rights, for example, understands under the rubric of religious freedom.

According to al-Qaraḍāwī's understanding, there is also absolutely no necessity: He is of the firm conviction that Jews and Christians in Islamic societies experience the greatest measure of freedom and tolerance, and enjoy a sure and free existence. Indeed, he is convinced that on the basis of the character of Islamic societies there are no encroachments which can even occur upon them but that Muslim minorities and occasionally even majorities in non-Islamic societies in Asia, Africa, and Europe are consistently oppressed.[430]

---

429 Also not so in his *fatwā* "fī mafhūm al-kufr wa-'l-kāfir wa-mauqif minhū," in which he warns in this issue that no one be prematurely raised up to mufti, judge, or executor, that no one may rashly speak judgment on the killing of a guilty individual and adminster it: al-Qaraḍāwī. *min hady al-islām,* Vol. 4, pp. 790-797, here p. 796.

430 He writes in the way indicated in the final remarks of his work: *ġair al-muslimīn,* p. 86.

For that reason, al-Qaraḍāwī calls for more justice. He proceeds to express his lack of understanding as to why "a Christian or a Jew should get upset about it when a thief has his hand cut off" (*yaqliqu masīḥī au yahūdī min qaṭc yad as-sāriq*)[431] be it a Muslim or a non-Muslim. Likewise, the same applies when it comes to a whipping administered to slanderers, adulterers, or drinkers, whether the punishment is administered to a Muslim or a non-Muslim. For a Muslim this is simply a component of his faith (*dīn*); this is a remark by which al-Qaraḍāwī's argumentation eludes criticism. At this point, there is nothing of true moderation which is recognizable with regard to administering capital punishment.

al-Qaraḍāwī moves in his theology within known Islamist and even Salifist patterns of argumentation, but he also moves within known Islamist and even Salifist patterns of argumentation with regard to his opinion pieces on apostasy. Among these maneuvers are repeatedly postulations about the superiority of Islam and its interests, which are to be categorically protected and have to be considered, along with the public welfare of the Islamic community, above all else. In the final event, as far as al-Qaraḍāwī is concerned, it is a matter of the contrast between Muslims and non-Muslims in all questions of social coexistence and more specifically, the resolution of this opposition through the transformation of the society by the *dacwa*.[432]

It is from this that the evaluation and condemnation of all phenomena are derived, and they either serve or run contrary to the maintenance and protection of the *umma*. In this connection, he postulates a dichotomous division of all worldviews and worldview positions into black and white, right and wrong, acceptable and objectionable.[433] Apostasy, as a significant notion nourished by Western working hypotheses, is for al-Qaraḍāwī one that is foreign to Islam and is an inimical position. Beyond that, it threatens

431 Ibid., p. 87.

432 David H. Warren and Christine Gilmore are pointing to the fact that al-Qaraḍāwī is mentioning a kind of citizenship which advocates equal rights for Muslims and Non-Muslims while referring to his concept of centrism (*wasaṭīya*): David H. Warren; Christine Gilmore. One Nation under God? Yusuf al-Qaradawi's Changing Fiqh of Citizenship, 2013. http://www.academia.edu/5357481/One_nation_under_God_Yusuf_al-Qaradawis_changing_Fiqh_of_citizenship (5.5.2014).

433 This dichotomy is also a mark of the writings of Sayyid Quṭb: Damir-Geilsdorf. *Herrschaft*, p 76.

the continuation of the *umma* and for that reason alone has no right to exist.

2.4.9. Outlook

Generally, for representatives of conservative Islamist discourse, and with respect to al-Qaraḍāwī in particular, it is not a matter of tracking with arguments which can speak in favour of religious freedom and freedom of worldview choice and of balancing their pros and cons. Instead, it is in fact something operating from the position of the scholar, or, as Jacob Høigilt formulates it, from that of the "judge"[434] possessing knowledge and instruction solely for the repulsion of what is "false" and to strengthen and maintain what is "right". In order to set forth "what is right" as an absolute value – with regard to apostasy – a type of fictitious debate is conducted. In the course of such a fictitious debate, arguments from history and their undesirable course of development, for example, are used in order for the deplorableness of a standpoint to be renounced (here: tolerance against other worldviews besides Islam) and the superiority of Islam to protrude all the more clearly.

One example has to do with a fictitious debate when al-Qaraḍāwī presents the cruelties of Christianity, the Reformation, and the Inquisition. He does not quote original European sources but rather Muslim apologists from the 19th and 20th centuries, such as Muḥammad ᶜAbduh and Aḥmad Šalabī. For their part, they mostly did not master any European languages. As a result, they did not use original sources and as a consequence handled history thoroughly imaginatively – for example, as far as the tremendously high numbers of victims of the crimes of the Inquisition are concerned.[435]

It is also a matter of a fictitious debate because no open-ended weighing of facts and arguments takes place in a pro and contra fashion. Rather, the result stands from the outset: The Islamic community has developed the highest degree of tolerance since it has allowed minorities to retain

---

434 Høigilt. *Rhetoric*, p 178.

435 For instance, this applies to al-Qaraḍāwī's work: *ġair al-muslimīn*, pp. 76-85. Additionally, the bibliography is unusable without the complete names of the authors as well as the essentially missing details regarding the place and date of publication of the reference works.

their beliefs which diverge from Islam.[436] All other possible "deficits" with respect to tolerance in countries shaped by Islam do not come into the field of view at all – also not in relation to apostasy and its punishment.

al-Qaraḍāwī finds himself in the middle of a battle. However, as he himself writes, this battle is nowadays not necessarily conducted in a way whereby people lose their lives.[437] Instead, it is a war of paradigms, of spiritual orientations, and worldviews. With al-Qaraḍāwī, what is involved is nothing less than to set down from which sources the young generation will nourish itself (from his point of view it should be the Quran, the *sunna*, and the interpretation offered by authorized scholars) and to which results they should come (namely a comprehensive socio-political Islam).

There was a question posed at the beginning: Does the al-Azhar scholar al-Qaraḍāwī have a practicable way to apply Sharia law by toning it down or by suspending it in Western modernity, or is he calling upon Western modernity to apply Sharia law? Against the backdrop of the analysis of all available texts by al-Qaraḍāwī on apostasy, it has to be answered that he is not prepared to make even slight cuts in the unconditional necessity for *ḥudūd* punishments, neither for the benefit of a Western context nor for reasons of principle relating to religious freedom and religious conversion in any direction.

With this huge chasm between the actual state of affairs and what is actually correct, al-Qaraḍāwī puts his hearers adrift on their own to draw their own conclusions, whereby he highlights the authority of his statements with the claim of divine direction. This tension does not resolve itself: Even when here and there he points out that there is no justification for vigilante justice but rather states that scholars and Sharia judges alone can assess whether one is dealing with a case of apostasy in the first place, he still neither discharges these authorities nor the community from the duty of applying God's law, nor does he in any way diminish the intrinsic justification of using *ḥudūd* punishments.

For al-Qaraḍāwī, as a reformed Salafist scholar, the start into the future can only be successful via a revitalization of the alleged ideal early days of Islam and an imitation of Muḥammad and his companions. When young people are instructed in what Islam actually is, they are put in a situation to shape a better future on the stage of history. In this play upon the stage, al-

---

436 Ibid., pp. 47-48.

437 al-Qaraḍāwī. *fiqh al-ǧihād*, Vol. 1, p. 43.

Qaraḍāwī apportions to himself the scriptwriting, the director's work, and the leading role by occupying all the important topics and areas of expertise with his publications and omnipresent remarks. He thus creates a "Qaraḍāwī'ian" reality which, on the basis of its ideological lack of contact with reality, only has a chance of survival in his own thoughts.

3. Abdullah Saeed's "Progressive" Position: Unlimited Religious Freedom

3.1. Abdullah Saeed: His Life and Work – Essential Principles of His Theology

The Muslim theologian, professor for Arab and Islamic Studies and holder of the Sultan of Oman Chair in Melbourne, Abdullah Saeed (b. 1960), is not only an extremely productive author, internationally sought after conference speaker, and political advisor for the Australian and other governments. Rather, he counts globally among the most dedicated representatives of religious freedom and universal human rights.

3.1.1. An Influential Academic and Advisor

This is not only brought to bear in his numerous publications. His standing is also evident through a number of his contributions to dialog events and human rights forums, such as his contribution as a speaker at the Deutsche Welle's Global Media Forum in Bonn from June 20-22, 2011 carrying the title "Human Rights in a Globalized World – Challenges for the Media."[1] In his lecture entitled "Freedom of Religion and Belief in the Age of Fundamentalism," Abdullah Saeed lamented the inadequate level of religious freedom in quite a number of Muslim majority countries and called for Muslim theologians to focus on the existing problematic topic of apostasy, to discuss it, and to distance oneself from the widespread practice of oppression of apostates seen up to now.

Beyond his numerous publications and addresses at conferences, Abdallah Saeed, who is referred to by the "Center for Research on Social Inclusion" at Macquarie University in Sydney, Australia as a "successful

---

1 Deutsche Welle Global Media Forum: *Human Rights in a Globalized World – Challenges for the Media*, 20.-22.6.2011. http://www.dw.de/saeed-prof-dr-abdullah/a-6503445 (10.6.2014).

Muslim academic,"[2] exercises a significant amount of influence at the academic as well as at the political level. With regard to the former, he has taught without interruption in two departments of The University of Melbourne since 1988. With regard to the latter, he has predominantly, although not exclusively, advised the Australian government and has expressed positions in the media as well as at numerous conferences on topics of public interest, such as with respect to questions surrounding terrorism, *ǧihād*, or Sharia courts in Australia.[3]

While there are a number of publications about the life and work of Abū l-Aᶜlā Maudūdī, who died around 35 years ago, and with respect to Yūsuf al-Qaraḍāwī, who for many decades has been involved indefatigably in publishing, preaching, and lecturing, the situation regarding Abdullah Saeed is essentially different:

Up until now and in all brevity, the person of Abdullah Saeed has been most frequently mentioned where what is involved are critical innovative approaches within Quranic studies by Muslim academics.[4] Besides such

---

2 *Political Participation of Muslims in Australia*, Final Report, June 2010. Centre for Research on Social Inclusion, Macquarie University, Faculty of Arts. http://www.crc.nsw.gov.au/__data/assets/pdf_file/0007/19726/2010_Political_Participation_of_Muslims_in_Australia.pdf (10.6.2014).

3 See in particular the article: Abdullah Saeed. "Reflections on the Establishment of Shari'a Courts in Australia" in: Rex Ahdar; Nicholas Aroney (eds.). *Shari'a in the West*. Oxford University Press: Oxford, 2010, pp. 223-238.

4 According to my research, the most comprehensive appraisal of Abdullah Saeed's academic work, which comprises around 1& pages, is found in Halim Ranes description of Abdullah Saeed's Quranic hermeneutics: Halim Rane. *Reconstructing Jihad amid Competing International Norms*. Palgrave Macmillan: New York, 2009, pp. 165-167; additionally, a Danish essay treats Abdullah Saeed's position on the Quran and exegesis of the Quran: Dorthe Maria Kodal. "Kritisk læsning af Koranen i muslimsk optik" in: *FTI* 1 (2006), pp. 1-12, here p. 7. In her section on the alternative interpretation of the Quran, the author presents Fazlur Rahman, Abū Zaid, and Abdullah Saeed in a nutshell. Furthermore, Abdullah Saeed's Quran hermeneutics is handled in a nutshell by Güney Dogan in his 2008 religious studies master thesis submitted at Linköping University in Sweden: Güney Dogan. "Tafsir, en religionshistorisk studie av koranexegetikens metodologi," pp. 3+15+23+27+34. Besides that, the number of brief references to Abdullah Saeed in academic publications is very manageable and is mostly limited to mere indications to one of his works in a bibliography or refers in the most absolute briefness to Abdullah und Hassan Saeed's work: *Freedom of Religion, Apostasy and Islam*,

brief mention, however, there has been no existing publication up to now which deals with the life and work of Abdallah Saeed, who has been performing intensive teaching, research, and publication activities for over 15 years. Nor is there mention of his function as an academic lecturer, as a political advisor, and as a proponent of dialog and encounter as well as an internationally involved advocate of positive and negative religious freedom and human rights. His academic work has not yet been rudimentarily discussed.[5] This circumstance first and foremost limits my academic discussion in the footnotes on Abdullah Saeed's life and work to the depiction and critical treatment of his theses on the basis of his own publications.

That the life and work of Abdullah Saeed, "one of the key Muslim thinkers in Australia/West"[6], have hardly been received in the Western ac-

Ashgate: Aldershot, 2004: Thus, for example, one has the dissertation submitted in 2005 at the University of Granada by Rafael Ortega Rodrigo. "Evolución del Islam Político en Sudán: De los Hermanos Musulmanes al Congreso Nacional," p. 177.

5 One of the very few brief mentions made of his person and attitude towards apostasy in a German publicatoin is found in Rotraud Wielandt. "Religionsfreiheit und Absolutheitsanspruch der Religion im zeitgenössischen Islam" in: Peter Krämer, inter alia (eds.). *Recht auf Mission contra Religionsfreiheit? Das christliche Europa auf dem Prüfstand*, Lit: Berlin, 2007, pp. 53-82, here pp. 70-71. For an additional brief mention of his person see Roswitha Badry. "Das Instrument der Verketzerung, seine Politisierung und der Bedarf nach einer Neubeurteilung der 'Scharia' und der Apostasiefrage im Islam" in: Thorsten Gerald Schneiders (ed.). *Islamverherrlichung. Wenn die Kritik zum Tabu wird.* VS Verlag: Wiesbaden, 2010, pp. 117-129, here p. 117. Outside of Germany (admittedly with the mistaken spelling "Saheed"), he is mentioned, for example, by Roger Trigg. *Religion in Public Life: Must Faith be Privatized?* Oxford: Oxford University Press, 2007, pp. 37+135. Also the US Study: *No Place to Call Home. Experiences of Apostates from Islam. Failures of the International Community.* Christian Solidarity Worldwide: New Malden, 2008, quotes and mentions Abdullah Saeed a number of times by name (pp. 28, 30, 32-33, 37-39, 120). There is likewise a study published in the USA by Aaron Tyler. *Islam, the West, and Tolerance. Conceiving Coexistence.* Palgrave Macmillan: New York, 2008, p. 33, quotes a small number of lines from Abdullah Saeed on the conflict between concepts of human rights from work: Abdullah Saeed; Hassan Saeed. *Freedom of Religion, Apostasy and Islam.* Ashgate: Aldershot, 2004, p. 13.

6 According to the notion of the Centre for Comparative Constitutional Studies upon the occasion of Melbourne Law School's conference "Law and Religion: Legal Regulation of Religious Groups, Organisations and Communities" on July 15-16,

ademic world is supposedly primarily due to the comparatively short period of time during which he has been publicly active. Additionally, it is perhaps due to the fact that his teaching and research activity is conducted in Melbourne, Australia, and is oriented towards the Pacific region. Admittedly, his publications and position, in particular as far as topics of international importance such as questions of human rights and religious freedom are concerned, have increasingly moved into focus in Europe and the United States. This is, for instance, readable from the continually increasing number of invitations he has received in these parts of the world. At the same time, via the fact that he holds the Sultan of Oman Professor of Arab and Islamic Studies chair, he has remained linked to the Arab world.

On the basis of what is a missing academic treatment of Abdullah Saeed's life and work, the statements made in this chapter (insofar as not otherwise remarked upon in the footnotes) are solely the result of my own study. There are all sorts of printed publications by Abdullah Saeed. Furthermore, there are publications which can be found on the internet, such as books, articles, addresses and reports given at conferences by and about Abdullah Saeed, locatable audio and video material related thereto, materials not made public up to now which were made available to me by Abdullah Saeed from his private collection as well as a recorded interview with him lasting several hours on June 19, 2011 which provided additional insights into the life and work of this author.

In my selection of and commentary on the publications from among Abdullah Saeed's rich publication activity, I have above all concentrated on titles which have a direct connection with the topics of religious freedom, human rights and civil rights and which receive a lot of attention from Abdullah Saeed. In the first instance, I considered publications which clarify the basic position of this author on questions of Islamic law and theology, with a view to being able to classify his observations on the question of apostasy within a larger framework. Since his publications relating to Islamic banking and finance are off the beaten path and contribute hardly anything to the examination of relevant socio-political topic groups, which make up the focus of his research work, I have only marginally considered such publications for the purposes of this study.

2011. http://www.olir.it/areetematiche/news/documents/news_2783_speaker_biographies.pdf (10.6.2014).

Hardly any biographical details on Abdullah Saeed are found in his own publications. For that reason, the information in this section – up to the time period covering the last two decades in which Abdullah Saeed, due to his teaching activity, published large parts of his résumé – is based to a lesser extent on information available on the author's website[7] and to a larger extent on remarks made by Saeed in the interview mentioned.

Abdullah Saeed, who is today "a leading Muslim scholar,"[8] was born on January 28, 1960 in the Maldives on Feydhoo Island in the Seenu Atoll. He is the oldest of five sons and was born into a traditional Muslim family. His father, who recognized the necessity of higher education and the lack of appropriate educational institutions on the Maldives, explored various possibilities for placing his son overseas in an institute of higher learning. In 1976 he was finally successful: Abdullah Saeed traveled at the age of 16 with a travel visa to Pakistan and found accommodation at an *Ahl-i-Ḥadīṯ madrasa* in Faisalabad. He thus found himself in a country where he neither mastered the language nor had relatives nor had a clear conception of the goal to which the traditional education there should lead.[9]

Learning for him there consisted primarily of learning by heart from what were – initially completely incomprehensible – textbooks in Urdu. Subsequent to his finding his bearings in the language and culture to some extent after about one and one half years, he was surprisingly presented with the opportunity to continue his education with a scholarship in Saudi Arabia. He again started to study in a new language and culture. From 1977-1979 he studied in Medina, initially in the Arabic language department within the Institute of Arabic Language of the Islamic University there. In 1982 he received admission to the Secondary Institute in Medina, and received a B.A. in Arabic and Islamic Studies from the Islamic University in Medina in 1986. After a total of nine years, he left Saudi Arabia in the direction of Australia due to the fact that, as he explained in conver-

7 http://www.abdullahsaeed.org/ (10.6.2014).

8 According to the idea in the Online publication "Public Discourse: Ethics, Law and the Common Good" in advance of an article by Abdullah Saeed: "The Quranic Case against Killing Apostates," 25.2. 2011. http://www.thepublicdiscourse.com/2011/02/2716 (10.6.2014).

9 These biographical details are based on statements made by Abdullah Saeed in a personal conversation.

sation, Australia offered the opportunity for an academic career and for simultaneously earning a living.

In 1987 he received an M.A. Preliminary in the area of Middle Eastern Studies, and from 1988-1992 he was tutor and lecturer for Arabic Language and Middle Eastern Studies at the University of Melbourne. In 1992 he received the degree of Doctor of Philosophy in Islamic Studies and in 1994 a Master of Arts in Applied Linguistics. In 2000 he became Associate Professor of Arabic and Islamic Studies in the Department of Applied Linguistics and Language Studies at the University of Melbourne, where in 1993 he had become Coordinator and in 1996 Senior Lecturer. From 1991-1995 he was additionally Coordinator and Consultant at the King Khalid Islamic College of Victoria. In 1999 he was Visiting Scholar at the School of Oriental and African Studies at the University of London.[10] From 1998-2005, Abdullah Saeed was the Deputy Director of The Melbourne Institute of Asian Languages and Societies (MIALS), from 2003-2004 Director of The Melbourne Institute of Asian Languages and Societies, and from 2005-2008 he was named Co-Director of the Centre for Islamic Law and Society (the prior Centre for the Study of Contemporary Islam) at The University of Melbourne.

Abdullah Saeed has held the position of an endowed professorship as the Sultan of Oman professor of Arab and Islamic Studies since 2003. According to an agreement between the Omani Minister of Higher Education, Dr. Yahya Mahfoodh Al Manthri, and the then Vice Chancellor of The University of Melbourne, Professor Alan Gilbert, the Sultan of Oman Chair in Arab and Islamic Studies was endowed with $US 1.5 million by the Sultan of Oman.[11]

From 2007-2010, Abdullah Saeed was Director of the Asia Institute at the University of Melbourne,[12] which comprises six academic programs: Arab and Islamic Studies as well as Indonesian, Chinese, Japanese and Asian Studies. Likewise, he has been Adjunct Professor since 2007 within the Faculty of Law at the University of Melbourne and Director of the

---

10 Comp. the statements on Abdullah Saeeds Webseite: http://www.abdullahsaeed.org/about-me (10.6.2014).

11 According to the official report on the establishment of the chair on the internet page of the University of Melbourne's Asia Institute: http://asiainstitute.unimelb.edu.au/study/islamic_studies/endowed_chair (10.6.2014).

12 http://asiainstitute.unimelb.edu.au/about/ (10.6.2014).

Australian National Centre of Excellence for Islamic Studies, which is supported annually with an amount of AUS $8 million by the Australian government.[13] The Australian National Centre of Excellence for Islamic Studies is a joint initiative of The University of Melbourne, the University of Western Sydney, and Griffith University in Brisbane.

One finds not only Arabic and Islamic Studies, Qur'an and Qur'an Hermeneutics, Islamic Banking and Finance, Muslim Intellectuals and Modernity, Great Empires of Islamic Civilization, Methodologies of Hadith und Methods of Islamic Law among the topics taught in Abdullah Saeed's various study programs. There are also the classes entitled Religious Freedom in Asia, Islam and Human Rights, and Islam and Muslims in Australia.[14]

Saeed has repeatedly attracted funding from the Australian Research Council. Since 1997 he has received numerous grants for research projects. For example, he received grants in 2001-2001 from the "Institute of Ismaili Studies" in Great Britain, in 2002 from the "Treub Society" in The Netherlands as well as in 2005 from the "Department of Immigration, Multicultural and Indigenous Affairs".[15] Since 2002 he has been a member of the "American Academy of Religion", since 2007 an honorary member of the "Australian Institute of International Affairs" as well as being a member of the "Association for Asian Studies" since 2007. In 2009 he was chosen as a Fellow of the "Australian Academy of Humanities".[16]

3.1.2. Publications

Abdullah Saeed has published and released around 20 independent works – among them a two volume Arabic grammar of modern standard Arabic.

---

13 At least according to the press report by Peter Day. "Islam in Australia," 26.1.2009. http:www.hudson-ny.org/246/islam-in-australia (10.6.2014).

14 According to Abdullah Saeed's notion on the webpage of the Majlis Ugama Islam Singapura (Islamic Religious Council of Singapore): http://www.muis.gov.sg/cms/Research/spResources_subpg.aspx?id=9868 (7.7.2011).

15 Comp. the comprehensive list of his research projects at http://www.linkroad.net/wp-content/uploads/2008/07/cv-saeed.pdf (10.6.2014). Abdullah Saeed expresses himself in the following manner: "I have played the lead role in attracting several million dollars for Islamic Studies at the University of Melbourne over the last ten years."

16 Comp. the details on the webpage ibid.

He has written around 50 articles and individual contributions, has held around numerous conference addresses and lectures, has given numerous interviews with the press and recently has begun with the release of videos on the internet. A number of addresses in the recent past as well as some of his videos on the internet are concerned with the questions of religious freedom and human rights, but they also relate to some very controversial topics such as homosexuality and apostasy, women's rights, and *ǧihād*. A number of his articles and books have been translated into Italian,[17] Portuguese,[18] and Indonesian.[19] Up to now, the author is not aware of any Arabic translations of his works.

The topics of his books and essays, which according to his own statements are equally directed at Muslims as well as non-Muslims, are concentrated on the relationship of Muslims to Western society and, more specifically, to Jews and Christians and their revelation, on the subject areas of the Quran, Quranic exegesis and tradition, *iǧtihād* (independent reasoning), the current role of the *ᶜulamā'* (scholars of Islam) and the Islamic educational system, concepts of political rule, human rights, religious freedom and apostasy, Islam in Australia and Indonesia, *ǧihād*, martyrdom, the question of the capacity for peace making within Islam, and the introduction of various Muslim reformers. Furthermore, his works discuss Islamic banking and finance, on which topic Abdullah Saeed has alone released multiple publications.[20] Additionally, Abdullah Saeed mentions about 25 radio, television, and print media interviews on his website.[21] A number of additional works have been released by Abdullah Saeed, such as a com-

---

17 Abdullah Saeed. "Tendenze fondamentali dell'odierna esegesi coranica e idee emergenti per un approccio contestuale all Corano" in: *Le religioni e il mondo moderno III (Islam)*. Giulio Einaudi: Torino, 2009, pp. 295-315.

18 Abdullah Saeed. *Introdução ao Pensamento Islãmico*. O Saber da Filosofia: Porto, 2010.

19 Abdullah Saeed. *Menyoal Bank Syariah: Kritik atas Interpretasi Bunga Bank Kaum Neo-Revivalis*. Jakarta: Paramadina, 2004.

20 In addition to the numerous essays and encyclopaedia articles which Abdullah Saeed published on this subject matter, among others, for EI, die EQ, and the EWIC, is his most significant treatment in the form of a comprehensive study: Abdullah Saeed. *Islamic Banking and Interest. A Study of the Prohibition of Riba and its Contemporary Interpretation*. E. J. Brill: Leiden, 1996.

21 See http://www.abdullahsaeed.org/about-me (10.6.2014) und http://www.linkroad.net/wp-content/uploads/2008/07/cv-saeed.pdf (10.6.2014).

prehensive four-volume, critically progressive collection of essays on the topics of the state, politics, and Islam in history and in the present day under the title *Islamic Political Thought and Governance.*[22] Furthermore, Abdullah Saeed belongs to a group of editors of various peer reviewed journals[23] which appear on three continents.

Due to their foundational treatment of individual questions such as the topic of *ǧihād*,[24] the various currents in Islam,[25] and the development of the Quran and its hermeneutic,[26] a part of Abdullah Saeed's publications fulfill the wish for basic knowledge and clarification and are in the first instance directed at Australian society. A number of publications are primarily directed at students of Islamic studies.[27]

In the process, there is no subject matter solely serving the inner-Islamic discussion or more specifically one's own existing standpoint, such as in the case of al-Qaraḍāwī with his document on the topic of *tauḥīd.*[28] This might be of interest to a very limited circle of Muslim theologians or theology students and is probably only able to a few external effects. Up to now, Abdullah Saeed has exclusively published on topics which address the Islamic community's dealings with the outside world (for instance his works on finance and banking), on topics which focus on the coexistence of Muslims and non-Muslims (such as his treatise on the relationship to Jews and Christians and, respectively, Western society) or on topics which

---

22 Abdullah Saeed (ed.). *Islamic Political Thought and Governance. Critical Concepts in Political Science.* 4 Vols., Abingdon: Routledge, 2011.

23 For instance according to the *Journal of Qur'anic Studies*, UK, the *Journal of Islamic Studies*, Pakistan, the *Journal of Arabic, Islamic and Middle Eastern Studies*, Australia und the *Jurnal Studi Qur'an*, Indonesia. http://www.linkroad.net/wp-content/uploads/2008/07/cv-saeed.pdf (10.6.2014).

24 Abdullah Saeed. "Jihad and Violence: Changing Understandings of Jihad among Muslims" in: Tony Coady; Michael O'Keefe (ed.). *Terrorism and Justice. Moral Argument in a Threatened World.* Melbourne University Press: Carlton South, 2002, pp. 72-86.

25 Abdullah Saeed. "Trends in Contemporary Islam: A Preliminary Attempt at a Classification" in: *MW* 97 (2007), pp. 395-404.

26 Thus for instance the essay: Abdullah Saeed. "Reading the Quran" in: Amyn B. Sajoo (ed.). *A Companion to the Muslim World.* I. B. Tauris Publishers: London, 2009, pp. 55-85.

27 According to the "Introduction,", p. vii, of the foundational introduction: Abdullah Saeed. *Islamic Thought. An Introduction.* Routledge: Abingdon, 2006.

28 See for instance his work: al-Qaraḍāwī. *ḥaqīqat.*

take up questions non-Muslims have of Muslims (such as, in particular, the question of the assessment of September 11, 2001 and the topic of terrorism in general).

From the beginning, the balance in Abdullah Saeed's publications, as regards style and content, is striking to the reader. While publications for an apologist such as al-Qaraḍāwī constantly have to do with presenting one's own point of view as the sole justified viewpoint without mentioning any other positions at all or not dealing with them on an equal footing, Abdullah Saeed, in most of his publications, presents several basic approaches and mentions the arguments for and against them. He expresses his own opinions, but he does not do so without referring to the spectrum of differing opinions.[29]

3.1.3. Abdullah Saeed's Position within Islamic Theology

Notwithstanding his very traditional religious education in Pakistan and Saudi Arabia, Abdullah Saeed is regarded as an advocate of comprehensive religious freedom and a champion of human rights and equal rights irrespective of religion, gender, or nationality. He is also regarded as a Muslim scholar who decidedly rejects the traditional Sharia position with respect to the judgment of apostasy but who would not characterize himself as either a "liberal" or as "secularized."

Abdullah Saeed's own confession of belief in Islam as well as his conviction that the Quran is God's revelation is expressed many times in his publications.[30] His criticism is primarily directed against a firmly cemented interpretation of the Quran and tradition from the early days of Islam by what was established theology up to the 10th century A.D. He is also critical of timelessly valid socio-political instructions derived from the aforementioned as well as being against the unquestioning and undeviating interpretations of – in his view – disputed or even unreliable texts of tradition.

---

29 A particularly good example for this carefully considered manner of argumentation is the mentioning of several arguments for and against the establishment of so-called Sharia courts in Australia and other countries: Abdullah Saeed. "Reflections on the Establishment of Shari'a Courts in Australia" in: Rex Ahdar; Nicholas Aroney (ed.). *Shari'a in the West*. Oxford University Press: Oxford, 2010, pp. 223-238.

30 Also according to his position in his work: Saeed. *Thought*, p. 17.

From Abdullah Saeed's viewpoint, however, not only tradition but also the Quran have to at least in part be opened to contemporary interpretation. In his essay "Rethinking 'Revelation' as a Precondition for Reinterpreting the Qur'an: A Qur'anic Perspective," Abdullah Saeed devotes himself to this line of questioning. Initially, he introduces the approach of the Anglican priest Kenneth Cragg, who pleads for a stronger inclusion of the historicity of revelation as well as consideration of Muḥammad's role as a fallible individual with limited knowledge in order to be able to open new space for a revised interpretation of the Quran.[31] Even if one were to take Muḥammad more strongly into focus as a human medium of revelation, as Saeed summarizes Cragg's view, this would in the end lead to benefit the standing of the Quran, for: "One would be able to avoid attributing any 'mistakes,', 'inaccuracies' or 'outdated views' to God." Would perhaps a "demythologizing" of the text according to the standards of Rudolf Bultmann be thereby conceivable?[32]

As is the case with all of his publications, Abdullah Saeed retains a sense of proportion as a believer and does not throw his basic understanding of the Quran as God's word into the ring. He flirts neither with an atheistic approach nor with a radical application of the historical-critical method in order to see an uninhibited enlightenment of Islam and demythologization of its sources where there are no taboos, nor does he take the standpoint of the agnostic or of the convinced secularist. In the choice of method, he is not dissimilar to al-Qaraḍāwī. Saeed seeks a middle ground and moderation – which he, however, does not see in a temporary postponement of elements of the Sharia which are not able to be executed or in certain exceptions for Muslims in the diaspora. Rather, he sees a compromise coming out of reconsideration and updating as well as coming out of tradition and textual preservation. This compromise he sees leads neither to ossification and an imitation of a 7th century society nor to giving up basic Islamic theological positions.

Thus he warns in his essay "Rethinking 'Revelation' as a Precondition for Reinterpreting the Qur'an: A Qur'anic Perspective" against overshooting the goal when considering the human component in the development

---

[31] Abdullah Saeed. "Rethinking 'Revelation' as a Precondition for Reinterpreting the Qur'an: A Qur'anic Perspective" in: *JQS* 1/1 (1999), pp. 93-114, here p. 93.

[32] Ibid., p. 94.

of the text of the Quran and placing revelation itself into question.[33] Indeed, with respect to ᶜUmar's codified text of the Quran, he states assuredly: "Its authenticity and reliability cannot be seriously questioned."[34]

Always gauging the extremes, Abdullah Saeed continues to discuss the topic in more detail. On the one hand, he emphasizes the ties between divine and human language: "God's speech is expressed in human form."[35] The human component in it does not exclude that it is a matter of revelation. Although God communicates in a language, which accommodates Muḥammad in the first place, there can be no doubt for him about its divine character. On the other hand, as Saeed emphasizes, Muḥammad was only a recipient of divine revelation. He was not, however, able to change it independently, so that it is not a human assemblage.[36]

At this point Saeed absolutely advocates shedding some light on the historical circumstances surrounding the reception of revelation. He also advocates a possible framework for what is, according to his opinion, the interpretation and application of the message given the changing circumstances in the case of Muḥammad and the first generations of Muslims. He seeks to do so without giving up on the text itself. As far as Abdullah Saeed is concerned, with the premise of its divine authorship, the text is set free for a reinterpretation without its development and inspiration being called into question per se.[37]

Saeed's basic orientation becomes clear in light of his statements on the role of women in modern society, when he defends the idea that the duty to support, to provide, and to prioritize men, which many theologians extract from Sura 4:34,[38] while reflecting an appropriate notion and practice for that former time, should be reconsidered on the basis of present day cultural circumstances.[39]

33 Ibid., p. 95.

34 Ibid., p. 106.

35 Ibid., p. 102.

36 Ibid., p. 111.

37 Ibid., p. 110.

38 There it is stated: "ar-riǧālu qawwāmūna ᶜalā n-nisā": "Men stand above women" (Rudi Paret. Der Koran. Kohlhammer: Stuttgart, 1980²) or "Men are responsible for women" (Harmut Bobzin. Der Koran: Aus dem Arabischen neu übertragen. C. H. Beck: Munich, 2010).

39 "Hence, the instructional teaching, 'men are maintainers of women,' reflects an idea and practice that was appropriate at the time . . . It is possible to conclude that

These directions from Sura 4:34 fall into the rubric of "instructional teachings" for Abdullah Saeed, dealing with certain questions arising in former times but which cannot or should not necessarily be retained. Which of these "ethico-legal teachings" are of universal significance is, according to Saeed, a highly complex question. He himself does not answer the question conclusively in any of his works.[40] This example likewise demonstrates what a personal conversation with Abdullah Saeed made clear, which is that even statements in the Quran are in the final event not untouchable. This is the case insofar as such statements are no longer realizable in our present day and, respectively, are not held to be universally valid. In the process, he does not turn against the text of the Quran per se or against its validity at the time of its revelation. Rather, in the case of individual topics, he assumes their temporally limited validity.

In one of his most important works with the title *Interpreting the Qur'ān. Towards a Contemporary Approach*,[41] Abdullah Saeed does not make any argument against the text of the Quran and its credibility or its reliable transmission per se. However, with respect to the topics of women's rights and human rights, the form of the state, the relationships of Muslims and non-Muslims as well as with respect to the question of peace and *ǧihād*, he expressly urges for a new interpretation of the text of the Quran adapted for the age in which we find ourselves.[42]

In the process, in his entire works he repeatedly speaks out against an undeviating interpretation of the Quran by literalists who reduce all exegesis to a sole allowed interpretation. On the contrary, it is Abdullah Saeed's goal to free the timeless, compulsory ethical commands of the Quran from the baggage of history and its chains of historically set exegesis, to consider social change, and thus to also preserve the message of the Quran in its relevance for the 21st century. His study of the Quran, according to Saeed, is

---

the teaching may be culturally specific and that its applicability should be considered in light of newly emerging circumstances." Abdullah Saeed. *The Qur'an. An Introduction*. Routledge: Abingdon, 2008, p. 170.

40 See for instance ibid., p. 173.

41 Abdullah Saeed. *Interpreting the Qur'ān. Towards a Contemporary Approach*. Routledge: Abingdon, 2006.

42 Ibid., p. 149. All of these are topics on which Abdullah Saeed has commented in his numerous publications and are topics where he has called for a new evaluation of classical theology's understanding.

> ". . . rather . . . an argument for releasing the ethico-legal verses from the legalistic-literalistic approach . . . the book is, first and foremost, a justification for using a different approach to the interpretation of the ethico-legal texts."[43]

This viable path between the foundational acknowledgement of God's revelation of the Quran, on the one hand, and the release from what is in his view an unjustified captivity to the past is for Abdullah Saeed a matter primarily to be achieved through being released from the claim of inscrutable tradition. This is due to a situation where ". . . the hadith would restrict the freedom of Muslim thinkers and scholars to a crippling extent in many areas," especially since tradition frequently contradicts itself. However, it is not only tradition but also the text of the Quran which not only has one single meaning. It can be newly interpreted by each generation, depending on the circumstances, with regards to the implementation of its ethical duties.[44]

Thus, for Abdullah Saeed the appropriate handling of the Quran does not lie in a sweeping acceptance derived from past exegesis dating from the early days of Islam. Rather, it above all lies in the production of a relationship between the text and the hearer, for in such manner the changing meaning of the text, depending on the epoch, is taken into account and the Quran is provided with practical relevance:[45] "The fundamental problem for us remains relating a sacred text from a distant 14 centuries ago to a world that has changed dramatically."[46]

Accordingly, Saeed sees it as problematic that a text can simply be read and its meaning undeviatingly set on the basis of linguistic or historical references to the early days of Islam without any additional reflection. This is a simplistic and reductionistic understanding of the "textualists," who hold firmly to a single, allegedly objective and literalistic meaning of the text of the Quran but in the process do not do justice to the text.[47]

---

43 Abdllah Saeed. *Interpreting the Qur'ān. Towards a Contemporary Approach.* Routledge: Abingdon, 2006, p. 1.

44 Ibid., pp. 19-20.

45 Ibid., pp. 93-94.

46 Ibid., p. 147.

47 Ibid., pp. 100-101+103.

By way of contrast, the "contextualists" are clear on the idea that there is not one true, objective exegesis of the text of the Quran, indeed, that the meaning of a verse in the Quran or text from tradition is first of all "indeterminate."[48] To start with, the background of the text and the historical development of the Quran has to be taken into account for each individual verse in order to be able to determine its meaning. As Abdullah Saeed emphasizes in several of his publications as well as in personal conversation, the core of Islam – as with all other religions – involves going beyond all texts, commands, and theologies to the personal relationship God has to humankind.[49]

As far as the ethical aspects of the Quran are concerned, according to Saeed there are various levels of values which exist: For a start, there are "obligatory values" which are undisputed and belong to the foundations of Islam with respect to belief and life and with respect to commands and prohibitions. The following layer comprises the "fundamental values," which define the protection of life, the family, and possessions. Among them are also religious freedom and additional civil rights and liberties, such as the freedom of speech or protection against torture, inhumane treatment, and arbitrary imprisonment.

What follows are additional subordinate levels of values which have varying degrees of importance according to how prominent a role they play as they appear within the Quran. The hierarchy of these value levels has to be kept in mind, according to Saeed, in order to not come to false conclusions and, for example, to falsely gauge the summons to kill an idolater higher than the value of protecting life and allowing religious freedom.[50]

With this essential approach to the text of the Quran and tradition, Abdullah Saeed, as he also confirms in personal conversations, counts himself among those scholars of the Quran who are called "progressive" or "New

---

48 ". . . the meaning of a particular Qur'anic verse (or hadith) is, to a large degree, indeterminate. Meaning, in this sense, is said to evolve over time, and is dependent upon the socio-historical, cultural and linguistic context of the text." Abdullah Saeed. The Qur'an. An Introduction. Routledge: Abingdon, 2008, p. 221.

49 "The Qur'an . . . emphasizes God's relationship to His creation, and all its teachings, legal or otherwise, must be viewed from the perspective of this relationship." Ibid., p. 171; see also p. 173.

50 Saeed. *Interpreting the Qur'ān*, pp. 133+143.

Ijtihadis."[51] For Saeed, this movement consists of a heterogeneous mixture of "Muslim modernists, liberals, feminists, and even reform-minded traditionalists."[52] What they have in common is a conception of the absolute necessity of reform in the traditional interpretation of Islamic law, of an *iǧtihād*,[53] which has to be shaped according to the demands of modernity. What is involved along with this is a critical distancing from dogmatism and a close bond with a certain school of legal thought as well as a strong commitment to gender equality and social justice, for human rights and the formation of peaceful relationships with non-Muslims.[54] Abdullah Saeed summarizes in the following manner:

"Progressive ijtihadis are both thinkers and activists . . . neither . . . ideologues nor . . . revolutionaries but . . . social critics."[55] The deal critically with their own tradition, rise up against terror and fanaticism and are involved in their society in order to practice justice and loving kindness there. They are politically engaged, substantiating a tradition of Islam which seeks to be able to be reconciled with the political, economic, social, technological, and philosophical convulsions in Western societies. For that reason, they welcome democracy and every type of civil right and liberty, gender equality, secular legislation, and equality before the law: "It is a product of a fusion of Islam with the Western environment, and Western secular liberal democratic values."[56] With respect to the meaning of this group of "New Ijtihadis" for the remaining Muslim community, Abdullah Saeed expresses the hope that they will increasingly take on the leadership in Western countries and soon exercise significant influence on the entire community of Muslims around the world.[57]

It is not the message of Islam per se, nor is it the revelation of the Quran or the definition of humanity as creatures of God which is thus scrutinized by Saeed. Rather, it is above all the domination of early Islamic scholars and their tradition of exegesis. It is not the claim of truth of

---

51 Saeed. *Thought*, p. 150.

52 Ibid.

53 Comp., for example, the early article by Abdullah Saeed: "Ijtihad and Innovation in neo-Modernist Islamic Thought in Indonesia" in: *ICMR* 8 (1997), pp. 279-295.

54 See the characterization in: Saeed. *Thought*, pp. 150-151.

55 Ibid., p. 151.

56 Ibid., p. 153.

57 Abdullah Saeed speaks here about "a significant impact:" Ibid., p. 153.

Quranic revelation which Saeed wishes to abolish, but rather the constrictions of their interpretation as the one "true" exegesis[58] and with it the absolutization of a single point of view which draws its justification solely from a normative past.[59]

3.1.4. Target Audience and Potential for Reception

In addition to his mother tongue, Dhivehi Abdullah Saeed also has a very good command of Urdu. Furthermore, he speaks and writes fluent Arabic due to the many years he spent in Saudi Arabia[60] and due to the fact that he primarily gave Arab language course instruction in the early years of his teaching activity in Melbourne. However, up to now he has never submitted any of his publications in Arabic. This is in spite of the fact that he has also published a multi-volume Arabic language textbook.[61] This alone demonstrates the aim of his publishing activity, which certainly is tied to

---

58 As a result, with reference to a justification of human rights based on Islamic tradition, for example, Abdullah Saeed advocates the inclusion of historical circumstances of the emergence of Islam in order to be able to adequately assess the conclusions of early Islamic legal experts: "This process is indeed difficult and it denies the possibility of one single 'Islamic view.'" Abdullah Saeed. "Creating a Culture of Human Rights from a Muslim Perspective" in: Swee-Hin Toh; Virginia F. Cawagas (eds.). *Proceedings of the International Symposium Cultivating Wisdom, Harvesting Peace. Education for a Culture of Peace through Values, Virtues, and Spirituality of Diverse Cultures, Faiths, and Civilizations*. Multi-Faith Centre, Griffith University: Brisbane, 2006, pp. 123-127, here p. 125.

59 For example, he writes: ". . . current movements in Islamic political thought are very much connected to the past." Abdullah Saeed. Introduction. "The Context of the Development of Islamic Political Thought" in: Abdullah Saeed. (ed.). *Islamic Political Thought and Governance. Critical Concepts in Political Science*. Vol. 1. *Roots of Islamic Political Thought: Key Trends, Basic Doctrines and Developments*. Routledge: London, 2011, pp. 1-12, here p. 1.

60 On his website http://www.abdullahsaeed.org/ he labels his Arabic language skills as "native or near native competency." Besides the mentioned languages, he also has a command of the basics of Indonesian.

61 In a personal conversation, Abdullah Saeed mentioned, however, that a number of his books were being translated into Arabic and placed on the internet. As far as Indonesian is concerned, he supposes that a number of his books had been published as pirated editions. However, he does not have any precise information. As far as the near future is concerned, he anticipates the official translation of a number of his titles into Indonesian and other languages.

the present geographical focus of his life and his many years of teaching in Melbourne. His aim is neither toward the traditional world of Islamic scholarship nor is it to maintain an inner-Islamic discourse. Rather, his aim is equally directed at Muslims and non-Muslims in English, the lingua franca.[62]

That the reception of his positions is most extensively and most comprehensively possible in English not only demonstrates the degree of globalization and fragmentation of authorities and scholars in the contest for followers within the global *umma*. Rather, since a large portion of Saeed's Asian as well as international audience and followers would surely not be able to be reached with statements and publications in Arabic, it also makes it clear which niches are filled by individual scholars within the Muslim community.

Abdullah Saeed, like Yūsuf al-Qaraḍāwī, does not have any political, religious, or (semi-) governmental apparatus at his disposal to serve for the backup and dissemination of his theological notions, such as would be the case with al-Azhar. For that reason, he has to exclusively solicit through efforts to persuade listeners in this global competition for interpretation and followers and seek to claim a certain spectrum of the *umma*. There are others, who due to their lack of access or language knowledge, are unable to advance. On the other hand, by exclusively publishing in English he has up to now avoided a direct confrontation with the classic Islamic world of scholarship.

In light of the style the author has chosen as well as the selection of topics with which Abdullah Saeed has concerned himself, what is reflected in his use of English becomes even clearer: It is observable that a number of Saeed's publications are expressly promoting appreciation of Muslims,

62 Nevertheless, Abdullah Saeed has not been spared completely from harsh criticism for his position and argumentation. Compare, for example, the review of one of his major works: Abdullah Saeed; Hassan Saeed. *Freedom of Religion, Apostasy and Islam*. Ashgate: Aldershot, 2004, by Muddathir ᶜAbd ar-Rahim. Abdullah Saeed and Hassan Saeed. Freedom of Religion, Apostasy and Islam" in: *IJMES* 37 (2005), pp. 614-615. Muddathir ᶜAbd ar-Rahim charges the authors with intellectual dishonesty, a lack of logic, arbitrariness as far as the selection of facts is concerned, exaggeration and ridiculing his opponents as well as abstruseness and flabbiness in his argumentation.

in particular given the echo of the events of September 11, 2001.[63] In other publications, the author appears rather to want to give members of the Muslim community advice and justification for affirming their permanent stay in Western society and participation in political life there.

While Abdullah Saeed might not have the Muslim scholar precisely in mind, al-Qaraḍāwī speaks and writes in the very traditional style of a conventional scholar and in the process reverts to content derived from his classical theological education – when for instance he utilizes specialist terminology or, without referring more specifically to the information about a person and work, mentions accepted sources of tradition in flowing text.[64] With that said, al-Qaraḍāwī directs himself either at key individuals who are theologically schooled within the Islamic community or at individual believers looking for instruction from a scholar.

Key persons as well as individuals are urged by al-Qaraḍāwī to change their behavior or more specifically to permanently apply the commandments of the Quran and *sunna*, in particular in the diaspora. Even given the fact of Arabic, which al-Qaraḍāwī uses universally due to a lack of alternative language abilities, insofar as his addressees are concerned – apart from the texts translated into English which are found on his website – one consistently thinks of a Muslim, Arabic speaking educated audience which at least has to bring along a certain prior knowledge in order to understand his rather theologically oriented publications in light of the specialist terminology and references to early Islamic authorities.

Abdullah Saeed, on the other hand, does not address himself exclusively to a Muslim audience. For that reason, as far as it is possible in his remarks about Islam, he combines academic neutrality with an explanation of theologically mainstream positions politically compatible with Western

---

63 A number of publications expressly mention this as the reason for writing and were suggested to Abdullah Saeed after the events of September 11, 2001, for instance his explanation of the foundations of Islam with a focus on Australia written for a broader audience: Abdullah Saeed. *Islam in Australia*. Allen & Unwin: Crows Nest, 2003, p. v.

64 For example, he thus mentions Ibn Kaṯīr and Ibn ᶜAbbās without any further explanation on p. 21 of his major work on apostasy: al-Qaraḍāwī. *ǧarīmat ar-ridda*.

societies.[65] In so doing, he also turns his attention to readers who up until now have acquired little knowledge about the topic of Islam.[66]

A great number of his articles have been expressly drafted to explain the history of Islam in Australia to non-Muslims,[67] to explain the basics of Islam or, more specifically, the character and orientation of Islamic community and thereby to build a bridge of understanding between the non-Muslim (predominantly: Australian) society and the Muslim minority there. As a general rule, Saeed does not use technical terms without explanation, and he explains notions found only within the inner-Islamic discussion. His statements are based on a Western line of reasoning and thus open a forum for discussion for Muslims as well as non-Muslims. In contrast to al-Qaraḍāwī's absolutely brief and, when viewed from an academic standpoint, incompletely noted references, Saeed's references to additional literature are correctly quoted, are available in customary libraries, and are thereby accessible for scientific review.

3.2. Abdullah Saeed's Significance

Abdullah Saeed's significance lies in his teaching activity, his publications, which have appeared under renowned publishing houses on three continents, Europe, Asia, and Australia, in his presence at numerous international conferences, his use of the media as well as his activity as a political and social advisor. Nowadays he counts as one of the most important

---

65 For example, comp. his essay: Abdullah Saeed. "Contextualizing" in: Andrew Rippin (ed.). *The Blackwell Commpanion to the Qur'ān*. Wiley-Blackwell: Chichester, 2009, pp. 36-50, here p 49.

66 For example, he notes this in the introduction to his generally understandable contribution: Abdullah Saeed. *Islam in Australia*. Allen & Unwin: Crows Nest, 2003, pp. vi-vii: "This book is intended for a general readership and attempts to give the reader a general understanding of Islam and the Muslim community life in Australia . . . This book attempts to avoid jargon, footnotes and references . . . its interest is in providing an overview."

67 For example, comp. the comments on the historical establishment of the Muslim community in Australia in Anthony Johns; Abdullah Saeed. "Muslims in Australia: The Building of a Community" in: Yvonne Yazbeck Haddad; Jane I. Smith (eds.). *Muslim Minorities in the West, Visible and Invisible*. Altamira Press: Walnut Creek, 2002, pp. 195-216, here pp. 197ff.

scholars on the topic of Islam in Australia.[68] It almost appears as if there is no foundational study on this topic on the fifth continent for which he is not responsible or has edited or in which he is not at least involved as an advisor.[69]

His national as well as international scope of activity as an academic and an intellectual, as a cultural intermediary and bridge builder, as an advocate of dialog and understanding, who not least embodies these characteristics through his own history of immigration, opens up a position as a prominent advocate of equality and peaceful coexistence between different nations, religions, and worldviews in the 21st century's multi-religious society.

3.2.1. Offices and Committees

Abdullah Saeed has been a member of the "UNESCO Commission of Australia" of the "Department of Foreign Affairs and Trade" as well as an examiner for "Texts and Traditions" of the "Victorian Curriculum and Assessment Authority", which reports to the Education Minister in the state of Victoria (VCAA) on the development, assessment, and standardization of curricula for high school students. At present he is, among others, a member of the "Academic Advisory Committee" of the "Centre for Cultural Materials Conservation", on the "Advisory Board" of the "Islamic

[68] For example, Peter Day, a former US correspondent for arguably the most important national newspaper, *The Australian*, who is critically inclined towards Abdullah Saeed, passes judgment in the following manner: "... perhaps the most high-profile Islamic Studies scholar in Australia." Day. Islam.

[69] Thus Abdullah Saeed appears as a member of the Board of Advisors in the disclosure of the "M(elbourne) U(niversity) P(ublishing) Studies Series," which published its first anthology: Samina Yasmeen (ed.). *Muslims in Australia. The Dynamics of Exclusion and Inclusion*. Melbourne University Press: Carlton, 2010. The *MUP Islamic Studies Series* is published by Saeed's colleague, Shahram Akbarzadeh, who is the Deputy Director of the National Centre of Excellence for Islamic Studies Australia at the University of Melbourne in cooperation with Griffith University and the University of Western Sidney. https://www.mup.com.au/page/Islamic_Studies_Series (10.6.2014). Comp. also the "Australia" entry in the third edition of the *Encyclopaedia of Islam* under Abdullah Saeed's authorship: Abdullah Saeed. "Australia" in: In: EI/3. http://referenceworks.brillonline.com/entries/encyclopaedia-of-islam-3/australia-COM_0023?s.num=172~s.start=160 (10.6.2014).

Women's Welfare Council" in Victoria, a member of the "Confucius Institute Executive Board" at the University of Melbourne, a member of the "Advisory Board" of the "Centre for Dialogue" at the LaTrobe University in Victoria as well as a "Research Associate" for the "Social Justice Initiative" on the Faculty of Law of the University of Melbourne.[70]

Abdullah Saeed plays a part in various dialog initiatives,[71] maintains contacts in the interreligious field, for instance on the Jewish Council of South Australia and, more specifically, is frequently invited to lectures as part of inter-religious activities: For example, in 2007 he held a lecture for the Dunedin Abrahamic Interfaith Group. The Dunedin Abrahamic Interfaith Group, together with the Otago University Chaplaincy, had invited him to speak at their Annual Peace Lecture on September 5, 2007. In his lecture he critically illuminated the sense of superiority and advocacy of violence by many an Islamic group and called for fresh thinking regarding their sources as well as a reappraisal of what is shared among religions.[72]

He likewise attends conferences which deal with the role of women and, more specifically, gender equality[73] and which propagate a progressive Islam having the following goals:

> "Justice, gender-equality, reclaiming Islam as a civilizational project, critical engagement with the Islamic tradition, and pluralism and inter-faith dialogue."[74]

---

70 Comp. the list of additional offices in his comprehensive résumé at: http://www.linkroad.net/wp-content/uploads/2008/07/cv-saeed.pdf (10.6.2014).

71 For example, he conducted a lecture at the "7th International Dialogue Australia Network Conference: Teaching the Abrahamic Religions: Christianity in Dialogue with Judaism and Islam" from April 15-17, 2009 in Canberra under the heading "The Role of the Quran in Contemporary Islam." http://www.australiansuficentre.org/talks-uni-school.htm (10.6.2014).

72 Abdullah Saeed lectured on the topic "Towards a more Inclusive View of the Religious 'Other'. A Muslim Perspective"; his lecture was at the same time the "Dunedin Abrahamic Interfaith Group and Otago University Chaplaincy 2007 Annual Peace Lecture," 5.9.2007. http://www.dunedininterfaith.net.nz/lecture07.php (10.6.2014).

73 Abdullah Saeed thus lectured at the "Global Meeting for Equality and Justice in the Muslim Family," a conference held by the Sisters of Islam from February 13-17, 2009 in Kuala Lumpur on the topic "Interpreting the Qur'an: Towards a contemporary approach." http://www.musawah.org/sites/default/files/Summary-Proceedings-EN.pdf (10.6.2014).

3.2.2. Advisory Activities for the Australian Government

Beyond his extensive publication, speaking, and teaching activities, Abdullah Saeed also exercises direct social and political influence through his public statements in favour of human rights and religious freedom as well as his advisory activities.[75] His advisory activities predominantly, but not exclusively, extend to the Australian government.[76]

Abdullah Saeed has conducted various projects either on behalf of, in cooperation with, or with the funding of the Australian government. For example, he was involved in advanced training on the topic of Islam for the Australian police authorities in a number of cities in Australia, was called in by the Assessment Authority of the "Department of Education" in the state of Victoria for the review of Arabic language exams as well as for the conception of teaching content on the topic of Islam for Australian upper school students. He has also advised Islamic schools such as the "Al Madina College" in New Zealand with respect to their study programs for Arabic and Islam as well as the Australian government's "Department of Immigration, Multicultural and Indigenous Affairs" in questions relating to integration.

Under Abdullah Saeed's authorship, an 80-page brochure was released in 2004 under the title *Muslim Australians: Their Beliefs, Practices and Institutions*,[77] which was published by the "Living in Harmony Initiative"

---

74 According to the report on Saeed's lecture "Progressive Muslims and the Interpretation of the Qur'an Today" at the "Progressive Islam and the State in Contemporary Muslim Societies" conference put on by the "Institute of Defence and Strategic Studies" (IDSS) as part of the Nanyang Technological University's S. Rajaratnam School of International Studies from August 7-8, 2008 in Singapore. http://www.rsis.edu.sg/publications/conference_reports/ProgressIslamConference06.pdf (10.6.2014).

75 Comp. the biographical details at http://www.abdullahsaeed.org/ (10.6.2014) and http://www.linkroad.net/wp-content/uploads/2008/07/cv-saeed.pdf (10.6.2014).

76 The "Australians All. Justice, Security, a Fair Go" website initiated by the Australian Prime Minister Malcolm Fraser in 2006 defines Abdullah Saeed's influence in the Australian government in the following manner: "His expert advice is regularly sought by both government and non-government agencies and institutions on complex Islamic issues." http://australiansall.com.au/archive/post/murderers-are-not-martyrs/ (10.6.2014).

77 Abdullah Saeed. *Muslim Australians: Their Beliefs, Practices and Institutions*. A Partnership under the Australian Government's *Living in Harmony* Initiative. Department of Immigration and Multicultural and Indigenous Affairs and Australian

of the Australian government's "Department of Immigration and Multicultural and Indigenous Affairs" (DIMIA) in cooperation with the Australian Multicultural Foundation and The University of Melbourne.[78] Drawing up the brochure goes back to carrying out the "Religion, Cultural Diversity and Social Cohesion Project" on assessing the role of religion in Australian society, which had been promoted by the "Department of Immigration and Multicultural and Indigenous Affairs".[79] Regardless of the title, the mentioned brochure consists in large part of a foundational presentation of Islam and only describes the Muslim community in Australia to a small degree. However, due to its publication on the internet, it has experienced high level of popularity and widespread distribution.

Abdullah Saeed was included in deliberations by the Australian government's "Department of Education, Science and Training" in 2005-2006 regarding the establishment of a form of education for religious leaders and teachers at Australian universities. This was to serve as a measure to combat extremism and to ensure peace within Australian society.[80] Moreover, at the beginning of 2010, in connection with a nationwide led discussion on de-radicalization strategies for Australian Muslims, the Australian government commissioned Abdullah Saeed to work out a strategy of effective measures in order to keep Muslims from making the trip to *jihādistic* training camps.[81] On the website "Australians All. Justice, Security, a Fair Go"[82] which was brought into being by the Australian Prime Minister

---

Multicultural Foundation in association with the University of Melbourne: Canberra, 2004. http://amf.net.au/library/uploads/files/Religion_Cultural_Diversity_Resource_Manual.pdf (10.6.2014).

78 On the Australian Parliament website, the reading matter relating to this study, under "Parliamentary Library," is recommended and expressly mentions Abdullah Saeed: http://www.aph.gov.au/About_Parliament/Parliamentary_Departments/Parliamentary_Library/Publications_Archive/archive/MuslimAustralians (10.6.2014)

79 According to the details in the foreword: Saeed. *Muslim Australians,* p. 4.

80 Australian Government, Department of Education, Science and Training. *Stocktake of Islamic Study at Australian Universities: 2006.* Collaboration Unit, Higher Education Group, September 2006. http://www.deewr.gov.au/HigherEducation/Programs/Equity/NCEIS/Documents/StockTakeReport.pdf (17.5.2011).

81 According to the report by Ben Packham and Philipp Hudson. "New National Security Blueprint says Threat of home-grown Terrorism has grown in past six years" in: *Herald Sun*, 23.2.2010.

82 http://australiansall.com.au/ (10.6.2014).

Malcolm Fraser in 2006 as a platform for combating all forms of racism and discrimination, Abdullah Saeed published an article with the title "Murderers are not Martyrs," in which in a very committed manner he denied suicide attackers any justification in invoking Islam.[83]

Abdullah Saeed has held courses on the topic of Islam for various governmental institutions, among them the "Department of Immigration and Multicultural Affairs" in Canberra. He has also advised the government in questions of imam education and, beyond that, has represented Australia in Brunei, Thailand, and the Philippines on behalf of the "Department of Foreign Affairs and Trade" (DFAT). His expert advice has already been called upon overseas, for example in Singapore, Indonesia, Thailand, and the United Arab Emirates.[84]

Under the umbrella of the "Department of Foreign Affairs and Trade", Abdullah Saeed is a member of the "Australian National Commission for UNESCO"[85] as well as being a member of the Advisory Board of the "Australia-Thailand Institute" of the Australian government's "Department of Foreign Affairs and Trade".[86] Besides working with the Australian government, he has worked for various publication and research projects with the government of New Zealand as well as with the "Qatar National Research Fund". Also, as a "distinguished international visitor", he has also visited the US Department of State and other establishments within the US government.

3.2.3. Use of the Media

Beyond using his activity as an academic and as an advisor, Abdullah Saeed uses additional channels in order to make his opinions known. He has not only published opinion pieces and articles in newspapers appearing nationwide, such as *The Australian*.[87] He has also begun to place 5-10 minute video addresses on his internet homepage[88] as well as on YouTube.[89]

---

83 Abdullah Saeed. "Murderers are not Martyrs," 28.11.2006. http://australiansall.com.au/archive/post/murderers-are-not-martyrs/ (10.6.2014).

84 Comp. the details at http://www.abdullahsaeed.org/ (10.6.2014) and http://www.linkroad.net/wp-content/uploads/2008/07/cv-saeed.pdf (10.6.2014).

85 http://www.dfat.gov.au/intorgs/unesco/members.html (10.6.2014).

86 Ibid.

87 For example, comp. his position statement: Abdullah Saeed. "Muslims don't need Separate Laws" in: *The Austalian*, 9.4.2008. http://www.theaustralian.com.au/

In the process, he appears to concentrate on current and intensively discussed topics with great potential for attention, such as the question of the prohibition on facial veils in Western societies,[90] gender equality and, more specifically, the problematic nature of domestic violence, political Islam and its representatives, and the disputed topic of homosexuality within the Muslim community. As Abdullah Saeed has asserted in personal conversations, he plans to substantially increase the number of his short lectures available on the internet in order to make his views known beyond the limited group of his readers and listeners. He also thereby seeks to convey to the Muslim community cause for thought regarding a foundational reorientation in the interpretation of the Quran.

On the basis of his extensive travel and lecturing activity on all continents, his engagement in inter-religious dialog, his far-flung advisory activity, and on the basis of a variety of channels in which he strives to dismantle prejudices and fears on both sides,[91] one could label Abdullah Saeed an activist who is not only a scholar but rather also someone who wants to make it clear to Western society that Muslims are democratically minded and freedom minded and thus are estimable members of the national as well as the international community. At the same time, he would like to move Muslims to an acceptance of their status quo, to involvement in Western societies, and through a re-evaluation of Islamic tradition and sources provoke a move from passive separation to active participation in Western societies.

higher-education/opinion-analysis/muslims-dont-need-separate-laws/story-e6frgcl o-1111116006923 (10.6.2014).

88 http://www.abdullahsaeed.org/media_reference (10.6.2014).

89 For example, comp. the address regarding the face veil, 2009: "Burqa debate is about choice." http://newsroom.melbourne.edu/studio/ep-33?video=1&play=1 (20.6. 2011).

90 For example, on the face veil in 2009 see: http://www.abdullahsaeed.org/media_reference/video-should-face-veil-burqa-be-banned-australia. (10.6.2014).

91 To dismantle the concerns of Australian society with respect to the allegedly hostilely minded Muslims is labeled by Abdullah Saeed as "one of the most important challenges for Muslim leaders" in Australia: Saeed. *Islam in Australia*, p. 211.

3.2.4. Abdullah Saeed as a Transnational Scholar

Not only on the basis of his own immigration history, his school education and training in three Asian Muslim majority countries, and his teaching activity on the continent of Australia, his extensive publishing activity as well as his increasing utilization of the Media, Abdullah Saeed is to be labelled a transnational scholar.

Beyond that, he has developed extensive travel activity for a period of around 15 years. Numerous international conferences identify him as one of the main speakers, and he has contributed articles and addresses to around 100 conferences. Frequent topics have been apostasy and religious freedom, human rights and women's rights, multiculturalism and democracy, non-Muslim religious communities, and inter-religious encounters, the question of the capacity for peace within Islam as well as concepts of tolerance and coexistence in Western society.[92]

3.3. Abdullah Saeed's Position on Apostasy in Islam

Apostasy, human rights, and civil rights and liberties are central themes for Abdullah Saeed, and in various contexts he has repeatedly taken them up over the years. Also in the years prior to 2004, when together with his brother Hassan Saeed he published his magnum opus on the topic of religious freedom entitled *Freedom of Religion, Apostasy and Islam*,[93] he had already grappled with this subject matter.

3.3.1. Freedom of Belief in Islam ("A Fresh Look at Freedom of Belief in Islam") – 1994

Over the course of years, Saeed has not essentially changed his position, but he has differed in his degree of emphasis and has continuously expanded his argumentation. As early as 1994, Abdullah Saeed published a basic essay on the topic of religious freedom with the title "A Fresh Look at

---

[92] See http://www.abdullahsaeed.org/ (10.6.2014) and http://www.linkroad.net/wp-content/uploads/2008/07/cv-saeed.pdf (10.6.2014).

[93] Abdullah Saeed; Hassan Saeed. *Freedom of Religion, Apostasy and Islam.* Ashgate: Aldershot, 2004.

Freedom of Belief in Islam."[94] Originally it was an address by Saeed at a conference entitled Difference and Tolerance: Ethnicity, Religion and Human Rights in Southeast Asia. The conference was held on September 11 and 12, 1993 by the Ethnic and Religious Conflict Group of the Deakin University Centre for Citizenship and Human Rights at Deakin University in the state of Victoria. It had the purpose of discussing the substantiation of the universality of human rights. The addresses made by speakers were later published in a collective volume.[95]

After he refers to the central role of the Quran and *sunna* in an understanding of human rights based on Islamic notions, Abdullah Saeed expressly emphasizes right at the start of his statements that what is involved cannot be a question of setting down a single interpretation of Islamic revelation as absolute: ". . . it could be said that there is no *one* "correct" and "final" interpretation of the Scripture, but possibly more than one, depending on the time, place or circumstance."[96]

According to Saeed, it is for that reason necessary to acknowledge the realities of modernity:

> ". . . taking into consideration . . . the reality of modern nation-states, the pluralistic nature of the societies in these nation-states and the emphasis on harmony and tolerance among communities."[97]

There are some significant keywords mentioned in this introduction which are repeatedly found in later publications on the topic of human rights and religious freedom: the relativization of truth claims on the part of theologians who appeal to a normative interpretation of early Islam, the acceptance of realities found in modernity, for instance societies which are culturally and religiously pluralistic in their composition, and the promotion of actively implemented tolerance via the expression of mutual esteem.

After this introduction, Abdullah Saeed justifies the compatibility of Islamic theology with the thought of religious freedom in four sections, and in four additional segments he explains why, according to his opinion, it is

---

94 Abdullah Saeed. "A Fresh Look at Freedom of Belief in Islam" in: Damien Kingsbury; Greg Barton (eds.). *Difference and Tolerance. Human Rights Issues in Southeast Asia*. Deakin University Press: Geelong, 1994, pp. 27-37.

95 Kingsbury; Barton (eds.). *Difference*.

96 Saeed. "A Fresh Look", p. 27 (emphasis in the original).

97 Ibid.

inappropriate when representatives of classical understandings of the Sharia revert to Islam for the justification of their assessment of apostasy.

As an introduction to the topic, Abdullah Saeed chooses a general affirmation of the universality of human rights[98] – such an explicit sanctioning of "The Universal Declaration of Human Rights" of 1948 is not to be found in any of al-Qaraḍāwī's literature, since for him neither the realities of pluralistic societies nor any declaration composed in Western countries could be the standard for dealing with the topic of apostasy. Abdullah Saeed, on the other hand, justifies the equality, the freedom of religion, and the freedom on the part of all people to decide as well as the sole otherworldly punishment for apostates with the Quran – for example, with Sura 2:256: "Let there be no compulsion in religion . . ." – as well as from tradition with Muḥammad's and ᶜUmar's practice on the basis of their various contracts concluded with non-Muslims.[99]

Abdullah Saeed explains here, among other points, the persisting conflict between a comprehensive understanding of religious freedom and the early Islamic Sharia-defined notion of apostasy: At this juncture the main point of criticism for Saeed is not at all that there is even persecution of apostates in Muslim majority societies. Rather, it is the fact that Islam, owing to the ruling understanding of apostasy, especially restricts the level of religious freedom for Muslims drastically. He refers to the numerous different definitions of apostasy, which prohibit claiming any absoluteness for the Sunnite, Shiite, or, for instance, the Mu'tazilite standpoint. In the process, he simultaneously strongly scrutinizes the possibility of an unassailable definition of apostasy.

Saeed now moves on to discussing the justification of the punishment of apostasy as unislamic.[100] To start with, he mentions several verses from the Quran which threaten apostates with an otherworldly punishment and concludes from them that the Quran does not at all intend a worldly punishment. The sole tradition which from his viewpoint deals with this topic, "Whoever changes his religion, kill him," is formulated so generally and transmitted in such varying textual variations that from it no course of action can be derived. Additionally, conversion between Judaism and Christianity, which purely theoretically could be meant by this wording, would

98 Ibid., p. 28.
99 Ibid., pp. 28-30.
100 Ibid., pp. 31-34.

then likewise be threatened with death – which indeed has never been the case. As a result, the prohibition against leaving Islam that is derived from this tradition is in Saeed's eyes strongly challenged.

As far as Saeed is concerned, since other traditions establish a connection between apostasy and separation from the Islamic community, the fact of fixing a punishment is only to be explained by the fact that it is originally the consequence of political strife on the side of the enemy against the Muslim community, not, however, that it was imposed for apostasy from Islam alone. It comes from a time in which it was not sufficient, according to Saeed, to formally declare adherence to the Islamic community. Rather, it was necessary in the battle for survival to go beyond that and demonstrate political loyalty.

This is also clear to Saeed due to the fact that Muḥammad, according to Saeed's understanding, dealt in an exceedingly forbearing manner with apostates who did not fight against the Muslim community and remained members of the Muslim community. At this point Saeed quotes a tradition by Imām al-Bayhaqī (d. 1066). Imām al-Bayhaqī expresses Muḥammads averseness to the execution of his companions who were regarded as "hypocrites." Saeed also quotes an additional *ḥadīṯ* text from the mouth of Muḥammad and delivered by Buḫārī, which forbade the execution of "hypocrites"[101], whereby the Quran, according to Saeed, sometimes equates the terms "hypocrite" and "apostate."

According to Saeed's understanding, this means that the punishment did not apply solely to apostasy, for "hypocrites" were to an extent the first apostates who were not necessarily mild-mannered opponents of Muḥammad. Saeed labels them as "opportunists living among the Muslims, constantly displaying their hatred of Islam, the Muslims and the Prophet."[102] This alone, however, does not apparently suffice in order to pronounce the death penalty as their judgment, according to Saeed. This was first the case when there was tangible opposition to the Muslim community, high treason, and schism:

> "It seems that the command to kill (in the *Hadith*) is only applicable when a Muslim repudiates Islam, rebels against the Community and attempts to create division in it. In any case, whether a person is a Muslim or not, rising

101 Ibid., p. 33.

102 Ibid., p. 34.

> against the Community is treason, and a violation which would incur severe punishment, possibly death . . ."[103]

Thus, treason against the state, as one could read between the lines, could definitely carry the death penalty, but mere apostasy is to be clearly delineated from fighting against the *umma*: the one offense does not automatically necessitate the other. By contrast, for al-Qaraḍāwī the terms apostasy and fighting against the *umma* are inseparable. An open display of apostasy is simultaneously aggression, which has to be punished accordingly. al-Qaraḍāwī cites the – from his point of view relentless – dealing on the part of Muḥammad with apostates as specific evidence for the killing of apostates as an appropriate handling of the problem of apostasy nowadays, while for Abdullah Saeed it is Muḥammad's tolerance towards those who think differently which stands in the foreground.

Finally, Abdullah Saeed refers to the unilinear development of the early history of Islamic theology. The result is the establishment of the death penalty for apostasy. At the same time, there is a lack of a clear definition of the term of what it means to be a non-believer or, more specifically, apostate, and then there are mutual recriminations seen between various groups within Islam. Nowadays, according to the author, some draw upon themselves the charge of apostasy by calling for equality for women, whereby Saeed implies that this term has nowadays experienced a shift in meaning which no longer has anything in common with the original charge of apostasy. He does not go directly into the argumentation of classical Sharia scholars on apostasy at this point.

At the end of the article, Saeed underscores again that for him no other conclusion is possible than that in Islam, as in the revealed religions prior to Islam, the principle of religious freedom and of the responsible decision on the part of each individual applies to the relationship between God and humankind. At another point he speaks unequivocally of a "relationship" between the Creator and creature[104] – even if apostasy, from his point of

[103] Ibid., p. 34.

[104] Abdullah Saeed. "Muslims in Secular States: Between Isolationists and Participants in the West." Lecture on November 30, 2003, Islamic Centre of Singapore. *MUIS Occasional Papers Series*: Majlis Ugama Islam Singapura/Islamic Religious Council of Singapore: Singapore, 2005, pp. 1-14, here p. 8.

view, is a wrong path to take.[105] Nevertheless, in his opinion, only those actions which directly bring damage to the community require political action as a defensive measure. Political action as a defensive measure is not, however, required when it comes to contravening religious practice with actions comparable to neglecting prayer or fasting.

With this argumentation, Abdullah Saeed has made a de facto division into two separate areas, with religion on the one side and politics and society on the other side. Likewise, he separates Muḥammad's role and mission as the enunciator of Islam from that of the political leader of its community: As the enunciator, Muḥammad urged unbelievers to repent, but he did not proceed against their unbelief (and against their hypocrisy and apostasy, respectively) in a military fashion. Saeed calls for the same action from the present day Islamic community: On the one hand, it is not an endorsement of the decision made by an apostate. On the other hand, no social or political verdict is allowed to be made.

With this attitude, Abdullah Saeed implicitly opposes the foundational concerns of political Islam and its understanding of the inseparability of the spiritual and worldly spheres as, for example, is unreservedly affirmed by al-Qaraḍāwī. From Saeed's viewpoint, it is possible in one area (the religious) to act wrongly as an apostate without drawing judgment upon oneself in another area (the sociopolitical). Belief thus becomes a private affair, the aims of which do not obligate the community to act. From this viewpoint, political judgment of an apostate appears illegitimate and unreasonable.

In Abdullah Saeed's argumentation, the desire expressed in numerous additional publications[106] that non-Muslims should not only view Islam from the perspective of violence, intolerance, and the events of September 11, 2001 also resonates: "What it all means is that Islam is not a draconian religion . . ."[107]

---

105 Saeed. "A Fresh Look", pp. 35-36.

106 See. For example, the articles Saeed. "Jihad and Violence", or Saeed. "Muslims in the West and their Attitudes to Full Participation in Western Societies: Some Reflections" in: Geoffrey Brahm Levey; Tariq Modood (eds.). *Secularism, Religion and Multicultural Citizenship*. Cambridge University Press: Cambridge, 2009, pp. 200-215.

107 Saeed. "A Fresh Look", p. 36.

3.3.2. Civil Rights Held by non-Muslims in an Islamic State ("Citizenship Rights of Non-Muslims in a Islamic State") - 1999

One way pursued by Saeed in order to campaign for his view of religious freedom and human rights is the presentation and discussion of articles on this debate as produced by other Muslim intellectuals. Thus, in 1999 he published a presentation of the most important theses on religious freedom by the Tunisian leader of the Nahḍa movement, Rāšid al-Ġannūšī (b.1941).[108] In particular, Abdullah Saeed particularly goes into Ġannūšī's criticism of the lack of equal handling of non-Muslims in Muslim majority countries, and he addresses his concept of justice as well as a number of his notions on the topic of religious freedom.

As early as in the introduction to his article "Rethinking Citizenship Rights of Non-Muslims in an Islamic State: Rashīd al-Ghannūshī's Contribution to the Evolving Debate,"[109] Abdullah Saeed points out that al-Ġannūšī's significance above all lies in the fact that as a Muslim intellectual he makes the attempt to subject traditional legal conceptions (at this point: with respect to the position of non-Muslims in Islamic states) to a reevaluation.[110]

In order to present al-Ġannūšī's viewpoint, Abdullah Saeed embeds his review of al-Ġannūšī's thoughts on human rights and individual freedoms in his own perspective: To start with, Saeed explains his concerns already expressed multiple times in other writings that the experience of the first Islamic community and the interpretational sovereignty derived from early Islamic scholars due to the special political circumstances of their time has led to specific conclusions which are not transferable to today. In particular, the socially and legally disadvantaged status of non-Muslims and the retention of this situation by "many traditionalists and neo-revivalists"[111] defies Saeed, and that especially in times of modernity in which secular-

---

[108] Abdullah Saeed. "Rethinking Citizenship Rights of Non-Muslims in an Islamic State: Rashīd al-Ghannūshī's Contribution to the Evolving Debate" in: *ICMR* 10/3 (1999), pp. 307-323.

[109] Ibid.

[110] Ibid., p. 307.

[111] Ibid., p. 309.

ists, modernists, traditionalists, and Islamists ("neo-revivalists") are at odds regarding the question of the appropriate (Islamic) model of the state.

Against this backdrop, Abdullah Saeed depicts important essential principles of Rāšid al-Ġannūšī's point of view, "one of the leading figures of the Islamist movement of the late twentieth century,"[112] as well as the principle of justice (*ᶜadl*), which Saeed explains in the following manner:[113] The goal of the application of the principle of justice in the case of Abdullah Saeeds interpretation of al-Ġannūšī is the establishment of a just order, equality of women and non-Muslims in Muslim majority states as well as complete positive and negative religious freedom.

With respect to the question of religious freedom, as Saeed summarizes al-Ġannūšī's point of view, Muḥammad only possessed the mandate of proclamation and not the task of forcing people to accept Islam. This is underscored by texts in the Quran, such as Sura 2:267. In elucidation of the frequently cited "verses of the sword," such as Sura 9:73, which orders Muḥammad to "strive hard against the unbelievers and the hypocrites, and [to be] firm against them", al-Ġannūšī resorts to a surprising construal: Verses such as this one are precisely not a call to battle and, more specifically, not a call to oppress non-Muslims. Rather, they are calls to protect them against oppression. They order battle against those who want to deny people their right to the freedom to come to their own conclusions! Thus, verses such as Sura 9:73, as Saeed summarizes al-Ġannūšī's viewpoint, do not allow war in order to limit religious freedom. Rather, the contrary is the cases, that battle serves the preservation of religious freedom:

> ". . . in order to provide protection against oppressors, so that all faiths may continue and have their place in society . . . Thus, the concept of fighting *(qitāl)* was instituted essentially to guarantee freedom of belief for both Muslims and non-Muslims."[114]

---

112 Ibid., p. 311.

113 This principle is presented in detail by al-Ġannūšī in his work: Rāšid al-Ġannūšī. *ḥuqūq al-muwāṭana. ḥuqūq ġair al-muslim fī 'l-muǧtamaᶜ al-islāmī.* al-maᶜhad al-ᶜālamī li-l-fikr al-islāmī/The International Institute of Islamic Thought: Herndon, 1979/1993, pp. 35ff. The principle of justice is based upon the assumption of the equality of all people owing to their common origin (*waḥdat al-aṣl al-bašarī*) (ibid., p.65) from which, according to al-Ġannūšī equal rights and duties arise for all people (ibid., p. 66).

114 Saeed. "Rethinking Citizenship Rights", p. 315.

For that reason, as Abdullah Saeed emphasizes, apostasy is also for Rāšid al-Ġannūšī an affair between God and man. As a consequence, according to Saeed, apostasy should not be rated as a *ḥadd* offense from al-Ġannūšī's perspective.[115]

With this pointed explanation of al-Ġannūšī's point of view, in particular with respect to the evaluation of Islamic sources as documents advocating human rights and civil rights and liberties, Abdullah Saeed places himself on al-Ġannūšī's side and to some extent allows him to emerge as an advocate of his own concerns. On the one hand, Saeed makes clear with the review of such a well known intellectual as al-Ġannūšī that he is in no way standing alone with his opinion of the necessity of a modified interpretation of sources. Rather, there are also other theologians – in this case even from the spectrum of Islamism – who defend a position which is comparable to his own notion.

Additionally, the presentation of al-Ġannūšī's position makes it clear that it is absolutely possible to come to alternative interpretive possibilities and to the justification of increased civil rights and liberties without a foundational critique and, more specifically, rejection of parts of the text of the Quran. That al-Ġannūšī is to be associated with the Islamist oriented Ennahḍa movement underscores Saeed's argument all the more and furthermore scrutinizes the interpretive sovereignty of the representatives of classic Sharia Islam.

To be sure, one could critically remark that Abdullah Saeed has likewise dismissed other aspects of the multi-faceted position of al-Ġannūšī, who was influenced by personalities such as Ḥasan al-Bannā, Sayyid Quṭb, and Abū l-Aᶜlā Maudūdī,[116] among others, on the status of non-Muslims in Muslim majority countries[117] as well as with respect to civil liberties, apos-

---

[115] Ibid., p. 316.

[116] The latter is documented by Maudūdī's biographer Roy Jackson. *Fifty Key Figures in Islam*. Routledge: London, 2006, pp. 232-233.

[117] al-Ġannūšī demands a declaration of loyalty by non-Muslim inhabitants prior to their acceptance as citizens as well as a prohibition against making influential positions in state service accessible to non-Muslims: al-Ġannūšī's biographer, Azzam S. Tamimi, summarizes al-Ġannūšī's writings in this manner: Azzam S. Tamimi. *Rachid Ghannouchi. A Democrat within Islamism*. Oxford University Press: Oxford, 2001, p. 77.

tasy,[118] *ǧihād*[119], and his position on a just societal order[120] and that Saeed solely presents the aspects where there is agreement with his own view of apostasy. As sources, Abdullah Saeed names al-Ġannūš's Werk *ḥuqūq al-muwāṭana,*[121] as well as an interview al-Ġannūšī had with the *Financial Times* and with *al-Shira.*[122] In both interviews al-Ġannūšī affirms religious

---

118 al-Ġannūšī's biographer, Azzam S. Tamimi, differentiates with reference to al-Ġannūšī's writings, that he did not plead for the death penalty for apostasy since he principally advocated responsibly configured civil rights and liberties as well as affirming freedom of expression. al-Ġannūšī does not consider *ridda* to be a religious but rather a political offense, and it is an offense of uprising, of rebellion, and of treason that is to be punished within the legal provisions of a state in order to protect law and order as well as the community: Ibid., pp. 78; 97; 191. – Nevertheless, it appears difficult to imagine that there could be true religious freedom in a state where apostasy from Islam is punished as a political offense.

119 Thus al-Gannusi has spoken out as an unrestricted advocate of Yusuf al-Qaraḍāwī's most recently presented comprehensive work on *jihād*: Yusuf al-Qaraḍāwī. *fiqh al-ǧihād. dirāsa muqarāna li-aḥkāmihī wa-falsafatihī fī ḍau' al-qur'ān wa-'s-sunna.* Maktabat wahba: al-Qāhira, 2009[1]; 2010[2]; 2011[3], in a review by al-Ġannūšī it is presented as a "masterpiece on Jihad" and its author as a "great scholar." Although in that work al-Qaraḍāwī glorifies Palestinian suicide attacks in great detail as heroic operations of martyrdom and calls for comprehensive and if need be violent battle against everyone opposing the worldwide spread of Islam, al-Ġannūšī judges as follows: "al-Qaradawi has opened a vast space for dialogue, tolerance, agreement and coexistence between Islam and other religions, human values, and international accords, enabling a response to the eternal Quranic call . . ." Rashid al Ghannushi. "Fiqh of Jihad: Book Review of Shaykh al-Islam al-Qaradawi's Masterpiece on Jihad," 13.12.2009. http://www.suhaibwebb.com/islam-studies/fiqh-of-jihad-book-review-of-shaykhul-islam-al-qaradawi's-latest-masterpiece-on-jihad-by-dr-rashid-al-ghannushi/ (10.6.2014).

120 As to al-Ġannūšī, a just societal order will come into existence in an Islamic state, but not in a secular one: Menno Preuschaft. Tunesien als islamische Demokratie? Rāšid al-Ġannūšī und die Zeit nach der Revolution. Waxmann: Münster, 2011, pp. 31ff.

121 al-Ġannūšī. *ḥuqūq al-muwāṭana.* In this work al-Ġannūšī indeed repeatedly emphasizes the voluntariness of belief which he sees completely achieved in Islam (ibid., pp. 67-68); an unlimited confession of complete religious freedom including affirmation of the freedom to turn from Islam and to turn to another religion without consequence, along with the freedom to openly communicate such is, however, sought after in this work in vain.

122 al-Ġannūšī's interview with the *Finanical Times* dated 10.2.1998 is no longer completely accessible on the internet, but it is quoted in part in the following arti-

freedom in principle[123] and leaves otherworldly punishment as the sole punishment for apostasy in force. However, al-Ġannūšī is also of the opinion that apostasy has never been a real problem in Islamic history, indeed that even in the West persecuted Christian minorities found refuge in Islamic areas:

> "Our history is full of proud moments when it comes to the question of religious tolerance and interfaith debates . . . When [sic; presumably intended: We] never had recourse to the question of apostasy and death (for someone's beliefs). This has never occurred in our midst. Some (esoteric) Christian movements can be found only in our land, after fleeing the West and the persecution of larger denominations."[124]

What, however, especially links al-Ġannūšī with Abdullah Saeed is an opinion shared by both. From the early days of Islam, it is their opinion that reports about the persecution of apostates only exist because these individuals were simultaneously insurgents and rebels who for that reason were fought. It was not owing to their turning away from Islam.[125] Both thus exclusively reduce the problematic issue of apostasy to a political

cle: "Rached Ghannouchi on Islamic Reformism. http://aliran.com/web-specials/2011-web-specials/rached-ghannouchi-on-islamic-reformism/ (10.6.2014); the interview with al-Shira in October 1994 (indirectly deducible that is was conducted between October 10 and October 12, 1994 in Beirut; exact details are missing), is on a website which can no longer be called up, but it is still accessible in an English translation entitled "Tunisia's Islamists are different from those in Algeria." http://www.library.cornell.edu/colldev/mideast/ghanush.htm (10.6.2014).

123 Nancy Gallagher, Associate Director for Research at the Center for International and Security Studies, Maryland (CISSM), also quotes al-Ġannūšī correspondingly: Nancy Gallagher. "Tunesian Coup Institutes First of Secular Islamists," 3.3.2011. Daily Nexus. http://www.dailynexus.com/2011-03-03/tunisian-coup-institutes-secular-islamists/ (10.6.2014).

124 Tunisia's Islamists are different from those in Algeria. http://www.library.cornell.edu/colldev/mideast/ghanush.htm (1.6.2011).

125 al-Ġannūšī is quoted in the following manner: ". . . when he [meaning Abū Bakr] fought the apostates, he fought them because of their political rebellion against Islam. It was not because of their position on creed. Allah is the sole judge of the apostate." "Tunisia's Islamists are different from those in Algeria." http://www.library.cornell.edu/colldev/mideast/ghanush.htm (1.6.2011) and Abdullah Saeed; Hassan Saeed. *Freedom of Religion, Apostasy and Islam*. Ashgate: Aldershot, 2004, p. 60.

moment, while al-Qaraḍāwī differentiates between a theological area of internal doubt and a political moment of agitation. However, al-Qaraḍāwī then views the latter as a given when the apostate speaks about his newly gained convictions.[126]

Additionally, the effort to find justification for peaceful coexistence with non-Muslims apparently links Abdullah Saeed with al-Ġannūšī, for he ranks al-Ġannūšī, who rejects a second class status for non-Muslims in Islamic societies, among "a number of Islamist figures [which] have displayed a conciliatory, justice-oriented attitude towards the non-Muslim 'other.'"[127] This is also Saeed's concern – even if it is from a non-Islamist perspective.

Besides al-Ġannūšī, Saeed deals multiple times with reform movements and individual personalities from along the Islamic spectrum.[128] In similar detail to al-Ġannūšī, he grapples with the rationalist approach of the Indonesian theologian Nurcholish Madjid. Nurcholish Madjid, like Saeed, does not proceed on the general idea that all tradition is flawless[129] and argues using the self-assertion of the threatened early Islamic community against today's application of the death penalty for apostasy.[130] Likewise, Abdullah Saeed addresses himself to the reform theology of Fazlur Rahman, who, as Saeed mentions in personal conversation, has perhaps

---

126 For instance, he justifies this in his work: Yūsuf al-Qaraḍāwī. *ǧarīmat ar-ridda wa-cuqūbat al-murtadd fī ḍau' al-qur'ān wa-'s-sunna*. Maktabat wahba: al-Qāhira, 2005³, p. 7, in like manner to his last work: Yūsuf al-Qaraḍāwī. *fiqh al-ǧihād dirāsa muqarāna li-aḥkāmihī wa-falsafatihī fī dau' al-qur'ān wa-'s-sunna*. Maktabat wahba: al-Qåhira, 2009¹, Vol. 1, pp. 180-182.

127 Abdullah Saeed. "Rethinking Citizenship Rights of Non-Muslims in an Islamic State: Rashīd al-Ghannūshī's Contribution to the Evolving Debate" in: *ICMR* 10/3 (1999), pp. 307-323, here p. 319.

128 Thus, for instance, in his article: Abdullah Saeed. "Introduction: The Qur'an, Interpretation and the Indonesian Context" in: Abdullah Saeed. (ed.). *Approaches to the Qur'an in Contemporary Indonesia*. Oxford University Press: Oxford, 2005, pp. 1-16.

129 Saeed sums up in this manner regarding Nurcholish Madjid's view on *aḥādīṯ*: Abdullah Saeed. "Ijtihad and Innovation in Neo-Modernist Islamic Thought in Indonesia" in: *ICMR* 8 (1997), pp. 279-295, here p. 287.

130 According to Abdullah Saeed, ibid., pp. 279-295 and Anthony H. Johns; Abdullah Saeed. "Nurcholish Madjid and the Interpretation of the Qur'an: Religious Pluralism and Tolerance" in: Suha Taji-Farouki (ed.). *Modern Muslim Intellectuals and the Qur'an*. Oxford University Press: Oxford, 2004, pp. 67-96, here p. 84.

shaped him most. He shares a bond with Fazlur Rahman with respect to sorrow at the "intellectual ossification" of the Islamic legacy as well as the call for a comprehensive reform and renewal of Islam on the basis of the Quran with tradition at the end of the queue putting tradition last.[131]

3.3.3. Abdullah Saeed's Primary Work on Apostasy: Freedom of Religion, Apostasy and Islam – 2004

Abdullah Saeed is one of the few Muslim theologians who not only treats the topic of apostasy in individual articles. Rather, he has also placed the topic in the center of an independent work. With his brother, the former Attorney General of the Maldives, Hassan Saeed, he published *Freedom of Religion, Apostasy and Islam* in 2004 via the renowned Ashgate Publishing House.[132] It is a comprehensive rebuttal of the notion of the legitimacy of the death penalty for apostasy in modernity, combined with a justification of the unconditional necessity of a critical reevaluation of the sources of apostasy from Islam.

Freedom of Religion as a Foundational Principle of Islam

The publication of the book in English via a renowned publishing house signifies a rejection of the monopoly of interpretation by the classical scholarly world, a summons to the experts to open the discussion as well as an effort to exert social influence for the benefit of increased religious freedom in Muslim majority countries. It was somewhat less suitable as a theological gauntlet, owing to the publication's chosen language and publishing house. On the other hand, it was definitely considered a socio-political gauntlet on the Maldives.[133]

---

[131] Abdullah Saeed. Fazlur Rahman: "A Framework for interpreting the Ethico-Legal Content of the Qur'an" in: Suha Taji-Farouki (ed.). *Modern Muslim Intellectuals and the Qur'an*. Oxford University Press: Oxford, 2004, pp. 37-66, here p. 40.

[132] Abdullah Saeed; Hassan Saeed. *Freedom of Religion, Apostasy and Islam*. Ashgate: Aldershot, 2004.

[133] Comp. the reports on the socio-political discussion on the Maldives relating to the publication as well as the intrigue of various political groups against the co-author of the work, Hassan Saeed, who at that point in time was a public figure, e.g., in: S. Chandrasekharan. "Maldives: On Dr. Hassan Saeed's Book on Freedom of Religion and Apostasy." South Asia Analysis Group. Paper no. 2747, 25.6.2008

On the one hand, this document, going by the title *Freedom of Religion, Apostasy and Islam*, presents the notions of intellectuals who have addressed themselves toward modernity. Just as is distinguishable in Abdullah Saeed's remaining publications, for him it is not simply a matter of negating the theological argumentation substantiated by the Quran and the *sunna*. Rather, it primarily has to do with a critical debate over the textual findings in the Quran and the sunna. This, however, leads him to come to other conclusions than, for example, Yūsuf al-Qaraḍāwī.

Just as Abdullah Saeed's remaining works, the list of literature cited in the appendix likewise shows an entire spectrum of information sources of varying orientations: Besides texts from the Quran and tradition, there are numerous works coming out of western Islamic studies, a compendia of traditional Shiite and Sunnite theologians and legal scholars, among them numerous Arabic titles, documents from the US Department of State on religious freedom and human rights, internet sources, newspaper reports, documentation from human rights organizations as well as autobiographical reports of former Muslims.[134]

The book *Freedom of Religion, Apostasy and Islam* is broken down into four parts. The first part from the pen of Abdullah Saeed comprises roughly one-half of the work and over the course of eight chapters essentially deals with the position of the Quran and tradition on apostasy and the conclusions to be drawn. The second part of the book, by Hassan Saeed, presents a critical evaluation of religious freedom in Malaysia against the background of constitutionally guaranteed religious freedom and the calls there to introduce apostasy legislation.[135] In a short, third section Abdullah

http://www.southasiaanalysis.org/%5Cpapers28%5Cpaper2747.html (6.5.2011); also comp. Judith Evans. "Supreme Council bans Hassan Saeed's Book," 18.6.2008. Minivan News. Independent News for the Maldives. http://www.minivannews.com/news/news.php?id=4605 (24.6.2010).

134 Abdullah Saeed; Hassan Saeed. *Freedom of Religion, Apostasy and Islam*. Ashgate: Aldershot, 2004, pp. 186ff.

135 As the authors explain in the foreword, Malaysia was chosen as an example of a virtually multi-religious society with a secular constitution guaranteeing religious freedom to all citizens; to date, it places apostasy under punishment in a few states and has to socially and politically grapple with a fraction of advocates of apostasy legislation as well as with opponents of such provisions at a federal level: Abdullah Saeed; Hassan Saeed. *Freedom of Religion, Apostasy and Islam*. Ashgate: Aldershot, 2004, p. 3.

Saeed calls for a reconsideration of existing "apostasy laws." The fourth and final part contains a legal text from the federal state of Perlis in Malaysia on religious freedom dating from 2000 as well as the text of Pakistan's "blasphemy laws."[136]

In my analysis which follows, I will limit myself to the foreword, for which Abdullah and Hassan Saeed were mutually responsible, as well as to the first, comprehensive part of the book from the pen of Abdullah Saeed. The latter contains essential observations on the topic. I will also deal with the third part of the book, a call to subject the traditional Sharia law judgment on apostasy to a critical reevaluation.

As early as in the foreword of the book, it becomes clear as to the direction in which the argumentation in the subsequent first part will develop. It has to do with scrutiny of a "pre-modern conception of apostasy and its punishment,"[137] which from Abdullah Saeed's point of view is an overdue reconsideration of a debate which for him in no way ended by the 10th century A.D. with the formulation of the known Sharia law guidelines for dealing with apostates.

According to the foreword, conducting this debate is absolutely no new thought and not something which is only limited to deliberations made by both the authors. Rather, it was launched by numerous scholars of the late 19th and early 20th centuries. Scholars of the 20th century, such as (the Chief Justice of Pakistan who in the meantime has retired) S. A. Rahman, Ḥasan al-Turābī, Rāšid al-Ġannūšī, Mohammad Hashim Kamali, Muḥammad Salīm al-ᶜAuwā, and Abdullahi An-Na'im continued these considerations, while at the same time a substantial number of Muslims whom Saeed does not mention here by name held firmly to defending the death penalty for apostates.

This approach of allowing both points of view, for and against the death penalty, of allowing advocates and opponents to present themselves, and to openly mention differences between the positions makes clear that Abdullah Saeed does not lecture in the form of a monologue as al-Qaraḍāwī does. From al-Qaraḍāwī's own perspective, he holds the one true

136 "Islamic Aqidah Protection (Perlis) Bill 2000" and "Pakistan's Blasphemy Laws" in: Abdullah Saeed; Hassan Saeed. *Freedom of Religion, Apostasy and Islam.* Ashgate: Aldershot, 2004, pp. 177-183 and 184-185.

137 Abdullah Saeed; Hassan Saeed. *Freedom of Religion, Apostasy and Islam.* Ashgate: Aldershot, 2004, p. 2.

viewpoint – making it clear why Saeed does not emerge as al-Qaraḍāwī with the authority of one who alone knows the truth and does not at all allow the other viewpoints to be expressed in a discussion conducted upon an equal footing.

In the process, it becomes clear in the foreword that Saeed does not reduce the debate to the Islamic scholarly world and not to the question of "right" or "wrong." Rather – and in complete contrast to al-Qaraḍāwī – he has the practical ramifications of the scholars' statements in view. Thus, he argues:

> "The death penalty is staunchly defended by a significant number of Muslims, but equally strongly opposed by an increasingly vocal group that includes some prominent Muslim thinkers and even Islamists," for: "Many Muslims are uncomfortable with the law of apostasy . . ."[138]

Thus, it is not only a question of scholars taking a position for or against the death penalty. Rather, it is that "Muslims" and Muslim societies still defend them as far as they have direct ramifications for the treatment of apostates.

It is the goal of the book to introduce religious freedom as a "fundamental principle of Islam" and to negate the justification of the death penalty for apostates, since they are to be brought into conformity with neither the Quran and the *sunna* nor "with the current ethos of human rights." Here it is a matter of an immanent argumentation placing the theological justification of the death penalty for apostasy into question as well as being a matter of questioning its justification in the face of internationally acknowledged standards of human rights. Does the call for the death penalty by "pre-Modern Muslim scholars" fit into modernity, or is it "outdated" and better abolished as many Muslims nowadays think?

And finally, the issue of the justification of the death penalty also contains an apologetic opportunity for Abdullah Saeed, since those who defend the death penalty for apostasy:

> "dominate the debate . . . they are armed with what they consider to be supporting texts from the Qur'an and *hadith* . . . as well as *fatwas* from conservative religious leaders today. This leaves opponents of the law of aposta-

---

[138] Ibid.

> sy largely defenceless against what appears to be unassailable and authoritative 'textual' evidence."[139]

Alone such a statement of the question would presumably be evidence of the apostasy of this author for Yūsuf al-Qaraḍāwī, since for scholars such as al-Qaraḍāwī no time limit is allowed on the eternally valid law of God and its authoritative interpretation by well-known scholars up to the 10th century.

The Context of the Current Debate

Abdullah Saeed opens the study with an outline of the human rights issue. To start with, he counters the claim that the call for the implementation of human rights is a question of an instrument of power of the West. This call is in point of fact inherent to Judaism, Christianity, and Islam, for it is plain and simple a question of people possessing rights on the basis of their being human. These rights have been formulated in numerous declarations with the collaboration of non-Western member nations of the United Nations – and among these declarations is The Universal Declaration of Human Rights dating from 1948.[140]

In the following, Saeed traces the history of the emergence of various human rights declarations up to The Universal Declaration of Human Rights in 1948. He expressly refers to every individual's right, as it is formulated there, to not only be included in a religion but also to have no religion, to practice a belief alone or with others openly, to convert, and thereby to not only foster concealed convictions within oneself which would otherwise never get through to the outside world.[141] Saeed makes it clear that he considers religious freedom to be the complete measure of negative as well as positive religious freedom, for convictions which are concealed possess little significance if they are not able to be expressed in actions.

With that said, Saeed unambiguously positions himself against the implied understanding of religious freedom coming out of the wording of numerous constitutions of Muslim majority countries. In such cases, it is implied that when individual convictions deviate from the interpretation of

139 Ibid.

140 Ibid., p. 9.

141 Ibid., p. 11.

Islam provided by the *ᶜulamā'* or governmental institutions, they are only allowed as internally concealed worldviews.

Saeed has also backed away from the traditional Sharia-influenced understanding of Islam as the only religion which allows comprehensive civil rights and liberties. This is something which has been defended by al-Qaraḍāwī. Saeed apparently does not want to award any religion the right to invite those who believe differently to join but then not grant them the right to leave. At no point in this first chapter does Saeed allow the perception that he would like to grant Islam special rights in the choir of religions.

Saeed continues in his explanation that generally with regard to religious freedom, practice remains far behind theory and that that is not only the case in Muslim majority societies. While cultural relativists reject the thought of universal human rights as an expression of Western neo-colonial imperialism, some Muslims find the values of The Universal Declaration of Human Rights in the Quran and Muḥammad's *sunna*. From their point of view – and it becomes evident from the argument developed on the following 100 pages that the author includes himself at this point – the rejection of free religious conversion is conditioned by "a misreading of the relevant sections of the Qur'an and a reliance on pre-modern Islamic law."[142] This "pre-modern Islamic law" – and this understanding belong to Abdullah Saeed's foundational convictions, which he repeats a number of times – together are neither "sacred" nor "immutable" but rather a "a human product constructed in a certain socio-historical context and therefore susceptible to change."[143]

With this said, Saeed differentiates between the Quran as God's revelation – which he does not subject to any essential scrutiny either at this point or elsewhere within his publications – and the law derived from it by people at a particular time when there were different parameters and thus no longer possesses any binding nature. Of course, with this the related notion of the value of religions and their adherents as believers (Muslims), *people of the book* with fewer rights (Jews, Christians, Zoroastrians), or, in turn, legally subordinated non-believers (all those who believe differently) has no basis.

---

142 Ibid., p. 13.

143 Ibid., p. 13.

Saeed notes correctly that this traditional notion not only means restrictions for non-Muslims – whereby he surely, given the remark that "the state does not generally discriminate against non-Muslims," sees their situation to be more positive than those involved would see it themselves in a number of states. Rather, it also only means freedom for Muslims "as long as they are not in conflict with the local 'orthodoxy.'"[144]

In what follows, Saeed points out that numerous Muslim majority states have anchored the commitment to religious freedom in their constitution and have outwardly defended the idea that already 1400 years ago the Quran formulated the principle of religious freedom in Sura 2:256. And nevertheless, numerous states have difficulties with the ratification of the corresponding UN documents on what is the freedom of religious conversion in every direction. This is due to the fact that the traditional theological understanding of the superiority of Islam as the most perfect of all religions is not to be relinquished.[145]

As an illustration of this point of view of the inferiority of other religions, which makes a conversion to adulterated Judaism or Christianity undesirable, Saeed quotes the Iranian Shiite theologian Sultanhussein Tabandeh as well as the Egyptian Sunnite representative Hassan Ahmad Abidin. Due to the fact that many theologians are shaped by this notion of the hierarchy of religions, Saeed concludes, they cannot warm to the thought that Muslims should also have the right to be allowed to turn away from Islam as the better religion. That is all the more the case since from their point of view neither the Quran nor tradition grants the possibility of apostasy.

With this said, Saeed ascribes the actual responsibility for the prohibition on turning away from Islam in Muslim majority societies to neither politics nor society, to neither lack of education nor the political domination of Western states. He has instead localized it in inner-Islamic discourse among theologians as opinion leaders who are not ready to revise the view of a "pre-modern Islamic legal view of religious freedom" in favour of – from his standpoint – universally valid human rights. The consequence of this for Saeed is the following:

---

144 Ibid.

145 "The argument of the superiority of Islam is ancient, found in classical sources of Islamic law." Ibid., pp. 15-16.

> "... many Muslims today argue that Islam is the true and final religion and that turning from this true religion to another which is, by definition, 'false' cannot be tolerated."[146]

Saeed thus views theologians as the actual forces spreading the "seed of the word."[147] As long as this is the case, the result, even if Islamic human rights declarations were to be formulated, can be nothing other than reduced human rights and individual freedoms.[148] This is so even if the concrete situations in the various Muslim majority states are very diverse. Despite all the commitments to religious freedom, it becomes critical when it has to do with the question of apostasy: It is prohibited almost everywhere and is often very severely punished, in some countries punishable even by death.[149]

Saeed summarizes his criticism of the specific understanding of religious freedom within classical Islamic theology as follows: In Muslim majority societies there is, on the one hand, a consensus to the effect that the conversion of a non-Muslim to a religion other than Islam is not permissible. The compulsion to lead an apostate back to Islam, however, definitely exists. That the right to religious freedom is indeed a universal conviction is accepted, but it is also accepted that this does not apply to Muslims.[150] Abdullah Saeed thus basically disputes the universal validity of argumentation from the formative period of Islam and the indisputability of interpretations of the Sharia on the question of apostasy which, as regards to the founders and followers of the four Sunnite as well as the most importance Shiite school of legal thought, are essentially in close proximity to each other.

---

146 Ibid., p. 16.

147 Thus the title of Hrant Dink's posthumously published articles after his murder in 2007 in Istanbul: Hrant Dink. *Von der Saat der Worte*. Verlag Hans Schiler: Berlin, 2008.

148 At this point, Abdullah Saeed formulates in a slightly ironic manner with respect to the Universal Islamic Declaration of Human Rights of the Islamic Council of Europe (which strictly limiting significant human rights) that this group had accepted the document "with much fanfare": Abdullah Saeed; Hassan Saeed. *Freedom of Religion, Apostasy and Islam*. Ashgate: Aldershot, 2004, pp. 16-17.

149 Abdullah Saeed names Saudi Arabia, Sudan, and Yemen as examples of countries which threaten apostates with the death penalty: Ibid., p. 19.

150 Ibid., p. 19.

The Historical Context of the Debate

In the second chapter, Abdullah Saeed addresses the historical causes of the classical understanding of apostasy. He describes the religious circumstances on the Arabian Peninsula at the time of the development of Islam and investigates in particular the then ruling understanding of tolerance. He sketches Muḥammad's essential acknowledgment of Judaism and Christianity as "religions of the book." However, he also refers to the Quran's criticism of the Jewish community as well as certain dogmatic statements from within Christianity, such as the Trinity.

The same level of respect is not shown to pre-Islamic heathenism (Saeed uses the rather derogatory term "idolatry" at this point) as is shown to the book religions. That does not mean, however, that from the point of view of the Quran not all people should be treated with respect regardless of their religion.[151] In a time which Saeed defines as lasting up to the year 630 A.D., all those who did not want to convert to Islam were not to be forced to do so. However, the political danger which emanated from these groups was to be averted. For that reason, since the "hostilities" on the part of these groups had to be brought to a halt, there were in part hostile formulations against those not belonging to the Islamic community from the early days of Islam after the year 630 A.D.

The caliphs also continued to practice tolerance during the subsequent spread of Islam, such that those conquered were able to retain their ancestral religions. According to the understanding of the author, apart from those few exceptions where there were cases of oppression of non-Muslims, what was principally religious freedom granted under Islamic rule expanded up to the abolishment of the caliphate in 1924, to include adherents of Judaism and Christianity as well as Zoroastrianism. Beyond that, it extended to "each other religious community under Muslim political rule," and a few lines later Saeed explicitly mentions Hinduism.[152]

Marked on the surface by tolerance, the Islamic community had numerous internal conflicts to fight which also included the question of the political rule of the community as well as who was actually to be viewed as a believer. What developed was a "'mainstream' outlook of the majority

[151] Ibid., p. 21.
[152] Ibid., p. 22.

of Muslims . . . it came to be conceived of as 'orthodoxy.'"[153] Orthodoxy, however, viewed the cases where various theological groups split off and ideological trends in early Islam such as Ḫāriǧītes, Shi'ites, Qadarites, Ǧabrīya, Murǧi'a, and Muᶜtazila, supplemented by Sufism, as either aberrant or even heretical, and Saeed sketches out their differing understandings of apostasy in all brevity

With this list, Saeed underscores the fact that there were very strongly opposing notions of "orthodoxy" and "heresy" in the formative period of Islam, and he simultaneously illustrates that already at that time no such thing as a single genuine interpretation of this question existed. Additionally, he emphasizes the relativity of a content-based definition of true Islam among the founders of the four Sunnite schools of legal thought and the most important Shiite school of legal thought, which in the end were able to assert their understandings as "orthodox."

Saeed detects growing intolerance among Muslims as well as mutual accusations of extremism and heresy which have continued into modernity in this age of increasing "proceedings" about the true interpretation of Islam. According to Saeed, this development was reinforced at the beginning of Umayyad rule by the intrusion of state force into questions of theology. The 9th century theological discussion and political dispute about the question of the (un)createdness of the Quran serves as an example for Saeed. In this connection, intellectuals, philosophers, and theologians were accused of and tortured for apostasy depending on the understanding of the respective ruling caliph, whereby at one time there was one reading and at another time another.

Saeed names a number of reasons for this development, such as the lack of a premier teaching authority within (Sunnite) Islam. As a result, there were a number of interpretations existing alongside each other which were the "only true" interpretation. Furthermore, he names the misuse of power by those who, owing to their positions, had the possibility of defining "true Islamic doctrine" as well as the power to undermine the existence of all those who opposed them.

For the period from the 8th to the 18th century, Saeed counts 14 scholars against whom there were charges of apostasy, heresy, severe sin, freethinking, and unbelief brought during their lifetime and who were either at-

---

153 Ibid., p. 27.

tacked, persecuted, imprisoned, and executed, while in later centuries they were considered role models and esteemed theologians. Among them are such noble names as Abū Ḥanīfa, Aḥmad Ibn Ḥanbal, and Ibn Taymīya.[154]

An increase in the condemnation and execution of individual dissenters, according to Saeed, is portrayed in accusing entire groups of apostasy. From Saeed's perspective, the Islamic community defined itself in the first three centuries by a strict separation between "inside" and "outside," between "true believers" and "heretics," and between "orthodox" and "apostates" much more strictly than the Quran, which takes as a basis a much broader understanding of the "believer." After the 10th century, an epoch of "blind following" came after the early figures of authority.[155]

Nowadays, according to Saeed, it is less the four schools of legal thought in Islamic societies which bring forward charges marked by intolerance against those who think differently. Nevertheless, a number of groups draw the opposition of the majority against them: Islamists, who aspire to establish an Islamic state, puritans who want to create as "pure" an Islam as possible and wish to avoid each and every reform, traditionalists who want to follow classical Sharia Islam as loyally as possible, "Ijtihadis" who demand reform and restoration of classical Sharia Islam, and secularists who reduce Islam to the realm of personal belief.[156]

With this chapter Abdullah Saeed illustrates how arbitrary and time-conditioned the respective understanding of "true" belief has been throughout the history of Islam and how closely linked it has been with the problematic issue of the abuse of power. This abuse of power allowed the instrument of denunciation in the hands of rulers to become a sharp weapon of combat against theological or political opponents.

For Abdullah Saeed, early Islamic history is thus not – as for instance is the case for Yūsuf al-Qaraḍāwī – an exemplary implementation of true faith to which the present day Muslim community has to return in order for Islam to be reinvigorated into its intrinsic, pure form and cope with modernity. A distant glance at achievements as well as undesirable developments underlies Saeed's analysis of early Islamic history and is thus a measure of self-criticism. This would perhaps never be uttered by a scholar of the likes of al-Qaraḍāwī, who tends in the direction of the Salafist spec-

154 Ibid., pp. 30-31.
155 Ibid., p. 33.
156 Ibid., pp. 33-34.

trum and who does not want to give up his point of reference for his actions, which is the unquestionable ideal of the primal Islamic community.

The Term Apostasy

In the following section[157] Saeed discusses the matter of the fluid terminology of apostasy and the difficulty arising out of it as far as the delimitation to blasphemy, heresy, hypocrisy, and unbelief is concerned. Saeed traces back the acceptance of the death penalty for apostasy in Islam to the influence of Judaism and Christianity. That is a development which in his opinion is fortified by the statements of the Quran and traditions regarding apostasy as well as from the experiences made by the first Muslim community with the movement of apostasy on the Arabian Peninsula after Muḥammad's death.

Saeed first of all discusses the term for apostasy (*ridda*): He points out that the Quran does not include the term *ridda* and that post-Quranic definitions of *ridda* indeed frequently contain descriptions such as the denial of the existence of God or of Muḥammad's mission. However, each attempt to organize apostasy into clear categories with respect to word, deed, or conviction ultimately remains indistinct.

Saeed continues his discussion by also mentioning the frequently brought charge of apostasy or the additionally brought charge of blasphemy (*sabb Allāh* bzw. *sabb ar-rasūl*). Similar to the charge of *ridda*, they can neither be found in the Quran nor handed down in the sayings of Muḥammad as an offense with a specific sentencing. They incriminate the individual who expresses such things, first and foremost for having committed a great sin, and in the eyes of numerous theologians it is also apostasy. There has been no consensus among Muslim theologians with respect to the question of whether blasphemers were to continue to be viewed as Muslim believers.

By means of a number of historical examples of diverse victims of charges of blasphemy, Saeed points to the arbitrariness of the charge. According to his understanding, this was especially employed by Muslim jurists as an abuse of power in the time after Muḥammad's death. Saeed's criticism is furthermore directed at the fact that an insult to Muḥammad

157 Ibid., pp. 334ff.

was threatened with a more severe punishment than an insult made towards God.[158]

Regarding charges against dissenters throughout the course of Islamic history, the term used for heresy (*zandaqa*) has not been a Quranic term. For that reason, the term has been filled with various sorts of content, frequently having meant to commit one of the *ḥudūd* offenses, politically to collaborate with the enemy, or theologically to deny the prophetic office of Muḥammad and the revelation of the entirety of the Quranic text. Nevertheless, the leeway for the misuse of power, according to Saeed, was in the case of this charge accordingly great, since it could only be refuted with much difficulty by the defendant.[159]

The circumstances surrounding the charge of hypocrisy (*nifāq*) are similar, and the effects of heresy are warned about in the Quran. However, from Saeed's point of view, there is as little calling for the death penalty for hypocrisy as there is in the case of blasphemers or apostates. Saeed traces the opinion of many scholars who consider hypocrites as serious dangers for the survival of the Muslim community back to political events of the 8th century A.D. At that time, Christians and Zoroastrians had formally converted to Islam, presenting a danger for the Abbasid caliphate that meant the hypocritical activities against the rulers were responded to with the death penalty.[160]

The circumstances are different in the case of unbelief (*kufr*). Most frequently, according to Saeed, unbelief is expressed in the denial (of the uniqueness) of God or of the prophetic office of Muḥammad. The circumstances are different insofar as the Quran does take up use of the term in a number of passages and mentions a number of marks of belief (such as the acknowledgment of God and of Muḥammad as a prophet but also the practice of Islam) but defines neither the unbeliever *(kāfir*) nor the believer (*mu'min*).[161]

From this Saeed concludes just how fluid the lines between the individual terms are and how possible it is for people who on the basis of a lack of clear criteria are then put into the position of having to conduct

---

158 Ibid., p. 39.

159 Ibid., p. 40.

160 Ibid., pp. 41-42.

161 Ibid., pp. 42-43.

"guesswork, ijtihad . . . and soul-searching."[162] According to Saeed, that is specifically what opens the floodgate to charging other Muslims or scholars deviating from one's own understanding with the anathema of apostasy or heresy and thereby politically muzzling them or summoning the Islamic community against them. And then, Saeed warns, if individual Muslims – or a corrupt regime supported by the "religious establishment" – exercised vigilante justice and killed the defendant on the basis of this obscurity of terms and with the opportunity for mutual accusation, then the Muslim community would even support this offense.

While Saeed warns against arbitrariness and the handing over of an innocent victim to rulers and theological authorities, it appears that one could at any rate conclude from the writings of al-Qaraḍāwī that, with an argumentum ex silentio, al-Qaraḍāwī sees no reason for concern. Since he does not mention such thoughts in his writings with as much as a word, al-Qaraḍāwī considers theological authorities, on the basis of their education in theology and law, to be competent, incorruptible, and free from error and a thirst for power.

In order to continue to clarify the character of judgment on account of apostasy, on the following pages Abdullah Saeed takes up four views held by four theologians from the 14th century and modernity along with their identifying features of apostasy.[163] Although there are numerous criteria about which there is broad consensus – such as the mockery of Islam, polytheism, or the failure to acknowledge the Quran – for other criteria there is less consensus demonstrated or items which largely elude objective inspection, such as the refusal to label Jews and Christians as non believers, the failure to practice Islam, or "to hate any aspect of Islam."[164]

The chapter closes with the consideration that by word or deed Muslims as well as non-Muslims could fall under the death penalty verdict on account of apostasy. According to Saeed, what one group, such as the Sunnites, considers apostasy can be interpreted by another group, for example the Shiites, as orthodoxy.

Regarding the "apostasy lists," Saeed notes critically that they are additionally suitable for totally controlling the thinking and actions of a person. With that said, those *ᶜulamā'* who do not differentiate between smaller sins

---

[162] Ibid., p. 43.

[163] Ibid., pp. 44-48.

[164] Ibid., pp. 46-48.

and severe sins with their criteria of orthodoxy, but rather count all the points of their self-prepared catalogue as capital offenses, have set their own limits tighter than those set by the Quran and the *sunna* and as a result are in the position to exercise considerable power to the detriment of others:[165]

> "Since the punishment of apostasy in Islamic law is a severe one, accusation of this offence can . . . be a powerful weapon in the hands of unscrupulous *ulama* or political authorities enabling them to eliminate their theological or political opponents."[166]

The very numerous warnings against the political misuse of power via the charge of apostasy have become reality in the life of both authors, in particular, however, for Hassan Saeed. This is due to the fact that after the publication of this book, Abdullah and Hassan Saeed were themselves confronted by members of the Islamic Democratic Party (IDP) on the Maldives with the charge of apostasy.[167]

Abdullah Saeed emphasizes that this judging mentality on the part of scholars is not according to Quranic revelation and that this "plethora of apostasy lists . . . can only be described as fluid, ambiguous, and highly problematic,"[168] for each scholar (Saeed points particularly to the example of Pakistan) produces a list according to his own discretion, places himself into an absolute position, is inscrutable, and thereby judges over the life and death of other people.

---

[165] Abdullah Saeed also critically occupies himself with the role of the scholar as well as with the conflictual link between the state and the *ᶜulamā'* at another point: Abdullah Saeed. "Islam and Politics. The official ulema and religious legitimacy of the modern nation state" in: Shahram Akbarzadeh; Abdullah Saeed (eds.). *Islam and Political Legitimacy*. Routledge: Abingdon, 2003, pp. 14-28.

[166] Abdullah Saeed; Hassan Saeed. *Freedom of Religion, Apostasy and Islam*. Ashgate: Aldershot, 2004, p. 49.

[167] Comp. the report by Judith Evans. "Supreme Council bans Hassan Saeed's Book," 18.6.2008. Minivan News. Independent News for the Maldives. http://www.minivannews.com/news/news.php?id=4605 (24.6.2010).

[168] Abdullah Saeed; Hassan Saeed. *Freedom of Religion, Apostasy and Islam*. Ashgate: Aldershot, 2004, p. 49.

The Punishment for Apostasy

In Chapter 4, Abdullah Saeed comes to the actual topic of apostasy and the justification for its punishment. Already at the beginning of this section, the author again expresses that he cannot accept punishing a sin (and be it even a severe sin), which from his point of view apostasy is, especially since the Quran itself does not mention punishment in this life. For that reason, it is problematic, according to Saeed, that a majority of early Islamic theologians who lean upon tradition almost unanimously speak out as advocates of the death penalty.

Saeed next reports on a number of criteria for determining apostasy in early Islamic theology, broken down according to legal schools. In the case of a charge, it can be determined by a confession or confirmed by the testimony of a witness. It can also be confirmed by a judge calling for the confession of faith to be spoken. Saeed names a number of civil law consequences of apostasy (such as disinheritance or divorce). He discusses the request to admit remorse as well as the question of who according to classical legal understanding is justified to carry out the death penalty on the accused. However, Saeed also makes a limitation here by saying that the frequent code of practice of premature action, which executes the apostate via vigilante justice, significantly endangers the life of a convicted individual.

In the second part of this chapter, the author critically addresses the reasons advocates have for the death penalty for apostasy. He does this by at first discussing why with respect to the death penalty there is nothing to be read out of verses from the Quran, such as Sura 5:54 and 16:109, as there is no imperative that can be read out from the frequently quoted texts of tradition in this connection.[169] For Saeed, these texts are no indication that the death penalty for apostasy belongs to the teaching of Islam, because if that were true, according to Saeed, any change of religion would be prohibited: "This, from the perspective of Islamic law, would be absurd,"[170] for the conversion from non-Muslim to Islam is, after all, one of the most desirable things of all.

For that reason, according to Saeed, early Islamic scholars already allowed an exception to this so absolute sounding rule (such as, for instance,

---

169 Ibid., pp. 56ff.

170 Ibid., p. 59.

the excusable turning from Islam under coercion), which did not lead to condemning the apostate. Likewise, there were some proponents of the death penalty who did not advocate the death penalty for apostasy until the apostate committed high treason against the Islamic community, i.e., until above all they became guilty of a political offense. This also describes the position of Yūsuf al-Qaraḍāwī, who admittedly with this admission of turning from Islam sees such high treason as pre-existing and, more specifically, judges that with the disclosure of this decision of conscience the destruction of the *umma* has already been accomplished. For Saeed, on the other hand, high treason is first recognizable when the apostate goes to the side of the enemy in the midst of acts of war and actively damages the *umma* by his actions.

At this point, Saeed does not actually argue that the apostate, who at the same time is acting militantly against the *umma*, has to be executed. However, he explains that this understanding of affirming the death penalty in the early days of Islam arose from the context of struggle for survival and is thereby explicable.[171]

In this Saeed recognizes a sensible explanatory model for the link between apostasy and the death penalty in the early days of Islam and correspondingly classifies a number of circumstances of early Islamic history, such as the execution of apostates after the taking of Mecca by Muḥammad's soldiers in 630 A.D. He also mentions other examples which report that individual apostates toward Muḥammad were forgiven. A third category of texts found in tradition are categorized by him as not reliable, so that from Saeed's point of view, there remains no example of a text which clearly documents that an apostate suffered the death penalty solely for turning from Islam.

An additional argument for the argumentation conducted by Abdullah Saeed is provided by the *ridda* wars at the time of the rule of Caliph Abū Bakr, who presents for him a virtually classical example of the political motive (at best relating to the threatened loss of tax revenues) and at any rate not lying in the religious motive for the execution of rebels who had

[171] Ibid., p. 60 formulated similarly by Shehrazad Hamit: "This sanctioning of violence against apostates was thus a specific strategy to help ensure the survival of Islam rather than one aimed at denying people the freedom of religion." Shehrazad Hamit. "Apostasy and the Notion of Religious Freedom in Islam" in: *MIJ* 1/2 (2006), pp. 31-38, here p. 3.

opposed the rule of Abū Bakr.[172] Like Yūsuf al-Qaraḍāwī,[173] Abdullah Saeed also considers that the early Islamic community would have gone under had it not been for the resistance of the *ridda* movement and he does not derive from this, in contrast to al-Qaraḍāwī, the conclusion that everyone who recognizably turns from Islam nowadays has to likewise be executed in order to not endanger the *umma*. Completely to the contrary, the *Ridda* wars offer for Saeed no justification for condemning apostates to death nowadays.[174]

After reading this fourth chapter, it is apparent that there can be no justification in Abdullah Saeed's eyes for executing those who think differently in a Muslim majority country. Also, there is no passage in the Quran or in tradition which is able to justify such a rigid punishment. It is Saeed's understanding that under no circumstances is it possible to derive a present day directive for the execution of apostates[175] from insufficiently documented texts coming from tradition.[176]

The Quran as a Charter of Religious Freedom

In the following chapter, Abdullah Saeed continues with his argumentation: According to his opinion, it is not only the case that there are no grounds for deriving a compulsory command from the Quran, tradition,

---

172 Abdullah Saeed; Hassan Saeed. *Freedom of Religion, Apostasy and Islam*. Ashgate: Aldershot, 2004, pp. 65-66.

173 Yūsuf al-Qaraḍāwī *fiqh al-ğihād dirāsa muqarāna li-aḥkāmihī wa-falsafatihī fī ḍau' al-qur'ān wa-'s-sunna*. Maktabat wahba: al-Qāhira, 2009[1], Vol. 1, p. 182.

174 Abdullahi Ahmed An-Na'im also argues completely similarly, ascribing the reports of the *sunna* on the punishment of apostates in the early days of Islam to "the special circumstances" and demands: "The legal concept of apostasy and all its civil and criminal consequences must be abolished." Abdullahi Ahmed An-Na'im. *Toward an Islamic Reformation. Civil Liberties, Human Rights, and International Law*. Syracuse University Press: New York, 1990, p. 109.

175 Abdullah Saeed; Hassan Saeed. *Freedom of Religion, Apostasy and Islam*. Ashgate: Aldershot, 2004, p. 68.

176 In this connection, Muddathir ᶜAbd ar-Rahim holds the view that Abdullah and Hassan Saeed discredit their opponents through exaggeration and caricature; in addition, they do not recognize tradition as a source of legislation, which is, after all, accepted by all schools of legal thought: Muddathir ᶜAbd ar-Rahim. Abdullah Saeed and Hassan Saeed. Freedom of Religion, Apostasy and Islam" in: *IJMES* 37 (2005), pp. 614-615, here p. 615.

and early Islamic history regarding the execution of apostates. His opinion is that there are far more reasons against it, and indeed, there is an outright ban on executing renegades.

As the line of argument for his thesis of prohibiting the death penalty for apostasy, Abdullah Saeed first of all concentrates in great detail on the Quran, about which, as a matter of principle, there is consensus with respect to its fundamental and complete validity.

Saeed directs his argumentation at the basic assumption that the Quran expressly opposes any invitation to Islam laden with coercion, for in Mecca as well as in Medina the message of God for people had to be conveyed "not by force but by discussion and persuasion."[177] Saeed quotes a total of 25 verses from the Quran from the Meccan as well as the Medinan time periods, for which the emphasis on the personal decision in questions of faith is held in common.

Not even in Medina, in a time when Muḥammad was able to increasingly develop military assertiveness, was coercion and force a means of spreading Islam, since the Quran, according to Saeed, already spoke about a diversity of religions, although it would have been easy for God to make all people Muslims so that only one religion exists on the earth (comp. Sura 10:99). For that reason, Muḥammad's task was that of a preacher whose responsibility did not include who received the message and who rejected it (see Sura 245:54).

At this point, Abdullah Saeed finds himself in a balancing act. On the one hand, he apparently does not want to directly take a position against the opinion that an own social order emerged in Medina through the emergence of the political community of the *umma* and the legal arrangements, above all in marital, family, and penal areas of the law.[178] Then again, he emphasizes that Muḥammad, in spite of his undeniable role as a legislator and commander, was only called to preach and that Meccans as well as Medinans were granted entire freedom to reject his message. With that

[177] Ibid., p. 69.

[178] He grants this at another point when he writes with reference to Muḥammad: "In his scheme, there was no distinction between a religious domain and a political domain." Abdullah Saeed. "Islam and Politics. The official ulema and religious legitimacy of the modern nation state" in: Shahram Akbarzadeh; Abdullah Saeed (eds.). *Islam and Political Legitimacy*. Routledge: Abingdon, 2003, pp. 14-28, here p. 15.

said, Islam is for him a religion which essentially rejects coercion from the very beginning. It is an argument which aggravates the justification of today's representatives for limiting religious freedom.

Muḥammad, as Saeed stresses, is not responsible for the decision of those to whom he preached the message of God (see, for instance, Sura 10:108). Those who rejected it are threatened by the Quran with punishment in the life hereafter (see, for instance, Sura 4:115). Nevertheless, God, in contrast to the angels, has provided humankind with freedom of the will.[179] Furthermore, according to Saeed, the Quran says in Sura 2:256, for instance, that it inviolably advocates religious freedom, since this verse has never been abrogated.[180] And Saeed, despite all of the interpretive variations, of which he lists several, holds firmly to this. Indeed, even Sayyid Quṭb is on his side in this question.[181]

At this point Saeed grants that in various verses the Quran orders the killing of polytheists who will not subjugate themselves to Muḥammd. However, since a group of polytheists at one point presented a political danger for the Muslim community, Saeed is of the opinion that these verses exclusively express the political circumstances at the end of Muḥammad's rule.

The formulation found in Sura 2:191, "And slay them wherever ye catch them," is, for that reason, viewed by Saeed as an expression of the necessary defensive stance allowed by Islam against those groups at Muḥammad's time who did not hold to peace treaties and agreements and injured Muslims and attacked their belief. The Quran itself warns at this point against oppression and aggression (Sura 2:190-193). Thus, Saeed viewed the verses in the Quran which broach the issue of fighting Muḥammad's adversaries as an expression of the legitimate defense against the political enemies of the *umma*; in no case was it in his opinion a matter of a one-sided aggression against non-Muslims or a matter of coercion with the goal of carrying out conversion.

In the final part of the chapter, Saeed turns to the question of punishing apostasy in the afterlife: He discusses several verses from the Quran which threaten God's punishment against those who initially were believers but

[179] Abdullah Saeed; Hassan Saeed. *Freedom of Religion, Apostasy and Islam*. Ashgate: Aldershot, 2004, p. 72.

[180] Ibid., p. 78.

[181] Ibid., pp. 73-75.

then turned from the faith (comp., e.g., Sura 3:86). In the process, he again underscores that these verses speak exclusively of hellfire. There is also mention of the absence of the forgiveness of God. However, there is never mention of a punishment in this world.[182] Also the example of Muḥammad, as Saeed continues, gives testimony to Muḥammad's lenient attitude towards apostates, to whom he only proclaims his message but is not authorized to force a positive reaction to it.

The same applies to the repeatedly mentioned "hypocrites" (e.g., in Sura 2:8-9), who according to the judgment of the Quran only pretended to have faith out of opportunism. However, at no point were they threatened with death, although the Quran labels them as liars, unbelievers, and authors of mischief. In order to underscore this statement, Saeed cites an *ḥadīṯ*, which reports on Muḥammad's leniency and forbearance with hypocrites as well as his strict prohibition against executing them.

If in his Ḥudaibīya armistice agreement concluded with the Meccans in 628 A.D. one sees that Muḥammad even allowed apostates to be given permission to return to Mecca, it is just as clear an argument for Saeed against Muḥammad's alleged desire to execute apostates as the claim from tradition, according to which Muḥammad is supposed to have said that he was not commissioned to delve into people's inward recesses.[183] Again and again, Abdullah Saeed intersperses names of Muslim scholars and early Islamic authorities which represent similar positions concerning certain individual points he holds.

In his closing remarks of this chapter, Abdullah Saeed again emphasizes that the death penalty for apostasy can really only hardly be derived from the Quran and the *sunna*, even if this was the honest opinion of numerous scholars: "The law of apostasy", as Saeed closes his remarks in this section, "was developed in Islam on the basis of a few isolated *hadith*, at a time and in circumstances that differ radically from today."[184]

At the time Islam emerged, there existed no national state and, with that said, no authority which would have defended the human rights of the individual; religious and family ties were the significant group building principles. Among believers and non-believers there were those who lived

---

[182] Ibid., pp. 80-81.

[183] Ibid., pp. 82-83.

[184] Abdullah Saeed; Hassan Saeed. *Freedom of Religion, Apostasy and Islam*. Ashgate: Aldershot, 2004, p. 85.

in peace with the Islamic community, and there were those who fought against them. Thus, in a time in which the existence of the Islamic community was threatened by non-believers, there arose a struggle for their survival in which several apostates went over to the enemies' side. The lack of belief alone, i.e., neither the refusal to turn to Islam, nor apostasy from Islam, could ever be a reason for using coercion to bring about conversion, to exercise oppression, and battle as well as the imposition of the death penalty, for non-believers will first be requited in the afterlife.

It is apparent in this chapter that Abdullah Saedd does not accept anything which is contradictory to his view of apostasy. He above all quotes from the Quran, tradition, and the theologies of individual theologians at points where he finds support for his view of things. He pieces these together to a whole which leaves no other possibility open than to recognize religious freedom as an inherent principle of Islam. Within the course of the individual chapters, at multiple times he repeats his opinion of the exclusive justification of retributive justice in the afterlife so that the reader is repeatedly confronted with Saeed's core tenets. An intensive debate with and argumentative refutation of the texts coming from tradition is found less than with argumentation against the theologians who advocate this view, and it is to their work which Abdullah Saeed frequently refers.[185]

The Discussion of Apostasy in Modernity

Abdullah Saeed turns his attention to modernity in Chapter 6, when in contrast to the early days of Islam there has been a greater range of variation with respect to opinions on the question of punishing apostasy. Abdullah Saeed names and discusses the three commonly recognizable contemporary positions: a) the classical position which has been inherited and has remained unchanged since the early days of Islam, b) the modified classical position, and c) the position of endorsing comprehensive religious freedom.

Still, Abdullah Saeed concedes, the majority of Muslim scholars who comment on the topic of apostasy follow the classic position of Sharia scholars from the early days of Islam. With this objectively correct and at the same time self-critical statement, Abdullah Saeed grants that his own

[185] He thus grapples in detail with Abū l-Aʿlā Maudūdī's position on apostasy: Ibid., pp. 90-92.

understanding (at least up to now) has played a marginal role, but he does not defend it in a manner that is any less convincing.

Saeed continues to explain that the adherents of the classical Sharia position adopt the conclusion of the early authorities in unchanged form for modernity. According to Saeed, this is as if these conclusions are not to be scrutinized. These scholars would also continue to hold firmly to the death penalty for apostasy today and would justify this position by using the argument that Islam definitely has to be protected from destruction.[186]

Theologians who defend a modified form of the classical position are of the opinion that a complete application of classical Sharia law is no longer possible in all cases nowadays. Nevertheless, they consider apostasy as a danger for the Muslim community. They identify apostasy with high treason – an expression which, admittedly, is hardly ever clearly defined as regards to contents. High treason cannot be tolerated in a political Islamic state structure and, for that reason, has to be punished. Many of the authors of this category differentiate between the apostate who can only be accused of unbelief but who lives in peace with the Islamic society and the apostate who causes turmoil and rebellion. Saeed mentions examples for both points of view.[187]

Finally, Saeed turns his attention to the third position, which defends the notion that endorsement of the death penalty in the case of apostasy emerged under completely different socio-political circumstances and no longer possesses any justification. The supporters of this view, for which he mentions a number of examples, have various ideological positions and range from secular to Islamist.

Saeed mentions supporters for all three orientations and explains their approaches. He places the focus with respect to detail and the number of mentioned names on the third group, to which he himself belongs. It becomes particularly clear how diverse, indeed contrasting, the judgment of apostasy is as depicted by Muslim theologians in modernity.

The Danger of false Charges

In Chapter 7 the author points out the particular potential danger of a possible misuse in the prosecution of apostates. Indeed, Yūsuf al-Qaraḍāwī

---

186 Ibid., pp. 88-89.
187 Ibid., pp. 90-93.

has warned in several of his writings that believers could be prematurely suspected and wrongly accused of apostasy. For al-Qaraḍāwī, the solution does not, therefore, lie in doubting the justification of the death penalty or in calling for a reevaluation of this set of problems. Instead, the solution lies much more in placing the judgment of apostates in the hands of competent scholars in Islamic law and theology who are able to pronounce an appropriate judgment – including the penalty of death.

Essentially, Abdullah Saeed argues differently at this point. For him the difficulty does not lie in the qualification of those who are to judge an apostate. The difficulty also does not lie in the question of whether a rumour or a fact is involved when there is suspicion of apostasy. For Saeed the difficulty lies in the historical perspective, which has to do with holding firmly to the death penalty after the early days of Islam, when battles against rebels served the survival of the community.

From a theological perspective, the difficulty lies in the lack of a reevaluation of a massively transformed society in modernity, as well as in the lack of a supreme teaching authority in Sunnite Islam. This makes improper accusation of apostasy against those who think differently simple, and it makes improper accusation of apostasy against victims of such charges almost unavoidable. This is due to the fact that in most cases the *ᶜulamā'* are civil servants and simultaneously, as the principal guardians of religion, exercise a great amount of social influence. With this they define – and the reader is reminded here of the case of Abū Zaid – as an extended arm of the state, what is correct belief, what is orthodoxy, and what is an aberration. For Abdullah Saeed, it is a dangerous accumulation of power.[188] For that reason, Saeed states that

> "... in a Muslim society, accusation of apostasy is one of the most dangerous and powerful tools available to an individual or a group to eliminate an opponent or a competitor (political or religious). Similarly it can be highly effective in suppressing dissent and maintaining the status quo."[189]

Additional factors which promote abusive handling of the apostasy issue and for that reason make a reorientation in the judgment of this question necessary are the modern media, global migration, and the resultant strong

---

188 Ibid., pp.. 99-100.

189 Ibid., p. 100.

diversification and pluralization of opinions within the Islamic community. This is an invitation for one group to charge another with aberrations.

Owing to these numerous factors which enable free actions on the part of individuals and which burden others due to selfish motives, incriminate others, or are even able to bring them into danger through *takfīr* (labelling them as unbelievers), extremist groups are encouraged or even comprehend it to be "their duty" to accuse those of apostasy whom they hold to be non-believers, Saeed continues. This is the case even if the courts concerned have not delivered any sort of judgment.[190]

With this said, Saeed points to the great danger to life and limb which threaten an individual who is unofficially condemned in public while his persecutors think – and at this point the reader is reminded of the Farağ Fūda case – that they are making a contribution to the protection of Islam with its stigmatization or even persecution. The consequence of this is that under certain circumstances, in the case of apostasy or blasphemy, society begins to act autonomously to the harm of the accused: "The community in which the act took place sometimes takes the law into its own hands."[191]

As a way to document this analysis, Abdullah Saeed mentions the persecution of the Aḥmadīya community, the badgering of Christians, and the badgering of Muslims deviating from the majority opinion in Pakistan in light of the possibility for anyone to file charges of apostasy with the police. He adds to this depiction of the situation by adding a number of concrete examples, such as the cases of Salman Rushdie and Taslima Nasreen.[192]

According to Saeed these are examples where apostasy law, owing to the function of Muslim scholars as role models and authority figures, can come to be applied in an unofficial way in situations where there are no national laws and opens the option of punishing an apostate. From the viewpoint of the author, this unofficial charge is a vastly more effective and, for the involved individual, more dangerous way of persecution than government legislation itself. This is especially so since scholars position

---

190 Ibid., p. 101.

191 Ibid., p. 100-101.

192 In the process he uses numerous sources, which, for instance, range from the Constitution of Pakistan to the human rights report produced by the US Department of State. Ibid., pp. 101-102.

themselves as lawyers for dealing with God's laws, and God's laws stand above each and every governmental regulation made by man.

In what follows, Abdullah Saeed goes into detail about the misuse of power by religious scholars and sheds light upon "extremists'" abuse and oppression of those who think differently. At this point, the author highlights Abū l-Aᶜlā Maudūdī and Sayyid Quṭb. Through the judgments they made about their governments, the political elite, and societies as pagan ("jahili"), they drew a sharp line between Muslims (by name) and true believers and in so doing provided the justification "to terrorize opponents, especially high profile or influential figures, and silence opposition to a particular political or religious agenda."[193]

Saeed then lists a number of victims of this vigilante justice, such as intellectuals who were permanently brought to silence with charges of apostasy and heresy: At this point Saeed mentions names such as Naṣr Ḥāmid Abū Zaid and ᶜAlī ᶜAbd ar-Rāziq and very briefly outlines the charges brought against them.

With respect to the possibility of placing book publications on a black list, Saeed particularly denounces the role of al-Azhar as a religious censor. As early as 1985, al-Azhar was given this role by law. It had already exercised this role before, however, with the condemnation of various publications, such as publications by Ṭāhā Ḥusain. From Abdullah Saeed's viewpoint, the damage for the society goes far beyond the direct prohibition against a certain work. This is due to the fact that censorship brings the intellectual and cultural life of a country to a standstill:

> "Accusations of apostasy in Egypt . . . appear to have created a climate of fear for its intellectuals, literary figures and liberal Islamic scholars. Censorship of books, films, plays and television programmes by the official religious establishment is on the rise, leading to a gradual stagnation of creative, intellectual and cultural work."[194]

Additional victims of censorship are, from Saeed's point of view, journalists and political office holders, who owing to their sense of reform are frequently designated as apostates in order to possibly be discredited. Saeed also mentions at this point a number of examples such as the found-

---

193 Ibid., p. 103.

194 Ibid., p. 106.

er of the Turkish Republic or the prior Egyptian President, Anwar al-Sādāt, who was assassinated by an extremist attack in 1981 in the wake of the Camp David Accords with arch enemy Israel.

In the closing words of this chapter, Saeed again underscores the danger that apostasy law can become a sharp weapon in the hands of any person by merely accusing another individual: "Harassment, intimidation and violence and even banishment from their community, without any redress" can be the consequence, with the potential "for injustice and wrongful accusation and destruction of life." For that reason, as Abdullah Saeed concludes the chapter, Muslim scholars should limit the existing possibilities for misuse by going through a readjustment with respect to this topic.[195]

For Saeed the difficulty with apostasy law lies neither in the function of Islam as a religion and legal order per se, nor in Islamic history alone, nor is it grounded in the aberrations of individuals or solely in the misuse of power. Rather, and above all, it is in the ossification of the legal practice of finding justice after the emergence of the legal schools up to the 10th century A.D., by which a necessary adaptation of legal sources became impossible. If one reverts to justifying the protection of the Islamic community in light of these foundations of violent subdual of upheaval brought about by the movement of early Islamic secession, then this mechanism becomes an instrument in the hands of extremists for the condemnation, persecution, and oppression of those who think differently.

Reasons for the Explosiveness of the Apostasy Debate

After this comprehensive discussion of the political reasons and consequences of charges of apostasy in Muslim majority countries, Saeed again turns to the religious components of the topic. Furthermore, he mentions factors which could explain why apostasy is such an awkward topic in countries marked by Islam. Here and there, between the lines, the author appears to want to hint at understanding and solidarity.

Unsettled by secularization and missionary activity as well as the painful experience of the crusades, the colonial period, and the abolition of the caliphate, a number of Muslims are again calling for the introduction of apostasy laws. A conversion to Christianity, which in the eyes of most theologians is a corrupted and superseded religion, appears to them to be tar-

[195] Ibid., p. 108.

geted, malicious criticism of the superiority of Islam. A conversion is therefore condemned as compelled or purchased proselytism involving impoverished layers of the population.[196]

In addition, according to Saeed, there are cases of inter-religious marriage as a reason for conversion and, as some Muslims believe, the lack of instruction to youth or instruction laced with too many prohibitions. The result is that youth increasingly distance themselves from Islam. Further reasons for distancing from Islam is its abuse by political authorities, the existence of atheism, materialism, and hedonism as well as philosophies and ideologies such as Marxism, socialism, and nationalism.

According to Saeed, Muslims are also unsettled and alienated with respect to their faith by numerous charges surrounding human rights and women's rights at the basis of present day debates, where Islam stands essentially in a conflict-laden tension with these rights.[197] Nowhere, however, does he draw the conclusion that a prohibition on conversion or, more generally, that a limitation on religious freedom could be justifiable.

At the end of the chapter the author again turns more intensively to the actual apostasy problem. From an internet forum, in which prior Muslims provide reasons for their conversion, he quotes a number of voices, among them also a critic who provides the problem of apostasy within Islam as a reason for his turning from Islam. From Saeed's point of view, such conversion reports, with which Islamic theology and society has up until now hardly grappled, should be the inducement for a modified response to these sceptics: "They represent a challenge to Muslim religious leaders in their efforts at conveying to these sceptical Muslims what Islam truly is and what it represents to people today."[198]

On the other hand, as Saeed continues in his next section, the particularly awkward relationship Muslims have toward apostasy is understandable or at least explicable if one considers that historically the topic has above all been burdened with the context of Christian mission and colonialism. The crusades, the Reconquista on the Iberian Peninsula, secularization, and Orientalism are all things, according to Saeed, which are emotionally unprocessed topics and, with that said, areas in which Muslims see themselves as losers in the competition with the West.

---

196 Ibid., pp. 109-110.

197 Ibid., pp. 112-114.

198 Ibid., p. 116.

In addition, there are the so very important concepts of loyalty and honor in Muslim majority countries. Through the conversion of Muslims to Christianity, they are threatened with damage in a race with the West, which possesses economic and political attractions and is also attractive in light of its civil rights and liberties and the intellectualism it offers. Saeed surely notices correctly in view of most documents within Islamic theology relating to apostasy that concern for the individual, who in giving up Islam loses his salvation, is of less immediate importance.[199]

Connected to this first portion of the book by Abdullah Saeed is a second part by Hassan Saeed with Chapters 9 to 12,[200] in which he critically describes the situation of religious freedom in Malaysia. The author explains the close link between Malaysian nationality and a confession of Islam. In spite of a general affirmation in the constitution with respect to religious freedom, this is strongly limited. This is seen when, for example, citizens who are accused of apostasy are called upon in prison to come back to Islam or even are imprisoned for a certain time for the purpose of forcing a return to Islam. Nevertheless, Hassan Saeed sees no developments in the direction of introducing the death penalty for apostates in Malaysia in the near future.[201]

A Call to rethinking the Debate on Apostasy

In Chapter 13 Abdullah Saeed again summarizes his statements made in the first eight chapters. He emphasized that the debate on human rights and religious freedom is also being conducted in Muslim majority countries and that in the process one sees that Muslims take very different positions. Saeed again comes to speak about the danger of the misuse of power which has been present throughout the entire history of Islam.

In conclusion he calls for rethinking the position on the death penalty on apostasy derived from classical Sharia legislation. This is due to the fact that laws which have developed out of a particular historical situation, such as the caliphate or slavery, are in his opinion not inviolable: "If these laws are no longer practicable or relevant for Muslims, there is a strong justifi-

199 Ibid., pp. 116-119.
200 Ibid., pp. 123ff.
201 Ibid., pp. 157; 163.

cation to reconsider them."[202] This means nothing other than that at least in parts Abdullah Saeed rejects the classical understanding of the Sharia. This also becomes clear because he holds the textual basis for a derivation of the mandatory death penalty to be conceivably narrow "on the basis of certain isolated *hadith*."[203]

At this point Saeed again emphasizes how foundationally the social and political circumstances in the early days of Islam differ from the present circumstances. By above all interpreting the original intention of apostasy legislation as political and as protective of the community and treating the religious components as rather secondary, he defuses the theological debate justifying punishment of apostasy in modernity. According to Saeed, this separation into secular and religious spheres also becomes visible in modern nation states, which grant Muslims as well as non-Muslims the same rights as citizens. That is to say, national identity and religious identity are separated, whereas this was not the case at the time of early Islam.

And finally, as Saeed pragmatically continues, there are nowadays no longer any closed Islamic societies. Instead, due to global media communication, migration, and pluralism, there are multi-religious and multicultural societies where the insistence on early Islamic legislation is of little help. Furthermore, particularly within a minority situation, it is completely meaningless: Conversion simply takes place de facto in one direction or the other.

In several of his publications, Saeed uses the argument of what is factual and uses guidelines from the realities of modernity for the purpose of muffling the idealistic or rather exaggerated expectations of Muslims as well as of non-Islamic societies in which these minorities live. With respect to the application of apostasy law, he also addresses "the unrealistic nature" of a large part of the debate and speaks of preserving ideas from the early days of Islam as "impractical and unrealistic."[204] It is one of the main features of Abdullah Saeed's writings that he always favors the way of seeing under existing circumstances what is feasible, where there are binding rules, and what comes from consensual agreement.

---

202 Ibid., p. 168.

203 Abdullah Saeed; Hassan Saeed. *Freedom of Religion, Apostasy and Islam*. Ashgate: Aldershot, 2004, p. 168.

204 Ibid., pp. 169; 170.

Nowhere in his criticism, however, does Abdullah Saeed go so far as to say that he would basically and flatly reject the historical justification of apostasy legislation in the early days of Islam. He makes a concession with respect to combating enemies, granting the legitimacy of such measures under the then prevailing circumstances of fighting for the survival of the Muslim community. However, he does not concede any justification for these regulations nowadays. As a result, Saeed above all directs himself against the a-historical adoption of early Islamic regulations in the present more than denying every justification to apostasy law in history.

Saeed thus concludes that is it imperative to find justification for the right to comprehensive religious freedom in harmony with the realities of the present time, with the religion of Islam, and with the very different local cultural situations. One should also take leave of concepts such as the caliphate, homogeneous Islamic societies, and the model of a *dār al-islām*.[205] In addition, Saeed sees a reality where there is a certain percentage of only nominal Muslims belonging to Islam, a number estimated to be at least 300 million people.[206] These are people who according to the classical Sharia understanding come very near to being regarded as apostate if they are not altogether regarded as apostate. With this he further undermines the idea of the practicability of apostasy law.

Saeed's argumentation is also pragmatically colored in view of religions' missionary components: Even if Muslims nowadays would like to hold to the prohibition on apostasy out of concern for the reduction in numbers in the Muslim community due to conversions, they are themselves calling upon others to convert to Islam. Saeed criticizes this double standard as not justified. By indicating that it is necessary for adherents of all religions to be given equal treatment, he gives up the classical viewpoint of the superiority and preemption of Islam before all other religions.[207]

---

205 Ibid., p. 170.

206 Ibid., p. 171. This thought is nowhere made a subject of discussion by al-Qaraḍāwī.

207 At another point he more explicitly develops his point of view of the advantageousness of a religiously plural society: "Pluralism . . . invites all people to engage with each other, despite their differences, and to work together towards a civil, fair and just society where being a human being is the key emphasis. It facilitates the creation of a harmonious society by acknowledging differences, ra-

His apprehension that Muslims who only from the force of circumstances remain Muslims but no longer consider Islam to be true and thus become hypocrites is an approach which places the individual in the center of consideration instead of the community. It is also foreign to the defendants of the classical position on apostasy from Islam, for instance that of al-Qaraḍāwī. If as a consequence more Muslims understand the religion "as covenant between an individual and God," that alone is justified, according to Saeed, since this is actually what corresponds to Islam's inherent understanding of the voluntary nature of belonging to this religion. Unfortunately, according to Saeed, only few Muslims have taken the step of wanting to basically reform apostasy law, which from Saeed's point of view is absolutely necessary in modernity.

The weaknesses of this approach to reforming apostasy law lies above all in its method: In Saeed's defense of religious freedom. what remains obscure is by which criteria he admits texts from tradition as instructions for today and which he holds to be obsolete as descriptions of political events in the past. This also applies in the end to Muḥammad's dealing with apostates and to his sayings which, apart from what are at least in part unanswered questions as to authenticity, by all means appear to be heterogeneous in what they purport. With that said, they can be variously interpretable.

Besides the more frequently repeated basic assumption that punishments for apostasy in the early days of Islam actually represented retaliatory punishment for political unrest and all statements and texts classified under this general guideline, Abdullah Saeed quotes no sources which would provide an unassailable foundation for his thesis. Given the diversity of texts from the early days of Islam and the historical imponderableness of their tradition, the results of this investigation of religious freedom in early Islam appear for that reason to be more strongly determined by previously made fundamental assumptions than by an incontestable result derived from available sources.

However, it has to be taken into account that a rejection of the notions of a large part of the early Islamic world of scholarship, with its extensive

ther than hiding it." Abdullah Saeed. "Foundations of Peace in the Qur'an." The Tasmanian Peace Trust 2010 Lecture, held at the Friends Meeting House, North Hobart, Sunday, 11.10.2010, pp. 1-12 (unpublished manuscript from the private collection of the author).

endorsement of the death penalty, requires an essential distancing from one of the pillars of Sharia law – namely the understanding of legal scholars up to the 10th century A.D. – so that its supporters would in the process automatically catapult themselves to the margins of the established world of scholarship and be in danger, threatened, or at least silenced. That is a risk which an English speaking author from Australia, who is economically and politically independent, can most likely take. For that reason, it is not merely by chance but rather downright symptomatic if up to now no supporter of classic Islamic theology has appeared to open the discussion of Abdullah Saeed's writings.

Since on the one hand tradition is not essentially rejected by Abdullah Saeed in its basic function for Sharia law, and yet a handy key to defusing the authority of texts which in his view are problematic is lacking, an actual dispute over the authority of the Sharia, solely questioning the justification of the death penalty for apostasy, has not yet been conducted. Saeed has repeatedly conceded that essential theory formation on the justification of a viewpoint of Islam compatible with the circumstances of Western societies has been lacking in his and in other progressive Muslims' work.[208]

The Prohibition of the Book

Hassan and Abdullah Saeed's book *Freedom of Religion, Apostasy and Islam* received little attention in Australia and other Western countries immediately after it appeared. Its publication, which was judged as "indeed . . . very bold,"[209] triggered political irritation on the Maldives close to four years after its appearance. Beforehand there had already been a dispute regarding the justification of the punishment for apostasy. The leader of the Religious Scholars' Council of the Adhaalath Party on the Maldives, Sheikh Abdul Majeed Abdul Bari, piped up with comments that he endorsed the death penalty for apostasy as well as for adultery involving married people and murder and the amputation of the hand for certain forms of theft, whereupon a "media furore" arose, in the wake of which the book

208 See for instance: Abdullah Saeed. "Muslims in the West Choose between Isolationism and Participation" in: *SangSaeng* 16 (2006), pp. 8-11, here p. 11.

209 S. Chandrasekharan. Maldives: "On Dr. Hassan Saeed's Book on Freedom of Religion and Apostasy" South Asia Analysis Group. Paper no. 2747, 25.6.2008. http://www.southasiaanalysis.org/%5Cpapers28%5Cpaper2747.html (6.5.2011).

Freedom of Religion, Apostasy and Islam by the Saeed brothers moved into the center of attention and protest.[210]

The protest against the book ignited in 2008 directly prior to the first free election in the Presidential Republic of the Maldives. The election was meant to put an end to the administration of President Maumoon Abdul Gayoom, who had been endowed with very far-reaching authority and had ruled since 1978. Since Abdullah Saeed's brother, Dr. Hassan Saeed (b. 1970), then envisaged his own candidacy for the office of President, it can be supposed that the motivation of those who suddenly crusaded against the book several years after its appearance lay perhaps in the political rather than in the theological realm.[211]

Hassan Saeed, at that time the head of the "Dhivehi Qaumee Party", had announced a desire to force his candidacy for President as an independent candidate in the run-up to the election.[212] Owing to differences, the former Justice Minister of the governing party, Mohamed Jameel Ahmed, turned his back against the ruling President and al-Azhar alumnus Gayoom in 2007. Together with Mohamed Jameel Ahmed and the former Minister of Foreign Affairs, Dr. Ahmed Shaheed, Saeed founded an organization with the name "Open Society". The "Open Society" organization morphed into a movement called the "New Maldives Movement", which later joined the "National Unity Alliance" opposition. Under its umbrella, the "National Unity Alliance" united the "Maldivian Democratic Party" (MDP), the "Islamic Democratic Party" (IDP), the "Adaalath Party" as well as the "Social Liberal Party".[213]

---

210 According to the report by Judith Evans. "Apostasy Punishable by Death: Top Adhaalath Scholar," 13.5.2008. Minivan News. http://www.minivannews.org/news_detail.php?id=4462 (5.5.2011).

211 This impression was confirmed by Abdullah Saeed during an interview conducted on 19.6.2011.

212 Comp. for instance his advertising message "Dr. Hassan Saeed for President" for his presidential candidacy at http://www.youtube.com/watch?v=eSQ1Kv6dRUo (part 1) and http://www.youtube.com/watch?v=MZ1P9WlFtaQ&feature=related (part 2) (20.6.2011).

213 S. Chandrasekharan. "Maldives: On Dr. Hassan Saeed's Book on Freedom of Religion and Apostasy." South Asia Analysis Group. Paper no. 2747, 25.6.2008. http://www.southasiaanalysis.org/%5Cpapers28%5Cpaper2747.html (6.5.2011) as well as Judith Evans. "Supreme Council bans Hassan Saeed's Book," 18.6.2008.

On the one hand, protests against the book arose from "Jamiyyatul Salaf", a non-governmental organization related to Wahhabism and Salafism, whose members charged the authors with attempts at destroying Islam and wanting to abet secularism among Muslims.[214] Protests were also made by the president of the "Islamic Democratic Party" (IDP), Umar Naseer, Hassan Saeed's opposing candidate, who argued that Hassan Saeed ". . . is inviting other religions to the country." He is the individual who also condemned the book and its author in a state television broadcast on the Maldives.[215] Moreover, he held a press conference in which he denounced the book as a concoction. After that he turned to the Supreme Council of Islamic Affairs with the call to have the book censored across the country. Indeed, Hassan Saeed likewise appealed to the public in an address,[216] and his brother Abdullah Saeed gave a radio interview in support of his brother. However, his political adversary's campaign soon afterwards showed success on several fronts:

On June 18, 2008 the highest religious authority in the country, the "Supreme Council of Islamic Affairs", who had been named by the President and stood in the service of the government, prohibited the book (although not documented with quotes from the publication) in an almost unique action. The following justification was given: "it contains phrases that may mislead the public"; "it violates Islamic principles."[217]

Minivan News. Independent News for the Maldives. http://www.minivannews.com/news/news.php?id=4605 (24.6.2010).

214 According to the report: "Dr. Hassan Saeed's Book on Apostasy Creates Controversy. Islamic Council Bans the Book." 12.8.2008. http://secularmaldives.blogspot.com/2008/08/drhassan-saeeds-book-on-apostasy.html (6.5.2011) with reference to the Jamiyyatul Salaf website in the Maldivian national language. Abdullah Saeed personally reports that members of Jamiyyatul Salaf even selectively translated parts of the book, composed a rebuttal a few days before the presidential election and placed it on the internet in order to depict Hassan Saeed as a danger for the Maldivian state.

215 Judith Evans. "IDP calls for Ban on Hassan Saeed's Book," 15.5.2008. Minivan News. http://www.minivannews.org/news_detail.php?id=4477 (5.5.2011).

216 Comp. Hassan Saeed's address on the "News conference on Dr. Hassan Saeed and Abdullah Saeed's Book" dated 24.5.2008 at http://www.youtube.com/watch?v=mmMIGZ6a8iA (20.6.2011).

217 Quoted by Judith Evans in her press report: "Supreme Council bans Hassan Saeed's Book," 18.6.2008. Minivan News. Independent News for the Maldives. http://www.minivannews.com/news/news.php?id=4605 (24.6.2010). Evans re-

After that the book was removed from the book market on the Maldives and the population called upon to turn in all copies in their possession. The possession, import onto the Maldives, and the dissemination of the book were all prohibited. Indeed, the possibility of withdrawing access to portions of the book accessible on the internet by blocking the relevant web pages was even debated. The prohibition of the book was traceable to repeated calls made by the "Islamic Democratic Party" (IDP), which labelled Hassan Saeed an "apostate" and "heretic" and suggested that he dispense with his presidential candidacy.[218] While Abdullah Saeed was already Professor for Arab and Islamic Studies at the University of Melbourne at the time of the publication of the book, Hassan Saeed had been a top judge known for his reform agenda and since 2003 the Attorney General of the Maldives before he entered the presidential candidacy in 2008.[219]

Hassan Saeed condemned the prohibition of the book as a "cowardly act" and as a political power play.[220] In moving to a counterattack, he said his adversaries did not understand English well enough at all to be able to competently judge the content of the book.[221] In the election which fol-

ports that in 2005 the Supreme Council temporarily prohibited the possession of the text of The Universal Declaration of Human Rights from the UN since in Articles 18 and 19 unlimited religious freedom infringes upon the Constitution of the Maldives and no Maldivian desires to practice a faith other than Islam. Comp. the text of The Universal Declaration of Human Rights at http://www.un.org/Overview/rights.html (6.5.2011).

218 Comp. the report by Judith Evans. "Supreme Council bans Hassan Saeed's Book," 18.6.2008. Minivan News. Independent News for the Maldives. http://www.minivannews.com/news/news.php?id=4605 (24.6.2010).

219 "Dr. Hassan Saeed . . . was the main architect of the road map for reforms agenda brought out by the Maldivian Government in the year 2006" (sic). S. Chandrasekharan. "Maldives: On Dr. Hassan Saeed's Book on Freedom of Religion and Apostasy." South Asia Analysis Group. Paper no. 2747, 25.5.2008. http://www.southasiaanalysis.org/%5Cpapers28%5Cpaper2747.html (6.5.2011).

220 Ibid.

221 According to the report: "Dr. Hassan Saeed's Book on Apostasy Creates Controversy. Islamic Council Bans the Book." Tuesday, 12.8.2008. http://secularmaldives.blogspot.com/2008/08/drhassan-saeeds-book-on-apostasy.html (6.5.2011), which maintained that, Hassan Saeed had spoken out against religious freedom per se. He is purported to have said that there would be no freedom for any religion other than Islam in his administration. The report quotes Hassan Saeed with the

lowed, Hassan Saeed lost, but he announced that he would run again as a candidate in 2013.[222]

3.3.4. "The Quranic Case against Killing Apostates" - 2011

Beyond the publications named heretofore, Abdullah Saeed additionally turned his attention to a broader (internet) audience with his justification for religious freedom based on the Quran and *sunna*: In February and April 2011 he published two articles[223] on this topic in Witherspoon Institute's[224] online publication *Public Discourse: Ethics, Law and the Common Good.*

The first of the two articles, "The Quranic Case against Killing Apostates,"[225] poses the question of the compatibility of human rights and Islam. This followed the condemnation of two Afghan converts to death for apostasy only a few years earlier. Abdullah Saeed argues here on the offensive; he labels Afghanistan's dealing with the question of apostasy a "regressive path" and the problematic issue of apostasy "a major problem," the negative ramifications of which lead to a situation where converts in some countries have to keep their conversion to another religion secret. This is done out of worry that they will be arrested or be put to death.

Corresponding to the platform of the internet, Abdullah Saeed argues here less scholarly than pragmatically. Conversions from and to Islam

---

words: "I have said before that I will not give any chance for a religion other than Islam in my government."

222 Maldives in Brief: Hassan Saeed Enters 2013 Presidential Race, 20.4.2010. In: Asian Tribune. http://asiantribune.com/news/2010/04/20/maldives-brief-hassan-saeed-enters-2013-presidential race (7.5.2011).

223 The following article was published by Abdullah Saeed on his website, which is dedicated to the topic of apostasy and collects voices of Muslim scholars and intellectuals who have spoken out negatively regarding the administration of the death penalty for apostasy: Abdullah Saeed. "A Fresh Look at Freedom of Belief in Islam." http://apostasyandislam.blogspot.com (13.4.2010). It is extracted from the following collective volume: Damien Kingsbury; Greg Barton (eds.). *Difference and Tolerance. Human Rights Issues in Southeast Asia.* Deakin University Press: Geelong, 1994, pp. 27-37.

224 See the website Witherspoon Institute located in Princeton, USA, http://thepublicdiscourse.com/ (3.2.2011).

225 Abdullah Saeed. "The Quranic Case against Killing Apostates." Published by: Public Discourse: Ethics, Law and the Common Good. 25.2.2011 http://www.thepublicdiscourse.com/2011/02/2716 (6.5.2011).

simply occur, according to Saeed, and the topic of human rights is on everyone's lips. How can the Islamic community continue to follow along the path of the "age-old 'law' of apostasy" and force converts to return to Islam upon the threat of the death penalty? Why should man play God and interfere in this personal affair between the Creator and the creature and do this in light of the fact that the Quran does not so much as spend a word on the punishment of converts in this world?

Saeed continues by pointing out that the situation converts face is absolutely different from country to country: In some countries converts are able to announce their new religious affiliation, while in others it is impossible. Saeed does not sketch a harmonious picture but rather points out the difficult situation for converts in a number of countries where persecution, intimidation, imprisonment, and even execution are threatened, such as in Saudi Arabia.

According to Saeed, even if "most Muslims" have no objections against the measure of religious freedom which Islam granted people 1400 years ago, this cannot satisfy anyone in a time in which many people in the West draw the conclusion from the restricted religious freedom in Muslim majority countries that "... 'Islam' appears to be in conflict with 'our' values today – including freedom of religion." Saeed argues here strongly from the standpoint of the reputation of Islam, which suffers from the fact that many people – Muslims included – have believed that the death penalty in Islam in the case of apostasy is a "divine law" which for that reason limits religious freedom.

Saeed now discusses briefly that the Quran does not have any such stipulation but instead assumes freedom of belief and limits Muḥammad's role to the proclamation of Islam. The problem of the persecution of apostasy only arose because within classical Islamic law an understanding prevailed that conversion was punishable. Today, however, according to Saeed, numerous scholars have rejected this position, and Saeed mentions several by name.[226] The position, however, is suitable for being utilized as

[226] Abdullah Saeed cites the professors Hashim Kamali from Malaysia as well as Salīm al-ᶜAuwā from Egypt, from the Islamist camp Ḥasan al-Turābī and Rāšid al-Ġannūšī as well as Sayyid Quṭb: Abdullah Saeed. "The Quranic Case against Killing Apostates." Published by: Public Discourse: Ethics, Law and the Common Good. 25.2.2011 http://www.thepublicdiscourse.com/2011/02/2716 (6.5.2011).

a tool of oppression against dissenting opinions, intellectual freedom, religious freedom, and minorities.

In conclusion, Saeed stresses that Islam professed religious freedom 1400 years ago in the Quran and that it was, however, limited by classical Islamic jurisprudence. With that said, Saeed again ascribes scholars of the formative period of Islam with what in his opinion is the primary responsibility for making manifestly inappropriate, argumentatively unjustified, and fatal misinterpretations of Islamic sources as far as their repercussions for converts and critics are concerned. The time up to the 10th century A.D., up to the end of the period of formative legal development, is thus seen to be an aberrant episode which obscured the real message of the Quran. For theologians such as al-Qaraḍāwī, who see themselves committed to this tradition, it must naturally be an unacceptable point of view.

In this article, Saeed does not really grapple with the theological arguments of his opponents. He also does not address the textual findings on apostasy in the Quran and *sunna*. However, he presents his opinion with a great deal of conviction. He concludes this essay with the call for Muslims to reflect on the legacy of the Quran and the principles set down there on religious freedom and mercy towards all people.

3.3.5. "Hadith (*ḥadīṯ*) and Apostasy" – 2011

In a second article, which Abdullah Saeed published only a few weeks later on the same internet forum, he primarily occupied himself with the refutation of the assumption expressed by a considerable number of theologians that tradition attests to the binding order of the death penalty for apostasy and that classical scholars unanimously endorsed the execution of apostates.[227]

This so apparent wing of consensus among early Islamic scholars is broken down by Saeed at the beginning by his emphasizing that this sort of unanimity never existed in the form asserted. Rather, dissenting opinions in the early days of Islam already existed. Saeed does not mention any names at this point, however.

227 Abdullah Saeed. Hadith and Apostasy. Published by: Public Discourse: Ethics, Law and the Common Good. 4.4.2011 http://www.thepublicdiscourse.com/2011/04/3082 (6.5.2011).

In the section which follows, Abduallah Saeed emphasizes that the Quran, although it reports on cases of apostasy in the Medina time period, exclusively speaks of punishment of apostates in the afterlife. That is not surprising, according to Saeed, since the Quran repeatedly emphasizes that belief is an affair between God and the individual.

With that said, Saeed makes two statements which are remarkable within the context of Islamic theology. In the cases of al-Qaraḍāwī and Maudūdī, they cannot be found anywhere. Moreover, on the basis of their theological position, they would not be expected to be found:

First of all, Abdullah Saeed calls for non-intervention in this "matter" between God and man, which he declares to be a private sphere which outsiders are not to judge. Secondly, Saeed speaks here of "the individual." When discussing the negative consequences of apostasy, al-Qaraḍāwī always mentions the interests of the community in the first place in a warning manner. For Saeed, community interests do not stand in the center of the discussion. Rather, it is the individual. Their concerns do not come up in any of the treatments by al-Qaraḍāwī and Maudūdī.

In contrast, Saeed speaks at no point in his publications on apostasy about the consequences for the community. He does not understand it as a coherent whole, and he does not see the existence of the community endangered through the apostasy of a few of its people. Rather, he presupposes the multicultural and multi-religious society as a reality from which Muslims can also profit. In contrast to al-Qaraḍāwī, Saeed lives in such a society. It has offered him a home for the past 25 years, the opportunity for social advancement, material security, and complete religious freedom. It is therefore not astonishing that Abdullah Saeed repeatedly highlights the positive sides of Australian society, in which Muslims make up an approximate 1.5% minority.[228] For him the one or the other conversion cannot essentially place the state of the Islamic community in question, much less

[228] Australia is "from a Muslim point of view . . . a generous and accommodating society that accepts people from all over the world . . . Australia gives people recognition and the freedom to practise, teach and even propagate their religion," which according to Saaed is not possible in most Islamic societies. Saeed. *Muslim Australians*, p. 9.

threaten it with "civil war" or "*fitna*," as al-Qaraḍāwī repeatedly outlines.[229]

Abdullah Saeed now turns to the question of whether tradition even decrees the death penalty at all, thus addressing the main pillar of the argumentation for capital punishment. More on the offensive than in earlier publications, Saeed doubts the justification of drawing this conclusion from the few statements which are attributed to Muḥammad.[230] In his view, their credibility rest upon such a fragile basis that in the face of this principle of religious freedom clearly set down in the Quran, the most extreme care is commanded. For this reason, the following applies for Saeed with respect to the saying attributed to Muḥammad on the killing of apostates:

> "Such sayings, while considered 'reliable', do not appear to reach the level of certainty that is required from textual evidence to justify the penalty of taking one's life . . . Given that the Quran, as the most important source for Islam, emphasises freedom of belief and does not appear to support the death penalty, any contrary sayings attributed to the Prophet should be read with a high degree of caution."[231]

Under the heading of fundamental doubt, Saeed now turns to the most quoted text in the context of the apostasy discussion: "Whoever changes his religion, kill him." More fundamentally than in earlier discussions on apostasy, he above all questions the authenticity of this saying attributed to Muḥammad – just as he questions the entire tradition at a lower level. His argument is that this material was first collected a number of decades after Muḥammad's death and was handed down by Ibn ᶜAbbās, who at the time of Muḥammad's death was still a child.

Saeed furthermore undermines the credibility of this tradition and its general validity by pointing out the imprecise formulation of the text, the exceptional rules which early Islamic legal practitioners allowed from this so general sounding rule as well as the historical context. For Saeed, this historical context allowed for punishment for apostasy in the wake of polit-

---

229 Comp., for example, al-Qaraḍāwī's remarks in his main work on apostasy: al-Qaraḍāwī. *ǧarīmat ar-ridda*, p. 6.

230 "a few sayings (hadith) attributed to the Prophet . . ." Saeed. "Hadith and Apostasy."

231 Ibid.

ical unrest and antagonism towards the Islamic community, not, however, solely as a lapse in faith.

At this point Abdullah Saeed makes an additional interesting assessment: He points out that membership in this group, or more specifically citizenship, is not coupled with religious affiliation: Instead, all the citizens in a modern nation state enjoy the same rights, independent of their religion. Abdullah Saeed views the political involvement of all citizens in such a state, regardless of their religion, to be a matter of course[232] and expressly distances himself from the thought that individual groups – Muslims, for example – could call for special political rights and privileges[233] on the basis of their religion.[234] He is thus talking of completely equal legal treatment. For Saeed, national affiliation is most decisive, which makes equals out of all citizens, independent of their religion.

For al-Qaraḍāwī, in contrast, Muslims have to be put in order ahead of non-Muslims. According to Sharia law, *people of the book*, on the basis of their faith, are always only second class citizens. For him, there is only one distinguishing characteristic between people, namely, whether the concerned individual belongs to the *umma* or not. For that reason, the place where a person lives has no far-reaching meaning for al-Qaraḍāwī. Completely to the contrary: al-Qaraḍāwī's activity is particularly aimed at determining a Muslim identity for youth living in Europe through education and instructions for conduct. This identity should be brought to bear as comprehensively as possible through participation in society. Religious affiliation should therefore also remain the decisive feature for their position in society in Western countries.

Abdullah Saeed closes this essay by declaring doubts with respect to a number of additional texts of tradition relating to apostasy. These texts have to do with advocating the death penalty for apostasy, and he mentions the names of a number of contemporary scholars who essentially follow him in this argumentation. He calls on all Muslims to let the Quran, which gives an unambiguous affirmative, have a chance to speak to questions of

232 Saeed. "Muslims in the West", p. 213.

233 Also according to his talk: Saeed. "Muslims in Secular States", p. 11.

234 Ibid.

religious freedom and, owing to its authority, overrides all other arguments.[235]

3.3.6. Miscellaneous Comments by Abdullah Saeed on Apostasy

In numerous other publications, Abdullah Saeed addresses the topics of religious freedom and human rights.[236] In several of his publications he concerns himself with concrete questions such as the configuration coexistence takes between Christians and Muslims and establishes that in non-Islamic societies Muslims should neither be disdained nor claim special rights for themselves.

Basic considerations with respect to the justification for living (permanently) in a non-Muslim community are lined up in an essay by Abdullah Saeed entitled "Muslims under Non-Muslim Rule. Evolution of a discourse:" he affirms this expressly.[237] In the process, he is conscious of the fact that this is not adhered to consistently among Muslims.

In his publications, Abdullah Saeed repeatedly breaks down the Muslim community living in the West and, more specifically, in Australia, into several groups or orientations. Within the realm of his dialog work and consulting activities, one motive could be the clearer differentiation be-

---

235 ". . . the Quran, which has supremacy over all other forms of evidence in Islamic norms and values." Saeed. "Hadith and Apostasy".

236 Comp., for instance, the very brief remarks in the study: *Muslim Australians*, p. 72. In this study Abdullah Saeed deals with the topic exclusively under the aspect of the prohibition of religious coercion in Islam, solely attributing the administration of the death penalty for apostasy on account of treason to the past, and speaks only about "threats of punishment on account of apostasy" in today's world. "The threat of punishment for apostasy exists and is often used as a political tool against people by their opponents." This drew the charge that he had indeed mentioned his own point of view, as likewise expressed and published in 2004 in *Freedom of Religion, Apostasy and Islam*, but had conveyed it as deviating from what he saw as the majority view of Muslim theologians, who nevertheless were predominantly advocates of the death penalty for apostasy. Comp. this criticism of Peter Day. "Australian Apologetics for Islam." Quadrant Online, 1.5.2009. http://www.quadrant.org.au/magazine/issue/2009/5/australian-apologetics-for-islam (10.6.2014).

237 Abdullah Saeed. "Muslims under Non-Muslim Rule. Evolution of a discourse" in: Anthony Reid; Michael Gilsenan (eds.). *Islamic Legitimacy in a Plural Asia.* Routledge: Abingdon, 2007, pp. 14-27.

tween Muslims in general and a radical minority as well as presenting in detail the capacity for peacemaking on the part of the Muslim majority.

Thus Saeed essentially frequently differentiates between (in part multiple sub-groups of) "isolationists," who at least in part pull back from the society into their "cultural and intellectual ghettos" and "participants" who are confronted in the west with equal rights and civil rights and liberties (among them religious freedom), with democracy and secular constitutions. The latter, however, understand this as a chance for development[238] and for that reason do not generate any essential reservations against the society. As a result, they get politically and socially involved as confessing Muslims,[239] whereby they could simultaneously play a decisive role in the development in inner-Islamic Reform.[240]

It cannot be overlooked that Abdullah Saeed favors the latter and, in the final event, practices it himself. From this perspective, he recognizes no problems at all in Western societies where Muslims come in contact with betting, prostitution, or the sale of alcoholic beverages, for example. This is due to the fact that in a free society no one is forced to consume these things. Nevertheless, Saeed sees Muslims participating in society attacked from two sides: If they show themselves to be open to Western society, they catch the criticism of isolationists, while from the outside they might frequently be excluded and "demonized." They thus might be fighting on two fronts.[241]

---

238 "Multiculturalism offers a valuable opportunity for Muslim communities and can assist in the development and consolidation of Islam in Australia." Shahram Akbarzadeh; Abdullah Saeed. "Searching for Identity: Muslims in Australia" in: Shahram Akbarzadeh; Abdullah Saeed (eds.). *Muslim Communities in Australia*. Universy of New South Wales Press Ltd.: Sydney, 2001, pp. 1-11, here p. 5.

239 Abdullah Saeed writes: "Muslims may retain their commitment to their religion, but also vote for the political party of their choice; take part in community life, contribute to the economy, buy their homes in average neighbourhoods and live essentially 'normal' lives." Saeed. *Islam in Australia*, p. 207; comp. likewise Saeed. "Muslims in the West Choose", pp. 8-10.

240 "Participant Muslim thinkers in the West have the potential to play a vital role in a reform project that is a concern for Muslims throughout the world." Saeed. "Muslims in Secular States", p. 12.

241 Abdullah Saeed. "Muslims in the West Choose", p. 11. At another point, Abdullah Saeed points out that one also finds gambling, pornography, and bordellos in Muslim majority societies; thus, this is no argument for saying that one cannot lead a

In this debate regarding the discussion of the majority society and Muslims, Abdullah Saeed defends the Muslim community against the general charge of militancy, separation, and an incapacity for freedom. He highlights their preparedness and ability to apply themselves in a peaceful manner in a non-Islamic society. Thus he answers the allegedly frequently discussed question in Australian society on the topic of Islam, counters presumptions and generalizations, and solicits understanding from both sides for the "others". Therefore, Saeed begins his essay "Muslims in the West Choose between Isolationism and Participation" with the following words:

> "It is widely assumed in countries like Australia that Muslims in the West constitute a serious problem for Western multicultural societies. The belief is that Islam, by its nature, is opposed to secular-liberal and multicultural values and that Muslims as a group will never adjust to the values on which Western societies today are based. Such a view could be described as alarmist, and indeed unfair . . ."[242]

Abdullah Saeed frequently speaks as a lawyer for Australia's Muslim community. On the other hand, he does not call for a privileged position for Muslims at any point. On the contrary, he expressly rejects this, while on the other hand urging non-Islamic societies to acknowledge and value Muslims as partners enjoying equal rights:

> "The sense of ownership and social responsibility among Muslim Australians is tied to the extent of their inclusion and participation in the multicultural project. That project is, by definition, a two-way process. Appreciation of the cultural and religious needs of Muslim communities by the mainstream of Australian society needs to be reciprocated by Muslims' commitment to the legal and political framework of the Commonwealth of Australia."[243]

---

life as a Muslim believer in Australian society: Abdullah Saeed. "Muslims must tackle Theology of Hate" in: *The Australian*, 7.8.2009. http://www.theaustralian.com.au/news/muslims-must-tackle-theology-of-hate/story-e6frg73o-1225758765963 (16.6.2014).

242 Saeed. "Muslims in the West Choose", p. 8.

243 Akbarzadeh; Saeed. "Identity", p. 6.

When, as Saeed remarked in 2008 in an article in the national newspaper *The Australian* under the heading "Muslims don't need separate laws,"[244] a Muslim minority defends the opinion that they can only truly feel at home and develop in a Muslim majority society, it is Saeed's opinion that they overlook that non-Islamic societies grant them much farther reaching freedoms than many a Muslim majority community.

Additionally, between the Australian laws and the Islamic commands and values such as "justice, equity and fairness," there is a lot of agreement, such that at its core Australian law could be judged to be Islamic:

> ". . . thus the Australian legal system for all practical purposes is Islamic in spirit; in fact, it is more Islamic than the laws in force in many Muslim-majority countries."[245]

As to Saeed, the majority of Muslims in Australia have understood this. Only a minority believe that there are actual differences which exist between the commands of Islam and Australian law. In the process, it is precisely religious freedom, according to Saeed, with makes life in the West much easier than in a Muslim majority society:

> "In fact, given the high degree of religious freedom that exists in Western countries, the fairness of the laws and legal system, the equality of citizens and – perhaps most important – the non-interference of the state in citizens' religious affairs, we might conclude it is far easier for a Muslim to remain committed and practising, and a decent human being, in a country such as Australia than in many Muslim-majority countries."[246]

Saeed exclusively judges religious freedom in non-Islamic societies in a positive manner for Muslims, while al-Qaraḍāwī can apparently only imagine a society in which religious freedom is practiced under the aspect of *fitna* or civil war. In connection with the permanent existence of the Islamic minority, Saeed nowhere in his publications addresses the thought of *daʿwa* (propagation of Islam), which could be offered as an argument in

244 This article is based on a lecture presented by Abdullah Saeed at a Griffith University entitled The Challenges and Opportunities of Islam in the West: The Case of Australia: Abdullah Saeed. "Muslims don't need separate laws".

245 Ibid.

246 Ibid.

favour of religious freedom and which offers Muslims, as al-Qaraḍāwī would view them, justification for a permanent stay in a non-Islamic society in the first place. For Abdullah Saeed, residence in such a society is not only allowed; rather, it is "perfectly normal, indeed desirable."[247] Instead of a threatening scenario, he sketches a picture of freedom.

Saeed's article "Muslims in the West and their Attitudes to Full Participation in Western Societies: Some Reflections"[248] is also an appeal to both sides to tear down prejudices and give up demarcations so that everyone can be understood to be members of modern society with equal rights.

He uses cautionary words to urge Western society to not pass judgment on "Islam" as "violent, fanatical and extremist." He also urges that Muslims not be viewed suspiciously as a type of "fifth column," who are unable to ever be loyal Western citizens, all owing to their faith, their alleged striving for power, and their loyalty to Islam. At the same time, Saeed grants that within Muslim societies there are "disturbing trends" with calls to demarcate and where the impossibility of successful co-existence is placed in the foreground.[249]

In this article, Saeed points out using pragmatic argumentation that Muslims are already living in the West in great numbers and apparently have affirmed the social, cultural, and political realities there. They accept democracy, human rights, equality and civil rights and liberties as well as the separation of the state and religion. According to Saeed, this is also true if in the first place it appeared to have been necessary due to sheer background conditions and only remains to be placed on theological-juridical grounds by the Islamic community. This fact that this latter commodity is in short supply, however, is particularly owing to the lack of a methodology.[250] Indeed, according to Saeed, there were early Islamic legal experts and theologians who frequently warned against permanently staying in a non-Islamic society. However, new answers have to be found.

---

247 Ibid.

248 Saeed. "Muslims in the West and their Attitudes".

249 At this point, Abdullah Saeed first mentions the names Oriana Fallaci, Jörg Haider, Pim Fortuyn, Hiryse Ali (sic), and Le Pen, who in his view poison the public climate but simultaneously turns against any walling off done by Muslim communities: Ibid., pp. 200-201.

250 Ibid. pp. 201+212.

In the following, Saeed discusses the motives of groups of Muslims[251] that are more likely to distance themselves in Western societies by following traditional juridical-theological opinions. Then again, there are others who participate in society with the call for enacting Sharia Islam.[252] And there are still others who on the basis of their enlightened view of Islam have freed themselves from the fetters of historical Sharia Islam of the four legal schools and live as citizens loyal to the state and its laws in Western societies and favorably link the civil rights and liberties there – including religious freedom – with the foundations of their faith.

Abdullah Saeed concludes this article with the far-reaching hope that precisely this last mentioned portion of the spectrum of Muslim community will take over leadership in the development of an Islam which will critically scrutinize and newly evaluate traditional methodologies, principles of jurisprudence, exegesis, and ethics.[253] At another point he speaks of the necessity to reassess conventional concepts of citizenship and the state, law and legislation, equal rights for the genders, and religious freedom.[254] On the basis of such remarks, it becomes clear that for Abdullah Saeed it is not only a question of peaceful coexistence. Rather, it has to do with foundational questions which, in relation to Islam, are at their core primarily of a theological nature.

In an address held on November 30, 2003 at the Islamic Centre of Singapore and later published by the Islamic Religious Council of Singapore with the title "Muslims in Secular States: Between Isolationists and Participants in the West,"[255] Abdullah Saeed emphasizes this change process through inculturation,[256] which, as a bridge builder, he would seek to promote. To this end, prejudices have to be successfully dismantled on both sides, and Islam as a religion has to be explained and understood in a way

251 Ibid., pp. 207ff.

252 Abdullah Saeed characterizes them as "heavily influenced by the Salafi trends that are closely connected with Hanbali-Wahhabi literalism and financed by sources in the Arabian Gulf . . . many of these hard-line isolationists have developed an ideology that is fanatical and extremist." Ibid., pp. 210-211.

253 Ibid., p. 215.

254 Saeed. "Muslims in Secular States", p. 2.

255 Ibid., pp. 1-14.

256 ". . . in the West, Islam and Muslims are undergoing a process of indigenization . . . it is leading to the emergence of a form of Islam that is in harmony with the social, political and intellectual context of the West." Ibid., p. 1.

which is not opposed to this suggestion but rather is advanced on the basis of the Quran.

Human Rights and Religious Freedom

Sounding out common ground and understanding stood in the center of a conference entitled "Cultivating Wisdom, Harvesting Peace" put on by Griffith University's Multi-Faith Centre in Brisbane, Australia. The conference was supported by, among others, UNESCO. Abdullah Saeed held an address on the topic of human rights under the heading "Creating a Culture of Human Rights from a Muslim Perspective."[257]

Saeed's concern is not only to be able to defensively make human rights compatible with the foundations of Islam. Instead, it is rather to take the offensive and derive them from the center of Islamic tradition. With that said, human rights become the "lingua franca"[258] of co-existence between Muslims and non-Muslims.

In his lecture, Abdullah Saeed names four key terms from Islamic theology which represent independent justification for human rights and include theological foundations of Islam and shape the interpersonal realm in a positive manner: "The Supreme Being, a common humanity, a common path to God and a set of universal ethical-moral values."[259] By treating the rights of God and the rights of human beings on one and the same level, Saeed hereby distances himself from the frequently formulated duty in classical Sharia law to first acknowledge God's law, to secondly acknowledge humankind's duty, and only to speak in the third place about human rights as defined by the Sharia.

At the beginning of this lecture, Saeed makes a number of remarks about the special value of human life, to which God has granted special dignity and protection. According to Saeed, however, although the aforementioned is undoubtedly the case, there are problems "within the Muslim tradition" from the viewpoint of the 21st century as far as gender questions, human rights, and religious freedom are concerned.

Also at this point Saeed mentions scrutiny towards the established interpretations of the early days of Islam as the key for achieving compati-

---

257 Saeed. "Culture".

258 According to Saeed. "Muslims in Secular States", p. 11.

259 Saeed. "Culture", p. 123.

bility between the civil rights and liberties mentioned and the tradition of Islam. Whoever dismisses the historicity of Islamic law – and Saeed does not mention the emotionally charged term "Sharia", although thematically it has precisely to do with this – will receive an abbreviated result. Although Muslims, according to Saeed, proceed on the assumption of the religious character of Islamic law, the regulations are not only based upon the Quran and Muḥammad's *sunna*. Rather, they are in part traced back to customary law, the specific historical circumstances at the time, and the culturally conditioned "conceptions of commonsense and fairness."[260]

With that said, Abdullah Saeed has implied that a part of the Sharia guidelines which have been considered by Islamic theologians to have remained unchanged since the 10th century are an expression of conclusions arising from prevailing circumstances and from underlying cultural tendencies and are thus of human origin and essentially corrigible. As is so frequently the case in Abdullah Saeed's publications, after a daring hypothesis, which he cloaks in as little a provocative wording as possible, he cites an example about which there can be little dispute:[261] It is slavery. Muslim legal experts have presented numerous publications on this topic which remain unnoticed because they have no significance at the present time. For that reason, according to Saeed, texts which were interpreted differently under other historical circumstances, have to be examined most carefully by taking the context into account.

Abdullah Saeed thus calls for careful differentiation between text and interpretation as well as a new *iǧtihād*, which is oriented towards the needs and conditions of modern society. However, this is done without openly mentioning the term by name. He apparently differentiates between revela-

---

260 Ibid., p. 125.

261 He proceeds similarly in the discussion about the question of whether the establishment of Sharia courts in Australia is sensible: Here he cites as an argument for Sharia courts a situation where a husband spends a long time at an unknown location overseas, such that his wife can only receive a divorce from a Sharia court. Since she could not receive this document in Australia, the circumstances would force her to conduct effortful travel to her country of origin for the purpose of receiving the document. Abdullah Saeed. "Reflections on the Establishment", p. 234.

tion and human – fallible – exegesis.[262] He does this in particular to reject equating an interpretation with a sole true interpretation.

Saeed repeatedly turns against this pretension of absolutism in his publications. In equal measure he apparently also endeavors to avoid emotionally laden terms (such as Sharia or *iǧtihād*) and instead of them to present his statements with predominantly positive formulations in the recognized terminology of classical Islamic theology in order to find a larger hearing – as his terms in part strongly deviate from classical Islamic theology:

> ". . . we have to 'contextualize' the rights debate within the religious community using the terminology and the language of the religious tradition. If we do that, there is a better chance of the rights debate being accepted within the broader community of Muslims."[263]

Just as al-Qaraḍāwī, Abdullah Saeed issues a summons to set modernity into relation with the text of revelation as well as to cede sufficient authority to revelation in order to derive options for action from it. Admittedly, this should not occur under the auspices of lining modernity up with early Islam and instructing youth, as with al-Qaraḍāwī, into an "Islamic awakening" and as precise an observance as possible of what is allowed and what is forbidden in order to completely orient them towards an ideal early Islam.

Instead, Abdullah Saeed goes in the opposite direction when he calls for scholars to choose and read the texts today in such a way so that individuals can experience a liberation which does justice to present circumstances. It is not the text which thus sets the standard for reality. Rather, it is reality which is the touchstone for the relevance and interpretation of the text:

> "Contemporary scholars and Muslim jurists have an obligation to read the texts which allows for the liberation of the human being in a manner that suits today's societies."[264]

---

262 In this connection, Saeed points out: ". . . the distinction between what the foundation texts, specifically the Qur'an, says about a particular issue . . . and what *we think* it says about that issue . . ." (emphasis in original). Saeed. "Culture", p. 125.

263 Ibid.

264 Ibid.

In this connection, Abdullah Saeed comes around to speak about religious freedom. Since the Quran has set down the general principle of the voluntary nature of belief (Sura 2:256), religious freedom is "an essential part of Islam."[265] That at other times and under other historical circumstances legal experts and theologians in the early days had to revert to political solutions does not make them authoritative for modernity according to the above mentioned principle and does not make them universally binding: ". . . there is no reason why new rights should not be created today."[266] On the foundation of this hermeneutical principle, there is of course no difficulty in justifying comprehensive human rights and civil rights and liberties.

In a completely similar fashion, Abdullah Saeed expressed himself in his recent publication on the human rights and religious freedom debate among Asian Muslims under the title "Muslim Debates on Human Rights and Freedom of Religion" in 2011.[267] Against the backdrop of Article 18 of the 1948 UN Declaration on Human Rights on the freedom of thought and conscience and the exercise of religion, Saeed discusses the diametrically opposed practice of early Islam of imposing the death penalty in the case of apostasy, which he declares is judging apostasy to be treason against the state.

That this classic point of view is nowadays increasingly scrutinized, according to Saeed, has to do with a number of factors, the first of which he mentions is "a changed contemporary socio-political context" or changed conditions when compared to the time of the emergence of Islam.[268] This factor is a point of departure for Abdullah Saeed. It is something which distinguishes him as one of a list of "liberal-minded Muslim theologians,"[269] and he names additional members on the list as he continues. Abdullah Saeed closes with the conviction that the opinion of "ultra-conservatives, traditionalists and political Islamists," whose standpoint of the legitimacy of the death penalty for apostasy is still shared by a "signifi-

265 Ibid., p. 126.

266 Ibid.

267 Abdullah Saeed. "Muslim Debates on Human Rights and Freedom of Religion" in: Thomas W. D. Davis; Brian Galligan (eds.). *Human Rights in Asia*. Edgar Elgar Publishing Limited: Cheltenham, 2011, pp. 25-37.

268 Ibid., p. 31.

269 Ibid.

cant section of the Muslim community," is increasingly questioned by progressive Muslims whose viewpoint is compatible with universal human rights.[270]

Terrorism and Islam's Capability for Promoting Peace

Completely in the spirit of bridge building and mutual appreciation, and subsequent to September 11, 2001, Abdullah Saeed published a short essay entitled "Religious and Human Freedoms." The gist was a call to tear down prejudices, fears, and insecurities in dealing with Muslims in Western societies.[271]

The short paper is less a programmatic document on justifying religious freedom in Islam, thus being a pragmatic call to levelheadedness and reflection in Australia's multi-religious society as well as a warning against marginalizing Muslims as an entire community on the basis of the terrorist activities of a few. Abdullah Saeed made a point to remind the reader that encounters between both religions had been marked by conflict and struggle but that there had also been peaceful coexistence and religious freedom for Muslims under Christian rule.

Saeed first briefly describes the magnitude and composition of the Muslim community in Australia, deals with differences in belief between Muslims and Christians, addresses peaceful as well as conflict-rife times, and concludes this historical review with a depiction of a number of initiatives for dialog in the 20th century.

In the last segment he treats irritations to the Christian-Muslim relationship due to the events of September 11, 2011. Saeed calls for mutual understanding as well as renouncing mistrust, stereotypes about Muslims, and mutual suspicion.[272] He laments undifferentiated media reporting on Muslims and warns of the "demonization" of an entire community owing to a small minority which admittedly has devised "destructive activities" and warns of a split in society as well as fear and hatred. Abdullah Saeed

---

[270] Ibid., p. 35.

[271] Abdullah Saeed. "Religious and human freedoms" in: *ES* 13/7 (2003), pp. 28-30.

[272] "We share the same neighbourhoods. Our children share the same schools. We share workplaces and, more importantly, we share the future of this country. Without understanding, we will continue to move towards the irrational, in the form of mistrust, stereotyping and suspicion." Ibid., p. 30.

concludes his brief treatise with a forecast of successful cooperation through resisting prejudices and blanket judgments.

However, with respect to the topic of terrorism, Abdullah Saeed does not limit himself to soliciting understanding for Muslims and warning against excluding them on the basis of fears of terror and prejudice. On the other hand, he uses media to also turn towards the Muslim community and emphatically calls on them to rise up against the minority of extremists so that their ideology does not spread further and their interpretation does not become the leading opinion among youth.[273] That would be devastating for the Muslim community in Australia. According to Saeed, this involves a concrete threat to Muslim majority societies, the religion (of Islam itself), and the entire world.

In the face of this challenge, silence and passivity on the part of the Muslim majority is particularly fatal.[274] This is due to the fact that it is precisely Muslims who have to oppose this "ideological-theological" challenge since security forces can only offer protection from violence. From Saeed's perspective, it is not sufficient to condemn attacks and terrorist activities or only to protect the community from the destructive repercussions of violence in order to stem the poisoning of society. According to Saeed, it is above all important to take a critical look at one's own community in order to stem ideology: ". . . to counter the threat of militant extremism and the hate-filled ideology of the extremists, and to save the younger generation of Muslims from this ideology."[275]

In the course of this article, Saeed repeats a total of four times that a condemnation of terrorists alone is not sufficient, instead, the ideology of "militancy" and "hate" on the part of Muslims has to be refuted at every opportunity in mosques, families, educational institutions, and youth camps, and the opinions of terrorists have to be expelled from society.[276] A

---

273 Saeed. "Muslims must tackle". The actual occasion for the composition of this article was, as can be seen from reports on the internet, the detention of a number of individuals in Australia suspected of terrorism which had occurred only a few days prior.

274 "That the number of these militant extremists is small is not a good reason for the majority of Muslims to remain silent." Ibid.

275 Ibid.

276 "Condemning the violence in the strongest terms is naturally the starting point, but it should not be the end of the story . . . The silent majority should strengthen its

condemnation of non-Muslims as "kuffar" (unbelievers) is unacceptable, for "non-Muslims and Muslims are brothers and sisters within the human family," where religious freedom is self-evident and justifiable from the Quran.[277]

Jihād and Religious Freedom

Especially after September 11, 2001, Abdullah Saeed has also turned explicitly to the topic of *jihād* and terrorism.[278] In his article "Jihad and Violence: Changing Understandings of Jihad among Muslims,"[279] Saeed initially attends to the different connotations of *jihād* in the Quran and in publications of classic Islamic theologians. This is a specialized article for explaining the classical teaching on *jihād* and its modern interpretation for a non-specified audience, one that is, however, supposedly predominantly non-Muslim.

According to the teaching of the Quran, militant *jihād*, in Saeed's opinion, could only be applied in the defense of Islam as well as in retaliation in the case of the breach of an agreement; for Abdullah Saeed, the main function of *jihād* lies in its use against "oppression and injustice" as well as in the defense of the *umma*.[280]

Saeed continues to historically discuss the topic of his essential rejection of the extremist interpretation of defensive and offensive *jihād* up to the present and emphasizes that indeed a number of legal experts allow for *jihād* in order to combat unbelief, that the Quran, however, does not know of battle as a means of forcing conversion, thus that *jihād* stands in no relation to the topic of religious freedom.[281]

campaign of undermining the militancy and hatred advocated by the extremists." Ibid.

277 Ibid.

278 As a foundational condemnation of terror in the name of Islam also see Saeed. "Murderers".

279 Saeed. "Jihad and Violence".

280 Ibid., p. 76.

281 Ibid., pp. 75+85.

The Assessment of other Religions

In a number of essays, Abdullah Saeed devotes himself to topics such as the existence of Muslim minorities in non-Muslim (Western) societies,[282] the evaluation of Jews and Christians[283] as "people of the book," and the evaluation of their revelation from the viewpoint of charges of Scriptural distortion.[284]

It appears that over the years, Abdullah Saeed has recognized increasing points of contact between Muslims and "people of the book" or, more specifically, he has increasingly spoken out for an appreciation for, instead of a denigration of, Judeo-Christian writings of revelation.

While in his 2002 essay entitled "The Charge of Distortion of Jewish and Christian Scriptures" he still considered the charge of distortion against the Scriptures of the Jews and Christians, above all with respect to their interpretation (or in any event relating to very slight textual changes),[285] in his most recent essay on this topic, which dates from 2011, no more mention of this type is made.

As early as 2002, Abdullah Saeed paid tribute to respectful statements in the Quran, for example in Sura 5:46 regarding the religions of the book, and emphasized that at no point does the Quran disparage the Scriptures of the Jews and Christians; they are reliable "books of God."[286]

For Muslims, the Quran is in a very literal sense God's direct revelation. It is "based on the dictation theory of revelation." Abdullah Saeed notes self-critically that from this point of view, it is rather simple to judge other forms of revelation as distorted when they do not share this understanding of revelation. This is especially the case since an understanding of revelation likened to that of Muslims would provide them with "an important psychological weapon" against the argument that also the *people of*

---

282 Saeed. "Muslims under Non-Muslim Rule".

283 Abdullah Saeed. "How Muslims View the Scriptures of the People of the Book: Toward a Reassessment?" in: Luca Anceschi; Anthony Camilleri; Ruwan Palapathwala; Andrew Wicking (eds.). *Religion and Ethics in a Globalized World. Conflict, Dialogue, and Transformation*. Palgrave Macmillan: New York, 2011, pp. 191-210.

284 Abdullah Saeed. "The charge of distortion of Jewish and Christian Scriptures" in: *MW* 92 (2002), pp. 419-436.

285 Ibid., p. 434.

286 Ibid., pp. 428-429+434.

the book belong to an undistorted religion.[287] Saeed concludes with the observation:

> "If the texts have remained more or less as they were in the seventh century CE, the reverence the Qur'ān has shown them at the time should be retained even today."[288]

In his 2011 essay entitled "Muslims View the Scriptures of the People of the Book: Toward a Reassessment?",[289] in which he again brings together a number of sections taken from 2002, there is only very little left from his earlier considerations about possible textual distortions among Jews and Christians.[290] Already in 2010 he had stated the following: "Muslims worship the same God as Jews and Christians."[291]

In his 2011 text,[292] Saeed differentiates more strictly between glorification of the Quran with respect to Scriptures revealed prior to the Quran and the statements of Muslim theologians. He argues that the Quranic demarcations towards Jews and Christians were only directed at individuals or groups of Jews and Christians and their actions but that their revelations were nevertheless considered to be God's word.[293] This applies regardless of the fact that a number of theologians, whose opinions strongly diverge with respect to the scope and specification of textual changes and are discussed here by Saeed, assume actual changes.[294] Indeed, Abdullah Saeed contemplates the possibility of an actual textual change in Jewish and Christian Scriptures. However, he simultaneously accepts arguments against textual distortion from the side of Christian theologians.[295]

---

287 Ibid., pp. 431+433.

288 Ibid., p. 434.

289 Saeed. "How Muslims View the Scriptures".

290 In a publication from 2004, Saeed expressed himself exclusively positively regarding the Jewish and Christian Scriptures: Saeed. *Muslim Australians*, p. 68.

291 Saeed. "Foundations of Peace".

292 Saeed. "How Muslims View the Scriptures".

293 In 2010 he wrote that the Quran mentions "in no place . . . disparaging remarks about these scriptures. It refers to them as scriptures that have come from God." Saeed. "Foundations of Peace", p. 5.

294 Saeed. "How Muslims View the Scriptures", pp. 193+194ff.

295 ". . . although there is the possibility of some textual distortion of the Jewish and Christian scriptures, it is possible to argue that distortion has mostly occurred through their interpretation." Ibid., pp. 202+203-204.

Abdullah Saeed concludes this essay with the thought that a renewed reconsideration of the reservations against the revelations of the respective others in the case of Jews, Christians, and Muslims would promote inter-religious dialog and tolerance and would tear down old feelings of superiority. He writes, "By treating their scriptures as authentic, Muslims, Christians, and Jews can better engage with one another and read their scriptures together," for since the Quran so respectfully speaks about older revelations, this should also be the appropriate attitude nowadays.[296] At this point, there is a recognizable development in Abdullah Saeed to a farther reaching acceptance of the revelational character of Jewish and Christian Scriptures, which, inter alia, is visible through his acceptance of apologetic arguments benefiting the credibility of Biblical texts.

3.4. Results: Abdullah Saeed's Position on Apostasy

Beyond his most importance piece of writing, "Freedom of Religion, Apostasy and Islam," Abdullah Saeed has frequently expressed thoughts on the topic of apostasy over the years. At no point can attempts be found to save even parts of the early Islamic provisions for punishing apostasy in modernity. All of Abdullah Saeed's references to an application of classical law regarding apostasy are ill-fated in modernity.

3.4.1. Abdullah Saeed's Scrutiny of Final Judgments

Abdullah Saeed's approach to the way human rights and civil rights and liberties are justified from an Islamic perspective is, on the one hand, marked by a repulsion of holistic and indisputable Sharia-based historical interpretation up to the 10th century, which he repeatedly characterizes as "pre-modern." In addition to this, his approach is marked by an attempt to newly exegete classical texts of the Quran and tradition by reanimating *iğtihād*.[297] Indeed, it is a call to reject the notion of a sole interpretation and

---

[296] Ibid., pp. 206-207.

[297] Saeed formulates it thus in light of the classical interpretation rooted in the *ribā* prohibition in the foreword to his study: Saeed. *Banking*, p. 3, as its direction: ". . . to highlight the importance of re-examining this interpretation in the light of the moral and humanitarian emphasis on the issue of *riba* as indicated in or understood from the Qur'ān and *sunna*."

particularly to avoid granting unseen validity in the present to historical instructions found in tradition. Along with this comes Abdullah Saeed's search for pragmatic, feasible solutions in the service of peace, humanity, and civil rights and liberties as well as rights of equality for all people in order to be able to harmonize Quranic guidelines with modernity.

A major statement in Saeed's book *Freedom of Religion, Apostasy and Islam* is that what appears so clearly accusable to some scholars as apostasy is, upon second glance, not at all the case. al-Qaraḍāwī's official statements on turning from Islam give the impression that he could precisely judge where the border lies between doubt and abandoning faith, between privately preserved freedom of thought and destructive desertion of the *umma*. Although Abdullah Saeed does not unambiguously define apostasy at any point in his writings, he goes in the opposite direction and relativizes this allegedly homogeneous and patently clear theological as well as political judgment of apostasy:

- He relativizes the justification for judging apostasy as a wrongdoing worthy of death according to Islamic theology. He does this by explaining that the genesis of the understanding of the appropriateness of the death penalty is actually non-Islamic in its origin.
- He relativizes stigmatizing those who throughout history were differently minded as apostates. He does this by pointing out the various ways the concept was imbued over the course of time.
- He scrutinizes the absolute nature of the authority of scholars. He does this by pointing to numerous examples of improper charges of apostasy for the sake of retaining one's own power.
- He relativizes the only apparent unambiguous interpretation and meaning of texts of tradition on apostasy by presenting them – with respect to their alleged historical lack of ambiguity – to be ambiguous and questionable with respect to content.
- He scrutinizes the self-aggrandizement of any individual scholar who raises himself up to be the measure of all things and makes his own judgment binding for all other Muslims.
- He relativizes the meaning of the early Islamic epoch as formative for all later periods of time when he argues for the idea that each generation views the Quran and the *sunna* with its own understand-

ing as marked by the circumstances of its time.[298] Therefore, in his opinion the early days of Islam are not an embodiment of "true Islam" per se. Rather, they are solely a temporary and other embodiment which has to justify itself in the present.

- And last but not least, Abdullah Saeed also scrutinizes the practical use of calling upon Sharia law in the question of apostasy and, more specifically, its operability in light of the present realities of multicultural and multi-religious societies.

It does not always become immediately clear which position Abdullah Saeed himself takes when he contrasts different opinions on various topics. Some of the statements are only reported on without evaluating them or by quoting another standpoint as for or against, without directly presenting his own opinion. While in al-Qaraḍāwī's works the reader receives a direct and unambiguous opinion, Abdullah Saeed does not himself take a stand on all points, even if the focus of his position is clearly recognizable on the whole.

3.4.2. Abdullah Saeed Holds Fast to the Quran as God's Revelation

At no point in Abdullah Saeed's magnum opus on the topic of apostasy – and in no other of his numerous writings – does one hear an essential criticism of Islam. Nowhere does he distance himself from the conviction with respect to the Quran as a divine revelation and of Muḥammad's practice. On the contrary: Abdullah Saeed campaigns for Muslims' needing to retain their faith in Western society.[299] He argues from the position of a believer

298 "Each generation appears to look at the Scripture and Islamic tradition from its *own* perspective, and interprets them considering the generation's *own* circumstances and *own* experiences" (emphasis in the original). Saeed. "A Fresh Look", p. 27.

299 "Participant Muslim thinkers in the West . . . are not diluting their 'Islam.' They hold on to the essentials of Islam but they adjust their understanding of what it means to be Muslims to the realities of the West . . . In this, they are not becoming carbon copies of non-Muslims." Saeed. "Muslims in Secular States", p. 12.

when he states that every individual who ridicules Islam or pokes fun at the truth of the revelation of Islam makes himself guilty of "major sins."[300]

His essential assessment of the Quran as God's word is also expressed in one of his major works entitled *The Qur'an – an Introduction*[301] in which he provides an overview of the genesis, contents, and the exegesis of the Quran over the course of twelve chapters. As Abdullah Saeed explains in the foreword, this study unites insights of Western Islamic studies with the inner-Islamic perspective of the Quran as God's revelation.[302]

As much as in his numerous publications he weighs up both sides and issues a rejection to the claim for a comprehensive political as well as extremist Islam, so little does he take up a "neutral" position with respect to the truth of the revelation of Islam and the validity of the "unambiguously" derived commands from the Quran and Muḥammad's practice.

Those instructions which are derivable as "unambiguous" from the Quran and the *sunna* are, as far as Abdullah Saeed is concerned and as he states in personal discussion, those actions which can be read from Muḥammad's practice in addition to being taken from the text of the Quran. This practice was still familiar to Muḥammad's contemporaries; a part of this description found its way into the collection of tradition. However, since later generations possessed no immediate access to Muḥammad and his practice, be it through the reports of later deliverers of tradition who only knew Muḥammad's words but had never experienced him themselves, there were some unreliable traditions which were absorbed. They were, therefore, recognizable as being in conflict with Muḥammad's practice (the "practice of the prophet").[303]

The legal regulations of the Quran, also those relating to penal law, are not criticized by Saeed at any point in his publications in any confrontational manner, even if they are not able to be brought into agreement with the realities of today's societies. His book composed after September 11, 2001, *Islam in Australia*, served to explain Islam to Australian society as well as to dismantle mistrust and fears over against the Muslim communi-

300 Saeed; Saeed. *Freedom of Religion*, p. 45.

301 Saeed. *The Qur'an. An Introduction.*

302 Ibid., pp. xiv+33.

303 This principle is also explained by him in detail, ibid., pp. 194-195. Admittedly, no objectively comprehensible criterion is named which belongs to these "distinct" practices described as actions in the Quran or in traditions relating to Muḥammad.

ty. In that book, he explains the various limitations on the application of the Islamic penal code, such as the evidence which can only be rendered with great difficulty as well as the exceptions which protect against punishment:

> "In fact, even the classical Islamic legal texts have laid out so many conditions to be met before any of these harsh punishmens can be carried out that, in practice, carrying out these punishments, becomes, in many cases, almost impossible. Thus, the importance of these punishments often lies in their symbolic deterrence value."[304]

With that said, Abdullah Saeed has again carefully considered both sides. Neither does he deny all justification for the Islamic penal law in a confrontational manner nor, on the other hand, can it be recognized that the application of Sharia law would in his eyes be desirable.

According to Saeed, there is surely an intensive debate underway among Muslims regarding the necessity and significance of these punishments. However, it is irrelevant in the Australian context. This is due to the fact that no one would listen to those who, if they did exist, called for such punishments.[305] With respect to the death penalty for apostates, Saeed also argues at another point that it would be "difficult" for Muslim scholars to justify true religious freedom in the event that the Quran would have given clear directions to kill apostates (which in his eyes is not the case).[306] It becomes clear from both statements that, at least publicly, Abdullah Saeed does not express any essential criticism of legal questions as they relate to the contents of revelation; however, he holds their early Islamic implementation to be unthinkable in today's world and, for that reason, the discussion regarding them to be unproductive.

Abdullah Saeed is thus no liberal theologian critical of the Quran such that he would suspend parts of the Quran. In contrast, he essentially holds

---

304 Saeed. *Islam in Australia*, p. 130.

305 "In any case, the debate on these punishments in the context of Australia is irrelevant . . . Even the most tradionalist Muslims do not entertain such ideas in Australia; even if some Muslims did, there is no possibility that such calls would be listened to in Australia." Ibid., p. 131.

306 Saeed. "Quranic Case".

fast to the truth of revelation.[307] However, in his work *Freedom of Religion, Apostasy and Islam*, he distances himself, as he also does in numerous other publications he has produced, from the a-historical, literary adoption of the opinions of classical Sharia scholars of the formative period of Islam. He also calls for incorporating the "socio-historical context,"[308] by which revelation was passed to Muḥammad, since this cannot readily be brought forward into modernity.

Hence, in Saeed's opinion, there is the necessity for a new manner of thinking about the sources. This has to orient itself toward social reality. Above all, however, it has to be oriented toward multi-religious societies. With this he differentiates between the Quran as God's revelation and what is for him, as far as traditional Sharia scholars are concerned, a legacy standing in contrast to that.[309] For instance there is, in his opinion, a disparaging view of other revelations as well as a political interpretation of theological issues. The Quran is for him the basis of belief, from which he derives civil rights and liberties as they are formulated in the constitutions of nation states, and for which reason, from his point of view, there cannot be any contradiction between Islam and life in a Western society.

3.4.3. Criticism of the Abuse of Power and Encrustation

It is apparent that Abdullah Saeed views the encrustation of classical Islamic legal theory and theology, with its essential orientation towards early Islamic authorities as well as their authoritatively claimed monopoly position in the construal of Islam, as a basic hindrance on the way to an interpretation of Islam that is able to provide appropriate, practical answers to circumstances found in modernity and which would be able to be experienced as promoting peace and coexistence.

---

307 For instance, in relation to the justification of and laying claim to comprehensive human rights by Muslims, Abdullah Saeed emphasizes: ". . . Muslims will be able to conceptualise standards of human rights practice and promote a culture of human rights. In so doing they are not required to compromise their religion or abandon their scripture, rather it requires engaging with the Qur'an and the broader Muslim tradition." Saeed. "Culture", p. 127.

308 Saeed. *The Qur'an. An Introduction*, p. 31.

309 ". . . these perspectives . . . left behind a legacy that was quite contrary to the original teachings and the principles of Islam." Saeed. "Foundations of Peace", p. 11

Abdullah Saeed believes that the cause for the limitations on religious freedom in Muslim majority countries can be seen in political power games. However, this is for him not a specifically Muslim set of problems: "I don't see it just as as Muslim problem," "it is essentially a political problem . . . it's actually a power issue."[310] The strong emphasis on the opinion that the disastrous consequences of the law against apostasy arise from the misuse of power and that in order to defuse the problematic set of issues surrounding apostasy the misuse of power has to be restrained has occasionally earned him the charge that he does not actually call the problem by its name.[311] Supposedly this remark is aimed at the fact that Abdullah Saeed nowhere frontally addresses himself to Sharia law.

Nevertheless, from my point of view, Abdullah Saeed's analysis is, for all intents and purposes, far-reaching and fundamental. He does not leave it at charges of the misuse of power and does not locate the problematic nature of the lack of religious freedom in undesirable political developments, educational policy or structural underdevelopment. He also does not locate it in the Western world as a hangover of the colonial era or in political dominance in the present.

Abdullah Saeed locates the set of problems in theology, which, in his opinion, already had lifted what was in part questionable tradition into the position of indisputable and timelessly valid regulations after Muḥammad's death. It also conveyed the then political and social background as instructions for action in modernity. All of that additionally opened the door for the misuse of power, which, however, is not the actual cause as far as he is concerned. Thus, Abdullah Saeed does not call for pragmatic rules alone. Rather, he calls for a theological solution, for a new *iǧtihād* with the goal of a new evaluation of sources which can provide

---

310 Abdullah Saeed commented in this manner in an interview during the following conference organized by the Australian government: 5th Regional Interfaith Dialogue in October 2009, which is summarized in the following report: Ana Marie Pamintua. "Living Laboratory," updated 30.10.2009. http://www.philstar.com:8080/opinion/518438/living-laboratory (10.6.2014).

311 For instance, Roxanne D. Marcotte criticizes in this manner with respect to the danger of the abuse of power in the application of apostasy law: "One of the qualms this reader has with such statements is that they do appear (probably "non" is missing here) to address the real problem." Roxanne D. Marcotte. "Freedom of Religion, Apostasy and Islam. Abdullah Saeed and Hassan Saeed" in: *SR* 34/2 (2005), pp. 291-292, here p. 292.

Muslims with a workable justification for peaceful, equitable co-existence with non-Muslims in Western societies and for their political engagement in that environment.

Abdullah Saeed recognizes basic approaches on the development of new ways of *iğtihād*, yet he concedes that they have up until now been methodically weakly developed and above all locally confined due to practical conditions (one could add: with only the slightest repercussions for theologians and authorities in the core Muslim majority countries). With respect to seeking justification for the increase in civil rights and liberties, he notes:

> "This trend among Muslims in the West is becoming quite common. It has no historical precedent, no clear-cut methodology to deal with Islamic law, no established grand narratives or writings. It is purely a product of a fusion of Islam with the West, western environment and western values . . . Its frame of reference is the local environment."[312]

3.4.4. Abdullah Saeed's Hopes for the Future

Numerous publications, such as speeches, close with an optimistic formulation and the hope for development within Islamic theology and society all the way to an affirmation of increased civil rights and liberties as well as a detachment from an ossified understanding of Sharia and history.[313] Abdullah Saeed especially expresses his hope that this development could become reality as it relates to aspects of equal rights for men and women and for human rights in countries marked by Islam.[314] In personal conversation, Abdullah Saeed added: "Political Islam has failed," such that from his point of view only the option remaining is to change towards more human rights and liberties.

---

312 Saeed. "Muslims in the West and their Attitudes", p. 212.

313 For instance, he thus expresses the hope that in place of the dispute carried out in 2010 regarding the establishment of religious courts of arbitration for cases of civil litigation among Muslims and the introduction of Sharia courts the insight might arise in Australia that commonalities between the ideas of both parties is large and for that reason might become more pronounced: Abdullah Saeed. "Reflections on the Establishment", p. 238.

314 Ibid., p. 238.

Abdullah Saeed views it as desirable that Muslims who have found their way to a pragmatic reconciliation of their belief with the conditions present in Western society become protagonists on the way to an essential renewal of Islam and exercise influence on the entire Muslim community.[315] The effectiveness of these Muslims

> "... will most likely lead to a rethinking of existing approaches, methods and principles in jurisprudence, Qur'anic exegesis and Islamic ethics ... Although, as an intellectual discourse, it is still in the early stages, it is making its mark on the wider Muslim discourse in the area of reform of Islamic law and thought."[316]

This step to a recognizably progressive disentanglement, from a past under the prerogative of interpretation by classical Sharia scholars which is no longer definitive for modernity, finds its counterpart in the fulfilled acceptance of the Muslim community in Australia. This community has gone beyond mere tolerance: "Even though pockets of intolerance still exist, the wider Australian community is not simply tolerant, but fully accepting of Muslims as persons . . ."[317]

For that reason, he already sees achievement in a portion of his vision of the future and in his efforts towards balance, moderation, and mutual engagement for a peaceful, equitable co-existence between Muslims and non-Muslims: "Give-and-take on both sides is essential if we are to see a harmonious Western society of which Muslims are full participants."[318]

According to Saeed, Muslims who come to Australia would have to first adopt this attitude since their theological training centers have not prepared them for life in Western societies. In this connection, Saeed criticizes curricula which demonstrate only a slight orientation towards modernity as well as the traditional authoritarian learning methods of classical Islamic educational institutions built upon repetition instead of creativity.

---

315 "These Muslims are using *ijtihad* to put forward bold solutions to contemporary concerns, while not turning their backs on their traditions. As yet restricted to the West, and little known to Westerners in general, this type of thinking is likely to have a significant impact on the wider Muslim world in time." Saeed. "Muslims in Secular States", p. 7.

316 Saeed. "Muslims in the West and their Attitudes", p. 215.

317 Johns; Saeed. "Muslims in Australia", p. 212.

318 Saeed. "Muslims in Secular States", here p. 11.

However, on the other hand, he keeps them safe from the charge that they are hotbeds for terrorism, which is often expressed in wholesale manner in the ongoing debate in the aftermath of September 11, 2001.[319] Every time he addresses problems within the Muslim community – for instance that of domestic violence – he at the same time points out that this is also a problem in the rest of society (here: Australian).[320]

3.4.5. Abdullah Saeed – Crossing the Borders between Cultures

Abdullah Saeed crosses borders between cultures, and this has been lastingly moulded by his own experience of migration over a number of continents. He had to adjust to three completely new situations, find his way into new environments, and get along in unfamiliar circumstances. To have been born in the Maldives and to have initially gone to Pakistan for school education, then to have moved to Saudi Arabia before long term residence in Australia finally became possible means areas with four different languages, four different traditions, and varying expressions of Islam. Abdullah Saeed's coming to Australia in 1985 had great implications for his view of Islam, as Ana Marie Pamintuan sums it up: "Those 24 years of intellectual freedom . . . led to his 'enormous' transformation as a Muslim."[321]

al-Qaraḍāwī, after moving to Qatar at the beginning of the 1960s, must have discovered comparable conditions to Egypt, and he continued to live in an Arabic language area in which Islam is the state religion and where a true debate with other religions and worldviews does not take place. On the other hand, Abdullah Saeed's migration proceeded on the basis of foundationally other circumstances and ended up in a Western society with only a very small Muslim minority enjoying all the freedoms of a Western society.

Abdullah Saeed – not least of all due to his own experience – has repeatedly emphasized in his publications that the classical manner in which

---

319 Saeed. "Islamic Religious Education and the Debate on its Reform Post-September 11" in: Shahram Akbarzadeh; Samina Yasmeen (eds.). *Islam and the West. Reflections from Australia.* University of New South Wales Press Ltd.: Sydney, 2005, pp. 63-76, here pp. 70-73.

320 Saeed. *Islam in Australia*, p. 173.

321 As cited by Pamintuan after an Interview with Abdullah Saeed. "Laboratory".

the *ᶜulamā'* is trained, which has only been slightly adjusted over the centuries, is hardly suitably for preparing Islamic scholars for the demands of modernity.[322] At a conference in 2005, he summarized that a particular set of problematic issues in the religious training of Muslims had to do with a lack of training in critical thinking for the necessary purpose of engaging with modernity: "A shortcoming in teaching, however, is the lack of training in critical thinking." He laments the abstract teaching of material, the rigidity of positions, and the irrelevance of the subject matter for the challenges of the present time:

> "Teaching and learning exist within an authoritative framework in which the teacher is dominant. The research process often consists merely of collecting segments of information and putting them together in an orderly but uncritical form . . . finally, the whole curriculum is driving largely towards producing graduates who, to a larger extent, rely on memorised knowledge, with no critical evaluations of that knowledge."[323]

Upon the occasion of the Conference of the Parliament of World Religions going by the title "Islam, Social Justice and Gender Justice," which took place from September 9-12, 2009 in Melbourne,[324] he personally reported on his very traditional education in Pakistan and Saudi Arabia, "where I ended up in one of the most conservative institutions for Islamic Studies." The answers which he adopted there were only applicable in the Islamic context, since it exclusively involved Islam and Muslim societies.

Having arrived in Australia's multi-religious landscape, this education did not help him in any way for conducting dialog with and understanding the non-Muslim majority society: "My training did not help me to basically engage with other religious traditions," according to Saeed. "I had to basically learn quite a bit when I came to Australia." Because religious leaders in a Western society have to fulfil various societal functions, Saeed recommends a comprehensive change in the education of Islamic scholars

---

322 Saeed. "Islam and Politics", p. 21.

323 Saeed. "Islamic Religious Education", pp. 68-69.

324 See that report at http://blogs.abc.net.au/religion/unrest_conflict_and_war (7.5.2011). He argued similarly in his lecture "Muslims, Multiculturalism and Democracy" at the National Ulama Conference of the Philippines (NUCP) on January 25-28, 2009. Comp. http://www.zabida.com.ph/index.php?option=com_content&task=view&id=416&ltemid=0 (7.5.2011).

and imams, who through the conventional manner of education are in no way prepared for life in a multi-religious society.[325]

3.4.6. A Comparison between Abdullah Saeed's Position and Yūsuf al-Qaraḍāwī's Position

Rootedness in the Western Context

In many respects, Abdullah Saeed's efforts can be viewed as being in exact diametrical opposition to al-Qaraḍāwī's endeavors, who wishes to prevent any enculturation of Islam and its finding a spiritual home as a Muslim minority in Western societies. al-Qaraḍāwī does so by defining Muslims as permanent "others" and by linking them closely to the Islamic doctrine of duty. al-Qaraḍāwī views a reconciliation of Islamic theology and jurisprudence with the conditions of modernity as an error. Indeed, with Saeed's calls for a new orientation in interpreting Islamic sources, al-Qaraḍāwī would presumably speak categorically of apostasy.

Abdullah Saeed as well as al-Qaraḍāwī justify Muslims' abiding residence in Western society. However, while Saeed's efforts go in the direction of seeing "an independent, authentic and unique expression of Islam"[326] emerge in Europe, for al-Qaraḍāwī this effort towards independence and culturally shaped self-reliance on the part of the Muslim diasporic community would be reprehensible and wrong.

While for Abdullah Saeed it is reality which provides an orientation for a reframing of Islamic theology and jurisprudence, for al-Qaraḍāwī it is theology and jurisprudence which prescribe how to deal with reality and modernity.[327] While al-Qaraḍāwī solely wishes to use Western society for his final goal of the complete implementation of the Sharia but neither awards any permanent right to existence nor gives a positive evaluation, Abdullah Saeed accepts Western societies not only out of necessity but ra-

325 Comp. the audio file at http://blogs.abc.net.au/files/abdullah-saeed.mp3 (10.6.2014).

326 Saeed. "Muslims in Secular States", p. 3.

327 Abdullah Saeed formulates as follows: "Much intellectual and creative energy is needed to construct a vision of Islam that is comfortable with the changes that are taking place in all areas of life today in the West: political, social, economic, technological and philosophical." Ibid., p. 6.

ther views them as room for manoeuvre in which "Islamic" values such as religious freedom, righteousness, and human rights can be implemented and thus where more rights and freedom can be granted than in Muslim majority countries. For this reason, the so necessary reshaping of society in al-Qaraḍāwī's view is dispensed with from Abdullah Saeed's perspective.

The Centrist Way and Moderation

Abdullah Saeed as well al-Qaraḍāwī call for moderation, alleviation, and adherence to a centrist position where extremes are avoided. However, when Abdullah Saeed states that the laws of a country which are based on "justice, equity, equality, fairness and public interest" are actually laws which can be labeled "Islamic,"[328] he is principally Islamizing modernity as al-Qaraḍāwī does. Saeed is not doing this, however, by dividing Sharia law judgments into spheres of what is forbidden and what is allowed and by trying to transform Muslim youth by binding them to tradition. Rather, he does so by declaring that the existing circumstances in free democratic societies are actually Islamic or, more specifically, by declaring them to be congruent with Islamic law, ethics, and theology.

Abdullah Saeed as well as al-Qaraḍāwī incorporate social change into their position and seek to set Islam into relation with modernity. But while al-Qaraḍāwī would like to reform modernity by orienting it towards classical Sharia law in a new embodiment of true Islam, Abdullah Saeed views modernity, along with its civil liberties, as the advantageous social and legal framework in which religious commands can be implemented.

The Role of the Quran and Fiqh

As is the case with al-Qaraḍāwī, Abdullah Saeed would also like to see the values of the Quran brought to bear in the life of Muslim society in the West, and he would like to produce a link between the revelation of Islam and its truth claim and the Muslim community in the 21st century. Saeed does not seek this by holding to an ideal desired status as a distant goal in spite of present circumstances in the diaspora and only by allowing for the suspension of certain Sharia regulations for tactical reasons alone. Instead, he accepts modernity with its pluralism and its multi-religious nature as the

328 Ibid., p. 8.

actual state of affairs and ponders pragmatically and flexibly how the ethical precepts of Islam can be implemented in modernity:

> "My main interest is how the meaning of the Qur'ān can be related to the life of the Muslim, in a sense of its application to day-to-day practicabilities in different times, circumstances and places, particularly as it relates to the concerns and needs of the modern period."[329]

If, according to Abdullah Saeed, a large number of the classical *fiqh* works no longer give believers answers to today's questions and challenges, then the danger exists that the mandatory ethical contents of the Quran will be considered irrelevant and, in the final event, pushed to the side.[330] This means that Abdullah Saeed, as is the case with al-Qaraḍāwī, recognizes the necessity of building a bridge between the time of revelation and modernity in order to gain a message that is pathbreaking for the present day generation. In contrast to al-Qaraḍāwī, he does not see the solution in loading down modernity with a seamless classification of every action as *ḥalāl* or *ḥarām*. On the contrary, Abdullah Saeed sees the solution in liberation from the mandatory instruction of the past and their time conditioned judgements in order to make the text of the Quran newly relevant in modern times.

The "Islamic Awakening"

As with Abdullah Saeed, al-Qaraḍāwī would like to see an "Islamic renaissance in the West."[331] Saeed does not, however, want to see classical Sharia Islam win ground in the West and then with corresponding successes in *da^c^wa* and immigration see the majority situation change in favour of an expression of this form of Islam. Rather, he would like to see it occur by Muslims' grasping the following in Western societies:

---

329 Saeed. *Interpreting the Qur'ān*, p. 1.

330 "This demonstrates that much of the earlier interpretatons of the ethico-legal content of the Qur'ān that exist in *fiqh* are no longer serving the needs of Muslims today. Therefore . . . the risk is that the ethico-legal content of the Qur'ān will gradually become ignored, or simply irrelevant, and Muslims will lose their connection to the Qur'ān in a significant way." Ibid., p. 3.

331 Saeed. "Muslims in Secular States", p. 11.

> "The intellectual freedom in the West provides a strong basis for Muslims to engage in a critical study of the Islamic texts. Their work has the potential to lead to a rethinking of methods and principles in jurisprudence, law, exegesis and ethics."[332]

Islam thus has to be renewed from the inside out, not Western societies: "A rethinking of Islamic law is necessary for Muslims living in the West."[333]

Like al-Qaraḍāwī, Abdullah Saeed urges taking a middle road demonstrating a balance between the extremes, not, however, in the sense that Islamic extremism has to be avoided – this is not up for discussion for Abdullah Saeed anyway. Rather, it is up to Muslims to demonstrate moderation in order to shape ethically exemplary behaviour.[334] Urging moderation serves self-critical reflection, which in the case of al-Qaraḍāwī above all serves to consider what can presently be accomplished in non-Islamic societies while at the same time retaining the opinion of superiority. Thus, both include the existing circumstances of modern times in their considerations, but they draw albeit very different conclusions from them.

Iǧtihād and Deontology

al-Qaraḍāwī affirms *iǧtihād* (independent reasoning) in order to substantiate his minority rights, with which assistance he allows exceptions and easing for a transitional period.[335] For Saeed, on the other hand, *iǧtihād* is a necessary instrument in order to produce a lasting reconciliation between Islamic identity and modernity. Beyond that, he advocates a critical evaluation of texts (in particular those of tradition), which on the basis of present day circumstances can no longer be applied. For this necessary reconciliation between Islam and modernity, modernity, from Saeed's point of view, does not have to be scrutinized – negative phenomena such as, for instance, immoral conduct can readily be avoided by Muslims in contemporary Western societies. Rather, the classical tradition of interpretation

332 Ibid., pp. 11-12.

333 Saeed. "Muslims under Non-Muslim Rule", p. 25.

334 "Muslims are told to take a 'middle path' by avoiding excess and extremism, and to refrain from improper conduct such as mistreating parents, backbiting or being tight-fisted." Saeed. *The Qur'an. An Introduction*, p. 73.

335 Comp. for a justification of al-Qaraḍāwī's affirmation of *iǧtihād* embedded in minority rights Schlabach, p. 119ff.

based on the sources of the Quran and *sunna* has to be reconsidered. With that said, al-Qaraḍāwī as well as Saeed – with different objectives – have installed the filter of their own authority between the text and the recipient, which relativizes the absolute validity of the Quran, *sunna*, and normative theology up to the 10th century.

Both Abdullah Saeed and al-Qaraḍāwī divide Islamic deontology into that which is dispensable and that which is essential. However, while according to al-Qaraḍāwī the assessment of that which on the basis of the diaspora, among others, deviates from classical Sharia law but temporarily counts as allowable is unconditionally reserved for qualified scholars, Abdullah Saeed nowhere grants Islamic scholars such a role. Indeed, the question remains open to him what his final criteria are for judging what falls into the categories of "the mutable and the immutable,"[336] which he primarily appears to define on his own in his writings. However, on the other hand, he does not explicitly insist on the special role of scholars.

Finally, Abdullah Saeed and al-Qaraḍāwī differ from each other with respect to the tone both take in their works. Abdullah Saeed does not appear as omniscient and superior to all others but rather objectively weighs[337] and incorporates differing viewpoints held by Muslim as well as non-Muslim academics.[338] Additionally, he speaks self-critically of a lack of theologically established methodology.[339] al-Qaraḍāwī, on the other hand, who mobilizes his entire authority as a legal scholar and *ᶜalīm*, and who from this position of superiority over against those who are ignorant either commends or reprimands, orders or dismisses, not infrequently uses emotional terms such as *fitna* in order to underscore what has been said without allowing for objections.

---

336 Abdullah Saeed. "Some Reflections on the Contextualist approach to ethico-legal texts of the Quran" in: *BSOAS* 71/2 (2008), pp. 221-237, here pp. 231-232.

337 He notes himself in the introduction to his foundational work: Saeed. *Islamic Thought*, "Introduction," p. vii: "In dealing with the topics covered I have tried my best to remain as neutral as possible," but at the same time emphasizes, that there is no true neutrality and that everyone brings his own perspective to the object of investigation." Ibid. pp. vii-viii.

338 "We could say that there is no consensus among Muslims on 'consensus' except on the fundamentals of Islam, such as the unity of God, the prophethood of Muhammad, the five daily prayers, the Qur'an as the word of God, fasting, and pilgrimage to Mecca." Ibid., p. 49.

339 For instance, comp. Saeed. "Muslims in the West Choose", p. 11.

3.4.7. Outlook

What one can read from the publication of Abdullah Saeed's works on religious freedom is that, on the one hand, the voices of Muslim scholars on the advocacy of complete religious freedom are increasing. Also, one notes that an inner-Islamic discussion on this topic is being conducted at an academic level. On the other hand, Abdullah Saeed's primary place of residence in Australia lies very much on the periphery of core Islamic countries. Also, until now, the English language has been the medium for study and daily communication for most of the representatives of classical Islamic theology to a very small extent. Furthermore, there is a connection with the well known fact that there has been limited freedom to express alternative points of view in the centers of Islamic scholarship. Abdullah Saeed has therefore primarily campaigned for his view of things at conferences and in the lecture halls of Western countries.

He does this by conveying the foundations of Islam via a mixture of objective, scientific means, for which he uses numerous works by Western Islamic scholars, and by personal opinion, in which he appears to be on a search for an appropriate methodology or looking for a key that can be applied to every text in order to interpret in a manner compatible with modernity. A deepened debate with the foundations of Islamic law, such as *asbāb an-nuzūl* (circumstances of revelation) or *maqāṣid aš-šarīʿa* (the purposes for which God's law has been given) hardly takes place in his publications. With that said, Abdullah Saeed indeed scrutinizes the interpretive monopoly and conclusions of classical scholars in important questions, such as the validity of classical Sharia law. However, he does not essentially unhinge either their methodology or their use of sources. Up to the present time, he has also not been in a position to draft an integrated and coherent alternative model for looking at source material.

From my point of view, this means that Abdullah Saeed's contribution to the academic discussion and the discussion of critical approaches to Islamic theology for the practical level of peaceful coexistence between people of different religions and worldviews has to be evaluated as highly significant. Also, his point of view, which he also confirmed in personal interviews, has hardly been received by theologians in core Arabic countries up to now. Admittedly, one can suppose that in the age of globalization and the internet as well as given the permanent establishment and increasing size of Muslim communities in Western countries, there may be dislocations and a pluralization of research approaches, also with respect to the Quran and Sharia law, and these events might have long-lasting effects.

4. Abū l-Aᶜlā Maudūdī's "Restrictive" Position: Religious Freedom is Self-Abandonment

4.1. Abū l-Aᶜlā Maudūdī: Life and Work – Essential Principles of His Theology

> "No one who wants to study seriously what is going on the Islamic world today can afford to neglect the writings and activities of Abul Ala Maududi and his supporters."[1]

4.1.1. Influential Politician and Activist

Abū l-Aᶜlā Maudūdī (1903-1979) was one of the most influential Islamic intellectuals, ideologues, and theologians in the 20th century. He was "one of the chief architects of contemporary Islamic resurgence."[2] He not only lastingly influenced Pakistan's self-image and ideological orientation as an Islamic state as, without doubt, the most prominent theological personality. Rather, he was also internationally active via numerous channels and gained for his understanding of Islam – above all, however, for his understanding of the Islamic state – a hearing within a global framework. Maudūdī worked as a journalist, author, commentator on the Quran, theologian, activist, and founder of the political movement and later *Jamāᶜat-i-Islāmī* party as well as working as an advisor for a number of Pakistani government administrations and counts as the most prominent intellectual pioneers of an established Islamic political system.

Via his addresses, articles, and books, in which he called for the creation of an Islamic state and societal order where Islam alone should be the identity and foundation of government, society, and the legal system,

---

1 Ralph Russell. *How not to write the History of Urdu Literature*. Oxford University Press: New Delhi, 1999, p. 206.

2 According to Maudūdī's understanding of the "Islamic Foundation" on the back jacket of his work: Abu A'la Mawdudi. *Human Rights in Islam*. The Islamic Foundation: London, 1976/1990².

Maudūdī exercised influence in a special way upon the formulation of the Constitution of Pakistan. Also, through his political agitation and his public work as a leading figure in the drafting of the first Pakistani Constitution, he surely has to count as an architect of Pakistan and its identity established on the basis of Islam.[3]

When the partitioning of India was looming, he initially spoke out against the thought of an independent state for Muslims. However, he changed his opinion after the national trauma of dramatic outbreaks of violence along with several hundred thousand deaths, which then saw the subsequent split of the subcontinent barely remaining under the direction of the former colonial power, Great Britain.[4] After the independence of India was announced on August 15, 1947, he moved to Lahore on August 29, 1947 and began campaigning for a reorganization of Pakistan into an Islamic state structure. Up to the present day, his notion of this state structure forms the essential foundation of Pakistan's ideological framework.

Maudūdī's influence manifests itself not only within Islamic theology and within Pakistan's intellectual history. Rather, he is also "one of the most significant Islamic ideologues"[5] in society and politics. As early as 1928, Maudūdī published a document entitled *risāla'i dīnīyāt*,[6] which summarized the foundational teachings of Islam and which, in its brief and

---

3 Maudūdī's agitation on the justification and establishment of an Islamic state of Pakistan is broken down into several phases in which Maudūdī attempts, after the partitioning of India, to win over the government and public for the formulation of an Islamic constitution; he later hoped to achieve political power with *Jamāᶜat-i-Islāmī* through participation in elections. At the end of his life, when he recognized that this way was not rewarded with success, he attempted to directly determine the course of Pakistani politics by his impact on the head of state Zia ul-Haqq. Comp. the explanation of the first three phases of Maudūdī's development in Saulat. *Maududi*, pp. 30-32.

4 Comp. the presentation by Yasmin Khan. *The Great Partition. The Making of India and Pakistan.* Yale University: New Haven, 2007.

5 John L Esposito; John O. Voll. Khurshid Ahmad: Muslim "Activist-Economist" in: *MW* 80/1 (1990), pp. 24-36, here p. 28.

6 Sayyid Abū l-Aᶜlā Maudūdī. *risāla'i dīnīyāt*. Hyderabad, 1932. The book was already published in English in 1940 with the title *Towards understanding Islam* and later translated into 13 additional languages. Comp. the details in Siddiqi; Aslam; Ahsan. "Bibliography", p. 9.

precise presentation in Urdu, filled a particular gap. It filled a gap not only through its application as a school book for Muslim children and college students. It also made its author well-known overnight.[7]

Maudūdī's view of ideological and totalitarian absoluteness of the Islamic state and social order and its abasement of all other religions, worldviews, and non-Islamic forms of government also become clear in his attitude towards human rights and religious freedom. His words were, in a sense, sown among his hearers and his 138 independent publications,[8] which were translated into numerous languages of Asia, the Near East, and Europe – among them his multi-volume commentary on the Quran, *Tafhīm al-Qur'ān,* "the first best-selling Urdu Qur'ān commentary"[9] – have had an intensive impact upon intellectual history up to the present day.

The sowing of Maudūdī's words also sprouted with the enactment of the "Blasphemy Laws" during the administration of General Zia ul-Haqq, who took power in Pakistan after a military putsch in 1977, pressed ahead with the Islamization of the country under Maudūdī's consultation and made a lasting impression on legislation – e.g., by introducing the Islamic penal code. The "Blasphemy Laws" were passed in 1980, 1982 and 1986 as § 295 B)-C) and § 298 A)-C) as parts of the Pakistani penal code, and since that time they have been employed against those who are different-minded, converts, minorities such as Christians or Aḥmadīya, and those who possess land or real estate. The laws have led to numerous court cases on account of blasphemy. In these court cases, statements made by non-Muslims are essentially unable to balance out statements made by Muslim accusers, and it has thus become a sharp and arbitrary weapon in the hand of unscrupulous oppressors.

Maudūdī, "who constructed the skeleton of the revivalist ideology . . . who set the parameters for revivalist discourse on state and society,"[10] exerted influence which was not only limited to Pakistan. Maudūdī's body of thought lastingly influenced leaders and intellectual pioneers in Islamist movements such as Sayyid Quṭb, and through him the Muslim Brotherhood, and via reception of their ideology wide swaths of the Islamist spec-

7 According to statements in Jackson. *Mawdudi*, pp. 41+45.

8 These numbers are at least named by Siddiqi; Aslam; Ahsan. "Bibliography".

9 Mir. "Features", pp. 234-235.

10 Seyyid Vali Reza Nasr. "Mawlāna (sic) Mawdūdī's Autobiography" in: *MW* 85/1-2 (1995), pp. 49-62, here p. 50.

trum up to the present day. Especially Maudūdī's concept of the "lordship of God" (*ḥākimīyat allāh*) has become deeply rooted in the world of Islamism through the Egyptian Muslim Brotherhood. Maudūdī's effect has nowadays been multiplied by internet sites,[11] through the translation of his works into more and more languages, and the distribution of his literature via numerous mosques' bookstores as well as online bookshops.

Although Maudūdī has already been the object of numerous investigations, it is striking how E. Platti fittingly noted in 1998[12] just how few studies up to now have addressed the ideological-theological aspects of his worldview and their ramifications. These ideological-theological aspects will be analyzed here using the example of Maudūdī's attitude towards apostasy on the basis of his polemic paper entitled *murtadd ki sazā islāmī qānūn mēn̠*[13] (*The Punishment of the Apostate according to Islamic Law*). The analysis of this document is complemented by an evaluation of Maudūdī's publications on the topic of human rights and minority rights, relating in particular to the Aḥmadīya movment. As is the case with Yūsuf al-Qaraḍāwī and Abdullah Saeed, Abū l-Aᶜlā Maudūdī was chosen as a representative of Islamic theology with an influence extending far beyond the normal circle of influence of a theologian in a mosque and *madrasa*. In his function as an activist, politician, and apologist, Maudūdī has lastingly affected the society and politics of Pakistan and has influenced Islamist and *Jihādist* movements up to the present day with his globally received writings.

---

11 For example, comp. the webpages http://abulala.com (25.11.2011) and http://www.maududi.org/ (10.6.2014), numerous additional pages carry Maudūdī's literature or videoclips of Maudūdī wie etwa http://tazkeer.org/ (10.6.2014) or http://wn.com.Mawdudi (25.11.2011).

12 "Ce qui me frappe en tout cela, c'est que d'une part, les études faites en Occident sont particulièrement attentives au côté sociopolitique de l'auteur; alors que le côté théologique qui en est le fondement est souvent laissé de côté." E. Platti. "La théologie de Abū l-Aᶜlā Mawdūdī" in: U. Vermeulen; D. De Smet. (eds.). *Philosophy and Arts in the Islamic World*. Uitgeverij Peeters: Leuven, 1998, pp. 243-251, here p. 244.

13 Abū l-Aᶜlā Syed Maudūdī. *murtadd ki sazā islāmī qānūn mēn̠*. markazi maktaba islāmī: Dihlī, 1980[5]. I follow DIN Norm 31635 for the transciption of Urdu: *Information und Dokumentation – Umschrift des arabischen Alphabets für die Sprachen Arabisch, Osmanisch-Türkisch, Persisch, Kurdisch, Urdu und Paschtu*. Deutsches Institut für Normung e. V.: Berlin, 2011.

Maudūdī is quoted here as a representative of an uncompromising call for applying the death penalty in the case of apostasy from Islam. Indeed, he refers to the authority of the Quran and *sunna* as well as significant early Islamic authorities for the justification of his position, equal to Yūsuf al-Qaraḍāwī and Abdullah Saeed. However, he deviates from al-Qaraḍāwī's viewpoint as essentially as he does from Abdullah Saeed's position. In this question, Maudūdī does not claim, as al-Qaraḍāwī does, that he is taking a middle of the road position and does not understand himself to be a representative of a progressive and yet Quran-based Islam such as Abdullah Saeed. For him it is not a question of adjusting Islamic law. Rather, it is its comprehensive implementation in modernity with the assistance of political tools, indeed encompassing a reshaping of modernity with the assistance of a comprehensive implementation of Islam which should comprise the state, religion, society, and legislation. Maudūdī places Western ideologies, for instance secularism or Marxism, over against his ideology of a holistic Islam. In order to establish the ideal society and to be able to eliminate all other regimes found in the world, he calls for complete devotion to the cause as well as freedom from all other things which bind.[14]

Maudūdī is in no way the sole Islamic theologian in the 20th century who unreservedly defends the call to apply the death penalty in the case of apostasy. Maudūdī is introduced at this point because he, owing to the impact and scope of his political and societal influence, like Yūsuf al-Qaraḍāwī and Abdullah Saeed, reaches far beyond a classical Islamic scholar as a worldview multiplicator and generator of ideas. This is due to the fact that he ". . . shaped the thinking not just of [his] . . . followers but Muslim intellectuals all over the world."[15]

That there are far fewer studies having to do with Abū l-Aᶜlā Maudūdī's activity in the political arena of Pakistan as well as relating to his theology and ideology than one could expect 36 years after the death of such an influential apologist, theologian, and politician may, among others, be due to the fact that Maudūdī originally composed most of his writings in Urdu. Only a limited number of these Urdu writings are available in German libraries. In the most recent past, however, Maudūdī has certainly

---

14 S. Abu A'la Mawdudi. *Jihād in Islam*. Islamic Publications Ltd.: Lahore, 1976/1980³, p. 5.

15 Merryl Wyn Davies. "The Legacy of Maududi and Shariati" in: *Inquiry* 2 (1985), pp. 34-39, here p. 34.

again attracted the attention of Western researchers,[16] for his broad based publications offer new starting points for conducting detailed studies up to the present day.

Maudūdī's writings treat a myriad of topics, among them studies of Islamic history, law, theology, philosophy, politics, and the economy. Among his most significant works are, doubtless, his foundational treatment of the Islamic state entitled *The Islamic Law and Constitution,*[17] a work which initially was published in three individual parts, later appeared in English, and thereafter found widespread dissemination; the same applies to his commentary on the Quran entitled *Tafhīm al-Qur'ān,*[18] which he composed over a time period of around 30 years between 1942 and 1972.

Numerous writings initially emerged as positions taken on current events, constituted addresses before parliament, contributions to discussions, or shorter individual essays. These writings were frequently published section by section in a journal edited by Maudūdī and entitled *Tarjumān al-Qur'ān* and later compiled and published as their own books. Others were radio addresses which Maudūdī used to appeal to a broad public. An example is the series entitled *Islām kā niẓām-i ḥayāt*, which was broadcast in 1948.[19] That was a time when radio was of great significance in Pakistan as a means of mass communication in what was overall a society where there was not a high degree of literacy.[20]

Antagonism against the hegemony of Western culture, Western civilization, and the Western mindset runs through all of Maudūdī's writings.[21]

---

16 For example, comp. the recently published scholarly biography by Jackson. Mawdudi, or Hartung. System.

17 S. Abu A'la Mawdudi. *The Islamic Law and Constitution*. Islamic Publications Ltd.: Lahore, 1955/1980^7.

18 Syed Abulala Maududi. *Tafheem ul-Quran*. [6 Vols., Lahore, 1949-1972]. http://tazkeer.org/quran/tafheemulquran/ (10.6.2014).

19 The foreword by Khurshid Ahmad mentions the year 1948. In: Sayyid Abul A'la Maududi. *Islamic Way of Life*. Islamic Publications Ltd.: Lahore, 1950/1965^3, pp. vii; Riaz Ahmad deviates and mentions 1947 for the beginning of the series of five programs: Ahmad. *Concept*, p. 107.

20 For the time after independence in Pakistan, Husain Haqqani assumes a literacy rate of only 16.4%; for 2003 35%: Husain Haqqani. *Pakistan between Mosque and Military*. Carnegie Endowment for International Peace: Washington, 2005, p. 313.

21 For instance, this intellectual threat sensed by Maudūdī is pointed out by Jān. "Critique".

He categorically wishes to see these broken. A second central thought is his desire for a complete implementation of the comprehensive Islamic system, superior as it is to the West, which should encompass the economy, child rearing, education, culture, society, and the state. Although an emotionally fierce rejection of everything which is Western is expressed in Maudūdī's writings, at the same time the influence of Western ideologies in his thinking becomes clear, for example the ideology of communism.

Maudūdī believes that the domination of Western civilization, which has come at the cost of the underlying existing supremacy of Islam, was only able to break fresh ground because Muslims have left the prescribed path of comprehensive observance of Islam.[22] For that reason, a return to this comprehensive form of Islam is only natural and has to have as its goal the whole world, for Islam is a universal and complete system (*niẓām*). Islam is founded upon its own societal order, its own culture, and its own political system. This system reflects the oneness and sovereignty of God.

4.1.2. Maudūdī's Parental Home, Formal Education, and Journalism

Abū l-Aᶜlā Maudūdī was born on September 25, 1903 in Aurangabad in the Indian State of Maharashtra in the south of India. The family of his mother, Ruqiah Begum, emigrated to India from Turkey in the 17th century and held influential positions under the Mughal. With the fall of the Mughal Dynasty, they lost these positions and, for that reason, were never able to reconcile with British rule.[23]

The ancestors on the father's side of the family are traceable back to notable personalities within the Chištī order, "the first important order, which was able to gain a foothold in India [in the 13th century]."[24] In the course of the 15th century, the family immigrated to India and in the 18th century came to Delhi. Maudūdī's grandfather was a Sufi *pīr* and possessed influence in the Mughal court. Maudūdī's family gained a reputa

22 For that reason the West took over leadership and Islamic societies lagged behind: Sayyid Abu A'la Mawdudi. *The Sick Nations of the Modern Age*. Islamic Publications Limited: Lahore, 1966¹/1979⁶, p. 10.

23 According to Nasr. "Mawdudi and the Jama'at-i Islami", p. 99.

24 Stephan Conermann. *Das Moghulreich. Geschichte und Kultur des muslimischen Indien*. Verlag C. H. Beck: München, 2006, p. 57.

tion within this dynasty, which was forfeited more and more over the course of British colonial rule. With the "mutiny" which occurred in 1857,[25] the family, in what was a parallel to the growing alienation of the British to the Muslim segment of the population, appeared to have finally positioned itself as anti-British.[26]

Maudūdīs father, Sayyid Aḥmad Ḥasan, was born in Delhi in 1855 and for a long time attended the Mohammedan Anglo Oriental College established by Sayyid Ahmad Khan (1817-1898) in 1875 in Aligarh. He attended until his father took him out of the school overnight because he had participated in a cricket match.[27] He later studied law and became an attorney. After he increasingly turned to Sufism, he was initiated into the Chištī order in 1900 after swearing the oath of loyalty (*baiᶜa*). For around three years, he practiced Sufism very intensively in Delhi. In 1907, however, he returned to his profession as an attorney. He died in 1920.

"The importance of his father's life on Mawdudi cannot be underestimated,"[28] according to the estimation of Roy Jackson. In this connection, he refers to Maudūdī's father's inner conflict between modernity, from which he disappointedly withdrew into Sufism, and the lost power and culture of the Mughal Empire. These experiences are echoed by Maudūdī when he passed judgment that modernity did not hold any answers for the current spiritual crisis.[29]

Maudūdī's father, in his desire to largely take away the influence of Western education and the English language, instructed his son in Arabic, Persian, Hindi, in the recitation of the Quran, in *fiqh* (jurisprudence), *ḥadīṯ* (Islamic tradition) und *manṭiq* (logic) in his early years at home.[30] This was done in an effort to presage the way for his being an Islamic scholar. He

[25] On the multi-layered causes for this military social national revolt on the way to Indian independence comp., for instance, the various aspects of the representative presentations by Yusuf A. Ali. *A Cultural History of India during the British Period*. AMS Press: New York, 1976; Rudrangshu Mukherjee. *Awadh in Revolt, 1857-1858. A Study of Popular Resistance*. Permanent Black: Delhi, 1984 or Peter Hardy. *The Muslims of British India*. Cambridge University Press: Cambridge, 1972.

[26] According to Jackson. *Mawdudi*, p. 11.

[27] Gilani. *'Maududi'*, p. 25.

[28] Jackson. *Mawdudi*, p. 17.

[29] Ibid.

[30] These subjects are mentioned by Jackson, ibid., p. 18.

and his siblings, as he later reported, were not allowed to play with other children. Not until he was eleven years old did he visit the Madrasa Fauqania in Aurangabad. There the family lived until 1915, at which time they moved to Hyderabad where Maudūdī was instructed in *dār al-ᶜulūm*.

Due to the early illness and death of his father, Maudūdī already had to begin to provide for his own living in 1918, and he decided to pursue journalism. For a short time in 1919, Maudūdī published the weekly newspaper *Tāj* in Jubalpur. In 1920 he so severely criticized the British colonial government that the newspaper had to be discontinued. For a brief time beginning in 1919, Maudūdī became involved in the Khilafat movement after World War I for the purpose of reinstalling the caliphate.

From 1920 onwards, Maudūdī worked in Jubalpur, initially for a weekly newspaper. From 1921 until it was discontinued in 1923, he was the editor of the newspaper *The Muslim*, which was an agent of *Jamᶜīyat ᶜUlamā-i-Hind* founded in 1919. During this time, Maudūdī studied Arabic, Quran exegesis, logic, philosophy, theology, and literature. He wrote verse, but left Delhi prior to his concluding his studies and went to Bhopal for one and one-half years.[31] Maudūdī must have come into contact with the *Ahl-i-Ḥadīṯ*[32] in Bhopal. They were inclined towards Wahhabism. He must have also picked up on their thinking with respect to the reestablishment of the prototypical Islam of Muḥammad's time. Disappointed, Maudūdī turned from the failed caliphate movement, which saw its final demise in 1924, as well as from the Indian Congress Party, which under Ghandi had increasingly taken on a Hinduistic orientation.

From 1924 (or 1925),[33] Maudūdī was the editor of the *Jamᶜīyat*, the newly originated body of the *Jamᶜīyat ᶜUlamā-i-Hind*, and he translated works from Arabic to Urdu, for example a history of the Fatimid dynasty under the Shafi'i scholar Ibn Ḫallikān. He later also translated from Persian.[34] From 1924 onwards, he was again in Delhi, where he took up studies again. This time his studies were at the Deobandi Mosque Fatihpuri,

---

31 Ibid., p. 27.

32 Comp. the explanations on the orientation of *Ahl-i-Ḥadīṯ* in Tariq Rahman. *From Hindi to Urdu. A Social and Political History*. Oxford University Press: Karachi, 2011, pp. 146-148.

33 The individual details differ occasionally; for instance, 1925 is mentioned by Ali. *Thought*, p. 154.

34 According to Jackson. *Mawdudi*, pp. 42-43.

where in 1926 under ᶜAbdussalām Niyāzī (d. 1966) he received his permission to teach *(iǧāza)* as an *ᶜālim*. Now he counted as a Muslim scholar, which he is said to have never publicly expressed. As a result, this qualification was first discovered at the time of his death.

Throughout his whole life, Maudūdī's relationship to the *ᶜulamā'* has to be described as ambivalent. On the one hand, he belonged to this group, drew his authority as a scholar from this tradition, and above all took his traditional interpretations of texts from this tradition. On the other hand, he frequently criticized the *ᶜulamā'* on account of its retreat from the field of politics and society and its backward-looking method of textual interpretation,[35] for which reason he saw it as not equal to the task of addressing the challenges of modernity.[36] For pragmatic reasons, Maudūdī was nevertheless able to build alliances with the *ᶜulamā'*. When what was involved was the building of as broad a front of support as possible in order to exert influence on the drawing up of Pakistan's first constitution at the end of the 1940s and the beginning of the 1950s, the areas of contact between Maudūdī and the *ᶜulamā'* became greater.

From the beginning, Maudūdī apparently did not intend to lead the life of a scholar. Rather, he planned to be politically active. In 1925 he was offered the first opportunity: After a Muslim assassin murdered Swami Shraddhanand, the leader of the monotheistic religious community Arya Samaj within the Shuddhi social reform movement, various Hindu players publicly denounced Islam as a militant religion.[37] This further exacerbated the already existing tensions between Hindus and Muslims.[38] Thereafter, for starters, Maudūdī published his first essential writings in Urdu in the *Jamᶜīyat ᶜUlamā-i-Hind* journal in several parts. It appeared in 1930 as an

---

35 Mawdudi. *Sick Nations*, pp. 11-12.

36 Seyyid Vali Reza Nasr supposes that Maudūdī's criticism of the *ᶜulamā'* is a type of retaliation for its very restrained acknowledgment of his scholarship: Nasr. *Mawdudi and the Making*, p. 116.

37 Gandhi, as well as a large number of Western oriented Muslims, is supposed to have spoken out critically about the potential for violence in Islam which had become visible through the murder: Lerman. "Concept", p. 493.

38 Comp. the depiction by Yoginder S. Sikand. "The *Fitna* of *Irtidad*: *Muslim Missionary Response to the Shuddhi of Arya Samaj in Early Twentieth Century India*" in: *JMMA* 17/1 (1997), pp. 65-82.

independent work[39] and, as a concise depiction of classical *Jihād* teaching in numerous editions and translations, it found broad dissemination.[40]

Maudūdī's writings are almost consistently politically programmatic writings, apologetic pamphlets, and calls to action more than being purely theological treatments. They were not primarily directed at the religious scholar class and were never drafted for purely academic purposes. Rather, they were above all an expression of Maudūdī's political lobbying work on the restructuring of society, which he underpinned with religious terms and concepts.

Roy Jackson made the time of the middle of the 1920s the time period when Maudūdī lost belief in democracy and, more specifically, he lost belief in the idea that the destiny of Muslims was well served in the hands of the increasingly Hindu oriented Indian National Congress.[41] Maudūdī now recognized and formulated the necessity of an Islamic awakening more and more clearly[42] since he feared that the Muslim minority would lose its identity in the ruins of the sinking colonial empire between the National Congress, Western influences, and the hostilities of Hindu groups.

In 1928 Maudūdī left *Jamᶜīyat ᶜUlamā-i-Hind* and, after being in Hyderabad, he moved to Andra Pradesh, where he became the editor of the periodical *Tarjumān al-Qur'ān* in 1932. He held this position until his death in 1979. The journal, as Roy Jackson indicates, never exceeded a circulation of more than 600, of which only around 100 went to individual subscribers. The remainder went to government and educational institutions as well as libraries.[43] And yet, for Maudūdī it was the most important

---

39 Abū l-Aᶜlā Maudūdī. *al-jihād fī al-islām*. Lahore, o.J. [Azamgarh, 1930].

40 From Maudūdī's disappointment at the floundering of the Khilafat Movement and the anti-Islamic resentment in face of Shraddhanand's murder, Seyyed Vali Reza Nasr concludes: ". . . the inability of Muslim intellectual leaders to defend their religion adequately, and the climate of helplessness and resignation that prevailed among Muslims impressed on Mawdudi the need for action." Nasr. *Mawdudi and the Making*, p. 22.

41 As formulated by B. P. Barua. *Eminent Thinkers in India and Pakistan*. Lancers Books: New Delhi, 1991, p. 90.

42 Tariq Rahman even names Maudūdī "the pioneer of revivalist Islam": Rahman. *Hindi*, p.151.

43 Jackson. *Mawdudi*, p. 48.

tool for the propagation of his increasingly political-ideological notions,[44] i.e., "the main vehicle of his ideas for the rest of his life."[45] It contributed to self-assurance among the Muslim minority and the repression of the influence of Western culture, and it contributed to the way of thinking about life for many Muslim intellectuals:[46]

> "The *Tarjuman* gave Mawdudi a place to air, test, refine, and rationalize his ideas and his vision and . . . cast him as a leader of the Muslim community in India."[47]

In 1937 Maudūdī married his cousin Mahmudah Begum, and since she was from a wealthy family, this marriage not only relieved Maudūdī of all material worries. It also placed him in the position of being able to support his political work with the income from his writings from that time forward.

Through his school education, which began late and then ended early due to the death of his father, Maudūdī acquired a good part of his knowledge as an autodidact. Thus, Maudūdī was, on the one hand, an Islamic theologian and yet not a typical member of the classic Sunni world of scholarship with a traditional education. That is a fact which is reflected in the characteristic style of his writings and made him appear to a number of scholars as an "intellectual outsider."[48]

In 1937 Maudūdī purchased a piece of property and planned, together with Muhammad Iqbal (1873-1938) to establish an educational institution, *Dār al-Islām*, in Pathankot in the province of Punjab, with the goal of equipping and training scholars in order to drive back Western influence owing to the British school system, which Maudūdī particularly viewed as

---

44 The time for the shaping of Maudūdī's political and ideological worldview is estimated by Sayyed Reza Vali Nasr to be between the years 1932 and 1937: Nasr. *Mawdudi and the Making*, p. 27.

45 F. C. R. Robinson. "Mawdūdī, Sayyid Abu'l A^clā" in *EI/2*, Vol. VI., pp. 872-874, here p. 872.

46 This is emphasized by Adam Muhammad Ajiri. "Some Aspects of Maududi's Contributions to Modern Islamic Thought" in: *MuEQ* 12/2 (1995), pp. 52-72, here p. 56.

47 Nasr. *Mawdudi and the Making*, p. 30.

48 As formulated by Reinhard Schulze. *Islamischer Internationalismus im 20. Jahrhundert. Untersuchungen zur Geschichte der Islamischen Weltliga*. E. J. Brill: Leiden, 1990, p. 323.

a given. Admittedly, the project came to a rapid end with the early death of Muhammad Iqbal in April 1938. Maudūdī left Pathankot a short time thereafter and turned his attention to Lahore.

In the following years, Maudūdīs interest in political work grew increasingly: From 1937 to 1941, he published a series of articles with political content in the journal *Tarjumān al-Qur'ān*. Prior to 1940, he appears to have voted neither for nor against the partitioning of India.[49] Admittedly, he supported the idea that Muslims constitute a different nation than Hindus.[50] For that reason, he vehemently rejected the ideas of national states as well as the nationalism propagated by Ali Jinnah and the Muslim League[51] – in addition to rejecting the partitioning of India under these guidelines.

However, after the partitioning of India was performed, Maudūdī invested all his efforts in promoting Pakistan's becoming an Islamic state, with a social order and legislation needing to be solely founded upon Sharia law. His activism maneuvered into what were in part bitter disputes with several administrations of the Pakistani government and became the cause of Maudūdī's multiple imprisonments: He was incarcerated for a period of about five years between 1948 and 1967,[52] and in 1963 he survived an attack upon his life.[53]

---

49 According to Omar Khalidi. "Mawlāna Mawdūdī and the Future Political Order in British India" in: *MW* 93/3-4 (2003), pp. 415-427, here p. 422.

50 In his work *Nationalism and India* Mawdūdī extensively discusses the difference between a community based on the idea of nationalism and an Islamic state: Abū l-Aᶜlā Maudūdī. *Nationalism and India*. Markazi Maktaba-Jama'at-e-Islami Hind: Dehli, 1965^4, pp. 4 ff.

51 Comp., for instance, the excerpt from Ali Jinnah's address on March 23, 1940 in which Muslims were labelled "a nation by any definition," warned against a future theocratic state, and sketched out a tolerant pluralism as the future of Pakistan. Jinnah said the following on August 11, 1947 before Pakistan's constituent assembly: "The Prophet was a great teacher . . . Thirteen hundred years ago he laid the foundations of democracy . . . You are free; you are free to go to your temples, you are free to go to your mosques or to any other place of whorship in this State of Pakistan . . . you will find that in course of time, Hindus would cease to be Hindus and Muslims would cease to be Muslims . . . in the political sense as citizens of the State" – a vision which in light of the following ideologization of the identity of Pakistan could not become a reality. Abdullah Adnan. "Pakistan: Creation and Genesis" in: *MW* 96/2 (2006), pp. 201-217, here pp. 204+213-214.

52 A number of the heads of Pakistan's government, for instance Zhulfiqar Bhutto, have attempted to control Maudūdī's agitation and the range of his activities and,

4.1.3. Jamā'at-i-Islāmī

Beyond Maudūdī's publications, his influence is primarily visible in politics through the founding of his own movement. He called it into existence and modeled it as a type of *umma*. Later, it entered the political stage as a party and up to the present day has remained, both within Pakistan as well as outside of the country, an influential voice of political Islam and of the political landscape of Pakistan. Up to the time of his death, the *Jamā'at-i-Islāmī,* "originally the brainchild of Mawlana Sayyid Abu'l A^c^la Mawdudi,"[54] comprised the most important forum of his political activism.[55]

When India's independence began to loom on the horizon, many Indians who were Muslims feared that they would henceforth begin to be marginalized in a country dominated by Hindus. In his writings, Maudūdī then began to describe the special character of Islamic community which could only unfold in an Islamic state. Only a few months after India was partitioned, the *Jamā'at-i-Islāmī* commenced its propaganda work in support of producing an Islamic state. This is due to the fact that at that time the public mood appeared to tend in favour of an Islamic state,[56] and Maudūdī set about taking on the leadership role on the way to propagating a complete Islamification of Pakistan.

With perhaps 70 adherents in Lahore,[57] Maudūdī founded the movement *Jamā'at-i-Islāmī*[58] on August 26, 1941 as a counterforce to Moham-

more specifically, to control the abrasiveness of his criticism of the government through his involvement and by co-opting him; the Pakistani government has at times attempted to prevent Maudūdī from foreign travel. Thus, for instance, all African countries were deleted from Maudūdī's passport when wanted to undertake a propaganda trip to South Africa. Comp. Saulat. *Maududi*, p. 52.

53 Nasr. *Mawdudi and the Making*, p. 44.

54 Seyyid Vali Reza Nasr. *The Vanguard of the Islamic Revolution. The Jama'at-i Islami of Pakistan*. University of California: Berkeley, 2004, p. 3.

55 "He was one of the first Islamic thinkers to develop a systematic political reading of Islam and a plan for social action to realize his vision." Nasr. *Mawdudi and the Making*, p. 3.

56 According to Adams. "Mawdudi", p. 106.

57 Abdul Rashid Moten even speaks about 75 founding members: Moten. Mawdūdī, p. 392; also according to Araghchi. Theo-Democracy, p. 775. Seyyid Vali Reza Nasr, a Maudūdī biographer, explains, however, that Maudūdī had indee invited

med Ali Jinnah's *All India League*. The basic considerations of *Jamā'at-i-Islāmī,* which moved its main office to Pathankot for five years, was the production of an elite. This elite, as an avant-garde, was supposed to erect and lead an Islamic state in order to hinder the demise and decay of the Muslim community in an India where there was a Hindu majority. The movement was a religious-ideological community,[59] which later became a party. It was, like a communist cadre party, strictly hierarchically organized.[60] It was a "pressure group" and simultaneously a concrete and demonstrative example of Maudūdī's planned world-scale Islamification project.[61]

One did not become a member in *Jamā'at-i-Islāmī* through one's own decision. This occurred only by being called, and mere membership in the family of Islam was not sufficient: The most important criteria, in addition to sound knowledge about Islam, were strength of character,[62] personal piety, ethical behavior, preparedness for sacrifice as well as loyalty and commitment to the movement, a solid knowledge of the Quran and the *sunna*, the Sharia, and Islamic history.[63] The members, who in the first

---

around 75 *ᶜulamā'* (learned men) to the founding but that "a handful replied, but only to register their disapproval" – he does not estimate, however, how many people it involved: Nasr. *Mawdudi and the Making*, p. 115.

58 Prior thereto, he had announced the founding in *Tarjumān al-Qur'ān*: N.N. Al-Mawudi (sic) (Abul-A'la): "Un Aperçu Biographique" in: *Sou'al* 5 (1985), pp. 123-129, here p. 124.

59 For instance, the internal composition and individual activities are described by Marc Gaborieau. "Le Néo-Fondamentalisme au Pakistan: Maududi et la Jamā'at-i-islāmī" in: Olivier Carré; Paul Dumont (eds.). *Radicalismes Islamiques.* Vol. 2. *Maroc, Pakistan, Inde, Yougoslavie, Mali.* Editions L'Harmattan: Paris, 1986, pp 33-76, here pp. 53ff.

60 Vanessa Martin points out that the strongly hierarchical structured Sufi orders were models for the *Jamāᶜat* and Muslim Brotherhood movements started by Maudūdī and Quṭb, respectiveley: Vanessa Martin. *Creating an Islamic State. Khomeini and the Making of a New Iran.* I. B. Tauris: London, 2003, pp. 134-135.

61 According to Moten. "Mawdūdī", p. 394.

62 The character test for an aspirant to membership could last a number of years: Ahmad. *Concept*, p. 81.

63 For instance, these criteria are mentioned by Khalid B. Sayeed. "The *Jama'at-i-Islami* Movement in Pakistan" in: *PA* 30/1 (1957), pp. 59-68, here p. 60 and Moten. "Mawdūdī", p. 393.

place had to say the *šahāda*, swore an oath and then had to give proof of their loyalty and dedication to erecting an Islamic society – thus a type of second conversion to Islam with a Maudūdī'ish adornment – were simultaneously the active supporters of the movement. An additional circle consisted of sympathizers as well as individuals who were loosely associated with the movement.

The majority of members came from the urban middle class, while few came from the lower class. With *Jamā'at-i-Islāmī*, Maudūdī conveyed a platform for actionism to this middle class, which appeared to move the community, the assignment, and appreciation as an elite with rule over Pakistan and the entire earth through the *Jamā'at-i-Islāmī* within reach. Additionally, the goals of the movement have been promoted by donors, for example from Saudi Arabia, who have provided targeted support to *Jamā'at-i-Islāmī* since the end of the 1960s.[64]

In comparison to the parent movement *Jamā'at-i-Islāmī*, there was a more radical student movement called *Jamᶜīyat-i-Talaba* which came into being as early as 1947. It was strongly influenced by the methods of the Egyptian Muslim Brotherhood and was enmeshed in violent actions and street fighting.[65] In addition, a women's division was founded in February 1948.

Nowadays, the *Jamā'at-i-Islāmī* possesses branches in India, Bangladesh, Kashmir, and Sri Lanka as well as in Southeast Asia, the Persian Gulf, and in Great Britain. Among the most important personalities are Khurshid Ahmad, the later editor and translator of numerous writings by Maudūdī, for which the "Jamaat i Islami . . . provided the inspiration, motivation, and context for his life's work."[66]

The *Jamā'at-i-Islāmī* was not just any party. Rather, for its adherents it counted as an instrument appointed by God in order to transform society

64 According to Khálid Durán; Munir D. Ahmed. "Pakistan" in: Werner Ende; Udo Steinbach (eds.). *Der Islam in der Gegenwart. Entwicklung und Ausbreitung, Kultur und Religion, Staat, Politik und Recht.* C. H. Beck: München, 2005[5], pp. 336-362, here p. 354.

65 As commented on by Haqqani. *Pakistan*, p. 24.

66 Comp., for instance, a short biography by the economist and Maudūdī's early adherent, the later member of the Pakistani Cabinet and Senate of the Pakistani government, Khurshid Ahmad; he became a full member of *Jamā'at-i-Islāmī* in 1956 and in 1968 founded the Islamic Foundation in Leicester, with goals closely linked to those of *Jamā'at-i-Islāmī*, in Esposito; Voll. Khurshid Ahmad, p. 27.

through revolution, to depose unjust rulers on earth and to install God's rule, or, in Maudūdīs words: "It is a party of God's soldiers [Hezbollah]. This party therefore, has no option but to take control of political power."[67] In the process, the *Jamā'at-i-Islāmī*, on the basis of its early instituted translations of Maudūdī's works in Persian and Pashtu, was "both model and mentor" for leaders of Afghani Islamism as well as a link to Islamic groupings in most Muslim majority countries.[68]

Jamā'at-i-Islāmī was led by an *amīr* – and, of course, Maudūdī himself filled this post. He successfully defended his absolute position for decades. An advisory board (*šūrā*) stood by his side. Important principles were obedience towards the *amīr*[69] and the management level as a way to emulate absolute obedience towards God within the hierarchical structure as well as strict discipline and mutual evaluation. Those who protested against the leadership or were viewed as deficient in their piety were excluded from the movement.[70]

Jamā'at-i-Islāmī viewed itself as a morally avant-garde in Pakistan, as a demonstrative example of a state within a state and a model-like recovery of the original Islamic community; there was no difference between the party and religious membership. A model that was based on obedience and accountability towards leadership and faithfulness to the Sharia, which Maudūdī had in mind for the overall society, was practiced here. The avant-garde of this movement was supposed to permeate society and islamify it by degrees through its exemplary actions in order for the Islamic state to become reality.

In the nine years from 1948 to 1946, until Pakistan had its first constitution, *Jamā'at-i-Islāmī* was the instrument which assisted Maudūdī in pitting all his influence so that Pakistan developed into an Islamic, non-

---

67 According to Abū l-Aᶜlā Maudūdī in *Tarjumān al-Qur'ān*, Mai 1939, p. 9; quoted in Jackson. *Mawdudi*, p. 129.

68 According to Haqqani. *Pakistan*, p. 171.

69 "Obedience" (*ṭāᶜat*) is, as Maudūdī repeatedly explains, a component of belief (*īmān*) and for that reason an unconditional "necessity" (*ẓarūrat*); comp. his remarks in his early work: Maudūdī. *risāla'i dīnīyāt*, pp. 25ff.

70 Roy Jackson references the exclusion of 300 members in 1944 on account of insufficient piety, which at that time was more than one-half of all the members: Jackson. *Mawdudi*, p. 68.

secular state with a Muslim majority population as had been originally drafted by its founding fathers.[71]

One of the instruments used by Maudūdī along the way was the exercise of pressure on the government through public appearances in which he emphatically called for the establishment of an Islamic state: On January 6 and on February 18, 1948, Maudūdī presented his legendary "Four Point Program"[72] towards which the constitution was supposed to be oriented:[73] The sovereignty of God, which was labeled here as higher than any rule, would obligate the government to act as its representative, to bring all laws into accord with the Sharia, to abolish all other laws, and, more specifically, not to pass such laws, and to entrust the dispensation of justice to Islamic authorities according to Sharia law. With these concrete demands, to which the "Islamic state" was to conform, Maudūdī put the government on the spot. In addition, he criticized the government on account of corruption and bribery.[74]

Maudūdī's calls were conveyed to the public via channels of the media and through a number of trips made by Maudūdī in the spring of 1948. According to statements by his biographer Syed As'ad Gilani, his first public address was held in Jahangir Park in Karachi in which he renewed his efforts of raising the four demands for implementing Islamification in Pakistan. Maudūdī's efforts – and those of his supporters and like-minded individuals – exhibited success:

> "The campaign launched by the neo-traditionalists and traditionalists for the enforcement of the Shariah was so forceful that the government had to take a decision relating to the introduction of the Shariah and an Islamic constitution in order to gain the support of the ulema and the masses."[75]

---

71 Robinson. "Mawdūdī", p. 872.

72 Mawdūdī made both addresses public in the same year with the title: *Islāmī qānūn mēṉ aur Pākistān mēṉ us kē nafāẕ kī ʿamalī tadābīr*, Lahore 1948 and already in English in 1955: S. Abu A'la Mawdudi. *The Islamic Law and its Introduction in Pakistan*. Islamic Publications Limited: Lahore, $1955^1/1983^4$.

73 See the presentation by Moten. "Thought", part. p. 181.

74 He now stood under the particular observation of the government. At that time, this circumstance made it clear that owing to his influence among the public, Maudūdī was already viewed as a potential threat. Comp. remarks by Ahmad. *Concept*, pp. 108-109.

75 Syed Mujawar Hussain Shah. *Religion and Politics in Pakistan* (1972-88). National Institute of Pakistan Studies: Islamabad, 1996, p. 44.

These four points were accepted in the form of an "objectives resolution" by the constitutional assembly of Pakistan on March 7, 1949,[76] and on March 12, 1949 the resolution was adopted as a preamble to the future Constitution of Pakistan.

With that said, the young state of Pakistan, under public pressure – and significantly so through Maudūdī and *Jamā'at-i-Islāmī* – had put a train upon the tracks, awakening expectations in every respect that Pakistan would position itself as an Islamic state and adopt a corresponding constitution. The partial victory of the acceptance of the "objectives resolution" counted as Maudūdī's "personal triumph."[77] This was hardly diminished by the fact that he was in custody from October 4, 1948 to May 20, 1950[78], which was owing to his statements regarding the then very recent Pakistani military intervention in Kashmir. His statements had been interpreted as pro-Indian partisanship, and *Jamā'at-i-Islāmī* had been interpreted as a form of sedition.[79]

However, after the acceptance of the "objectives resolution," Maudūdī remained in charge in the mobilization of additional scholars and activists who have continually kept the topic awake in the mind of the public: After the acceptance of the "objectives resolution," additional key points were set for the future constitution by representatives of various groups, among them the Barelvi, Deobandi, Ahl-i-Hadith, and Shi'ites at a gathering in Karachi in 1951. However, in the case of this group of individuals, it in no way involved representatives chosen by the people. They defined Pakistan as an Islamic state and in a 22-point program professed commitment to the "sovereignty of Allah" and to legislation on the basis of the Quran and the *sunna*.[80]

---

[76] Gilani. *'Maududi'*, pp. 396-397. Ali mentions March 9, 1949: Ali. *Thought*, p. 228.

[77] Allahbukhsh K. Brohi. "Mawlānā Sayyid Abul Aᶜlā Mawdūdī: The Man, The Scholar, the Reformer" in: Khurshid Ahmad; Zafar Ishaq Ansari Ishaq (eds.). *Islamic Perspectives. Studies in Honour of Mawlānā Sayyid Abul Aᶜlā Mawdūdī*. The Islamic Foundation: London/Saudi Publishing House: Jeddah, 1979, pp. 289-312, here p. 296.

[78] Ali. Thought, p. 228.

[79] See further explanations in: Nasr. Mawdudi and the Making, p. 42.

[80] For instance, comp. the wording of the suggestions summarized into 22 points in: Brohi. Mawdūdī, p. 296-297.

This gathering was under the leadership of Maudūdī. He played a key role in the formulation of the 22 points and put forward all individual points which were voted upon. Even after that, in particular in 1952, he continued his campaign by making public appearances[81] and by offering a new 8-point program with the call for an Islamic constitution. *Jamā'at-i-Islāmī* supported him with demonstrations, the distribution of informational material, and the organization of events.[82] With the formulation of these programmatic points, the yardstick for the future constitution of Pakistan was publicly laid out.

In 1952, when the assembly to produce the constitution still did not appear to be moving in the direction of adopting a constitution, *Jamā'at-i-Islāmī* again increased its pressure and called for the implementation of Maudūdī's 8-point program. Above all, this concentrated on aligning all national laws with Sharia law.[83] When the first Constitution of Pakistan was finally adopted in 1956, it was characterized by *Jamā'at-i-Islāmī's* massive influence and by Maudūdī's activity in the background.[84] Up until that time came, he was able to solicit for his vision of an Islamic state on state radio.[85]

In 1957, *Jamā'at-i-Islāmī* became an official political party and decided to participate in the 1958 elections. A number of scholars who had supported Maudūdī in years past criticized this.[86] Maudūdī had been under the illusion at the time of the founding of *Jamā'at-i-Islāmī* that *Jamā'at-i-Islāmī* would rapidly become a mass movement and could come to rule all of India, where the population would rapidly turn to Islam.[87] He also hoped for great victories in a number of elections after the partitioning of India,

---

81 A summary of his public addresses in Karachi in November 1952, in which, in the search for supporters, he targeted his communication regarding the foundations of an Islamic state to members of the educated class, was published in the following document: Sayyid Abū l-Aʿlā Maudūdī. *Islāmī dastūr kī tadwīn* [Lahore 1952].

82 According to Ali. *Thought*, pp. 230-232.

83 Comp. the text of this 8-point in Gilani. *'Maududi'*, pp. 399-400.

84 Charles J. Adams subsumes: "Mawdudi seemed to feel that the majority of his demands had been met in the Constitution": Charles, J. Adams. "The Ideology of Mawlana Maududi" in: Donald Eugene Smith (ed.). *South Asian Politics and Religion*. Princeton University Press: Princeton, 1966, pp. 371-397, here p. 378.

85 According to Haqqani. *Pakistan*, p. 25.

86 According to Euben; Qasim Zaman (eds.). *Readings*, p. 83.

87 Sayeed explains this thought: "*Jama'at-i-Islami*", pp. 61-62.

and he hoped for that not only for Pakistan but all over the world.[88] However, the party was still only achieving moderate victories. Nevertheless, its ideological influence was considerable.

In 1977, *Jamāʿat-i-Islāmī* again interfered massively in politics. Maudūdī, for whom the national-socialist oriented government of Ali Bhutto was a thorn in the side, called for the toppling of Bhutto's government. Together with *Jamāʿat-i-Islāmī*, Maudūdī pursued Bhutto's arrest, the imposition of martial law, and Bhutto's death sentencing. In the end, Bhutto was hanged on April 4, 1979 and, with that said, the way was freed for intensive political influence on the part of Maudūdī and of *Jamāʿat-i-Islāmī* under Bhutto's successor, Zia ul-Haqq.

The assumption of power by General Zia ul-Haqq was successfully achieved in 1977. He counted as a member of the Islamist branch of the spectrum and was supported by Islamic parties. The help provided by Islamic parties served to ensure his political survival and attempted to legitimate his rule by calling a comprehensive Islamification into being[89] and declaring Sharia law to be the foundation of all legislation.

Maudūdī influenced, supported, and legitimated him as his official consultant, while Zia ul-Haqq demonstrated himself to be Maudūdī's true devotee and promoter.[90] Via Zia ul-Haqq's government, *Jamāʿat-i-Islāmī* was able to record significant growth in power and achieve large social influence, while for its part it supported the government of Zia ul-Haqq and kept it alive.

When Abū l-Aᶜlā Maudūdī died in the USA on September 22, 1979, where he had traveled to undergo medical treatment, he had become one of the most influential theologians and activists of an Islamist stripe. Supposedly there were one million people who lined up and passed by at the time of his burial.[91] The Iranian government, the leaders of which had sent numerous messages of condolence, asked to take over the return of the corpse

---

88 "The ultimate goal of Islam is a world-state." Maudoodi. *Nationalism and India*, p. 9.

89 Comp., for instance, the detailed presentation in John L. Esposito. "Islamization: Religion and Politics in Pakistan" in: *MW* 72/3-4 (1982) pp. 197-223.

90 "La dottrina di Abul A'la Maududi . . . avrebbe influenzate notevolmente il programma di islamizzazione di Zia." Elisa Giunchi. *Radicalismo Islamico e Condizione Femminile in Pakistan*. L'Harmattan Italia: Torino, 1999, p. 42.

91 This number is mentioned by Nasr. "Mawdudi and the Jama'at-i Islami, p. 118.

from the USA to Pakistan.[92] Numerous prominent individuals paid last respects to Maudūdī – among them Zia ul-Haqq[93] – and commemorated him as "a 'reformer' (*mujaddid*) of Islam in the 20th century."[94] The requiescat was given by Yūsuf al-Qaraḍāwī,[95] who labeled his death a great loss for the entire Islamic world.[96] The University of Punjab, colleges, and schools closed their doors on the day of his burial. Maudūdī's widow, Begum Maudūdī, expressed her desire to be allowed to have Maudūdī buried in Medina in Saudi Arabia, a request which highlighted Maudūdī's importance.[97]

4.1.4. The Rule of God and "Theodemocracy"

The concept of the sole sovereignty and rule of God (*ḥākimīyyat allāh*) is in the center of Maudūdī's theology. Maudūdī derived it from the unique oneness of God (*tauḥīd*), and it is designated the sole form of legitimate rule on earth in numerous writings he produced.[98] Humankind has erroneously departed from this and instead placed other rulers, e.g., kings, in God's place. Such rulers are usurpers, their reign is illegitimate, and the acknowledgement of their rule is polytheism (*širk*). The rule of God only emerges at that point where those in power implement God's law, i.e., put the Sharia into practice.

---

92 H. Mintjes. "Mawlana Mawdudi's Last Years and the Resurgence of Fundamentalist Islam" in: *al-mushir* 22 (1980), pp. 46-73, here p. 61.

93 According to Haqqani. *Pakistan*, p. 139.

94 Durán; Ahmed. "Pakistan", p. 354.

95 Masudul Hasan. *Sayyid Abul A'Ala Maududi* (sic) *and His Thought.* 2 Vols., Islamic Publications Ltd: Lahore, 1984+1986, here Vol. 2, p. 484.

96 According to Saulat. *Maududi*, p. 166. See there the list of numerous prominent domestic and foreign condolence visitors (ibid., pp. 166-167), as well as a number of obituaries from various media and individuals (ibid., pp. 169-184).

97 Mintjes. "Mawlana Mawdudi's Last Years", p. 71. Begum Sahiba is supposed to have suggested a burial site for him on an own piece of property in Lahore as an alternative. According to Saulat. *Maududi*, p. 168.

98 Yvonne Y. Haddad assumes that the term *ḥākimīya* in Arabic first came into circulation through the translation of Maudūdī's own works and that Sayyid Quṭb did not pick it up until after that: Yvonne Y. Haddad. Sayyid Qutb: "Ideologue of Islamic Revival" in: John L. Esposito (ed.). *Voices of Resurgent Islam.* Oxford University Press: New York, 1983, pp. 67-97, here p. 89.

Maudūdī saw Islam as a comprehensive system which leads humankind on the path of faith, on the path of a peaceful societal order as well as on the path of just state legislation. This legislation is to be drawn from the Sharia, such that a community which is superior to all other emerges.[99]

This comprehensive form of Islam is to be implemented with the help of an avant-garde of truly believing Muslims, at the forefront of which is a male Muslim who is a mature, spiritually healthy member of Islamic society. He acts as the *amīr*,[100] who is the leading statesman: "il capo dello stato, chiamato *amīr* . . . [lui] simboleggia la sovranità divina, è cioè vice-reggente di Dio."[101] He and his committee of consultants are chosen, and for that reason, according to Maudūdī's understanding, this model of the state is in the final event a matter of a democratic system.

Due to the fact that this state is an ideological state, only those who share this ideology have the right to codetermination. The council, to which neither women nor non-Muslims may belong, advise the leading statesman and can be overthrown if it deviates from the Sharia. It should be distinguished by its piety and good moral behaviour (admittedly Maudūdī always remained vague as to what that means in concrete terms).

All people in this system, without exception, are "vice regents", i.e., representatives or caliphs of God.[102] They choose the avant-garde of the

---

99 Comp. in part. Maudūdī's political ethics: See Mawdudi. *Islamic Law and Constitution*, pp. 123ff. It is supposedly a matter of Maudūdīs best known work of all, in which he brought together several less comprehensive exploratory works at the time of the apex of his influence. To a significant extent, Maudūdī composed this state theory between the years 1953 and 1955 for the English-speaking educated class as a type of compendium – on the eve of the enactment of the Constitution of Pakistan – when he was imprisoned on account of the agitation he directed toward the Aḥmadīya movement.

100 These four conditions for the leader of a state are described and explained by Maudūdī in his work: Maudūdī. *Islāmī dastūr kī tadwīn*, pp. 39ff.

101 In English: "The head of the state, called *amīr* . . . symbolizing divine sovereignty, is rather God's vice regent". Roberto Bellani. "Lo Stato Islamico: Postulati Fondamentali di Abū l-Aᶜlā l-Mawdūdī" in: *AION* 42 (1987), pp. 593-603, here p. 598.

102 ". . . the status of man is in this world is that of an ᶜabd (God's servant and slave) who is also Khalifat-ul-Allah (Allah's deputy and viceregent) . . . God has appointed him as his vice-regent giving him the power to use these objects for his benefit." S. Abul A'la Maududi. *Ethical Viewpoint of Islam*. Islamic Publications Ltd.: Lahore 1966²/1967³, p. 26.

elite and only distinguish themselves from each other in their character or in their abilities; otherwise, they are completely equal before God.[103] On the basis of their own complete implementation of Islam and submission to God, they ensure that the best representatives are chosen. Such a society is the realization of the ideal community. There is neither injustice nor oppression nor hatred nor greed in this community, for through devotion to God humanity can overcome his arrogance and keep his egoism under control. Through absolute loyalty in following God, humanity becomes free from all other dependencies and constructs a centrist community (*umma wasaṭa*).[104]

In this state, laws are not made by people, since God has already given his perfect law, the Sharia, to humanity. The Sharia is only to be interpreted and put into practice through analogy. For that reason, parties are unnecessary in such a system. This is due to the fact that the political orientation has already been prescribed by God's law. States, which do not implement this system, are on the path to *ǧāhilīya*.

Maudūdī, who does not see himself as obligated to any particular school of legal thought, calls this system "theodemocracy"[105] or a "democratic caliphate." This is due to the fact that the highest echelon is democratically elected and through the people it receives the mandate of Islamizing the state from the ground up. God possesses the highest sovereignty in such a state – not the people as is the case in Western democracy, which from Maudūdīs point of view means tyranny and despotism.

Nevertheless, the people in such a state possess limited freedom, in dependence upon God's law, to regulate things which do not unambiguously arise from the sources of Islam: While the religion (*dīn*) has been revealed for all times and is unchanging, tradition can change (*šarīᶜa*), i.e., the rules

---

103 In this connection, Jan-Peter Hartung points to fractures in Maudūdī's ideology in light of this repeatedly emphasized equality of all people; which, however, he at other points denies to minorities, apostates, and women and awards only reduced rights: Hartung. *System*, p. 187.

104 Moten summarizes Maudūdī's concept of vice regency in this manner: Moten. "Thought", pp. 176-178.

105 Comp. the discussion of this "theo-democracy" in his work: Abū l-Aᶜlā Maudūdī. *Islām kā naẓarīya-'i siyāsī*. [Lahore, 1939] as well as in Abu A'la Mawdudi. *Political Theory of Islam*. Islamic Publications Limited: Lahore, $1960^1/1993^8$, pp. 22ff.

of behavior or the rites of honouring God. They can be interpreted differently at different times,[106] however always in accordance with revelation.

Maudūdī does not entertain any considerations with respect to the question of how a misinterpretation of God's law by the highest holder of power and his counsellors is to be addressed[107] or, more specifically, how the correct interpretation and application of the Sharia is to be determined; Maudūdī apparently assumed that the "correct" (Maudūdīish) interpretation of Islam was so apparent for the experts that there could not be any disagreement. According to Maudūdī's understanding, the personal integrity, belief, morality, fear of God, and complete loyalty towards God and his law automatically prevent arbitrary or irregular action.

Maudūdī also does not address the question of how the Islam he proclaims, which is a strictly regulating interpretation of Islam, is to be implemented throughout an entire society and how expected resistance is to be addressed. Maudūdī assumes that peace and unity will self-adjust under the Sharia in such a state. This is due to the fact that adherence to (true) Islam, obedience and submission thereto, would cause all differences and discrepancies to disappear. Islam is politics, politics is the implementation of ethics and morality,[108] and citizenship is membership in the *umma*: "Islam, the umma and the state are inseparable."[109] With this, Maudūdī proclaims that piety is the remedy for all social problems; with a complete implementation of Islam, they come to a halt.

The implementation of the Islamic state occurs via the means of education and instruction, throught legislation by capable representatives of the people, and through the implementation of Islamic norms and laws according to the Sharia. From Maudūdī's point of view, Islam cannot be effected without legal implementation: Individually lived out piety alone cannot

[106] Comp. the discussion of this differentiation by Maudūdī between *dīn* und *šarīᶜa* in Ron Geaves. "A Comparison of the Ideas of Maulana Mawdudi (1903-1980) and Shah Wali-Allah (1703-1762): A Pure Islam or Cultural Heritage" in: *IQ* 41/3 (1997), pp. 167-186, here p. 174. Also comp. Maudūdī's explanation: Abū l-Aᶜlā Maudūdī. *Towards Understanding Islam*. The Islamic Foundation: London, 1980, pp. 129-130.

[107] Ahmad also refers to this. *Islam and Modern Political Institutions*, p. 165.

[108] For instance, comp. Maudūdī's explanation about "Das Moralische System des Islam" in his work: *Maududi. Islamic Way of Life*, pp. 31ff.

[109] Ishtiaq Ahmed. *The Concept of an Islamic State. An Analysis of the Ideological Controversy in Pakistan*. Pinter: London, 1987, p. 202.

bring about the Islamic state. Ideally, people desire the implementation of Sharia legislation, and, if necessary, force must be used as a final means.

4.1.5. Maudūdī's Criticism and Acceptance of the Spirit of the Age

Maudūdī was of the opinion that he taught the pure form of Islam from the Quran and *sunna*, but he was apparently hardly aware of the fact of how strongly his understanding of Islam was shaped by his own culture and time. It appeared to him, as is repeatedly clear from his writings, that there is only a true and a false point of view, the "Islamic" and the "non-Islamic". He ignored differences within Islam.

Just how little Maudūdī reflected upon his own interpretation of Islam and his culture becomes particularly clear in Maudūdī's writing on the position of women. In his writings, he uses numerous details in going into the question of what women are allowed to do and what is prohibited, and he sets this in contrast to (from his point of view) aberrations which have appeared in the West. He expounds the problems of equal rights between men and women in the West, the freedom women have to pursue professional life outside of the home, the neglect of their families which arises as well as their economic independence, which leads to moral wrongdoing. Maudūdī sketches a caricature of a Western society and explains the apparently scientifically demonstrated instable female constitution in such drastic terms that for him the compelling conclusion is that women are actually only well served when they are within the house.[110] Maudūdī also advocates wife beating in case of disobedience.[111]

Maudūdī explains that a limited education is sufficient for women and that the Indian-Pakistani practice of wearing a veil and segregation, "purdah," is a compulsory norm on the way to establishing Islamic society.[112] He holds this view without it being clear in his mind that a portion of his

---

[110] Maudūdī explains that at times women return the wrong change as tram conductors, can only drive cars very slowly, and as secretaries make a lot of typing errors, indeed, that they are so nervous that they are inclined to commit crimes and even commit suicide: Abul A^cla Maudūdī. *Purdah and the Status of Woman in Islam.* Islamic Publications Limited. Lahore 1972/1979, pp. 115-117.

[111] Comp. Shehadeh Lamia Rustum's explanation: The Idea of Women in Fundamentalist Islam. University Press of Florida: Gainesville, 2003, pp. 34ff.

[112] Maudūdī even suggested that in order to preserve the purdah, women should only visit mosques when it is dark. Maudūdī. *Purdah*, p. 205.

instructions correspond more to the cultural norms of his time and his location than the consensus of Muslim scholars.[113]

Maudūdī's so vehemently rejected influence of culture and the 20th century spirit of the age and his radical rejection of all forms of secularism, in particular communism and Marxism, are found in several of his writings to go hand in hand with echoes of the vocabulary borrowed from these worldviews and their contents. Beyond that, there are recognizable borrowings from Wahhabism and Salafism, from Ibn Taymīya (1263-1328), Ğamāl ad-Dīn al-Afġānī (1838-1897) as well as Rašīd Riḍā (1865-1935).[114]

As far as Maudūdī's dealings with the normative sources of early Islam are concerned, not even a subliminal criticism is to be found in his writings, neither towards the founders of the four schools of legal thought nor towards the scholars of early Islam, nor towards the Quran, nor towards individual traditions handed down. According to Roy Jackson, in taking recourse to sources, Maudūdī chooses a central path between *iğtihād* (independent reasoning) and *taqlīd* (imitation):

> "He has one foot in independent reasoning, and one foot in blind imitation: a schizophrenic ijtihad-taqlid figure struggling with contrasting ideologies, ideals and methods."[115]

On the other hand, Maudūdī appears to only quote those texts which he can draw upon to corroborate his theses. His interpretation of the Quran is above all a justification of his world outlook as it relates to the rule of God, and Islam for him is less a spiritual than it is a political program. His reference to decisions of the first four caliphs and companions of the Prophet are not presented in an academic fashion. Rather, they are primarily tinted with apologetics and presented in a narrative and preaching style. Above all, however, Maudūdī is his own authority. He only mentions other authorities where they confirm his opinions.

---

[113] This work, carrying the title *Parda*, appeared initially in 1939 in Urdu and saw 13 editions up to the year 1972: Ibid., p. iv.

[114] These worldview borrowings by Maudūdī are discussed in detail by Jackson. *Mawdudi*, pp. 95ff.

[115] Ibid., p. 106.

4.1.6. Maudūdī's Understanding of *ǧāhilīya* and *Jihād*

As the first author of modernity, Maudūdī formulates a – albeit as far as content is concerned rather indeterminate – call to *Jihād*[116] with the goal of establishing a just political order over all the earth.[117] This order is to rest upon the three principles of *tauḥīd* (the oneness of God), the *risāla* (the sending of Muḥammad), and the *ḫilāfa* (the caliphate).[118] The goal of *Jihād* is to produce a sole Islamic community around the world, the communal life of which is completely permeated by Islam, the law of which is exclusively God's commands, and which applies[119] the penal code, family law, and commercial law[120] stipulated in the law of God. Islam does not strive for growth in power as imperial powers do. Rather, it solely pursues liberation, truth, and justice.

From Maudūdī's point of view, *Jihād* does not mean to conquer with the sword and by violent revolution.[121] Rather, it means the successive implementation of Islamic order over the entire earth. He designates this successive implementation a revolution (*inqilāb*) which abolishes the tyrannical rule of people over people, the non-Islamic state structure, and which introduces a new and perfect order: "In reality Islam is a revolutionary ideology and programme which seeks to alter the social order of the whole world."[122]

116 Comp. his comprehensive early work: Abū l-Aᶜlā Maudūdī. *al-jihād fī al-islām*. Lahore, year not indicated, [Azamgarh, 1930] and a summary presentation of its contents in Hasan. *Maududi* Vol. 1, pp. 51-53. On April 13, 1939, "Iqbal Day," he gave a lecture on this topic in the Lahore Town Hall, in which he summarized significant thoughts relating to this thinking on *Jihād*: Mawdudi. *Jihād in Islam*.

117 "In reality Islam is a revolutionary ideology and programme which seeks to alter the social order of the whole world." Ibid., p. 5.

118 Comp. his remarks on these three foundations of Maudūdī's politico-Islamic objectives in his work: Maududi. *Islamic Way of Life*, pp. 49ff.

119 Comp. Nasr. "Autobiography", p. 51.

120 For a summary of Maudūdī's understanding of the economic structure of the Islamic state see, for instance, Ahmad. *Maulana Maududi and the Islamic State*, pp. 129ff.

121 Seyyed Abbas Araghchi points out that Maudūdī does not essentially reject or exclude violence; however, on the other hand, he does not call directly for the use of violence but rather to transform the society: Araghchi. "Theo-Democracy", p. 789.

122 Mawdudi. *Jihād in Islam*, p. 5.

This concept of revolution in order to reorganize society[123] breathes of the Marxist body of thought,[124] since the Revolution should bring about the consummate condition of society: "Mawdudi's concept of jihad amounts to a well-planned *putsch* launched to replace one government with another."[125] Maudūdī traces the command for revolution, however, directly back to Muḥammad, who likewise set a revolution in motion in Arabia with the proclamation of Islam.[126]

Maudūdī dedicated a separate publication to the necessity of an Islamic revolution. It had the title *Islāmī ḥukūmat kis ṭarḥ qā'im hōtī hai?*[127] In that publication, he initially explained that the leadership of a nation has to be placed in the hands of Muslims exhibiting exemplary character.[128] Only such individuals could effect change through obedience and moral behavior.[129] This revolution is a gradual ethical reconfiguration of society through influential people who implement Islam according to the axample of the prophets, for "all the Prophets of God . . . without exception were revolutionary leaders."[130] This ethically exemplary leadership elite is comprised of officers authorized to issue directives to the people, and in this manner the people are freed from oppression, exploitation, and injustice.[131]

The Muslim community might slowly be restructured through morality and legislation. Nevertheless, towards non-Muslims (including *people of the book*) who do not believe in God and the Day of Judgment, Islam pre-

---

123 "Mawdudi's understanding of jihad is not as 'war' but rather as 'liberation,' a 'struggle' for peace and justice." Jackson. *Mawdudi*, p. 157.

124 For instance, this is documented with textual references by Lerman. "Concept", p. 500.

125 Choueiri. *Fundamentalism*, p. 138.

126 Mawdudi. *Islamic Law and Constitution*, pp. 125 ff.

127 Abū l-Aᶜlā Maudūdī. *Islāmī ḥukūmat kis ṭarḥ qā'im hōtī hai?* Lahore, [1941]. This document already apppeared a few years later in English and went through seven editions up to the time of Maudūdī's death: S. Abul A'la Maududi. *The Process of Islamic Revolution*. Islamic Publications Ltd.: Lahore, 1947/1980[8].

128 Abū l-Aᶜlā Maudūdī. *Islāmī ḥukūmat*, pp. 17-19.

129 Ibid., pp. 39-40.

130 In an address, which Maudūdī held in 1939 in the Lahore Town Hall, he traced his concept of "revolution" (*inqilāb*) back to the time of the emergence of Islam: Mawdudi. *Jihād in Islam*, p. 15.

131 "Mawdudi's notion of revolution is more ethical in nature, rather than social or political." Jackson. *Mawdudi*, p. 146.

scribes *Jihād*. This is due to the fact that through their godless life they deny Islam. They have to be subjugated and *ǧizya* has to be paid, since in Maudūdī's view there are only two spheres which exist, those of unbelief and of belief, those of the West and of Islam.[132] As long as both of these spheres exist, *Jihād* is not a duty limited in time. Rather, it is a permanent order upon all Muslims. For it is unthinkable that Muslims would live under non-Islamic rule.[133] Additionally, *Jihād* serves to defend Islam against enemy powers: "L'histoire même est pour lui essentiellement une lutte continue entre l'islam et la *jāhilīya*."[134]

Maudūdī frequently uses the term *ǧahilīya*.[135] In Maudūdī's thought, *ǧahilīya* means the opposite of the rule of God, i.e., everything which directs itself against the comprehensive concept of Islam in theology and practice. The term *ǧahilīya* means ignorance and self-determination, but it also means polytheism and pantheism.[136] According to Maudūdī's understanding, people persisted for a large portion of history in this condition of *ǧahilīya* after they turned their back on the ideal early days of Islam and turned away from its comprehensive practice.

The situation of *ǧahilīya* is overcome when the state and society are subjugated to Islamic law, the unity of state and religion is produced, and the leadership of Islamic community is entrusted to a ruler which is simultaneously the religious leader: Humanity then returns to true Islam. Thus it

---

132 According to how Idris incisively determines: Idris. "Reflections", p. 548.

133 Mawdudi. *Jihād*, p. 19.

134 As summarized by Jacques Waardenburg. "Le Renouveau Islamique, vu à travers un *Festschrift*" in: *ASSR* 50/2 (1980), pp. 191-204, here p. 195.

135 Comp. the definition of this muli-layered term used by Maudūdī in Hartung. *System*, pp. 64ff. It is no longer disputed that Sayyid Quṭb adopted this term from Maudūdī. Thus Sabine Damir-Geilsdorf assumes that Quṭb came into contact with the term *ǧāhilīya* in Abū l-Ḥasan ᶜAlī al-Nadwī, who already used it in the middle of the 1940s. Damir-Geilsdorf. *Herrschaft*, p. 86. Sayed Khatab even supposes that Quṭb already used this term in the 1930s: Sayed Khatab. *The Political Thought of Sayyid Qutb. The theory of jahiliyyah*. Routledge: London, 2006, pp. 63+171.

136 Thus there are by all means differences between Maudūdī's and Quṭb's notions of *ǧāhilīya*: For instance, comp. on Quṭb's understanding of this term Khatab. *Political Thought*. A few differences between both protagonists are mentioned by William E. Shepard. "Sayyid Qutb's Doctrine of *Jāhiliyya*" in: *IJMES* 35 (2003), pp. 521-545, here pp. 524ff.

is not only religion in Maudūdī's view but rather, at the same time, the socio-political order which can be read from the Quran and the *sunna* and can be produced through obedience to God's law. It is not until this comprehensive Islamic order is again able to be erected that it is possible for an individual to orient himself towards the commands of God.

4.1.7. Maudūdī's Agitation with the Aḥmadīya Movement

Maudūdī's influence on the course of Pakistani politics is not only limited to its co-creation of the content of the first Pakistani constitution. At the beginning of the 1950s, he prominently intervened in the debate regarding the legal status of the Aḥmadīya movement in Pakistan.

A debate had erupted at the beginning of the 20th century regarding the assessment of the Aḥmadīya movement after propagators of the Aḥmadīya movement had been brought before court on account of apostasy, charged, and executed in Afghanistan in 1924.

The Aḥmadīya movement first arose in 1889. When Mīrzā Ġulām Aḥmad (1835-1908) accepted oaths of allegiance from a number of his followers, the movement gained momentum. At first, Mīrzā Ġulām Aḥmad had merely labeled himself a recipient of revelation. Soon, however, he strengthened his claim to the effect that along with the incarnation of Christ, Krishna, and Mahdi he amounted to a prophet sent by God, even if he had not been sent with a law-giving scripture such as Moses, Jesus, or Muḥammad. Indeed, God has not sent another prophet with Scripture after Muḥammad, but God continutes to remain in contact with his community by sending prophetic elaborations (*kamālāt*). In 1904 Mīrzā Ġulām Aḥmad ultimately identified himself as a reappearance of Muḥammad. His second successor, from 1914 onwards, was his son Mīrzā Bashīr ad-Dīn Maḥmūd Aḥmad. Under Mīrzā Bashīr ad-Dīn Maḥmūd Aḥmad the movement split.

The opinions regarding the continuation of the prophetic office split one of the two groups of the Aḥmadīya movement, the Qādyānī, who revered Mīrzā Bašīr ad-Dīn Maḥmūd Aḥmad as the second caliph after the founder. They considered non-Aḥmadīya to be unbelievers. The smaller group of Lāhōrī, who were adherents of Maulānā Muḥammad ᶜAlī and Kh̲wāja Kamāl al-Dīn, considered the founder Mīrzā Ġulām Aḥmad to merely be a renewer (*muǧaddid*).

As early as after the execution of a number of Aḥmadīya followers at the beginning of the 20th century, the Deoband scholar Maulānā Šabbīr Aḥmad U̱smānī published a pamphlet in which he labelled Aḥmadīya followers as apostates. This pamphlet was republished in 1950. It is possible that the insistent pro-British attitude demonstrated by the Aḥmadīya played an additional role in their condemnation in Pakistan.

The dispute began in 1931 with the founding of a group called Majlis-i-Aḥrār-i-Islām (MAI), "religiously motivated men," a spin-off of the Congress and "a politico-religious movement,"[137] which on May 1, 1949 renewed their 1936 requests to declare that Aḥmadīya adherents were a non-Muslim minority.[138] At the same time, they requested the resignation of the Minister of Foreign Affairs Chaudhri Zafrullah Khan, who was an Aḥmadīya adherent, as well as the removal of all Aḥmadīya adherents from all political offices. A number of *ᶜulamā'*, who in part belonged to *Jamā'at-i-Islāmī*, associated themselves with these requests. It appears that with their affiliation, the agitation against the Aḥmadīya took on an alarming form:[139]

In January 1953, the strengthened group set an ultimatum before the Prime Minister K̲h̲wāja Nāẓim-ud-Dīn in the name of the existing Muttaḥida Majlis-i-ᶜAmal (MMA), which consisted of several Islamic groups. In the ultimatum, they called for Aḥmadīya to be declared non-Muslims. The Prime Minister ignored this request and had a number of members of the Muttaḥida Majlis-i-ᶜAmal arrested, whereupon unrest broke out in 1953 in Punjab[140] and lasted until the middle of April 1953. A number of people – among them Aḥmadīya adherents were killed and martial law was imposed.[141]

On the one hand, Maudūdī did not join the agitation against the Aḥmadīya at the beginning. On the contrary, he issued a warning with the

---

137 Ahmad. *Islam and Modern Political Institutions*, p. 97.

138 The depiction of the agitation originating from the Aḥrār is explained in detail by Leonard Binder. *Religion and Politics in Pakistan*. University of California Press: Berkeley, 1963², pp. 261ff.

139 This is described ibid., p. 262: "The agitation really achieved alarming proportions when the ᶜulamā' joined forces with the Aḥrār."

140 That the unrest on account of the conflict between *ᶜulamā'* und Aḥmadīya adherents erupted does not exclude that the outbreak of the unrest also "reflected profound social conflicts in Pakistani society." Schulze. *Internationalismus*, p. 363.

141 According to the description by Stahmann. *Menschenrechtskonzepte*, p. 135.

suggestion that a course of action against the Aḥmadīya would reduce the prospects for adopting an Islamic constitution that was most urgently expected by *Jamā'at-i-Islāmī*. Five years after the partitioning of India, an Islamic constitution was still not in place.[142] Therefore, after the constitution being adopted – as Maudūdī's has been understood – "it would automatically solve the Qadiani problem"[143] – thus, toleration of the Aḥmadīya movement was thus never on Maudūdī's agenda.

In the final event, however, since he basically shared the goals of agitation against Aḥmadīya,[144] Maudūdī not only joined the actions against Aḥmadīya. Rather, he placed himself at the pinnacle[145] of the group of a total of 33 *ᶜulamā'*[146] dealing with this question. He became the leading figure of this group at the beginning of 1953 after the publication of his position on the Aḥmadīya movement, which was entitled *Qādiyānī mas'ala*[147] (*The Aḥmadīya Question*). In that publication, he designated adherents as apostates and requested that his assessment of this group be declared binding for all Muslims.

According to Maudūdī, it is not only the fact that the founder of the movement, Mīrzā Ġulām Aḥmad, said he was a prophet sent by God which made the group essentially distinguishable from Muslims. Rather, Maudūdī holds, their entire faith was erroneous and wrong. This judgment rests upon their own actions for which they would themselves have to be responsible. Throughout his entire document, Maudūdī argues in a way in

---

142 As explained by Ali. *Thought*, p. 236.

143 Hasan. *Maududi*, Vol. 1, p. 444.

144 Leonard Binder sums up with respect to Maudūdī's initial delay in moving against the Aḥmadīya and then joining the group consisting of Aḥrār und *ᶜulamā'*: "... There is no question but what he agreed with the doctrinal bases of the demands." Binder. *Religion*, p. 263.

145 According to Adams. "Mawdudi", p. 110.

146 This number is mentioned by Maudūdī himself in his work: Abū l-Aᶜlā Maudūdī. *Qādiyānī mas'ala*. [Karachi, 1953]/Lahore 1996/1998, p. 4.

147 Maudūdī. *Qādiyānī mas'ala*. This document was also translated into Arabic and widely disseminated: Abū l-Aᶜlā Maudūdī. *mā hiya 'l-qādiyānīya? dirāsa šāmila wa-ᶜarḍ ᶜilmī li-l-qādiyānīya wa-madā tā'ṯīrihā fī 'l-muǧtamaᶜ al-'islāmī*. dār al-qalam: Kuwait, 1969. An English translation appeared with the title S. Abul A'la Maududi. *The Qadiani Problem*. Islamic Publications (Pvt.) Limited: Lahore, 1979¹/1991³ just as the Urdu edition for the first time in 1953: According to statements in Siddiqi; Aslam; Ahsan. "Bibliography", p. 9.

which the responsibility for the later exclusion of the group from the community of Muslims is shifted to the Aḥmadīya movement itself. In the reading of this treatment, the sharp tone and the disparaging choice of words forcefully catch the reader's attention as an instrument of denunciation of this movement.

On the basis of the unrest which had broken out in Punjab, the responsible judge, Muhammad Munir, Chief Justice of the Lahore High Court and later Chief Justice of Pakistan[148] had a so-called "Report of the Court of Inquiry,"[149] also called the "Munir Enquiry Report," produced and published on April 10, 1954. This report contained an investigation of the reasons for the outbreak of unrest in Punjab. The investigating commission took up its work on July 1, 1953, held 117 meetings, and concluded their inquiries on February 28, 1954. The report was presented in written form in the middle of 1954.

This report was followed by an almost as comprehensive and forceful a commentary entitled "An Analysis of The Munir Report. A Critical Study of the Punjab Disturbances Inquiry Report" in which the *Jamā'at-i-Islāmī* expressed with sharp wording its disappointment regarding the course of the judicial inquiry and its results.[150] It above all criticized the fact that the report considered the establishment of an Islamic state to be an impossible undertaking.[151] And finally, Aḥmadīya adherents also published a position paper. In that paper they likewise established that the Aḥrār were the driving force in the proceedings against them. However, they also raised fierce allegations against Maudūdī and summed up their statements by saying that Maudūdī had an insatiable power hunger and that he was "totally ob-

148 According to Daniel P. Collins. "Islamization of Pakistani Law: A Historical Perspective" in: *SJIL* 24 (1988), pp. 511-584, here p. 553.

149 *Report of the Court of Inquiry, Constituted under Punjab Act II OF 1954 to Enquire into the Punjab Disturbances of 1953*," Printed by the Superintendent, Government Printing: Lahore, Punjab, 1954.

150 For instance, *Jamā'at-i-Islāmī* commented on the "Munir Enquiry Report" with the following: "The report indulges in a discussion of the nature and the prospects of the Islamic state and vomits out a lot of venom on this point." Khurshid Ahmad (ed.). *An Analysis of The Munir Report. A Critical Study of the Punjab Disturbances Inquiry Report*. Jamaat-e-Islami Publications: Karachi, 1956, p. 2.

151 Ibid., p. 6.

sessed with political authority." For that reason, he was the actual speaker and motor of the agitation against them.[152]

Martial law was imposed in Punjab on March 6, 1953 due to unrest, which Maudūdī vehemently criticized. Thereafter, on March 28, 1953, he was arrested and on May 11, 1953 he was sentenced to death.[153] The charges against him read: "promoting feelings of enmity and hatred between different groups in Pakistan."[154]

Thereafter such massive protests arose all over Pakistan and far beyond – e.g., in Indonesia, Iraq, the Palestinian territories, and Egypt[155] – that Maudūdī's sentencing was initially changed into lifelong imprisonment and then shortened to a 14-year prison sentence. Finally, the sentence was suspended with the result that Maudūdī was released on May 25, 1955, around two years later, and was said to have been welcomed by 10,000 people.[156] He had even emphatically rejected filing a plea for clemency. His sentencing as well as his pardon can be interpreted as indicators of his then far-reaching power, his great popularity, and his far-reaching influence in politics and society. "Already a hero, he quickly became the spokesman for a religious alliance whose zeal he was determined to rekindle."[157]

That the Aḥmadīya movement was made out to be an alleged troublemaker to a homogeneous Islamic order, that it was ostracized, discriminated against, its existence threatened, and persecuted all the way to the inclusion of death has to at least in part be attributed to Maudūdī's activity as an agitator and the activity of *Jamāʿat-i-Islāmī*. In the 1950s, Maudūdī had at

152 "But it was Maulana Abul Ala Maududi . . . who became their voice." Hazrat Mirza Tahir Ahmad. *Murder in the Name of Allah*. Lutterworth Press: Cambridge, 1989, pp. 44+VII.

153 This was supposedly due to the fact that, although the dispute between Aḥrār-i-Islām and a number of other religious groups and *ᶜulamā'* was led, the government viewed the support of the *Jamāʿat-i-Islāmī* in this matter "with greater alarm and as more invidious than the provocative activities of the Ahrar": Nasr. Mawdudi and the Making, p. 43.

154 According to the journal *Tasnim,* February 28, and March 7, 1953, quoted by Nasr. *Vanguard*, p. 137.

155 Masudul Hasan lists the individual voices of protest: Hasan. *Maududi*, Vol. 1, p. 449.

156 This number is mentioned Masudul Hasan, ibid., Vol. 1, p. 461.

157 Nasr. *Vanguard*, p. 141

his disposal, aside from all official political offices, such great popularity when the political debate regarding the judgment of the Aḥmadīya acutally took its dramatic turn, that through his appearances and writings he was in a position to decisively co-determine public political opinion with reference to the Aḥmadīya.[158]

Thus, a good portion of the responsibility has to be ascribed to him for the proceedings which set in, at the end of which the adherents of this movement were prohibited from labeling themselves as Muslims, from having the call to prayer sounded out, and from having their places of assembly referred to as mosques. Aḥmadīya adherents were at that time already pushed to the margins of society and up to the present day have frequently been the victims of formal charges, mistreatment and even deadly attacks. Admittedly, it must also be mentioned that the *ᶜulamā'*, who also participated in this anti-Aḥmadīya movement, were not any milder in their appraisal of this movement than Maudūdī.[159] To be sure, he was the prominent sociopolitical speaker of these scholars, and he provided a detailed justification for ostracising and excluding the Aḥmadīya movement from the Muslim community. Also, within the *Jamā'at-i-Islāmī,* the clear direction of which he set as *amīr*, he was the absolute leading figure and figure of respect whom all the members owed absolute obedience.

In 1973 Maudūdī again condemned the Aḥmadīya as apostates, and in 1974 the *Jamā'at-i-Islāmī* student movement urged on a new anti-

158 Roy Jackson also judges as follows: "Some blame must be placed on Mawdudi for inflaming the passions of many Muslims against the Ahmadi in the first place." Jackson. *Mawdudi*, p. 36.

159 According to the "Report of the Court of Inquiry," there were among the *ᶜulamā'* virtually no dissension – they judged in a "practically unanimous" manner – that apostasy in an "Islamic State" was to be punished by death and likewise judged just as little that Aḥmadī were apostates; indeed, the report even echoes the notion defended by these *ᶜulamā'* that those who used to be Muslims and had converted to the Aḥmadīya movement, such as the Foreign Minister, Muhammad Zafrullah Khan, who belonged to the movment, should actually be executed. Maudūdī did not go this far in his judgment of the Aḥmadīya question in his work: Abū l-Aᶜlā Maudūdī. *Qādiyānī masᶜala*. [Karachi, 1953]: *Report of the Court of Inquiry Constituted under Punjab Act II OF 1954 to Enquire into the Punjab Disturbances of 1953*. Printed by the Superintendent, Government Printing: Lahore, Punjab, 1954, pp. 218ff.

Aḥmadīya campaign[160] to the point that finally in 1974 the Aḥmadīya were declared to be a subversive, heretical sect and excluded from the community of Muslims. This occurred with Saudi support – one of the important financiers behind *Jamā'at-i-Islāmī* – at the first "Conference of Islamic World Organizations" of the Islamic World League. In the English language journal of the World League, the *Muslim World League Journal*, a campaign against the Aḥmadīya, among others, was triggered, in which Maudūdī was one of the participants.[161]

On September 7, 1974, the Pakistani National Assembly finally declared the movement to be a non-Islamic community by the addition of the Second Amendment Bill to Article 260 of the 1973 Constitution of Pakistan. The Islamic World League,[162] and movements such as many branches of the Muslim Brotherhood and prominent personalities from Muslim majority countries, congratulated the Pakistani President. Nowadays members of the Aḥmadīya movement are among the most frequent victims of lawsuits involving blasphemy as well as attacks outside of court, even including executions in the streets. This is due to the fact that they can be charged at any time with slandering Muḥammad according to the existing legal situation, and for such offense, according to the 1991 amended §295-C of the Pakistani penal code, the death penalty applies. Maudūdī has to at least be considered one of the spiritual fathers of this decision by the Pakistani National Assembly.

It is possible that the motives of Maudūdī's vehement agitation against the Aḥmadīya were less than purely theological in nature and not primarily to be found with their belief in the continuation of the prophetic office after Muḥammad, with Jesus' journey to Kashmir, and in their pacifistic reinterpretation of the teaching of *Jihād*. It is possible that the reason for Maudūdī's decisive actions against them is to be found more in the fact that he saw in them a disturbing factor in the establishment of the purely Islamic community he was urging for. Their existence hindered the genesis of an Islamic state.

Maudūdī himself acted as a messianic figure and understood himself to be a type of savior for the insecure, straying Islamic community, which

160 Jackson. *Mawdudi*, p. 164.

161 Schulze. *Internationalismus*, p. 365.

162 Ibid.

was caught in the *ǧāhilīya* because it no longer knew true Islam.[163] Now that the Islamic community needed Maudūdī as its true leader, the thought of eliminating any competition was not far removed. At least in his later years, Maudūdī saw himself increasingly as a renewer (*mujaddid*) of the umma, who in his own view united numerous outstanding character qualities.

> "Though a mujaddid is not a prophet, yet in spirit he comes very close to prophethood. He is characterized by a clear mind, penetrating vision, unbiased straight thinking, special ability to see the Right Path clear of all extremes ... he ... must be a perfect Muslim in thought and attitude ... (p. 36) He will ... change mental attitudes of the people, and initiate a strong movement which will at once be cultural and political. 'Ignorance' will muster all its forces and strength and come out to crush him, but he will eventually put it to out and estrablish a powerful Islamic State."[164]

4.1.8. Criticism of Maudūdī

Maudūdī declared Aḥmadīya adherents to be heretics on the basis of the claim that their founder, Mīrzā Ġulām Aḥmad, had been sent as a prophet. For his part, he was condemned by a number of Deobandi *ᶜulamā'* as *kāfir* because they were of the opinion that with his claim to be a renewer and a Mahdi-type leader figure he had moved too much into the proximity of being a prophet.[165] Other scholars criticized Maudūdī because he supposedly possessed too little knowledge of the Quran and of tradition[166] and had a

---

163 As a result, 90% of Muslims do not know Maudūdī and follow a blind faith, 5% are Western elites and only 5% know actual Islam and are fit to assume executive: That is the way A. Rashid Moten summarizes Maudūdī's estimation of the number of "true" Muslims in a society: Moten. "Ideology", p. 234; however, Maudūdī is supposed to have in part named even lower percentages; according to Roy Jackson. *Fifty Key Figures in Islam*. Routledge: London, 2006, p. 193.

164 Sayyid Abū l-Aᶜlā Maudūdī. *A Short History of the Revivalist Movement in Islam*. Islamic Publications Limited: Lahore, 1963/1976³, pp. 36+45 and Sayyid Abū l-Aᶜlā Maudūdī. *tajdīd-o iḥyā'i dīn*. [Lahore 1952], pp. 45+54.

165 This is how Laurent Murawiec summarizes in: Laurent Murawiec. *The Mind of Jihad*. Cambridge University Press: New York, 2008, p. 263.

166 Charles J. Adams reports on a meeting with a number of *ᶜulamā'* in Pakistan in 1969, who presented him with several books which condemned Maudūdīs use of texts of tradition. Comp. the list of works in: Charles J. Adams. "The Authority of

thirst for power as a motor behind his activity.[167] More specifically, it was thought he reinterpreted Islam as a political ideology[168] and preached the purpose of the revelation of Islam to be the establishment of a political ideology and not the promotion of piety.[169] In 1952 the *dār al-ᶜulūm* in Deoband initiated a *fatwa* campaign,[170] in which several scholars joined and charged Maudūdī with "unorthodox" Quran and *ḥadīṯ* interpretations, insufficient respect of Muḥammad and his companions, a tendency towards Wahhabism, and even sympathizing with the Aḥmadīya movement![171]

4.2. Abū l-Aᶜlā Maudūdī's Significance

> ". . . Maududi [turned] into the pinnacle and center of the world, the decisive historical figure of the age, which in turn gave him unlimited rights. He 'was' Islam . . . His party was the the party of God."[172]

the Prophetic *Ḥadīth* in the Eyes of some Modern Muslims" in: Donald P. Little (ed.). *Essays on Islamic Civilization, presented to Niyazi Berkes*. E. J. Brill: Leiden, 1976, pp. 25-47, here pp. 35-36.

167 Altaf Gauhar judges as follows: "All he wanted was power for himself and was using Islam as a convenient political platform. This is how the ruling *élite* analysed and understood the role of Mawlānā Mawdūdī." Altaf Gauhar. "Mawlānā Abul Aᶜlā Mawdūdī – A Personal Account" in: Khurshid Ahmad; Zafar Ishaq Ansari (eds.). *Islamic Perspectives. Studies in Honour of Mawlānā Sayyid Abul Aᶜlā Mawdūdī*. The Islamic Foundation: London/Saudi Publishing House: Jeddah, 1979, pp. 265-288, here pp. 268-269.

168 This criticism is reported on byAfsaruddin. "'Theo-Democracy'", pp. 324-325. Maudūdī actually declares "power, suzerainty and control" to be components of Religion *(dīn)*: Sayyid Abū l-Aᶜlā Maudūdī. *The Religion of Truth*. Islamic Publications Limited: Lahore, 1967/1978, p. 2.

169 According to Seyyid Vali Reza Nasr, he is criticized in this manner by the Deobandi scholar Muhammad Manẕūr Nu'mānī in his work *Tablīġī Jamāᶜat, Jamāᶜat-i-Islāmī, aur Barelvī ḥaḍrāt*. al-Furqan Buk Dipo: Lucknow, 1980: Nasr. *Mawdudi and the Making*, p. 59.

170 This is described by Seyyid Vali Reza Nasr, ibid., pp. 117-118.

171 Comp. the summary presentation of Maulānā Waḥīduddīn Khān's criticism against Maudūdī in Aaron Tyler. *Islam, the West, and Tolerance. Conceiving Coexistence*. Palgrave Macmillan: New York, 2008, pp. 225ff. Also comp. the internet presence of the al-Risāla movement http://www.alrisala.org/ (26.11.2011).

172 Murawiec. *Mind*, p. 263.

4.2.1. Maudūdī's Influence as a Theologian

Abū l-Aᶜlā Maudūdī could be counted as one of the most influential theologians of modernity and without a doubt as "one of the most widely read Muslim authors of today."[173] An understanding of his influence is not to be gathered from his publications alone, in which he took positions on a number of topics and with which he stepped into the social as well as political controversies of his time, for example the debate over the Aḥmadīya movement. His influence is also exercised in his function as one of the main activists the 20th century's "Islamic Awakening."[174] F.C.R. Robinson has correctly remarked that as an apologist and an activist, as a politician, and as a party leader, Maudūdī "has influenced in his turn men ranging from the leaders of Islamic movements in Egypt, Syria and Iran to many ordinary Muslims throughout the Islamic World."[175]

His influence also grew through heavyweight financial sponsors and supporters coming from the Arab world. Thus, one of Maudūdī's more frequent travel destinations between 1956 and 1969 was Saudi Arabia, where he participated in an advisory fashion in the planning and the establishment of the Islamic University in Madinah[176] and the establishment of the Islamic World League.[177] In 1979 he was the first recipient of the King Faisal International Prize in Saudi Arabia. There, as "the greatest scholar of the century,"[178] he was given this formal recognition for his efforts with respect to Islam.

---

173 Moten. "Thought", p. 177.

174 He is appraised as such by, for instance, David Cook. *Understanding Jihad*. University of California Press: Berkeley, 2005, p. 99.

175 According to Robinson. "Mawdūdī", p. 873.

176 In his correspondence with Maryam Jameelah, Maudūdī mentions the invitation extended to him by the then Saudi King Saᶜūd Ibn ᶜAbd al-ᶜAzīz Āl Saᶜūd and his visit there in order to consult during the planning process for the Islamic University in Madinah: Maryam Jameelah aur Maulānā Sayyid Abū l-Aᶜlā Maudūdī. *kī murāsalat*. markazī maktaba islāmī publišrz, Neu Dehli, 2010, p. 9.

177 Comp. the list of members of the advisory council of the World League in Schulze. *Internationalismus*, pp. 158+187.

178 As quoted by Mintjes. "Mawdudi's Last Years", p. 57; comp. also the report at: http://www.globalwebpost.com/farooqm/writings/islamic/maududi-faisalprize.htm (10.6.2014).

It is particularly notable that this honor was given in one of the most important centers of Islamic scholarship and that Maudūdī received this honor as a non-Arab and largely self educated individual. After Saudi Arabia took away Egypt's right to annually provide new draping (*kiswa*) for the Ka'ba, this exceedingly prestigious duty was given to Maudūdī personally.[179]

Maudūdī's influence reaches far beyond his lifespan and the borders of Pakistan. That is not only made clear due to the number of Maudūdī's independent works, 138,[180] or the translations of numerous writings into a number of the languages of Asia and Europe.[181] Rather, it is also due to the prominent forums which Maudūdī was offered for his activities within an international framework: For instance, in 1977 he composed a 21-page introduction to the American Trust Publications' second edition of "The Holy Qur'ān, Translation and Commentary" for The Muslims Students' Association.[182] It is perhaps the most widespread translation of the Quran and was conducted by Yusuf Ali.

Jamā'at-i-Islāmī, which was started by Maudūdī, is still active in Pakistani politics, and the missions works founded by it dominate the British Islamist scene,[183] as for instance is the case with the UK Islamic Mission.[184] Additional multiplicators up to the present mentioned by Ron Geaves, which are popular with young Muslims, are those linked to

179 Mintjes. "Mawdudi's Last Years", p. 57.

180 This number is mentioned by Siddiqi; Aslam; Ahsan. "Bibliography".

181 Thus the "Index Translationum" by itself lists 59 translations in an unspecific keyword search using "Maududi" and "Islam"; among them are numerous translations from recent dates in Asiatic languages such as Telugu, Indonesian, Malay, Tamil, Bengali, but also, for instance, Japanese, Dutch, Albanian, and Turkish. http://www.unesco.org/xtrans/ (10.6.2014).

182 According to statements about the edition of this Quran translation not available in Germany in Abul Ala Mawdudi. *The Punishment of the Apostate According to Islamic Law*, translated and annotated by Syed Silas Husain and Ernest Hahn. The Voice of the Martyrs. Mississauga, 1994, Introduction, p. 8.

183 According to David Rich. "The Very Model of a very British Brotherhood" in: Barry Rubin (ed.). *The Muslim Brotherhood. The Organization and Policies of a Global Islamist Movement*. Palgrave Macmillan: New York, 2010, pp. 117-136, here p. 117.

184 Comp. e.g.: http://ukim.org/dawah/islamic-books; http://kitaabun.com/shopping3/index.php?manufacturers_id=54 (10.6.2014).

Jamā'at-i-Islāmī and include the Islamic Foundation, The Muslim Educational Trust, Young Muslims UK, and the Islamic Society of Britain.[185]

With this prominent role as a political activist, apologist, and as an architect of politics and society in Pakistan with respect to the history of ideas, Maudūdī belongs among the most influential leaders with respect to the attitudes of Muslim theologians towards religious freedom, apostasy, and human rights.

4.2.2. Maudūdī's Influence as an Author

Maudūdī was supposedly not only "by the time of his death . . . the most widely read Muslim author of our time" in the eyes of his adherents.[186] This rests upon the composition of innumerable pamphlets, speeches, sermons, radio and parliamentary addresses as well as his numerous independent publications and their enormously wide distribution up to the present day. His first book publication, *risāla'i dīnīyāt*, dating from 1932,[187] was used as a school textbook and experienced enormous distribution and produced Maudūdī's status as a religious scholar (Maulānā), author, and intellectual.[188]

The reception of Maudūdī's thinking on the Indian subcontinent and, more specifically, in what later became Pakistan is illustrated by numerous translations of this work into languages such as Bengali, Hindi, Pashtu, Sindhi, and Tamil. The translation of the same work into Arabic and Persian during Maudūdī's lifetime illustrates his influence in the international Muslim community, while the translation of this document into German, French, Italian, Portuguese, Indonesian, and Japanese – many of them were published prior to his death in 1979 – illustrates the reach of this author.

After Maudūdī had come into contact with Masᶜūd Ālam in the 1940s via Abū l-Ḥasan ᶜAlī al-Nadwī,[189] Masᶜūd Ālam began with the translation

---

185 This organization is mentioned by Geaves. "Comparison", p. 178.

186 Khurshid Ahmad. "Preface" in: Mawdudi. *Human Rights*, p. 5.

187 Maudūdī. *risāla'i dīnīyāt*. Hyderabad, 1932. The English edition: Abū l-Aᶜlā Maudūdī. *Towards Understanding Islam* has been translated into 13 languages.

188 According to Lerman. "Concept", p. 494.

189 According to Hartung. *System*, p. 193f.

of Maudūdī's work into Arabic.[190] Reception of Maudūdī's books was superb in the Arab speaking realm, because "such a fresh, profound perspective found an enthusiastic audience in the educated Arab youth."[191] Thus, Kurshid Ahmad's and Zafar Ishaq Ansari's commemorative publication entitled *Islamic Perspectives* recorded the translation of 27 works by Maudūdī into Arabic. This occurred while Maudūdī's was still alive.[192]

The translation of Maudūdī's works also achieved great influence by their being translated into English. A small number of the works appeared exclusively in English.[193] The English versions – excluding those for foreign countries – were of particular importance for the upper class in Pakistan, which also had a preference for the English language after the partitioning of India:

> "The *élite* insisted on keeping English as the official language. This was the language they knew, and more importantly, the language which the people did not know."[194]

The English versions of Maudūdī's writings had a much broader sphere of impact than the Urdu versions. This was due to the fact that at the time of the partitioning of India, Urdu was absolutely a minority language. According to Jamal Malik, at that time only 2% of the people spoke Urdu as their mother language.[195] However, the importance of Urdu as lingua franca and language of education is nowadays increasing.

---

190 According to Fathi Osman, it is a matter of a "small publishing committee under the name Lajnat al-Shabāb al-Muslim (The Committee of Muslim Youth in Cairo), which has dedicated itself to the translation and distribution of Maudūdīs works in Arabic. In later years translations were also published in Beirut, Damascus, Kuwait, and Jeddah: Osman. "Mawdūdī's Contribution", p. 466.

191 Ibid., p. 468.

192 Siddiqi; Aslam; Ahsan. "Bibliography".

193 The number of titles translated into English or composed in English during his lifetime are numbered at 61 in Maudūdī's commemorative publication: Ibid. Wherever individual works by Mawdūdī appeared exclusively in English, initially in English, or as an English translation during Mawdūdī's lifetime and were authorized by him, I have treated these editions as as well as the Urdu versions as originals.

194 Gauhar. "Mawdūdī", p. 267.

195 Jamal Malik. *Islam in South Asia. A Short History*. E. J. Brill: Leiden, 2008, p. 379.

Maudūdī himself recognized early on that only having publications in Urdu would greatly limit his sphere of influence:

> "If Muslims restrict their literature and public speaking only to Urdu for parochial reasons, they stand to be isolated, and will not able (sic) to influence the larger society."[196]

Other writings by Maudūdī, which were translated into Norwegian, Dutch, Russian, Albanian, Bulgarian, and Hungarian, illustrate that his international influence extended into Europe. Today, this influence, in particular due to more recent translations of his works into Asian languages such as Indonesian, Malay, Assamese, and Turkish, encompasses a constantly growing geographic sweep. This is also being complemented by the printing and distribution of Maudūdī's works in different countries in Africa.[197]

From the middle of the 1950s to the beginning of the 1970s, Maudūdī undertook a number of trips to different countries in Africa and in Europe. He also visited the USA and Arab countries, participated in conferences, held lectures and talks and thereby became known around the world. His writings were received and discussed, whereby his body of thought became spiritual sources for various Islamist-*Jihādist* movements in Arab countries, in Asia, and in Africa. Generally speaking, they were the quarry dug for political Islam.[198] Thus, from 1952 onwards, they served this function for the Sudanese Muslim Brotherhood.[199]

In particular, students in Turkey, Syria, Iraq, Indonesia, Malaysia, Sri Lanka, Bangladesh, Nigeria, South Africa, and Kenya,[200] additionally fostered by the circumstances which included a shortage of literature in English about Islam, were recipients of Maudūdī's body of thought. Maudūdī's greatest influence was exerted among the upper class in Malaysian in the

---

196 Quoted in Omar Khalidi. *Between Muslim Nationalists and Nationalist Muslims: Mawdudi's Thought on Indian Muslims*. Institute of Objective Studies: New Delhi, 2004, p. 76, unfortunately only with the imprecise source citation: "Tarjuman al-Quran, June 1947."

197 See for instance the close to 200 translations at http://portal.unesco.org/culture/en/ev.php-URL_ID=7810&URL_DO=DO_TOPIC&URL_SECTION=201.html (10.6.2014) for Mawdūdī's listed works.

198 According to Cook. *Jihad*, p. 99.

199 Ahmad. "Mawdūdī's Concept", p. 533.

200 These countries are mentioned by Ahmad, ibid.

1970s and 1980s owing to the fact that his writings were obtainable in English in Kuala Lumpur in the 1960s as well as due to the fact that his books were used in the English language education sector there. However, it is also the case that students come into contact with Maudūdīs writing in Europe, particularly in Great Britain, but likewise in the USA.[201]

4.2.3. Maudūdī's Influence in the Islamist Movements of the 20th Century

Undoubtedly, Maudūdī is counted among the most influential theologians and activists of the 20th century and was, for his part, influenced by the forefathers of Islamism, such as the Hanabilite theologian Ibn Taymīya (d. 1328).[202] At the high point of Maudūdī's socio-political activism, roughly from the time of 1950 to 1970, simultaneously a high time for "Islamic awakening," a number of participants from the Islamist and Salafistic spectrum mutually influenced each other, studied the writings of the movements and their leading personalities closest to them, and let their thoughts flow into their own writings, partly in modified form. Althugh there are a number of points of reference for mutual influence, it is hardly possible to precisely determine who influenced whom in which year. In any event, Maudūdī played a key role in the process. David Cook formulates it appropriately: "Mawdudi to a large extent provided the intellectual framework for the Muslim 'revival' of the latter half of the twentieth century."[203]

Maudūdī's Influence on the Muslim Brotherhood

F. C. R. Robinson operates on the idea that Maudūdī adopted the thinking of Ḥassan al-Bannā[204] and was influenced by him, especially since al-

---

201 According to M. Kamal Hassan, Maudūdī's writings are used as textbooks at Malaysian universities up to the present day: M. Kamal Hassan. "The Influence of Mawdūdī's Thought on Muslims in Southeast Asia: A Brief Survey" in: *MW* 93/3-4 (2003), pp. 429-464, here pp. 430-432+435.

202 According to R. Hrair Dekmejian. *Islam in Revolution. Fundamentalism in the Arab World*. Syracuse University Press: Syracuse, 1985, p. 41.

203 Cook. *Jihad*, p. 99.

204 Robinson. "Mawdūdī", p. 874. Also comp. David Bukay. *From Muhammad to Bin Laden. Religious and Ideological Sources of the Homicide Bombers Phe-*

Bannā's drafts on the mandate and organization of the Muslim Brotherhood were rather similar to the foundational thinking of *Jamā'at-i-Islāmī*: For both organizations, the thinking was essential that through a hierarchically configured, ideal primal community practicing the holistic implementation of Islam, a standard would arise for the entire society. However, in the case of the Muslim Brotherhood, the thought of social care, in the beginning, appeared to be more formative. Both groups posed the question of whether a retreat from society or political participation via elections would lead to a greater accumulation of power.

Maudūdī's influence on the guiding spirit of the Muslim Brotherhood,[205] Sayyid Quṭb, is directly traceable through textual references. Sayyid Quṭb was particulary impressed by Maudūdī's thoughts of a vanguard transforming a Muslim majority society into a truly Islamic state.[206] Maudūdī's concept of the rule of God (*ḥākimīyat allāh*) was also assumed.[207] Even if Quṭb is supposed to have "only vaguely referred to Maudūdī" in hearings in 1964/65,"[208] he was, as was circulated by his sister Āmina Quṭb, indeed "a great admirer" of Maudūdī[209] and drew signifi-

nomen. Transaction Publishers: New Brunswick, 2008, p. 212; Martin. *State*, p. 144, assumes mutual influence from al-Bannā and Maudūdī an.

205 Gilles Kepel mentions Mawdūdī as a source of a number of terms found in Quṭb; he calls Quṭb "un lecteur de Mawdudi," "son héritier spiritual": Gilles Kepel. *Le Prophète et Pharaon. Les mouvements islamistes dans l'Egypte contemporaine*. La Découverte: Paris, 1984, pp. 50-51+64.

206 For instance, comp. the remarks on Quṭb's view of this vanguard in Ibrahim, M. Abu-Rabi^c. *Intellectual Origins of Islamic Resurgence in the Modern Arab World*. State University of New York Press: Albany, 1996, pp. 140ff.

207 At least in John Calvert. *Sayyid Qutb and the Origins of Radical Islamism*. Hurst and Company: London, 2010, p. 213. Calvert assumes that Quṭb took this concept from Maudūdī's work *al-muṣṭalaḥāt al-arba^{c}a* (Englisch: *The Four Key Concepts of the Qur'an*), which was already translated into Arabic in 1955.

208 According to Krämer. *Staat*, p. 218.

209 With the words "Sayyid Qutb . . . is a great admirer of you and specially recommended your books to me," the Jewish convert and pupil of Maudūdī, Maryam Jameelah, quotes Āmina Quṭb, who responded to correspondence by Maryam Jameelah directed to the incarcerated Quṭb: Correspondence between Abi-l-A'la Maudoodi and Maryam Jameelah. Presidency of Islamik Researlh, Ifta and Propagation (sic): Riyad, 1982, p. 35; comp. the corresponding reference in the Urdu translation of the original correspondence which was surely conducted in English: Maryam Jameelah aur Maulānā Sayyid Abū l-A^{c}lā Maudūdī, p. 47.

cant thoughts from his writings.[210] Additionally, Quṭb generated additional resonance in the Arabic-speaking realm forwhat was Maudūdī's stylistic and geographically more peripheral body of thought.

Beyond Quṭb, Yūsuf al-Qaraḍāwī also points to Maudūdī's body of thought in his writings, for instance to his model of "God's rule" (*ḥākimīyat allāh*).[211] In his autobiography,[212] al-Qaraḍāwī describes Maudūdī's January 15, 1960 visit to Egypt,[213] describes Maudūdī as an exeedingly learned man (*al-ustāḏ al-kabīr al-ᶜallāma*), and explains in particular the honors which were bestowed upon Maudūdī at al-Azhar. As al-Qaraḍāwī explains, Maudūdī had undertaken a tour in order to visit all the places he had referred to in his Quran commentary without ever having seen.

David Bukay makes Maudūdī responsible for the concept of *Jihād* adopted by Ḥassan al-Bannā and Sayyid Quṭb (according to which *Jihād* is the mandatory conduct of all Muslims) as well as for the Arab resentment of Zionism and the existence of the state of Israel.[214] However, whether in Quṭb's writings such a prominent concept of *ǧāhilīya* is directly traceable back to Maudūdī appears to at least be doubtful. According to Youssef Choueiri, the concepts originate instead in the writings of Muslim Indian authors in the 1930s and 1940s. They were initially oriented against the beliefs of the Hindus, who were judged to be pagan, and later came to be expanded to apply to all non-Islamic religions.[215]

This *ǧāhilīya* concept is supposed to have most significantly come into Quṭb's field of vision[216] through the Indian author Abū l-Ḥasan ᶜAlī al-Nadwī (1914-1999/2000). He was ascribed to the Salafist part of the spec-

---

210 This influence is also assumed by Dekmejian. *Islam*, p. 91.

211 For example, in his work: al-Qaraḍāwī. *ǧarīmat ar-ridda*, e.g., p. 35.

212 al-Qaraḍāwī. *Ibn al-qarya*, Vol. 2, pp. 285-286.

213 This visit is dated and described by Maudūdī's biographer Hasan. Maududi,Vol. 2, pp. 93-98.

214 Bukay. *Muhammad*, p. 212. Aaron Tyler argues likewise with respect to Sayyid Quṭb: "What is more, Maududi's influence is evident in Qutb's practical strategy of *jihad* . . . war is justified against those who refuse such submission, as they are opposing God's will and prohibiting all of humanity from experiencing the justice and tranquility that only come from an Islamic way of life." Tyler. *Islam*, p. 103.

215 Choueiri. *Fundamentalism*, p. 94.

216 al-Nadwī and Quṭb are supposed to have met together for the first time in Cairo in spring of 1951: Schulze. *Internationalismus*, p. 322.

trum.[217] al-Nadwī, a classical scholar and rector of the "ᶜUlama Institute" in Lucknow, "one of the best known Muslim chroniclers of history,"[218] arguably brought Maudūdī into contact with the Muslim Brotherhood in 1951.[219] al-Nadwī had himself also profited from Maudūdī's thinking.[220] At the same time, which was at the beginning of the 1950s, al-Nadwī's also siezed upon Quṭb's thesis of the demise of Muslim society in his own writings.[221]

Not all concepts of *ǧāhilīya* and *Jihād* have been identically interpreted by diverse central characters in their respective contexts. Thus, Maudūdī was far more reserved than Quṭb with his indictment of Islamic society as a pre-Islamic and pagan *ǧāhilīya* community. This was not the case, however, because he had a less radical view of the world, as Youssef M. Chouerie assesses it, but rather out of the desire and the necessity to strengthen the Pakistani *umma* as an independent nation and not to undermine it.[222]

Certainly, the background of differing personal experiences by both Quṭb and Maudūdī are to be included: Quṭb saw the way to transformation from a pagan society into a God-fearing society to be realized through the devotion of the individual to true, holistic Islam. However, Quṭbt did not concede a decisive role to the state in this process (for many years Quṭb was imprisoned and up to the time of his execution was subjected to persecution, torture, and repression by the Egyptian state powers). Maudūdī (who had considerable political influence to bring about change via the *Jamā'at-i-Islāmī)* saw the key to societal transformation to lie in the implementation of Islam via state and legal means.[223]

---

217 According to the assigmnent made ibid., p. 157.

218 Michael Gottlob (ed.). *Historisches Denken im modernen Südasien* (1786 until the present), Vol. 3. Humanities Online: Frankfurt, 2002, p. 385.

219 Hartung, however, leaves the possibility open that at this point Quṭb already knew Maudūdī's works, since at that time a number of his writings had already been translated into Arabic and were accessible in Cairo: Hartung. *System*, p. 194.

220 Johann Calvert even calls Maudūdī al-Nadwī's "mentor": Calvert. *Sayyid Qutb*, p. 158.

221 According to Choueiri. *Fundamentalism*, p. 94-95.

222 Ibid., p. 96.

223 This difference is pointed out by Geert Hendrich. *Islam und Aufklärung. Der Modernediskurs in der arabischen Philosophie*. Wissenschaftliche Buchgesellschaft: Darmstadt, 2004, p. 225.

The thought of *ḥakimīya*, God's rule, is also adopted by Quṭb from Maudūdī, to whom he refers by name[224] in his most famous work *maᶜālim fī 'ṭ-ṭarīq*.[225] Quṭb introduces this legacy into the Muslim Brotherhood movement, which emerged prior to *Jamā'at-i-Islāmī* and ushered in a radical phase of abasement and excommunication of large parts of the Muslim community via Maudūdī's body of thought. Maudūdī's differentiation between nominal and truly believing Muslims is for Seyyed Vali Reza Nasr the soil upon which Quṭb's later radical messge and excommunication thrived, the end product of which was militant *takfīr* groups.[226]

Maudūdī's Influence on Ruḥollāh Khomeinī

Maudūdī's influence goes beyond the realm of the Muslim Brotherhood to include additional movements and individual personalities. According to Roy Jackson, this includes, for instance, the Palestinian *Jihādist* theologian ᶜAbdallāh Yūsuf ᶜAzzām,[227] while David Bukay believes he even recognizes Maudūdī's influence in ᶜAzzām's mentor, Usāma bin Lādin as well as beyond that in "the global Islamic jihad groups."[228]

A number of authors assume a direct influence by Maudūdī on Ruḥollāh Khomeinī – this is due to the fact that in 1963 Khomeinī and

---

[224] In a footnote on p. 47 of his work *maᶜālim fī ṭ-ṭarīq*, no location provided, 1964, Sayyid Quṭb, in connection with his discussion of the rule of God (*ḥākimīyat allāh)* and the *ǧāhilīya* in his work *maᶜālim fī ṭ-ṭarīq*, points to the work of Sayyid Abū l-Aᶜlā Maudūdī. *mabādi' al-islām*. maktabat aš-šabāb al-muslim: [al-Dimašq], 1954¹/1961²/dār al-anṣār: al-Qāhira, [1977]; also in his work hāḏā 'd-dīn, Quṭb quotes extensively from Maudūdī's work *al-ǧihād fī 'l-islām* in discussing the essence of *Jihād*: According to Hartung. *System*, p. 209.

[225] Comp. the analysis of this work by Quṭb as well as a comparison of the central terms in Quṭb und Maudūdī such as *ḥākimīya, ǧāhilīya, Jihād*, or martyrdom in Leonard Binder. *Islamic Liberalism: A Critique of Development Ideologies*. The University of Chicago Press: Chicago, 1988, pp. 170-205.

[226] Seyyid Vali Reza Nasr. "Communalism and Fundamentalism: A Reexamination of the Origins of Islamic Fundamentalism" in: *CO* 4/2 (1995), pp. 121-139, here pp. 128-129.

[227] Jackson. *Mawdudi*, p. 2. David Bukay judges likewise, who views ᶜAzzām as influenced by Quṭb and Maudūdī with respect to his understanding of the necessity of a violent revolution against the secular governments of Islamic states, which persist in *ǧāhilīya*: Bukay. *Muhammad*, pp. 256-257.

[228] Ibid., pp. 214+261.

Maudūdī are supposed to have met[229] in Mecca on a pilgrimage. Others formulate it more generally and believe they are able to recognize an indirect influence by Maudūdī on Khomeinī's "increasing utilitarianism."[230] This is at least recognizable in the influence of the message of "unity and power" in Khomeinī's goal of a Sharia state achieved via revolution.[231]

However, the question arises as to whether what Ervand Abramian supposes applies to Khomeinī ("Khomeini's real entry into politics came in 1962-63"),[232] and if, as Youssef M. Choueri assumes, Khomeinī, when he was sent into exile in 1964 by Shah Reza Pahlavi, actually completed a turn of events in his viewpoint regarding his own role during the "great concealment" of the Twelfth Imam. If with respect to this he had not yet come to final conclusions by that time,[233] then his opinion of the duty to bring about revolution (not laid out in classical quietistic Twelver Shi'ite Islam) could have been foundationally transformed by a contact between Maudūdī and Khomeinī.[234]

Said Amir Arjomand is of the opinion that the "revolutionary slogans and pamphleteering" as well as the application of the term *ṭāġūt* to the Shah's regime by Khomeinī indeed make Maudūdī's und Quṭb's influence clear, not, however, Khomeinī's desire to found an Islamic state. The roots

---

229 According to Saulat. *Maududi*, p. 113 with a reference to the daily Karachi newspaper *Jasarat* dated January 21, 1979; likewise Mintjes. "Mawlana Mawdudi's Last Years", p. 60, without a source citation, perhaps leaning upon Saulat.

230 In regard to Khomeinī's reference to Maudūdī, Daniel Brumberg reflects carefully: "Finally, his [Khomeinī's] increasing utilitarianism may reflect the ideas of Seyyed Abu al-'Ala Maududi." Daniel Brumberg. *Reinventing Khomeini. The Struggle for Reform in Iran*. The University of Chicago Press: Chicago, 2001, p. 61.

231 For instance, Vanessa Martin does not want to be tied down to a single provider of ideas from the Islamist spectrum at the middle of the 20th centuries. She only accepts the influence of Ǧamāl ad-Dīn al-Afġānī's (1838-1897) on Khomeinī as verified: Martin. *State*, pp. 44+103.

232 Ervand Abrahamian. *Khomeinism. Essays on the Islamic Republic*. I. B. Tauris: London, 1993, p. 10.

233 As supposed by Choueiri. *Fundamentalism*, p. 70.

234 In regard to Khomeini's about-turn from what was in principle recognition of the Iranian monarchy to his unconditional advocacy of a revolution and overthrow of the monarchy: "The reasons for his change of opinion are not known." Walter Posch. "Islam und Revolution in Iran oder Schiismus als Politik" in: Walter Feichtinger; Sibylle Wentker (eds.). *Islam, Islamismus und Islamischer Extremismus. Eine Einführung*. Böhlau Verlag: Wien, 2008, pp. 99-121, here p. 104.

of this thinking, Arjomond believes, is to be accounted for in Shi'ite Islam itself.²³⁵ The fact is that in the middle of the 1960s, K͟homeinī again strongly stepped up his criticism of the regime, which now included the direct call to overthrow the monarchy, because "in the late 1960s, K͟homeini began to think seriously about an Islamic government."²³⁶

It is undisputed that K͟homeinī came into contact with representatives and writings of other Islamist movements. Thus, according to Amir Taheri, K͟homeinī became acquainted with the body of thought of the Muslim Brotherhood as early as 1937. This occurred upon his return from a pilgrimage in Najaf, during which he met with Mohammad Nawāb-Ṣafavī. Mohammad Nawāb-Ṣafavī belonged to the Muslim Brotherhood. An activist who propagated military action against the "enemies of Islam," Mohammad Nawāb-Ṣafavī founded Fedayin-e Islam in 1946 and was executed in 1956.²³⁷ By referring to Amir Taheri, others assume that in 1937 Ruḥollāh K͟homeinī even came into contact with the writings of Ḥasan al-Bannā.²³⁸ What appears to be correct is that Seyyed Vali Reza Nasr reports that in 1937 there actually was contact made between K͟homeinī and Maudūdī. However, it was in Mecca where Maudūdī was holding a lecture which is supposed to have impressed K͟homeinī so much that he sought out Maudūdī for a discussion.²³⁹

What is in any case certain is that K͟homeinī had several of Maudūdī's works translated into Persian.²⁴⁰ Likewise, there were a number of Quṭb's works which were translated into Persian in the 1960s and 1970s.²⁴¹ Still

---

²³⁵ Said Amir Arjomand. *The Turban for the Crown. The Islamic Revolution in Iran.* Oxford University Press: New York, 1988, p. 104-105.

²³⁶ Ibid., p. 98.

²³⁷ Unfortunately, Amir Taheri does not give a source citation: Amir Taheri. *The Spirit of Allah.* Hutchinson: London, 1987, p. 97.

²³⁸ Brumberg. *K͟homeini*, p. 61 points to the source of this assertion as Amir Taheri. *The Spirit of Allah.* Hutchinson: London, 1987, pp. 97-98, who does not, however, express this thought there.

²³⁹ Nasr. *Vanguard*, p. 154 with reference to a report in the journal *Awaz-i Jahan*, November 1989, pp. 33-34.

²⁴⁰ Arjomand also assumes this: Arjomand, p. 97.

²⁴¹ See the list of five works released by Quṭb between 1955 and 1970 and six works by Maudūdī published between 1964 and 1971 – which in part were even furnished with a foreword by ᶜAlī Ḥāmene'ī – which according to information from the National Library of Iran in Teheran have been translated into Persian: Martin.

prior to 1979, at the time of the Parisian exile, Maudūdī is said to have directed a letter to Khomeinī in which he offered his support in the Iranian Revolution. Upon the visit of an eight-man delegation, which was the first to be received by the Iranian regime after the outbreak of the Revolution in 1979, the then *amīr* of the *Jamā'at-i-Islāmī*, Miyān Ṭufayl Muḥammad, presented a written statement from Maudūdī.[242] Upon the occasion of this delegation's visit, the then Prime Minister Mehdī Bāzargān is supposed to have emphasized that four Muslim thinkers had had a significant part in the success of the Iranian Revolution. He named Maudūdī among them. After Maudūdī's death, Khomeini's deputy, Ayatollah Noorī, who called Maudūdī "the sword and the spokesman of Islam," also emphasized Maudūdī's deep influence on the Iranian people.[243]

Maudūdī's Influence on Individual Islamist and Central Jihādist Characters

Beyond what has been mentioned, Maudūdī exercised some influence on numerous individuals: For instance, Fathi Osman mentions the positive appreciation of Maudūdī by Rāšid al-Ġannūšī,[244] who at the end of the 1960s took up Maudūdī's thought (as well as al-Bannā's and Quṭb's) and disseminated it in Tunesia.[245] Roy Jackson names Ahmad Shah Massoud (1953-2001), one of the key military figures of the Mujahiddin in the battle against the Soviet occupation of Afghanistan, as a student of Maudūdī. Beginning in 1992, Shah Massoud was the Defense Minister under

State, pp. 144-145 (Fn 87,88). Baqer Moin adds to this that ᶜAlī Ḫāmene'ī even translated at least one of Quṭb's works into Persian without, however, naming the title: Baqer Moin. *Khomeini. Life of the Ayatollah*. I. B. Tauris: London, 1999, p. 246.

242 Mintjes. "Mawlana Mawdudi's Last Years", p. 60 with reference to press reports by the *Pakistan Times* dated January 20 and 21, 1979.

243 Ibid., pp. 60-61 with reference to reference to press reports by the *Pakistan Times* dated February 27, 1979 and October 3 and 9, 1979.

244 Fathi Osman describes, inter alia, Maudūdī's intensive influence on Sayyid Quṭb; however, he errs when he assumes that Sayyid Quṭb never directly refers to Maudūdī: Osman. "Mawdūdī's Contribution", p. 479-480.

245 According to Martin Kramer. "Fundamentalist Islam at Large: The Drive for Power" in: *MEQ*, June 1996, pp. 37-49.

Burhanuddin Rabbani.[246] During his studies in Kabul, he came into contact with *Jamā'at-i-Islāmī*'s student organization and, according to Roy Jackson, counts as "a genuine disciple of Mawdudi."[247]

An additional student of Maudūdī named by Roy Jackson is Gulbuddin Hekmatyar (b. 1947), who in the 1990s was twice Prime Minister of Afghanistan as well as the founder of the Ḥizb-i Islāmī Party, a Mujahiddin group which was strongly supported from abroad in the Afghanistan War. As Roy Jackson argues, Hekmatyar reverted to Maudūdī-like terminology in his call for a vanguard of Islamic intellectuals in the fight against the communist regime, especially, according to Jackson, in that the existence of the *Jamā'at-i-Islāmī* and Maudūdī's ideology were a stimulus and a role model for the Afghan fighters.[248]

The undisputed fact is that numerous Islamist movments and individual personalities in the second half of the 20th century found their ideological and political breeding ground in Maudūdī's und Sayyid Quṭb's writings, whose thoughts were taken up and in part modified and integrated into the regionally various circumstances. Even if the occupation with Maudūdī's individual thoughts turn out to be quite critical in the case of many takers,[249] the circumstance shows that the world of Arab-speaking intellectuals and scholars – among them scholars such as ᶜUmar ᶜAbd al-Raḥmān – generally grappled with the self-educated Maudūdī. Youssuf Choueiri thus judges as follows regarding these movements:

> "The ideology of these groups, be they in Malaysia, Indonesia, Afghanistan or Nigeria, is invariably a local offshoot of Sayyid Qutb's theoretical analysis, or a mixture of Mawdudian and Qutbist formulas",[250]

while Seyyed Vali Reza Nasr makes Maudūdī out to be the essentual influential factor in the realm of Islamism:

---

246 Rabbani was one of the leaders of the Afghan resistance against the Taliban and during the time of Taliban rule was commander of the "United Islamic Front for the Salvation of Pakistan."

247 Jackson. *Mawdudi*, p. 172.

248 Ibid., p. 173.

249 Hartung above all demonstrates this critical dispute with respect to the application of the terms *ḥakimīya* and *ǧāhilīya* for Ḥasan al-Huḍaybī: Hartung. *System*, p. 222+257f.

250 Choueiri. *Fundamentalism*, p. 78.

"Still Mawdudi's contribution is singularly significant. For, it was he who constructed the scaffolding of the fundamentalist ideology, set the parameters of its discourse, clarified its agenda and gave its ideas their distinct flavor . . . Over the years, Islamic fundamentalism has developed along many trajectories; still, as an ideological corpus, it is in large measure the product of Muawdudi's works . . . many of the defining features of Islamic fundamentalism can be better understood in the context in which Mawdudi first shared them . . ."[251]

Maudūdī's Influence on the National Self-understanding of Pakistan

Due to Maudūdī's "major influence on the politics of Pakistan,"[252] he can be seen as one of the most important sources of ideas and shapers of modern Pakistan. He belongs to the circle of scholars which various Pakistani governments summoned in order to receive consultation in political and religious questions. Beginning in 1948, Maudūdī played a key role in the coloring of Pakistan as an Islamic state in that he exercised enormous pressure on the formulation of the "Objectives Resolution," the foundation of the first Constitution of Pakistan in 1956.

Additionally, as a prominent speaker and leader of the *ᶜulamāʿ*, Maudūdī was able to achieve a situation whereby in January 1951 their representatives were able to agree upon 22 principles of an Islamic state and which were to be demonstrated to be influential for the formulation of the first Constitution of Pakistan in 1956 and beyond. Even before that, with the dispute with the Aḥmadīya movement beginning in 1952, in which Maudūdī had played the major role, these 22 principles had been applied. It was thanks to Maudūdī's lobbying work and influence that this first constitution in 1956 designated the state to be the "Islamic Republic of Pakistan" and was formulated as follows in the preamble:

"The Muslims of Pakistan should be enabled individually and collectively to order their lives in accordance with the teachings and requirements of Islam, as set out in the Holy Quran and Sunnah."

And in Article 25 one reads the following:

---

251 Nasr. "Communalism", p. 123.

252 Robinson. "Mawdūdī", p. 872.

> "(1) Steps shall be taken to enable the Muslims of Pakistan individually and collectively to order their lives in accordance with the Holy Quran and Sunnah. (2) The State shall endeavour, as respects the Muslims of Pakistan, . . . (b) to make the teaching of the Holy Quran compulsory; (c) to promote unity and the observance of Islamic moral standards."[253]

Maudūdī and the die *Jamā'at-i-Islāmī* hailed the first Constitution of Pakistan with a countrywide campaign after its enactment: Maudūdī appeared in Peshawar, Rawalpindi, and Daska[254] and continued to remain present on the political stage after his success. After the adoption of the constitution, he turned his efforts to implementing its principles socially and politically.

> "Mawdudi was also among the most influential of those reminding successive Pakistani governments of what the constitutions – in part under his own influence – had laid down regarding the public implementation of Islamic norms."[255]

For a period of decades, he remained the guiding spirit of political Islam in Pakistan. He was someone who always had a say in political events and continually made his influence felt in the direction of a strengthened Islamization of Pakistani society and politics.

From the time of the emergence of Pakistan and up to 1977, the day on which Zia ul-Haqq came to power and Maudūdī finally was able to hope for the implementation of large-scale Islamization, the *Jamā'at-i-Islāmī* and Maudūdī had conducted their lobbying efforts for the benefit of this goal and . . . "continued to exert pressure on the federal government for inclusion of Islamic contents in the constitution."[256] However, Maudūdī not only exercised influence upon Zia ul-Haqq. Earlier heads of state were also not able to ignore him. Rather, they saw the necessity of involving Maudūdī in their politics. Thus, for example, he was received by President Ayub Khan in his residence in Rawalpindi in September 1965 with several other individuals, and Maudūdī was asked to include the Kashmir conflict

---

[253] Comp. the complete text of the 1956 Constitution of Pakistan at http://therepublicofrumi.com/archives/56_00.htm (10.6.2014).

[254] Ali. *Thought*, p. 239.

[255] Euben; Qasim Zaman (eds.). *Readings*, p. 83.

[256] As summarized by Surendra Nath Kaushik. *Politics of Islamization in Pakistan. A Study of Zia Regime. South Asian Publishers*: New Dehli, 1993, p. 11.

in his prayers and to publicly declare the war against India to be *Jihād*.[257] And in an additional meeting between the two, a weekly radio address was offered as well as Maudūdī's being offered to be brought into the ranks as an official advisor to Ayub Khan's administration.[258]

When General Zia ul-Haqq came to power by ousting Zulfiqar Ali Bhutto in 1977 in a military putsch, this was the first regime which was prepared to give Maudūdī a full measure of support. While Maudūdī had advocated Zia ul-Haqq's request to execute Zulfiqar Ali Bhutto, on whose overthrow Maudūdī had cooperated,[259] Zia ul-Haqq named Maudūdī as the "Senior Statesman" and advisor, whose statements now dominated the headlines of the daily newspapers. Zia ul-Haqq set a comprehensive program of Islamization into motion, disseminated writings via the official channels of government, and used Maudūdī's popularity and influence for his own retention of power. He thus had Maudūdī's work *Understanding the Qur'an* distributed among members of the army as the winnings for a competition and suggested using the contents of the book in the testing of army officers.[260]

Zia ul-Haqq pursued the Islamization of Pakistan by including various personalities from the Islamist spectrum: On February 10, 1979, he pronounced the introduction of the "Islamic system" (*niẓām-i Islām*) in Pakistan. What followed was the adoption of the Hudood Ordinance and Islamic courts of justice in 1979 and the abolishment of non-Islamic civil legislation.

In the penal code, property crimes, sexual offences, slander in connection with sexual offences and consumption of alcohol were able to be repaid with corporal punishment from that time onward. Apostasy was not covered in this catalog of criminal law, which offered the occasion for discussion and criticism.[261] Sharia benches were established in High Courts, and a Sharia chamber of appeals was established within the Supreme Court in order to check for conformity with the Sharia. The result was numerous whippings (which were boycotted by physicians) and the ordering of am-

---

257 According to Nasr. *Mawdudi and the Making*, p. 45.

258 As described by Gauhar. "Mawdūdī", p. 269-270.

259 Nasr. "Mawdudi and the Jama'at-i Islami", p. 118.

260 Jackson. *Mawdudi*, p. 167.

261 According to Muhammad Munir. *From Jinnah to Zia*. Vanguard Books Ltd.: Lahore, 1980[2], pp. 124-125; 133-134.

putations.[262] Furthermore, commercial law was also Islamized.[263] Zia ul-Haqq, ideologically and financially supported by Saudi Arabia,[264] officially declared the Sharia to be the foundation of all legislation, as well as the foundation of the educational system, culture, the administration of justice, and religion.

Maudūdī's influence in the background to the passage of Hudood laws becomes clear in that congratulations not only reached Zia ul-Haqq but Maudūdī as well after their adoption, "because the whole world knows that he is the pioneer of Islamic movement in Pakistan"[265] (sic). In the face of Maudūdī's long-held expectations of this government, which now appeared to be coming true, Harry Mintjes has written: "Mawdūdī leek op zijn oude dag Pakistans ongekroonde koning te zijn geworden."[266] In November 1978, Maudūdī, who in the meantime had become seriously ill, drafted a ten point plan for the comprehensive implementation of Islam in the state and society.[267]

The Islamization of Pakistan, which for decades had been propagated and advanced by Maudūdī and the *Jamā'at-i-Islāmī* by the time Zia ul-Haqq came to power, received enormous thrust through the combination of ideology and political power. According to Muhammad Khalid Masud, this was reflected in the educational sector and the press and in the founding of thousands of *madāris*, of which a number of them supported the *Jihād* in Afghanistan in the 1980s as well as in an increasing militancy

262 According to remarks with respect to the set punishments in John L. Esposito and John O. Voll. *Islam and Democracy*. Oxford University Press: Oxford, 1996, p. 111.

263 Comp. Jamal Malik. *Die Islamisierung der Wirtschaft in Pakistan unter Zia ul Haqq*. Deutsche Stiftung für internationale Entwicklung: Bad Honnef, 1998.

264 Thus Zia ul-Haqq invited so-called charitable organizations from Saudi Arabia and the Gulf States to open mosques and *madāris* in Pakistan: Haqqani. *Pakistan*, p. 190.

265 Saulat. *Maududi*, p. 112.

266 Harry Mintjes. "Pakistan: Mawdūdī, de Jamā'at-i-Islāmī en Zia ul-Haqq's Programma van Islamisiering" in: K Wagtendonk; P. Aarts (eds.) *Islamitisch Fundamentalisme*: Dick Coutinho: Muiderberg, 1986, pp. 26-40, here p. 28.

267 This plan reached from a reform of education to the implementation of effective measures to promote morality (e.g., by establishing a number of educational institutions for girls and censoring of the press all the way to a economic program for the just distribution of goods: Comp. Saulat. *Maududi*, pp. 110-111.

among youth. *Jamā'at-i-Islāmī*, as Muhammad Khalid Masud judges it, "was the main supporter of Zia's regime . . . a primary influence of this shari'a politics, which no liberal organization was able to challenge in the public domain."[268] Thus it was that under Zia ul-Haqq an additional and weighty development took its course.

The Adoption of Blasphemy Laws

It is not only Islamization of society which advanced under Zia ul-Haqq. Rather, legislation also advanced. Under his regime, the Indian Penal Code of 1860, which had been adopted as the Pakistan Penal Code[269] at the time of the founding of Pakistan, was decisively strengthened by a number of addendums and amendments and reshaped into an instrument of power against minorities such as the Aḥmadīya, Christians, converts, and progressive Muslim intellectuals.

The Indian Penal Code was originally and essentially traceable back to Lord Macaulay – his common name being Thomas Babington Macaulay. He was the main person responsible[270] for the formulation of §295 to §298, which had been drafted to effectively protect the adherents of various religions within India from mutual deliberate defamation and to protect the society from disputes arising out of conflicts owing to the religious diversity of India. Thus, §295 of the Indian Penal Code, for instance, prohibits defiling places of worship of other religions as a way of offending the re-

---

268 Muhammad Khalid Masud. "Communicative Action and the Social Construction of Shari'a in Pakistan" in: Armando Salvatore; Mark LeVine (eds.). *Religion, Social Practice, and Contested Hegemonies. Reconstructing the Public Sphere in Muslim Majority Societies*. Palgrave Macmillan: New York, 2005 pp. 155-179, here p. 173.

269 The text of the Indian Penal Code with all amendments dating from 1860 up to the present can be found at: http://www.netlawman.co.in/acts/indian-penal-code-1860.php (10.6.2014); the text of the Pakistan Penal Code with all with all amendments up to the present can be found at http://www.pakistani.org/pakistan/legislation/1860/actXLVof1860.html (10.6.2014). All paragraphs in the following text refer to both of these editions.

270 According to Tarik Jan et al. *Pakistan between Secularism and Islam. Ideology, Issues and Conflict*. Institute of Policy Studies: Islamabad, 1998, pp. 200-201; also comp. Theodor Gabriel. *Christian Citizens in an Islamic State. The Pakistan Experience*. Ashgate Publishing Limited: Aldershot, 2007, p. 59.

spective religions. §298 prohibits offending religious feelings "with deliberate intent." In 1927, §295-A was amended, which in a certain sense represented a doubling of §298 and prohibited each and any degrading word and gesture directed against other religions and faith convictions under threat of imprisonment.

The standing formulations, as they were already in place, strengthened the "Blasphemy Laws". Indeed, they were first added following Maudūdī's death in the years 1980, 1982, 1984, and 1986 as three Amendments and an additional law to the Pakistan Penal Code. They were consequences of the course of Islamization under Zia ul-Haqq and had the breath of Maudūdī's intolerant attitude toward minorities, in particular towards Aḥmadīya adherents.

§298-A was adopted in 1980. It made degrading remarks about the caliphs, the women, the family, and Muḥammad's companions punishable. In 1982, §295-B was added to the penal code, which threatened dirtying, destroying, or desecrating the Quran punishable with lifelong imprisonment. §295-C followed in 1986, which threatened the disparagement of Muḥammad with the death penalty or lifelong imprisonment in addition to a financial penalty. On July 29, 1991, the Federal Sharia Court (FSC) exhorted the government to exclusively impose the death penalty for this latter offense.[271] In 1992, the Parliament of Pakistan resolved to correspondingly change§295-C.[272]

In 1984, owing to massive pressure from Tehrik-i-Khatm-i-Nabuwwat (The Finality of Prophethood), a separate law, the Anti-lslamic Activities of Quadiani Group, Lahori Group and Ahmadis (Prohibition and Punishment) Ordinance, XX, was passed against the Aḥmadīya movement. It supplemented the Pakistan Penal Code's §298-B and §298-C.

§ 298-B (1) prohibits adherents of the Aḥmadīya movemenrt from speaking about the "companions of the Prophet", Muḥammad's "wives", his family, and the "Caliphs", and from referring to the places of prayer as

---

271 Asad Ali Ahmed lists the groups which were the force behind the most recent intensification of the "Blasphemy Laws": Asad Ali Ahmed. "Specters of Macaulay. Blasphemy, the Indian Penal Code, and Pakistan's Postcolonial Predicament" in: Raminder Kaur; William Mazzarella (eds.). *Censorship in South Asia. Cultural Regulations from Sedition to Seduction*. Indiana University Press: Bloomington, 2009, pp. 172-205, here p. 174.

272 See Gabriel. *Citizens*, p. 60.

"Masjid". § 298-B (2) prohibits them from sounding a call to prayer or anything which is reminiscent of a call to prayer. §298-C prohibits Aḥmadīya adherents from labeling themselves as "Muslims" and from calling their religion "Islam", from soliciting people for their faith, or from doing anything which would hurt the feelings of Muslims. Infringements against §298-B and C are punishable with three years of imprisonment and a fine.[273]

While there were only few charges brought against individuals under the earlier provisions of the Indian Penal Code and after the founding of Pakistan, respectively, and from 1927 to 1986 only seven charges of blasphemy were supposedly registered as having been taken to court, this number rose drastically after the corresponding paragraphs were expanded up to 1986 under Zia ul-Haqq. From 1986 to 2007, there was said to be over 4,000 charges registered on account of blasphemy.[274]

Up to now, in spite of repeated sentencing by lower courts, a death sentence has never been administered. Higher courts, above all the Supreme Court, have up to now regularly acquitted defendants on account of an uncertain body of evidence or procedural errors that have occurred in the cases. Admittedly, this does not mean that such a case has remained without consequences. A number of the defendants were executed while in custody or in broad daylight.[275] Whoever incurs the charge of blasphemy loses his civic existence, his family and his possessions, and he has to go underground or even leave the country.

Repercussions of the "Blasphemy Laws"

The "sowing of the word" – of Maudūdī's words, among others – works itself out in the application of the "Blasphemy Laws." Under the pretext of prophetic slander or Quranic desecration, rumors are put into circulation, recriminations made, and charges brought on account of blasphemy against those who think differently, adherents of minorities, converts and socially

---

273 Comp. remarks in Martin Lau. *The Role of Islam in the Legal System of Pakistan*. Martinus Nijhoff Publishers: Leiden, 2006, pp. 114-115.

274 At any rate, these numbers are mentioned by Gabriel. *Citizens*, p. 66.

275 Comp. the description of a number of cases Marshall; Shea. Apostasy, pp. 83ff.

disadvantaged in the fight for power, influence, and belongings.[276] As a general rule, this usually brings great harm to those affected.

This not only entails a frequent multi-year prison sentence – with the real danger that over the course of which, owing to the charge of blasphemy, life may be lost due to attacks by the police, fellow inmates, or guards[277] – and a costly if not seldom set of multi-year proceedings, mostly involving a multitude of authorities. In a number of cases, it can also mean the death of the accused through vigilante justice prior to or in spite of the dismissal of the individual.[278] Release in return for payment of a bond is basically not offered in cases where the charge is blasphemy, and the testimony of Muslims against Christians cannot be legally invalidated. Frequently, when it comes to the killing of an accused, there are no targeted investigation efforts made in order to determine the culprit. Many cases run aground, in particular when with respect to the victims it is not a matter of influential members of the society.

Around 25 years after their having been strengthened, the criticism of these very easily instrumentalized "Blasphemy Laws" or, more specifically, the few attempts made to lighten the laws are, for all intents and purposes, taken to be as extensive an offense as blasphemy itself. When in April 2000 President Pervez Musharraf announced a revision of the "Blasphemy Laws" owing to the potential that they could be abused, there were bitter protests by Islamist groups. By the middle of May 2000, he had to retreat from the proposal he put forward.[279]

In recent history, the attempt to weaken the "Blasphemy Laws" has claimed two additional prominent victims. The prior Governor of Punjab and close friend of President Asif Ali Zardari, Salman Taseer, was shot by his bodyguard, Malik Mumtaz Hussein Qadri, at a market in Islamabad;

---

276 In 2010 alone, Amnesty International knew of 98 court cases on account of blasphemy, of which 67 cases were directed against members of the Aḥmadīya community: *Amnesty International Report 2011. Zur weltweiten Lage der Menschenrechte*. S. Fischer: Frankfurt, 2011, p. 364.

277 Comp. the description of a number of cases in Gabriel, pp. 61ff.

278 For instance, on July 19, 2010 Pastor Rashid Emanuel and his brother Sajid Emanuel were shot and killed in Faisalabad in front of the court building after being indicted for blasphemy: *Amnesty International Report 2011. Zur weltweiten Lage der Menschenrechte*. S. Fischer: Frankfurt, 2011, p. 364.

279 Owen Bennett-Jones. "Pakistan's Blasphemy Law U-Turn," BBC News, 17.5.2000. http://news.bbc.co.uk/2/hi/south_asia/751803.stm (10.6.2014).

the remaining members of Taseer's security unit did not intervene. The background to the incident was that Governor Taseer had visited Asia Bibi in prison, a Christian who had been sentenced to death by hanging on account of blasphemy. Governor Taseer had agreed to offer her his support.[280] When Qadri was brought before a court, he was sentenced to death on October 1, 2011. Lawyers had rose leaves showered upon him as a sign of their reverence.[281] Hundreds of demonstrators excitedly celebrated him, many people kissed him and shouted out calls which praised his action. Prior thereto, over 500 mullahs and scholars of the *Jamāʿat Ahl-e Sunna* had praised the action of the assassin with grand remarks and publicly an-

280 Asia Bibi had been condemned on November 8, 2010 by a court in the Province of Punjab on account of allegedly insulting Muḥammad. A year earlier, as a day laborer on an estate, she had fetched water for female Muslim workers. Before accepting the water, they asked her to convert to Islam because the water was otherwise "impure," to which Asia Bibi is supposed to have answered with her confession that Jesus Christ is the true prophet – Asia Bibi later disputed, however, that she had ever said those words. A number of days later demagogic slogans were propagated against her over loudspeakers from the mosque. Inhabitants of the village thereupon sought to take her by force. This was prevented by the police by their arresting her, stating that this was done for her protection. Under pressure by Islamic academics, a charge was brought against Asia Bibi on account of blasphemy, and she did not receive defense counsel. On November 8, 2010, in the court of first instance, she was sentenced to pay two and one-half years' salary and condemned to death by hanging. While human rights organizations have advocated her release, the influential Ittehad Council warned President Asif Zardari not to pardon her. There were alternating protest campaigns and demonstrations. Asia Bibi's husband Ashiq Mashi and her children have now gone underground and frequently change their housing. Asia Bibi is still in custody; the case, however, is still pending before the court, and the death penalty has not been lifted, but has been confirmed recently. Comp., for example, the reports: Pakistan: Asia Bibi darf nicht sterben. Pakistanischer Konsul nimmt 2000 Unterschriften entgegen, 7.1.2014. http://www.igfm.de/ne/?tx_ttnews%5Btt_news%5D=2823~cHash=d6b5333d51929392aa4b4be7d57fcbf6 (10.6.2014) und Hasnain Kazim. Gotteslästerung in Pakistan. Christin soll am Galgen sterben, 11.11.2010. http://www.spiegel.de/pano rama/gesellschaft/0,1518,728521,00.html (10.6.2014).

281 In 2000 one of the judges of the Lahore High Court, Nazir Akhtar, publicly announced that every Muslim has the religious duty to execute an apostate and need not wait for court proceedings: Marshall; Shea. *Apostasy*, p. 88.

nounced that no one was allowed to regret Taseer's death and participate in his burial.[282]

In Rawalpindi there were numerous larger-than-life posters hung out in public with the picture of the assassin and banners with sayings such as "Mumtaz Qadri, we praise your courage" and "Long live the soldier of the Prophet" upon them. While this occurred, Qadri's older brother received multitudes of visitors on a daily basis who brought their best wishes."[283] One lawyer offered to defend Mumtaz Qadri on a pro bono basis, a prior Chief Justice of the Lahore High Court publicly placed himself in support of the culprit, and everywhere in the country there were violent protests calling for the death penalty to be reversed.[284] The judge who had sentenced the culprit to death had to take refuge in Saudi Arabia; in 2011 a mosque had been erected in honour of Mumtaz Qadri in Islamabad.[285]

The second prominent victim who announced that he wanted to see the "Blasphemy Laws" softened was Shabaz Bhatti, the Minister for Religious Minorities and a member of the ruling Pakistan Peoples Party (PPP). After the announcement of his desire to see the "Blasphemy Laws" revised, he was pulled out of his car by three assassins on the way to his ministry offices in Islamabad on March 2, 2011 and executed in public. According to

---

282 According to the report: Pakistani Lawyers Salute Taseer's Killer. http://arabnews.com/world/article229955.ece (10.6.2014); also comp. the report: "500 Islamic Clerics and Religious Scholars in Pakistan Issue Statement Justifying the Assassination of Governor Salman Taseer: 'Prophet [Muhammad] had Ordered the Killing of An Apostate for Committing Blasphemy Right Inside Masjid Al-Haram [Mecca Mosque]'". *MEMRI Special Dispatch* No 3491, 5.1.2011. http://www.memri.org/report/en/0/0/0/0/0/0/4896.htm (10.6.2014).

283 Andreas Spalinger. "Von der Vision des Staatsgründers Jinnah weit entfernt. Der unter dem Militärdiktator Zia ul-Haqq gross gewordenen jungen Generation in Pakistan ist religiöse Toleranz fremd." *NZZ Online*, 3.3.2011. http://www.nzz.ch/nachrichten/politik/international/von_der_vision_des_staatsgruenders_jinnah_weit_entfernt_1.9749775.html (10.6.2014).

284 According to the report by Aftab Afribi. "Release of Mumtaz Qadri." Pak Tea House, 19.10.2011 http://pakteahouse.net/2011/10/19/release-of-mumtaz-qadri/ (10.6.2014). The Website established for Mumtaz Qadri at http://mumtazqadri.net/ (27.11.2011) enjoys active professions of sympathy.

285 Comp. the report of Silke Mertins. Wo Attentäter zu Helden werden. In Islamabad wird eine Moschee für Mumtaz Qadri gebaut, der einen Gouverneur erschoss. Szenen aus einem Hochrisikostaat. In: Financial Times Deutschland, 5.12.2011, p. 13.

statements, he was the sole minister who did not have an armoured vehicle. The terrorist group Tehrik-i Taliban Pakistan (TTP) claimed responsibility for the deed. Thereafter, the Ministry for Religious Minorities was abolished by the government. The ruling Pakistan Peoples Party (PPP) only hesitantly condemned the acts. After fierce street protests, the Pakistan People's Party, which in the meantime was in the Parliament of Pakistan, withdrew their proposal for revising the "Blasphemy Laws". The court proceedings did not end up in a lawsuit sentencing the four suspects – all of them members of the extremist group Tehrik-i Taliban – who had been temporarily imprisoned before. The brother of the victim, Paul Bhatti who had strongly advocated the continuation of the lawsuit had to leave Pakistan temporarily due to several death threats against life and limb.[286]

As becomes clear from the last two cases of extra-legal executions of high-ranking politicians (Shabbaz Bhatti even belonged to the ruling party), the "Blasphemy Laws", at least as far as a number of groups understood them, were taken to be a carte blanche to condemn and kill undesirable individuals independent of their social status. Also, what is more calamitous is that it meets with a social climate which is a mixture of fear, indifference, and agreement that appears to have little to set against such an outgrowth. In addition to many a faulty political and economic development, the role of the religious ideology of political Islam in this radicalization process, along with its promoters and providers of ideas, cannot be overlooked.

4.3. Abū l-A'lā Maudūdīs Position on Apostasy from Islam

As in the case of both of the prior protagonists, in the choice and treatment of Maudūdī's publications I am limiting myself to those titles which stand in direct connection with the topics of apostasy, religious freedom, human rights, and civil liberties.

4.3.1. Maudūdī as an Architect of a Homogeneous Society

Maudūdī's position on apostasy from Islam is of far-reaching significance for the self-understanding of Pakistan due to Maudūdī's active involve-

[286] Comp. the following report: http://www.thenews.com.pk/Todays-News-6-231409-Shahbaz-Bhatti-murder-case-suffers-setback, 9.2.2014 (10.6.2014).

ment in the orientation and drafting of the first constitution, his involvement in the politics of Pakistan, and the influence arising from such involvement. At the time of the end of British colonial rule in India, the final demise of Moghul rule manifested itself, the caliphat movement finally failed, and many Muslims faced the concern of an unequal weighting of power in Hindu-Muslim coexistence after independence was achieved. Maudūdī was thus in the situation of filling this vacuum, which demonstrated a search for orientation and self-assurance with a hopeful vision of the future for a political Islam.

With utopian idealistic outlines for an Islamically drafted state, which Maudūdī derived from his vision for a comprehensive, socio-political Islam, he not only profoundly influenced the spiritual and political history of Pakistan in the second half of the 20th century. Up to the present day, he has also influenced well-known Islamist movements and individual personalities from Arab, Iranian, and Asian cultural circles as well as the global *umma* with over 130 books, writings, expert opinions, *fatāwā*, and articles in numerous languages.

An analysis of Maudūdī's point of view with respect to his judgment of apostasy from Islam is for that reason not only an item of historical interest: Above all, his views have taken on such a form through Maudūdī's agitation against the Aḥmadīya movement and their stigmatization as apostates from Islam as well as in the strengthening and new formulation of the "Blasphemy Laws" in the 1980s under Maudūdī's protégé, Zia ul-Haqq, that he lives on up to the present day through his writings, through the movement and political party founded by him, *Jamāᶜat-i-Islāmī*, as well as through his influence on Islamist doyens and movements.

On the whole, Maudūdī did not express himself very frequently on the topic of apostasy from Islam.[287] When he took up this question, he answered it in an unmistakeable manner. Already at the time prior to the partitioning of India, i.e., at a time when the founding of an Islamic state was

[287] What applies for the topic of apostasy is supposedly what Seyyed Vali Reza Nasr has noticed with regard to Maudūdī's relatively seldom dealing with the role and rights of minorities in an Islamic state, namely that Maudūdī was of the opinion that in a state with an Islamic constitution this question would resolve itself; against the background of Maudūdī's politicized understanding of Islam with respect to minorities and their legal disadvantage this would mean their execution for apostasy. Nasr. *Vanguard*, p. 131.

in no way foreseeable and the Muslim minority in India, in light of a strengthening Hindu imprint on Indian politics, appeared to be standing on the losing side of power, he spoke out with a fundamental treatment of apostasy.

As early as in the first document on the topic, which he composed at the beginning of the 1940s, he pointed to the idea that turning away from the Islamic community was political disloyalty and high treason. He did not give up this attitude over the course of his life, nor did he weaken it. Also in a number of his other works he would now and then come around to speaking on the topic of apostasy from Islam. In every individual case, he decidedly placed himself in opposition to the idea that after accepting Islam a Muslim believer was allowed to turn his back upon the faith.

4.3.2. Abū l-Aᶜlā Maudūdī's Main Work on Apostasy: The Punishment of Apostates according to Islamic Law ("murtadd ki sazā islāmī qānūn mēṉ") - 1942/1943

Abū l-Aᶜlā Maudūdī's main work on the topic of apostasy appeared for the first time in Urdu in the journal he published over the course of many years, *Tarjumān al-Qur'ān*. The text was, as the author explained in his foreword,[288] published there as a two-part answer to a question in October 1942 and June 1943.

Occasion and Significance of this Written Work

In this piece of writing, Maudūdī speaks with a great degree of implicitness as if an Islamic state in which religion, society, and legislation are oriented towards a comprehensive form of Islam and build a unity. Indeed, he refines his idea of the implementation of this model by using only a few examples – when for instance he calls for the forced practice of the Islamic doctrines of duty in such a state.[289] Mostly, however, he remains general and only postulates instead of explaining. This also applies to his treatment of the topic of apostasy.

---

288 Maudūdī. *murtadd*, p. 3.

289 Ibid., p. 60.

Maudūdī's two-part answer to the question from his journal *Tarjumān al-Qur'ān*, entitled *murtadd ki sazā islāmī qānūn mēṉ*, appeared for the first time in Urdu in 1953 as an independent document comprising 64 pages. Since that time it has been issued a number of times[290] and is also accessible on the internet nowadays.[291]

That this expert opinion from Maudūdī's pen at the beginning of the 1950s appeared as an independent publication should, according to Tim Green, not be judged to be something which happened by chance.[292] Rather, it should be judged in connection with Maudūdī's reaction against the Aḥmadīya movement in 1953, the marginalization and ostracization of which Maudūdī dedicated himself to with great attention. One could assume that Maudūdī concludes his argumentation against the Aḥmadīya with this writing on apostasy. He had already referred to them as unbelievers in his written work entitled *Qādiyānī masᶜala*[293] and, more specifically, stigmatized them as apostates. His writing entitled *murtadd ki sazā islāmī qānūn mēṉ* explains how these apostates are to be treated in an Islamic society.

On the whole, his writing *murtadd ki sazā islāmī qānūn mēṉ* has more the character of a political polemic than a theological treatment. Maudūdī argues only little with the Quran and *sunna*. His considerations are above all directed at the socio-political consequences of apostasy, against which he warns with forceful words.

Maudūdī justified his seeing himself needing to present his own position on the question of apostasy by the fact that there was a bitter dispute surrounding the topic and the unrest arising from discussions on the question. This can supposedly be understood as a direct indication of a dispute over the Aḥmadīya movement which had never really come to rest since the 1920s.

This also appears conceivable due to the fact that in the case of the position presented by Maudūdī, there is hardly a balanced discussion of the question of which criteria a person or group is to be judged as having fall-

---

290 Pertinent library directories mention editions from 1953, 1963, 1976, 1980, and 1981.

291 For example, see the slightly edited textual verion at http://www.scribd.com/doc/51556657/Murtad-Ki-Saza-Syed-Abul-A-la-Maududi (19.9.2011).

292 Green. *Factors*, p. 28.

293 Abū l-Aᶜlā Maudūdī. *Qādiyānī masᶜala*.

en away from Islam and which various opinions exist within Islamic theology. Instead, it is more of a proclamation and justification for administering the death penalty for turning away from Islam as well as an uncompromising call for applying this penalty against anyone who is guilty of apostasy, regardless of what the individual's motives are.

The Title of the Work

The orientation is clear from the title of the work: It does not involve a discussion of the question of apostasy per se. Rather, it has to do with the "punishment" (*sazā*) of an apostate. It is not the weighing of various points of view which is the topic. Rather, it is the presentation of that which is ordered "in Islamic law" (*islāmī qānūn mēn̠*).

By using the term "Islamic law," the impression is conveyed that it is a matter of the Sharia in the form of a legal codex and not a collection of interpretable legal guidelines for which a wealth of various interpretations exist. In so doing, the formulation of the title implies that the punishment of an apostate is a religious command. Indeed, it is even more. It is a compulsory law of God. This formulation corresponds to Maudūdī's understanding of one clearly recognizable law of God for true Muslim members of the *umma*, which does not require any interpretation.

Topic and Contents

Maudūdī's writing on apostasy is introduced by the question posed by a reader who is looking for justification for the punishment of execution in the case of apostasy. Whether this form of questioning was actually brought before Maudūdī or whether it is a matter of a fictitious question, is something which in the final event must remain open.

What sets the tone for Maudūdī's entire treatment is the fact that the anonymous initial question is neither calling for a definition of apostasy nor is it looking for an assessment on the basis of relevant sources of Islam. Instead, it is the legitimacy of the compulsory death penalty as the punishment based on Sharia law and the evidence for this punishment.[294] With that said, the topic of "apostasy" from the beginning of the discussion

---

294 Maudūdī. *murtadd*, p. 3.

is strongly oriented towards the question of its penalty and not on the derivation or justification of a prohibition of apostasy from relevant sources.

A second part of the initial question is directed towards the limits of religious freedom for non-Muslims, which is broken down into "unbelievers" (*kuffār*) and "*people of the book*" (*ahl-e-kitāb*). Also at this point it is not a question of which rights non-Muslims have in Muslim majority countries. Rather, it has to do with the question of which justification can be offered for refusing them the dissemination of their faith. The segment of this multi-part question closes with what seems like a strongly schematic request made of Maudūdī for an explanation of the facts surrounding the condemnation of apostates. In the questioner's judgment, based on the questioner's knowledge of the subject, the condemnation of apostates is neither spoken about clearly in the Quran nor in the *sunna*. There is also a request for publication of an answer in light of what is an admitted uncertainty on the part of the questioner with respect to the appropriate standpoint from the perspective of Islam.

The Necessity of the Application of the Death Penalty for Apostates

The actual text of Maudūdī's writing on apostasy is broken down into three main chapters and a brief closing chapter. The first chapter treats the reasons which speak for a duty to execute apostates. The second chapter addresses the necessity of preventing the spread of unbelief in an Islamic state, and the third chapter handles the right of the state to defend itself. The final chapter again briefly formulates the impossibility of providing space for the propagation of unbelief in such an Islamic state.

At the beginning[295] it above all has to do with determining the unconditional application of the death penalty for apostates. As early as the first sentence, Maudūdī emphatically underscores the idea that it is "no secret" (or: "not concealed") (*pošīda nahīṉ hai*) that "according to Islamic law" (*islāmī qānūn se*) an apostate receives the death penalty. Doubts regarding this situation first arose in the course of the 19th century. These doubts were basically something which appeared in modernity while the Muslim

[295] Ibid., p. 5ff.

community had been in agreement for the prior twelve hundred years. Indeed, there had never been a lack of agreement regarding this stance.

With this introduction, Maudūdī has already anticipated the form of the entire treatise from the start. In his writing there is no point at which a balanced presentation of possible pro and contra arguments takes place. It is not a matter of looking at objections against their possible legitimacy, much less to address the rights of those who think differently or to even mention the motives of those who turn away from Islam. For Maudūdī it is solely a question of a decisive repudiation of possible doubts regarding the legitimacy of no alternative other than the death penalty for apostates. Their actions are emphatically condemned in his writing.

At the same time, there is a recognizable theme running through this document, which is visible throughout the entirety of his writings: The dichotomy between belief and unbelief, between Muslims and unbelievers, between a true Islamic state and the Western world, between a noble disposition and immorality, and between submission to God and materialism.[296] He also expresses his dual-pole view of the world in this treatment, without at any point reconciling both extremes. He also does not include the realities found in a multi-religious society in his deliberations – particularly in India prior to the partitioning of the country, where conversions into various streams occur.

This dichotomy in Maudūdī is clear from the start in the first chapter of the work, when he speaks of those who have been influenced by modernity and now emerge with a body of thought which stands in contradiction to that which has been transmitted as a consensus by Muḥammad, the four rightly guided caliphs, the companions of the Prophet, their successors, the outstanding *muǧtāhidūn*, and Sharia scholars: the unconditional necessity of executing apostates. According to Maudūdī, if one opens the door to a counterargument in spite of these numerous witnesses from the past, it would be the beginning of the end, for soon thereafter it would be the

296 An example of such a dichotomous presentation is Maudūdī's work: Sayyid Abul A'la Maududi. *Come let us Change this World*. Markaza Maktaba Islami: Delhi, 1991/1996. Therein he broaches the issue of the ideological "foundations of Western civilization" and in the end traces back all the evil in the world to a single cause: "Wheresoever evil is found in the world, at its root is one thing alone: acceptance of supremacy and overlordship other than of Allah. That is the source of all mischief and the seed of all evil." (ibid., p. 69).

Quran, ritualistic prayer, or fasting which could be up for discussion. Indeed, the sending of Muḥammad would also not be immune from scrutiny. In other words: Those who set themselves apart from the apparently so clear assessment of the apostasy question from the past endanger the continuation of Islam in a foolhardy manner.[297]

With that said, Maudūdī has already made clear on the first page of his treatment on judging apostasy that, from his point of view, a discussion about the question of the legitimacy of execution of an apostate is impermissible. This is particulary the case since not once has there ever been a debate on this over the course of history up to the present – a supposition which is not correct when one takes a look at sources from the 14th century with respect to Islamic history and theology. It is difficult to make out whether Maudūdī is aware of this fact and deliberately overlooks it or whether he is actually lacking profound knowledge of Islamic history and theology.

At this point, Maudūdī gives his own opinion the greatest authority by reverting to Muḥammad as well as to the central foundational personalities within Islamic theology and law, and he does so without past evidence for such a far-reaching supposition of unassailable advocacy of the execution of apostates. He even goes a step further and compares an individual who is not prepared to accept what is obvious in his religion (namely that Islam calls for the death penalty for apostates) with someone who has distanced himself from the right path of his religion and is only holding to it out of tradition, thus only being a nominal adherent of his religion.

The Quran and Tradition on Apostasy

In the following five sections,[298] Maudūdī makes a few citations from the Quran and tradition in support of his point of view. He complements this with remarks from the first four caliphs as well as the founders of the four legal schools completely in the sense of his unrestricted advocacy of the death penalty.

Initially, Maudūdī emphasizes at the outset that any doubts regarding the unambiguous nature of the directive to execute an apostate from Islam

297 Maudūdī. *murtadd*, pp. 5-6.

298 Ibid., pp. 6-23.

have to be owing to a lack of insight into the sources.[299] In order to rebut possible doubts, he quotes Sura 9:11-12. That is a verse calling for combating those who "break their oath" (*nakaṯū aimānahum*) after having concluded a contractual relationship, after having prior thereto joined the community of Muslims, after having conducted the ritual prayer, and after having paid the alms tax. Maudūdī emphasizes that this verse does not speak of a political break of loyalty. Rather, it should become clear from the context that prior adherents of Islam, which now incite apostasy, should be combated (*iqrār-e-islām-sē phir jānā*).[300]

Regardless of the diversity and content-related multidimensional nature of a number of verses from the Quran on the topic of unbelief and of turning from it, Maudūdī discusses no additional verses. Rather, one is left with this single textual reference. He also does not go into the very diverse interpretations of this or other verses from the Quran.

In the following section, Maudūdī provides somewhat more detail about "evidences" (*ṯubūt*) cited from tradition[301] regarding the unconditional necessity of imposing the death penalty. He quotes a number of the best known traditions in Urdu and Arabic, such as the text passed down from sources like Abū Bakr and ᶜUṯmān which states, "He who changes his religion, kill him." There is also a report going back to ᶜĀ'iša, according to which Muḥammad is said to have only allowed the killing of a Muslim in three cases, among them apostasy.

By mentioning these names from the first generation of Muslims and companions of the Prophet, respectively, Maudūdī views the "scholarly" justification for the mandatory execution of an apostate as satisfied. Questions regarding the simple reference or multiple reference of the tradition texts are touched upon as little as is engagement with considerations regarding the credibility of those who have transmitted the tradition.

He also does not cite any alternative *aḥādīṯ* which allow contrary statements about cases of apostasy in the early days of Islam, nor does he name texts which could prompt the advocacy of religious freedom. Instead, Maudūdī emphasizes that there was not a single voice raised against the authority of an ᶜUṯmān in the early days of Islam calling for the killing of an apostate in the presence of a large crowd of people. But even here there

299 Ibid., p. 6.

300 Ibid., p. 7.

301 Ibid., pp. 7-13.

remains a bare assertion of the facts which rest solely upon Maudūdī's depiction without providing source citations.

Maudūdī continues by quoting four additional transmitted accounts from tradition dating from the early days of Islam. They likewise hand down the sentencing of apostates to death. There is also one text cited with the direct order to execute a female apostate,[302] without Maudūdī's pointing to the lack of a consensus among Muslim scholars with respect to the execution of women in the case of apostasy.[303] As a consequence, Maudūdī draws a one-sided and exceedingly uniform picture from the early days of Islam in both of these sections which actually claims to provide a multilayered finding of texts in the Quran and tradition. He does this without allowing the objections which the texts themselves offer. He also does not pursue the justification others have for doubts regarding the authenticity of the statements nor does he address the assertions of such statements nor reproduce the objections of diverse central characters.

The Early Days of Islam

In the following section on the assessment of apostasy at the time of the rule of the rightly guided caliphs,[304] Maudūdī lists ten additional cases of apostasy and the sentences of death issued against those involved – among them also cases of conversion to Christianity. According to none of the accounts mentioned by Maudūdī was there a case where the execution was suspended or deferred. Thus, also in the case of this section the impression is left of an unambiguous assessment of cases from the early days of Islam. Maudūdī additionally underlines the idea that the condemned meet their death exclusively on the basis of their apostasy and were not found guilty owing to another offense.

The following fourth section[305] is dedicated to how apostasy was combated by the first of the four rightly guided caliphs. Here it also becomes clear by the heading that for Maudūdī it is not a matter of weighing the divergent reports – which are also contained in the collections of tradition

302 Ibid., p. 12.

303 The different notions of the four Sunnite schools of legal thought regarding this question are mentioned, for instance, by Khoury. *Toleranz im Islam*, p. 112.

304 Maudūdī. *murtadd*, pp. 13-16.

305 Ibid., pp. 16-19.

judged to be authentic – against each other. Instead, it has more to do with inseparably linking the rule of the caliphs under the topic of *Jihād* against the apostates.

Maudūdī continues his argumentation according to this pattern in order to further develop his argumentation: After initial disagreement about *Jihād* against apostates, "the entire community of the Prophet's companions" participated in it (*is men̲ ṣaḥāba-e-karām kī pūrī jamāᶜat šarīk thī*).[306] Owing to their direct proximity to Muḥammad, they were united by the desire to defend against those who in their apostasy had opposed Islamic rule. At this point, Maudūdī interprets the battle against apostates as a necessary means to self-preservation.

At this point Maudūdī takes up the intra-Islamic discussion about the justification of the prosecution of apostates, insofar as he goes into the question of whether apostates in the early days of Islam were fought against due to their political opposition to the *umma*. In particular, he goes into whether it was resistance against the *zakāt* tribute imposed by Muḥammad's successors that elicited the prosecution. This is an argument which is frequently brought up by advocates of complete religious freedom in order to document that renegades in the early days of Islam were not prosecuted due to apostasy. Rather, their prosecution was owing to the political unrest that they caused – something which Maudūdī, however, resolutely denies.

From his point of view, apostates' actual offense in the early days of Islam was their turning away from Islam. Their prosecution was brought about by this offense and not due to political disputes between different groups or individuals. Maudūdī's argument for this point of view goes as follows: in connection with the movement of apostasy in the early days of Islam, it is not, for instance, the term for "rebellion" (*baġāwat*) and "rebels" (*bāġī*) which is employed. Rather, it is the term for "apostasy" (*irtidād*) and for "apostate" (*murtadd*). From this situation it is thus clear that the actual offense which was punishable with the death penalty was apostasy and not rebellion.[307]

In order to underpin his point of view, which is that the *ridda* wars were the prosecution of religiously defined offenses, Maudūdī cites a saying by Abū Bakr. However, he does not take the trouble to provide a

306 Ibid., p. 17.

307 Ibid., pp. 17-18.

source citation or characterize the account as a quote.[308] In the final event, then, he maintains his position on the basis of his own authority and in this manner removes any possibility for representatives of other standpoints to engage in an objective and source-based controversy.

In particular, owing to this strongly preconceived form of argumentation and the lack of discussion of opposing historical testimony, as well as the simplified, unilinear conclusions in which connection neither a counterargument nor objections are allowed, the conclusion is suggested that what is merely "proved" by this form of argumentation is what already stood firm for the author prior to composing the section or even the entire treatment. Namely, insofar as the author provides a definition of apostates, their condemnation solely on the grounds of their turning from Islam is the only justified point of view from the perspective of Islam.

In the last section of this first chapter,[309] what is addressed is the agreement among Muslim scholars from the formative era of Islam with respect to the condemnation of apostasy and with respect to the extent of the punishment imposed upon the apostate. Regarding the various aspects of this question, Maudūdī mentions that among the founders of the four legal schools there are indeed various understandings which to be found when it comes to details. However, he says that they all call for the execution of the apostate. At this point, Maudūdī quotes excerpts from compendia from the three legal schools which without exception speak out for the execution of the individual involved.

Maudūdī again underscores the idea that there can be no doubts that according to this unanimous testimony from times past execution for apostasy was ordered for the turning away from Islam and that it was carried out. Its administration was not, however, applied as a penalty for another offense.[310]

At this point, Maudūdī again takes up an apparent counterargument and, again however, does not conduct any actual discussion: "A number of people" (*haᶜz̤ log*) – whom Maudūdī does not specify more precisely defend the opinion, irrespective of what are from Maudūdī's point of view the unambiguous facts, that the Quran does not call for the execution of

[308] Ibid., p. 18. In the following section Maudūdī quotes Ibn Kaṯīr, albeit without providing a location and year for his work *al-bidāya wa-'n-nihāya*.

[309] Maudūdī. *murtadd*, pp. 19-23.

[310] Ibid., p. 22.

apostates. But then, according to Maudūdī, there still remain the traditions and the opinions of the rightly guided caliphs as well as the significant legal specialists from the formative period. In particular, their texts are called in with respect to legal questions as well as by calling upon social and political concerns. Furthermore, their texts have been viewed as binding by the entire Muslim community as well as by judges and legal scholars over the course of thirteen centuries. Does this fact have stronger weight or does the opinion of those who in modern times have been influenced by non-Islamic bodies of thought and foreign civilizations and cultures and have no education in the respective disciplines?

With that said, Maudūdī marginalizes as ignorant all those who would take up opposing positions to his understanding. Furthermore, they are suspected of having distanced themselves from Islam by borrowing from non-Islamic positions. In this way, Maudūdī polarizes, indicating that there is an appropriate, Islamically justified point of view and an errant position deviating from Islam. At the same time, he presents his own standpoint as the actual and sole justified understanding based on Islamic sources. All other standpoints, the arguments of which he has up to now nowhere seriously taken into account, have for him no justification due to the fact that they transport foreign bodies of thought from outside of Islam.

With his presentation, Maudūdī draws a picture of harmony and of absolute agreement with the formative period of Islam, which is awakened to new life when the death penalty is imposed. In this manner, Maudūdī constructs the illusion of a continuation of the practices from an ideal early time into modernity and thereby catapults over 13 centuries of very diverse Islamic history which have occurred. According to his depiction, the Quran, tradition, the rightly guided caliphs, and early Islamic legal experts have, in referring to Muḥammad, without exception called for the execution of apostates in such a way that any doubt brought forth nowadays is reprehensible. No text which reads otherwise is mentioned by Maudūdī, no divergent opinions by Muslim theologians from the centuries between the time of early Islam and modern times are named, and no interpretive variations of texts from the Quran which speak out in favour of religious freedom or could at least be interpreted as approving freedom from punishment in the case of apostasy are considered.

Moreover, Maudūdī dedicates himself with not so much as a word to the strongly divergent understandings on the part of religious critics and apostates. Without a word, he differentiates between personal questions and doubts of an individual who still counts himself as an adherent of Islam but stands at a critical distance to it and an individual who openly confesses to no longer belonging to Islam. He does not differentiate between the individual who has given up the practice of Islam, the individual who has made a sympathetic declaration of atheism or agnosticism, and the individual who has converted to another religion or even solicits for his newly found faith. Indeed, he does not even differentiate him from one who actually runs over to the camp of the enemy and advances militarily against a Muslim majority country.

Irrespective of the pressure he places upon the unconditional necessity of imposing the death penalty, Maudūdī provides no definition of apostasy, nor does he justify the reprehensibility of apostasy from Islam in any actual sense. He offers no concrete description of either its consequences or the forms of its appearance. Thus, terms such as "apostasy," "rebellion," or "offense" remain equally empty of content, sterile, artificial; simultaneously, apostasy is labelled a great danger for the Islamic community.

The Limits of Religious Freedom for non-Muslims

In a short second chapter with five sub-chapters,[311] Maudūdī discusses the position of non-Muslims in an Islamic state and the limits of religious freedom under which they are placed. He again does this by taking a glance at the practice found in the early days of Islam.

At the beginning, he again underscores that Muslims possess no rights allowing them to leave Islam; he sets this "within the limits of our authority" (*ham apnē ḥudūd-e-iqtidār mē̱n*). No Muslim can lay claim to the right to give up Islam once an individual has accepted it in order to take up a new religion (*maẕhab*) or to strike out on a new path (*maslak*).

From this it can be derived that the announcement and dissemination of another religion which is opposed to Islam is not to be permitted. For this first to be allowed and then, however, to place the conversion of a Muslim to this religion under a punishment is in itself a contradiction. From the unambiguous directive on the execution of an apostate, there is a conclusion to be drawn of a prohibition on missionary efforts by other religions, to which at this point Maudūdī allocates the synonyms of "unbelief" or

311 Ibid., pp. 24-30.

"heathenism" (*kufr*).[312] Maudūdī also does not respect the differentiation made by classical Islamic theology between *people of the book* and adherents of other religions. Rather, he subsumes all religions besides Islam under the heading of unbelief. Muslims have to be protected against their propagation within the borders of an Islamic area. The following three chapters have to do with this protection for Muslims from the spread of unbelief.

As early as in the first subchapter entitled "The Topic of Investigation" (*mas'ala kī taḥqīq*),[313] Maudūdī underscores the absolute nature and completeness of Islam which offers the individual a "way" (*rāsta*), proclaims this as truth, and rejects all other ways as errant. However, in the process it is not a matter of just any way but rather the way upon which the weal and woe of the entirety of humanity is decided since all other ways lead directly into "destruction" (*barbādī*). For that reason, all people are to be advised to give up this errant way and to join Islam.

Maudūdī emphasizes that every way of thinking and doing which arises from or is traceable back to non-Muslims is in the end "misdirection" (or: misleading) (*gamrāhī*)[314] and whoever follows this way can only lose. With these words, Maudūdī not only directly and straightforwardly rejects every other religion and world view. Rather, in a wholesale manner he insinuates that their adherents are primarily able to produce nothing but misdirection and ruin. Indeed, this is solely for the reason that they are non-Muslims.

Islam, Maudūdī continues, leaves no room for doubt that it is the sole truth and, over and above that, there is no other way of salvation for humanity. In all explicitness, Islam points out to people that all other ways lead to hellfire. Since that, however, is the case, according to Maudūdī, it is hardly bearable that people should be subjected to other messages which for certain will surely make them fall victim into destruction. These messages, which lead people into destruction, cannot be additionally promoted by freedoms which are granted to their propagators. It is difficult to accept that people would have to be left with the choice between Islam and the way of self-destruction. According to Maudūdī, that is only thinkable be-

312 Ibid., p. 24.

313 Ibid., pp. 25-27.

314 Ibid., p. 25.

cause it is simply not possible to evoke belief in a person by exercising coercion.

Interestingly, Maudūdī differentiates between mere membership in a religion and the internal conviction of an individual which could induce him to leave Islam. He could have recommended holding to formalism so that the individual who no longer possesses faith (in Islam) would at least formally continue to belong. Instead, however, he apparently assumes that the lack of conviction to acknowledge truth can prompt an individual to separate from the community.

If it were possible, Maudūdī continues, to remove unbelief through countermeasures, then people would have to be prevented by force from lapsing. However, even if it is impossible to keep people from unbelief who have so decided – Maudūdī calls this decision against Islam drinking the "cup of poison" (*zahr kā pailā*)[315] – this does not mean, on the other hand, that Islam allows it or acquiesces without comment if people take this path of self-destruction. Unbelief has to be staved off, and the involved individual has to be brought back to Islam. However, this can only occur if the involved individual acknowledges that his thinking and his actions are wrong and turns back to Islam of his own accord. Exercising coercion is futile.

However, even if there is no way of keeping a person from lapsing into unbelief, it is altogether unthinkable to surrender to him the chance to try and solicit others and take them with him on the path to destruction. He has to by all means be stopped from this.

Where Islam is not able to exercise any state power, this cannot be enforced. However, where Islam has control, it may not allow things which injure people, such as misuse of drugs, prostitution, or theft – how could it approvingly put up with the much more dangerous dissemination of "unbelief" (*kufr*), "polytheism" (*širk*), "atheism" (*dahrīyat*), "rebellious opposition towards God" (*ḫodā sē baġāwat*)?[316]

In this chapter, Maudūdī repeatedly personalizes "Islam" as if Islam it self possesses courses of action it could take. Islam does not allow anyone to be lured away. Islam has the power to do this or that, or it offers the individual the way to salvation. With that said, "Islam" is introduced as a unit and not as a wide-ranging phenomenon touching upon legal, religious,

---

315 Ibid., p. 26.

316 Ibid., pp. 26-27.

social as well as political questions. In all these aspects and for its adherents, Islam presents itself as exceedingly diverse. On the other hand, it is in this way that "Islam" is suggested to be an acting subject in which its own judgments, opinions, and courses of action reside and which has to defend Islam's existence. By claiming that his own position has the authority of "Islam" and speaks for "Islam," Maudūdī revokes any justification for possible contradictions and from the outset deprives critics of defending their viewpoint of "Islam." At the same time, he polarizes by making the reader or, more specifically, the believer decide for or against "Islam" as it is presented here in absolute terms, coterminous with Maudūdī's point of view.

In this section, Maudūdī uses terms which are neither useful for conveying an objective overview of the facts nor are neutral about other religions and still less speak neutrally about those who turn away from Islam. He uses emotionally laden terms[317] in order to underscore all the more distinctly the error and the destructive power of rejecting Islam.

The Rule of Islam

The second subheading of this chapter[318] provides an explanation of the character of Islamic rule. At the outset, Maudūdī quotes two verses from the Quran which make the *umma's* battle against unbelievers as well as Muslims' witness (at the judgment) against people the subject of discussion. From this, Maudūdī derives the goal of sending Muḥammad to be the rule and conquest of Islam over all other worldviews. Wherever this mission is fulfilled, there cannot be any competition between God's religion and another religion or worldview. Additionally, according to Maudūdī, where Islam holds the position of power, it has a certain responsibility before God, who will call his servants to account if they have allowed evil to gain power.

The following subheading[319] places the borders of freedom for the *ḏimmī* within Islamic territories. With all brevity, Maudūdī names a number of well known pillars coming from the provisions of Sharia law with respect to subjects, or wards, such as the payment of the *ǧizya*, which

[317] Ibid., p. 26.

[318] Ibid., pp. 27-28.

[319] Ibid., pp. 28-29.

stands opposite the protection of life, possessions, and their practice of their own religion.[320]

On the one hand, Maudūdī emphasizes that the freedom to retain one's own religion means, however, unconditionally maintaining the border which is transgressed by human subjects each time there is an attempt to usurp rule and push through their interests. This may in no way be tolerated by an Islamic government, for according to Sura 9:29 the individual subjects should be "subdued" and respect prescribed Sharia law limitations. For that reason, their status is defined and they are not allowed to reach for heights and to exercise power. Foreigners as well, who for economic or political reasons live in a territory of Islam, have to respect this limitation and are not allowed to propagate their religion. This is due to the fact that God has allocated to Muslims the mandate to stem unbelief, thereby showing themselves as thankful to God.

It is blatantly obvious that for Maudūdī there is principally no equality when it comes to religions under Islamic rule, neither religious freedom nor legal or social equal status. For all other religions except Islam, there are no other terms than unbelief as far as Maudūdī is concerned. Non-Muslims are considered to be tolerated in an Islamic state. They are controlled with respect to their room for maneuver and have to be consistently directed, but in no way are they on an equal footing with full civil liberties and rights to develop themselves.

In the final segment,[321] Maudūdī refers to the legal position of subjects in territories where there was Islam after Muḥammad's death. In books by *fiqh* scholars, according to Maudūdī, there is no indication of the apparent right for non-Muslims to propagate their religion in an Islamic area.[322] Islam's opinion that such freedom is not within the realm of possibility is not suspended by worldly-minded leaders' nevertheless affording individuals this right. This fact speaks solely against the involved powers that be but for Muslims cannot count as an argument. According to Maudūdī, it can be pointed out with pride that to non-Muslims the freedoms afforded by these

---

320 For instance, Maudūdī speaks in detail about the rights of *people of the book* in the Islamic state in his writing. Sayyid Abu A'la Mawdudi. *First Principles of the Islamic State*. Islamic Publications Limited: Lahore, 1960²/1983⁶. pp. 66ff.

321 Ibid., p. 29-30.

322 Ibid., p. 30.

rulers changes nothing about the fact that their actions are considered to be "offenses" (*jarā'im*), and as such have to be held against those rulers.[323]

Arguments for the Death Penalty in the Case of Apostasy

In the third part of his treatment, the most extensive chapter of this work, Maudūdī now turns to a detailed explanation of two themes: the degree of penalty for apostates, execution, and a justification of the prohibition on propagating unbelief.[324]

To start with, it involves the justification of the unconditional necessity of the death penalty for the apostate.[325] Maudūdī takes up an explanation of his understanding of four objections against the execution of apostates. He addresses each of these objections one by one in individual sections but does not refute them.

The four objections listed here against the duty to execute apostates do not, however, represent an existential discussion of the topic. The objections do not touch upon any foundational questions, such as ones of reliability or conclusions to be drawn from individual reports of tradition. A list of interpretive variations of the relevant verses from the Quran is also not to be found here, just as little as there is any reference to Islamic scholars who have diverging understandings with respect to religious freedom or only with respect to the degree of penalty applicable to apostates.

The four objections which Maudūdī brings up basically direct themselves towards the question of which weight can be conceded to freedom of conscience against the backdrop of as far as Maudūdī is concerned the doubtless established – instructions in Islam to impose the death penalty on the apostate. What is Islam's stance with respect to freedom of conscience if it threatens people who turn their back on the faith with death and does not confront them with arguments? Is not the expression of faith of an individual to be considered sheer hypocrisy if he refrains from turning from Islam only in view of an impending execution, all the while having internally long since become an unbeliever?

Is it still a matter of faith in any actual sense if this faith is only externally sustained by the threat of existential violence while the heart and rea-

323 Ibid., p. 30.
324 Ibid., p. 31-60.
325 Ibid., p. 31-34.

son are no longer satisfied? Does staying formally in the Muslim community serve the interests of the community, and does it make the individual pleasing to God? And would it be practical if other religions were to speak out for a prohibition on turning away and for the prosecution of apostates such that it would then be hardly possible for non-Muslims to turn to Islam? How does the call for applying the death penalty agree with Suras 2:256 and 18:29, two verses which apparently advocate the freedom of choice to an individual in questions of religion? And does not the pressure exercised from threatening the death penalty induce Muslims to hypocrisy, even as it is simultaneously disapproved of by several texts in the Quran? Additionally, one could also argue, isn't it in the end untenable that Islam condemns non-Muslims for wanting to prevent their fellow believers from converting to Islam but threatens those who want to leave Islam with the death penalty?[326]

Maudūdī emphasizes that by no means are all Muslims in the situation of being able to deal with these critical questions. According to Maudūdī, in the face of this critical set of questions there is one group, which he admittedly does not mention by name, which takes refuge in maintaining that execution does not have anything to do with religion. Another group is indeed aware of the duty to take penal action against apostates but is not in the position of being able to rationally justify this. The result is that it has negative ramifications for the Muslim community. At this point, Maudūdī cites an example from the past. He does not elaborate on it, but in this connection even Muslim scholars are not proficient enough in Islam to be able to convincingly refute the objections brought forward against the death penalty.

Islam as a Comprehensive System

In the next section,[327] Maudūdī gets around to speaking about one of his standard topics, which from his point of view is also of great significance for his assessment of apostasy. Namely, this has to do with the essence and character of Islam, the explanation of which is found in several other writings by Maudūdī in a similar form. Indeed, this counts as one of his most frequent topics of all.

---

[326] Ibid.

[327] Ibid., pp. 34-36.

Actually, for Maudūdī, the explanation for Islam's intolerance towards apostates lies in the essence of Islam, for Islam is not only a simple "religion" (*mazhab*),[328] comparable to other religions. If this were to be the case, then execution in the case of apostasy would, as a matter of fact, not make any sense. If Islam were to be something like a faith or a worldview, then it would only have to do with things in the hereafter, such as the question of salvation after death. The reason is that such a construct would correspond to the character of a religion. Why should one of its adherents not be allowed to change his mind if he believes he finds salvation in another religion? If Islam were thus a religion, there would be nothing "more absurd" (*ziyāda nā maᶜqūl bāt*)[329] than to invite people who believe differently to come to Islam but to threaten those with death who turn their back on it.

Maudūdī turns the expected argument on its head: He does not discuss the justification of the death penalty in the case of apostasy. Rather, he takes this factor to be an irrefutable fact and the point of departure for his additional considerations. Since execution in the case of apostasy is a mandatory directive, Islam cannot be a mere religion. Since the execution of an apostate makes sense, it has to mean Islam is more than solely a belief. When Maudūdī argues that the justification of the intolerance of Islam towards apostasy lies in the essence of Islam as a comprehensive order, he divests any counterargument against the death penalty of its grounds of legitimacy, for abandoning the death penalty means to destroy Islam. And if the essence of Islam – the religion of God – does not allow any other course of action, who would want to raise any objections against it?

By no means is Islam only a religion, as Maudūdī continues. It is, "rather, a complete life order" (*balki ek pūrā niẓām-e-zindagī*).[330] Islam does not only regulate issues relating to the hereafter but also issues relating to the here and now. It orders life prior to death, indeed linking salvation in the afterlife with life in this mortal world. Islam has provided humankind a system which regulates all of individual and community life.

For this reason Islam's mandate also has far-reaching consequences. The consequences relate to society and the state, because in the final event, Maudūdī believes, the survival of human civilization and community is

---

[328] Ibid., p. 32.

[329] Ibid., p. 34.

[330] Ibid., p. 35.

dependent upon the continued existence of Islam: This is due to his view that both of them rest upon Islam as their foundation. This foundation cannot be jeopardized by individuals and their momentary leanings towards or away from Islam. If Islam, as the basic foundation of society, is shaken, the stability of its superstructure, namely the state and the society, is directly affected and with it the lives of millions of people are acutely endangered. Can faith be allowed to become a "plaything" (*khilaunā*) of the free decision of individuals?[331]

Maudūdī no longer argues here, as for instance Yūsuf al-Qaraḍāwī and Abdullah Saeed do, from within a theological discourse. Maudūdī does not establish why Islam is not only a religion but rather a social and a political order. He places Islam in a much more essential disposition as the foundation of society and of the state: Maudūdī does not discuss whether Islam contains social and political aspects at all. Rather, he argues that the state and society are even unthinkable without Islam as their foundation.

The self-Defense of the Umma

In the following shorter section,[332] Maudūdī further explains this idea of the stability of a society: A state which has chosen a particular form of organization cannot afford to offer freedom to those within the state who deviate from the foundations of the state or reject them. From Maudūdī's point of view, Islam grants at this point the greatest freedoms by allowing each individual the freedom to decide and by forcing no one to conformism. With that said, Islam practices a measure of tolerance like no other system when compared to representatives of deviating opinions, but in granting freedom it cannot go so far that it endangers its own existence.

Behind the liberalness and patience of the Islamic state is the hope of adaptation on the part of the obstinate, so that they might still be won over by the positive experiences they make with an Islamic society and its advantages. As for the individual who closes his heart, although he has heard about Islam and thereby shows himself to be absolutely unwilling to integrate into the societal order, the only appropriate way to proceed exists in removing that individual from society. This is due to the fact that under no

331 Ibid., p. 36.

332 Ibid., pp. 36-37.

circumstances can an individual be allowed to jeopardize an entire community.

With that said, Maudūdī has placed religious confession on a par with a political stance for or against the state and raised it to a standard for constitutional allegiance. It is completely independent of the behaviour of an individual citizen and his legal compliance: It is a stance which he also expressed in the position he took on the Aḥmadīya movement. Thus, all non-Muslims become potentially dubious allies, and all those who change religions are declared to be usurpers. With the assistance of such logic, Maudūdī ascribes responsibility for the execution of the apostate to the apostate himself. The apostate veritably provokes it by his undiscerning actions. In the process, Maudūdī divides all citzens into three categories: The Muslim citizen who is a buttress for the society, who enjoys full rights, the person of the book, and the apostate traitor who has no place in this state on account of his or a danger for the general public. With that said, Maudūdī divides all citizens into three categories: the Muslim, who is a supportive citizen for the community and enjoys full rights, a person of the book who is tolerated and has limited rights, and the apostate traitor for whom there is no place in the state on account of his being a potential danger. No more justification is needed for the fact that in such a totalitarian state model there is no place for worldview or religious pluralism, and no place for tolerance and religious freedom.

In the fourth subsection of this chapter,[333] Maudūdī turns his attention towards possible objections towards this point of view. Again he underscore the fact that in imposing the death penalty, it is by no means something that merely has to do with a change in religion. Instead, it is an indispensable countermeasure for the protection of the (Islamic) state. The apostate has made clear, as Maudūdī explains it, that there is no hope that he could him to become a loyal citizen through complete assimilation in the future. Since in this work Maudūdī at no point speaks about the possibility of repentance and the apostate's return to Islam, he appears to defend the opinion that falling away a single time is sufficient justification for immediate execution.

In order to be able to effectively establish the necessary protection in society from the corruptive influence of apostates, according to Maudūdī

333 Ibid., pp. 37-40.

there are three paths to consider: The first is for the apostate to emigrate from the state, as he is no longer able to agree on its foundation. If he is not prepared to emigrate, the second path is to withdraw all the individual's rights as a citizen (thus experiencing social death), and the third path is execution. If one considers paths two and three as Maudūdī's "proposed solutions" for dealing with apostates, in light of the fact that Maudūdī condemned the adherents of the Aḥmadīya movement as such, it is understandable why he was sentenced to death in 1953 for composing his book *Qādiyānī mas'ala*.

The Necessity of Executing Apostates

According to Maudūdī, execution is by far the most desirable solution, since in the final event existence for an individual who has no rights as citizens is torturous. Additionally, the apostate endangers the community if he is kept alive. He is a "permanent offense" (or: harm) (*ek mustaqill fitna*)[334] and causes more harm if he infects the remaining healthy members of society with his "poison" (*pailā*). For that reason, according to Maudūdī, it is better to punish the apostate with death and to put an end to his own miserable situation (*muṣībat*) and to end the danger for society. Execution is interpreted here as an act of mercy, and at the same time as a necessary way to avert danger.[335] The strongly emotionally colored and inhuman terms which Maudūdī uses here underscores the content of his message. The apostate appears as a dangerous, contagious bacillus who has to be hindered in his pernicious activities, removed from society, or better still, has to be physically destroyed.[336]

---

[334] Ibid., p. 37.

[335] In light of this argumentation Maudūdī uses, Norman Anderson's supposition appears too euphemistic: ". . . I think, he [Maudūdī] would regard the death penalty as the maximum, rather than the mandatory, penalty for apostasy." Norman Anderson. *Law Reform in the Muslim World*. University of London: The Athlone Press, 1976, p. 180.

[336] In examining this argumentation by Maudūdī, Tārik Jān's position on Maudūdī's attitude towards apostasy does not appear to go to the heart of the matter when he silently ignored Maudūdī's condemnation of apostates to death; he merely summarizes Maudūdī's attitude as one that is "irrational" if one questions one's faith after having joined the religious community: Jān. "Critique", p. 506.

From what has been said is becomes clear that Maudūdī in no way wastes any thoughts on the individual who changes religion or is an atheist. Neither the individual's motives are of interest to Maudūdī, which would induce the individual to pay such a high price for his decision, nor do the consequences called for appear to touch him in any way, i.e., the social ostracism, banishment, and death. A "seed of the word" seems to have worked itself out in the "Blasphemy Laws" in Pakista approximately a decade after the exclusion of the Aḥmadīya movement from the Islamic community and its persecution. The passage of the "Blasphemy Laws" in the 1980s seems to have led to around 100 arrests as well as 2,000 charges and indictments on file on account of apostasy and blasphemy solely against adherents of the Aḥmadīya movement[337] by the mid-1990s.

In the following, Maudūdī grapples with the charge that the threat of the death penalty in the case of apostasy leads to coercion or even to hypocrisy. This thought is from his point of view unable to be substantiated: For the sake of its self-preservation, society protects itself from the weak-mindedness of individuals, who owing to personal instability make such a serious thing as the welfare of a complete community a plaything for their caprice. Society cannot be built upon this. Society needs committed members for its self-preservation. At this point the reader is reminded of the obligation on the part of committed members of *Jamāᶜat-i-Islāmī* to the comprehensive implementation of Islam.

Neither with this thought nor in the adjoining considerations – that each individual who joins this community should carefully consider it since there is no opportunity to turn back does it come up as a question for discussion that not everyone has a free choice when it comes to joining Islam. For instance, this is the case when a child is born into the Islamic community. A number of lines later, Maudūdī takes up this topic again and underscores that Sura 2:256 ("Let there be no compulsion in religion . . .")

[337] This number is mentioned in the middle of the 1990s by Said Amir Arjomand. "Religious Human Rights and the Principle of Legal Pluralism in the Middle East" in: Johan D. Van der Vyver; John Jr. Witte (ed.). "Religious Human Rights in Global Perspective. Legal Perspectives." Martinus Nijhoff Publishers: Den Haag, 1996, pp. 331-347, here p. 340; there are, however, also higher estimates of 5.000 legal actions between 1984 and 2004; 2/3 of the accused are said to have been killed outside the courts: http://www.pakistanblasphemylaw.com/?page_id=15 (10.6.2014).

correctly emphasizes that no one can be forced into entering Islam. He interprets this verse from the Quran such that every convert to Islam should take time to calmly consider his step.

Once again Maudūdī emphasizes that other religions are not comparable to Islam and that they can hold their doors open for entry and exit. Indeed, it would be nonsensical if they would forbid a change of religion. However, in the case of a religion which is the foundation of the state and society, this sort of freedom is unthinkable if the demise of the community has to be taken into account.

At this point it is not only Maudūdī's understanding of Islam as a state structure which becomes clear. With this demarcation to other religions, Maudūdī also classifies Islam so that it is in its own category. He allows it a special role which does not apply to any other worldview. He withdraws it from any and all criticism and every comparison. Additionally, with that said, he also eliminates the right to evaluate it according to the standards used for other religions or worldviews. Assessments which might possess validity when it comes to (other) religions do not apply to Islam since it is not only the one true religion but also unique in its essence.

Maudūdī again turns against the charge that moving against apostates could bring about hypocrisy (*nifāq*)[338] from their side. At this point, he argues again that someone who turns his back on his community, although he knows that this possibility is not at all open to him, has himself caused the consequences which in the final event arise from it. The "error" (*quṣūr*) lies with him alone. And if he should be so truly concerned about his possible hypocrisy, then he can courageously come forth and receive the (appropriate) punishment for his apostasy!

At this point Maudūdī becomes downright cynical when he assigns the actual guilt for the consequences of apostasy to the apostate himself. It is not the punishment for the change of belief which is at this juncture the topic of critical examination. Rather, it is the internal attitude of the one who has changed religions and the question of whether he possesses adequate courage to willingly take upon himself the death penalty coming to him or whether, as Maudūdī implies, he is too much of a coward to do so.

338 Maudūdī. *murtadd*, p. 39.

Islam is not Merely a Religion

The section closes with an examination of the argument of whether the attitude of allowing a conversion to Islam or between others religion but prohibiting the conversion from Islam to another religion does not constitute a contradiction in terms. Maudūdī answers in the negative with the rationale that Islam views itself as the truth and for that reason cannot be compared with other religions. A contradiction would first emerge if Islam were to be considered a religion like all others. For that reason, an acceptance of the truth (a conversion to Islam) and a turning from the truth (a conversion from Islam to another religion) are in no way to be compared with each other. Whoever prevents the involved individual who is in the process of injuring himself and others from turning his back on the truth may in no way be rebuked for he is objectively acting correctly. It is obvious that an examination of the argument against the duty to execute the apostate in light of this absolute premise of the peerlessness of Islam and the absoluteness of its position is only a mock discussion.

Maudūdī again underscores this fundamental difference between a "mere religion" (*muǧarrad maẕhab*) and a "religious community" (*maẕhabī riyāsat*)[339] in the following section in which Islam is not only a worldview but rather a foundation of the state and of the society. Indeed, Maudūdī emphasizes that where Islam only has the character of a religion, he himself also rejects execution as the punishment to be applied in the case of apostasy. Islam's penal code can only be applied in an Islamic state.

As early as the years 1942/1943 – at the time of the original composition of these statements by Maudūdī – the thought that an Islamic state in which Islam shapes religion, society, and legislation, is a condition for the implementation of true Islam. This is a concern that Maudūdī pursued in founding the *Jamāᶜat-i-Islāmī* party, in exercising his influence on Pakistani politics, and in ostracizing the Aḥmadīya movement.

In his transition to the sixth segment of this chapter,[340] Maudūdī brings up the question of whether individuals in an Islamic state in which Islam is the foundation for legislation, who assure the state of their "obedience and loyalty" (*ṭaᶜāt wa wafā-dārī*) but later relinquish this, can be held account-

339 Ibid., p. 40.

340 Ibid., pp. 41-42.

able. Maudūdī insistently answers in the affirmative.[341] This is because the state has the right to condemn courses of behaviour which endanger its existence. This right, according to Maudūdī, is also claimed by democratic states which solely on the grounds of their having had negative experiences with the papacy react so disagreeably to the idea of an "Islamic state".

At this point Maudūdī again directly equates a change in religious affiliation with political action. He maintains that apostasy per se is conduct subversive to the state. He does so without providing arguments, whereby a citizen who was yesterday a Muslim believer and today a confessing atheist or Christian presents a danger for the state and society, for law and legislation, and for family and the community. He also does not explain why there are Muslims who are not good citizens. Because Maudūdī fails to explain how apostasy endangers the community, he also cannot explain how using the death penalty protects the community so that apostasy no longer arises. In the final event, states in which those who change religions have to reckon with their execution (e.g., Saudi Arabia, Iran) nevertheless record a certain rate of converts. Indeed, in some countries the number rose with the commencement of punishing conversion compared to times when there was religious freedom.[342]

Maudūdī explains that Western states also avail themselves of this right to self-preservation, and, as examples, he discusses what this self-preservation means in the context of England and the United States.[343]

With both examples, Maudūdī equates citizenship with adherence to Islam and thus creates a type of "Muslim nation" or, more specifically, opts for an Islamization of the concept of the nation state. To begin with, it is an understanding which leads him to reject the partitioning of India. He does not define where the dividing line runs between a Muslim and a prior Muslim who has not explicitly declared that he holds a position of apostasy and who is no longer to be counted within Islam. However, by his comparison

---

341 Ibid., p. 41.

342 Comp. the case of the Iranian convert to Christianity Yousuf Nadarkhani who had been sentenced to death for apostasy in Iran on September, 22, 2010, but astonishingly had been released after international protests on September 8, 2012: http://www.igfm.de/mach-mit/appelle/was-ist-aus-ihnen-geworden/iran-freispruch-fuer-pastor-nadarkhani/ (10.6.2014).

343 Maudūdī. *murtadd,* pp. 42-48.

with the unambiguously documentable national citizenship, he awakens the impression that Islamic identity is likewise clearly definable.

Following this argumentation, Maudūdī cites the example of England's conspicuous differentiation between nationals and foreigners. Leaning upon his earlier affirmation that there is a free choice to join Islam but that one has to carefully consider it since leaving Islam is not thereafter allowed, Maudūdī emphasizes that accepting English citizenship is likewise a deliberate step which the applicant himself initiates. Then, however, as long as the individual lives within a state, he does not acquire this citizenship today and change it tomorrow. Rather, this is only possible if the individual leaves the country. Again, in leaning upon his judgment of apostasy as political unrest, he emphasizes the duty of a subject to demonstrate loyalty and obedience.

Apostasy Means Giving up Citizenship

Maudūdī escalates this arbitrary argumentation further. He does so by maintaining that a British citizen who in time of war is living outside of a country and applies for citizenship in an enemy country and provides support to that country against his own can be executed for high treason. Likewise an individual who threatens the king or attempts to undermine the laws or the religion of a country exposes himself to the death penalty, i.e., in short, he calls the existence of the state into question in some way. With that said, Maudūdī equates an attack on the life and limb of the head of state in a Western country with the change of religion in a Muslim majority country.

The comparison chosen by Maudūdī falls even farther out of balance with respect to its argumentation when he equates an example of England's foreigners with group of "wards" in an Islamic State and equates nationals with Muslims: Furthermore, he equates God and, more specifically, Muḥammad with the position of an English king (and the government and constitution of the United States of America): At this point it becomes clear from Maudūdī's point of view that it is impossible to tolerate a change of religion in an Islamic state because it corresponds to this enemy's desertion to the side of another country. At the same time, he has hereby implied that an attack on the head of state in the Western context corresponds to an attack on God himself or on Muḥammad. Only in the case where an apostate flees to the protection of another state with which the Islamic state has a contractual relationship will the individual be considered only as an unbeliever (*kāfir*)[344] and not as an apostate.

It is difficult to make out anything at all in this comparison which applies, as there is nothing common between a change of religion and the attempted assassination of a head of state in a Western democracy or monarchy. It becomes clear how Maudūdī perceives wards essentially as foreign bodies within Islamic societies who are guests more than as members of their own community. In addition to wards and citizens, Maudūdī defines a third category, the category of traitor, who possesses no legal status at all and for whom even the comparison to a deserter in time of war does not offer an adequate corresponding form. Furthermore, it becomes clear in equating an English king (and the United States' government and constitution) with Muḥammad or God just how little Maudūdī must have known of the political relationships in Europe or how little prepared he was to acknowledge facts when what was involved was finding arguments to undergird his point of view.

In addition, Maudūdī does not consider the fact that foreigners in Western countries are not second class citizens, in contrast to wards in Muslim majority countries. Rather, they enjoy the same human rights and have the same legal status. Furthermore, Maudūdī equates the special case of desertion of soldiers in the event of war and their punishment with a change of citizenship. And last but not least, Maudūdī – wrongly – compares laws passed as part of the democratic process (such as the Constitution of the United States) or the position of heads of state in constitutional states – even if they are dynastically legitimate – with the position of God or Muḥammad in an Islamic country.

Here[345] Maudūdī alters the argument of the right of every state to protect itself against disloyalty on the part of any citizens into a charge against the secular state when he argues that a secular state rests upon a "wrong foundation" (*bātil banā*) anyway and for that reason its existence represents "an offense" (*ek jurm*).[346] This offense becomes greater if the state resorts to force in order to form itself or to maintain itself. A comparison between an Islamic and a non-Islamic state is also unable to be made in this regard.

344 Ibid., p. 47.
345 Ibid., pp. 48-49.
346 Ibid., p. 49.

Maudūdī segues from the difference between an Islamic and a non-Islamic state to the difference between an unbeliever who never belonged to the Muslim community and an apostate:[347] Why does one of them receive rights as a *dimmī* (ward) and the other, as a *murtadd* (apostate), not?

The decisive difference, as Maudūdī remarks, lies in previous affiliation and the then complete separation from the community which naturally elicits strong resentment against such a person. Owing to the prior existing trust and bond, the treason weighs that much heavier, which adds dramatic harm to the community. It is no miracle that such a damaged community would demonstrate such a violent reaction and that as a reaction of it a "battle" (*jang*) breaks out.[348] According to Maudūdī, whoever shows himself to be treacherous has to be punished at all costs.[349] Strong emotions owing to a change of religion thus justify the use of force against those who think differently, and a changed conviction in the question of religion justifies the execution of the individual involved. This is Maudūdī's message.

At this point, Maudūdī resorts to the picture of the career soldier who voluntarily enters the army and for that reason cannot simply leave it at his discretion. If he nevertheless does so, according to Maudūdī he will be treated as a "criminal" (*mujrim*)[350] and can be imprisoned with a life sentence. If he flees the army in times of battle, he will be executed. If parts of an individual state split off into independent state structures, war is the consequence.

With that said, Maudūdī has again implied a certain inevitability with respect to the drastic consequences to be expected in the case of separation tendencies and a responsibility for one's own death that lies upon the victim for these consequences. The war-like actions arising are also shifted off to him without explaining wherein the harm to the community caused by the apostate lies and where the harm so emphatically attested to by Maudūdī exists in detail. Additionally, he suggests a comparison between the apostate and a deserter in time of war, such that Maudūdī perceives the Islamic state to be in a sort of state of war with non-Islamic states. It is a time when the lines have to be held closed because otherwise Islam would

347 Ibid., pp. 49-53.

348 Ibid., p. 50.

349 Ibid.

350 Ibid.

go under. This basic assumption can be documented in numerous other writings by Maudūdī.[351]

The reason for the fierce reaction to treason and separation is, according to Maudūdī, the necessity of building up trust and stability which gets lost through these jolts and then endangers the entire nation. Freedoms for such behaviour could be provided where nothing is at stake (Maudūdī chooses the example of a children's playground). However, where the weal and the woe of the community is decided – Maudūdī mentions the state, the military, and political parties[352] – no treason can be tolerated in order to prevent worse occurrences.

The danger of later separation, Maudūdī believes, can be effectively met by in this case by indicating prior to joining that there is an expected execution, such that the undecided are deterred from withdrawal. What is more, those who nevertheless insist on dissociation should be killed. Likewise, all of those in the future who believe that they have to take this path should be killed. Of course, such a procedure does not come into question for oppressive systems which would only increase their power through such a manner of behaviour. What is meant is doubtless the Islamic state called for by Maudūdī.

In this section Maudūdī employs a war-like, truculent choice of words. His words are anticipatory given the threatened execution with which he robs a concerned person of all dignity and every freedom of conscience and autonomy to decide and deprives him of any honest motivation. From Maudūdī's point of view, the motives for turning away from Islam could only be treason and malice as well as the desire to bring instability, chaos, and conflict upon an entire community. The result is that the community's countermeasures have to be solely seen as defense for the purpose of self-preservation and thus understandable.

A Comparison with Western Society

In the eleventh, comprehensive section of the chapter,[353] Maudūdī again turns in more detail to the view that the prohibition of apostasy would then

---

[351] For instance, his writing follows this characteristic style: Abū l-Aᶜlā. Maudūdī. *jihād fī 'l-sabīl allāh*. [Lahore, 1962].

[352] Maudūdī. *murtadd*, p. 52.

[353] Ibid., p. 53-57.

be a difficulty for the Islamic community if other religious communities threaten their adherents with death and thus make a conversion to Islam impossible, i.e., if Islam were not the only religion prohibiting apostasy. According to Maudūdī, this thought is not so relevant since all religions around the world prohibit apostasy where they have the opportunity to do so.

Needless to say, "all Christian nations" (*kull ʿīsā'ī qaumeṉ*) no longer punish apostasy nowadays.[354] Rather, they grant religious freedom. This leads to a situation where all people there no longer perceive apostasy as an offense. However, Christianity is only a religion and not an all-encompassing order for the state and society. It also does not become such an order of things even if influential powers are adherents of Christianity. This is due to the fact that the state concerned is nevertheless not a Christian state. For that reason, apostasy from Christianity is far less significant because it does not unsettle the foundations of the society and is thereby acceptable. Christianity is in such a state not the source of laws. Instead, the nation state and the constitution are the highest authorities upon which the state powers are based and from which dissociation is not tolerated.

What is striking at this point is how vague Maudūdī expresses himself when he speaks about circumstances in Western nations and how frequently he leaves things in abeyance. Indeed, in a number of cases he misleadingly argues, for example when he hints at the idea that a practicing Muslim believer in the Western context who rejects the foundations of Western states and associates himself with another community can likewise expect execution.

The partially irrelevant comparison may in some measure be attributable to his meager state of knowledge about the politics, society, and history of Western countries. Simultaneously, the rather coarse nature of the implied and sweeping nature of the alleged comparisons between the Western and the Islamic state as Maudūdī describes it in this work offers him the opportunity to summarily postulate a basis for comparison. He does this instead of keeping to differentiation and allowing arguments which would describe the circumstances in Western states according to their own self-understanding. At this point, Maudūdī treats Islam primarily as a political and social order; it only marginally appears as a religion.

---

[354] Ibid., p. 53.

With respect to the topic of apostasy, what is involved in the final large section of this chapter[355] is in the end the question of whether a differentiation has to be made between Muslims who converted to Islam at a later time and Muslims born into a Muslim family. Interestingly, at this point Maudūdī takes up the question of whether it is unjust if a child of Muslim parents, who has never made a decision for Islam, might under certain circumstances later want to leave Islam but then on account of the threatened punishment be unable to make this step and thus becomes a hypocrite.

According to Maudūdī, no difference can be made between children of Muslim parents and later converts – other religions also demand that members gained through birth practice the religion. In turn, Maudūdī makes an irrelevant comparison to other religions in which, indeed, the continuation of tradition might be expected but where the death penalty might not be a corresponding option for the individual who does not meet these expectations. Additionally, there might hardly ever be an authoritative religious and legal source available to postulate mandatory execution of the convert.

Also, from Maudūdī's point of view it would be practically impossible and intellectually utter nonsense (*ye bāt ᶜamalan nā-mumkin aur ᶜaqlan bil-kull laġw hai*)[356] to first raise children without religious education or without linking them to community life and then later to leave them to make an independent decision as to whether they want to associate with the religion or the state in which they have grown up. There is the simple reason that the community is dependent upon the following generation for its stability. For that reason, such a thought is to be decidedly rejected and in addition, Maudūdī believes, not practiced by any religion, community, or state on earth. This is due to the fact that every community would like to propagate its traditions, culture, and foundations to a new generation.

Those few, who nevertheless do not want to conform to the continuation of the aforesaid (Maudūdī assumes that given the proper rearing of youth this number should be under 1,000[357]) have the choice of either leaving this state or putting their life at risk. Thus, if a child of Muslim parents, as Maudūdī again emphasizes, wanted to turn his or her back on Islam, then that child is also to be executed as one who had converted to Islam

355 Ibid., pp. 57-60.
356 Ibid., p. 58.
357 Ibid.

and then later wanted to retract. There seems to be no dissent among Muslim legal experts and Sharia experts on this point. Maudūdī leaves nothing open to apostates other than to unconditionally call for execution.

As background to this discussion, Maudūdī points to foreign bodies of thought seeping in due to the educational system influenced by the West during colonial times. This led to increased resistance to and rejection of Islam. However, as Maudūdī adds almost threateningly at this point – approximately five years prior to the founding of Pakistan – once Islamic order is established at some point in the future, then the execution of apostates will have a legal anchor. Children of Muslim parents (Maudūdī hints between the lines here that he means those who do not truly practice Islam in a loyal manner and for that reason, as hypocrites, present a threat to the community) have to be thrown in prison, and if they leave Islam, they have to be executed.

With that said, Maudūdī no longer threatens actual apostasy without exception with the most severe penalty. Rather, he also threatens the attitude of those who as children of Muslim parents continue to belong to the Muslim community but are possibly not truly and completely rooted in Islam. Maudūdī does not mention any investigative instrument which there might be as an aid in determining such an attitude. However, the threats he verbalizes are of a fundamental nature.

How does the implementation of such measures look for Maudūdī after an Islamic order has been established? After the inhabitants have been subjected to the teaching and practice of Islam, apostates should be given one year to emigrate. Whoever has left Islam should make this publicly known and then separate themselves from the community. Whoever remains within the borders of the Islamic states would be treated as a believing Muslim after the expiration of one year and made subject to Islamic laws. Indeed, they would be forced to follow Islamic doctrine.[358] Whoever refuses to follow the duties of the faith and positions himself outside of the Islamic community has to unavoidably suffer the death penalty.

It becomes clear at this point that in Maudūdī's eyes the failure to fulfil the obligatory doctrine means apostasy. Apostasy does not only mean one's own confession of it. Maudūdī naturally means that as many children as possible have to be saved from the claws of unbelief. However, where

358 Ibid., p. 60.

that is unsuccessful, they have to be executed, as sad as that may be (!). After this act of "purification" (*aᶜmal-e-taṯhīr*),[359] Maudūdī notes in ideological armumentation that a new stage of life could then begin for Islamic society, for only true, practicing Muslims would live in such a state.

The Prohibition on Missions Work for non-Muslims

A short fourth and final chapter is added by Maudūdī to these three comprehensive chapters.[360] It answers the last part of the question posed at the outset by the reader. It involves the justification for refusing non-Muslims the right to propagate their faith, which Maudūdī classifies here as "unbelief" (*kufr*). This is due to the fact that if non-Muslims may freely propagate their faith, apostasy will be the result.

On the one hand, Maudūdī observes, non-Muslims are allowed to teach their faith in their own community. Additionally, Islam has no objections if an *ḏimmī* exchanges his religion for another non-Islamic faith. However, what is strictly forbidden in an Islamic area is the establishment of an organization which has the intention of soliciting Muslims to join another religion. A secular state can tolerate such action, for after all it tolerates wickedness, immorality, and deviation from religion. There one solely proceeds against those who challenge the authority of the state and is otherwise only interested in materialistic issues. However, in the interest of the well-being of God's servants, the Islamic state can tolerate neither the promotion of another political order nor the propagation of error and immorality.

Since Islam is simply the truth, an individual who preaches something else cannot be given permission to spread falsehood and insanity. There can be no discussion about this at all. And although Islam only brings what is good and agreeable to humanity, it has frequently been humiliated and is mentioned in the same breath with other (false) religions. Soon, however, Islam, the religion of truth, with its true adherents and heralds, will humble the "*ṭāġūt*" (idols, corrupters, Satan)[361] and see the truth conquer. With this triumphalistic outlook for the future, Maudūdī's work closes on the topic of the "punishment of apostates according to the law of Islam."

---

359 Ibid.

360 Ibid., pp. 61-64.

361 Ibid.

Summary: Maudūdī's View of Apostasy

In the center of Maudūdī's work *murtadd ki sazā islāmī qānūn mēn̠* is the question of the preservation and continued existence of the Islamic state. From Maudūdī's point of view, this Islamic state is threatened from without – above all through invasion by Western powers, but also propagated through ideologies, materialism, and godlessness. It has to be defended and protected in order to not be undercut and weakened. Possible dangers have to be repelled with complete resolve. If the community of "wards" remains within the framework of their own limited freedom of movement, as subjects who have been vanquished into humility, they do not represent such a danger. However, the case of apostasy is essentially different because such individuals have made up their minds to be rebellious and, with that said, move outside of all prescribed bounds of legal existence. They bring adverse effects upon the social structures regulated by the Sharia simply through their existence. For that reason, the topic of apostasy is for Maudūdī first of all not a set of religious or theological questions. Rather, it is above all a politically motivated attack on the Islamic state.

With this treatise, Maudūdī expresses himself very fundamentally and uncompromisingly on the topic of apostasy, religious freedom, and freedom of speech in an Islamic state, and he places very strict limits on everyone who deviates from his definition of an Islamic state. Even the title of this treatise makes it clear that Maudūdī is not describing his personal opinion but rather desires to speak with the authority of "Islamic law," i.e., the Sharia. However, he does this without considering various statements from the sources (Quran and *sunna*) upon which the Sharia is based and various theological viewpoints. Maudūdī only cites a few names in order to reinforce his presentation; he is himself the most important authority for his argumentation.

Time and time again, he repeats his central statements and essential thoughts. What are intellectually not very profound explanations are repostulated over and over in an inflammatory manner. As a result, neither the scholar nor the theologian Maudūdī becomes hardly visible in this work. Maudūdī barely uses theological vocabulary. It is, rather, the political activist and demagogue who demands, asserts himself, proclaims, condemns, and calls for action by above all things authoritatively throwing himself and his powers of persuasion on the scales. In the process it becomes clear that with respect to the practical application of his understanding of an ideal Islamic state – where there can be no dissent concerning the appropriate implementation of Islam – Maudūdī makes practically no statements. Throughout his life, Maudūdī defended the position that this Islamic state would emerge on its own where all of the citizens obey the law of God.

For Maudūdī, the Islamic community consists not only of the community of believers, the *umma*, who assemble for Friday prayer. Rather, it consists of the state structure in which Islam is legally anchored and is comprehensively applied. For Maudūdī, correctly understood Islam necessitates the application of the Sharia including the penal code, since a reduction of Islam to the realm of private faith contradicts what, from his point of view, Islam was from its beginnings: a comprehensive life and legal order. For that reason, the deciding question is not – as it indeed is for al-Qaraḍawī – whether the apostate takes the offensive and speaks about his new worldview or keeps it quietly to himself. What counts is the fact that he exists at all within the bounds of an Islamic state and thereby endangers this state. This is due to the fact that he has broken out of the designed order, independent of whether he additionally propagates his view or not.

It is striking in this connection that Maudūdī has no view for the realitites of modernity, with its multi-religious societies, the free exchange of worldviews independent of national borders, or migrations of entire people groups with other religious affiliation. Especially at the end of his work on apostasy, it becomes clear that he conceives of an almost homogeneous society within which borders ideally only Muslims live or at best the subjugated *people of the book* should be tolerated.

Because he so consistently dismisses reality, he also nowhere describes concretely in this work what religious freedom means for tolerated non-Muslims and minorities: To which degree may their faith be made visible in the public sphere – through religious instruction, for instance, the building of churches or temples, processions, and celebrations? What would happen if Muslisms seek out discussions with other religious communities? Is dialog allowed or only *daᶜwa*? Is apostasy from Islam first bound up with an acceptance ritual conducted with respect to the other religion (baptism, for example) or are there other, unambiguous characteristics of apostasy? Who would be in a legitimate position to issue a sentence and to execute it? Also, the question frequently discussed throuout the centuries of whether the apostate should be offered the opportunity to repent does not arise anywhere in Maudūdī's writing. For that reason, this publication is more of an ideological verdict than a set of practical directions on how to act.

From Maudūdī's perspective, Islam requires not only the mosque for its correct implementation. Rather, it also requires the state and society. Indeed, the Islamic state first of all provides him the precondition for an individual's life that can conform to Islam. The renewal of the Islamic society happens from the bottom up in the case of al-Qaraḍāwī, i.e., through building conscious awareness, through education, and through equipping the individual with knowledge and self-confidence so that slowly its ability grows to conduct *daʿwa* and to take up key positions in the non-Islamic community. At the same time, in Maudūdī's view the renewal has to occur from the top down. This is due to the fact that the state first has to produce the framework for a life conforming to Islam, whereupon the citizens of the state then fulfil this space with behaviour conforming to the norms.

Nowhere does Maudūdī define or account for what is to be understood by "Islam," as if there was only one understanding of what makes up the core of Islam and how it should be implemented. He speaks frequently of "Islam" in a personalized manner. He does this as if one were dealing with an autonomously acting subject as well as a clearly defined entity in which there are no differences at all with respect to the differing schools of legal thought, "denominations" such as Sunnis and Shi'ites, or theological traditions. Furthermore, nowhere does he point to the legitimacy of divergent understandings. Additionally, he builds a direct bridge between the early days of Islam and modernity by linking both poles through the topic of the necessity of a life conforming to Islam. However, he does so by completely dismissing the checkered Islamic history between both of these poles.

Maudūdī makes no difference between the quiet doubter and the open propagandist for a newly gained disposition. He does not differentiate between personal religious freedom and religious affiliation. The "apostate" remains a faceless being, a usurper and destroyer who deserves no understanding and forbearance. The apostate's possible motives in no way concern Maudūdī. According to Maudūdī's opinion, changed attitudes can only come from outside through the harmful operations of foreign powers. Why, however, people can become apostates in spite of the threatened dramatic consequences, does not at all come into Maudūdī's field of vision.

According to Maudūdī's presentation, the apostate is a being about whom hardly anything remains human. He labels him a danger, as morbid bacteriam which radiates "poison" and brings destruction upon the society. For that reason, the apostate's activities cannot be tolerated. He has to either be caused to emigrate or executed. If a Muslim citizen converts, the individual, who beforehand was endowed with all civil rights, becomes an ogre who has given up his citizenship and can no longer claim any rights at all – not even the right to life. Wherever this degrading, destructive characterization is made of fellow human beings and has hatred and persecution as its result, it is reminiscent of the memory of Hrant Dink's death and his legacy of the "seed of the word" as well as the deaths of many additional victims of hatred and intolerance which have been preceded by such destructive words.

Maudūdī limits his stigmitization of the "apostate" so that there is much room left for the reader to individually fill this term and open the flood gates for their own interpretations. The verdict of execution is absolutely formulated. However, in the end the "how" and the "why" remain uncertain so that this work, in the hands of unscrupulous self-appointed Sharia watchmen, could even serve ideological justification for autonomous judgments or, under certain circumstances, could even serve independent actions against those who think differently, especially since any warning against vigilante justice is missing.

The combination of the content of ambiguously defined terminology and the very emphatically stated demand for the death penalty provide an idealogically rich breeding ground for the condemnation of those who think differently, minorities, atheists, or those who change religions. Since Maudūdī only speaks very generally about apostasy and simultaneously sets his own understanding of Islam in an absolute sense while not considering other understandings found within Islamic theology, this work virtually invites diverging opinions to be subsumed under this verdict, especially since Maudūdī expresses many sweepingly negative prejudices against Western societies and non-Muslims. With that said, he strongly generalizes and disparages "the others" within his black and white classification.

With respect to apostasy, there is for Maudūdī no bridge of understanding and free space for peaceful coexistence, no moderation, and no middle way for him. On the contrary, for Maudūdī it is solely a matter of the uncompromising application of Islamic law, within which bounds he perceives an indispensible duty to execute apostates. Everything else, according to his perspective, is harmful influence from the outside and in the final event abandons God's order.

Maudūdī's work can be labeled as having more of the character of a polemic, which in a dualistic and in part aggressively disparaging manner only acknowledges one law, namely the right of the Islamic community to recognition of its prominent status and its unique character. Derived from this is its worthiness of being protected from destabilization. Maudūdī argues acutely sweepingly and without differentiation. He posits and threatens. His argumentation is strongly ideologically colored, and with respect to its ability to monitor worldviews, it is idealistic out of touch with reality with respect to the "maintainance of the purity" of the Islamic community.

4.3.3. The Rights of non-Muslims in an Islamic State ("Islāmī ḥukūmat mēn̲ d̲immīyōn̲ kē ḥuqūq") – 1948

In a number of his works, Abū l-Aᶜlā Maudūdī discusses the legal position of non-Muslims in an Islamic state. As early as 1948, i.e., at the time of the formation of Pakistan, Maudūdī composed his program agenda *Islāmī ḥukūmat mēn̲ d̲immīyōn̲ kē ḥuqūq* (*The Rights of non-Muslims in the Islamic State*). From 1961 to 1982 it was published in seven English editions[362] and above all, after it had appeared as part of an anthology entitled *The Islamic Law and Constitution*, was counted among the most renowned and most widely disseminated of all of Maudūdī's works.[363]

This work, which compares the special features of the Islamic state with (Western) nation states that always oppress their minorities and are even out to see their extermination, was developed in 1948. It was developed as a response to a questionnaire which had been presented by the constituent assembly to various "experts" in preparation for a constitution defining the position of non-Muslims in an Islamic state. Maudūdī had initially published his opinions in 1948 in his internal publication *Tarjumān al-Qur'ān* and also within the same year as an independent document.

362 S. Abu A'la Mawdudi. *Rights of Non-Muslims in Islamic State* (sic). Islamic Publications Limited: Lahore, 1961/1982[7].

363 This work of Maudūdī had been inserted later into the following anthology: Mawdudi. *Islamic Law*, pp. 273-299.

Sharia Standards Regarding the Position of non-Muslims

Since at that time Maudūdī took his very strong starting point to be the imminent realization of an Islamic state, he primarily treated the topic within the question of which Sharia standards are to be observed by non-Muslims in a completely Islamized society. In the process, he exclusively bore "essentially an ideological state"[364] in mind when considering the minority situation of non-Muslims in an Islamic state.

According to Maudūdī, all people in the state are judged pursuant to their faith and their relationship to the ideological foundations of the Islamic state. Since non-Muslims do not share these ideological foundations, they cannot basically enjoy an equal coexistence. Rather, they can only claim reduced legal status. From Maudūdī's point of view, this contractual relationship is, on the one hand, above all characterized by the guarantee of protection and possession for the *ḏimmī*, the guarantee of honor, and the freedom to be able to practice one's own religion since the Islamic state guarantees freedom of belief and freedom of conscience as well as protection from tyranny.[365] This relationship of protection becomes legally binding through the payment of the *ǧizya* r, and the refusal to do so brings punishment, such as prison sentences.

Of course, non-Msulims are not able to participate in the formation of policy in an Islamic state. Their principle participation in the "leglislative assembly" is possible as long as they do not attempt to infringe upon the ideological foundations of the state. They may not form policy,[366] and they are not able to assume socially influential positions. Additionally, they are prohibited from publishing and disseminating teaching which is opposed to Islam. The Islamic state defines the ideology to which everyone must adapt, and non-Muslims have to at least adapt through loyal behaviour. Equitable pluralism, however, is not tolerated by this state.

Non-Muslims as Contractual Partners and Subjects

Maudūdī subdivides all non-Muslims into three different groupings:[367] contractual partners which acknowledge the Islamic state and enter into a

---

364 Mawdudi. *Rights of Non-Muslims*, p. 1.

365 Ibid., pp. 7-9.

366 Ibid., p. 2.

regulated relationship with Islam through an agreement, non-Muslims who owing to their defeat in war against Muslims are now subjects, and non-Muslims who in another way have come to be domiciled in an Islamic country. Places of worship and shrines can be captured. However, it is more honourable to leave them untouched. Muslims and non-Muslims are subject to the same penal code in an Islamic state. Wards do not lose their status through lawbreaking. Rather, they lose it through leaving the territory and defecting to enemies or though open revolt against the state with the goal being its destruction.[368]

As far as the extent of religious freedom is concerned, wards are free to practice their faith in their own residential areas. However, in Muslim residential areas there are limitations with respect to the exercise of religion in public and ceremonies which are held there. Their places of worship and shrines may be maintained but no new ones are allowed to be erected. This should definitely be allowed in non-Muslim residential areas.

Non-Muslims are not able to be elected as state leaders and cannot become members of the *Šūrā*. Likewise, they may not participate in setting state policies and for that reason may not be placed in influential government offices and ministries. In a modern legislative body or parliament not representing a *Šūrā*, non-Muslims can participate, provided that all laws are passed in conformity with the Quran and the *sunna* and non-Muslims do not call the ideological basis of the state into question. Another possibility is the establishment of a parliament that only consists of non-Muslims and only regulates their affairs.[369]

Non-Muslims, as Maudūdī continues, have the same freedom of conscience, freedom of opinion, and freedom to express these opinions – even to express thoughts which are critical of Islam – to the same measure which Muslims themselves have. They are even allowed to criticize the governement and its representatives. Non-Muslims may change their religion among themselves – of course, however, no Muslim can convert to one of their religions.[370]

Accordingly, only Muslims have the full set of rights in an Islamic state, whereby men are legally favored over women. Non-Muslims who

---

367 Ibid., pp. 6ff.
368 Ibid., p. 15.
369 Ibid., pp. 27-30.
370 Ibid., pp.27-29.

acknowledge the sovereignty of the Islamic state possess limited rights, and groups not fulfilling these criteria, such as adherents of the Aḥmadīya movement and apostates, possess no rights at all in an Islamic state.

4.3.4. The Aḥmadīya Question ("Qādiyānī mas'ala") – 1953

The story of the development of this work[371] in connection with Maudūdī's political activity with the goal of transforming Pakistan into an Islamic state has already been discussed in Section 4.1.7. I would like to concentrate here on the significant contents of this comprehensive treatise on the justification of the exclusion of the Aḥmadīya movement from the community of Muslims owing to the charge of apostasy.

The Aḥmadīya Movement as an independent religio-political Group

This work opposes the branch of the Aḥmadīya movement which, on account of its being located in Qādiyān, is labelled Qādiyānī. It held firmly to the claims of the founder of the movement Mīrzā Ġulām Aḥmad that he was not a recipient of a revelatory document but of a message of God. The more moderate Lāhōrī group (named after their whereabouts in Lāhōr) only labelled their founder a "reformer" (*mujaddid*).

In the first part of his work *Qādiyānī mas'ala*, Maudūdī goes into what from his point of view are the theological as well as politically objectionable and dangerous ambitions of the Qādiyānī. Throughout his entire work, his intention appears to be to portray the Qādiyānī as primarily a political group who consummated a break from the Muslim *umma* of their own accord and is highly dangerous for it in a political respect.

By bringing in numerous quotes from Qādiyānī publications, Maudūdī initially vehemently opposes their rejection of the finality of the sending of Muḥammad.[372] This is a point of view which is to be flatly rejected. He charges the Qādiyānī group with claiming that all who do not share their opinion are unbelievers, with delimiting themselves from Muslims with respect to their beliefs and their religious practices, and as having defined themselves as an independent group. For this Maudūdī repeatedly quotes

[371] Maudūdī. *Qādiyānī mas'ala.*

[372] Ibid., pp. 4ff.

from the publications of the movement itself. On account of their differentiation, the Qādiyānī, according to Maudūdī, have declared themselves to be their own *umma*, "another religion" (*judā madhab*).[373] With these words, it is from the very beginning that Maudūdī ascribes to the Qādiyānī, as a group separating itself from Islam, the responsibility for their non-recognition as Muslims and all of the consequences resulting from that.[374]

However, he does not leave it at that. He demands that the Qādiyānī be made an example and separated from the umma by the Muslim community so that other groups do not dare take similar steps.[375] This preventive measure against a further fragmentation of the umma – thus the avoidance of the political danger of a weakening of the Muslim nation – is the strongest argument for declaring the Qādiyānī to be non-Muslims, as he discusses in the following: Their plan is to found their own Qādiyān ī state within the state of Pakistan, thus committing treason.[376] For that reason, the majority of Muslims want separation from the Qādiyānī, since it is the majority who suffer the actual "damage" (*nuqṣān*) through the propaganda of the minority.[377] And this was all the more the case when the Qādiyānī exhibited loyalty towards the British colonial rulers and thereby committed another breach of loyalty.

The Aḥmadīya Adherents as Collaborators and State Founders

Maudūdī next summarizes the four significant charges against the Aḥmadīya adherents, the Qādiyānī, by occasionally interspersing charges against the Pakistani government and leaders, respectively, in the following manner:[378] a) They condemned everyone who does not believe in what they maintain to be a continuation of the prophetic office by Mīrzā Ġulām Aḥmad; b) they thereby created a new category of belief and unbelief within Islam and organized themselves into a new umma; c) over against the British colonial rulers they behaved loyally, thereby promoting colonial rule and declared this attitude as an expression of their faith; and d) the

373 Ibid., p. 9.
374 Ibid., pp. 17-18.
375 Ibid., p. 13.
376 Ibid., pp. 22-24.
377 Ibid., p. 24.
378 Ibid., pp. 33-36.

British recognized the Qādiyānī as a Muslim group, which led to an increase in their numbers, since many Muslims did not understand that joining the Qādiyānī was identical with giving up Islam.

Sponsored in this way, the Qādiyānī, according to Maudūdī, were able to secure numerous posts, for instance in the army and in the police forces, and to place adherent of its religious community in additional positions. If they were able to become stronger, according to Maudūdī, they would threaten Muslims' existence. Muslims would then not be able to achieve anything without the Qādiyānī who were placed in influential positions, and they would no longer be able to establish an independent state.

The Aḥmadīya Adherents as "Cancers" and Unbelievers

It is apparent that Maudūdī – according to his depiction – saw himself personally threatened by the strengthening Qādiyānī community in his yearlong efforts, which at this time had been to call an Islamic state into life. He insinuates that they are pursuing separatism, the formation of their own polity within Pakistan, political dominance, and collaboration with the enemy. This is an insinuation which is understandable based on Maudūdī's equating religious affiliation and citizenship. As Maudūdī concludes this argumentation, excluding the Qādiyānī from the community of Muslims is, for that reason, inevitable. This is because they are like a "cancer" (*saraṭān*).[379] As a consequence, they may not hold any influential posts, and Minister Zafrullah Khan, who was among their adherents, had to be pushed out of ministerial position.

In this work, Maudūdī repeatedly reverts to polemics, bitter charges and accusations against the rulers of Pakistan and leaders of the state. He calls upon them to present their arguments if they deviate from his. Indeed, Maudūdī distances himself from all forms of pressure which are utilized in order to bring about action from the government in the course of the 1953 unrest. On the other hand, however, he simultaneously formulates a bitter charge against those who are ruling. From his point of view, they do not want to recognize the true problematic situation with respect to the Aḥmadīya movement.

In the second part, the work contains four excerpts from addresses which are mentioned under 4.1.7. The excerpts are from Maudūdī's hear-

[379] Ibid., p. 36.

ing before the "Court of Inquiry" and are from statements by a number of politicians and *ᶜulamā'* on the topic of the Aḥmadīya.[380]

In his first address, Maudūdī again emphasized the condemnation by the Qādiyānī of all such Muslims not sharing their understanding of the sending of Mīrzā Ġulām Aḥmad as "unbelievers" (*kāfir*).[381] As a consequence and according to Maudūdī, Muslims from all theological schools viewed the Qādiyānī as unbelievers. He discusses that the conflict between Qādiyānī and Muslims began with the Qādiyānī. They sought to win adherents from among the Muslims and at the same time, for their part, had drawn a line of separation between themselves and Muslims (for instance with respect to marriage and ritualistic prayer).

The Aḥmadīya Movement Justifies Being Seen as a "new Religion"

The second and third attachments consist of a statement by a group of 33 adherents of the *ᶜulamā'*, at the head of which Maudūdī placed himself for his campaign against the Aḥmadīya movement. As a result of its consultations on the conflict, this group presents the solution that the Qādiyānī should exist with the classification of an independent religion.

Attachment three consists of various statement by Muhammad Iqbal (d. 1938), in which he warned in the past of the danger of a conflict caused by the Qādiyānī and stated his endorsement of a separation between Muslims and this "new community"[382]. Furthermore, a text by Jawaharlal Nehru is added, which labelled the Qādiyānī as a danger to the Muslim community. The attachment closes with the depiction of a Muslim married couple from Bahawalpur and their divorce judgment. It dates from 1935 and became legally binding after the conversion of the husband to the Aḥmadīya movement and judicially determined apostasy was the result. This incident serves Maudūdī as an additional puzzle piece in the chain of evidence which he constructed in order to demonstrate that what one was dealing with in the matter of the Qādiyānī group was non-Muslims.[383]

---

380 Ibid., p. 38ff.

381 Ibid., p. 39.

382 Appendix two and three are exclusively found in the English edition of the text: Maududi. *The Qadiani Problem*, p. 65.

383 Ibid., pp. 59-76.

The last part of the treatment consists of a summary of a second and third statement of opinion by Maudūdī before the "Court of Inquiry."[384]

In the first of the two texts, Maudūdī justifies why Zafrullah Khan was removed from his ministerial post and Qādiyānī essentially were unable to receive access to influential positions and, more specifically, why they were to be removed from posts already held. Maudūdī emphasizes that in this connection it is not only a matter of a theological question. Rather, it involves a "conflict issue" (*nizāᶜ*) with "social" and "political" reach. For that reason, a political solution had to be found.[385] Zafrullah Khan misused his position in order to confer advantages upon the Qādiyānī in the way other members of this community attempt to fill as many government positions as possible and take the government (*ḥukūmat*) of Pakistan into their hands![386]

At this point, Maudūdī sketches the picture of a threatening socio-political conquest by Qādiyānī adherents throughout all the country who are out to serve their own interests and are subversive and strategically animated by the desire to achieve a position of power. Therefore, to defend oneself against them in order to ensure one's own survival is a valid approach. Theologially, according to Maudūdī, their convictions are really a matter of a new notion that is not compatible with the foundational teachings of Islam.

The Inescabability of Excluding the Aḥmadīya Movement from Islam

For this reason, Maudūdī's concluding judgment in his second address before the "Court of Inquiry" reads that in order to avoid the inescapably looming conflict between both groups, it is imperative that the Qādiyānī either give up their adherence to Mīrzā Ġulām Aḥmad and/or exist outside of the *umma* as an independent community. Maudūdī does not only call for a pragmatic solution at this point but rather simultaneously a legal provision.[387] This can by all means be interpreted as a preannouncement of what

384 Maudūdī. *Qādiyānī mas'ala*, pp. 53ff.

385 Ibid., p. 53.

386 Ibid., p. 58.

387 Ibid., pp. 69-70.

later ensued as the exclusion of this movement from the community of Muslims.

Maudūdī closes this segment by explaining instructions for a process of exclusion of those who have lapsed into unbelief: This is unambiguously the case among the Qādiyānī, and their exclusion from Islam is compulsory. This is due to the fact that it is not possible for Muslims, as believers, to be associated with them, as unbelievers, in one *umma*. Maudūdī's basic understanding of a community again becomes clear at this point. It is an understanding which is religious and political at the same time. Indeed, it is one where there is no place for minorities not moving within the framework of the categories of "Muslim" or "tolerated *people of the book*" and even exercise political power and canvass for converts.[388]

In his concluding third statement before the "Court of Inquiry", Maudūdī concentrates more robustly on a theological justification for the exclusion of the Qādiyānī from the community of Muslims and on a polemical and derogatory condemnation of their theological specifics, in particular their understanding of the sending of Mīrzā Ġulām Aḥmad and their interpretation of the return of the Messiah.[389]

In order to justify the social and political marginalization and the exclusion of the Qādiyānī from the community of Muslims, which Maudūdī calls for, he argues at this point very strongly with what is, according to his understanding, the Qādiyānī's already consummated separation as well as its *takfīr* of all other Muslims. With that said, the exclusion of, or more specifically the marginalization of, the Qādiyānī is only declared to be a reaction to a threatened, perhaps even soon to be minority community of Muslims. As a result, Maudūdī calls upon the community of believers to employ their political power against rebels. In the process, he leaves no doubt that from his point of view he is unambiguously dealing with unbelievers (*kāfir*) when it comes to the Qādiyānī.[390]

Interestingly, Maudūdī does not argue here that the Qādiyānī used to be Muslims, thus being apostates in the actual sense. He merely labels them as "unbelievers." With that said, after he divides all remaining citizens into wards, they are without rights in an Islamic state. The consequence of their

---

388 Ibid., p. 73.

389 Ibid., pp. 79ff.

390 Ibid., p. 55. Maudūdī does not use the term *murtadd* (apostate) but rather consistently *kāfir* (unbeliever).

unbelief, however, which would be the unconditionally imposed death penalty, and which Maudūdī names in his work *murtadd ki sazā islāmī qānūn mēn̲* in all explicitness, is not mentioned anywhere here. Does this happen because Maudūdī fears his arrest when he directly calls for the execution of his fellow human beings? After all, a member of the government, among them Zafrullah Khan, is to be found among them.

On the other hand, Maudūdī was able to dispense with the call for the death penalty without weakening his message, when his work on apostasy, *murtadd ki sazā islāmī qānūn mēn̲*, had appeared for the first time in 1942/43 in the journal *Tarjumān al-Qur'ān*. Although Maudūdī does not directly speak of "apostasy" and explicitly demand the execution of Qādiyānī, the government must have taken Maudūdī's condemnation of this movement as well as his bitter criticism of the government so seriously that they had Maudūdī arrested for it – expressly for composing this work – and had him sentenced to death.[391]

This work on the Qādiyānī presumably counts among Maudūdīs most politically influential works. As early as 1953, the year of the "Punjab Disturbances," i.e., the unrest which broke out over the question of how to evaluate the Qādiyānī, it was simultaneously published in English and Urdu. In the 1960s, a refutation of the central thoughts of Qādiyānī theology additionally appeared under Maudūdī's authorship in Arabic.[392]

In 1975, there was likewise a written statement published by the World League – admittedly hardly theologically argued – with the title *Der Qadjanismus. Destruktive Bewegungen.*[393] It is noteworthy that a refutation of

---

[391] According to Kalim Bahadur, the writing was not forbidden irrespective of that fact, and as early as March 23, 1953 the *Jamāᶜat-i-Islāmī* indicated that 57,000 copies had already been sold: Kalim Bahadur. *The Jama'at-i-Islami of Pakistan. Political Thought and Political Action.* Chetana Publications: New Dehli, 1977, p. 72.

[392] The Arabic version available to me originated in 1969: Abū l-Aᶜlā Maudūdī. *mā hiya 'l-qādiyānīya? dirāsa šāmila wa-ᶜarḍ ᶜilmī li-l-qādiyānīya wa-madā tā'ṯīrihā fi 'l-muǧtamaᶜ al-'islāmī.* dār al-qalam: Kuwait, 1969.

[393] Mohammed Al Khoder Hussein; Abu Al Aala Al Mawdudi; Abu Al Hassan Ali Al Hassani Al Nadwi. *Abhandlungen über den Qadjanismus.* Liga der Islamischen Welt: Mekka, 1975. This treatment, tainted with numerous errors of expression and grammar consists of four parts: The first comes from the pen of Ḥassanein Muḥammad Maḫlūf, one of the constituent members of the World League who comments polemically about the "destructive movement of the Qadianis these

the Aḥmadīya movement would appear in the face of its being a conflict located in Pakistan. Did this occur because many of its adherents had turned towards Germany due to persecution of the movement in Pakistan and had published a German-Arabic edition of the Quran as early as 1954,[394] which then represented something absolutely novel as far as its bilingual format was concerned?

4.3.5. "Let there be no compulsion in religion" (Sura 2:256) – 1955

An additional, rather comprehensive, statement from Maudūdī's pen on the complex of problems surrounding apostasy stems from the middle of the 1950s: In June 1955, the historian Freeland K. Abbott posed fifteen written questions to Maudūdī with the request that they be answered personally.

---

saboteurs" (ibid., p. 5) and whom he invalidates as apostates and labels the founder of the movement "mentally ill," addicted to drugs, and a "big liar" (ibid., p. 6+9-10). As the occasion for his opinion, he mentions the World League's review of the translation of the Quran by the Qādiyānī, which he judges to be completely distorted. The second part consists of a comprehensive position statement by Abū l-Ḥasan ᶜAlī al-Nadwī on the unrest in 1953, in which connection he sharply criticizes the arrest of the *ᶜulamā'* by the government (ibid., p. 36), defines the Qādiyānī movement as an "invention of English politics in India" (ibid., p.20) and their publications as "meager, daft literature in which one only comes across a pale style, scurrilous words, indecent insults, blatant contradictions, unvarnished lies . . . preposterous and childish interpretations." al-Nadwī's polemic increases when he speaks of the "nest of espionage . . . headquarters of the fifth column in the Islamic world and the bordello of of all whores," of the "source of decay . . . the disease in the body of the Islamic world" (ibid., pp. 44-45); finally, he declares: "Hence, Qadianism was a crime against all of humanity," "an impardonable . . . wrongdoing against the dignity of all people (ibid., p.46). –Such a use of language corresponds to justifying every denunciation of the movement and prepares the ideological soil for a physical annihilation of those who allegedly wreak so much damage. Part four consists of Maudūdī's writing: Abū l-Aᶜlā Maudūdī. "Qādiyānī mas'ala." [Karachi, 1953] (ibid., pp. 47-95). In the final part, Muḥammad Ḥoḍr Ḥussein helps himself to language which is rich in contrast when he threatens that the "conceited ignoramuses . . . [would] soon have their tongues cut out" (ibid., p. 97) before then dedicating himself to a very apologetically derogatory presentation of the founder and the faith of the Qādiyānī ("stupidness," "nonsense," "contortions," "diabolical insinuations"; ibid., pp. 108+111+112+124).

[394] Hazrat Mirza Nasir Ahmad. Der Heilige Qur'ân. Ahmadiyya-Bewegung, no location provided, 1980[4].

Ten of those questions had to do with the topic of apostasy. At that time, Maudūdī already held an influential position; for one thing, there was his successful activity in support of a constitution which was to define Pakistan as an Islamic state. Additionally, however, was his having successfully placed himself at the head of the anti-Aḥmadīya movement. At the time of the correspondence between Abbott and Maudūdī, it was only two years after the dispute with this movement.

Although Freeland K. Abbott's questions were very direct and critically formulated, it was only a few months later that he received answers from Maudūdī. Maudūdī had published the answers prior thereto in his journal *Tarjumān al-Qur'ān*. Three years later, in 1958, Freeland K. Abbott's questions as well as Maudūdī's answers were published in the journal *The Muslim World*.[395]

Does not the Execution of an Apostate Mean "Compulsion"?

The first eight questions and the last two questions are interesting for the topic of religious freedom and apostasy. The first eight questions revolve around the significance and the interpretation of Sura 2:256: "Let there be no compulsion in religion." Abbott inquires about the substantive meaning of the term "compulsion" as well as the theological significance and practical application of the rejection of "coercion" in "religion." Does compulsion exist when, for example, conversion to Islam offers financial advantages? Did the persecution of the Bahā'ī in Iran and the 1953 unrest in Pakistan in connection with the Aḥmadīya occur in conformity with this verse or in contradiction to it? How does the message in Sura 2:256 relate to political power and majority conditions?

Question six is ultimately aimed at the complex of problems relating to apostasy. Would the execution of an apostate practiced in an Islamic state not mean "compulsion in religion"?[396]

Questions nine to thirteen involve the permission to engage in polygamy, the principles of interpretation in light of – from Abbott's point of view – contradictory verses in the Quran, the question of justifying authoritative interpretations of the Quran, the justification of recruiting for Islam

[395] Freeland K. Abbot. "Maulānā Maudūdī on Quranic Interpretation" in: *MW* 48/1 (1958), pp. 6-19.

[396] Ibid., p. 8.

among those tho think differently in light of Sura 2:256, and the effects of scientific knowledge on the interpretation of the Quran.

On the other hand, the last two questions relate to the topic of apostasy and religious freedom: Question 14 relates to the charge of corruption of the Scriptures by Muslim theologians, and Question 15 exposes the problems of a voluntary acceptance of Islam in light of inherited religious affiliation through birth.

No One can be Forced to Accept Islam

Initially, Maudūdī places an introductory text before his answer.[397] In the introductory text, he generally discusses a way to approach the text of the Quran. For example, he does this by occupying himself with the Arabic original, through an examining the context in detail, or by comparing the text with related verses. He emphasizes that indeed the unconditional truth of the existence of God is not up for discussion but that according to Sura 2:256 no individual is forced to turn to this belief, even if in the final event the individual doing so harms himself.

Admittedly, according to Maudūdī, there is no freedom with respect to true offenses and trespasses: The Quran contains unambiguous instructions having to do with this, and indeed "in regard to various crimes."[398] In order to enforce what is commanded there and to repress what is forbidden, the application of coercion with the help of state force or moral pressure exerted within society is indispensable. In this respect, coercion thus by all means exists and is legitimate.

The formulation "no coercion in religion" is thus exclusively limited to the question of whether a person can be forced to accept Islam, which Maudūdī expressly denies. This assumption can only occur of one's own complete accord. Muḥammad and his companions also never forced anyone to convert. Whoever wanted to retain his beliefs possessed full rights ("unabridged freedom in matters of faith").[399] Whoever becomes a Muslim is, as a consequence, by all means placed in the position of being able to be forced to keep the commands of Islam. Indeed, this can also be done with the aid of state force.

---

[397] Ibid., pp. 8-9.

[398] Ibid., p. 9.

[399] Ibid., p. 10.

In what follows, Maudūdī goes into each of the individual fifteen questions with a separately identified section: He does not comment on the situation of the Bahā'ī in Iran. With respect to the Aḥmadīya movement, Maudūdī speaks of a "gross misunderstanding," for no one in Pakistan would ever have called for them to be displaced from the country or for them to be extinguished, nor that they should renounce Qadianismus or that they would be robbed of their "normal civic rights." It solely has to do with legally recognizing the separation which the Qādiyānī themselves had long since carried out. It also had to do with the Qādiyānī not possessing any right to consider themselves as part of the Muslim community. Admittedly, Maudūdī does not spend a single word discussing the consequences of their condemnation as apostates, for whom he very emphatically demands the death penalty in his work *murtadd ki sazā islāmī qānūn mēṉ*.

Maudūdī strongly rejected the idea that "no coercion in religion" could mean that a group, such as the Qādiyānī, could remain a part of the Muslim community. Admittedly, this decision is not a matter of force: During the 1953 unrest, a number of Qādiyānī became the target of violence because in police and military uniform they killed Muslims and, as a result, Muslims then defended themselves. Maudūdī thus depicts the Muslim community as endangered by the machinations of the Aḥmadīya movement and not as initiators of their exclusion.

It is apparent that in this text Maudūdī finds no justification at all for equitable co-existence. He also finds no justification for pluralism or for religious freedom in a comprehensive sense of the word. Against the background understanding that "Islam" always also means affiliation with a political order, Islam means an expression of loyalty as well as a precondition for complete civil rights for Maudūdī. Simultaneously, Maudūdī reduces his pleading for exclusion and social ostracism of the Aḥmadīya movement down to a theological question, although their denunciation in Pakistan in 1953 had profound social consequences for them.

Answers to the remaining questions continue to eminate from the absolute point of view of the assumption of the truth of Islam. Thus, the Islamic practice of taxation does not offer any disadvantages for non-Muslims, according to Maudūdī: "There is no discrimination between Muslims and non-Muslims in an Islamic state in the matter of taxation," for where a non-Muslim pays *ǧizya*, a Muslim certainly pays *zakāt*.[400]

The Execution of Apostates for Reasons of Self-Defense

The next question, question 6, is interesting as it has to do with the execution of apostates: Is not the execution of an apostate tantamount to coercion, that no one is allowed to turn their back on Islam? Maudūdī responds in the negative: "Actually it is not so,"[401] for this law only serves to protect Islamic society, "the bedrock of the Islamic State" so that it does not dissipate. In turn, Maudūdī compares affiliation and joining the umma with citizenship in a Western country.

At least as important as what Maudūdī mentions here on apostasy is what he does not say: There is no word of limitation with respect to the application of the death penalty, no regrets, no attenuation with respect to the existence of multi-religious societies in the 20th century, no admissions with respect to the particular life situations individuals find themselves in, and a fortiori there is no essential renunciation of the death penalty for conversion. As is the case in earlier publications, Maudūdī likewise gives a sterilely dogmatic response, without creating a link to reality, to his circle of readers, or to publications in which his responses have been published.

Maudūdī answers question 14, which targets the corruption of the Jewish and Christian Scriptures, in a manner that naturally works upon the assumption that their transmission has not remained true to the text. Indeed, it does not even want to commit to whether Jews and Christians possessed "Scriptures" in any actual sense at the time of Muḥammad's life, while the Quran has been transmitted in its original wording up to the present day.[402]

Freedom of Belief for the Children of Muslim Parents

The final question – expressed by Freeland K. Abbott on another occasion but attached here to the text – is about the voluntary nature of religious af-

---

400 Ibid., p. 11.
401 Ibid., p. 12.
402 Ibid., p. 16.

filiation as it relates to an individual born into belief. It receives the most comprehensive response of all.[403]

Maudūdī gives a two-part response to this: As a matter of principle, he points out, no differentiation can be made between an individual born into the "system" and an individual who converts at a later time, for the system can only survive when it is bolstered by its adherents and their permanent affiliation. For that reason, it is not possible that "citizenship," which Maudūdī equates with affiliation with Islam without any further explanation, could be an issue which could lie at the root of a desire for a change, even in the case where the person involved only possesses this citizenship as a result of birth. That is the principle.

According to Maudūdī, the entire issue is, however, much less dramatic, since most "citizens" added through birth do not at all stop to think about wanting to give up this citizenship. The principle can also naturally not be given up "for the sake of a handful of such individuals"[404] who would then endanger the entire community. Even if they possess steadfast convictions – and this argumentation strongly resembles Maudūdī's discussions in his work *murtadd ki sazā islāmī qānūn mēṉ* in which he summons the obstinate convert to still readily suffer death in the case of deep conviction[405] – it is then free for them to either leave the community or else put their life in jeopardy. If the person in question, who by all means wishes to change his loyalty, remains within the country, he commits high treason.

In what follows, Maudūdī – as a response to imaginary critics – again discusses that Islam is not merely a religion. Rather, it is "a state system . . . an ideology and order of life and its principles."[406] Wherever that is the case, Islam is the law and thus also has the right to punish those who have sworn loyalty and obedience to Islam. At this point, Maudūdī completely equates the state and Islam, when he discusses that states everywhere have the right to impose sanctions against dissidents, also against those who change their citizenship in times of war.

Maudūdī now provides sketches of various groups within an Islamic state – likewise in accord with earlier publications: He mentions temporary

403 Ibid., pp. 16-19.
404 Ibid., p. 17.
405 Maudūdī. *murtadd*, p. 39.
406 Abbot. "Maudūdī", p. 17.

visitors and wards who acknowledge the sovereignty and authorization and instruction on the part of the Islamic state ("if they agree to abide as obedient and faithful subjects").[407] However, according to Maudūdī, the complete rights of citizens are only enjoyed by Muslims who have immigrated into an Islamic state or who were born there and who for their part demonstrate loyalty and obedience towards God and his Messenger.

Since a "different attitude" exists between believers and unbelievers, it has to be all too understandable, according to Maudūdī, that secession can lead to war. For this purpose, Maudūdī cites the American Civil War as well as the 19th century Sonderbund war in Switzerland. In this one can see where freedom leads to separation:

> "Hence a state, an army, and parties formed for the high purpose of serving important social ideals and undertaking hazardous tasks . . . are compelled to slam the doors on those who wish to retrace their steps."[408]

The best method to prevent secession and disloyalty is, for that reason, the emphatic warning about the seriousness of this step of association and the explanation that the death penalty follows separation. Maudūdī, in the process, contradicts the remarks he has just made since a child born into the community simply cannot be warned. This serious warning can only be made by an institution having instruments of power at its disposal, for example the power of legislation – while "an unwholesome and evil system" cannot achieve this and only produces even more injustice by coercing its adherents to remain associated.

Regardless of the fact that Maudūdī's response was published in an Islamic studies journal in the USA, he has not deviated from his attitude in this treatment of religious freedom and apostasy. He proclaims and postulates a state that is composed in an Islamic manner, which per se defines and practices the appropriate measure of civil rights and liberties for Muslims as well as non-Muslims. Maudūdī understands this neither as "coercion" nor as a lack of religious freedom.

---

407 Ibid., p. 18.

408 Ibid., p. 19.

4.3.6. Human Rights in Islam – 1976

In his writing entitled *Human Rights in Islam*, Maudūdī has commented most comprehensively on the the topic of "human rights" and thus on individual civil rights and religious freedom,[409] which was exclusively published in English. In view of this fact as well as the topic, it can be concluded that it is directed at a Western or, more specifically, international audience and is geared towards sketching out a picture of Islamic theology and Maudūdī's attitude on human rights which is compatible with human rights as defined by the UN.[410]

Human Rights and Civil Rights in an Islamic State

This work, as numerous other later published works by Maudūdī, consists of what were originally public addresses. Also like numerous others, it was originally two public addresses. It is presented in five chapters. Furthermore, in this case, it has to do with two addresses given by Maudūdī published together, the dates of which lie thirty years apart. The first chapter carries the title "The Political Framework of Islam" and was originally a radio address by Maudūdī which was broadcast on Radio Pakistan in Lahore on January 20, 1948. Chapters two to five consist of the text of a lecture which Maudūdī held on November 16, 1975 upon the invitation of the "Civic Rights and Liberty Forum" in Lahore.[411]

In this document, which in a manner of speaking could be viewed as a counterweight to Maudūdīs treatment of apostasy, Maudūdī names and establishes a catalog of eight human rights which he indeed presents from the perspective of the Quran and the *sunna*. He simultaneously avoids naming the intended punishments based on the Sharia.

In spite of the general tenor of the compatability of this work with Western conceptions of human rights, Maudūdī also does not deviate at

409 Mawdudi. *Human Rights*.

410 Also as concluded by Alf Tergel. *Human Rights in Cultural and Religious Tradition*. Uppsala University Library: Uppsala, 1998, p. 90.

411 Chapter 2 to 5 were published at a number of additional locations, for example, in a journal published in Teheran, *al-Tawḥīd: A Quarterly Journal of Islamic Thought and Culture* 4/3 (1987), pp. 59-89; for instance, a copy of this journal can be found at: http://islamworld.net/docs/hr.txt (10.10.2011).

this point from his basic theological convictions which run through his writings as a common theme. For instance, there is the absolute sovereignty of God, to whose will and system of order everything is to be subordinated. Also at this point, he holds out the strengths of the practices of the Islamic state in his theory compared to the numerous weaknesses of Western societies, even if he does so in an overall less combative manner than in a number of his other writings. It again becomes clear in this document that Maudūdī understands affiliation with Islam as religiously defined citizenship which a Muslim acquires when entering an Islamic territory:

> "A Muslim *ipso facto* becomes the citizen of an Islamic state as soon as he sets foot on its territory with the intention of living there and thus enjoys equal rights along with those who acquire its citizenship by birth."[412]

A type of citizenship in an Islamic state is absolutely intended for the non-Muslim, although it is the citizenship of only a second class ward (*d̲immī*) with whom a contract is entered into in order to guarantee basic rights. However, on the other hand the limits of his freedom are simultaneously defined. Maudūdī interestingly emphasizes expressly and generally – in contrast to his remarks in the work on apostasy, *murtadd ki sazā islāmī qānūn mēn̠* – that non-Muslims possess the right to propagate their faith, indeed "they are even entitled to criticize Islam." However, in an additional clause there is a limitation placed on this: "within the limits laid down by law and decency."[413] Admittedly, Maudūdī does not define these "limits" in detail.

Granted legal rights can under no circumstances be taken from non-Muslims unless they, for their part, rescind the contract guaranteeing them their citizenship. In the event that Maudūdī has the case of apostasy in mind as a type of revocation of the contractual agreement, he does not mention it with a single word. Instead, he points out that the rights of non-Muslims cannot under any circumstances be violated. Even if Muslims are wronged in non-Islamic states in dramatic ways, indeed if all Muslims

---

412 "... even if all the Muslims outside the boundaries of an Islamic state are massacred ... Mawdudi. *Human Rights*, p. 12.

413 Ibid.

were "slaughtered" there,[414] the blood of not a single non-Muslim would be allowed to be shed in an Islamic state.

To a large extent, this treatment involves a political declaration as a theological explanatory statement of a position. In the first section of the text of Maudūdī's 1948 radio address, he explains the foundations of the political system of the Islamic state in all brevity. The three principles of its foundation are the oneness of God (*tauḥīd*), the prophetic office (*risāla*), and the caliphate ((*ḫilāfa*). After that, Maudūdī unfolds his essential understanding of the lordship of God, which justifies his position as a legislator and his demand for obedience, worship, and submission from people.

There is no single individual who is entitled to rule as a caliph. Rather, it is the polity of all Muslims which performs this task as vice-regents. Maudūdī labels this participatory rule by believers "democracy"[415] – however not as a theo-democracy as in many of his other writings – since all citizens have are on an equal footing in their share of rule. As far as Maudūdī is concerned, the crucial difference to Western democracy, in which all power originates with the people and in which the will of the people is implemented, is that the origin of power is God himself and his law, the Sharia.[416] The Islamic state should base its activity on justice, truth, and forthrightness and may not tolerate evil, falsehood, and injustice.[417]

This Islamic state is guided through the implementation of the law of God by commanders (*amīr*) at the top supported by a consultative assembly (*šūrā*). This is similar to the president or the prime minister of a Western country, at least Maudūdī maintains that this is the case.[418] That Maudūdī chooses the same term for leaders which he himself held within his own movement, the *Jamāᶜat-i-Islāmī*, points to the fact that Maudūdī,

---

414 Ibid.

415 Ibid., p. 10.

416 Comp. his complete rejection of Western democracy, which to his understanding has nothing in common with Islam, for instance in his work Mawdudi. *Political Theory*, pp. 21ff.

417 "... the state should base its policies on justice, truth and honesty. It is not prepared ... to tolerate fraud, falsehood and injustice ..." Mawdudi. *Human Rights*, p. 11.

418 Ibid., p. 13.

in his view had established a miniature model state through the creation of *Jamāᶜat-i-Islāmī*. Indeed, it also points to the fact that he viewed himself as a capable leader of the entire structure of this state. In any case, at this point he emphatically points out that the leader should unite fear of God and statesmanlike abilities, thus principles which were indispensable for membership in *Jamāᶜat-i-Islāmī*.

At the end of the first chapter, Maudūdī again refers to the topic of human rights by stating that "in Islam" the only courts that can be involved are those introduced by the state. The directions they are to follow are to be exclusively drawn from the law of God. At this point it again becomes clear, particularly owing to a complete lack of consideration regarding possible divisiveness or differing interpretations of God's law, that Maudūdī's blueprints for life in an ideal Islamic state never got beyond the stage of an edifice of ideas that never had to stand the test in practice. In this point, Maudūdī's approach is similar to that of Yūsuf al-Qaraḍāwī, who in large part in his argumentation is lacking in a distinction between *fiqh* und *šarīᶜa* and for that reason – similar to Maudūdī – proclaims that his ideas bring absolute application of "the law of God".

According to Maudūdī, since the Islamic state is based upon the law of God, the topic of human rights is in no way a matter of the Islamic state wanting to limit rights and privileges. It is quite the contrary. In an Islamic state, "universal human rights for humanity,"[419] for example the rights to life or protection of the aged, the sick, women, minors, and the injured, are unambiguously defined and set down. These rights are to be preserved under all circumstances.

In the final three chapters, Maudūdī turns to a concrete explanation of these human rights. In the second chapter, which is placed before the final chapter as a short introduction, Maudūdī argues in brevity in a way that is polarizing and ideological but not aggressive. He argues that Western states only discovered the thought of human rights in modern times and that the problem then existed: "More often than not these rights existed only on paper."[420] On the other hand, in Islam human rights are given by God which cannot be infringed upon by any individual.

---

419 Ibid., p. 11.

420 "More often than not these rights existed only on paper". Ibid., p. 15.

Basic Human Rights in Islam

Maudūdī now turns in more detail to individual human rights which are guaranteed in Islam. He lists eight individual human rights and discusses their significance and their content using verses from the Quran and illustrations from the history of Islam. These are, specifically, the right to life (which in the history of non-Muslims has been disregarded in wars of extermination and genocide but has always been fully vouchsafed by Islam), the right to assistance for the saving of life and aid in every emergency situation, the right to respect for the integrity of individuals, and the protection of women.

It is precisely on the topic of women where Maudūdī again falls into his recurrent attempt at a black and white formula. This occurs when he maintains that the protection of women in Western nations is trampled under foot because women have been subjected to mistreatment by their own army or by surrounding countries, while this has "never occurred" under an Islamic army since ". . . the history of the Muslims, apart from individual lapses, has been free from this crime against womanhood."[421]

Maudūdī now turns to the question of every individual's personal civil liberties. However, he does not give positive justification for which civil rights and liberties people possess. Rather, under the heading of "The Individual's Right to Freedom,"[422] he first of all goes into the slave trade in Western nations in an accusatory manner in order to finally depict with praise how Islam and individual personalities in Islamic history have worked towards the freeing of slaves. According to Maudūdī's depiction, the rightly guided caliphs and their successors were responsible for the freeing of numerous slaves and exchanged them for prisoners of war – a practice which non-Islamic countries seem to have finally learned from Islam: "the problem of the slaves of Arabia was thus solved in under 40 years."[423]

The final three sections are treated under the mantle of Sharia-defined "rights" with the catchwords "The Right to Justice," "The Equality of Hu-

---

421 "It has never happened that after the conquest of a foreign country the Muslim army has gone about raping the women of the conquered people." Ibid., p. 18.

422 Ibid., p. 19.

423 Ibid., p. 20.

man Beings," and "The Right to Co-operate and not to Co-operate"[424] without filling these terms with respect to content. For all three subject areas Maudūdī predominantly quotes verses from the Quran without discussing their meanings and possible socio-political application, apart from making general statements that Muslims should behave "justly" towards all people. Does "just" mean for Maudūdī that Muslims are to follow all existing laws? How is this terminology to be filled with content if Muslims are living as a minority in a non-Islamic country? That they are to behave justly in the sense of Sharia law, i.e., that Muslims and non-Muslims are to be treated according to different legal standards with respect to religious freedom or marital law? There are no concrete questions which in any way come up for discussion.

Even if in the following section Maudūdī states that ""Islam" is based on "absolute equality between men irrespective of colour, race or nationality,[425] it is not only the lack of mentioning religion which catches one's eye. Rather, it is the absence of discussion of the content of what "equality" means. Maudūdī gives an indication inasmuch as he explains that the superioritiy of people over other people would be exclusively possible on the basis of "God-consciousness, purity of character and high morals."[426] This indeed hints at Muslims' being superior to non-Muslims, whereby in the final event these words are only replaced by other words – and not by tangible content.

In the final section of the chapter, one finds the same way of dealing with assertions and explanations when Maudūdī warns that "the wicked and vicious person" cannot be the beneficiary of support from the side of Muslims even if it is their own brother. On the other hand, Muslims could be friends and helpers to him "who is doing deeds of virtue and righteousness"[427] or at least could be well-disposed to him. It does not need to be especially emphasized that as far as content is concerned, these generally formulated terms of "friend" or "enemy" can be very differently interpreted, depending on the circumstances.

424 Ibid., p. 22.
425 Ibid., p. 21.
426 Ibid., p. 22.
427 Ibid.

Those in Power as Administrators of the Sharia

The fourth chapter takes up the topic of human rights in fifteen sub-points. In this chapter, Maudūdī again quotes verses from the Quran in every section. Besides that, in every section there are also texts from tradition.

Maudūdī's argumentation under the heading of the "Right to Life and Possessions"[428] is interesting because Maudūdī again concedes that only "during wars or insurrection" may the life of a person be taken. Simultaneously, he emphasizes that no court can come to such a decision which does not at all attempt to implement the will of God. Rather, this can only be done by a government acting in agreement with the stipulations of the Sharia: "Only a just and righteous government, which follows the *sharī'a*, can decide whether the taking of a life is justified."[429] Does Maudūdī consider apostasy to fall within the classification of "insurrection" at this point?

With this said, Maudūdī locates the power to decide about the appropriate application of the Sharia within the government and those in power, respectively. In contrast to al-Qaraḍāwī, who very strongly ascribes the role of interpreter of divine commands to the *ᶜulamā'*, Maudūdī does not speak about Islamic scholars. Furthermore, he warns that the state is not allowed to kill those "citizens" who criticize the state for its incorrect actions. According to Maudūdī, that would truly be "a crime." However, who has the right to evaluate the state and its actions? All of these statements remain too general and not precise at this point so that they appear to be applicable to every and no action on the part of the government.

In both of the following sections, Maudūdī emphasizes how clearly the prohibition against damage to Islam's reputation is superior to corresponding Western regulations and the provisions Muḥammad made in order to effectively protect the private sphere of the individual, e.g., of the women of the home.

The next two sections regarding the right to protest against tyranny as well as the "Security of personal Freedom" have to do with protection against arbitrary arrest, complemented by narrative additions of several parts belonging to tradition without any historically verifiable correlation. Here, however, the formulations once again remain at a level of superfi-

[428] Ibid., pp. 23-24.

[429] Ibid., p. 23.

cial, general appeals such as the call to not arrest anyone merely on the basis of rumours.[430]

Section six is of direct significance for the topic of human rights and comes under the heading of "Freedom of Expression."[431] Maudūdī again operates by utilizing empty phrases, which within the context of a politically understood Islam are indeed meaningful. However, under certain circumstances and in the context of a supposedly predominant Western readership coming from another socio-cultural background, they could be understood less restrictively. Maudūdī emphasizes that all citizens of an Islamic state, under the condition that they pursue positive intentions, possess "the right of freedom of thought and expression on the condition that it is used for propagating virtue and not for spreading evil."[432] Indeed, to propagate accountability and "righteousness" are duties.

What is meant by "virtue" and "evil" in an Islamic state is not defined here. Against this background, in particular with respect to the call he unmistakably made elsewhere to "command the good and to forbid that which is reprehensible" (*al-amr bi-'l-ma^crūf wa-'n-nahy ^can al-munkar*), whereby Maudūdī points to Sura 3:110, it can be concluded that Maudūdī demands the community to limit the freedom of proclamation for wards of the state and issue a complete prohibition against the propagation of unbelief and apostasy. However, the total permeation of the community by Islam is favored, for he continues by explaining that the rejection of this right leads the involved individual into a "state of war with God."[433] This underscores the conclusion of the section, in which he points out that "all true Muslims" have the duty "to try to persuade people along the paths of righteousness."[434]

This obligation to proclaim Islam is complemented by a section carrying the heading of the right to organize oneself. This is something which, as Maudūdī emphasizes, represents a duty. Admittedly, the intent and purpose of this form of organization is exclusively to proclaim Islam. From Maudūdī's point of view, when society has abandoned the mandate intend-

---

430 Ibid., pp. 25-28.

431 Ibid., pp. 28-29.

432 Ibid., p. 28.

433 "Anyone who tries to deny this right to his people is openly at war with God." Ibid.

434 Ibid., p. 29.

ed for it, it is of paramount importance that at least a group within the Islamic community exists which then fulfils this duty.

With these words, the conclusion is then strongly suggested that Maudūdī is referring to the *Jamāᶜat-i-Islāmī* as the effective group within the community of Muslims to follow its designated assignment to propagate Islam. This especially appears to be the case since just a few lines later Maudūdī suddenly harshly judges the Pakistani government, which in 1975, at the time this text was composed, was headed by Prime Minister Zulfiqar Ali Bhutto. Maudūdī laments that "in a Muslim country" it is unfortunate that the "association" which has been founded for the propagation of evil also possesses the power to rule the country. At the same time, the "association" which was called into existence for the propagation of good and virtue had to fear for its survival and had to fear prohibition. This is a danger which *Jamāᶜat-i-Islāmī* continually saw itself exposed to up to the time Zia ul-Haqq assumed power.

Maudūdī leaves no doubt as to how he sees these roles distributed: The *Jamāᶜat-i-Islāmī* fulfils the role intended for it, while ruling powers are oriented towards promoting evil: "directed to spreading evil, to corrupting and morally degrading and debasing people."[435] This is the case even though the involved Muslims are, according to Maudūdīs understanding, not actual Muslims but rather only nominal adherents of Islam. Here again Maudūdī's viewpoint of a form of nationalism based on religious affiliation is made clear. This was seen in not viewing Pakistan to be an Islamic country when the government there, as was the case under Zulfiqar Ali Bhutto, did not pursue a decided course of Islamization.

Freedom of Conscience and Religious Freedom

These general instructions with respect to the unconditional duty to propagate Islam are complemented by the following two sections on freedom of conscience and freedom of one's convictions as well as the protection of religious feelings:[436]

In mentioning freedom of conscience, and by referring to Sura 2:256, Maudūdī emphasizes the free choice of every individual person to join Is-

[435] Ibid.

[436] Ibid., p. 30.

lam of one's own accord. In spite of the fact that Islam is the truth, no coercion is allowed to be exercised upon anyone.

At this point, a reader not acquainted with Maudūdī's other writings cannot recognize that as far as Maudūdī is concerned, the refusal to accept Islam is linked to a certain disparagement, including reduced rights for *people of the book*, a duty to submit, and a limitation on non-Islamic religious practice as well as the denial of leadership functions for the body politic. Since at this point Maudūdī ends the section, the impression arises that according to Maudūdī's definition, total religious freedom actually obtains in an Islamic state. This is an impression that is even fortified through the following section on the prohibition against injuring the religious feelings of other religious communities.

Maudūdī again uses the following section, under the heading of protection against arbitrary arrest, in order to demonstrate his displeasure with circumstances in the state of Pakistan, where this right has been trampled under foot. He endeavors to bring forth a concrete example, that of exercising pressure on the defendant by incarcerating family members. Owing to such conduct, Maudūdī labels those responsible at the head of the country "tyrants" who commit "crimes" and essentially scrutinizes their affiliation to Islam: "They disgrace and humiliate humanity – and then they claim that they are Muslims."[437]

Maudūdī now turns to the right to be supplied with things essential to life, which he takes as a given through the arrangement of *zakāt* donations as well as the general duty to provide welfare to those in need in an Islamic state.

As Maudūdī now proceeds to make the right to equality before the law a topic of discussion,[438] this section, which goes under the heading of "equality before the law", primarily presents a proclamation of inequality between people by what is not expressed. Immediately at the outset of this section, Maudūdī assumes that the Quran, along with tradition, substantiates the equality and brotherliness of all Muslims. In the case of converts to Islam, there is also no distinction made between converts and Muslims who have grown up in Islam, and the lives and possessions of wards of the state are inviolable.

---

437 Ibid., p. 31.

438 Ibid., pp. 31-32.

With this paragraph, Maudūdī draws a clear line of separation between individual social groups – between Muslims and non-Muslims, and *people of the book* – in an Islamic state. Brotherliness, solidarity, and protection are limited to one's own faith community, even if wards within the state are not allowed to be attacked. However, through the special duty of solidarity, but particularly through legal discrimination against non-Muslims, which is not made a topic of discussion, equal treatment in an Islamic state can at most mean only treatment according to Sharia law.

What is involved in the next section is the application of the same legal standards to managers of the state, which Maudūdī derives from the exemplary behaviour on the part of Muḥammad as an equal among equals as well as from the option of lodging complaints against the heads of the state at the time of the caliphate rule.[439] According to Maudūdī, this subordination under the law, also by superiors, is expressed by leaders of the state not being allowed to command any citizen to overstep the law of God or, more specifically, by leaders not having the right to flout such ordinances.

In the final section of this chapter, Maudūdī again discusses his concept of splitting society into Muslims and non-Muslims.[440] Only Muslims – but for that matter not only one's own community but rather the entire Muslim community – have the right to exercise representation (*ḫilāfa*) of God on earth. In this they are on a par with each other.

Maudūdī now points out that the "how" of government is explained by Sura 42:38. That is a verse which mentions "consultation" (*šūrā*) among believers. Because the Quran recommends consultation, it is appropriate that each Muslim either directly expresses himself regarding the affairs of the state or can do this via a representative; it is a very vague statement supplemented by a number of brief demands that the people choose the government in free and independent elections that demonstrate a majority. The situation within the country – and along with that the abilities of the government – have to be able to be assessed together in an unimpeded manner.

Maudūdī again follows his dichotomous division of society into Muslims and non-Muslims found in a number of his other works, and at this point he concedes no voice at all to the latter in political affairs. Admittedly, without specifically pointing it out, he equates a "citizen" whose human

---

439 Ibid., pp. 32-33.

440 Ibid., pp. 33-34.

rights were treated in the preceding paragraphs with a "Muslim." This corresponds to his basic conviction that only Muslims are citizens in the fully entitled sense of the word.

Maudūdī concludes this chapter with a warning against the abuse of power by usurpers since God has awarded all Muslims the right to reign.

The final chapter of this treatment on the topic of human rights addresses the topic of "Rights of Enemies in War."[441] After a brief introduction, in which Maudūdī points out the first-time introduction of humane rules of war by Islam, he addresses his attention to the discussion of the rights of enemies. Indeed, his attention also addresses combatants as well as civilians who are able to call upon protection from torture, abuse, withholding assistance, destruction and plundering, the robbing of dead people, breach of contract as well as attacks prior to declarations of war. He does this without again pointing out that Muslims – frequently in contrast to the other warring parties – have observed these commands. With that, Maudūdī concludes his treatment of "human rights in Islam."

Evaluation

If one considers Maudūdī's treatment of "human rights in Islam," it appears as if in his text he is leaning upon The Universal Declaration of Human Rights, adopted by the UN on December 10, 1948. This is not, however, pursued without at the same time either withholding significant civil and equal rights formulated there or, far more commonly, modifying them in a way that they are robbed of their actual contents. Overall, what appears to be more meaningful than what was said is what was not said. In composing this document, Maudūdī had the scenario of an (ideal) Islamic state in mind where Islam forges society, public life, and applicable laws.

Maudūdī's text at no point advocates equal rights for men and women, equality for Muslims and non-Muslims, or rights to equality for people of different religions (postulated in Article 2 by the Universal Declaration of Human Rights of 1948).[442] He says nothing about protection against discrimination (Article 7), which he automatically proclaimed via legal discrimination against certain groups in an Islamic state, and the same goes for equal treatment for everyone before the law (Article 7). Additionally,

441 Ibid., pp. 35-39.

442 http://www.un.org/depts/german/grunddok/ar217a3.html (10.6.2014).

Maudūdī distances himself from the right to change one's religion as formulated in the UN's declaration, the right to the free choice of a religious confession, the right to publicly practice any kind of religion and worldview (Article 18) as well as the right to freedom of speech (Article 19).

At no point in this work on the topic of human rights does the author become concrete with respect to the question of which inalienable rights people possess, independent of their religious affiliation. In the final event, all remarks remain vague and uncertain. The first paragraph, which concedes an unlimited right to life, could count as an exception were there not the reference to Sura 6:151 which forbids killing – besides killing in cases allowed by Sharia-law (which are not presented in detail). With that said, the author, according to all probability, wishes to express that killing in cases defined by the Sharia is allowed – which again he does not define. Due to the fact that Maudūdī frequently reverts to texts from the Quran, but beyond that appears in his exegetical conclusions to exclusively lecture on his own views, the impression could arise for the reader that Maudūdī's point of view quite simply represents "the" Islamic point of view.

As a result, this work by Maudūdī is to be viewed more as a proclamation of the superiority of Islam and its values more than a justification of concrete human rights, let alone a grappling with understandings which diverge. One can agree with Seyyid Vali Reza Nasr, who with respect to Maudūdī has observed the following:

> "The basic human right was the right to demand an Islamic order and to live in it, not the right to differ with the rulers of the Islamic state or defy its authority."[443]

All in all Maudūdī presents a very limited, unilinear, and on top of that superficial point of view on things, while at the same time one can recognize his efforts to offer critical considerations as small a target as possible. To a certain degree, there are concessions made with respect to civil rights and rights of self-determination. However, he does not depart from the framework of Sharia-defined values. Nowhere does he deny the justification of Sharia law, which forms the background of his writing. However, on the other hand he does not explain this in his delimiting or condemning state-

443 Nasr. *Mawdudi and the Making*, p. 92.

ments. This writing represents the attempt to present human rights in Islam, as Maudūdī defines them, with as little controversy surrounding them as possible and by deviating from Western understandings of human rights as little as possible.

In his work it is not the fact of being human which for Maudūdī is the source of human rights. Rather, it is Islam, which accedes complete human rights to its believers and limited human rights to its contractual partner, "wards of the state," (which, however, he only hints at here). At no point is it made clear that Maudūdī would be prepared to deliberate about Sharia-based guidelines against the background of cultural influence and contemporary history, e.g., with respect to his understanding of women's rights.

Again and again what is expressed is Islamic superiority and a certain triumphalism on the part of the author, for example when he maintains that non-Muslims also recognize nowadays that Islam can better cope with the difficulties of coexistence than all other religions.[444] Above all, this work does not present any dispute with positions outside of classical Sharia law, which he only now and again hints at without actually setting them forth. "That which is not said" will less clearly catch the eye of a reader unfamiliar with this specialized area than an individual who is familiar with Sharia law.

Throughout Maudūdī's entire work on the topic of human rights, the first and sole point of reference consists of the Quran and the *sunna*. They are brought forward as the argument for the sole justification for or against individual rights and are interpreted within the framework of Maudūdīs worldview. Admittedly, this occurs without it being recognizable that Maudūdī would be prepared to discuss the interpretive variations or the difference between *fiqh* and *šarīʿa*. "Islam" appears, as it does in Maudūdī's other writings, as the acting protagonist in which principles, resolution, and the will to shape society inhere.

What Maudūdī does is to simply proclaim without reference to reality. Maudūdī's writing has little to do with actual present day life, which for many Muslims means permanent residency in territories that are non-Islamic. He has no instructions at all ready for the diaspora situation. With that said, a scenario emerges in which the rule of Islam is a norm and ideal

444 Mawdudi. *Human Rights*, p. 22.

to strive for in all areas of life. And there is no alternative to it – at least there is no alternative which can be discerned from Maudūdī's writing.

Since Maudūdī repeatedly lets the framework of Sharia law shimmer through as the absolute frame of reference, it is apparent that from his point of view no religious change is possible. More specifically, a change of religion does not belong among the inalienable rights. Maudūdī does not directly take up the topic of the death penalty but depicts how Muslims and non-Muslims are treated differently as well as how the legal subordination of those who do not belong to Islam looks.

The right to change religions – something which is a matter of course in the Western context in which this work was published – is not made a topic of discussion, but what is emphasized is the duty of an Islamic state to keep everything which is destructive, that which is "evil," at a distance. For that reason, it is by no means the case that this work by Maudūdī represents a justification of religious freedom and human rights. Rather, it is aimed more at their limitation.

4.3.7. Maudūdis Other Remarks on Apostasy

Beyond the cited texts, there are relatively few of Maudūdī's remarks which directly address the topic of apostasy. Thus, his Quran commentary *Tafhīm al-Qur'ān* only contains a few statements on the lawfulness of execution of those who fight against an Islamic state and turn from it (Sura 17:33; quite similar to his commentary on Sura 6:151).[445]

A further work by Maudūdī, which occupied itself with contesting the orthodoxy of the Aḥmadīya movement, appeared in 1962 in Urdu with the title *Ḫatm-i nubūwat* and in 1963 in English as *The Finality of Prophethood.*[446] In this work Maudūdī makes the unjustified assertion of a continuation of the prophetic office after Muḥammad (in all probability he is alluding to the Aḥmadīya movement[447]) as one of the main causes of division of the *umma* in the past. The Muslim community is so helplessly

---

445 Maududi. *Tafheem ul-Quran.*

446 Abū l-Aᶜlā Maudūdī. *Ḫatm-i nubūwat.* [Lahore: 1963], no location provided, 1985.

447 The Aḥmadīya movement is not expressly mentioned in this piece of writing; there are only two allusions made to it: See Abul A'la Maududi. *The Finality of Prophethood.* Lahore, 1962, p. 27.

placed at the mercy of this deception since the community is not sufficiently instructed with respect to Muḥammad's prophetic office. Maudūdī denounces every individual who accepts a prophetic office after Muḥammad as an apostate who does not belong to the Muslim community.[448] His argumentation is above all theological and less politically directed.

4.4. Conclusion: Abū l-Aᶜlā Maudūdī's Position on Apostasy

After abū l-Aᶜlā Maudūdī entered the political stage on the Indian subcontinent in the middle of the 20th century, he shaped the ideological orientation of Pakistan like almost no other individual as a journalist, activist, theologian, and politician with his eclectic picture of history, his narrow dualistic worldview, his polarized understanding of Islam, and his activist millenarianism.

4.4.1. The Prohibition against Apostasy on the Way to an Islamic Social Order

Beyond what has been addressed up to now, Maudūdī also became an idea generator for significant leading personalities within the Islamist movement into the Near and Middle East. Maudūdī's own biographical and contemporary historical background shines as fierce antagonism against everything which is Western and non-Islamic as well as does his summons to a dedicated struggle to implement a political Islamic state structure: It reflects the loss of reputation and influence of his family in connection with the inexorable downfall of the Mogul empire and its Persian-shaped high culture, British colonial rule with its social and legal culture shaped by European and Christian influences, and the marginalization of Muslim community owing to the nationalism and secularism of the Hindu majority, which manifest itself in its dominance of the Indian National Assembly at the threshold of the emergence of the Indian nation state.

His battle against the threat from within and from without by everything that is non-Islamic in an Islamic state structure where Islam determines the exercise of religion, social life, education, and legislation and

448 Ibid., p. 10.

politics is what gave Maudūdī his orientation in the topics of apostasy, religious freedom, and human rights:

Maudūdī operated from a comprehensively Islamic perspective combined with tireless activism. In order to save the Islamic community from impending disintegration, ignorance, enslavement, tyranny, and meaningless by returning to true, holistic Islam, Maudūdī found it inconceivable to allow developments which would hinder the implementation of these goals and prevent or delay the formation of an Islamic state.

In addition to diverse external threats, Maudūdī above all perceived the Aḥmadīya movement as an internal threat attempting to split Islam from within as well as every type of apostate who made the construction of a homogeneous, internally firmly integrated polity impossible.[449] For that reason, apostates are for Maudūdī not only religious "deviants." Rather, they are above all political traitors who want to prevent the Islamic community from living up to its actual task as the guidepost and paradigm for all people and who hamper the realization of the Sharia as God's just order on earth. Maudūdī musters up neither appreciation nor indulgence for such politically active revolutionaries.

The *people of the book* do not disturb this harmony insofar as they move within the divine order, acknowledge the sovereignty of Islam and due to their submission to the state do not place its ideological orientation into question. This is absolutely the case when it comes to apostates (and adherents of the Aḥmadīya movement), since according to Maudūdī' they rebel against the divine order and through the withdrawal of their loyalty work towards its overthrow. Considering that it was Maudūdī's central concern to regain the leading position of Islamic community which had been seen as lost, he viewed everything as a threat which could inhibit returning the Islamic community to this. In the process, apostates' possible motives are of no consequence. They are merely uninteresting for Maudūdī since he makes sweeping insinuations about apostates with respect to wickedness, treason, and cunning.

[449] In his writing: itteḥād-i ᶜālam-i islāmī (Lahore, no year provided), Maudūdī discusses as the actual difference between Western ideologies, other religions, and Islam the idea that only the latter is in the position to bring humanity together "into a family": S. Abul A'la Maududi. *Unity of the Muslim World.* Islamic Publications Ltd.: Lahore, 1967[1]/1982[5], pp. 11ff.

4.4.2. Maudūdī's Blueprint for a Homogeneous Society

Maudūdī sets his alternative plan of a homogeneous community over against a world crumbling into numerous religious, political, and social groups. This community follows the law of God as a whole and is hierarchically structured through and through, bringing education and instruction to the ignorant but keeping destructive deviants – e.g., apostates – from their midst in order to maintain the stability of the community.

At the same time, one of the keys for Maudūdī's broad reception in the post-colonial era arguably lies in his uncompromising rejection of the West and its ideologies and values. He sets a comprehensive, self-confident, autonomous, solution-oriented Islam predestined for imminent victory over against what appears to have been an overwhelming invasion of Western culture. This becomes a voice of reassurance of self-identity and of defense against evil from without.

Maudūdī not only defends the community against evil. He is at the same time a spearhead for what is good and right. He leads this battle, "an apocalyptic battle between the forces of good and evil,"[450] with all means so that the good wins over evil, so that godlessness has to yield and that by necessity a just society emerges. This is because it is structured according to correct foundations and is led by a capable, God-fearing *amīr*.

Maudūdī, a forward-looking individual and conveyor of what is right and necessary on the way to the establishment of a completely just and peaceful society, becomes a messianic figure who can lead the Muslim community. Indeed, in the final event he becomes a messianic figure who can lead the entire world to the implementation of this just society under the law of God. He initially conveys this knowledge to a capable elite which in turn, due to its piety and fear of God, is in a position to take on responsibility for applying the principles of Islam in society, legislation, and in the dispensation of justice worldwide. In the process, as an *amīr*, Maudūdī plays the role of an infallible father figure who, for his part, is obligated to follow the commands of Islam and to whom all others owe their unconditional obedience.

At the same time, Maudūdī persists within the framework offered to him by his training, which is that of a traditional scholar. This framework

---

[450] Jackson. *Mawdudi*, p. 94.

offers him a solution for coping with the problems of the 20th century, which is nothing more than an ever stricter implementation of the rules coming from the Quran and the *sunna*, as he defines them. Additionally, Maudūdī, in the same way as al-Qaraḍāwī, uses these means to claim special authority for himself.[451] Maudūdī recognizes the sole sound bridge on the way into modernity to be the establishment of a hierarchically constructed community according to the guidelines of his views – justified in the final event by his personal authority. For instance, as far as the role of women is concerned, these guidelines consist of his culturally defined demarcation between what is allowed and what is forbidden.

Maudūdī's just society, which by necessity emerges by itself from the complete implementation of Islam, does so because Islam allows people to become just, generous, and benevolent.[452] It is in the position to cope with all challenges,[453] such as poverty and injustice, by correctly implementing Islam.[454] Without possessing the special knowledge to qualify himself, Maudūdī comments on a list of topics from the fields of economics, sociology, medicine, and technology, and he argues with the assistance of pseudo-scientists. Even then, he employs what are in part antiquated arguments,[455] often "totally bizarre" ones.[456] He claims holistic solutions under

---

451 Daniel W. Brown has pointed out that Maudūdī was of the opinion that scholars particularly gifted by God (*fuqahā'*) who had spiritually delved into the Quran, the *sunna*, and Muḥammad's being in a particular way, were able to intuitively sense which traditions were to be taken as authoritative and, more specifically, which texts stem from Muḥammad and which do not. Daniel W. Brown. *Rethinking Tradition in Modern Islamic Thought*. Cambridge University Press: Cambridge, 1996, p. 127.

452 This inevitable mechanism, which is set into motion as soon as the ruler obediently submit themselves to the commands of God, is explained in detail in his writing: *taḥrīk-i islāmī kī aḫlāqī bunyāden̲* [Lahore, 1945], p. 1+7.

453 Sheila McDonough formulates it as follows: "The conversion of hearts brought ready solutions to formerly insoluble problems." Sheila McDonough. *Muslim Ethics and Modernity. A Comparative Study of the Ethical Thought of Sayyid Ahmad Khan and Mawlana Mawdudi*. Wilfried Laurier University Press: Waterloo, 1984, p. 65.

454 For that reason, Merryl Wyn Davies speaks of a "mechanical" solution, which Maudūdī offers to deal with all societal problems as soon as Islam is applied: Davies. "Legacy", p. 36.

455 A particularly impressive example for this is Maudūdīs work: Maulānā Sayyid Abū l-Aᶜlā Maudūdī. *salāmatī ka rāsta*. [Lahore, 1940] (*The Road to Peace and*

a complete Islamic order, which at its core contains an Islamized Western concept (formulated in the context of communism, for example), which he indeed rejects (democracy, for instance) to only a little time later present it with a supposedly Islamic re-definition ("theo-democracy") as a genuinely Islamic notion.

His education, practically exclusively achieved through autodidactic efforts, results in his viewing the past as well as the present from a vantage point that dovetails with his political objectives. When he invokes the early days of Islam, in which people comprehensively oriented their life towards Islam and Islam was fully implemented in society and politics, it is for him not a matter of a scholarly differentiated review of Islamic history. Rather, it has solely to do with a confirmation of his worldview and a justification of the reason why an Islamic constitution is nowadays indispensable in order to defeat the evil found in the present.

Maudūdī also places combating apostates in this context, which from his point of view is a political threat to the community of believers as in the early days of Islam. Based on his guidelines of how Islam and the homogeneous Islamic community must have looked, Maudūdī defines terms such as religious freedom according to his conceptions from an early Islam, which he then projects into the future as an ideal target.

4.4.3. The Islamic State as a Model of Hierarchy and Authority

Nothing besides the Quran and *sunna*, Muḥammad and the companions of the Prophet, the Sharia, and the caliphate should possess authority in this religiously defined state structure. The Medina *umma* is the flawless role model which has to be implemented anew. The life of everyone, when oriented towards the Quran and the *sunna*, is where the answer to all the challenges of modernity is found and how all injustices are done away with. In the process, Maudūdī transfers what he has as a focus for the Islamic state back onto the original community in Medina. That is where he apparently "rediscovers" his utopian notion of the future – within which is his notion of the uncompromising persecution and invariable execution of apostates.

Salvation), in which he explains that nature can only function because it has only a single sovereign Lord and Creator who rules everything. Humanity has to acknowledge this for its own benefit and submit itself completely to it.

[456] Davies. "Legacy", here p. 36.

In his draft of an Islamic state, Maudūdī avoids all discussion about how those responsible at the top gain their knowledge and, more specifically, who defines this path to a complete Islamic state. At the same time, absolute power in decision-making is conceded to them in the religious as well as political realms. All of this serves to show the ideologically utopian and totalitarian character of the religiously hierarchical state authority Maudūdī has in mind.[457]

All other considerations, all concepts coming from without and relating to civil and human rights, equal rights, and religious freedom have to be subordinated to an ideal of prototypical Islam. Everything that is not compatible with Maudūdī's interpretation of history is dismissed. And yet Maudūdī defines this coopting and constriction as "freedom." The term freedom can only be what the law of God prescribes and, more specifically, what Maudūdī stipulates as such.

Should the model of the state not be genuinely Islamic, then all true Muslims should campaign for a replacement of this order by an Islamic order. Whoever puts up with a non-Islamic government or pulls himself out of politics and society counts as a sinner for Maudūdī if the individual can be counted as a Muslim believer at all. This is the case even if Maudūdī does not call for penal consequences or the death penalty for the individual. With that said, Maudūdī creates a new parameter for assessing belief and unbelief. What is involved is no longer affiliation with or the practice of Islam. It is the question of participation in political upheaval at the end of which the Islamic state stands. That is what differentiates true Muslims from nominal Muslims.[458]

---

[457] Even Maudūdī's student and admirer Maryam Jameelah attests that Maudūdī has an illusionary worldview: "Searching for an earthly utopia, the Maulānā was convinced that his movement vastly could improve on anything previously known." Maryam Jameelah. "Modern Ideas and Concepts in the Work of Maulānā Sayyid Abul Aᶜlā Mawdūdī" in: *IS* 42/2 (2003), pp. 347-352, here p. 350.

[458] In a number of his works, Maudūdī asks his readers the question of whether they can even call themselves Muslim if the live in a self-determined manner and to not acknowledge the rule of God over their lives and do not stand for the renewal of Islam. This question also dominates a number of his Friday sermons, which he held near Pathankot in Punjab beginning in 1938 and which were later published under the title *Ḫutbāt*: Maulānā Sayyid Abū l-Aᶜlā Maudūdī. *Ḫutbāt*. Lahore [1957].

Since secularly defined Western states, with their comprehensive religious freedom, have no permanent right to exist as far as Maudūdī is concerned, the thought does not even arise that the civil rights there could possibly function as a model for Muslim majority countries or that the civil rights there could be desirable. Since for Maudūdī the worldview orientation lying at their base is testimony to their godlessness and obliquity, the resulting misorientations have to be overcome by the – ultimately global – victory of Islam. However, their freedoms do not need to become standards for Islamic states.

4.4.4. The Islamic State as a Precondition for Piety

Nowhere in Maudūdī's remarks is it visible that he looked beyond the "ideal" Islamic state of Pakistan, and it was for the realization of such in Pakistan which he campaigned for during his lifetime. Indeed, he proclaimed the creation of a global and uniform Islamic community, but it cannot be recognized that he includes circumstances which strongly deviate from Pakistan into his considerations.

Maudūdī's life's work was an effort to establish an Islamic state, for life according to God's commands can only first begin only through the founding of this state. A state oriented towards God's law is the necessary precondition. It provides the framework which first of all makes it possible for the believer to practice submission and obedience. This state becomes a reality when the power lies in the hands of true believers. For that reason, politics and the way to political power, respectively, are for Maudūdī not addendums but rather an elementary necessity so that the *umma* can take shape. Politics and the acquisition of power are direct ways to piety.

Maudūdī judges apostasy to be a political threat which he would like to completely remove by exterminating it from the true Islamic community. However, Maudūdī's definition of religious freedom and his prohibition on apostasy remains an edifice of ideas, a pseudo solution which would not eliminate the reality of religious conversions from the world. Maudūdīs "solution," the execution of apostates, is totalitarian and authoritarian in its orientation, a "religiously-tinged magic formula"[459] for a supposed rapid

[459] This is how Asma Afsaruddin labels Maudūdī's ideologically colored suggestions at a solution, with which he attempts to push back the ideology of his time: Afsaruddin. "Mawdūdī's 'Theo-Democracy'", p. 319.

and lasting elimination of all threats. It requires the merciless condemnation of those who think differently, their condemnation beyond doubt and without a court of appeals.

On the path to the realization of true Islamic community, Maudūdī continually speaks about "revolution." And yet, he does not mean a violent overthrow.[460] Rather, he repeatedly points out that only a gradual transformation of society into an Islamic one can be crowned with success. For that reason, from Maudūdī's perspective, instruction and education of the elite is the first step[461] to then, in turn, being in the right situation to assist in implementing Islam in the state, government, and society and to enforce it.

4.4.5. Comparison of the Positions Held by Abū l-Aᶜlā Maudūdī, Yūsuf al-Qaraḍāwī and Abdullah Saeed

iǧtihād

How the three authors Yūsuf al-Qaraḍāwī, Abdullah Saeed, and Abū l-Aᶜlā Maudūdī define the relationship between the Sharia and modernity is of great importance for the question of whether the death penalty, as it was advocated with broad agreement in the formative period of Islam by influential scholars, is today still legally and politically significant.

al-Qaraḍāwī und Abdullah Saeed would like to define the application of the Sharia in modernity through the use of *iǧtihād* (independent reasoning). However, they come to very different conclusions with the help of the use of *iǧtihād*. al-Qaraḍāwī and Abdullah Saeed direct their efforts in the direction of building a bridge between the past and the present, and they do so by modifying the circumstances of early Islam for use in modernity. For al-Qaraḍāwī, the result of these considerations is the duty to execute apostates who not only doubr Islam but rather simultaneously stir up turmoil. For Abdullah Saeed, a change of religious affiliation does not entail any

460 For that reason, Seyyed Vali Reza Nasr has rightly pointed out that Maudūdī's idea of "revolution" differs essentially from the understanding of revolution of someone of the likes of Ruḥollāh Khomeinī: Nasr. "Autobiography", p. 52.

461 Thus in 1948 he had already drafted a detailed program for the establishment of an academy for the training of future leaders: Mawdudi. *The Islamic Law and its Introduction*, pp. 55ff.

punishment at all. And for Maudūdī, a change of religion is to be punished in every case with the death penalty. The result of which elements from the time of Islam's founding have to be applied are in the end set by the three authors on their own individual authority.

Maudūdī also seeks to do some bridge building between the past and the present. However, for his part, this can only happen by comprehensively importing the early Islamic set of conditions into modernity and through uncompromisingly applying Sharia law. It would be unacceptable for Maudūdī to think that there are portions of the Sharia which in light of life in the diaspora could in part be disregarded for the sake of practicality, much less that there could be a suspension of certain contents of Sharia law on the basis of their limited application in the early days of Islam, which is what Abdullah Saeed postulates. Still, Maudūdī recognizes that with the complete application of early Islamic Sharia law one has reached an important milestone in the realization of true Islamic community.

Dealing with the Legal Sources

As far as the question of apostasy is concerned, the preliminary decision of dealing with early Islamic legal sources and assessing and weighing diverse remarks also affects the basic direction these three authors take.

As far as the al-Azhar scholar al-Qaraḍāwī is concerned, in light of the normative authority of early Islamic legal sources taught in classical theology regarding the discussion of tradition and legal decisions, it is in the best case a matter of a few interpretive variations (which in his case, for instance, comes down in the form of a warning to not precipitously execute the doubter). There is an unrestrained position of advocating the execution of apostates in the case of political unrest, which is automatically a given for al-Qaraḍāwī when there is overt apostasy. As far as he is concerned, it is predetermined because it can be derived from the legal sources.

In contrast, Abdullah Saeed enjoyed his school education and early university education in the Pakistani and Saudi Arabian educational systems. Thereafter, he received his advanced degrees in Australia, began his professional career there and found his ultimate home in a Western democracy with a multi-religious society, a Muslim minority, and complete religious freedom. He has adopted a differentiated attitude on the universal duty to apply the resolutions of the early Islamic legal community and society. In the final event, he measures legal sources against the reality of the society in which he currently lives. From this perspective, Abdullah Saeed sees the meaning of the condemnation of apostasy in early Islamic legal texts reduced to a religious moment, namely that of a sin in light of Islam's task, which nowadays no longer entails any legal consequences at all. For him it is not classical theology's guidelines on how to view legal texts which stand in the foreground. Rather, it is the pragmatic justification for having peaceful, equitable coexistence between Muslims and non-Muslims in the Western context.

For Abū l-Aᶜlā Maudūdī, neither form of access to the texts and realities of the 20th century is worthy of consideration. Neither with the comprehensive theological and judicial competence of a classical scholarly education nor armed with the openness to enable reconciliation between the early days of Islam and modernity through a depoliticization of the Sharia's claims, Maudūdī neither immerses himself in the subtleties of a credibility discussion regarding texts of tradition, such as is the case with al-Qaraḍāwī, nor in consideration of the merits of Western societies where there is complete religious freedom as is the case with Abdullah Saeed. Instead, he calls more for the uncompromising outworkings from the supposed ideal early days of Islam. That means that after a certain waiting period, every apostate had to reconsider the consequences of his attempts at political overthrow (which is always the case as Maudūdī sees it) and flee or otherwise accept the inevitable death sentence.

The Islamic Awakening

All three authors are of the opinion that the Islamic faith community urgently requires an Islamic awakening.

For Abdullah Saeed, however, it is an awakening which would lead to more Muslims turning away from traditional Sharia Islam and its interpretation, more Muslims discovering the freedom-oriented message of peace, tolerance and equality in the Quran and, accordingly, becoming active in society for the well being of their fellow citizens.

As far as al-Qaraḍāwī is concerned, the Islamic awakening, supported by instruction and education of youth, is above all an approach adapted for modernity. It is a middle path, one of moderation and the temporary suspension of certain rules owing to the minority situation Muslims have in

Western societies. However, this is done without essentially giving up Sharia claims. For al-Qaraḍāwī, the "Islamic awakening" means the assumption of a leadership and pioneering role in Western societies as well as the fulfilment of the task of *da^cwa*.

Maudūdī, in contrast, consistently assumes the majority situation of the Muslim community in which it dictates the social order and the political system. At the same time, Non-Muslims, who can only enjoy reduced rights in an Islamic state, have to submit and adapt. Maudūdī also pleads for a practical attitude in instruction and education of the ignorant. He also pleads for an explanation of the foundations and principles of Islam in an understandable language (he takes a dim view of purely traditional scholarship without reference to a practical orientation) in order to promote Islamic awakening. From Maudūdī's point of view, those who are instructed have to be placed at the loci of power in order to transform society according to the guidelines of Islam and enable people to lead a life pleasing to God.

Activism and Involvement

Abdullah Saeed calls for Western societies to dismantle their mistrust of Muslim minorities and give them the chance to participate in society. On the other hand, members of the the Muslim community should take advantage of the opportunities Western environment offers them. For Saeed, this is primarily all a matter of peaceful coexistence and a recognition of the actual state of affairs one finds in 21st century multi-religious societies.

al-Qaraḍāwī also calls for acquiring education, becoming involved, and demonstrating political participation. He does this not in order to accept the plurality of worldviews. Rather, it is so that the avant-garde of Muslim believers can be enabled to reconquer their vanguard role in Western societies which they have lost due to Western dominance.

Maudūdī likewise calls for the world to be actively refashioned in order to make it into an ideal community. According to Maudūdī, whoever only passively watches possesses a dubious faith.[462] For him it is by no means a matter of reconciliation between Western and Islamic living environments. Rather, in the 20th century, in which there is only good and evil, only peo-

[462] Sayyid Abul A'la *Mawdudi. The Islamic Movement. Dynamics of Values, Power and Change*. The Islamic Foundation: Leicester, 1984, pp. 120-121.

ple who act completely justly or absolutely objectionably, God's rule or paganism, obedience toward or rebellion against God,[463] it is a matter of the establishment of a correct way, of the one truth and the one appropriate practice of Islam as defined by Maudūdī.

Maudūdī as well as al-Qaraḍāwī assume the idea of an avant-garde which is equipped with pre-eminent knowledge of Islam and the necessary consciousness for activism in modernity in order to be able to shift the fortune of the Muslim community. On the contrary, Abdullah Saeed accepts Australian's secular 21st century society. He appears to align his standards and judgments of what is actually "Islamic" with those circumstances rather than to do the reverse.

Maudūdī as well as al-Qaraḍāwī defend the opinion that the current generation of Muslims are neither equipped with sufficient knowledge about Islam nor practice it sufficiently comprehensively in order to be able to accept the challenges of modernity. For that reason, both have established their own educational institutions in order to be personally involved in the equipping of this avant-garde.

In the reformation of society, which Abdullah Saeed never makes a point of discussion, Maudūdī as well as al-Qaraḍāwī, to a certain extent and in a comparable manner assume a slow reshaping of society. Both are of the opinion that overthrow and violence are not the means of choice but rather slow change. And knowledge is the key for its implementation. While admittedly al-Qaraḍāwī assumes that society will become increasingly Islamized with the comprehensive implementation of Islam adapted to its respective time and environment, even if the laws of a land do not change, Maudūdī believes that comprehensive Islam, when the avant-garde has recognized it to be the true practice of belief, will have to be asserted by social as well as legal implementation and not solely produced through the example of individuals who practice it.

One's Own Authority as the Standard

Although all three authors refer to the Quran, *sunna*, and the significant theologians and legal experts from the early days of Islam in order to underpin their remarks, in the final event they make their own authority the

[463] For example, comp. the detailed explanations of both sides in Maudūdī's work: *The Islamic Law and its Introduction*, pp. 10ff.

decision-making body with regard to texts and their application in today's societies.

After considering early Islamic texts, there can be no other conclusion for Abdullah Saeed regarding the execution of apostates than to see the practice deactivated and recognized for its non-practicability in modernity. On the other hand, as it relates to al-Qaraḍāwī and Maudūdī, this is precisely what cannot be involved. Instead, al-Qaraḍāwī and Maudūdī, find the texts to provide a justification for the execution of apostates in certain cases and, as the case may be, essentially mandatory execution.

Maudūdī, "the terrible simplificateur,"[464] needs to grapple with non-Islamic worldviews and thinkers as little as al-Qaraḍ āwī, and for that matter there is also no need to grapple with other Islamic theologians. He alone is authority enough and charged and warranted to work towards education, instruction, admonition, and the layout of politics for the implementation of an Islamic state. In the process, as *amīr*, Maudūdī plays the role of someone who is practically suspended above the human level as a messianic figure and as an eschatological savior of the marginalized, weakened Islamic community. For his part, Maudūdī is indeed obligated to follow the commandments of Islam. Yet he interprets and defines them himself, while all others owe unconditional obedience to him.

Autonomy and Obedience

While Abdullah Saeed esteems the autonomy of the mature believer as an important instrument for freeing oneself from a politicized understanding of the Sharia, Maudūdī, similar to al-Qaraḍāwī, recognizes obliquity in man's autonomy, through which man is released from God's law and gives up his complete loyalty, his obedience, and his devotion which make him into a true believer in the first place. According to Maudūdī's understanding, this devotion first applies to God. After that it applies to the *amīr* and to the leadership elite, demanding obedience and submission, not independence and individual responsibility. By virtue of this, Maudūdī as well as al-Qaraḍāwī claim for themselves an exceptional authority.

Maudūdī is of the opinion that autonomy and self-determination are dangerous for people. This is due to the fact that they lead them into inde-

464 Murawiec. *Mind*, p. 261.

pendence from God's law and his dictates; indeed, Maudūdī defends the idea that the God-fearing individual completely gives up his autonomy.

al-Qaraḍāwī would also like to lead the believer to permanent dependence upon the scholars authorized to lead, among whom al-Qaraḍāwī occupies a special status. He clearly makes a far-reaching instructive leadership claim over the global *umma*. This is also expressed in his worldwide involvement in umbrella organizations, financial institutions, and the media.

State and Society

Abdullah Saeed publishes his statements about human rights and religious freedom before the backdrop of the free, multi-religious, and multi-cultural society of Australia, and in the process enters into a reciprocal relationship with the Australian state of sponsorship and support via a university setting and diverse advisory boards. al-Qaraḍāwī, in contrast, has composed a number of publications for the Muslim minority in the European diaspora, which he knows from his own experience through activities in quite a few scholarly and financial boards domiciled in the Western world. It is not foreseen in Maudūdī's worldview that Muslims live as a minority in a state which is not ruled by Islam. Only an Islamic government and legislative apparatus can offer a Muslim believer a home.

On the contrary, the state is not the precondition for a life as a Muslim believer for al-Qaraḍāwī. From his point of view, the actual precondition is educating and instructing believers so that through their formation a new consciousness and a good knowledge of Islam can become a forerunner and set of role models for the penetration of society with Islam.

As far as Maudūdī is concerned, there is no differentiation whatsoever between that which is religious and that which is political in a state in which Islam is applied in its fullness. The two are the same. For that reason, there is no "private sphere" at all – also not with respect to apostasy from Islam – all actions simultaneously have a religious as well as a political character. While al-Qaraḍāwī expressly concedes this private sphere to the apostate, one in which he is allowed to harbour doubts about Islam and remains exempt from punishment as long as he does not go public about his convictions and try to promote them, Maudūdī has no realm at all which is not affected by society and the state order. The apostate always acts in a political manner since he always undermines the state order with his apostasy. There is no neutrality. In the process, Maudūdī remains true to the frame of reference of traditional scholars given him by his training. This frame of reference offers nothing else as an answer to the questions of the 20th century (e.g., the dispute with other religions and worldviews) than an even more rigorous implementation of the prescriptions of the Quran and *sunna*, as he defines them himself.

Abdullah Saeed has completely decoupled citizenship from religious affiliation. From his point of view, democratic, Western society can also become home for Muslims.

For al-Qaraḍāwī, the question of citizenship has no recognizable meaning. From his standpoint, one's actual identity lies in rootedness in the *umma* as well in following the commands of Islam which Muslims can implement in every society, including those societies in the West. However, Maudūdī couples citizenship and a confession of faith by assuming that only Muslims can be fully entitled citizens and by having a confession to belief in Islam as simultaneously equivalent to citizenship.

Abdullah Saeed acknowledges democracy. He sees himself obligated to its laws and views its ethical values as agreeing with those of Islam. In this sense, democracy counts for him as an Islamic state.

al-Qaraḍāwī criticizes Western society, which according to his understanding is immoral. However, he uses democracy for purposes of the *daʿwa*, and in the process remains committed to God's law. In the final event, Maudūdī completely rejects democracy and the laws of Western nations as a system of unbelief: He only accepts their Islamized form, which is "theo-democracy."

A Comprehensive Understanding of Islam

While Abdullah Saeed divides the message of Islam into politico-social and ethical-religious components and views the former as no longer obligatory and universally valid in our present time, neither Maudūdī nor al-Qaraḍāwī conduct such a division. Abdullah Saeed expressly encourages critical engagement with the historical legacy of Islam and a distancing from political content which a number of groups justify with Islam.

Maudūdī and al-Qaraḍāwī defend the view that Islam has to be lived out in a comprehensive manner and that its claim to regulate all personal and socio-political spheres may not be curtailed. However, where this comprehensive form of Islam has not been lived out (yet) or, more specifically, the society is determined by other values, al-Qaraḍāwī hopes that after a time of compromise and of moderation there will be a dissipation of these contradictions due to a gradual Islamization of the society by youth educated and trained in Islam. For Maudūdī, in contrast, the implementation of Islam has as its precondition legislation and politics in order for Islam to be lived out at all. Indeed, this is a precondition for being able to be a true believer. An Islam which only exists as a private belief is for Maudūdī no Islam at all, and a believer who does not take a stand for change in societal conditions through "revolution" has already abandoned Islam.

Life in Modern Society

Maudūdī views an environment which is not completely Islamized, which is pervaded by a Western body of thought and is inimical and blighted, as one where the complete implementation of Islam would bring about a rebirth into a peaceful, just, and moral society. al-Qaraḍāwī, on the other hand, does not plead for combating the environment in which Muslims find themselves living as a minority. Rather, he pleads to utilize the good – e.g., the opportunities there for education – without taking on the measures of value belonging thereto.

Abdullah Saeed pleads for an unreserved mutual acceptance of Muslims and non-Muslims. Additionally, he pleads for the discovery of common values which he perceives to be the core of religion for both Islam and Christianity and which he sees as realized in Australia's society.

According to Abdullah Saeed, neither religious conviction nor cultural reasons are acceptable bases for calling for segregation. In contrast, al-Qaraḍāwī pleads, as does Maudūdī, for clear distancing from everything which is not Islamic and is objectionable. al-Qaradāwī particularly does this with respect to the minority situation in the diaspora, while Maudūdī does so more with regard to the Islamic region that is geographically separated from West and its omnipresent ideologies.

With co-opting Islamic society for its own goals, al-Qaraḍāwī and Maudūdī fill a vacuum: It is a vacuum in the third generation of migrants who find themselves in the diaspora with respect to their identity and standpoint. It creates a new self-assured identity (al-Qaraḍāwī) or, as the case may be, fills the vacuum of knowledge which is lacking about Islam and of the trauma of disempowerment after the end of the Mogul period, the humiliation of the colonial period, and the abolishment of the caliphate (Maudūdī).

4.4.6. Outlook

Maudūdī can under no circumstances be lined up with *Jihādist* movements proclaiming suicide and martyrdom. He has nowhere called for political overthrow in connection with implementing the Sharia, nor have there been calls for terror or suicide attacks. For, as one author has stated: "Maududi was no backwater fanatic."[465]

On the other hand, it is obvious that Maudūdī not only clearly positioned himself against pluralism, the equal rights of Muslims and non-Muslims or men and women.[466] Rather, he spoke out with recourse to the ideal of an Islamic state for a comprehensive application of the Sharia, including the Islamic penal code. For Maudūdī, when it came to applying this to apostates, it meant to unconditionally administer the death penalty. Just as he wanted to revitalize and reform Islam,[467] and wanted to have Islam resurrected in a renewed form through the role model function of *Jamāᶜat-i-Islāmī*, he did not want to see the entire society contaminated by those who from his point of view had politically rebellious intentions and wanted to accomplish the opposite, as, for instance, the apostates.

As far as what the execution of individuals who change their worldview means in a society in its practical application, Maudūdī does not say a single word. He devotes himself solely to the theoretical side of this topic. He does not explain who would be entitled to determine apostasy in the case of an individual charged and who should condemn and execute him. He only assesses that in this state there is no place for individuals who think differently, and there is no place for comprehensive religious freedom as well as religious conversion in any direction. This is due to the

465 Collins. "Islamization", p. 532.

466 Riaz Ahmad has correctly noted that there are three categories of people in Maududi's ideal state, namely Muslim men, Muslim women, and non-Muslims, to which various rights belong: Ahmad. *Maududi and the Islamic State*, p. 154.

467 Maudūdī is, among other things, labelled a "restorer": Ahmed. *Concept*, p. 112.

fact that the stability of the state as a community of believers would thereby be subverted.[468] Maudūdī's idea of the state and society is characterized by totalitarianism and intolerance.

With his demand to execute an apostate living within the national territory no matter what, without considering any mitigating circumstances or looking for other solutions – since due to an apostate's sheer existence he presents a political danger – Maudūdī prepares an ideological breeding ground for intolerance among religious communities, for persecution, ostracism, and the attack upon life and limb of those who think differently

The seed in this breeding ground has continued to come up since Maudūdī's death, co-determined by a number of political, economic, and undesirable social developments. The situation for adherents of minorities such as the Aḥmadīya, Christians,[469] or progressive Muslims continues to be precarious. Whoever has low social status, little education, or little professional legal help and gets crushed under the wheels of a charge of apostasy is threatened today more than ever with arbitrariness, incarceration, and violence.[470]

The way Pakistan deals with minorities and those who think differently is to a large extent a barometer of the absent positive foundation for tolerance and pluralism as well as a characteristic of what continues to be an

---

[468] Also in his writing entitled *taḥrīk-i islāmī kī aḫlāqī bunyāden̲* [Lahore, 1945], Maudūdī explains that that individual who revokes his "obedience" *(ṭāᶜat)* towards God and gives up his membership in the community deserves the death penalty *(qatl)*, even if he formally remains a believing Muslim: Sayyid Abū l-Aᶜlā Maudūdī. *taḥrīk-i islāmī kī aḫlāqī bunyāden̲* [Lahore, 1945], p. 3.

[469] M. G. Chitkara laments that, for instance, several voices call today for classifying Christians in Pakistan as *ḏimmī*, thus as conquered alien residents and as tolerated, less privileged second class citizens in Islamic regions, although in all probability they were already endemic there long before the arrival of Islam in the 8th century A.D.: M. G. Chitkara. *Human Rights in Pakistan.* A.P.H. Publishing Corporation: New Dehli, 1997, p. 158.

[470] In March 2013, after unsubstantiated rumor was spread in Lahore that the Christian Sawan Masih had uttered blasphemous remarks against Muḥammad, 3.000 Muslims are reported to have plundered and burnt down the Christian quarter of the city. Several Hundreds of Christian families had to flee from their homes. It is believed that the background of the incident was the desire to capture the land of Sawan Masih. Comp. the report: Pakistan. Todesurteil wegen Blasphemie, 7.4.2014. https://www.opendoors.de/aktiv-werden/informiert-bleiben/gemeindebrief_news/2014/april_pakistan/ (10.6.2014).

unresolved question of the role Islam should play in the country. The question of Pakistan's identity appears to continue to be unanswered. Because his strongly ideological understanding of the state and his ahistorical, utopian model of applying the Sharia offered no practical answers at all for coping with the pending problems of modernity or a sensible ordering of society, Maudūdī contributed nothing to a constructive answer to this question.[471] Rather, his understanding further polarized society – in particular with regard to minorities such as the Aḥmadīya.

Maudūdī never held an official political position in Pakistan and was only firmly rooted in *Jamāᶜat-i-Islāmī*, which since its formation was a minority movement and was never successful on the political stage and as far as political participation was concerned. Nevertheless, Maudūdī's body of ideas and his interpretation of Islam has left deep traces in society, the constitution, and even in the compendium of laws found in the Pakistani penal code. This is the case even if he was above all a generalist, tracing out broad lines in his remarks and often leaving his reader at a loss with respect to the question of how his postulates should be implemented in practice. Nevertheless, his painting black and white pictures of issues, the intensive lobbying work, the indefatigable production of books, and the emphatic demands made by Maudūdī' and his movement have all shaped intellectual history and the international Islamist movement.

At the present time, the crises of the past in Pakistan, the "country of the pure", appear to be less mastered than ever before. Instead, they appear to have intensified and new threats for the stability of the country have come along. Up to now, there has not been a single condemned victim of the "Blasphemy laws" who has actually been executed. However, it speaks volumes that it is even possible that the mere assertion of an accuser can mean the incarceration of the individual charged with blasphemy. It can also mean exposure to violence and abuse in custody or assassination attempts in broad daylight. Along with this, one possible consequence is that in the case of acquittal, the accused and his family have to go underground

[471] One of his utopian suggestions was, for instance, that after the erection of a "block of Muslim countries", complete passport and visa limitations could go into effect for Muslims: Maududi. *Unity of the Muslim World*, p. 32.

and as a general rule lose their possessions, home, work, safety, their family, and local community.[472]

It is not only the perennial reports of violence against members of minorities and against those who think differently, the arbitrary charges of blasphemy against the defenseless, and attacks against high-ranking officials who take a stand for victims. It is also the inaction of police forces in the case of attacks on victims and the unwillingness of the judicial apparatus to track down the guilty and to impose still penalties.[473] In short, there is the following: the failure of politics in light of an apparently growing intolerance and deterioration of the situation for the defenseless victims of arbitrariness, the abuse of power, and religious extremism. Added to that are further problems such as the desolate economic situation, exacerbated by a number of natural catastrophes in recent years, the plight of education, corruption up into the circles of government, a military sector

[472] The legal attempt to defuse the abuse potential of the "Blasphemy Laws" and to threaten a false charges with up to ten years of imprisonment had to be withdrawn. After a revision of the law, since 1995 the credibility of an accuser has to be demonstrated before a charge can be accepted. However, in practice this has had little impact and has encountered stubborn opposition among religious groups: According to Gabriel. *Citizens*, pp. 9+64-65.

[473] In a terrorist attack made on two Aḥmadīya mosques in Lahore on May 28, 2010, around 90 people were killed and 120 injured. The attack lasted for three hours and was unhindered by security forces. Such events, as was uttered locally, were the consequence of the ideologization and Islamification of society under Zia ul-Haqq in the 1980s and the "Blasphemy Laws" which were intensified at that time. There were calls made by "Mullahs . . . in the mosques for the murder of Ahmadi which went unpunished." Andreas Spalinger. "Von der Vision des Staatsgründers Jinnah weit entfernt. Der unter dem Militärdiktator Zia ul-Haqq gross gewordenen jungen Generation in Pakistan ist religiöse Toleranz fremd." *NZZ* Online, 3.3.2011. http://www.nzz.ch/nachrichten/politik/international/von_der_vision_des_staatsgruenders_jinnah_weit_entfernt_1.9749775.html (10.6.2014). – In another case, there were two lawyers for the Aḥmadīya movement who wanted to apply for the release of an incarcerated convert to the Aḥmadīya movement in return for bail and who were outright executed outside of the courtroom while police forces unmovingly observed the events unfolding; the culprits were not prosecuted: According to Dominic Moghal. "The Status of Non-Muslims in the Islamic Republic of Pakistan. A Confused Identity" in: Dominic Moghal; Jennifer Jivan (eds.). *Religious Minorities in Pakistan: Struggle for Identity*. Christian Study Centre: Rawalpindi, 1996, pp. 21-30, here p. 21.

which is in part ailing and has ties to extremists, the traditional enmity to India, and the continuing unresolved Kashmir conflict. Beyond that, however, there is increasing radicalization due to a number of the factors mentioned but also due to influential voices promoted by the world of scholarship. Maudūdī's "seed of the word" has sprouted – not only his wordsDa, but also his words.

5. Concluding Remarks: Paths to an Increase in Religious Freedom?

After having just discussed and summarized the individual positions held by Yūsuf al-Qaraḍāwī, Abdullah Saeed, and Abū l-Aᶜlā Maudūdī on the topic of apostasy in Sections 2.4, 3.4, and 4.4, and then having compared them with each other, this short concluding chapter is dedicated to addressing the question of possible future developments on the path to increased freedom of religion in Muslim majority societies. This question arises in light of the fact that as a general rule religious freedom only exists there to a limited degree.[1] Furthermore, what is mostly a one-sided freedom to turn to Islam but not, however, to be able to turn from it is defended by influential theologians as indispensable and defended as a position justified by Sharia law.

From the perspective of Western democracies, unlimited religious freedom, and the reality of multi-religious societies of the 21st century which are additionally pluralized through the globalization of the media, this could suggest that personalities such as Yūsuf al-Qaraḍāwī or Abū l-Aᶜlā Maudūdī, who speak out for the execution of apostates in the case of apostasy from Islam, are nowadays on the fringes of Islamic theology and that their opinions find little approval in Muslim majority societies. However, this is not the case.

Most of the statements coming from the spectrum of the classic Islamic *ᶜulamā'* fall within the range of Yusuf al-Qaradawi's reduced endorsement of religious freedom as an internal freedom of conscience.[2] Perhaps this comes with the limitation that not all advocates of this point of view speak out so emphatically for the administration of the death penalty as soon as the apostate speaks about his religious conversion. However, as Gudrun

---

1 Comp. as a comprehensive overview the study by Paul Marshall; Nina Shea. *Silenced. How Apostasy & Blasphemy Codes are Choking Freedom Worldwide.* Oxford University Press: Oxford, 2011.

2 Significant representatives of reform Islam, such as Rašīd Riḍā, defended this middle position: Jomier J. *Le Commentaire Coranique du Manār. Tendences Modernes de L'Exégèse Coranique en Égypte.* Éditions G.-P. Maisonneuve & Cie: Paris, 1954, pp. 290-291.

Krämer has appropriately noted: "The hard line [meaning the uncompromising endorsement of the death penalty] also still has numerous supporters,"[3] over against which there are a few advocates of complete religious freedom[4] on the other side.

Indeed, there are perceptible voices of those Muslim intellectuals who like Abdullah Saeed speak out for complete religious freedom and promote this notion at conferences and in their publications. The mere fact that this understanding of the compatibility of Islam and complete religious freedom is promoted does not mean that it appears to have been pushed through on a broad front. Apparently, the established scholarly world holds too firmly to the traditional position defined by the Sharia, and this position is defended with the entire authority of scholars and with reference to the authoritative source texts – with considerable consequences for the involved individuals.

In light of the discrepancy between the state (predominantly secular) penal code and that which is preached by traditional scholars with reference to the Quran and tradition as God's law (namely the duty to kill apostates), the apostate can also not be certain about the safety of his life where there is a lack of state legislation. This is due to the fact that apart from the diverse consequences according to civil law, the individual can either be attacked on the street or the judge can interpret "Sharia law according to the demands of public interest" and can punish the individual according to his own discretion.[5]

If an apostate has suffered at the hands of private individuals, this can entail no criminal prosecution or only slight prosecution in a number of countries (e.g., in Pakistan or Iran). Quite a few theologians have even ex-

---

3 Krämer. *Staat*, p. 155.

4 See, for instance, the comprehensive justification for complete religious freedom by Shaikh Abdur Rahman. *Punishment of Apostasy in Islam*. Institute of Islamic Culture: Lahre, 1978². Shaikh Abdur Rahman, former Chief Justice of the Supreme Court of Pakistan first submitted this comprehensive rationale for complete freedom of religion in Islam, arguing primarily on the basis of the Quran and tradition, in 1977.

5 This possibility is mentioned by Lukas Wick as a possibility for punishing "infringements against God's commandments . . . if they are not at all more precisely defined in the penal code." Lukas Wick. *Islam und Verfassungsstaat. Theologische Versöhnung mit der politischen Moderne?* Ergon: Würzburg, 2009, pp. 132-133.

pressly declared that it is the duty of every Muslim believer to kill an apostate if the government does not perform this duty.[6]

What individual scholars say on the topic of apostasy and the fact that overall so few advocates of religious freedom speak out are not the only things which have a fatal impact. It is also the fact that so many people do not take a position against the punishment of apostates even if, as Saira Malika supposes, they themselves would not advance against an apostate.[7] Nevertheless, they do not actively reject the Sharia's claim of the death penalty. Overall, there are still very few theologians who fundamentally challenge the position of the advocates of the death penalty.

One of the problems along the way to greater religious freedom in Muslim majority societies is the fact that through the early Islamic *ridda* wars the topic of apostasy is linked with rebellion, schism within the Muslim community, and political unrest. For those reasons, up to the present day it is not only seen as a theological problem. Rather, it is also seen as political agitation. Additionally, Sharia law counts unreservedly as part of divine revelation and it is taught as such up to the present day. Criticism of this view easily exposes the involved individual to suspicion of heresy.

A further set of problems arises out of the fact that the death penalty was "... set at this early time and this punishment ... [was] not contested in any epoch of Islamic history."[8] In other words, up to the time of the formation of Sharia law in the 10th century, the most influential theologians' rather unanimous call for the death penalty was never essentially declared to be invalid, abolished, or superseded by the four Sunni schools and the significant Twelver Shiite legal school from within the Shiite domain. For that reason, those calling for increased civil rights and liberties for those who think differently either doubt the hermeneutics of their forefathers, mask out the far-reaching consensus in this question up to the 10th century, or, as Abdullahi an-Na'im, call for a systematic reorientation in reaching legal rulings. This is due to the fact that:

> "... apostasy and related notions cannot simply be abolished through purely secular legislation without sufficient Islamic justification because of the paramount moral and social authority of Shari'a among Muslims ... Achieving

---

6 According to Forstner. "Menschenrecht", p. 116 on ᶜAbd al-Qādir ᶜAudā.

7 Malik. "Analysis", p. 222.

8 Griffel. "Anwendung", pp. 353-354.

> the necessary degree of Islamic reform also requires the reformation of *usul al-fiqh*, because traditional as well as alternative interpretations of the Qur'an and Sunna are necessarily the product of the historical context of the Muslim society of a specific time and place."[9]

A further problem on the path to increased religious freedom lies in the fact that apostasy is so closely linked to legal consequences in civil law (e.g., with compulsory divorce or disinheritance according to Sharia law) and to stirring up social furor. Along with that, a change of religion appears to itself be an unlawful action. In this connection, Nisrine Abiad speaks of the "criminalization of apostasy."[10]

Furthermore, according to classical Sharia law, apostasy is linked to a change in the legal status of the involved individual: The apostate changes from a respected citizen who enjoys all the rights of a citizen and the solidarity of community to an outcast who in a number of societies no longer possesses any legal status at all, indeed not even being able to claim the limited rights of a *ḏimmī*. Rather, at least theoretically, the person counts as a condemned outlaw according to Sharia law.

Even if the apostate does not become the victim of violent attacks, it is especially his voluntary abandonment of the Islamic community, when linked to a conversion to another religion judged to be inferior, such as Christianity, which can in many cases be viewed as a great disgrace to one's own family. Repudiation of the apostate can also be the response if not even persecution by one's own family.[11] In short, Apostasy as a general rule is viewed as a social wrong or injustice, and in a number of countries it is even viewed by the majority as a severe offense.

According to comprehensive data collection undertaken the "Pew Research Center for the People and the Press", an opinion research insti-

---

9 Abdullahi Ahmed An-Na'im. *Islam and the Secular State. Negotiating the Future of Shari'a*. Harvard University Press: Cambridge, 2008, pp. 123-124.

10 Nisrine Abiad. Sharia, *Muslim States and International Human Rights Treaty Obligations: A Comparative Study*. British Institute of International and Comparative Law: London, 2008, p. 27.

11 Comp., for instance, the autobiographical account of the convert to the Catholic faith: Joseph Fadelle. *Das Todesurteil. Als ich Christ wurde im Irak*. Sankt Ulrich Verlag: Augsburg, 2011.

tute,[12]in Washington, D.C. in the middle of 2010, a survey of around 8,000 people in Muslim majority countries showed that 84% of all Muslims in Egypt, 86% of all Muslims in Jordan, and 76% of all Muslims in Pakistan advocated the death penalty for apostasy.[13]

Thus, as Lorenz Müller has declared, it only appears that "the matter of fact of apostasy – and in most cases also the mentioned legal consequences – for the majority of Islamists"[14] is something which is abided by; at least in a number of regions, it also appears to have become a substantial part of their worldview in the middle of society. This is the case even if it is not to be assumed that every one of these advocates would personally act in the case of real persecution of an apostate.[15]

This high percentage of affirmation of norms under Sharia law is not to be understood as agreement with existing national law, which in almost all Muslim majority countries is secular in nature. Instead, it is more important to ask about the influence of opinion leaders, in particular of theologians from the Islamist spectrum. Their notions are apparently clearly apprehended by the public – particularly if one bears in mind the example of the killing of Farağ Fūda in 1992. Also, they appear to have an aggravating effect on the street[16] more than theologians advocating liberal approaches have been able to effect a reorientation of traditional theology or

---

12 Pew Research Center for the People and the Press: http://people-press.org/ (10.6.2014).

13 In Turkey, on the other hand, 91% rejected it, in Lebanon 86%, and in Indonesia 64%. Comp. the results of the study at http://pewglobal.org/2010/12/02/muslims-around-the-world-divided-on-hamas-and-hezbollah/ (10.6.2014).

14 Müller. *Islam*, p. 151.

15 In a television debate on Al-Risala TV on November 5, 2007, the Kuwaiti Sheik Tareq Al-Sweidan and two Egyptian scholars Gamal 'Allam and Gamal Al-Bana discussed the question of freedom of religious conversion in Kuwait. The viewers, who were included via a survey, rejected freedom for Muslims to leave Islam by a margin of 76%; demands for the death penalty were also made from among the callers. Gamal 'Allam expressed the opinion that in the case of a Muslim who is not convinced of Islam, "there is something wrong in his head . . . Anybody who is insane should go to a mental asylum, or else if he is insane, his head should be removed so that it does not contaminate the heads of others." "Muslim Scholars in TV Debate on Apostates in Islam." MEMRI Special Dispatch No 1781, 7.12.2007. http://www.memri.org/report/en/0/0/0/0/0/0/2477.htm (10.6.2014).

16 Ami Ayalon formulates the body of thought they propagated: "The main battlefield is the street." Ayalon. *Quest*, p. 26.

bring about moderate societal treatment of converts. Book markets, mosques, universities, and the modern media apparently offer Islamist-oriented opinion leaders a larger forum for exercising influence than reform oriented intellectuals have been able to mobilize.

Consequently, there is the question of how the voices of those theologians who have the effect of a moderating influence or, more specifically, endorse unlimited civil rights and liberties could find a better hearing. In order to move classical theology to a reorientation, is it enough for moderate voices to take up opposite positions to theologians who carry a great amount of weight and have classical scholarly training, such as Yūsuf al-Qaraḍāwī, and who refer to the normative interpretations of scholars up to the preliminary closure of the manner of ascertaining justice in the 10th century? Which authority can be placed in the balance by progressive theologians such as Abdullah Saeed when they want to put limitations on the customary source interpretations by founders and students of the four legal schools?

One could arguably express agreement with scholars such as Abdullahi an-Na'im that a reorientation of classical Islamic theology only appears conceivable via a discussion of the basic validity of Sharia law, of the sources regarding the finding of justice under Sharia law, and of interpretive principles. The result is that more theologians come to the viewpoint, as did an-Na'im, that *ḥadd* punishment for apostasy and its legal consequences are seen as part of the Medinan period and the death penalty for apostasy is viewed as abrogated.[17]

Owing to the distinctive features of Sharia law with respect to its character and its provenance, it appears to be difficult to imagine that comprehensive civil rights and liberties could develop regarding the issues of religious affiliation, of religious conversion, of the historical-critical reconsideration of Islam, or regarding the issue of a lack of religious affiliation without a foundational re-examination of the Sharia by the theological establishment: "This is due to the fact that Islamic law, as the Quran itself, holds apostasy to be the gravest sin of all and to be an attack upon God and the community."[18]

---

17 According to An-Na'im's understanding, there are no legal consequences which arise from apostasy, and no *ta'zīr* (discretionary) punishment may be imposed: An-Na'im. *Reformation*, p. 109.

18 Khoury. *Toleranz*, p. 111.

In terms of the effects European powers had on the Ottoman Empire in the middle of the 19th century, by which diplomatic efforts the administration of the death penalty for apostasy was suspended, Ahmet Mumçu consequently concludes the following on the relationship between theology and practice:[19] "The problem remained – and remains in many an Islamic country nowadays where Islamic law applies – theoretically and theologically unresolved."[20] This is due to the fact that according to the predominant theological opinion, there is a command to kill that is inherent in the Quran and formulated as imperative in tradition and would require a theological justification for it to be permanently eliminated from society.

As a consequence, Armin Hasemann's conclusion also appears – specifically nowadays around the time of the Arab revolutions – to continue to be relevant:

> "Whether the problem of apostasy will be defused in the future or not is ultimately and unquestionably dependent upon the result of the struggle between radical Islamic forces and progressive forces and will be determined by the Islamic masses' acceptance of confining religion to the private sphere and the extent to which their consciousness detaches from tradition."[21]

---

19 Comp. the description in: Subaşı. "Apostasy", pp. 1-34.

20 Mumçu. "Lage", p. 98.

21 Hasemann. "Apostasiediskussion", p. 119.

6. Bibliography

Book titles and names of authors have been compiled according to the transcription of the respective publications, even if one has to accept that names such as Abū l-Aᶜlā Maudūdī are recorded in the bibliography under several spellings (e.g., Sayyid Abū l-Aᶜlā Maudoodī; S. Abu A'la Mawdudi, or Maulana Abul Ala Maududi). Details in brackets have been indirectly deduced.

6.1. Sources

6.1.1. Sources Relating to Yūsuf al-Qaraḍāwī

"Group of Muftis. Source of the Punishment for Apostasy", 26.07.2003. http://www.onislam.net/english/ask-the-scholar/crimes-and-penalties/apostasy/169569.html (15.04.2014)

al-Qaraḍāwī, Yūsuf. *al-ḥalāl wa-'l-ḥarām fi 'l-islām*. dār iḥyā' al-kutub al-ᶜarabīya: al-Qāhira, 1960/dār al-iᶜtiṣām: al-Qāhira, 1974⁸/maktab al-islāmī: Dimašq: 1980¹³/dār al-ta'āruf: Beirut, 1993

al-Qaraḍāwī, Yūsuf. *ẓāhirat al-ġulūw fi 't-takfīr*. dār al-ǧihād/dār al-iᶜtiṣām: [al-Qāhira, 1978]

al-Qaradawi, Jusuf. *Erlaubtes und Verbotenes im Islam*. SKD Bavaria: München, 1989

al-Qaraḍāwī, Yūsuf. *al-awlawīyāt al-ḥaraka al-islāmīya fi 'l-marḥala al-qādima*. maktabat wahba: al-Qāhira, 1990

al-Qaraḍāwī, Yūsuf. *malāmiḥ al-muǧtamaᶜ al-muslim allaḏī nanšuduhū*. maktabat wahba: al-Qāhira, 1993

al-Qaraḍāwī, Yūsuf. *al-iǧtihād wa-'l-muᶜāṣir baina 'l-inḍibāṭ wa-'l-infirāṭ*. dār at-tauzīᶜ wa-'n-našr al-islāmīya: al-Qāhira, 1994

al-Qaradawi, Yusuf. *The Lawful and the Prohibited in Islam (Al-Halal Wal Haram Fil Islam)*. Hindustan Publications: Delhi, 1998

al-Qaraḍāwī, Yūsuf. *al-iḫwān al-muslimūn.70 ᶜāman fi 'd-daᶜwa wa-'t-tarbiya wa-'l-ǧihād*. maktabat wahba: al-Qāhira, 1999

al-Qaraḍāwī, Yūsuf. *ṯaqāfatunā baina 'l-infitāḥ wa-'l-inġilāq*. dār aš-šurūq: al-Qāhira, 2000

al-Qaraḍāwī, Yūsuf. *fī fiqh al-aqallīyāt al-muslima. ḥayāt al-muslimīn wasaṭ al-muǧtamaᶜāt al-uḫrā*. dār aš-šurūq: al-Qāhira, 2001 al-Qaraḍāwī, Yūsuf. *al-ḥall al-islāmī, farīda wa-ḍarūra*. maktabat wahba: al-Qāhira, 2001[5]

al-Qaradawi, Yusuf. "Freedom of expression from an Islamic perspective", 10.06.2002. http://www.onislam.net/english/ask-the-scholar/shariah-based-systems/imamate-and-political-systems/174717-freedom-of-expression-from-an-islamic-perspective.html?Political_Systems= (15.04.2014)

al-Qaradawi, Yusuf. "How Islam views Secularism", 22.06.2002. http://www.onislam.net/english/ask-the-scholar/ideologies-movements-and-religions/175438-how-islam-views-secularism.html?Religions= (05.05.2014)

al-Qaradawi, Yusuf. "Donating Organs to non-Muslims", 24.06.2002. http://www.onislam.net/english/ask-the-scholar/health-and-science/medicine/174946 (05.05.2014)

al-Qaraḍāwī, Yūsuf. "Le danger de l'apostasie ... et la lutte contra la zizanie", 30.12.2002. http://www.islamophile.org/spip/Le-danger-de-l-apostasie-et-la.html (15.04.2014)

al-Qaraḍāwī, Yūsuf. *ibn al-qarya wa-'l-kuttāb. malāmiḥ sīra wa-masīra*, 4 Vols., dār aš-šurūq: al-Qāhira, 2002-2011

al-Qaradawi, Yusuf. "Fatwa on Intellectual Apostasy", 24.03.2003. http://www.onislam.net/english/ask-the-scholar/crimes-and-penalties/apostasy/175287.html (05.5.2014)

al-Qaraḍāwī, Yūsuf. "Bringing Religions Closer: Is that Possible?" 29.05.2004. http://www.onislam.net/english/ask-the-scholar/dawah-principles/dawah-to-non-and-new-muslims/174432.html?New_Muslims= (15.04.2014)

al-Qaradawi, Yusuf. "Does Inability to Treat Wives Equally Prohibit Polygamy?" 27.07.2004. http://www.onislam.net/english/ask-the-scholar/family/polygamy/170404.html (15.04.2014)

al-Qaraḍāwī, Yūsuf. *ġair al-muslimīn fi 'l muğtamaᶜ al islāmī*. maktabat wahba: al-Qāhira, 2005[4]

al-Qaraḍāwī, Yūsuf. *ğarīmat ar-ridda wa-ᶜuqūbat al-murtadd fī ḍau' al-qur'ān wa-'s-sunna*. silsilat rasā'il taršīd aṣ-ṣaḥwa, Nr. 6. maktabat wahba: al-Qāhira, 2005[3]

al-Qaraḍāwī, Yūsuf. "al-ḥurrīya ad-dīnīya wa-'l-fikrīya", Nachschrift der Sendung aš-šarīᶜa wa-'l-ḥayāt, 06.02.2005. http://www.qaradawi.net/site/topics/article.asp?cu_no=3841&version=1&template_id=105&transparent_id=16 (16.02.2011)

al-Qaraḍāwī, Yūsuf. *al-islām wa-'l-ᶜunf*. dār aš-šurūq: al-Qāhira, 2005

al-Qaraḍāwī, Yūsuf. *aṣ-ṣaḥwa al-islāmīya baina 'l-ğumūd wa-'t-taṭarruf*. dār aš-šurūq: al-Qāhira, 2005[2]

al-Qaraḍāwī, Yūsuf. "ḫuṭūrat ar-ridda wa-ᶜuqūbat al-murtadd", 27.03.2006. http://www.onislam.net/arabic/ask-the-scholar/8397/8320/43372-2004-08-01%2017-37-04.html (15.04.2014) al-Qaradawi, Yusuf. "Apostasy: Major and Minor", 13.04.2006. http://www.onislam.net/english/shariah/contemporary-issues/islamic-themes/413125.html (15.04.2014)

al-Qaradawi, Yusuf. "Palestinian Women Carrying out Martyr Operations", 06.11.2006. http://www.onislam.net/english/ask-the-scholar/international-relations-and-jihad/jihad-rulings-and-regulations/175306.html?Regulations= (15.04.2014)

al-Qaraḍāwī, Yūsuf. *ḥaqīqat at-tauḥīd*. maktabat wahba: al-Qāhira, 2006[8]

al-Qaraḍāwī, Yūsuf. *al-islām wa-'l-ᶜalmānīya wağhan li-wağh*. maktabat wahba: al-Qāhira, 2006[2]

al-Qaradawi, Yusuf. "Duties of Muslims Living in the West", 27.05.2007. http://www.onislam.net/english/ask-the-scholar/dawah-principles/dawah-to-non-and-new-muslims/175226.html?New_Muslims= (15.04.2014)

al-Qaraḍāwī, Yūsuf. "ḥurma ad-dimā'", 25.10.2007. http://www.qaradawi.net/ßnew/articles/1267-2012-02-05-19-28-41 (05.05.2014)

al-Qaraḍāwī, Yūsuf. *al-ḥurrīya ad-dīnīya wa-'t-taᶜaddudīya fī naẓar al-islām*. maktab al-islāmī: Bairūt, 2007

al-Qaraḍāwī, Yūsuf. "al-muğtamaᶜ al-muslim wa-muwāğahat ar-ridda", 28.02.2008. http://mdarik.islamonline.net/servlet/Satellite?c=ArticleA_C&cid=1175010105612&pagename=Zone-Arabic-MDarik%2FMDALayout (03.08.2010)

al-Qaraḏāwī [sic], Yūsuf. *Fatwā Contemporaines*. Maison d'Ennour: Paris, 2009

al-Qaraḍāwī, Yūsuf. *fiqh al-ğihād. dirāsa muqārana li-aḥkāmihī wa-falsafatihī fī ḍau' al-qur'ān wa-'s-sunna*. maktabat wahba: al-Qāhira, 2009[1]; 2010[2]; 2011[3]

al-Qaraḍāwī, Yūsuf. *min fiqh ad-daula fī 'l-islām. makānatuhā . . . maᶜālimuhā . . . ṭabīᶜatuhā . . . mauqifuhā min ad-dīmuqrāṭīya wa-'t-taᶜaddudīya wa-'l-mar'a wa-ġair al-muslimīn*. dār aš- šurūq: al-Qāhira, 2009[5]

al-Qaraḍāwī, Yūsuf. *min hady al-islām. fatāwā al-muᶜāṣira*. 4 Vols., dār al-qalam li-n-našr wa-'l-tauzīᶜ bi-l-Kūwait/al-Qāhira, 2009[11]

al-Qaraḍāwī, Yūsuf. "fī mafhūm al-kufr wa-'l-kāfir wa-mauqif minhū". In: Ders. *min hady al-islām. fatāwā al-muᶜāṣira*. dār al-qalam li-n-našr wa-'t-tauzīᶜ bi-l-Kūwait/al-Qāhira, 2009[11], Vol. 4, pp. 790-797

al-Qaradawi, Yusuf. "Deserting Worldly Sciences for Religious Studies", 04.02.2010. http://www.onislam.net/english/ask-the-scholar/morals-and-manners/social-manners/170426.html (15.04.2014)

al-Qaradawi, Yusuf. "Qaradawi Critisizes al-Azhar for Condemning Jerusalem Attacks", 04.12.2010. http://www.islamonline.org/English/News/2001-12/05/article6.shtml (17.04.2011)

Quardhaoui, Docteur Youcef [sic]. *Le Licite et l'Illicite en Islam*. Okad Editions: Paris/Ets. Rayhane: Maroc, 1990

6.1.2. Sources Relating to Abdullah Saeed

Printed Sources

Akbarzadeh, Shahram; Saeed, Abdullah. "Searching for Identity: Muslims in Australia". In: Akbarzadeh, Shahram; Saeed, Abdullah (Eds.). *Muslim Communities in Australia*. University of New South Wales Press Ltd.: Sydney, 2001, pp. 1-11, accessible at http://www.abdullahsaeed.org/sites/abdullahsaeed.org/files/Searching_for_identity.pdf (10.06.2014)

Akbarzadeh, Shahram; Saeed, Abdullah. "Islam and Politics". In: Akbarzadeh, Shahram; Saeed, Abdullah (Eds.). *Islam and Political Legitimacy*. Routledge: Abingdon, 2003, pp. 1-13

Celermajer, Danielle; Yasmeen, Samina; Saeed, Abdullah. "Introduction, Special Edition: Australian Muslims and Secularism". In: *AJSI* 42/1 (2007), pp. 3-6

Johns, Anthony; Saeed, Abdullah. "Muslims in Australia: The Building of a Community". In: Yazbeck Haddad, Yvonne; Smith, Jane I. (Eds.). *Muslim Minorities in the West, Visible and Invisible*. Altamira Press: Walnut Creek, 2002, pp. 195-216, accessible at http://www.abdullahsaeed.org/sites/abdullahsaeed.org/files/Muslim_Minorities.pdf (10.06.2014)

Johns, Anthony H.; Saeed, Abdullah. "Nurcholish Madjid and the Interpretation of the Qur'an: Religious Pluralism and Tolerance". In: Taji-Farouki, Suha (Ed.). *Modern Muslim Intellectuals and the Qur'an*. Oxford University Press: Oxford, 2004, pp. 67-96

Saeed, Abdullah. "Australia". In: *EI/3*. http://referenceworks.brillonline.com/entries/encyclopaedia-of-islam-3/australia-COM_0023?s.num=172&s.start=160 (10.06.2014)

Saeed, Abdullah. "Islamic Banking in Practice: A Critical Look at the Murabaha Financing Mechanism". In: *JAIMES* 1 (1993), pp. 59-79

Saeed, Abdullah. "A Fresh Look at Freedom of Belief in Islam". In: Kingsbury, Damien; Barton, Greg (Eds.). *Difference and Tolerance. Human Rights Issues in Southeast Asia*. Deakin University Press: Geelong, 1994, pp. 27-37, accessible at http://www.globalwebpost.com/farooqm/study_res/islam/freedom/a_saeed_freedom_of_faith.html (10.06.2014)

Saeed, Abdullah. "The Moral Context of the Prohibition of *Ribā* in Islam Revisited". In: *AJISS* 12/4 (1995), pp. 496-517

Saeed, Abdullah. "Islamic Banking in Practice: The Case of Faisal Islamic Bank of Egypt". In: *JAIMES* 2/1 (1995), pp. 28-46

Saeed, Abdullah. *Islamic Banking and Interest. A Study of the Prohibition of Riba and its Contemporary Interpretation*. E. J. Brill: Leiden, 1996[1]; 1999[2]

Saeed, Abdullah. "Ijtihad and Innovation in Neo-Modernist Islamic Thought in Indonesia". In: *ICMR* 8 (1997), pp. 279-295

Saeed, Abdullah. "Idealism and Pragmatism in Islamic Banking: The Application of *Shari'ah* Principles and Adjustments". In: *JAIMES* 4/2 (1998), pp. 89-111

Saeed, Abdullah. "Indonesian Islamic Banking in Historical and Legal Context". In: Lindsey, Timothy (Ed.). *Indonesia. Law and Society*. The Federation Press: Leichhardt, 1999, pp. 323-338, accessible at http://www.abdullahsaeed.org/sites/abdullahsaeed.org/files/Law_and_Society.pdf (10.06.2014)

Saeed, Abdullah. "Rethinking Citizenship Rights of Non-Muslims in an Islamic State: Rashīd al-Ghannūshī's Contribution to the Evolving Debate". In: *ICMR* 10/3 (1999), pp. 307-323, accessible at http://www.abdullahsaeed.org/sites/abdullahsaeed.org/files/Rethinking_citizenship_rights.pdf (10.06.2014)

Saeed, Abdullah. "Rethinking 'Revelation' as a Precondition for Reinterpreting the Qur'an: A Qur'anic Perspective". In: *JQS* 1/1 (1999), pp. 93-114

Saeed, Abdullah. "Towards Religious Tolerance through Reform in Islamic Education: The Case of the State Institute of Islamic Studies of Indonesia". In: *IMW 79* (1999), pp. 177-191

Saeed, Abdullah. "Islamic Banking: Moving towards a Pragmatic Approach". In: *ISIM* Newsletter 3 (1999), p. 7. https://openaccess.leidenuniv.nl/bitstream/handle/1887/11959/newsl_3.pdf?sequence=1 (10.06.2014)

Saeed, Abdullah; Kamal, Muhammad; Mayer, Christina. *Essential Dictionary of Islamic Thought*. Seaview Press: Adelaide, 2001

Saeed, Abdullah. "The Muslim Community Cooperative of Australia as an Islamic Financial Service Provider". In: Akbarzadeh, Shahram; Saeed, Abdullah (Eds.). *Muslim Communities in Australia*. University of New South Wales Press Ltd.: Sydney, 2001, pp. 188-205, accessible at http://www.abdullahsaeed.org/sites/abdullahsaeed.org/files/Muslim_Communities.pdf (10.06.2014)

Saeed, Abdullah. "Jihad and Violence: Changing Understandings of Jihad among Muslims". In: Coady, Tony; O'Keefe, Michael (Eds.). *Terrorism and Justice. Moral Argument in a Threatened World*. Melbourne University Press: Carlton South, 2002, pp. 72-86, accessible at http://www.abdullahsaeed.org/sites/abdullahsaeed.org/files/Terrorism_and_Justice.pdf (10.06.2014)

Saeed, Abdullah. "The Charge of Distortion of Jewish and Christian Scriptures". In: *MW* 92 (2002), pp. 419-436, accessible at http://www.quranandinjil.org/sites/default/files/pdfs/The-Charge-of-Distortion-of-Jewish-and-Christian-Scriptures_Abdullah%20Saeed.pdf (10.06.2014)

Saeed, Abdullah. "Economics". In: *EQ*, Vol. II, pp. 5-9

Saeed, Abdullah. *Islam in Australia*. Allen & Unwin: Crows Nest, 2003

Saeed, Abdullah. "Islam and Politics. The Official Ulema and Religious Legitimacy of the Modern Nation State". In: Akbarzadeh, Shahram; Saeed, Abdullah (Eds.). *Islam and Political Legitimacy*. Routledge: Abingdon, 2003, pp. 14-28

Saeed, Abdullah. "Religious and Human Freedoms". In: *ES* 13/7 (2003), pp. 28-30, accessible at http://www.uniya.org/talks/saeed_jss03.html (10.06.2014)

Saeed, Abdullah; Saeed, Hassan. *Freedom of Religion, Apostasy and Islam*. Ashgate: Aldershot, 2004

Saeed, Abdullah. *Muslim Australians. Their Beliefs, Practices and Institutions. Department of Immigration and Multicultural and Indigenous Affairs and Australian Multicultural Foundation in Association with the University of Melbourne:* Canberra, 2004. http://amf.net.au/library/uploads/files/Religion_Cultural_Diversity_Resource_Manual.pdf (10.06.2014); http://www.abdullahsaeed.org/book/muslim-australians-their-beliefs-practices-and-institutions (10.06.2014)

Saeed, Abdullah. Menyoal Bank Syariah: *Kritik atas Interpretasi Bunga Bank Kaum Neo-Revivalis*. Jakarta: Paramadina, 2004

Saeed, Abdullah. "Ribā". In: *EI*/2, Vol. XII, pp. 690-692

Saeed, Abdullah. "Ṣarrāf". In: *EI*/2, Vol. XII, pp. 710f.

Saeed, Abdullah; Fazlur Rahman: "A Framework for Interpreting the Ethico-Legal Content of the Qur'an". In: Taji-Farouki, Suha (Eds.). *Modern Muslim Intellectuals and the Qur'an*. Oxford University Press: Oxford, 2004, pp. 37-66

Saeed, Abdullah. "Islamic Banking and Finance: In Search of a Pragmatic Model". In: Hooker, Virginia; Saikal, Amin (Eds.). *Islamic Perspectives on the New Millenium*. Institute of Southeast Asian Studies: Singapore, 2004, pp. 113-129, accessible at http://www.abdullahsaeed.org/sites/abdullahsaeed.org/files/Islamic_Perspectives.pdf (10.06.2014)

Saeed, Abdullah. "Umma". In: *EIMW*, Vol. II., Macmillan Reference USA: New York, 2004, pp. 705f.

Saeed, Abdullah. "Introduction: The Qur'an, Interpretation and the Indonesian Context". In: Saeed, Abdullah (Ed.). *Approaches to the Qur'an in Contemporary Indonesia*. Oxford University Press: Oxford, 2005, pp. 1-16

Saeed, Abdullah. "Islamic Religious Education and the Debate on its Reform Post-September 11". In: Akbarzadeh, Shahram; Yasmeen, Samina (Eds.). *Islam and the West. Reflections from Australia*. University of New South Wales Press Ltd.: Sydney, 2005, pp. 63-76, accessible at http://www.abdullahsaeed.org/sites/abdullahsaeed.org/files/Islamic_religious_education_post_911.pdf (10.06.2014)

Saeed, Abdullah. "Muslims in Secular States: Between Isolationists and Participants in the West", Lecture, 30.11.2003. Islamic Centre of Singapore. MUIS Occasional Papers Series: Majlis Ugama Islam Singapura/Islamic Religious Council of Singapore: Singapore, 2005, pp. 1-14. http://www.muis.gov.sg/cms/uploadedFiles/MuisGovSG/Research/MOPS1.pdf (10.06.2014)

Saeed, Abdullah. *Islamic Thought. An Introduction*. Routledge: Abingdon, 2006

Saeed, Abdullah. "Muslims in Australia". In: Mansouri, Fethi (Ed.). *Australia and the Middle East: A Front-Line Relationship*. Tauris Academic Studies: London, 2006, pp. 73-83

Saeed, Abdullah. *Interpreting the Qur'ān. Towards a Contemporary Approach*. Routledge: Abingdon, 2006

Saeed, Abdullah. "Murderers are not Martyrs", 28.11.2006 (First published in: *The Australian*, 16.07.2005). http://australiansall.com.au/archive/post/murderers-are-not-martyrs/ (10.06.2014)

Saeed, Abdullah. "Muslims in the West Choose Between Isolationism and Participation". In: *SangSaeng* 16 (2006), pp. 8-11. http://apceiu.org/data/file/sangsaeng/740725887_ef5d14c1_060906_ss_vol16_total.pdf (10.06.2014)

Saeed, Abdullah. "Creating a Culture of Human Rights from a Muslim Perspective". In: Toh, Swee-Hin; Cawagas, Virginia F. (Eds.). *Proceedings of the International Symposium Cultivating Wisdom, Harvesting Peace. Education for a Culture of Peace through Values, Virtues, and Spirituality of Diverse Cultures, Faiths, and Civilizations*. Multi-Faith Centre, Griffith University: Brisbane, 2006, pp. 123-127, accessible at http://www.abdullahsaeed.org/sites/abdullahsaeed.org/files/Creating_a_Culture_of_Human_Rights.pdf (10.06.2014)

Saeed, Abdullah. "Trends in Contemporary Islam: A Preliminary Attempt at a Classification". In: *MW* 97 (2007), pp. 395-404, accessible at http://www.abdullahsaeed.org/sites/abdullahsaeed.org/files/Trends_in_Contemporary_Islam.pdf (10.06.2014)

Saeed, Abdullah. "Economics: Islamic Banks". In: *EWIC*, Vol. IV, pp. 196-198

Saeed, Abdullah. "Muslims under Non-Muslim Rule. Evolution of a Discourse". In: Reid, Anthony; Gilsenan, Michael (Eds.). *Islamic Legitimacy in a Plural Asia*. Routledge: Abingdon, 2007, pp. 14-27

Saeed, Abdullah. "Towards a more Inclusive View of the Religious 'Other'. A Muslim Perspective". Annual Peace Lecture der Dunedin Abrahamic Interfaith Group und der Otago University Chaplaincy, 05.09.2007. http://www.dunedininterfaith.net.nz/lecture07.php (10.06.2014)

Saeed, Abdullah. *The Qur'an. An Introduction*. Routledge: Abingdon, 2008

Saeed, Abdullah. "Some Reflections on the Contextualist Approach to Ethico-Legal Texts of the Quran". In: *BSOAS* 71/2 (2008), pp. 221-237

Saeed, Abdullah. "Muslims Don't Need Separate Laws". In: *The Austalian*, 09.04.2008. http://www.theaustralian.com.au/higher-education/opinion-analysis/muslims-dont-need-separate-laws/story-e6frgclo-1111116006923 (10.06.2014)

Saeed, Abdullah. "Contextualizing". In: Rippin, Andrew (Ed.). *The Blackwell Companion to the Qur'ān*. Wiley-Blackwell: Chichester, 2009, pp. 36-50

Saeed, Abdullah. "Muslims Must Tackle Theology of Hate". In: *The Australian*, 07.08.2009. http://www.theaustralian.com.au/news/muslims-must-tackle-theology-of-hate/story-e6frg73o-1225758765963 (16.06.2014)

Saeed, Abdullah. "Reading the Quran". In: Sajoo, Amyn B. (Ed.). *A Companion to the Muslim World*. I. B. Tauris Publishers: London, 2009, pp. 55-85

Saeed, Abdullah. "Tendenze Fondamentali dell'Odierna Esegesi Coranica e Idee Emergenti per un Approccio Contestuale all Corano". In: *Le Religioni e il Mondo Moderno III (Islam)*. Giulio Einaudi: Torino, 2009, pp. 295-315

Saeed, Abdullah. "Muslims in the West and Their Attitudes to Full Participation in Western Societies: Some Reflections". In: Levey, Geoffrey Brahm; Modood, Tariq (Eds.). *Secularism, Religion and Multicultural Citizenship*. Cambridge University Press: Cambridge, 2009, pp. 200-215

Saeed, Abdullah. "Reflections on the Establishment of Shari'a Courts in Australia". In: Ahdar, Rex; Aroney, Nicholas (Eds.). *Shari'a in the West*. Oxford University Press: Oxford, 2010, pp. 223-238

Saeed, Abdullah. *Introdução ao Pensamento Islãmico*. O Saber da Filosofia: Porto, 2010

Saeed, Abdullah. "Foundations of Peace in the Qur'an". The Tasmanian Peace Trust 2010 Lecture, held at the Friends Meeting House, North Hobart, 11.10.2010, pp. 1-12 (unpublished manuscript, from the private collection of the author)

Saeed, Abdullah (Ed.). *Islamic Political Thought and Governance. Critical Concepts in Political Science*. 4 Vols., Abingdon: Routledge, 2011

Saeed, Abdullah. "Introduction". In: Saeed, Abdullah (Ed.). *Islamic Political Thought and Governance. Critical Concepts in Political Science*. Vol. 1: Roots of Islamic Political Thought: Key Trends, Basic Doctrines and Development. Routledge: Abingdon, 2011, pp. 1-12

Saeed, Abdullah. "How Muslims View the Scriptures of the People of the Book: Toward a Reassessment? " In: Anceschi, Luca; Camilleri, Anthony; Palapathwala, Ruwan; Wicking, Andrew (Eds.). *Religion and Ethics in a Globalized World. Conflict, Dialogue, and Transformation*. Palgrave Macmillan: New York, 2011, pp. 191-210

Saeed, Abdullah. "The Quranic Case Against Killing Apostates". Published by: *Public Discourse: Ethics, Law and the Common Good*, 25.02.2011. http://www.thepublicdiscourse.com/2011/02/2716 (10.06.2014)

Saeed, Abdullah. "Hadith and Apostasy". Published by: *Public Discourse: Ethics, Law and the Common Good*, 04.04.2011. http://www.thepublicdiscourse.com/2011/04/3082 (10.06.2014)

Saeed, Abdullah. "Muslim Debates on Human Rights and Freedom of Religion". In: Davis, Thomas W. D.; Galligan, Brian (Eds.). *Human Rights in Asia*. Edgar Elgar Publishing: Cheltenham, 2011, pp. 25-37

Saeed, Abdullah. "Rethinking Classical Muslim Law of Apostasy and the Death Penalty". In: Marshall, Paul; Shea, Nina. Silenced. *How Apostasy & Blasphemy Codes are Choking Freedom Worldwide*. Oxford University Press: Oxford, 2011, pp. 295-303

Saeed, Abdullah. "Ambiguities of Apostasy and the Repression of Muslim Dissent". In: *RFIA* 9/2 (2011), pp. 31-38

Saeed, Abdullah. "The Self-Perception and the Originality of the Qur'ān: 2:23-24; 3:44; 10:15; 69:38-47". In: Marshall, David (Ed.). *Communicating the Word: Revelation, Translation, and Interpretation in Christianity and Islam*. Georgetown University Press: Washington 2011, pp. 98-106

Saeed, Abdullah. "Authority in Qur'ānic Interpretation and Interpretive Communities". In: Marshall, David (Ed.). *Communicating the Word: Revelation, Translation, and Interpretation in Christianity and Islam*. Georgetown University Press: Washington 2011, pp. 115-123

Saeed, Abdullah. Adapting "Understanding of Riba to Islamic Banking: Some Developments". In: Ariff, Mohamed; Iqbal, Munawar (Eds.). *The Foundations of Islamic Banking: Theory, Practice and Education*. Edward Elgar Publishing: Cheltenham, 2011, pp. 51-64

Saeed, Abdullah. "Pre-Modern Islamic Legal Restrictions on Freedom of Religion, with Particular Reference to Apostasy and its Punishment". In: Emon, Anver M.; Ellis, Mark S.; Glahn, Benjamin (Eds.). *Islamic Law and International Human Rights Law: Searching for a Common Ground?* Oxford University Press: Oxford, 2012, pp. 226-246

Saeed, Abdullah (Ed.). *Islam and Human Rights*, Vol. 1. Key Issues in the Debate. Edward Elgar Publishing: Cheltenham, 2012

Saeed, Abdullah; Salah, Omar. "History of Sukuk: Pragmatic and Idealist Approaches to Structuring Sukuk". In: Ariff, Mohamed; Iqbal, Munawar; Mohamad, Shamsher (Eds.). *The Islamic Debt Market for Sukuk Securities: The Theory and Practice of Profit Sharing Investment*. Edward Elgar Publishing: Cheltenham 2012, pp. 42-66

Video Files by Abdullah Saeed

On the face veil, 2009: "Should Face Veil (Burqa) be Banned in Australia?" http://www.abdullahsaeed.org/media_reference/video-should-face-veil-burqa-be-banned-australia (10.06.2014); comp. the same speech also under the following title: "To Ban or not to Ban Face Covering Veil": http://www.youtube.com/watch?v=nU0MLhV3IvI (10.06.2014)

On the face veil, 2009: "Burqa Debate is about Choice". http://newsroom.melbourne.edu/studio/ep-33?video=1&play=1 (10.06.2014)

On Abū l-A^c^lā Maudūdī, 2009: ""Introduction to Mawlana Mawdudi"

Part 1: http://www.abdullahsaeed.org/media_reference/video-introduction-maw lana-mawdudi-part-1-3

Part 2: http://www.abdullahsaeed.org/media_reference/video-introduction-maw lana-mawdudi-part-2-3

Part 3: http://www.abdullahsaeed.org/media_reference/video-introduction-mawlana-mawdudi-part-3-3 (10.06.2014)

On the existence of multi-religious societies, 2009: "No Clash of Civilisations, Obama's Address Paves the Way for Peace". http://newsroom.melbourne.edu/studio/ep-26?video=1&play=1 (10.06.2014)

On the question of gender equality, 2010: "Can Gender Equality be Compatible with Islamic Norms? "

Part 1: http://www.youtube.com/watch?v=E79GjaUU50Y

Part 2: http://www.youtube.com/watch?v=UHnR32JBqWo (10.06.2014)

On Muslim minorities in Western societies: "Muslims in the West between Participants and Isolationists", 2010:

Part 1: http://www.youtube.com/watch?v=C4iEN8kdj7s

Part 2: http://www.youtube.com/watch?v=dEVMeW-s6xU (10.06.2014)

On domestic violence: "Islam and Domestic Violence", 2011:

Part 1: http://www.youtube.com/watch?v=p_Vo4NkfddY

Part 2: http://www.youtube.com/watch?v=p_Vo4NkfddY

Part 3: http://www.youtube.com/watch?v=rmOBWf7YhT0

Part 4: http://www.youtube.com/watch?v=NAnBVfT2DkA

Part 5: http://www.youtube.com/watch?v=5b13aNUsQQY (10.06.2014)

Audio Files by Abdullah Saeed

On traditional Education in Islamic educational Facilities, 2009: http://blogs.abc.net.au/files/abdullah-saeed.mp3 (10.06.2014)

6.1.3. Sources Relating to Abū l-Aᶜlā Maudūdī

Correspondence between Abi-l-A'la Maudoodi and Maryam Jameelah. Presidency of Islamik Researlh [sic], Ifta and Propagation: Riyadh, 1982

Hussein, Mohammed Al Khoder; Al Mawdudi, Abu Al Aala; Al Nadwi, Abu Al Hassan Ali Al Hassani. *Abhandlungen über den Qadjanismus*. Liga der Islamischen Welt: Mekka, 1975

Maryam Jameelah aur Maulānā Sayyid Abū l-Aᶜlā Maudūdī. kī murāsalat. markazī maktaba islāmī publišrz: Neu Dehli, 2010

Maududi, Sayyid Abul A'la. *Jihad fi Sabilillah (Jihad in Islam)*. U. K. I. M. Dawah Center: o. O. o. J., accessible at http://teachislam.com/dmdocuments/Maulana_Maududi_Jihad_Fi_Sabilillah_Translated_by_Khurram_Murad.pdf (10.06.2014)

Maududi, Abul Al'a [sic]. "Economic and Political Teachings of the Qur'an". In: Sharif, M. M. (Ed.). *A History of Muslim Philosophy*. Low Price Publications: Delhi, o. J. http://www.al-islam.org/historyofmuslimphilosophy/ (10.06.2014)

Maudūdī, Abū l-A^clā. *al-jihād fī 'l-islām*. Lahore, o. J. [Azamgarh, 1930], accessible at http://www.scribd.com/doc/19033799/07-Al-Jihad-Fil-Islam-By-Maududi- (10.06.2014)

Maudūdī, Sayyid Abū l-Aᶜlā. *risāla'i dīnīyāt*. Hyderabad, 1932, accessible at http://www.scribd.com/doc/50455471/Risalah-Deeniyat-Abul-Ala-Maududi (29.07.2011)

Maudūdī, Abū l-Aᶜlā. *islām kā naẓarīya-'i siyāsī*. [Lahore, 1939]

Maudūdī, Maulānā Sayyid Abū l-Aᶜlā. *salāmatī ka rāsta*. [Lahore, 1940], accessible at http://www.teachislam.com/dmdocuments/140/28%20SALAMTI%20KA%20RASTA.pdf (10.06.2014)

Maudūdī, Abū l-Aᶜlā. *islāmī ḥukūmat kis ṭarḥ qā'im hōtī hai?* Lahore, [1941], accessible at http://www.scribd.com/doc/48787906/Islami-Hukumat-Kis-Tarah-Qaim-Hoti-Hai-Maulana-Syed-Abul-A-la-Maududi (29.07.2011)

Maudūdī, Sayyid Abū l-Aᶜlā. *taḥrīk-i islāmī kī aḫlāqī bunyādeṉ* [Lahore, 1945], accessible at http://www.teachislam.com/dmdocuments/140/20%20Threek_e_Islami%20ki%20ikhlaqi%20bunyadain.pdf (10.06.2014)

Maududi, S. Abul A'la. *The Process of Islamic Revolution*. Islamic Publications Ltd.: Lahore, 1947/1980[8]

Maudūdī, Abū l-Aᶜlā. *islāmī ḥukūmat mēṉ ḏimmīyōṉ kē ḥuqūq* [Lahore, 1948]

Maududi, Syed Abulala. *tafheem ul-Quran*. [6 Vols., Lahore, 1949-1972], accessible at http://tazkeer.org/quran/tafheem-ul-quran/ (10.06.2014)

Maududi, Sayyid Abul A'la. *Islamic Way of Life*. Islamic Publications Ltd.: Lahore, 1950/1965[3]/1986

Maudūdī, Sayyid Abū l-Aᶜlā. *tajdīd-o iḥyā'i dīn*. [Lahore, 1952], accessible at http://www.teachislam.com/dmdocuments/140/05%20Tajdeed%20O%20Ahyaa%20E%20Deen.pdf (10.06.2014)

Maudūdī, Sayyid Abū l-Aᶜlā. *islāmī dastūr kī tadwīn*. [Lahore, 1952], accessible at http://www.scribd.com/doc/48936503/Islami-Dastoor-Ki-Tadween-Maulana-Maududi- (29.07.2011)

Maudūdī, Abū l-Aᶜlā. *Qādiyānī mas'ala*. [Karachi, 1953]/Lahore, 1996/1998, accessible at http://openlibrary.org/works/OL293636W/Qadiyani_mas'alah (29.07.2011)

Maudūdī, Sayyid Abū l-Aᶜlā. *Qur'ān kī cār bunyādī iṣṭilāḥēṉ. ilāh, rabb, ᶜibādat aur dīn*. Lahore, 1953, accessible at http://www.teachislam.com/dmdocuments/140/01%20Quran%20ki%204(four)%20%20Bunyadi%20Istilahain.pdf (10.06.2014)

Maudūdī, Sayyid Abū l-Aᶜlā. *mabādi' al-islām*. maktabat aš-šabāb al-muslim: [ad-Dimašq,] 1954[1]/1961[2]/dār al-anṣār: al-Qāhira, [1977]

Mawdudi, S. Abu A'la. *The Islamic Law and Constitution*. Islamic Publications Ltd.: Lahore, 1955/1980[7]

Mawdudi, S. Abu A'la. *The Islamic Law and its Introduction in Pakistan*. Islamic Publications Limited: Lahore, 1955[1]/1983[4]

Maudūdī, Maulānā Sayyid Abū l-Aᶜlā. *ḫutbāt*. Lahore, [1957], accessible at http://www.teachislam.com/dmdocuments/140/04%20Khutbaat.pdf (10.06.2014)

Maudoodi, Syed Abul Ala. "The Family Law of Islam (The Questionnaire & its Reply)". In: Ahmad, Khurshid (Ed.). *Studies in the Family Law of Islam*. Chiragh-e-Rah Publications: Karachi, 1959/1961², pp. 13-34

Mawdudi, Sayyid Abu A'la. *First Principles of the Islamic State*. Islamic Publications Limited: Lahore, 1960²/1983⁶

Mawdudi, Abu A'la. *Political Theory of Islam*. Islamic Publications Limited: Lahore, 1960¹/1993⁸

Maudūdī, Abū l-Aᶜlā. *tadwīn ad-dustūr al-islāmī*. dār al-fikr: [Dimašq, ca. 1960]

Mawdudi, S. Abu A'la. *Rights of Non-Muslims in Islamic State* [sic]. Islamic Publications Limited: Lahore, 1961/1982⁷

Maududi, S. Abul A'la. *The Finality of Prophethood*. Lahore, 1962; accessible at http://www.teachislam.com/dmdocuments/Maulana_Maududi_Finality_of_Prophethood.pdf (10.06.2014)

Maudūdī, Abū l-Aᶜlā. *jihād fi 'l-sabīl allāh*. [Lahore, 1962]

Maudūdī, Abū l-Aᶜlā. *ḫatm-i nubūwat*. [Lahore, 1963]

Maududi, S. Abul A'la. *The Road to Peace and Salvation*. Islamic Publications Ltd: Lahore, 1963/1988⁶

Maudūdī, Sayyid Abū l-Aᶜlā. *A Short History of the Revivalist Movement in Islam*. Islamic Publications Limited: Lahore, 1963/1976³/[1992⁷] (without cover)

Maudoodi, Sayyed Abulala (sic). *Nationalism and India*. Markazi Maktaba-Jama'at-e-Islami Hind: Dehli, 1965⁴

Maududi, S. Abul A'la. *Ethical Viewpoint of Islam*. Islamic Publications Ltd.: Lahore, 1966²/1967³

Mawdudi, Sayyid Abu A'la. *The Sick Nations of the Modern Age*. Islamic Publications Limited: Lahore, 1966¹/1979⁶

Maududi, S. Abul A'la. *Unity of the Muslim World*. Islamic Publications Ltd.: Lahore, 1967¹/1982⁵

Maudūdī, Abū l-Aᶜlā. *The Meaning of the Qur'ān*. Lahore, 1967ff., accessible at http://www.englishtafsir.com (10.06.2014)

Maudūdī, Sayyid Abū l-Aᶜlā. *The Religion of Truth*. Islamic Publications Limited: Lahore, 1967/1978

Maudūdī, Abū l-Aᶜlā. *mā hiya 'l-Qādiyānīya? dirāsa šāmila wa-ᶜarḍ ᶜilmī li-l-qādiyānīya wa-madā tā'ṯīrihā fi 'l-muğtamaᶜ al-islāmī*. dār al-qalam: Kuwait, 1969

Maudūdī, Abū l-Aᶜlā. "The Necessity of Divine Government for the Elimination of Oppression and Injustice; The Moral Foundations of the Islamic Movement", trans. by Charles J. Adams. In: Ahmad, Aziz; von Grunebaum, G. E., (Eds.).

Muslim Self-Statement in India and Pakistan 1857-1968. Otto Harrassowitz: Wiesbaden, 1970, pp. 156-166

Maudūdī, Abū l-A^{c}lā. *naẓarīyat al-islām al-siyāsīya*. dār al-fikr: [Bairūt, ca. 1970]

Maududi, Abul A'la. *Purdah and the Status of Woman in Islam*. Islamic Publications Limited: Lahore, 1972/1979^{4}

Maudūdī, Abū l-A^{c}lā. *al-islām al-yaum*. dār al-turāṯ al-^{c}arabī: al-Qāhira, [1975]

Maudūdī, Abū l-A^{c}lā. *šahādat al-ḥaqq*. mū'assassat ar-risāla: [Bayrūt,] 1975

Maudūdī, Sayyid Abū l-A^{c}lā. *dīn-i ḥaqq*. Dehli, 1975/1995

Mawdudi, S. Abu A'la. *Fundamentals of Islam*. Islamic Publications Limited: Lahore, 1975/1980^{4}

Mawdudi, Abu A'la. *Human Rights in Islam*. The Islamic Foundation: London, 1976/1990^{2}, accessible at http://www.teachislam.com/dmdocuments/Maulana_Maududi_Human_Rights_in_Islam.pdf (10.06.2014)

Mawdudi, S. Abu A'la. *Jihād in Islam*. Islamic Publications Ltd.: Lahore, 1976/1980^{3}

Maududi, S. Abul A'la. *The Moral Foundations of the Islamic Movement*. Islamic Publications Ltd: Lahore, 1976^{1}/1982^{3}

Maudūdī, Abū l-A^{c}lā. *Niẓām al-ḥayāt fī 'l-islām*. mū'assassat ar-risāla: [Bayrūt, 1977]

Maudūdī, Abū l-A^{c}lā. *minhāǧ al-inqilāb al-islāmī*. dār al-anṣār. al-Qāhira, [1977]

Maudūdī, Abū l-A^{c}lā. *al-ḫilāfa wa-'l-mulk*. dār al-qalam: Kuwait, 1978

Mawdudi, Syed Abul A'la. *System of Government under the Holy Prophet*. Islamic Publications Limited: Lahore, 1978/1989^{2}

Maudūdī, Abū l-A^{c}lā. *ḥuqūq ahl aḏ-ḏimma fī 'd-dawlat al-islāmīya*. dār al-anṣār: al-Qāhira, [1979]

Maududi, S. Abul A'la. *The Qadiani Problem*. Islamic Publications (Pvt.) Limited: Lahore, 1979^{1}/1991^{3}

Maudūdī, Abū l-A^{c}lā. *Towards Understanding Islam*. The Islamic Foundation: London, 1980

Maudūdī, Abū l-A^{c}lā Syed. *murtadd ki sazā islāmī qānūn mēṉ*. markazi maktaba islāmī: Dihlī, 1980^{5} (further editions in Urdu: Rampur 1952, Lahore, 1953, Lahore, 1963^{4}, Lahore, 1976), accessible at http://www.scribd.com/doc/51556657/Murtad-Ki-Saza-Syed-Abul-A-la-Maududi (01.12.2011)

Mawdudi, Sayyid Abul A'la. *The Islamic Movement. Dynamics of Values, Power and Change*. The Islamic Foundation: Leicester, 1984

Mawdudi, Sayyid Abu A'la. *Let us be Muslims*. The Islamic Foundation: London, 1985

Mawdudi, Sayyid Abu A'la. *The Islamic Way of Life*. The Islamic Foundation: London, 1986

Mawdudi, Sayyid Abu A'la. *Witnesses unto Mankind. The Purpose and Duty of the Muslim Ummah*. The Islamic Foundation: London, 1986

Maudūdī, Abū l-Aᶜlā. *al-jihād fī 'l-islām*. Lahore, 1988/1996

Maududi, Sayyid Abul A'la. *Come Let us Change this World*. Markaza Maktaba Islami: Delhi, 1991/1996

Maudūdī, Abū l-Aᶜlā. *islāmī riyāsat. falsafah, niẓām-i kār aur uṣūl-i hukmzānī*. Islāmik buk fā'ūndešan: Na'ī Dihlī, 1991

Maudoodī, Sayyid Abū l-Aᶜlā. *Weltanschauung und Leben im Islam*. International Islamic Federation of Student Organizations: Kuwait, 1992

Mawdudi, Abul Ala. *The Punishment of the Apostate According to Islamic Law*. The Voice of the Martyrs: Mississauga, 1994

Mawdudi, Sayyid Abu A'la. *Als Muslim leben*. Cordoba: Karlsruhe, 1995

Maududi, Sayyid Abul A'la. *Islamische Lebensweise*. I. I. F. S. O.: o. O., 1997

Mawdudi, Sayyid Abu A'la. *Das Leben nach dem Tode*. Vorträge über den Islam Nr. 8. Informationszentrale Dār-us-Salām: Garching, 1998

Mawdudi, Sayyid Abul A'la. *The Islamic Movement. Dynamics of Values, Power and Change*. The Islamic Foundation: Leicester, 1998

Maudūdī, Abū l-Aᶜlā. *Warum ausgerechnet Islam?* Cordoba: Karlsruhe, 1999

Maududi, Sayyid Abu l-A'la. "Self-Destructiveness of Western Civilization". In: Moaddel, Mansoor; Talattof, Kamran (Eds.). *Modernist and Fundamentalist Debates in Islam*. Palgrave Macmillan: London, 2000, pp. 325-331

Maudoodi, Maulana Abul A'ala (sic). *The Laws of Marriage and Divorce in Islam*. Islamic Book Publishers: Safat, 2000[3]

Maudūdī, Sayyid Abū l-Aᶜlā. *Four Key Concepts of the Qur'ān*. The Islamic Foundation: Markfield, 2006

6.2. Secondary Literature

Abbot, Freeland K. "Maulānā Maudūdī on Quranic Interpretation". In: *MW* 48/1 (1958), pp. 6-19

Abd al-Monein, Said Aly; Wenner, Manfred W. "Modern Islamic Reform Movements: The Muslim Brotherhood in Contemporary Egypt". In: *MEJ* 36/3 (1982), pp. 336-361

ᶜAbd ar-Rahim, Muddathir. "Abdullah Saeed and Hassan Saeed. Freedom of Religion, Apostasy and Islam". In: *IJMES* 37 (2005), pp. 614f.

Abdul-Aziz, Islam. "Proceedings of the 19th Session of the International Islamic Fiqh Academy: Apostasy: Scholars differ on the Penalty". (o. J.) http://www.onislam.net/english/shariah/shariah-and-humanity/applying-shariah/413128.html (10.06.2014)

Abdullah, Eman. "Qaradawi Honored as Islamic Personality of the Year", 17.12.2000. http://gulfnews.com/news/gulf/uae/general/qaradawi-honoured-as-islamic-personality-of-the-year-1.437003 (15.04.2014)

Abdur Rahman, Shaikh. *Punishment of Apostasy in Islam*. Institute of Islamic Culture: Lahore, 1978[2]

Abiad, Nisrine. *Sharia, Muslim States and International Human Rights Treaty Obligations: A Comparative Study*. British Institute of International and Comparative Law: London, 2008

Abou El Fadl, Khaled. "Islamic Law and Muslim Minorities: The Juristic Discourse on Muslim Minorities from the Second/Eighth to the Eleventh/Seventeenth Centuries". In: *ILS* 1 (1994), pp. 141-187

Abou El Fadl, Khaled. *Rebellion and Violence in Islamic Law*. Cambridge University Press: Cambridge, 2003

Abrahamian, Ervand. *Khomeinism. Essays on the Islamic Republic*. I. B. Tauris: London, 1993

Abu-Rabi[c], Ibrahim, M. *Intellectual Origins of Islamic Resurgence in the Modern Arab World*. State University of New York Press: Albany, 1996

Abu Zaid, Nasr Hamid. *Ein Leben mit dem Islam*. Herder: Freiburg, 1999

ACSJC Position Paper: *Blasphemy & Death Penalty in Pakistan*. Australian Catholic Social Justice Council Position Paper, published by the Australian Catholic Bishops Conference. Sydney, 2001

Adam, Raoul J. "Relating Faith Development and Religious Styles: Reflections in Light of Apostasy from Religious Fundamentalism". In: *APS* 20 (2008), pp. 201-231

Adams, Charles J. "The Ideology of Mawlana Maududi". In: Smith, Donald Eugene (Ed.). *South Asian Politics and Religion*. Princeton University Press: Princeton, 1966, pp. 371-397

Adams, Charles J. "The Authority of the Prophetic *Ḥadīth* in the Eyes of some Modern Muslims". In: Little, Donald P. (Ed.). *Essays on Islamic Civilization, Presented to Niyazi Berkes*. E. J. Brill: Leiden, 1976, pp. 25-47

Adams, Charles J. "Mawdudi and the Islamic State". In: Esposito, John L. (Ed.). *Voices of Resurgent Islam*. Oxford University Press: New York, 1983, pp. 99-133

Adams, Charles J. "Kufr". In: *OEMIW*, Vol. II. Oxford University Press: Oxford, 1995, pp. 439-443

Adang, Camilla. "Belief and Unbelief". In: *EQ*, Vol. I. E. J. Brill: Leiden, 2001, pp. 218-226

Adil, Mohamed Azam Mohamed. "Law of Apostasy and Freedom of Religion in Malaysia". In: *AJCL* 2/1 (2007), pp. 1-36

Adnan, Abdullah. "Pakistan: Creation and Genesis". In: *MW* 96/2 (2006), pp. 201-217

Afribi, Aftab. "Release of Mumtaz Qadri. Pak Tea House", 19.10.2011 http://pakteahouse.net/2011/10/19/release-of-mumtaz-qadri/ (10.06.2014)

Afsaruddin, Asma. "Mawdūdī's "Theo-Democracy": How Islamic is it Really?" In: *OM* 87/1 (2007), pp. 301-325

Afshar, Mandana Knust Rassekh. "The Case of an Afghan Apostate – The Right to a Fair Trial between Islamic Law and Human Rights in the Afghan Constitution". In: Max Planck Year Book of United Nations Law (UNYB) 10 (2006), pp. 591-605, accessible at http://www.remep.mpg.de/files/student_body/knust-mandana/Knust_-_Case_of_an_Afghan_Apostate.pdf (15.04.2014)

Ahmad, Anis. "Mawdūdī's Concept of Sharīʿah". In: *MW* 93/3-4 (2003), pp. 533-545

Ahmad, Aziz. "Mawdudi and Orthodox Fundamentalism in Pakistan". In: *MEJ* 21 (1967), pp. 369-380

Ahmad, Aziz. *Islamic Modernism in India and Pakistan 1857-1964*. Oxford University Press: London, 1967

Ahmad, Aziz; Grunebaum, G. E., von (Eds.). *Muslim Self-Statement in India and Pakistan 1857-1968*. Otto Harrassowitz: Wiesbaden, 1970

Ahmad, Hazrat Mirza Tahir. *Murder in the Name of Allah*. Lutterworth Press: Cambridge, 1989

Ahmad, Irfan. "Genealogy of the Islamic State: Reflections on Maududi's Political Thought and Islamism". In: *JRAI* 15/1 (2009), pp. 145-162

Ahmad, Khurshid (Ed.). *An Analysis of the Munir Report. A Critical Study of the Punjab Disturbances Inquiry Report*. Jamaat-e-Islami Publications: Karachi, 1956

Ahmad, Khurshid; Ansari, Zafar Ishaq. *Mawlānā Sayyid Abul Aʿlā Mawdūdī. An Introduction to his Vision of Islam and Islamic Revival*. The Islamic Foundation: Leicester, 1986; also published in: Ahmad, Khurshid; Ansari, Zafar Ishaq (Eds.). *Islamic Perspectives. Studies in Honour of Mawlānā Sayyid Abul Aʿlā Mawdūdī*. The Islamic Foundation: London/Saudi Publishing House: Jeddah, 1979, pp. 359-383

Ahmad, Khurshid; Ansari, Zafar Ishaq. *Mawdūdī: An Introduction to his Life and Thought*. The Islamic Foundation: Leicester, 1979/1986/Markazi Maktaba Islami: Delhi, 1992

Ahmad, Khurshid. "Pakistan: Vision and Reality, Past and Future". In: *MW* 96/2 (2006), pp. 363-379

Ahmad, Riaz. *The Concept of the Islamic State as Found in the Writings of Abul A'la Madūdī*. Ph. D. Thesis, o. O., 1969

Ahmad, Sayed Riaz. *Maulana Maududi and the Islamic State*. People's Publishing House: Lahore, 1976

Ahmad, Sayed Riaz. *Islam and Modern Political Institutions in Pakistan. A Study of Mawlana Mawdudi*. Ferozsons Ltd.: Lahore, 2004

Ahmad, Syed Barakat. "Conversion from Islam". In: Bosworth, C. E. et al. (Eds.). *The Islamic World from Classical to Modern Times*. The Darwin Press: Princeton, 1989, pp. 3-25

Ahmed, Asad Ali. "Specters of Macaulay. Blasphemy, the Indian Penal Code, and Pakistan's Postcolonial Predicament". In: Kaur, Raminder; Mazzarella, William (Eds.). *Censorship in South Asia. Cultural Regulations from Sedition to Seduction*. Indiana University Press: Bloomington, 2009, pp. 172-205

Ahmed, Ishtiaq. *The Concept of an Islamic State. An Analysis of the Ideological Controversy in Pakistan*. Pinter: London, 1987

Ahmed, Ishtiaq. *State, Nation and Ethnicity in Contemporary South Asia*. Pinter: London, 1996

Ahmed, Munir D. "Ausschluss der Ahmadiyya aus dem Islam. Eine umstrittene Entscheidung des Pakistanischen Parlaments". In: *Orient* 1 (1975) pp. 112-143

Ahmed, Munir D. "Islamisierung in Pakistan". In: Conrad, Dieter; Zingel, Wofgang-Peter. *Pakistan. Zweite Heidelberger Südasiengespräche*. Franz Steiner: Stuttgart, 1992, pp. 69-76

Ahmedov, Aibek. "Religious Minorities and Apostasy in Early Islamic States: Legal and Historical Analysis of Sources". In: *JISP* 2/3 (2006), pp. 1-17

Ahsan, Abdullah. "Pakistan since Independence: An Historical Analysis". In: *MW* 93/3-4 (2003), pp. 351-371

Ajiri, Adam Muhammad. "Some Aspects of Maududi's Contributions to Modern Islamic Thought". In: *MuEQ* 12/2 (1995), pp. 52-72

Akyol, Mustafa. *Islam without Extremes. A Muslim Case for Liberty*. W. W. Norton & Company: New York, 2011

Albrecht, Sarah. *Islamisches Minderheitenrecht. Yūsuf al-Qaraḍāwīs Konzept des fiqh al-aqallīyāt*. Ergon: Würzburg, 2010

Aldeeb Abu-Sahlieh, Sami Awad. *L'Impact de la Religion sur l'Ordre Juridique, Cas de l'Egypte, Non-Musulmans en Pays d'Islam*. Editions Universitaires: Fribourg, 1979

Aldeeb Abu-Sahlieh, Sami A. "Le Délit d'Apostasie Aujourd'hui et ses Conséquences en Droit Arabe et Musulman". In: *ISCH* (20) 1994, pp. 93-116

Aldeeb Abu-Sahlieh, Sami A. *Les musulmans Face aux Droits de l'Homme. Religion & Droit & Politique. Étude et Documents*. Dr. Dieter Winkler: Bochum, 1994

Aldeeb Abu-Sahlieh, Sami A. *Muslims in the West (Caught between Rights and Duties) Redefining the Separation of Church and State*. Shangri-La Publications: Warren Center, 2002

Alhomayed, Tariq. "The Political Activist Yusuf al-Qaradawi", 21.01.2010. http://www.alarabiya.net/views/2010/01/21/98050.html (10.06.2014)

Ali, Sheikh Jameil. *Islamic Thought and Movement in the Subcontinent. A Study of Sayyid Abu A'la Mawdudi and Sayyid Abul Hassan Ali Nadwi*. D. K. Printworld Ltd: New Delhi, 2010

Ali, Yusuf A. *A Cultural History of India during the British Period*. AMS Press: New York, 1976

Almirzanah, Syafa'atun. "On Human Rights and the Qur'anic Perspective: Freedom of Religion and the Rule of Apostasy". In: *AJ* 45/2 (2007), pp. 367-388, accessible at http://journal.aljamiah.org/index.php/AJ/article/view/101 (10.06.2014)

Altikriti, Anas Osama (Übers.). *European Council for Fatwa and Research. First Collection of Fatwas*. o. J. www.e-cfr.org/data/cat30072008113814.doc (15.04.2014)

al-Alwani, Taha Jabir. *Towards a Fiqh for Minorities. Some Basic Reflections*. International Institute of Islamic Thought: London, 2003

Amjad-Ali, Christine. "Update on Minority Issues". In: *al-mushir* 34 (1992), pp. 85-91

Amnesty International Report 2010. *Zur weltweiten Lage der Menschenrechte*. S. Fischer: Frankfurt, 2010

Amnesty International Report 2012. *Zur weltweiten Lage der Menschenrechte*. S. Fischer: Frankfurt, 2012

Amor, Abdelfattah. "Addendum 2 of the Interim Report on the Elimination of all Forms of Religious Intolerance Relating to a Visit to the Sudan." United Nations General Assembly, Fifty-first session, Agenda Item 110 (b). 11. 11.1996, A/51/542/Add.2. http://un.org/documents/ga/docs/51/plenary/a51-542add2.htm (15.04.2014)

Anderson, Jon W. "Muslim Networks, Muslim Selves in Cyberspace: Islam in the Post-Modern Public Sphere". NMit Working Papers on New Media & Information Technology in the Middle East, 5.-8.10.2001. http://www.mafhoum.com/press3/102S22.htm (15.04.2014)

Anderson, Jon W. "The Internet and Islam's New Interpreters". In: Eickelmann, Dale F.; Anderson, Jon W. (Eds.). *New Media in the Muslim World. The Emerging Public Sphere*. Indiana University Press: Bloomington, 2003, pp. 45-60

Anderson, Norman. *Law Reform in the Muslim World*. University of London: The Athlone Press, 1976

Androme, Mary Jane. "Nawal El Saadawi's Memoirs from the Women's Prison: Women Closing Ranks". In: Emenyonu, Ernest N.; Eke, Maureen N. (Eds.). *Emerging Perspectives on Nawal El Saadawi*. Africa World Press: Trenton, 2010, pp. 79-91

Ansari, M. Abdul Haq. "Mawdūdī's Contribution to Theology". In: *MW* 93/3-4 (2003), pp. 521-531

Araghchi, Seyed Abbas. "Islamic Theo-Democracy: The Political Ideas of Abul A'la Mawdudi". In: *IJIA* 8/4 (1997), pp. 772-797

Arif, General Khalid Mahmud. *Working with Zia. Pakistan's Power Politics 1977-1988*. Oxford University Press: Karachi, 1995

Arjomand, Said Amir. *The Turban for the Crown. The Islamic Revolution in Iran*. Oxford University Press: New York, 1988

Arjomand, Said Amir. "Religious Human Rights and the Principle of Legal Pluralism in the Middle East". In: Van der Vyver, Johan D.; Witte, John Jr. (Eds.). *Religious Human Rights in Global Perspective. Legal Perspectives*. Martinus Nijhoff Publishers: Den Haag, 1996, pp. 331-347

Ashour, Omar. *The De-Radicalization of Jihadists. Transforming Armed Islamist Movements*. Routledge: London, 2009

El-Awa, Mohamed. *Punishment in Islamic Law: A Comparative Study*. American Trust Publications: Indianapolis, 1993

Ayalon, Ami. *Egypt's Quest for Cultural Orientation*. The Moshe Dayan Center for Middle Eastern and African Studies: Tel Aviv University, 1999

Ayoub, Mahmoud. "Religious Freedom and the Law of Apostasy in Islam". In: *ISCH* 20 (1994), pp. 75-91

Aziz, Zahid. "Maudoodi on *Takfir* (Calling Muslims as *kafir*)". In: *The Light & Islamic View* 73/6 (1996), accessible at http://www.muslim.org/light/96-6.htm (10.06.2014)

Badawi, Jamal. "Is Apostasy a Capital Crime in Islam?" 26.04.2006. http://www.onislam.net/english/shariah/contemporary-issues/islamic-themes/425673.html (15.04.2014)

Badri, Malik B. "A Tribute to Mawlāna Mawdūdī from an Autobiographical Point of View". In: *MW* 93/3-4 (2003), pp. 487-502

Badry, Roswitha. "Das Instrument der Verketzerung, seine Politisierung und der Bedarf nach einer Neubeurteilung der 'Scharia' und der Apostasiefrage im Islam". In: Schneiders, Thorsten Gerald (Ed.). *Islamverherrlichung. Wenn die Kritik zum Tabu wird*. VS: Wiesbaden, 2010, pp. 117-129

Bälz, Kilian. "Submitting Faith to Judicial Scrutiny through the Family Trial: The 'Abū Zayd Case'". In: *WI* 37/2 (1997), pp. 135-155

Bälz, Kilian. "Die 'Islamisierung' des Rechts in Ägypten und Libyen: Islamische Rechtsetzung im Nationalstaat". In: *RabelsZ* 62 (1998), pp. 437-463

Bälz, Kilian. "Islamic Banking and Interest. A Study of the Prohibition of Riba and its Contemporary Interpretation. By Abdullah Saeed". In: *JLR 15* (2000), pp. 481f.

Bahadur, Kalim. *The Jama'at-i-Islami of Pakistan. Political Thought and Political Action*. Chetana Publications: New Dehli, 1977

Baker, Barbara G. "Blasphemy 'Convict' Shot Dead in Pakistani Jail", 14.06.2002, http://www.worthynews.com/462-blaspemy-convict-shot-dead-in-pakistani-jail?wpmp_switcher=mobile (15.04.2014)

Baker, Raymond William. "Invidious Comparisons: Realism, Postmodern Globalism, and Centrist Islamic Movements in Egypt". In: Esposito, John L. *Political Islam. Revolution, Radicalism, or Reform?* Lynne Rienner Publishers: Boulder, 1997, pp. 115-133

Baker, Raymond William. *Islam without Fear. Egypt and the New Islamists*. Harvard University Press: Cambridge, 2003

Baker, Raymond William. "'Building the World' in a Global Age". In: Salvatore, Armando; LeVine, Mark (Eds.). *Religion, Social Practice and Contested Hegemonies. Reconstructing the Public Sphere in Muslim Majority Societies*. Palgrave Macmillan: New York, 2005, pp. 109-133

El Baradie, Adel. *Gottes-Recht und Menschen-Recht. Grundlagenprobleme der islamischen Strafrechtslehre*. Nomos: Baden-Baden, 1983

Barraclough, Steven. "Al-Azhar: Between the Government and the Islamists". In: *MEJ* 52/2 (1998), pp. 236-249

Barua, B. P. *Eminent Thinkers in India and Pakistan*. Lancers Books: New Delhi, 1991

Baumann, Herbert; Ebert, Matthias (Eds.). *Die Verfassungen der Mitgliedsländer der Liga der Arabischen Staaten*. Berlin Verlag: Berlin, 1995

Bellani, Roberto. "Lo Stato Islamico: Postulati Fondamentali di Abū l-A^{c}lā l-Mawdūdī". In: *AION* 42 (1987), pp. 593-603

Benard, Cheryl. *Civil Democratic Islam. Partners, Resources, and Strategies*. Rand Corporation: Santa Monica, 2003

Bennett-Jones, Owen. "Pakistan's Blasphemy Law U-Turn". BBC News, 17.05.2000. http://news.bbc.co.uk/2/hi/south_asia/751803.stm (10.06.2014)

Berger, Maurits S. "Apostasy and Public Policy in Contemporary Egypt: An Evaluation of Recent Cases from Egypt's Highest Courts". In: *HRQ* 25 (2003), pp. 720-740

Besson, Sylvain. *La Conquête de L'Occident. Le Projet Secret des Islamistes*. Éditions du Seuil: Paris, 2005

Bielefeldt, Heiner. *Philosophie der Menschenrechte. Grundlage eines weltweiten Freiheitsethos*. Wissenschaftliche Buchgesellschaft: Darmstadt, 1998

Bielefeldt, Heiner. "Religionsfreiheit – ein 'sperriges' Menschenrecht". In: Heimbach-Steins, Marianne; Bielefeldt, Heiner (Eds.). *Religionen und Religionsfreiheit: Menschenrechtliche Perspektiven im Spannungsfeld von Mission und Konversion*. Ergon: Würzburg, 2010, pp. 37-45

Bielefeldt, Heiner. *Streit um die Religionsfreiheit: Aktuelle Facetten der internationalen Debatte*. Friedrich-Alexander-Universität Erlangen-Nürnberg: Erlangen, 2012

Binder, Leonard. *Religion and Politics in Pakistan*. University of California Press: Berkeley, 1963[2]

Binder, Leonard. *Islamic Liberalism: A Critique of Development Ideologies*. The University of Chicago Press: Chicago, 1988

Bindra, S. S. *Politics of Islamisation, with Special Reference to Pakistan*. Deep & Deep Publications: Delhi 1990

Bobzin, Hartmut. *Der Koran: Aus dem Arabischen neu übertragen*. C. H. Beck: München, 2010

Bonney, Richard. *Jihād. From Qur'ān to Bin Laden*. Palgrave: Macmillan, 2004

Broadbridge, Anne F. "Apostasy Trials in Eighth/Fourteenth Century Egypt and Syria: A Case Study". In: Pfeiffer, Judith; Quinn, Sholeh A. (Eds.). *History and Historiography of Post-Mongol Central Asia and the Middle East. Studies in Honor of John E. Woods*. Harrossowitz: Wiesbaden, 2006, pp. 363-382

Brohi, Allahbukhsh K. "Mawlānā Sayyid Abul A^c^lā Mawdūdī: The Man, the Scholar, the Reformer". In: Ahmad, Khurshid; Ansari, Zafar Ishaq (Eds.). *Islamic Perspectives. Studies in Honour of Mawlānā Sayyid Abul A^c^lā Mawdūdī*. The Islamic Foundation: London/Saudi Publishing House: Jeddah, 1979, pp. 289-312

Brown, Daniel W. *Rethinking Tradition in Modern Islamic Thought*. Cambridge University Press: Cambridge, 1996

Brumberg, Daniel. *Reinventing Khomeini. The Struggle for Reform in Iran*. The University of Chicago Press: Chicago, 2001

Bryson, Jennifer S. "Does Islam Require Killing Apostates?" http://www.firstthings.com blogs/firstthoughts/2011/04/does-islam-require-killing-apostates (10.06.2014)

Buchta, Wilfried. *Die iranische Schia und die islamische Einheit 1979-1996*. Deutsches Orient-Institut: Hamburg, 1997

Bukay, David. *From Muhammad to Bin Laden. Religious and Ideological Sources of the Homicide Bombers Phenomenon*. Transaction Publishers: New Brunswick, 2008

Bunt, Gary R. Virtually Islamic. *Computer-Mediated Communications and Cyber Islamic Environments*. University of Wales Press: Cardiff, 2000

Bunt, Garry R. *Islam in the Digital Age. E-Jihad, Online Fatwas and Cyber Islamic Environments*. Pluto Press: London, 2003

Bunt, Gary R. "The Digital Umma". In: Sajoo, Amyn B. (Ed.). *A Companion to the Muslim World*. I. B. Tauris Publishers: London, 2009, pp. 291-310

Burkhart, Grey E.; Older, Susan. *The Information Revolution in the Middle East and North Africa*. Rand Corporation: Santa Monica, 2003

Burr, J. Millard; Collins, Robert O. *Revolutionary Sudan. Hasan al-Turabi and the Islamist State, 1989-2000*. E. J. Brill: Leiden, 2003

Caeiro, Alexandre; al-Saify, Mahmoud. "Qaraḍāwī in Europe, Europe in Qaraḍāwī? The Global Mufti's European Politics". In: Skovgaard-Petersen, Jakob; Gräf, Bettina (Eds.). *Global Mufti. The Phenomenon of Yusuf al-Qaradawi*. Hurst & Company: London, 2009, pp. 109-148

Caeiro, Alexandre. "The Power of European Fatwas: The Minority Fiqh Project and the Making of an Islamic Counterpublic". In: *MES* 42 (2010), pp. 435-449

Caeiro, Alexandre. "Transnational Ulama, European Fatwas, and Islamic Authority. A Case Study of the European Council for Fatwa and Research". In: van

Bruinessen, Martin; Allievi, Stefano (Eds.). *Producing Islamic Knowledge. Transmission and Dissemination in Western Europe*. Routledge: London, 2011, pp. 121-141

Cahen, Cl.; Talbi, M. "ḥisba". In: *EI*/2, Vol. III, pp. 485-489

Calvert, John. *Sayyid Qutb and the Origins of Radical Islamism*. Hurst and Company: London, 2010

The Center for Human Rights Legal Aid (CHRLA). "From Confiscation to Charges of Apostasy. The Implications of the Egyptian Court Decision Ordering the Divorce of Dr. Nasr Hamed Abu-Zeid from his Wife, Dr. Ibthal Younis". In: *Dossier. Women Living Under Muslim Laws* 14-15 (1996), pp. 33-44

Chamberlain, Michael. *Knowledge and Social Practice in Medieval Damascus, 1190-1350*. Cambridge University Press: Cambridge, 1994

Chandrasekharan, S. Maledives: "On Dr. Hassan Saeed's Book on Freedom of Religion and Apostasy". South Asia Analysis Group. Paper no. 2747, 25.06.2008. http://archive.today/Qrap (10.06.2014)

Chengappa, Bidanda M. *Pakistan. Islamisation, Army and Foreign Policy*. A. P. H. Publishing Corporation: New Dehli, 2004

Chitkara, M. G. *Human Rights in Pakistan*. A. P. H. Publishing Corporation: New Dehli, 1997

Choueiri, Youssef M. *Islamic Fundamentalism*. Pinter Publishers: London, 1990

Choueiri, Y. M. "Theoretical Paradigms of Islamic Movements". In: *PC* 41/1 (1993), pp. 108-116

Collins, Daniel P. "Islamization of Pakistani Law: A Historical Perspective". In: *SJIL* 24 (1988), pp. 511-584

Conermann, Stephan. "Maudūdī, Abū l-Alā al-". In: Elger, Ralf; Stolleis, Friederike (Eds.). *Kleines Islam-Lexikon. Geschichte, Alltag, Kultur*. Beck: München, 2001, likewise licensed edition Bundeszentrale für politische Bildung: Bonn, 2002, pp. 192-193; accessible at http://www.bpb.de/popup/popup_lemmata.html?guid=M8XOM5 (10.06.2014)

Conermann, Stephan. *Das Moghulreich. Geschichte und Kultur des muslimischen Indien*. C. H. Beck: München, 2006

Conring, Hans-Tjabert. "Der Islam und das Menschenrecht der Religionsfreiheit". In: *KuR* 2/1 (1996), pp. 1-10

Cook, David. *Understanding Jihad*. University of California Press: Berkeley, 2005

Cook, David. "Apostasy from Islam: A Historical Perspective". In: *JSAI* 31 (2006), pp. 248-288

Cook, Michael. *Commanding Right and Forbidding Wrong in Islamic Thought*. Cambridge University Press: Cambridge, 2000

Croitoru, Joseph. "Islamismus nach dem 11. September. Bedingt selbstkritisch: Arabische Intellektuelle äußern sich in einer Umfrage der Zeitschrift 'Al-Hayat'". In: FAZ, 20.09.2004, p. 33

Crone, Patricia. "Islam and Religious Freedom". Festvortrag anlässlich der Eröffnungsfeier des 30. Deutschen Orientalistentags, 24.9.2007. http://orient.ruf.uni-freiburg.de/dotpub/crone.pdf (15.04.2014)

Damir-Geilsdorf, Sabine. *Herrschaft und Gesellschaft. Der islamistische Wegbereiter Sayyid Quṭb und seine Rezeption*. Ergon: Würzburg, 2003

Damir-Geilsdorf, Sabine. "Der islamische Fundamentalismus und seine muslimischen Gegner". In: Achtner, Wolfgang; Böckel, Holger; Kreuzkamp, Doris (Eds.). *Notwendige Fundamente – gefährlicher Fundamentalismus?* Gießener Hochschulgespräche & Hochschulpredigten der ESG WS 03/04, Gießen 2004, pp. 71-95

Dankowitz, A. "Accusing Muslim Intellectuals of Apostasy". *MEMRI:* The Middle East Media Research Institute, 18.02.2005. http://www.memri.org/report/en/0/0/0/0/0/114/1321.htm (15.04.2014)

Davies, Merryl Wyn. "The Legacy of Maududi and Shariati". In: *Inquiry* 2 (1985), pp. 34-39

Davis, Joyce M. *Between Jihad and Salaam. Profiles in Islam*. Macmillan: Houndmills, 1997

Day, Peter. "Islam in Australia", 26.01.2009. http://www.gatestoneinstitute.org/246/islam-in-australia (10.06.2014)

Day, Peter. "Australian Apologetics for Islam". *Quadrant Online*, 01.05.2009. http://www.quadrant.org.au/magazine/issue/2009/5/australian-apologetics-for-islam (10.06.2014)

Dekmejian, R. Hrair. *Islam in Revolution. Fundamentalism in the Arab World*. Syracuse University Press: Syracuse, 1985

Deringil, Selim. "'There is no Compulsion in Religion:' On Conversion and Apostasy in the Late Ottoman Empire: 1839-1856". In: *CSSH* 42/3 (2000), pp. 547-575

Dessouki, Ali E. Hillal (Ed.). *Islamic Resurgence in the Arab World*. Praeger Publishers: New York, 1982

Dink, Hrant. *Von der Saat der Worte*. Hans Schiler: Berlin, 2008

Dogan, Güney. *Tafsir, en Religionshistorisk Studie av Koranexegetikens Metodologi*. http://liu.diva-portal.org/smash/get/diva2:208209/FULLTEXT01 (20.06.2011).

Donohue, John J.; Esposito, John L. (Eds.). *Islam in Transition. Muslim Perspectives*. Oxford University Press: New York, 1982

Duncker, Anne. *Menschenrechte im Islam. Eine Analyse islamischer Erklärungen über die Menschenrechte*. Wissenschaftlicher Verlag: Berlin, 2006

Dunckern, Ursula-Charlotte. "Allah will deinen Tod". In: *Der Freitag*, 21.09.2001. http://www.freitag.de/autoren/der-freitag/allah-will-deinen-tod (15.04.2014)

Durán, Khálid; Ahmed, Munir D. "Pakistan". In: Ende, Werner; Steinbach, Udo (Eds.). *Der Islam in der Gegenwart. Entwicklung und Ausbreitung, Kultur und Religion, Staat, Politik und Recht*. C. H. Beck: München, 2005[5], pp. 336-362

Dwyer, Kevin. *Arab Voices. The Human Rights Debate in the Middle East*. Routledge: London, 1991

Ebert, Hans-Georg. *Das Personalstatut arabischer Länder. Problemfelder, Methoden, Perspektiven*. Peter Lang: Frankfurt, 1996

Edge, Ian. "A Comparative Approach to the Treatment of Non-Muslim Minorities in the Middle East, with Special Reference to Egypt". In: Mallat, Chibli; Connors, Jane (Eds.). *Islamic Family Law*. Graham & Trotman: London, 1993, pp. 31-53

Eickelman, Dale F.; Piscatori, James. *Muslim Politics*. Princeton University Press: Princeton, 1996

Eickelman, Dale F.; Anderson Jon W. "Print, Islam, and the Prospects for Civic Pluralism: New Religious Writings and their Audiences". In: *JIS* 8/1 (1997), pp. 43-62

Eickelman, Dale F.; Anderson, Jon W. "Redefining Muslim Politics". In: Eickelman, Dale F.; Anderson, Jon W. (Eds.). *New Media in the Muslim World. The Emerging Public Sphere*. Indiana University Press: Bloomington, 2003, pp. 1-18

Eickelman, Dale F. "Communication and Control in the Middle East: Publication and its Discontents". In: Eickelman, Dale F.; Anderson, Jon W. (Eds.). *New Media in the Muslim World. The Emerging Public Sphere*. Indiana University Press: Bloomington, 2003, pp. 33-44

Eickelman, Dale F. "Clash of Cultures? Intellectuals, their Publics, and Islam". In: Dudoignon, Stéphane A.; Hisao, Komatsu; Yasushi, Kosugi (Eds.). *Intellectuals in the Modern Islamic World*. Routledge: London, 2006, pp. 289-304

Eltahawy, Mona. "Qaradawi Damages Palestine's Cause by Turning Global Issue into Islamist Weapon". In: Craze, Joshua; Huband, Mark (Eds.). *The Kingdom. Saudi Arabia and the Challenge of the 21st Century*. Hurst & Company: London, 2009, pp. 286-290

Ende, Werner. "Wer ist ein Glaubensheld, wer ist ein Ketzer?" In: *WI* 23-24 (1984), pp. 70-94

Ende, W. "Rashīd Riḍā". In: *EI*/2, Vol. VIII, pp. 446-448

Ennafifer, H'mida. "De la Foi à la Conscience d'un Paradoxe: Un Cas de Conflit entre le Droit d'Origine Révélée et les Droits de l'Homme: le Châtiment en Cas d'Apostasie de l'Islam (le *ridda*)". In: *Foi et Justice. Un défi pour le Christianisme et pour l'Islam*. Centurion: Paris, 1993, pp. 104-113

Erdodan, Mustafa. "Religious Freedom in the Turkish Constitution". In: *MW* 89/3-4 (1999), pp. 377-388

Esposito, John L. "Islamization: Religion and Politics in Pakistan". In: *MW* 72/3-4 (1982) pp. 197-223

Esposito, John L. (Ed.). *Voices of Resurgent Islam*. Oxford University Press: New York, 1983

Esposito, John L.; Voll, John O. "Khurshid Ahmad: Muslim Activist-Economist". In: *MW* 80/1 (1990), pp. 24-36

Esposito, John L.; Voll, John O. *Islam and Democracy*. Oxford University Press: Oxford, 1996

Esposito, John L. *Political Islam. Revolution, Radicalism, or Reform?* Lyenne Rienner Publ.: Boulder, 1997

Esposito, John L. "Practice and Theory. A Response to 'Islam and the Challenge of Democracy'". In: *BR* April/May 2003. http://bostonreview.net/archives/BR28.2/esposito.html (10.06.2014)

Euben, Roxanne L.; Qasim Zaman, Muhammad (Eds.). *Princeton Readings in Islamist Thought. Texts and Contexts from al-Banna to Bin Laden*. Princeton University Press: Princeton, 2009

Evans, Judith. "Apostasy Punishable by Death: Top Adhaalath Scholar", 13.05.2008. *Minivan News*. http://www.minivannews.org/news_detail.php?id=4462 (05.05.2011)

Evans, Judith. "IDP Calls for Ban on Hassan Saeed's Book", 15.05.2008. *Minivan News*. http://www.minivannews.org/news_detail.php?id=4477 (05.05.2011)

Evans, Judith. "Supreme Council Bans Hassan Saeed's Book", 18.06.2008. *Minivan News*. Independent News for the Maledives. http://www.minivannews.com/news/news.php?id=4605 (24.06.2010)

Fadelle, Joseph. *Das Todesurteil. Als ich Christ wurde im Irak*. Sankt Ulrich: Augsburg, 2011

Fähndrich, Hartmut. "Der Kasus Farag Foda". In: *Du. Islam – Die Begegnung am Mittelmeer*. 640 (1994), pp. 55-57

Fautré, Willy; Schubert, Jan Nils; Vaiya, Alfiaz (Eds.). *Freedom of Religion or Belief. World Report 2012*. Human Rights Without Frontiers Int.: Brussels, [2013]

Feichtiner, Walter; Wentker, Sibylle (Eds.). *Islam, Islamismus und Islamischer Extremismus. Eine Einführung*. Böhlau: Wien, 2008

Feldman, Noah. "Shari'a and Islamic Democracy in the Age of al-Jazeera". In: Amanat, Abbas; Griffel, Frank (Eds.). *Shari'a. Islamic Law in the Contemporary Context*. Stanford University Press: Stanford, 2007, pp. 104-119

Fishman, Shammai. *Fiqh al-Aqalliyyat: A Legal Theory for Muslim Minorities*. Research Monographs on the Muslim World, Series No. 1, Paper No. 2, October 2006. Hudson Institute: Washington, 2006, pp. 1-18. http://www.hudson.org/content/researchattachments/attachment/1148/20061018_monographfishman2.pdf (10.06.2014)

Flores, Alexander. "Secularism, Integralism, and Political Islam: The Egyptian Debate". In: Beinin, Joel; Stork, Joe (Eds.). *Political Islam. Essays from Middle East Report*. University of California Press: Bekeley, 1997, pp. 83-94

Flores, Alexander. "Ägypten". In: Ende, Werner; Steinbach, Udo (Eds.). *Der Islam in der Gegenwart*. C. H. Beck: München, 2005[5], pp. 477-489

Forstner, Martin. "Das Menschenrecht der Religionsfreiheit und des Religionswechsels als Problem der islamischen Staaten". In: *Kanon. Kirche und Staat im Christlichen Osten. Jahrbuch der Gesellschaft für das Recht der Ostkirchen*. Verlag des Verbandes der wissenschaftlichen Gesellschaften Österreichs: Wien, 1991, pp. 105-186

Forte, David F. *Studies in Islamic Law. Classical and Contemporary Application*. Austin & Winfield Publishers: Lanham, 1999

Freyer Stowasser, Barbara. "Yūsuf al-Qaraḍāwī on Women". In: Skovgaard-Petersen, Jakob; Gräf, Bettina (Eds.). *Global Mufti. The Phenomenon of Yusuf al-Qaradawi*. Hurst & Company: London, 2009, pp. 181-211

Friedmann, Yohanan. *Tolerance and Coercion in Islam. Interfaith Relations in the Muslim Tradition*. Cambridge University Press: Cambridge, 2003

Fuchs, Simon Wolfgang. *Proper Signposts for the Camp. The Reception of Classical Authorities in the Ǧihādī Manual al-ᶜUmda fī Iᶜdād al-ᶜUdda*. Ergon: Würzburg, 2011

Fūda, Faraǧ. *al-ḥaqīqa al-ġā'iba*. dār wa-maṭābiᶜ al-mustaqbal: al-Iskandarīya, 2003[2]

Furman, Uriah. "Minorities in Contemporary Islamist Discourse". In: *MES* 36/4 (2000), pp. 1-20

Gaborieau, Marc. "Le Néo-Fondamentalisme au Pakistan: Maududi et la *Jamāᶜat-i-islāmī*". *In: Carré, Olivier; Dumont, Paul (Eds.). Radicalismes Islamiques. Vol. II. Maroc, Pakistan, Inde, Yougoslavie, Mali*. Editions L'Harmattan: Paris, 1986, pp. 33-76

Gabriel, Theodore. *Christian Citizens in an Islamic State. The Pakistan Experience*. Ashgate Publishing Limited: Aldershot, 2007

Gallagher, Nancy. "Apostasy". In: *EWIC*, Vol. II, pp. 7-9

Gallagher, Nancy. "Tunesian Coup Institutes First of Secular Islamists", 03.03.2011. Daily Nexus. http://www.dailynexus.com/2011-03-03/tunisian-coup-institutes-secular-islamists/ (10.06.2014)

Gamlem, Anne-Liv. *Islamic Discourse of Difference: A Critical Analysis of Maulana Mawdudi's Texts on Kāfirs and Dhimmīs*. Masteroppgave i Sør-Asiastudier. Institutt for Kulturstudier og Orientalske Språk: Universitetet i Oslo: Høsten 2008, accessible at http://www.duo.uio.no/publ/IKOS/2008/83331/ALGamlem _Master.pdf (10.06.2014)

al-Ġannūšī, Rāšid. *ḥuqūq al-muwāṭana. ḥuqūq ġair al-muslim fī 'l-muǧtamaᶜ al-islāmī*. al-maᶜhad al-ᶜālamī li-l-fikr al-islāmī: [Herndon,] 1993[2]

Le Gassick, Trevor (Ed.). *Critical Perspectives on Naguib Mahfouz*. Three Continents Press: Washington, 1991

Gauhar, Altaf. "Mawlānā Abul Aᶜlā Mawdūdī – A Personal Account". In: Ahmad, Khurshid; Ansari, Zafar Ishaq (Eds.). *Islamic Perspectives. Studies in Honour of Mawlānā Sayyid Abul Aᶜlā Mawdūdī*. The Islamic Foundation: London/Saudi Publishing House: Jeddah, 1979, pp. 265-288

Geaves, Ron. "A Comparison of the Ideas of Maulana Mawdudi (1903-1980) and Shah Wali-Allah (1703-1762): A Pure Islam or Cultural Heritage". In: *IQ* 41/3 (1997), pp. 167-186

Gebauer, Matthias. "Im Knast der armen Teufel". Spiegel Online, 27.03.2006. http://www.spiegel.de/politik/ausland/0,1518,408290,00.html (15.04.2014)

al-Ghannushi, Rashid. "Fiqh of Jihad: Book Review of Shaykh al-Islam al-Qaradawi's Masterpiece on Jihad", 13.12.2009. http://www.suhaibwebb.com/islam-studies/fiqh-of-jihad-book-review-of-shaykhul-islam-al-qaradawi's-latest-masterpiece-on-jihad-by-dr-rashid-al-ghannushi/ (10.06.2014)

Gilani, Syed As'ad. *'Maududi'. Thought and Movement*. East & West Publishing Company: Karachi, 1978[5]

Giunchi, Elisa. *Radicalismo Islamico e Condizione Femminile in Pakistan*. L'Harmattan Italia: Torino, 1999

Giunchi, Elisa. *Il Pakistan tra Ulama e Generali*. Franco Angeli: Milano, 2002

Gottlob, Michael (Ed.). *Historisches Denken im modernen Südasien (1786 bis heute)*, Vol. 3. Humanities Online: Frankfurt, 2002

Gräf, Bettina. *Islamische Gelehrte als politische Akteure im globalen Kontext. Eine Fatwa von Yusuf ᶜAbdallah al-Qaradawi*. Diskussionspapiere 93. Klaus Schwarz: Berlin, 2003

Gräf, Bettina. "Yusuf al-Qaradawi and the Foundation of a 'Global Muslim Authority'", 29.04.2005. http://en.qantara.de/content/the-international-association-of-muslim-scholars-yusuf-al-qaradawi-and-the-foundation-of-a (15.04.2014)

Gräf, Bettina. "Yūsuf al-Qaradāwī: Das Erlaubte und das Verbotene im Islam". In: Amirpur, Katajun; Ammann, Ludwig (Eds.). *Der Islam am Wendepunkt. Liberale und konservative Reformer einer Weltreligion*. Herder: Freiburg, 2006, pp. 109-117

Gräf, Bettina. "Sheikh Yūsuf al-Qaradāwī in Cyberspace". In: *WI* 47 (2007), pp. 403-421

Gräf, Bettina. "IslamOnline.net: Independent, interactive, popular". In: *AMS* 4 (2008). http://www.arabmediasociety.com/?article=576 (05.05.2014)

Gräf, Bettina. "The Concept of Wasaṭiyya in the Work of Yūsuf al-Qaraḍāwī". In: Skovgaard-Petersen, Jakob; Gräf, Bettina (Eds.). *Global Mufti. The Phenomenon of Yusuf al-Qaradawi*. Hurst & Company: London, 2009, pp. 213-238

Gräf, Bettina. *Medien-Fatwas@Yusuf al-Qaradawi. Die Popularisierung des islamischen Rechts*. Klaus Schwarz: Berlin, 2010

Gräf, Bettina. "Media fatwas, Yusuf al-Qaradawi and Mediated Authority in Islam". In: *Orient* 51/1 (2010), pp. 6-15

Grami, Amel. *Apostasy in Contemporary Islamic Thought*. [Centre National de la Traduction: Tunis, 2009[2]] [title in Arabic: Āmāl Qrāmī. *qaḍīyat ar-ridda fī fikr al-islāmī*. Tūnis, 1997]

Green, Tim. *Factors Affecting Attitudes to Apostasy in Pakistan*. Unpublished M. A. Thesis. School of Oriental and African Studies: London, 1998

Griffel, Frank. "Die Anwendung des Apostasieurteils bei aš-Šāfiʿī und al-Ġazālī". In: Wild, Stefan; Schild, Hartmut (Eds.). *Akten des 27. Orientalistentages: Norm und Abweichung*. Ergon: Würzburg, 1998, pp. 353-362

Griffel, Frank. *Apostasie und Toleranz im Islam. Die Entwicklung zu al-Ġazālīs Urteil gegen die Philosophie und die Reaktionen der Philosophen*. E. J. Brill: Leiden, 2000

Griffel, Frank. "Apostasy". In: *EI*/3. http://referenceworks.brillonline.com/entries/encyclopaedia-of-islam-3/apostasy-SIM_0044?s.num=7 (15.04.2014)

Grim, Brian J.; Finke, Roger. *The Price of Freedom Denied. Religious Persecution and Conflict in the Twenty-First Century*. Cambridge University Press: Cambridge, 2011

Haddad, Yvonne Y. "Sayyid Qutb: Ideologue of Islamic Revival". In: Esposito, John L. (Ed.). *Voices of Resurgent Islam*. Oxford University Press: New York, 1983, pp. 67-97

Haddad, Yvonne Y. "Muslim Revivalist Thought in the Arab World: An Overview". In: *MW* 76/3-4 (1986), pp. 143-167

Hafez, Kai. *Mass Media, Politics, and Society in the Middle East*. Hampton Press: Cresskill, 2001

Hagemann, Ludwig; Khoury, Adel Theodor. *Dürfen Muslime auf Dauer in einem nichtislamischen Land leben?* Echter: Würzburg, 1997

Hallaq, Wael B. "Ifta'and Ijtihad in Sunni Legal Theory: A Development Account". In: Masud, Muhammad Khalid; Messick, Brinkley; Powers, David S. (Eds.). *Islamic Legal Interpretation. Muftis and Their Fatwas*. Harvard University Press: Cambridge, 1996, pp. 33-43

Hallaq, Wael. "Apostasy". In: *EQ*, Vol. I. E. J. Brill: Leiden, 2001, pp. 119-122

Hallaq, Wael. B. *Sharīʿa. Theory, Practice, Transformations*. Cambridge University Press: Cambridge, 2009

Hamad, Ahmed Seif al-Islam. "Legal Plurality and Legitimation of Human Rights Abuses. A Case Study of State Council Rulings Concerning the Rights of Apostates". In: Dupret, Baudouin; Berger, Maurits; al-Zwaini, Laila (Eds.). *Legal*

Pluralism in the Arab World. Kluwer Law International: Den Haag, 1999, pp. 219-228

Hamit, Sherazad. "Apostasy and the Notion of Religious Freedom in Islam". In: *MIJ* 1/2 (2006), pp. 31-38. http://digitalcommons.macalester.edu/cgi/viewcontent.cgi?article=1018&context=islam (10.06.2014)

Haqqani, Husain. *Pakistan between Mosque and Military*. Carnegie Endowment for International Peace: Washington, 2005

Hardy, Peter. *The Muslims of British India*. Cambridge University Press: Cambridge, 1972

Harms, Florian. "Der Prophet ruft aus dem Cyberspace. Formen islamischer Mission im Internet". In: Brückner, Matthias; Pink, Johanna. *Von Chatraum bis Cyberjihad. Muslimische Internetnutzung in lokaler und globaler Perspektive*. Ergon: Würzburg, 2009, pp. 169-212

Hartung, Jan-Peter. *A System of Life. Maudūdī and the Ideologisation of Islam*. Hurst & Company: London, 2013

Hasan, Masudul. *Sayyid Abul A'Ala Maududi [sic] and his Thought*. 2 Vols., Islamic Publications Ltd.: Lahore, 1984+1986

Hasemann, Armin. "Zur Apostasiediskussion im Modernen Ägypten". In: *WI* 42/1 (2002), pp. 72-121

Hashemi, Kamran. *Religious Legal Traditions, International Human Rights Law and Muslim States*. Martinus Nijhoff Publishers: Leiden, 2008

Hassan, Kamal M. "The Influence of Mawdūdī's Thought on Muslims in Southeast Asia: A Brief Survey". In: *MW* 93/3-4 (2003), pp. 429-464

Hassan, Riaz. *Inside Muslim Minds*. Melbourne University Press: Carlton, 2008

Hatina, Meir. "Historical Legacy and the Challenge of Modernity in the Middle East: The Case of al-Azhar in Egpyt". In: *MW* 93/1 (2003), pp. 51-68

Heffening, W. "Murtadd". In: *EI*/2, Vol. VII. E. J. Brill: Leiden, 1993, pp. 635-636

Hefny, Assem. "Hermeneutik, Koraninterpretation und Menschenrechte". In: Elliesie, Hatem (Ed.). *Beiträge zum islamischen Recht VII: Islam und Menschenrechte/Islam and Human Rights/al-islām wa ḥuqūq al-insān*. Peter Lang: Frankfurt, 2010, pp. 73-97

Heimbach-Steins, Marianne; Bielefeldt, Heiner (Eds.). *Religionen und Religionsfreiheit: Menschenrechtliche Perspektiven im Spannungsfeld von Mission und Konversion*. Ergon: Würzburg, 2010

Heimbach-Steins, Marianne. *Religionsfreiheit. Ein Menschenrecht unter Druck*. Ferdinand Schöningh: Paderborn, 2012

Heinrich-Böll-Stiftung (Ed.). *Iran nach den Wahlen. Eine Konferenz und ihre Folgen*. Westfälisches Dampfboot: Münster, 2001

Helfont, Samuel. *Yusuf al-Qaradawi, Islam and Modernity*. Moshe Dayan Center for Middle Eastern and African Studies: Tel Aviv University, 2009

Heller, Erdmute; Mosbahi, Hassouna (Eds.). *Islam, Demokratie, Moderne. Aktuelle Antworten arabischer Denker*. C. H. Beck: München, 1998

Hendrich, Geert. *Islam und Aufklärung. Der Modernediskurs in der arabischen Philosophie*. Wissenschaftliche Buchgesellschaft: Darmstadt, 2004

El-Hennawy, Noha. "Islamist Presidential Candidate Declares Conversion Permissible", 16.05.2011. http://www.egyptindependent.com//news/islamist-presidential-candidate-declares-conversion-permissible (15.04.2014)

Hoffmann, Christiane. "Willkommene Munition. Streit im Iran um eine Konferenz in Berlin". In: FAZ, 20.04.2000, p. 5

Høigilt, Jacob. "Varieties of Persuasion in Modern Forms of Islamic Proselytizing in Egypt". In: *RMM* 124 (2008), pp. 243-262

Høigilt, Jacob. "Rhetoric and Ideology in Egypt's *Wasaṭiyya* Movement". In: *Arabica* 57 (2010), pp. 251-266

Høigilt, Jacob. *Islamist Rhetoric. Language and Culture in Contemporary Egypt*. Routledge: London, 2011

el-Houshi, Riham. "Qaradawi Centre Vows to Fight Extremism". In: *Gulf Times*, 12.09.2011. http://www.gulf-times.com/site/topics/article.asp?cu_no=2&item_no=314242&version=1&template_id=57 (13.10.2011)

Hroub, Khaled. "Yusuf al-Qaradawi and Minorities: Learned Intolerance", 12.02.2010. http://en.qantara.de/content/yusuf-al-qaradawi-and-minorities-learned-intolerance (15.04.2014)

Hussain Shah, Syed Mujawar. *Religion and Politics in Pakistan (1972-88)*. National Institute of Pakistan Studies: Islamabad, 1996

Ibn Taymīya, al-Shaykh al-Imām. *Public Duties in Islam. The Institution of Ḥisba*. The Islamic Foundation: London, 1982

Ibn Warraq (Ed.). *Leaving Islam. Apostates Speak Out*. Promotheus Books: Amherst, 2003

Idris, Sajjad. "Reflections on Mawdūdī and Human Rights". In: *MW* 93/3-4 (2003), pp. 547-561

IOL Shari'h Researchers. "Islamic Fixed Penalties: Striking Balance between Causes & Results", 17.01.2002. http://www.islamonline.net/servlet/Satellite?cid=1119503544834&pagename=IslamOnline-English-Ask_Scholar%2FFatwaE%2FFatwaEAskTheScholar (30.07.2010)

Ismail, Salwa. "Confronting the Other: Identity, Culture, Politics, and Conservative Islamism in Egypt". In: *IJMES* 30 (1998), pp. 199-225

Jackson, Roy. *Fifty Key Figures in Islam*. Routledge: London, 2006

Jackson, Roy. *Mawlana Mawdudi & Political Islam. Authority and the Islamic State*. Routledge: London, 2011

Jameelah, Maryam. "An Appraisal of some Aspects of Maulana Sayyid Ala Maudoodi's Life and Thougt". In: *IQ* 31/2 (1987), pp. 116-130

Jameelah, Maryam. "Modern Ideas and Concepts in the Work of Maulānā Sayyid Abul A^{c}lā Mawdūdī". In: *IS* 42/2 (2003), pp. 347-352

Jan, Tarik et al. *Pakistan between Secularism and Islam. Ideology, Issues and Conflict*. Institute of Policy Studies: Islamabad, 1998

Jān, Tārik. "Mawdūdī's Critique of the Secular Mind". In: *MW* 93/3-4 (2003), pp. 503-519

Johansen, Baber. "Wahrheit und Geltungsanspruch: Zur Begründung und Begrenzung der Autorität des Qadi-Urteils im Islamischen Recht". In: *La Giustizia nell'Alto Medioevo* (Secoli IX-XI), 11.-17.4.1996, Vol. II. Presso la Sede del Centro: Spoleto, 1997, pp. 975-1065

Johansen, Baber. "Apostasy as Objective and Depersonalized Fact: Two Recent Egyptian Court Judgements". In: *SoR* 70/3 (2003), pp. 687-710

Johansen, Baber. "Zwischen Verfassung, kodifiziertem Recht und Šarī^{c}a: Die Apostasiegesetzgebung und Rechtsprechung einiger arabischer Staaten". In: Tellenbach, Silvia; Hanstein, Thoralf (Eds.). *Beiträge zum Islamischen Recht IV*. Peter Lang: Frankfurt, 2004, pp. 23-43

Jomier, J. *Le Commentaire Coranique du Manār. Tendences Modernes de L'Exégèse Coranique en Égypte*. Éditions G.-P. Maisonneuve & Cie: Paris, 1954

Jürgensen, Carsten. *Demokratie und Menschenrechte in der arabischen Welt. Positionen arabischer Menschenrechtsaktivisten*. Nomos: Baden-Baden, 1999

Jürgensen, Carsten. "Die Menschenrechtsdebatte". In: Faath, Sigrid (Ed.). *Politische und gesellschaftliche Debatten in Nordafrika, Nah- und Mittelost. Inhalte Träger, Perspektiven*. Deutsches Orient-Institut: Hamburg, 2004, pp. 295-318

Jurkiewicz, Sarah. *Al-Jazeera vor Ort. Journalismus als ethische Praxis*. Frank & Timme: Berlin, 2009

Kamali, Mohammad Hashim. *Freedom of Expression in Islam*. Islamic Texts Society: Cambridge, 1997

Kaplony, Andreas. "Fernseh-Philologie: Form, Sprache und Argumentation einer Sendung von aš-Šarī^{c}a wa-l-ḥayāt mit Yūsuf al-Qaraḍāwī". In: Marzolph, Ulrich (Ed.). *Orientalistische Studien zu Sprache und Literatur. Festgabe zum 65. Geburtstag von Werner Diem*. Harrassowitz: Wiesbaden, 2011, pp. 417-434

Karg, Dieter. "Asylgutachten. Besitz der Satanischen Verse", 13.06.2000. http://aidrupal.aspdienste.de/umleitung/2000/deu06/080?print=1 (15.04.2014)

Karg, Dieter. "Asylgutachten. Gefährdung von Teilnehmern an der Iran-Konferenz der Heinrich Böll-Stiftung in Berlin vom 7.-9. April 2000", 29.08.2000. http://www.amnesty.de/umleitung/2000/deu06/100 (15.04.2014)

Kauser, Zeenath. "Mawdudi on Democracy: A Critical Appreciation". In: *IQ* 47/4 (2003), pp. 303-331

Kaushik, Surendra Nath. *Politics of Islamization in Pakistan. A Study of Zia Regime (sic)*. South Asian Publishers: New Dehli, 1993

Kazim, Hasnain. "Gotteslästerung in Pakistan. Christin soll am Galgen sterben, 11.11.2010. http://www.spiegel.de/panorama/gesellschaft/0,1518,728521,00.html (10.06.2014)

Keller, Nuh Ha Mim. "Which of the Four Orthodox Madhhabs has the most Devloped Fiqh for Muslims Living as Minorities?" http://www.masud.co.uk/ISLAM/nuh/fiqh.htm (15.04.2014)

Kepel, Gilles. *Le Prophète et Pharaon. Les Mouvements Islamistes dans l'Egypte Contemporaine*. La Découverte: Paris, 1984

Kermani, Navid. *Offenbarung als Kommunikation. Das Konzept waḥy in Naṣr Ḥāmid [sic] Abū Zayds Mafhūm an-naṣṣ*. Peter Lang: Frankfurt 1996

Kerr, Malcolm H. Islamic Reform. *The Political and Legal Theories of Muḥammad ᶜAbduh and Rashīd Riḍā*. University of California Press: Berkeley, 1966

Khalidi, Omar. "Mawlāna Mawdūdī and the Future Political Order in British India". In: *MW* 93/3-4 (2003), pp. 415-427

Khalidi, Omar. *Between Muslim Nationalists and Nationalist Muslims: Mawdudi's Thought on Indian Muslims*. Institute of Objective Studies: New Delhi, 2004

Khalil, Mohammad Hassan; Bilici, Mucahit. "Conversion out of Islam: A Study of Conversion Narratives of Former Muslims". In: *MW* 97/1 (2007), pp. 111-124

Kahlil Samir, Samir [sic]. "Le Débat autour du Délit d'Apostasie dans l'Islam Contemporain". In: Donohue, John J.; Troll, Christian W. (Eds.). *Faith, Power, and Violence. Muslims and Christians in a Plural Society, Past and Present*. Pontificio Istituto Orientale: Rom 1998, pp. 115-140

Khan, Qamaruddin. *The Political Thought of Ibn Taymiyah*. Adam Publishers & Distributors: New Delhi, 2009

Khan, Yasmin. *The Great Partition. The Making of India and Pakistan*. Yale University: New Haven, 2007

Khatab, Sayed. *The Political Thought of Sayyid Qutb. The Theory of jahiliyyah*. Routledge: London, 2006

Al-Khateeb, Mostafa. "Hudud (Penalties) in Contemporary Legal Discourse. A Review of Sheikh Qaradawi's Program on Hudud on Al-Jazeera". http://www.onislam.net/english/shariah/contemporary-issues/interviews-reviews-and-events/450554-hudud-in-the-contemporary-fiqhi-discourse.html?Events= (05.05.2014)

al-Khateeb, Motaz. "Yūsuf al-Qaraḍāwī as an Authoritative Reference (Marjiᶜiyya)". In: Skovgaard-Petersen, Jakob; Gräf, Bettina (Eds.). *Global Mufti. The Phenomenon of Yusuf al-Qaradawi*. Hurst & Company: London, 2009, pp. 85-108

Khomeini, Imam Ruhullah. "The Pillars of an Islamic State". In: Moaddel, Mansoor; Talattof, Kamran (Eds.). *Modernist and Fundamentalist Debates in Islam*. Palgrave Macmillan: London, 2000, pp. 247-250

Khomeini, Imam Ruhullah. "The Necessity of Islamic Government". In: Moaddel, Mansoor; Talattof, Kamran (Eds.). *Modernist and Fundamentalist Debates in Islam*. Palgrave Macmillan: London, 2000, pp. 251-262

Khoury, Adel Theodor. *Toleranz im Islam*. Chr. Kaiser: München, 1980

Khoury, Adel Theodor (Übers.). *Der Koran, Arabisch-Deutsch. Übersetzung und wissenschaftlicher Kommentar*. Gütersloher Verlagshaus: Gütersloh, 1991 (Vol. 2); 1995 (Vol. 6)

Khoury, Adel Theodor. *Christen unterm Halbmond. Religiöse Minderheiten unter der Herrschaft des Islams*. Herder: Freiburg, 1994

Khoury, Adel Theodor. *Toleranz und Religionsfreiheit im Islam*. J. P. Bachem: Köln, 1995

Khoury, Adel Theodor. "Toleranz und Religionsfreiheit im Islam". In: *KuG* 216 (1995), pp. 3-15

Khoury, Adel Theodor. "Abfall vom Glauben im Koran und im Rechtssystem". In: Khoury, Adel Theodor; Heine, Peter; Oebbecke, Janbernd. *Handbuch Recht und Kultur des Islams in der deutschen Gesellschaft. Probleme im Alltag, Hintergründe, Antworten*. Gütersloher Verlagshaus: Gütersloh 2000, pp. 237-242

Kingsbury, Damien; Barton, Greg (Ed.). *Difference and Tolerance. Human Rigths Issues in Southeast Asia*. Deakin University Press: Geelong, 1994

Klingberg, Max. *Abfall vom Islam in der Islamischen Republik Iran. Rechtslage nach der Präsidentschaftswahl vom 12. Juni 2009*. Unveröffentlichter Bericht, Internationale Gesellschaft für Menschenrechte (IGFM): Frankfurt, [2010] (Copy from the collection of IGFM)

Klingberg, Max. *Mohammed Hegazy. Hintergrundinformationen*, Stand 28.04.2010. Unveröffentlichter Bericht, Internationale Gesellschaft für Menschenrechte (IGFM): Frankfurt, [2010] (Copy from the collection of IGFM)

Knüppel, Katharina. *Religionsfreiheit und Apostasie in islamisch geprägten Staaten*. Peter Lang: Frankfurt, 2010

Knysh, Alexander. "'Orthodoxy' and 'Heresy' in Medieval Islam: An Essay in Reassessment". In: *MW* 83/1 (1993), pp. 48-67

Kodal, Dorthe Maria. "Kritisk Læsning af Koranen i Muslimsk Optik". In: *FTI* 1 (2006), pp. 1-12. http://www.islamforskning.dk/Tidsskrift_1_2006/Kodal-Kritisk_læsning.pdf (20.06.2011)

Köndgen, Olaf. *Das islamisierte Strafrecht des Sudan. Von seiner Einführung 1983 bis Juli 1992*. Deutsches Orient-Institut: Hamburg, 1992

Krämer, Gudrun. *Gottes Staat als Republik. Reflexionen zeitgenössischer Muslime zu Islam, Menschenrechten und Demokratie*. Nomos: Baden-Baden, 1999

Krämer, Gudrun. "Drawing Boundaries: Yūsuf al-Qaraḍāwī on Apostasy". In: Krämer, Gudrun; Schmidtke, Sabine (Eds.). *Speaking for Islam. Religious Authorities in Muslim Societies*. E. J. Brill: Leiden, 2006, pp. 181-217

Krämer, Gudrun. "'New Fiqh' Applied. Yūsuf al-Qaraḍāwī on Non-Muslims in Islamic Society". In: *JSAI* 36 (2009), pp. 489-515

Krämer, Gudrun. *Hasan al-Banna*. Oneworld Publications: Oxford, 2010

Kraemer, Joel. "Apostates, Rebels and Brigands". In: *IOS* 10 (1980), pp. 34-73

Krämer, Klaus; Vellguth, Klaus (Eds.). *Religionsfreiheit. Grundlagen – Reflexionen – Modelle*. Herder: Freiburg, 2014

Kramer, Martin. "Fundamentalist Islam at Large: The Drive for Power". In: *MEQ*, June 1996, pp. 37-49. http://www.meforum.org/304/fundamentalist-islam-at-large-the-drive-for-power (15.04.2014)

Krawietz, Birgit. "Der Mufti und sein Fatwa. Verfahrenstheorie und Verfahrenspraxis nach islamischem Recht". In: *WO* 26 (1995), pp. 161-180

Kruse, Hans. "Takfīr und Ǧihād bei den Zaiditen im Jemen". In: *WI* 23-24 (1984), pp. 424-457

Kuran, Timur. "The Genesis of Islamic Economics: A Chapter in the Politics of Muslim Identity". In: *SoR* 64/2 (1997). https://www.mtholyoke.edu/acad/intrel/kuran.htm (15.04.2014)

Kursawe, Janet. "Yusūf ᶜAbdallāh al-Qarāḍawī [sic] (Yusuf Abdallah al-Qaradawi)". In: *Orient* 44/4 (2003), pp. 523-530

Kurzman, Charles. *Liberal Islam. A Sourcebook*. Oxford University Press: Oxford, 1998

Larsson, Göran. "Yusuf al-Qaradawi and Tariq Ramadan on Secularisation: Differences and Similarities". In: Marranci, Gabriele (Ed.). *Muslim Societies and the Challenge of Secularization: An Interdisciplinary Approach*. Springer: Dordrecht, 2010, pp. 47-63

Lau, Martin. *The Role of Islam in the Legal System of Pakistan*. Martinus Nijhoff Publishers: Leiden, 2006

Layish, Aharon; Warburg, Gabriel R. *The Reinstatement of Islamic Law in Sudan under Numayrī. An Evaluation of a Legal Experiment in the Light of its Historical Context, Methodology, and Repercussions*. E. J. Brill: Leiden, 2002

Lecker, M. "Al-Ridda". In: *EI*/2, Vol. XII, Suppl., pp. 692-695

Lemke, Wolf-Dieter. *Maḥmūd Šaltūt (1893-1963) und die Reform der Azhar. Untersuchungen zu Erneuerungsbestrebungen im ägyptisch-islamischen Erziehungssystem*. Peter Lang: Frankfurt, 1980

Lerman, Eran. "Mawdudi's Concept of Islam". In: *MES* 17/4 (1981), pp. 492-509

Levy, Leonard W. *Blasphemy. Verbal Offense against the Sacred, from Moses to Salman Rushdie*. The University of North Carolina Press: Chapel Hill, 1995

Lewis, Bernard. "Some Observations on the Significance of Heresy in the History of Islam". In: *SI* 1 (1953), pp. 43-63

Lewis, Bernard. *Die politische Sprache des Islam*. Europäische Verlagsanstalt: Hamburg, 2002

Longva, Anh Nga. "The Apostasy Law in the Age of Universal Human Rights and Citizenship. Some Legal and Political Implications". The Fourth Nordic Conference on Middle Eastern Studies: The Middle East in Globalizing World [sic]. Oslo, 13.-16.08.1998. http://www.hf.uib.no/smi/pao/longva.html (15.04.2014)

Longva, Anh Nga. "Apostasy and the Liberal Predicament". *ISIM Newsletter*, 8 (2001), p. 14. https://openaccess.leidenuniv.nl/bitstream/handle/1887/17500/ISIM_8_Apostasy_and_the_Liberal_Predicament.pdf?sequence=1 (15.04.2014)

Longva, Anh Nga. "The Apostasy Law in Kuwait and the Liberal Predicament". In: *CD* 14/3 (2002), pp. 257-282

Lumbard, Joseph; Nayed, Aref Ali (Eds.). "The 500 Most Influential Muslims 2010". The Royal Islamic Strategic Studies Centre: (Amman), 2010. http://www.rissc.jo/docs/0A-FullVersion-LowRes.pdf (15.04.2014)

Lynch, Marc. *Voices of the New Arab Public. Iraq, Al-Jazeera, and Middle East Politics Today*. Columbia University Press: New York, 2006

Malik, Jamal. *Islamisierung in Pakistan 1977-84. Untersuchungen zur Auflösung autochthoner Strukturen*. Steiner: Wiesbaden, 1989

Malik, Jamal. *Die Islamisierung der Wirtschaft in Pakistan unter Zia ul Haqq. Deutsche Stiftung für internationale Entwicklung:* Bad Honnef, 1998

Malik, Jamal. "Maududi, Abu l-A[c]la". In: *EIMW*, Vol. II. Macmillan Reference USA: New York, 2004, pp. 443-444

Malik, Jamal. *Islam in South Asia. A Short History*. E. J. Brill: Leiden, 2008

Malik, Saira. "An Analysis of Apostasy/*irtidād*: Considerations for Muslims in Contemporary Western Societies". In: *JILC* 11/3 (2009), pp. 211-223

Malik, Zafer. "The Religious Minorities in the Historical Context of Pakistan". In: Moghal, Dominic; Jivan, Jennifer (Eds.). *Religious Minorities in Pakistan: Struggle for Identity*. Christian Study Centre: Rawalpindi, 1996, pp. 1-20

Malti-Douglas, Fedwa. *Men, Women and God(s). Nawal El Saadawi and Arab Feminist Poetics*. University of California Press: Berkeley, 1995

Mandaville, Peter. *Transnational Muslim Politics. Reimagening the Umma*. Routledge: London, 2001

Marcotte, Roxanne D. "Freedom of Religion, Apostasy and Islam. Abdullah Saeed and Hassan Saeed". In: *SR* 34/2 (2005), pp. 291-292

Maréchal, Brigitte. *The Muslim Brothers in Egypt. Roots and Discourse*. E. J. Brill: Leiden, 2008

Mariani, Ermete. "Youssef Al-Qaradawi: Pouvoir Médiatique, Économique et Symbolique." In: Mermier, Frank (Ed.). *Mondialisation et Nouveaux Médias dans l'Espace Arabe*. Maisonneuve & Larose, Paris, 2003, pp. 195-203

Mariani, Ermete. "The Role of States and Markets in the Production of Islamic Knowledge On-line: the Examples of Yusuf al-Qaradawi and Amr Khaled". In:

Larsson, Göran. *Religious Communities on the Internet*. Proceedings from a Conference. Swedish Science Press: Uppsala, 2006, pp. 131-149

Mariani, Ermete. "Cyber-Fatwas, Sermons and Media Campaigns: Amr Khaled and Omar Bakri Muhammad in Search of New Audiences". In: Bruinessen, Martin, van; Allievi, Stefano (Eds.). *Producing Islamic Knowledge. Transmission and Dissemination in Western Europe*. Routledge: London, 2011, pp. 142-168

Marshall, Paul; Shea, Nina. *Silenced. How Apostasy & Blasphemy Codes are Choking Freedom Worldwide*. Oxford University Press: Oxford, 2011

Martin, Vanessa. Creating an Islamic State. Khomeini and the Making of a New Iran. I. B. Tauris: London, 2003

Masud, Muhammad Khalid; Messick, Brinkley; Powers, David S. "Muftis, Fatwas and Islamic Legal Interpretation". In: Masud, Muhammad Khalid; Messick, Brinkley; Powers David S. (Eds.). *Islamic Legal Interpretation. Muftis and Their Fatwas*. Harvard University Press: Cambridge/MA, London 1996, pp. 3-32

Masud, Muhammad Khalid. "Apostasy and Judicial Separation in British India". In: Masud, Muhammad Khalid; Messick, Brinkley; Powers, David S. (Eds.). *Muftis, Fatwas and Islamic Legal Interpretation*. Harvard University Press: Cambridge, 1996, pp. 193-203

Masud, Muhammad Khalid. "Communicative Action and the Social Construction of Shari'a in Pakistan". In: Salvatore, Armando; LeVine, Mark (Eds.). *Religion, Social Practice, and Contested Hegemonies. Reconstructing the Public Sphere in Muslim Majority Societies*. Palgrave Macmillan: New York, 2005, pp. 155-179

Masud, Muhammad Khalid; Peters, Rudolph; Powers, David S. "Qāḍīs and their Courts: An Historical Survey". In: Masud Muhammad Khalid; Peters, Rudolph; Powers, David S. (Eds.). *Dispensing Justice in Islam. Qadis and their Judgements*. E. J. Brill: Leiden, 2006, pp. 1-46

Mayer, Ann Elizabeth. "The Fundamentalist Impact on Law, Politics, and Constitution in Iran, Pakistan, and the Sudan". In: Marty, Martin E.; Appleby, R. Scott (Eds.). *Fundamentalism and the State. Remaking Polities, Economics, and Militance*. The University of Chicago Press: Chicago, 1993, pp. 110-151

Mayer, Ann Elizabeth. *Islam and Human Rights. Tradition and Politics*. Westview Press: Boulder, 1995[2]

Mazrūᶜa, Muḥammad. *aḥkām ar-ridda wa-'l-murtaddīn min ḫilāl šahādatai al-Ġazālī wa-Mazrūᶜa*. al-Qāhira, 1994

McDonough, Sheila. *Muslim Ethics and Modernity. A Comparative Study of the Ethical Thought of Sayyid Ahmad Khan and Mawlana Mawdudi*. Wilfried Laurier University Press: Waterloo, 1984

Mertins, Silke. "Wo Attentäter zu Helden werden. In Islamabad wird eine Moschee für Mumtaz Qadri gebaut, der einen Gouverneur erschoss. Szenen aus einem Hochrisikostaat". In: *Financial Times Deutschland*, 05.12.2011, p. 13

Michot, Yahya M. "Qaradawi's Tahrir Square Sermon: Text and Comments". http://www.onislam.net/english/shariah/contemporary-issues/interviews-reviews-and-events/451341-the-tahrir-square-sermon-of-sheikh-al-qaradawi.html?Events= (15.04.2014)

Al-Mikhlafy, Abdo Jamil. *Al-Jazeera. Ein regionaler Spieler und globaler Herausforderer*. Schüren: Marburg, 2006

Miller, Ruth A. "Apostates and Bandits: Religious and Secular Interaction in the Administration of Late Ottoman Criminal Law". In: *SI* 97 (2006), pp. 155-178

Mintjes, H. "Mawlana Mawdudi's Last Years and the Resurgence of Fundamentalist Islam". In: *al-mushir* 22 (1980), pp. 46-73

Mintjes, Harry. "Pakistan: Mawdūdī, de Jamā^cat-i-Islāmī en Zia ul-Haqq's Programma van Islamisiering". In: Wagtendonk, K.; Aarts, P. (Eds.). *Islamitisch Fundamentalisme*. Dick Coutinho: Muiderberg, 1986, pp. 26-40

Mir, Mustansir. "Some Features of Mawdudi's Tafhīm al-Qur'ān". In: *AJISS* 2 (1985), pp. 233-244

Moghal, Dominic. "The Status of Non-Muslims in the Islamic Republic of Pakistan. A Confused Identity". In: Moghal, Dominic; Jivan, Jennifer (Eds.). *Religious Minorities in Pakistan: Struggle for Identity*. Christian Study Centre: Rawalpindi, 1996, pp. 21-30

Moin, Baqer. *Khomeini. Life of the Ayatollah*. I. B. Tauris: London, 1999

Moten, A. Rashid. "Pure and Practical Ideology: The Thought of Mawlana Madudi (1903-1979)" In: *IQ* 28/3 (1984), pp. 217-240

Moten, Abdul Rashid. "Mawdūdī and the Transformation of Jamā^cat-e-Islāmī in Pakistan". In: *MW* 93/3-4 (2003), pp. 391-413

Moten, Abdul Rashid. "Islamization of Knowledge in Theory and Practice: The Contribution of Sayyid Abul A^clā Mawdūdī". In: *IS* 43/2 (2004), pp. 247-272

Moten, Abdul Rashid. "Islamic Thought in Contemporary Pakistan: The Legacy of ^cAllāma Mawdūdī". In: Abu-Rabi', Ibrahim (Ed.). *The Blackwell Companion to Contemporary Islamic Thought*. Blackwell Publishing: Malden, 2006, pp. 175-193

Moustafa, Tamir. "Conflict and Cooperation between the State and Religious Institutions in Contemporary Egpyt". In: *IJMES* 32 (2000), pp. 3-22

Mozzafari, Mehdi. "The Rushdie Affair: Blasphemy as a New Form of International Conflict and Crisis". In: *TPV* 2 (1990), pp. 415-441

Müller, Lorenz. *Islam und Menschenrechte. Sunnitische Muslime zwischen Islamismus, Säkularismus und Modernismus*. Deutsches Orient-Institut: Hamburg, 1996

Mukherjee, Rudrangshu. *Awadh in Revolt, 1857-1858. A Study of Popular Resistance*. Permanent Black: Delhi, 1984

Mullally, Siobhán. "Women, Islamisation and Human Rights in Pakistan: Developing Strategies of Resistance". In: Rehman, Javaid; Breau, Susan C. (Eds.). *Religion, Human Rights and International Law. A Critical Examination of Islamic State Practices*. Martinus Nijhoff: Leiden, 2007, pp. 379-408

Mumçu, Ahmet. "Die rechtliche Lage der nichtmuslimischen Bürger im Osmanischen Reich im 19. Jahrhundert". In: *Kanon* 12 (1994), pp. 85-103

Munir, Muhammad. *From Jinnah to Zia*. Vanguard Books Ltd.: Lahore, 1980[2]

Murawiec, Laurent. *The Mind of Jihad*. Cambridge University Press: New York, 2008

Nafi, Basheer M. "Fatwā and War: On the Allegiance of the American Muslim Soldiers in the Aftermath of September 11". In: *ILS* 11/1 (2004), pp. 78-116

Nafi, Basheer M. "The Rise of Islamic Reformist Thought and its Challenge to Traditional Islam". In: Taji-Farouki, Suha; Nafi, Basheer M. (Eds.). *Islamic Thought in the Twentieth Century*. I. B. Tauris: London, 2004, pp. 28-60

Nagel, Tilman. "Abkehr von Europa. Der ägyptische Literat Ṭāhā Ḥusain (1889-1973) und die Umformung des Islams in eine Ideologie". In: *ZDMG* 143 (1993), pp. 383-398

Nagel, Tilman. *Das Islamische Recht. Eine Einführung*. WVA Skulima: Westhofen, 2001

Nagel, Tilman. *Allahs Liebling. Ursprung und Erscheinungsformen des Mohammedglaubens*. 2 Vols., R. Oldenbourg: München, 2008

Nagel, Tilman. *Mohammed. Zwanzig Kapitel über den Propheten der Muslime*. Oldenbourg: München, 2010

An-Na'im, Abdullahi Ahmed. "The Islamic Law of Apostasy and its Modern Applicability. A Case from the Sudan". In: *Religion 16* (1986), pp. 197-224

An-Na'im, Abdullahi Ahmed. "Religious Minorities under Islamic Law and the Limits of Cultural Relativism". In: *HRQ* 9 (1987), pp. 1-18

An-Na'im, Abdullahi Ahmed. *Toward an Islamic Reformation. Civil Liberties, Human Rights, and International Law*. Syracuse University Press: New York, 1990

An-Na'im, Abdullahi Ahmed (Ed.). *Human Rights in Cross-Cultural Perspectives. A Quest for Consensus*. University of Pennsylvania Press: Philadelphia, 1992

An-Na'im, Abdullahi Ahmed. "Islamic Foundations of Religious Human Rights". In: Van der Vyver, Johan D.; Witte, John Jr. (Eds.). *Religious Human Rights in Global Perspective. Religious Perspectives*. Martinus Nijhoff Publishers: Den Haag, 1996, pp. 337-359

An-Na'im, Abdullahi Ahmed. *Islam and the Secular State. Negotiating the Future of Shari'a*. Harvard University Press: Cambridge, 2008

Naim, C. M. (Ed.). *Iqbal, Jinnah, and Pakistan*. Jinnah Publishing House: Dehli, 1982

Najjar, Fauzi M., "The Debate on Islam and Secularism in Egypt". In: *ASQ* 18/2 (1996), pp. 1-21

Najjar, Fauzi M. "Islamic Fundamentalism and the Intellectuals: the Case of Naguib Mahfouz". In: *BJMES* 25/1 (1998), pp. 139-168

Nasir Ahmad, Hazrat Mirza. *Der Heilige Qur'ân*. Ahmadiyya-Bewegung, o. O., 1980[4]

Nasr, Seyyid Vali Reza. "Mawdudi and the Jama'at-i Islami: The Origins, Theory and Practice of Islamic Revivalism". In: Rahnema, Ali (Ed.). *Pioneers of Islamic Revival*. Zed Books: London, 1994, pp. 98-124

Nasr, Seyyid Vali Reza. "Mawlāna [sic] Mawdūdī's Autobiography". In: *MW* 85/1-2 (1995), pp. 49-62

Nasr, Seyyid Vali Reza. "Communalism and Fundamentalism: A Reexamination of the Origins of Islamic Fundamentalism". In: *CO* 4/2 (1995), pp. 121-139

Nasr, Seyyid Vali Reza. *Mawdudi and the Making of Islamic Revivalism*. Oxford University Press: Oxford, 1996

Nasr, Seyyid Vali Reza. *The Vanguard of the Islamic Revolution. The Jama'at-i Islami of Pakistan*. University of California: Berkeley, 2004

Nickel, Gordon. "Apostasy: V. Islam". In: *EBR*, pp. 470-471

N. N. "Al-Mawudi [sic] (Abul-A'la): Un Aperçu Biographique". In: *Sou'al* 5 (1985), pp. 123-129

No Place to Call Home. Experiences of Apostates from Islam. Failures of the International Community. Christian Solidarity Worldwide: New Malden, 2008

Nurlaelawati, Euis. "Zakat and the Concept of Ownership in Islam. Yusuf Qaradawi's Perspective on Islamic Economics". In: *AJ* 48/2 (2010), pp. 365-385

Oevermann, Annette. *Die "Republikanischen Brüder" im Sudan. Eine islamische Reformbewegung im Zwanzigsten Jahrhundert*. Peter Lang: Frankfurt, 1993

Özsoy, Ömer. "Zum Ethos der Religionsfreiheit in muslimischer Perspektive". In: Heimbach-Steins, Marianne; Bielefeldt, Heiner (Eds.). *Religionen und Religionsfreiheit: Menschenrechtliche Perspektiven im Spannungsfeld von Mission und Konversion*. Ergon: Würzburg, 2010, pp. 57-60

Olsson, Susanne. "Apostasy in Egypt. Contemporary Cases of Ḥisbah". In: *MW* 98/1 (2008), pp. 95-115

Ortega Rodrigo, Rafael. "Evolución del Islam Político en Sudán: De los Hermanos Musulmanes al Congreso Nacional". http://hera.ugr.es/tesisugr/15826284.pdf (10.06.2014)

Osman, Fathi. "Mawdūdī's Contribution to the Development of Modern Islamic Thinking in the Arab-Speaking World". In: *MW* 93/3-4 (2003), pp. 465-485

O'Sulliva, Doctor P. "The Comparison and Contrast of the Islamic Philosophy, Ideology and Paradigms of Sayyid Qutb, Mawlana Abul A'la Mawdudi and Fazlur Rahman". In: *IQ* 42/2 (1998), pp. 99-124

O'Sullivan, Declan. "The Interpretation of Qur'anic Texts to Promote or Negate the Death Penalty for Apostates and Blasphemers". In: *JQS* 3/2 (2001), pp. 63-93

O'Sullivan, Declan. "Egyptian Cases of Blasphemy and Apostasy against Islam: *Takfir al-Muslim* (Prohibition against Attacking those Accused)". In: *IJHR* 7/2 (2003), pp. 97-137

'Oudah Shaheed, Abdul Qader. *Criminal Law in Islam*. 3 Vols., International Islamic Publishers: New Delhi, 1991

Ourghi, Mariella. *Muslimische Postionen zur Berechtigung von Gewalt. Einzelstimmen, Revisionen, Kontroversen*. Ergon: Würzburg, 2010

Packham, Ben; Hudson, Philipp. "New National Security Blueprint says Threat of Home-Grown Terrorism has Grown in Past Six Years". In: *Herald Sun*, 23.02.2010. http://www.heraldsun.com.au/news/new-national-security-blueprint-says-threat-of-home-grown-terrorism-has-grown-in-past-six-years/story-e6frf7jo-1225833204676 (10.06.2014)

Palmer, Alasdair. "Hanged for Being a Christian in Iran", 11.10.2008. http://www.telegraph.co.uk/news/worldnews/middleeast/iran/3179465/Hanged-for-being-a-Christian-in-Iran.html (15.04.2014)

Pamintuan, Ana Marie. "Living Laboratory", 30.10.2009. http://www.philstar.com:8080/opinion/518438/living-laboratory (10.06.2014)

Paret, Rudi. "Sure 2,256: la ikrāha fi d-dīni. Toleranz oder Resignation?" In: *DI* 45 (1969), pp. 299-300

Paret, Rudi. *Der Koran*. Kohlhammer: Stuttgart, 2010[11]

Patel, Rashida. *Islamisation of Laws in Pakistan?* Faiza Publishers: Karachi, 1986

Paxton, E. H. (Übers.) *An Egyptian Childhood. The Autobiography of Taha Hussein*. George Routledge & Sons: London, 1932

Paz, Reuven. "The Coronation of the King of the Golden Path: Sheikh Qaradawi Becomes Imam Al-Wasatiyyah and a School and Movement by Itself". Global Research in International Affairs (GLORIA) Center: The Project for the Research of Islamist Movements (Prism), Occasional Papers Vol 5/3 (2007). http://www.e-prism.org/images/PRISM_no_3_vol_5 - _Qaradawi_-_August07.pdf (15.04.2014)

Peters, Rudolph; De Vries, Gert J. J. "Apostasy in Islam". In: *WI* 17 (1976-1977), pp. 1-25

Peters, Rudolph. *Crime and Punishment in Islamic Law. Theory and Practice from the Sixteenth to the Twenty-First Century*. Cambridge University Press: Cambridge, 2005

Petersohn, Alexandra. *Islamisches Menschenrechtsverständnis unter Berücksichtigung der Vorbehalte muslimischer Staaten zu den UN-Menschenrechtsverträgen*. Dissertation der Rheinischen-Friedrich-Wilhelms-Universität: Bonn, 1999

Pink, Johanna. "A Post-Qur'ānic Religion between Apostasy and Public Order: Egyptian Muftis and Courts on the Legal Status of the Bahā'ī Faith". In: *ILS* 10/3 (2003), pp. 409-434

Pink, Johanna. *Neue Religionsgemeinschaften in Ägypten. Minderheiten im Spannungsfeld von Glaubensfreiheit, öffentlicher Ordnung und Islam*. Ergon: Würzburg, 2003

Pink, Johanna. "Der Mufti, der Scheich und der Religionsminister. Ägyptische Religionspolitik zwischen Verstaatlichung, Toleranzrhetorik und Repression". In: Faath, Sigrid (Ed.). *Staatliche Religionspolitik in Nordafrika/Nahost. Ein Instrument für modernisierende Reformen?* GIGA Institut für Nahost-Studien: Hamburg, 2007, pp. 27-56. http://liportal.giz.de/fileadmin/user_upload/oeffentlich/Marokko/40_gesellschaft/wuquf_2007_staatliche_religionspolitik.pdf (15.04.2014)

Piscatori, James P. *Islam in a World of Nation-States*. Cambridge University Press: Cambridge, 1986

Platti, E. "La Théologie de Abū l-A^c^lā Mawdūdī". In: Vermeulen, U.; De Smet, D. (Eds.). *Philosophy and Arts in the Islamic World*. Uitgeverij Peeters: Leuven, 1998, pp. 243-251

Polanz, Carsten. *Yūsuf al-Qaraḍāwīs Konzept der Mitte bei der Unterscheidung zwischen Jihad und Terrorismus nach dem 11. September 2001*. EB: Berlin, 2010

Polka, Sagi. "The Centrist Stream in Egypt and its Role in the Public Discourse Surrounding the Shaping of the Country's Cultural Identity". In: *MES* 39/3 (2003), pp. 39-64

Posch, Walter. "Islam und Revolution in Iran oder Schiismus als Politik". In: Feichtinger, Walter; Wentker, Sibylle (Eds.). *Islam, Islamismus und islamischer Extremismus. Eine Einführung*. Böhlau: Wien, 2008, pp. 99-121

Preuschaft, Menno. *Tunesien als islamische Demokratie? Rāšid al-Ġannūšī und die Zeit nach der Revolution*. Waxmann: Münster, 2011

Quṭb, Sayyid. *ma^c^ālim fi 'ṭ-ṭarīq*. o. O., 1964

Qasim Zaman, Muhammad. *The Ulama in Contemporary Islam. Custodians of Change*. Princeton University Press: Princeton, 2002

Qasim Zaman, Muhammad. "The Ulama of Contemporary Islam and their Conception of the Common Good". In: Salvatore, Armando; Eickelman, Dale F. (Eds.). *Public Islam and the Common Good*. Brill: Leiden, 2004, pp. 129-155

Qasim Zaman, Muhammad. "The Scope and Limits of Islamic Cosmopolitanism and the Discursive Language of the 'Ulama'". In: Cooke, Miriam; Lawrence, Bruce B. (Eds.). *Muslim Networks from Hajj to HipHop*. The University of Carolina Press: Chapel Hill, 2005, pp. 84-104

Racius, Egdunas. "Limits of Application of the Šarī'a in Modern Kuwait: The Case Study of Apostasy of Ḥusayn Qambar ^c^Alī, a Convert from Islam to Christianity". In: *SAI* 7 (1999), pp. 5-21

Rafat, M. (Übers.) "Moudoodi on Science". In: *JISc* 10/2 (1994), pp. 111-115

Rahman, Tariq. *From Hindi to Urdu. A Social and Political History*. Oxford University Press: Karachi, 2011

Raja, Masood Ashraf. *Constructing Pakistan. Foundational Texts and the Rise of Muslim National Identity, 1857-1947*. Oxford University Press: Oxford, 2010

Rane, Halim. *Reconstructing Jihad amid Competing International Norms*. Palgrave Macmillan: New York, 2009

Rathmell, Andrew; Schulze, Kirsten. "Political Reform in the Gulf: The Case of Qatar". In: *MES* 36/4 (2000), pp. 47-62

Refworld. "The Leader in Refugee Decision Suppport: Pakistan: Conviction of Ahmadis under Ordinance XX or the Blasphemy Laws and their Prevalence; Penalties Handed out", 26.11.2007. http://www.refworld.org/cgi-bin/texis/vtx/rwmain?page=country&category=&publisher=IRBC&type=&coi=Pak&rid=&docid=47d654712d&skip=0 (15.04.2014)

Rehman, I. A. "A Critique of Pakistan's Blasphemy Laws". In: Tarik, Jan et al. *Pakistan between Secularism and Islam. Ideology, Issues and Conflict*. Institute of Policy Studies: Islamabad, 1998, pp. 195-207

Rehman, Javaid. "Nation-Building in an Islamic State: Minority Rights and Self-Determination in the Islamic Republic of Pakistan". In: Rehman, I.A.; Breau, Susan C. (Eds.). *Religion, Human Rights and International Law. A Critical Examination of Islamic State Practices*. Martinus Nijhoff: Leiden, 2007, pp. 409-439

Remien, Florian. *Muslime in Europa: Westlicher Staat und islamische Identität. Untersuchungen zu Ansätzen von Yūsuf al-Qaraḍāwī, Tariq Ramadan und Charles Taylor*. EB: Schenefeld, 2007

Report of the Court of Inquiry, Constituted under Punjab Act II OF 1954 to Enquire into the Punjab Disturbances of 1953. Printed by the Superintendent, Government Printing: Lahore, Punjab, 1954, accessible at http://www.thepersecution.org/archive/munir/index.html (15.04.2014)

Rich, David. "The Very Model of a Very British Brotherhood". In: Rubin, Barry (Ed.). *The Muslim Brotherhood. The Organization and Policies of a Global Islamist Movement*. Palgrave Macmillan: New York, 2010, pp. 117-136

Richter, Jan. *Sayyid Quṭb – Spiritus Rector einer islamistischen Avantgarte?* Unpublished master thesis at the Ruprecht-Karls-Universität Heidelberg: Heidelberg, 2009

Roald, Anne Sofie. "The Wise Men: Democratization and Gender Equalization in the Islamic Message: Yūsuf al-Qaraḍāwī and Aḥmad al-Kubaisī on the Air". In: *Encounters* 7/1 (2001), pp. 29-55

Robbers, Gerhard. "Mission und Religionswechsel als Gewährleistungsinhalte der Religionsfreiheit". In: Heimbach-Steins, Marianne; Bielefeldt, Heiner (Eds.). *Reli-*

gionen und Religionsfreiheit: Menschenrechtliche Perspektiven im Spannungsfeld von Mission und Konversion. Ergon: Würzburg, 2010, pp. 37-45

Robinson, F. C. R. "Mawdūdī, Sayyid Abu'l A^c^lā". In: *EI/2*, Vol. VI., pp. 872-874

Rohe, Mathias. *Das islamische Recht. Geschichte und Gegenwart.* C. H. Beck: München, 2009

Rubin, Barry. *The Long War for Freedom. The Arab Struggle for Democracy in the Middle East.* John Wiley & Sons: Hoboken, 2006

Rubin, Barry (Ed.). *The Muslim Brotherhood. The Organization and Policies of a Global Islamist Movement.* Palgrave Macmillan: New York, 2010

Russell, Ralph. *How not to Write the History of Urdu Literature.* Oxford University Press: New Delhi, 1999

Ruxton, F. H. "The Convert's Status in Maliki Law". In: *MW* 3 (1913), pp. 37-40

Ryad, Umar. *Islamic Reformism and Christianity. A Critical Reading of the Works of Muḥammad Rashīd Riḍā and His Associates (1898-1935).* E. J. Brill: Leiden, 2009

El Saadawi, Nawal. *A Daughter of Isis.* Zed Books: London, 1999

Safwat, Safia M. "Offences and Penalties in Islamic Law". In: *IQ* 26/3 (1982), pp. 149-181

al-Salih, Huda. "Al-Qaradawi: I Call for making Sufism into Salafi, and making Salafi into Sufi". In: *Al-Sharq al-Awsat Online*, 23.12.2010, zitiert nach: N. N. Shaykh Yusuf al-Qaradawi on Muslim Brotherhood, Salafi Tendency, Shiism, Women. http://www.biyokulule.com/view_content.php?articleid=3171 (15.04.2014)

Salvatore, Armando. *Islam and the Political Discourse of Modernity.* Ithaca Press: Reading, 1997

Aṣ-Ṣāmit, Scheich ^c^Abdullāh; Bubenheim, Frank; Elyas, Nadeem (trans.) *Der edle Qur'ān und die Übersetzung seiner Bedeutungen in die deutsche Sprache.* König-Fahd-Komplex zum Druck vom Qur'ān [sic]: Medina, 2005

Sanasarian, Eliz. *Religious Minorities in Iran.* Cambridge University Press: Cambridge, 2000

Saulat, Sarwat. *Maulana Maududi.* International Islamic Publishers: Karachi, 1979

Sayeed, Khalid B. "The *Jama'at-i-Islami* Movement in Pakistan". In: *PA* 30/1 (1957), pp. 59-68

Schirazi, Asghar. *The Constitution of Iran. Politics and the State in the Islamic Republic.* I. B. Tauris: London, 1997

Schlabach, Jörg. *Scharia im Westen. Muslime unter nicht-islamischer Herrschaft und die Entwicklung eines muslimischen Minderheitenrechts für Europa.* Lit: Berlin, 2009

Scholz, Jorge. "Staat zwischen Aufbau und Zerfall – Grundzüge der pakistanischen Geschichte seit 1947". In: Chiari, Bernhard; Schetter, Conrad (Eds.). *Wegweiser zur Geschichte Pakistans*. Ferdinand Schöningh: Paderborn, 2010, pp. 57-71; accessible at http://www.mgfa.de/html/einsatzunterstuetzung/downloads/meupakistangesamt internet.pdf (15.04.2014)

Schulze, Reinhard. *Islamischer Internationalismus im 20. Jahrhundert. Untersuchungen zur Geschichte der Islamischen Weltliga*. E. J. Brill: Leiden, 1990

Schwartländer, Johannes. *Freiheit der Religion. Christentum und Islam unter dem Anspruch der Menschenrechte*. Matthias-Grünewald: Mainz, 1993

Schweizer, Ursi. *Muslime in Europa. Staatsbürgerschaft und Islam in einer liberalen und säkularen Demokratie*. Klaus Schwarz: Berlin, 2008

Sevea, Terenjit. "Islamist Questioning and Colonialism. Towards an Understanding of the Islamist Oeuvre". In: *TWQ* 28/7 (2007), pp. 1375-1400

Shah, Niaz A. "Freedom of Religion: Koranic and Human Rights Perspectives". In: *AJHL* 6/1-2 (2005), pp. 69-88

Shakir, Chaudhry Naeem. "Fundamentalism, Enforcement of Shariah and Law on Blasphemy in Pakistan". In: *al-mushir* 34/4 (1992), pp. 113-129

Shamsie, Kamila. *Offence. The Muslim Case*. Seagull Books: London, 2009

Shari'ah Staff. "Islamists Should Participate in Every Election in Pursuit of Reform. Sheikh Qaradawi's First Interview with Onislam.net." http://www.onislam.net/english/shariah/contemporary-issues/interviews-reviews-and-events/449388-sheikh-qaradawis-first-interview-with-onislamnet (15.04.2014)

Shavit, Uriya. "Should Muslims Integrate in the West?" In: *MEF* 4/14 (2007), pp. 13-21 http://www.meforum.org/1761/should-muslims-integrate-into-the-west (15.04.2014)

Shehadeh, Lamia Rustum. *The Idea of Women in Fundamentalist Islam*. University Press of Florida: Gainesville, 2003

Shepard, William. "Satanic Verses and the Death of God: Salmān Rushdie and Najıb Maḥfūẓ". In: *MW* 82/1-2 (1992), pp. 91-111

Shepard, William E. "Sayyid Qutb's Doctrine of *Jāhiliyya*." In: *IJMES* 35 (2003), pp. 521-545

Al Sherbini, Ramadan. "Top Cleric Denies 'Freedom to Choose Religion' Comment", 24.07.2007. http://gulfnews.com/news/region/egypt/top-cleric-denies-freedom-to-choose-religion-comment-1.191048 (15.04.2014)

Siddiqi, Mohammad Iqbal. *The Penal Law of Islam*. International Islamic Publishers: New Delhi, 1994

Siddiqi, Moḥammad Nejatullah. "A Meeting with Mawlāna Mawdūdī". In: *MW* 95/1 (2005), pp. 121-124

Siddique, Osama; Hayat, Zahra. "Unholy Speech and Holy Laws: Blasphemy Laws in Pakistan". In: *MJIL* 17/2 (2008), pp. 303-385

Siddiqi, Qazi Zulqadr; Aslam, S. M; Ahsan, M. M. "A Bibliography of Writings by and about Mawlānā Sayyid Abul A^clā Mawdūdī". In: Ahmad, Khurshid; Ansari, Zafar Ishaq (Eds.). *Islamic Perspectives. Studies in Honour of Mawlānā Sayyid Abul A^clā Mawdūdī*. The Islamic Foundation: London/Saudi Publishing House: Jeddah, 1979, pp. 3-14

Sikand, Yoginder S. "The *Fitna* of *Irtidad*: Muslim Missionary Response to the *Shuddhi* of Arya Samaj in Early Twentieth Century India". In: *JMMA* 17/1 (1997), pp. 65-82

Sikand, Yoginder. "Shaikh Yusuf al-Qaradawi's Approach to Shia-Sunni Dialogue". In: Rafiabadi, Hamid Naseem (Ed.). *Challenges to Religions and Islam. A Study of Muslim Movements, Personalities, Issues and Trends*. Sarup: Dehli, 2007, pp. 1454-1459

Šisler, Vit. "Islamic Jurisprudence in Cyberspace. Construction of Interpretative Authority in Muslim Diaspora". In: Polćāk, R.; Škop, M.; Šmahel, D. (Eds.). *Cyberspace 2005 Conference Proceedings*. Masaryk University: Brno, 2006, pp. 43-50, accessible at http://www.digitalislam.eu/article.do?articleId=1420 (15.04.2014)

Sivan, Emmanuel. *Interpretations of Islam. Past and Present*. The Darwin Press: Princeton, 1985

Skovgaard-Petersen, Jakob. "The Global Mufti". In: Schaebler, Birgit; Stenberg, Leif (Eds.). *Globalization and the Muslim World. Culture, Religion and Modernity*. Syracuse University Press: New York, 2004, pp. 153-165

Skovgaard-Petersen, Jakob; Gräf, Bettina (Eds.). *Global Mufti. The Phenomenon of Yusuf al-Qaradawi*. Hurst & Company: London, 2009

Skovgaard-Petersen, Jakob. "Yūsuf al-Qaraḍāwī and al-Azhar". In: Skovgaard-Petersen, Jakob; Gräf, Bettina (Eds.). *Global Mufti. The Phenomenon of Yusuf al-Qaradawi*. Hurst & Company: London, 2009, pp. 27-53

Slomp, Jan. "Mawdudi, Ideologist of Revivalist Islam". In: *BHMIS* 10/1 (1991), pp. 28-38

Soage, Ana Belén. "Faraj Fowda, or the Cost of Freedom of Expression". In: *MERIA* 11/2 (2007), pp. 26-33, accessible at http://www.gloria-center.org/2007/06/soage-2007-06-03/ (15.04.2014)

Soage, Ana Belén. "Shaykh Yusuf Al-Qaradawi: Portrait of a Leading Islamic Cleric". In: *MERIA* 12/1 (2008), pp. 51-68, accessible at http://www.gloria-center.org/2008/03/soage-2008-03-05/ (15.04.2014)

Soage, Ana Belén. "Rashīd Riḍā's Legacy". In: *MW* 98/1 (2008), pp. 1-23

Soage, Ana Belén. "Yusuf al-Qaradawi: The Muslim Brothers' Favorite Ideological Guide". In: Rubin, Barry (Ed.). *The Muslim Brotherhood. The Organization and Policies of a Global Islamist Movement*. Palgrave Macmillan: New York, 2010, pp. 19-37

Soage, Ana Belén. "Sheikh Yūsuf al-Qaraḍāwī: A Moderate Voice from the Muslim World?" In: *RC* 4/9 (2010), pp. 563-575

Spalinger, Andreas. "Von der Vision des Staatsgründers Jinnah weit entfernt. Der unter dem Militärdiktator Zia ul-Haqq gross gewordenen jungen Generation in Pakistan ist religiöse Toleranz fremd". NZZ Online, 03.03.2011. http://www.nzz.ch/nachrichten/politik/international/von_der_vision_des_staatsgruenders_jinnah_weit_entfernt_1.9749775.html (10.06.2014)

Stahmann, Christian. *Islamische Menschenrechtskonzepte. Islamische Menschenrechtskonzepte und das Problem sogenannter "islamischer" Menschenrechtsverletzungen in Pakistan seit 1977.* Ergon: Würzburg, 2005

Stalinsky, Steven; Yehoshua, Y. "Muslim Clerics on the Religious Rulings Regarding Wife-Beating". *MEMRI:* The Middle East Media Research Institute, 22.03.2004. http://www.memri.org/report/en/0/0/0/0/0/0/1091.htm (10.06.2014)

Stetkevych, Suzanne Pinckney. *The Mantle Odes. Arabic Praise to the Prophet Muḥammad.* Indiana University Press: Bloomington, 2010

Stowasser, Barbara. "Old Shaykhs, Young Women, and the Internet: The Rewriting of Women's Political Rights in Islam". In: *MW* 91/1&2 (2001), pp. 99-119

Strauss, E. "L'Inquisition dans l'État Mamlouk". In: *RSO* 25 (1950), pp. 11-26

Subaşı, Turgut. "The Apostasy Question in the Context of Anglo-Ottoman Relations, 1843-1844". In: *MES* 38/2 (2002), pp. 1-34

as-Suyūfī, Aḥmad. *muḥākamat al-murtaddīn. al-malaff al-kāmil li-šahādatai al-Ġazālī wa-Mazrūʿa fī qaḍīyat Farağ Fūda wa-kāffat rudūd al-afʿāl allatī fağarat qaḍīyat ar-ridda.* al-Qāhira, 1994

Swaine, Lucas. "Demanding Liberation: Political Liberalism and the Inclusion of Islam". In: *JILC* 11/2 (2009), pp. 88-106

Syrjänen, Seppo. *In Search of Meaning and Identity. Conversion to Christianity in Pakistani Muslim Culture.* The Finnish Society for Missiology and Ecumenics: Helsinki, 1984

Tafner, Georg. *Konversion und Apostasie in den abrahamitischen Religionen.* Grin: München, 2008

Taha, Mahmoud Mohamed. *The Second Message of Islam. Translation and Introduction by Abdullahi Ahmed an-Na'im.* Syracuse University Press: Syracuse, 1987

Taheri, Amir. *The Spirit of Allah.* Hutchinson: London, 1987

Taji-Farouki, Suha; Nafi, Basheer M. (Eds.). *Islamic Thought in the Twentieth Century.* I. B. Tauris: London, 2004

Talbi, Mohamed. "Religious Liberty: A Muslim Perspective". In: *ISCH* 11 (1985), pp. 99-113

Talbi, Mohamed. "Religionsfreiheit – eine muslimische Perspektive". In: Schwartländer, Johannes. *Freiheit der Religion. Christentum und Islam unter dem Anspruch der Menschenrechte.* Matthias-Grünewald: Mainz, 1993, pp. 53-71

Tamimi, Azzam S. *Rachid Ghannouchi. A Democrat within Islamism*. Oxford University Press: Oxford, 2001

Tammam, Husam. "Yūsuf al-Qaraḍāwī and the Muslim Brotherhood". In: Skovgaard-Petersen, Jakob; Gräf, Bettina (Eds.). *Global Mufti. The Phenomenon of Yusuf al-Qaradawi*. Hurst & Company: London, 2009, pp. 55-83

Taylor, Paul M. *Freedom of Religion. UN and European Human Rights Law and Practice*. Cambridge University Press: Cambridge, 2005

Tellenbach, Silvia. "Neues zum iranischen Strafrecht". In: *ZAA* 18 (1998), pp. 38-42

Tellenbach, Silvia. "Die Apostasie im islamischen Recht". 2006 http://www.gair.de/pdf/publikationen/tellenbach_apostasie.pdf (15.04.2014)

Tergel, Alf. *Human Rights in Cultural and Religious Tradition*. Uppsala University Library: Uppsala, 1998

Ternisien, Xavier. "Al-Qaradāwi [sic] l'Islam à l'Écran". In: *Le Monde*, 31.08.2004, accessible at http://www.lemonde.fr/cgi-bin/ACHATS/ARCHIVES/archives.cgi?ID=2227aac3529430e8246cc12167f181f9497f22456afa40ac (16.10.2011)

Thielmann, Jörn. *Naṣr Ḥāmid Abū Zaid und die wiedererfundene ḥisba. Šarī'a und Qānūn im heutigen Ägypten*. Ergon: Würzburg, 2003

El-Tigani, Mahmoud Mahgoub. *State and Religion in the Sudan. Sudanese Thinkers*. The Edwin Mellen Press: Lewiston, 2003

al-Tikriti, Nabil. "Kalam in the Service of State. Apostasy and the Defining of Ottoman Islamic Identity". In: Karateke, Hakan T.; Reinkowski, Maurus (Eds.). *Legitimizing the Order: The Ottoman Rhetoric of State Power*. E. J. Brill: Leiden, 2005, pp. 131-149

Trigg, Roger. *Religion in Public Life: Must Faith be Privatized?* Oxford: Oxford University Press, 2007

Tyler, Aaron. *Islam, the West, and Tolerance. Conceiving Coexistence*. Palgrave Macmillan: New York, 2008

Ucar, Bülent. "Die Todesstrafe für Apostaten in der Scharia. Traditionelle Standpunkte und neuere Interpretationen zur Überwindung eines Paradigmas der Abgrenzung". In: Schmid, Hansjörg et al. (Eds.). *Identität durch Differenz? Wechselseitige Abgrenzungen in Christenum und Islam*. Friedrich Pustet: Regensburg, 2007, pp. 227-244

Uphoff, Petra. *Untersuchung zur rechtlichen Stellung und Situation von nichtmuslimischen Minderheiten im Iran*. Internationale Gesellschaft für Menschenrechte: Frankfurt, 2012

Usmani, Muhammad Taqi. "The Islamization of Laws in Pakistan: The Case of *Hudud* Ordinances". In: *MW* 96/2 (2006), pp. 287-304

Vidino, Lorenzo. "The Muslim Brotherhood's Conquest of Europe". In: *MEQ* 12/1 (2005), pp. 25-34, accessible at http://www.meforum.org/687/the-muslim-brotherhoods-conquest-of-europe (15.04.2014)

Vidino, Lorenzo. "Aims and Methods of Europe's Muslim Brotherhood". In: *Current Trends in Islamist Ideology. Vol. IV*. Hudson Institute: Washington, 2006, pp. 22-44, accessible at http://mail.currenttrends.org/research/detail/aims-and-methods-of-europes-muslim-brotherhood (05.05.2014)

Virkama, Anna Kristina. *Discussing Moudawana. Perspectives on Family Law Reform, Gender Equality and Social Change in Morocco*. M. A. Thesis, University of Joensuu, 2006. http://joypub.joensuu.fi/publications/masters_thesis/vir kama_discussing/virkama.pdf (21.07.2011)

Vogel, Gereon. *Blasphemie. Die Affäre Rushdie in religionswissenschaftlicher Sicht. Zugleich ein Beitrag zum Begriff der Religion*. Peter Lang: Frankfurt, 1997

Waardenburg, Jacques. "Le Renouveau Islamique, Vu à Travers un *Festschrift*." In: *ASSR* 50/2 (1980), pp. 191-204

Wahdat-Hagh, Wahied. *Religionsfreiheit im Iran am Beispiel der Christen und Baha'i. Iran-Reader 2012*. Konrad-Adenauer-Stiftung: St. Augustin: 2012

al-Waqfī, Ibrāhīm Aḥmad. *tilka ḥudūd Allāh*. aš-šu'ūn ad-dīnīya: ad-Dauḥa/Qaṭar, 1977

Wardeh, Nadia. *Yūsuf al-Qaraḍāwī and the "Islamic Awakening" of the late 20th century*. M. A.thesis der McGill University: Montreal, 2001. http://digitool.lib rary.mcgill.ca/R/?func=dbin-jump-full&object_id=32950&local_base=GEN01-MCG02 (05.05.2014)

Warren, David H.; Gilmore, Christine. "One Nation under God? Yusuf al-Qaradawi's Changing Fiqh of Citizenship", 2013. http://www.academia.edu/5357481/ One_nation_under_God_Yusuf_al-Qaradawis_changing_Fiqh_of_citizenship (05.05.2014)

Wasserstein, David. "A *Fatwā* on Conversion in Islamic Spain". In: *SMJR* 1 (1993), pp. 177-188

Watt, W. Montgomery. "ᶜAḳīda". In: *EI*/2, Vol. I, pp. 332-336

Weiner, Mark S. "Religious Freedom and the Rule of the Clan in Muslim Societies". In: *RFIA* 9/2 (2011), pp. 39-45

Weiss, Bernard G. *The Spirit of Islamic Law*. University of Georgia Press: Athens, 2006

Wensinck, A. J. *Concordance et Indices de la Tradition Musulmane*. 7 Vols., E. J. Brill: Leiden 1936-1969

Wentker, Sybille. "Historische Entwicklung des Islamismus". In: Walter Feichtinger; Wentker, Sybille (Eds.). *Islam, Islamismus und Islamischer Extremismus*. Böhlau: Wien, 2008, pp. 45-60

Wenzel-Teuber, Wendelin. *Islamische Ethik und moderne Gesellschaft im Islamismus von Yusuf al-Qaradawi*. Dr. Kovać: Hamburg 2005

Wenzel-Teuber, Wendelin. "Yūsuf al-Qaraḍāwī – Wenn ein arabischer Fernsehprediger das Denken übernimmt". In: Schneiders, Thorsten Gerald (Ed.). *Islamver-*

herrlichung. Wenn die Kritik zum Tabu wird. VS: Wiesbaden, 2010, pp. 277-285

Wick, Lukas. *Islam und Verfassungsstaat. Theologische Versöhnung mit der politischen Moderne?* Ergon: Würzburg, 2009

Wiederhold, Lutz. "Blasphemy against the Prophet Muḥammad and his Companions *(sabb al-rasūl, sabb al-ṣaḥābah)*: The Introduction of the Topic into Shāfiʿī Legal Literature and its Relevance for Legal Practice under Mamluke Rule". In: *JSS* 42/1 (1997), pp. 39-70

Wiedl, Nina. "Dawa and the Islamist Revival in the West". In: *Current Trends in Islamist Ideology. Vol. IX*. Hudson Institute: 2006, Washington, pp. 120-150, accessible at http://www.hudson.org/content/researchattachments/attachment/1179/20100108_ct9forposting.pdf (05.05.2014)

Wiedl, Nina. *Da'wa – Der Ruf zum Islam in Europa*. Hans Schiler: Berlin, 2008

Wielandt, Rotraud. "Zeitgenössische ägyptische Stimmen zur Säkularisierungsproblematik". In: *WI* 22 (1982), pp. 117-133

Wielandt, Rotraud. "Religionsfreiheit und Absolutheitsanspruch der Religion im zeitgenössischen Islam". In: Krämer, Peter et al. (Eds.). *Recht auf Mission contra Religionsfreiheit? Das christliche Europa auf dem Prüfstand*. Lit: Berlin, 2007, pp. 53-82

Winer, Stephanie. "Dissident Watch: Mohammed Hegazy". In: *MEQ*, 17/1 (2010), p. 96, accessible at http://www.meforum.org/2631/dissident-watch-mohammed-hegazy (15.04.2014)

Wise, Lindsay. "Amr Khaled vs Yusuf Al Qaradawi: The Danish Cartoon Controversy and the Clash of Two Islamic TV Titans". In: Media on the Front Lines: Satellite TV in Iraq. Transnational Broadcasting Studies, Vol 2, Nr. 1. The American University in Cairo Press: Cairo, 2006, pp. 43-49. http://www.tbsjournal.com/wise.htm (23.08.2010)

Yasmeen, Samina. "Pakistan and the Struggle for 'Real' Islam". In: Akbarzadeh, Shahram; Saeed, Abdullah. (Eds.). *Islam and Political Legitimacy*. Routledge: Abingdon, 2003, pp. 70-87

Yasmeen, Samina (Ed.). *Muslims in Australia. The Dynamics of Exclusion and Inclusion*. Melbourne University Press: Carlton, 2010. http://www.mup.com.au/uploads/files/acmo/MuslimsinAustralia-Preface.pdf (20.06.2011)

Yousif, Ahmad. "Islam, Minorities and Religious Freedom: A Challenge to Modern Theory of Pluralism". In: *JMMA* 20/1 (2000), pp. 29-41

Zainiy Uthman, Muhammad. "Approaches to the Qur'ān in Contemporary Indonesia, by Abdullah Saeed". In: *JIS* 18/3 (2007) pp. 408-410

Zakzouk, Mahmoud. *Fragen zum Thema Islam*. Shorouk Intl. Bookshop: [Kairo,] 2004 http://www.el-hikmeh.net/de/fragen_zum_thema_islam.html (15.04.2014)

Zeghal, Malika. *Gardiens de l'Islam. Les Oulémas d'Al Azhar dans l'Égypte Contemporaine*. Presses de la Fondation Nationale des Sciences Politiques: Paris, 1996

Zwemer, Samuel. "The Law of Apostasy". In: *MW* 14 (1924), pp. 373-391

Zwemer, Samuel M. *Das Gesetz wider den Abfall vom Islam*. C. Bertelsmann: Gütersloh, 1926

6.3. Internet Articles and Internet Documents not Ascribed to an Author

"Ägypten: Muslimische Autoritäten fordern Enthauptung von Konvertiten", 31.08.2007. http://www.kath.net/detail.php?id=17614 (15.04.2014)

"Afghan Tried for Christianity, West Concerned". http://www.islamonline.org/English/News/2006-03/21/article09.shtml (14.04.2011)

"Ali Hussain Sibat, 46-jähriger libanesischer Staatsbürger, zweiter Mann nur bekannt als 'Magier der TV-Moderatorinnen'", 09.12.2009. http://www.amnesty.de/urgent-action/ua-328-2009/todesurteil-wegen-hexerei (15.04.2014)

[Antidefamation League]. "Sheik Yusuf al-Qaradawi: Theologian of Terror", 03.05.2013. http://www.adl.org/main_Arab_World/al_Qaradawi_report_20041110.htm (15.04.2014)

"Apostasy in Islam: Any Chance in the Contemporary Context?" 27.03.2006 http://livedialogue.islamonline.net/livedialogue/english/Browse.asp?hGuestID=Gz9HCK (14.04.2011)

Australian Government, Department of Education, Science and Training. *Stock-Take of Islamic Study at Australian Universities*: 2006. Collaboration Unit, Higher Education Group, September 2006. http://www.deewr.gov.au/HigherEducation/Programs/Equity/NCEIS/Documents/StockTakeReport.pdf (17.05.2011)

"The Bahā'ī Question. Cultural Cleansing in Iran". http://news.bahai.org/documentlibrary/TheBahaiQuestion.pdf (15.04.2014)

"Berlusconi: Rahman in Italien eingetroffen", 30.03.2006. http://www.faz.net/artikel/C31325/religionsfreiheit-berlusconi-rahman-in-italien-eingetroffen-30070029.html (15.04.2014)

"Critcism of Sheikh al-Qaradhawi's 'Islamist Democracy' Doctrine". *MEMRI* Special Dispatch No 740, 07.07.2004. http://www.memri.org/report/en/print1166.htm (15.04.2014)

"Dr. Hassan Saeed's Book on Apostasy Creates Controversy. Islamic Council Bans the Book", 12.08.2008. http://secularmaldives.blogspot.com/2008/08/drhassan-saeeds-book-on-apostasy.html (06.05.2011)

"Drohende Folter und Misshandlung/Gewaltlose politische Gefangene. Iran: Akbar Ganji, Journalist", 25.04.2000. http://www.amnesty.de/umleitung/2000/mde13/007?lang=de&mimetype=text/html (15.04.2014)

"Dr Younus Shaikh Free! International Humanist and Ethical Union. The World Union of Humanist Organizations", 23.01.2004. http://iheu.org/dr-younus-shaikh-free/ (15.04.2014)

"Egypt: Muslim Authorities Call for Beheading of Convert. Minister for Religion Approves Death Penalty for Defection from Islam – The ISHR Appeals to President Mubarak to Protect Converts", 30.08.2007. http://www.ishr.org/Detailansicht.861+M5b2895cd995.0.html (15.04.2014)

"500 Islamic Clerics and Religious Scholars in Pakistan Issue Statement Justifying the Assassination of Governor Salman Taseer: 'Prophet [Muhammad] had Ordered the Killing of An Apostate for Committing Blasphemy Right Inside Masjid Al-Haram [Mecca Mosque]'". *MEMRI* Special Dispatch No 3491, 05.01.2011. http://www.memri.org/report/en/print4896.htm (15.04.2014)

"Former Qatar University Dean of Islamic Law Dr. Abd Al-Hamid Al-Ansari in AAFAQ Article Responds to Fatwa Calling for Two Saudi Writers' Killing". *MEMRI* Special Dispatch No 1888, 07.04.2008. http://www.memri.org/report/en/0/0/0/0/0/0/2699.htm (15.04.2014)

"Gay and Lesbian Humanist Association: Response to the Mayor of London's Dossier Concerning Sheikh Yusuf Al-Qaradawi", February 2005. http://www.galha.org/briefing/qaradawi.html (31.07.2010)

"Gelehrter: Todesstrafe für Muslim, der Christ wurde", 16.08.2007. http://www.welt.de/welt_print/article1109387/Gelehrter_Todesstrafe_fuer_Muslim_der_Christ_wurde.html (15.04.2014)

"Gesundheitszustand/Haft ohne Kontakt zur Aussenwelt/ Iran", 23.03.2006. Iran: Akbar Ganji, 45jähriger Journalist. http://www.amnesty.de/umleitung/2006/mde13/029 (15.04.2014)

"Islamische Republik Iran: Freispruch und Haftentlassung für Pastor Youcef Nadarkhani", 10.09.2012. http://www.igfm.de/ne/?tx_ttnews%5Btt_news%5D=1762&cHash=743035d888280393bb9157a2fed6dede (15.04.2014)

[Italian Muslim Assembly]. "A Warning for the Ummah against the Heretic Yusuf al-Qaradawi" [ca. 1999]. http://www.amislam.com/qaradawi.htm (03.08.2010)

"Kritische Stimmen gegen Islamisierung nicht zum Schweigen bringen! Afghanistan: Freilassung eines wegen Gotteslästerung verhafteten Journalisten gefordert", 05.10.2005. http://www.gfbv.de/pressemit.php?id=304&highlight=blasphemie (15.04.2014)

"Kuwait – Constitution, Adopted: 11.11.1962". http://www.servat.unibe.ch/icl/ku00000_.html (15.04.2014)

"Leading Sunni Sheikh Yousef Al-Qaradhawi and Other Sheikhs Herald the Coming Conquest of Rome". *MEMRI* Special Dispatch No 447, 06.12.2002. http://www.memri.org/report/en/0/0/0/0/0/0/774.htm (15.04.2014)

"Maledives in Brief: Hassan Saeed Enters 2013 Presidential Race", 20.04.2010. In: Asian Tribune. http://asiantribune.com/news/2010/04/20/maldives-brief-hassan-saeed-enters-2013-presidential-race (10.06.2014)

"Muslim Scholars in TV Debate on Apostates in Islam". *MEMRI* Special Dispatch No 1781, 07.12.2007. http://www.memri.org/report/en/0/0/0/0/0/0/2477.htm (10.06.2014)

"Pakistan: Aus Rache der Blasphemie bezichtigt. Baumaterialien für Moscheebau ausgeliehen, nach Forderung auf Rückgabe Blasphemie vorgeworfen. Fünffache Mutter inhaftiert". http://www.igfm.de/ne/?tx_ttnews%5Btt_news%5D=2169&cHash=3c03817d73f67cdda032a8494513cd6c (15.04.2014)

"Pakistan: Christlicher Minister ermordet", 02.03.2011. http://www.igfm.de/news-presse/aktuelle-meldungen/detailansicht/?tx_ttnews%5Btt_news%5D=1124&cHash=5e123624fab76a858610a6a1a39a42c3 (15.04.2014)

"Pakistan: Asia Bibi darf nicht sterben. Pakistanischer Konsul nimmt 2000 Unterschriften entgegen", 07.01.2014. http://www.igfm.de/ne/?tx_ttnews%5Btt_news%5D=2823&cHash=d6b5333d51929392aa4b4be7d57fcbf6 (10.06.2014)

"Pakistan Penal Code (Act XLV of 1860), 06.10.1860". http://www.pakistani.org/pakistan/legislation/1860/actXLVof1860.html (15.04.2014)

"Pakistani Lawyers Salute Taseer's Killer", 06.01.2011. http://www.arabnews.com/node/364725 (10.06.2014)

"Pakistan. Todesurteil wegen Blasphemie", 07.04.2014. https://www.opendoors.de/aktiv-werden/informiert-bleiben/gemeindebrief_news/2014/april_pakistan/ (10.06.2014)

"Political Participation of Muslims in Australia, Final Report", June 2010. Centre for Research on Social Inclusion, Macquarie University, Faculty of Arts. http://www.crc.nsw.gov.au/__data/assets/pdf_file/0007/19726/2010_Political_Participation_of_Muslims_in_Australia.pdf (10.06.2014)

"Prisoner of Conscience Appeal Case. Hamid Pourmand: Imprisonment Due to Religious Belief". September 2005. http://www.amnesty.org/en/library/asset/MDE13/060/2005/en/26a13a09-d4a7-11dd-8a23-d58a49c0d652/mde130602005en.html (15.04.2014)

"Qaradawi Critisizes al-Azhar for Condemning Jerusalem Attacks". http://www.islamonline.org/English/News/2001-12/05/article6.shtml (05.02.2011)

"Qardawi, Yusuf." [sic] Oxford Islamic Studies Online. http: www.oxfordislamicstudies.com/article/opr/t125/e1923?_hi=5&pos=56 (15.04.2014)

"Profile: Shaykh Yusuf al-Qaradawi". Minaret Research Network. The IOS Minaret, an Online Islamic Magazine. An Initiative of Institute [sic] of Objective Studies, New Delhi, India. Vol. 5/20, 01.-15.03.2011. http://www.iosminaret.org/vol-5/issue20/pofile.php (15.04.2014)

"Rached Ghannouchi on Islamic Reformism", 07.02.2011. http://aliran.com/web-specials/2011-web-specials/rached-ghannouchi-on-islamic-reformism/ (10.06.2014)

"Reactions to Sheikh Al-Qaradhawi's Fatwa Calling for the Abduction and Killing of American Civilians in Iraq". *MEMRI* Special Dispatch No. 794, 06.10.2004. http://www.memri.org/report/en/0/0/0/0/0/0/1231.htm (05.05.2014)

"Reading in Qaradawism. Part 3: Statements of Apostasy". http://www.spubs.com/sps/sp.cfm?subsecID=NDV16&articleID=NDV160003&articlePages=1 (n.d.) (15.04.2014)

Report of the Court of Inquiry Constituted under Punjab Act II of 1954 to Enquire into the Punjab Disturbances of 1953, Lahore, 1954. http://www.thepersecution.org/archive/munir/index.html (10.06.2014)

"Sheikh Yousef al-Qaradhawi. 'There is No Dialog between Us and the Jews Except with the Sword and the Rifle.'" *MEMRI* Special Dispatch No. 753, 27.07. 2004. http://www.memri.org/report/en/0/0/0/0/0/0/1181.htm (05.05.2014)

"Statement by the Middle East Centre for Women's Rights on the Terrorist Attacks in London". In: *Al-Nisa* 9, August 2005, pp. 12ff. http://www.mecwr.org/resources/Al-Nisa9-+English-+Aug+05.pdf (31.07.2010)

"Stop Terror Sheikhs, Muslim Academics Demand". In: *Arab News*, 30.10.2004. http://www.arabnews.com/node/257332 (15.04.2014)

"Syrian Jihadist Scholar Abu Basir Al-Tartusi: Sheikh Youssef Al-Qaradhawi is an Apostate". *MEMRI* Special Dispatch No 2162, 24.12.2008. http://www.memri.org/report/en/print3018.htm (15.04.2014)

"A Talk with Shaikh Yusuf al-Qaradawi". In: *Asharq alawsat*, 08.04.2008. http://www.aawsat.net/2008/04/article55259331 (15.04.2014)

"Tunisia's Islamists are Different from those in Algeria". http://www.library.cornell.edu/colldev/mideast/ghanush.htm (10.06.2014)

"Urgent Action. Todesstrafe/Unfaires Gerichtsverfahren. Saudi-Arabien, Sabri Bogday, 30-jähriger türkischer Staatsbürger", 23.04.2008. http://www.amnesty.de/umleitung/2008/mde23/014 (15.04.2014)

"Die Verfassung der islamischen Republik Afghanistan vom 27.01.2004". http://www.mpipriv.de/files/pdf4/verfassung_2004_deutsch_mpil_webseite.pdf (05.05.2014)

"Verfolgung von Muslimen und Christen in Pakistan stoppen". http://www.gfbv.de/inhaltsDok.php?id=317 (15.04.2014)

"Which Countries Still Outlaw Apostasy and Blasphemy?" http://www.pewresearch.org/fact-tank/2014/05/28/which-countries-still-outlaw-apostasy-and-blasphemy/, 28.05.2014 (10.06.2014)

"Zum Christentum übergetreten: Herr Mahmoud Matin, 52jähriger Bauingenieur, Herr Arasch Basirat, 44 Jahre", 17.09.2008. http://www.amnesty.de/urgent-action/ua-151-2008-2/drohende-todesstrafe (15.04.2014)

6.4. Abbreviations

AION: Annali Orientale di Napoli
AJ: l-Jāmi'ah: Journal of Islamic Studies
AJCL: Asian Journal of Comparative Law
AJHL: Asia Pacific Journal on Human Rights and the Law
AJISS: The American Journal of Islamic Social Sciences
AJSI: Australian Journal of Social Issues
AMS: Arab Media & Society
APS: Archive for the Psychology of Religion
ASQ: Arab Studies Quarterly
ASSR: Archives des Sciences Sociales des Religions
BHMIS: Bulletin of the Henry Martyn Institute of Islamic Studies
BJMES: British Journal of Middle Eastern Studies
BR: Boston Review
BSOAS: Bulletin of the School of Oriental and African Studies
CD: Cultural Dynamics: Insurent Scholarship on Culture, Politics and Power
CO: Contention: Debates in Society, Culture and Science
CSSH: Comparative Studies of Society and History
DI: Der Islam
EBR: Encyclopaedia of the Bible and its Reception
EI/2: Encyclopaedia of Islam, 2. Aufl.
EI/3: Encyclopaedia of Islam, 3. Aufl. (Online-Version)
EIMW: Encyclopaedia of Islam and the Muslim World
EQ: Encyclopaedia of the Qur'ān
ES: Eureka Street
EWIC: Encyclopaedia of Women and Islamic Cultures
FAZ: Allgemeine Zeitung
FTI: Forfatteren og Tidsskrift for Islamforskning – Danske koranstudier
HRQ: Human Rights Quarterly
ICMR: Islam and Christian-Muslim Relations
IJHR: International Journal of Human Rights
IJIA: The Iranian Journal of International Affairs

IJMES: International Journal of Middle East Studies
ILS: Islamic Law and Society
IMW: Indonesia and the Malay World
IOS: Israel Oriental Studies
IQ: The Islamic Quarterly
IS: Islamic Studies: Journal of the Islamic Research Institute of Pakistan
ISCH: Islamochristiana
ISIM: Institute for the Study of Islam in the Modern World
JAIMES: Journal of Arabic, Islamic and Middle Eastern Studies
JILC: Journal of Islamic Law and Culture
JIS: Journal of Islamic Studies
JISc: Journal of Islamic Science
JISP: Journal of Islamic State Practices in International Law
JLR: Journal of Law and Religion
JMMA: Journal of Muslim Minority Affairs
JQS: Journal of Qur'anic Studies/mağallat ad-dirāsat al-qur'ānīya
JSAI: Jerusalem Studies in Arabic and Islam
JSS: Journal of Semitic Studies
KuG: Kirche und Gesellschaft
KuR: Kirche und Recht
MEF: Middle East Forum
MEJ: The Middle East Journal
MEQ: The Middle East Quarterly
MERIA: The Middle East Review of International Affairs
MES: Middle Eastern Studies
MIJ: Macalester Islam Journal
MJIL: Minnesota Journal of International Law
MuEQ: Muslim Education Quarterly
MW: The Muslim World
NZZ: Neue Zürcher Zeitung
OEMIW: The Oxford Encyclopaedia of the Modern Islamic World
OM: Oriente Moderno
PA: Pacific Affairs
PC: Political Studies
RabelsZ: Rabels Zeitschrift für ausländisches und internationales Privatrecht
RC: Religious Compass

RFIA:	The Review of Faith and International Affairs
RMM:	Revue des Mondes Musulmans et de la Méditerranée
JRAI:	Journal of the Royal Anthropological Institute
RSO:	Rivista degli Studi Orientali
SAI:	Studia Arabistyczne i Islamistyczne
SI:	Studia Islamica
SJIL:	Stanford Journal of International Law
SMJR:	Studies in Muslim-Jewish Relations
SoR:	Social Research
SR:	Studies in religion: SR; revue canadienne = sciences religieuses
TPV:	Terrorism and Political Violence
TWQ:	Third World Quarterly
UNYB:	Max Planck Year Book of United Nations Law
WI:	Die Welt des Islams
WO:	Die Welt des Orients
ZAA:	Zeitschrift für Ausländerrecht und Ausländerpolitik

www.ingramcontent.com/pod-product-compliance
Lightning Source LLC
Chambersburg PA
CBHW080528300426
44111CB00017B/2643